SO-BIW-975

THE ART OF
ACCOMPANIMENT
FROM A
THOROUGH-BASS

American Musicological Society
Music Library Association Reprint Series

Dover Publications, Inc., New York, in cooperation with the American Musicological Society and the Music Library Association, has undertaken to bring back into print a select list of scholarly musical works long unavailable to the researcher, student, and performer. A distinguished Committee representing both these professional organizations has been appointed to plan and supervise the series, which will include facsimile editions of indispensable historical, theoretical and bibliographical studies as well as important collections of music and translations of basic texts. To make the reprints more useful and to bring them up to date, new introductions, supplementary indexes and bibliographies, etc., will be prepared by qualified specialists.

Sir John Hawkins, *A General History of the Science and Practice of Music*
W. H., A. F., and A. E. Hill, *Antonio Stradivari, His Life and Work*
Curt Sachs, *Real-Lexikon der Musikinstrumente,* new revised, enlarged edition
The Complete Works of Franz Schubert (19 volumes), the Breitkopf & Härtel
    Critical Edition of 1884-1897 *(Franz Schubert's Werke. Kritisch
    durchgesehene Gesammtausgabe.)*
Charles Read Baskervill, *The Elizabethan Jig and Related Song Drama*
George Ashdown Audsley, *The Art of Organ-Building,* corrected edition
Emanuel Winternitz, *Musical Autographs from Monteverdi to Hindemith,*
    corrected edition
William Chappell, *Popular Music of the Olden Time,* 1859 edition
F. T. Arnold, *The Art of Accompaniment from a Thorough-Bass as
    Practised in the 17th and 18th Centuries*
The Breitkopf Thematic Catalogue, 1762-1787, with new introduction and
    indexes by B. S. Brook
Otto Kinkeldey, *Orgel und Klavier in der Musik des 16. Jahrhunderts*
Andreas Ornithoparcus, *Musice active micrologus,* together with
    John Dowland's translation, *A. O. his Micrologus, or Introduction,
    Containing the Art of Singing*
O. G. T. Sonneck, *Early Concert-life in America (1731-1800)*
Giambattista Mancini, *Practical Reflections on the Figurative Art of Singing*
    (translated by Pietro Buzzi)
Denis Stevens, *Thomas Tomkins, 1572-1656*
Thoinot Arbeau, *Orchesography* (translated by Mary Stewart Evans)
Edmond vander Straeten, *La Musique aux Pays-Bas avant le XIXe siècle*
Frits Noske, *La Mélodie française de Berlioz à Duparc* (translated
    by Rita Benton)
Board of Music Trade, *Complete Catalogue of Sheet Music and Musical Works*
    (1870)

THE ART OF ACCOMPANIMENT

FROM A

THOROUGH-BASS

AS PRACTISED IN THE
XVIITH & XVIIITH CENTURIES

BY F. T. ARNOLD, M.A. (CANTAB.)

WITH A NEW INTRODUCTION BY

DENIS STEVENS

IN TWO VOLUMES

Volume I

DOVER PUBLICATIONS, INC., NEW YORK

This Dover edition, first published in 1965, is an unabridged and unaltered republication of the work first published by Oxford University Press in 1931. The work, originally in one volume, has been divided into two volumes in this edition.

A new Introduction has been written specially for this edition by Denis Stevens.

Standard Book Number: 486-21442-7
Library of Congress Catalog Card Number: 65-24022

Manufactured in the United States of America

Dover Publications, Inc.
180 Varick Street
New York, N. Y. 10014

This edition is dedicated
to the memory of

FRANCK THOMAS ARNOLD

INTRODUCTION TO THE
DOVER EDITION

When Franck Thomas Arnold, a university professor of German language and literature, was devoting his leisure hours to collecting, translating, and compiling the basic theoretical materials that gradually gave generous shape to a book still unsurpassed for its scope and erudition, the word "baroque" was rarely (if ever) mentioned in connection with music, unless in the context of speculative musicological writings. The seventeenth century, and the greater part of the eighteenth, were known to the majority of historians and critics as the period of the thorough-bass, and it is only in recent years that the term "baroque" came to be accepted as a part of our legal musico-terminological tender.

At first, the essentially pejorative overtones of the word seemed to lie outside the normal auditory range of musicians, both amateur and professional; but after a time the inevitable reaction set in, and enthusiasts joined with iconoclasts to ask whether the drenching downpour of sonatas, concertos, and concerti grossi—especially of the Italian school—would ever come to an end. On the air and on disc, in concerts and in festivals, on tape and on television, this flood of baroque music threatened to engulf the world of music and drown it in a sea of pompous puerilities.

There was a stage when Arnold's book could have done something to save the situation, but as luck would have it, stocks were exhausted and copies could only be consulted in libraries. In consequence, the one genuinely creative contribution to a performance of a baroque instrumental or vocal work—the artistic and imaginative realization of the continuo part—was all too often conspicuous by its absence, which did not (as far as the true connoisseur was concerned) make the heart grow fonder. Indeed, baroque music began to fall into disrepute, although there began to emerge in certain countries a select group of organists, harpsichordists, and lutenists capable of enlivening a continuo part in keeping with the style and spirit of the age. They, like their fellow musicians, realized not only the thorough-bass; they realized that a vast proportion of the newly fashionable baroque repertory had been primarily created for the performer, not the listener. All over Europe, the devotees of the accademia, the collegium musicum, the orchestral society, the concert spirituel, demanded newly composed instrumental music suitable for immediate performance, and the evidence points to the fact that they were more than satisfied, if not satiated.

Musicians today have this lesson to learn: that much of this material can still be played for enjoyment, but that full enjoyment will come only when the soloists learn the gentle art of tasteful embellishment of a melodic line, and when continuo players learn that their role, far from being a subsidiary one of mere accompaniment, is perhaps the most important in the entire ensemble. A constant and concentrated study of Arnold's monumental work will greatly assist in bringing about a true appreciation and knowledge of the art of continuo playing, and of the way in which it can transform a mediocre work into an acceptable one, and a pedestrian performance into one full of lightness and grace.

Figured basses were going out of fashion in Italy during Vivaldi's lifetime, yet they were retained in Germany until the time of Beethoven, the autograph of whose *Emperor Concerto* contains vestigial traces of figures used for harmonic filling in the tutti passages. When the German violinist Pisendel asked Vivaldi to figure the bass of a concerto he had just received, the Italian declined with the derisive and (for a priest) none too proper exclamation "per i coglioni." But today's continuo player must learn the figures before he can forget them, even if in doing so he is guilty of a monstrous pun on the poet's *musicus qui numerans nescit se numerare.*

Many of the authorities quoted by Arnold have since become more extensively available in facsimiles, extracts, or complete translations.* These

* Among the more important publications since 1931 are the following, each dealing with one authority: J. Adlung, *Anleitung zu der musikalischen Gelahrtheit* (facsimile; Kassel, 1953); A. Agazzari, *Del sonare sopra'l basso* (facsimile; Milan, 1934); J. H. d'Anglebert, "Principes de l'accompagnement" in *Pièces de clavessin*, ed. M. Roesgen-Champion (Publications de la Société Française de Musicologie, Series I, Volume 8; Paris, 1934); C. P. E. Bach, *Essay on the True Art of playing Keyboard Instruments*, translated by William J. Mitchell from the *Versuch über die wahre Art das Clavier zu spielen* (New York, 1949); "On the keyboard accompaniment to Bach's Leipzig Church Music," by Arthur Mendel (*The Musical Quarterly*, Vol. 36, New York, 1950); A. Banchieri, *Conclusioni nel suono dell'organo* (facsimile; Milan, 1934); "Francesco Corbetta und das Generalbass-Spielen," by M. Schulz (*Die Musikforschung*, Vol. IV, 1951); F. Gasparini, *The Practical Harmonist at the Harpsichord*, translated by F. S. Stillings from *L'armonico pratico al cimbalo* (New Haven, 1963); J. D. Heinichen's *Der General-Bass in der Composition—A Critical Study with Annotated Translation of Selected Chapters* by G. J. Below (Ph.D. dissertation, New York University, 1961); Johann Mattheson's *Forty-Eight Thorough-Bass Test-Pieces —Translation and Commentary* by H. P. Reddick (Ph.D. dissertation, University of Michigan, Ann Arbor, 1956); J. J. Quantz, *Versuch einer Anweisung die Flöte traversière zu spielen* (facsimile; Kassel, 1953); J. J. Quantz's *Versuch . . ., A Translation and Study* by E. R. Reilly (Ph.D. dissertation, University of Michigan, Ann Arbor, 1958); *Der Generalbass bei Heinrich Schütz*, by G. Kirchner (Kassel, 1960); G. P. Telemann, *Singe-, Spiel- und Generalbass-Übungen* (Kassel, 1935).

Recent works of general interest include: R. Donington, *The Interpretation of Early Music* (London, 1963); N. Fortune, "Continuo Instruments in Italian Monodies" (*Galpin Society Journal*, Vol. V, 1953); E. Harich-Schneider, *Die Kunst des Cembalo-Spiels* (Kassel, 1939; translated as *The Harpsichord*, St Louis, Mo., 1954); R. Matthes, "Generalbass-Probleme in der modernen Aufführungspraxis" (*Schweizerische Musikzeitung*, Vol. XI, 1957); F. Oberdörffer, *Der Generalbass in der Instrumentalmusik des ausgehenden 18. Jh.* (Kassel, 1939); O. Strunk, *Source Readings in Music History* (New York, 1950); E. Ulrich, *Studien zur deutschen Generalbass-Praxis in der ersten Hälfte des 18. Jh.* (Kassel, 1932).

too should be studied and put to practical use, for they will add to the store of information in Arnold without in any way making his observations out of date. He could not have known that the *canto llano* at the bottom of p. 5 was a basse-danse, "Il Re di Spagna"; but on the other hand he often gave a lead which has been ignored by later generations of scholars—in the remarks about the Tenbury copies of Praetorius' *Syntagma Musicum* (unique examples of the 1618 edition) which were not mentioned in the "Nachwort" of the facsimile published in the series *Documenta Musicologica*.

Some system of investigation is often of value when a large and complex work demands our attention. There are many ways of reading Arnold; no single system will be convenient for every scholar and performer. But the following may serve to draw the reader into the framework of the book and place him on advantageous terms with its fascinating multitude of ideas: chapter XXV, then III, II, and XVIII; after these have made their due impression, chapters IV, I, and—slowly but surely—the main technical section, V–XVII. Finally the chapters dealing with special subjects, XIX–XXIV, may be approached. Then, and only then, can the contemporary exponent of thorough-bass say with the sage cited by Christoph Schröter, "All that pertains to it I carry with me."

Columbia University, New York   DENIS STEVENS

PREFACE

§ 1. THE first object of the present work is to give adequate information concerning the way in which the accompaniment founded on a *Basso continuo*, or Thorough-Bass, was actually treated during the period, extending over wellnigh two centuries, when such an accompaniment was, with few exceptions, a necessary part of every musical performance, solo or concerted, vocal or instrumental.

§ 2. To any one who has made some progress in the art of playing from a figured Bass an immense storehouse of music is opened which can be enjoyed in no other way. Many works of the old masters, chiefly, perhaps, those written for a single Violin or Violoncello, have appeared in modern editions with an accompaniment arranged from the original figured Bass, but in too many instances these accompaniments are as different from those which a contemporary musician would have played as is the music of the nineteenth century from that of the seventeenth and eighteenth, and, quite apart from this, no one who has once tasted the delight of playing an *ex tempore* accompaniment from the figures, as the composer intended it to be played, could ever again become reconciled to dependence on the taste of an 'arranger'. It may be objected that the old editions are difficult to acquire and often costly, and this is, no doubt, to some extent true; but, on the other hand, there are many delightful works which are constantly appearing in second-hand catalogues, and which may be obtained for a moderate price, as, for example, Corelli's forty-eight Sonatas for two Violins and Bass (*Opera prima, seconda, terza, quarta*), than which no more fitting nucleus for a collection of old chamber-music can be found.

There are also a certain number of modern editions, as, for example, Joachim and Chrysander's edition of Corelli's works (Augener & Co.) and the publications of the *Bach-Gesellschaft* (Breitkopf & Härtel), in which the figured Bass is given in its original form.

§ 3. At the present day, when an awakened interest in J. S. Bach has caused so many of his compositions to be performed over and over again in the different musical centres, it is particularly important that Organists and Pianists should be independent of arranged accompaniments, which, in many instances, have been compiled from the vocal or instrumental score without reference to, or comprehension of, the figures.

§ 4. Above all, it is necessary that the misunderstanding which unfortunately exists in many quarters with regard to the necessity for a chordal accompaniment on a keyed instrument, in cases where the harmony is supplied (though often in an incomplete form) by the vocal or instrumental parts,

should be removed once and for all. The present writer has heard performances of the St. Matthew Passion in which not a single chord was played
upon the Organ during the whole of the first chorus: not even when the
Chorale "O Lamm Gottes unschuldig" enters as a ninth part, sung in unison
by a separate choir of Trebles! Upon one occasion he ventured to inquire
the reason of this and was assured by the conductor, a musician of great and
well-deserved eminence, that, had Bach had similar instrumental forces at his
command, he would not have troubled about any accompaniment from the
figured Bass. It would be interesting to learn what comment Bach himself
would have made on this statement!

This idea, that the Organ—or Harpsichord—accompaniment was ever
regarded as a means of covering the defects of an inadequate performance, is
as pernicious as it is unfounded. For one thing, though every interval
indicated by the figures may be present in the instrumental or vocal parts, or
both, the chord, as a whole, is often hardly distinguishable among the passing
notes: an important interval may be represented by no more than a single semiquaver; a chordal accompaniment on a keyed instrument, on the other hand,
presents a clear, though unobtrusive, picture of the harmony, and forms a
background to the filigree-work of the moving parts. For another thing, and
this is, after all, the more important consideration, *there is not a single indication, in any one of the contemporary treatises on the subject, that the figured Bass
accompaniment was ever regarded as, in any sense, optional.*

Its importance, in Bach's choral works in particular, is picturesquely defined
by Wilhelm Rust in his preface to a volume of that composer's Church Cantatas [1]; he writes: ". . . just as, in historical paintings, a background, however
simple, is an absolute necessity for the grouping of the figures, so, too, is the
harmonic background on which, like characters in action, Bach's polyphonic
parts move with the utmost freedom. And, just as figures removed from their
painted background lose their collective effect, even though drawing, colour-
ing, and character remain, so, too, in Bach's compositions, if they are stripped
of their harmonic background, the full effect is lost."

§ 5. Thanks to our Cathedrals, the figured Bass tradition was kept alive in
England, though in a limited circle, until comparatively recent years.

Such Organists as Goss, Turle, and Hopkins had Boyce's Cathedral Music,
and other old editions of the Services and Anthems of the seventeenth and
eighteenth centuries, in their Organ-lofts, and knew full well how to use
them. In Germany, on the other hand, the tradition was practically dead
before the middle of last century. Robert Franz, in his famous "Open letter
to Edward Hanslick" (Leipsic, 1871), gives an account of performances of
Bach's works as he remembered them in his earlier days; he writes as follows: "At that time, I am speaking of the early forties, one had to get on as

---

[1] B. G. ed., *Jahrgang* (annual issue), xxii (1875), Church Cantatas, vol. x, p. xiv.

best one could, according to the dictates of circumstances. Handel's Oratorios were confined, for us, to those adapted for performance (*bearbeitet*) by Mozart and Mosel; Bach's Cantatas and Masses to the editions prepared by Marx. We performed the works as presented in the texts in question, and assumed, innocently enough, that, in them, the whole contents (*Inhalt*) of those works of art were reproduced in their entirety (*völlig erschöpft*). It is true that the audience sometimes opened their eyes when, in a Bach Cantata, a strange duologue between Flute and Double-Bass was performed, or when the *Continuo* gave them a long grumbling monologue,—but that kind of thing did not trouble us further, and was put down to the account of the good old times, which we thought we had to accept as they were."

The appearance of the great edition of Bach's works issued by the *Bach-Gesellschaft* seems to have come as nothing short of a revelation to Franz, who writes: "Bach's Cantatas certainly presented an entirely different appearance from that which they did in the editions of Marx (*nahmen sich . . . ganz anders aus als bei Marx*): everywhere full figurings, which could not, after all, be there without a purpose, and which permitted definite conclusions with regard to an art-practice (*Kunstpraxis*) formerly in vogue."

Now the conditions are entirely changed. In Germany the problems arising in connexion with accompaniment from a Thorough-bass have been studied anew, and there has been a great revival of the old traditions, especially fostered by the New Bach Society (*Neue Bach-Gesellschaft*) and the annual festivals given under its auspices. In our own country the reverse has been the case. The old editions have disappeared from the Organ-lofts of many of our Cathedrals and Collegiate Chapels, and the tendency is to do away with tests in playing from, or even setting out, a figured Bass, as part of the Organist's *curriculum* in our Schools of Music; many of the younger generation even grudge the trouble of acquiring more than a very bare acquaintance with the C clefs, perfect familiarity with which is absolutely essential to the accompanist who plays from a figured Bass. Such is the general tendency, though, happily, we do not entirely lack exponents of the art of accompaniment as it was understood in the old days. Mr. Arnold Dolmetsch, who for many years past has made England his home, has done pioneer work of inestimable value, both in research and in the practical revival of the music of a bygone age, rendered, in every detail, in strict accordance with the practice of the time. Again, Professor Donald Tovey's accompaniment, on the Pianoforte, of a Solo in one of Bach's Cantatas (a supreme test) is a thing not to be forgotten. In listening to it one is reminded of Daube's words, used in reference to Bach himself: "Enough! any one who has not heard him has missed much."[1] The names of Sir Henry Walford Davies, too, and Dr. Harold Darke will occur to those who have been privileged to hear them.

[1] Cf. Ch. iii, § 8 *f*, note 5 *ad fin.*

§ 6. The present treatise represents the labour of many years, and its compilation would have been impossible had not the writer been fortunate enough to acquire gradually all but a very few of the works (both didactic and musical) to which reference is made in its pages. He has pleasant memories of a little shop in St. Martin's Lane, long since closed, where second-hand music was sold, among which treasures were sometimes to be found, and acquired at prices very different from those which rule to-day.

Early attempts at accompaniment from the old figured Basses soon convinced him that they presented certain problems to which modern text-books provided no clue. What was to be done when the downward resolution of a succession of discords brought the hands too close together? Did the composer expect contrapuntal devices (imitation, &c.) to be employed? Did 8ves between one of the upper parts of the accompaniment and a principal part come under the heading of forbidden consecutives?

The best way of answering these and other similar questions seemed to be a careful study of contemporary treatises. One of the first of these to be acquired was the exceedingly rare First Part of Niedt's *Handleitung*, with the delightfully quaint semi-allegorical narrative which constitutes the Introduction.[1] Heinichen's *General-Bass*[2] soon followed, and then came, as a veritable revelation, Ph. Em. Bach's *Versuch*.[3]

The information derived from these and many other sources was sorted and arranged by the writer for his own benefit, together with examples from the works of a great variety of composers. The idea of publishing the results of these inquiries had never occurred to him till it was suggested by his friend Dr. E. H. Fellowes, at whose instance he resolved to undertake the task of embodying them in a book. Here he found himself confronted with two alternatives, that of treating the subject from a purely practical point of view, with no more than a brief reference to the early history of the art of accompaniment from a Bass, and that of tracing the latter to its first beginnings and following its subsequent development throughout the seventeenth century, as recorded in the rules and instructions embodied in the prefaces, &c., to musical works, as well as in separate treatises. The latter alternative was chosen.

§ 7. The attention of the writer has been called by the learned librarian of the Brussels *Conservatoire*, M. Charles van den Borren, to the fact that an important book on the early history of accompaniment from a Thorough-Bass, by Professor Max Schneider, appeared as early as 1918. He decided, however, rightly or wrongly, that it was better to postpone acquaintance with its contents till after the completion of his own attempt.

M. van den Borren had mentioned that several of Viadana's *concerti* were quoted *in extenso* by Professor Schneider, and, at the writer's request, he

---

[1] Cf. Ch. i, § 25. [2] Cf. Ch. ii, § 5. [3] Cf. Ch. ii, § 9.

kindly supplied a list of these, in order that different ones might be selected for inclusion in the present work.

§ 8. A few words must be said concerning the plan which has been adopted in certain particulars:

(1) To some it may seem that, in the explanation of certain chords and progressions, the principle of inversion has been carried to extreme lengths. But it must be remembered that the classification of a certain harmony as an 'inversion' does not necessarily imply the priority of its 'root position', or, indeed, its *existence in actual practice*. If a $\frac{6}{4}$ chord on the Subdominant had been in use a century before the Dominant Seventh, it would, none the less, be convenient to classify the former as the third inversion of the latter.

(2) All examples are given (except in the comparatively rare cases in which only a later reprint of the *editio princeps* has been available) with the figuring used by the composer, or the author of the treatise from which they were taken. Thus, in an example from Purcell, and in one from Leclair, an augmented Fourth is figured ♯4 and ×4, respectively. In the writer's own examples he has, of set purpose, refrained from adhering to one standard. The first inversion of a Dominant Seventh may be figured $\frac{6}{5}$, $\frac{6}{5\flat}$, $\frac{6}{5}$, 5♭, or 5; but no really *exceptional* figuring is used in any of the examples, old or new, without an explanatory reference.

(3) So, too, with regard to the clefs, all examples from extant works are given with the original clefs, and, in all other cases, the old principle of avoiding, as far as possible, the use of leger lines has generally been followed.

Any reader who shrinks from the extra trouble involved had better at once abandon the idea of a first-hand acquaintance with the old figured Basses (and the vocal or instrumental *solo* parts printed above them) in which three of the four C clefs (Tenor, Alto, and Soprano) are used with the utmost freedom, not to speak of the Barytone and Contrabass F clefs (on the middle and top line, respectively) and the 'French' G clef (on the bottom line) to which some composers are addicted.

§ 9. It remains for the writer to express his gratitude to all who have, in various ways, helped him in his task: in particular to Dr. Fellowes, without whose constant encouragement it would have been abandoned long ago; to M. Charles van den Borren of Brussels, who has ungrudgingly given much invaluable assistance; to M. Lionel de la Laurencie, who most kindly procured a transcript of the Tenor volume of Viadana's *Cento Concerti* (lacking in the British Museum) from the National Library in Paris; to Professor Vatielli of the *Liceo Musicale* at Bologna, to whom the writer is indebted for a transcript of Biancardi's *Breve Regola*, together with a photograph of the ornamented title, as well as for much valuable information; to Professor Breul of Cambridge for kind assistance in the elucidation of problems arising in connexion with the translation of passages from the German authorities, and other matters; finally to the staff of the British Museum, and especially to Mr. William C. Smith, now in charge of the printed music, and to Mr. C. B. Oldman, for their unvarying courtesy and kindness.

Since the above was written, especial gratitude has become due to Dr. Fellowes, Dr. C. Sanford Terry, and M. Van den Borren for the sacrifice of precious time to the arduous task of reading the proofs, and for many valuable suggestions.

TABLE OF CONTENTS

VOLUME I

CONTENTS

LIST OF SUBSCRIBERS

CHAPTER I

THE BEGINNINGS OF THE *BASSUS CONTINUUS* AND FIGURED BASS

THE BEGINNINGS OF THE *BASSUS CONTINUUS* AND FIGURED BASS

§ 1. *Viadana's 'Cento Concerti'*.

It used to be commonly stated that the method of notation known as a 'figured Bass' (*Basso numerato, Basse chiffrée, bezifferter Bass*, &c.) was the invention of Lodovico Grossi (1564–1645), generally known by the name of his birthplace as Lodovico da Viadana.

The incorrectness of this assumption has, however, long since been recognized, for, in the first place, there are figured Basses of Peri, Caccini, and Cavalieri, of a date slightly anterior to the publication of that work of Viadana on which his claim as an inventor is based,[1] and, in the second, Viadana's Basses do not exhibit a single figure,[2] the nearest approach thereto being an occasional ⨉ or ♭ above the Bass note, generally denoting its sharpened or flattened Third, but with a further significance which will be explained in due course.

The work in question was entitled *Cento Concerti Ecclesiastici, a Una, a Due, a Tre, & a Quattro voci. Con il Basso continuo per sonar nel Organo Nova inventione commoda per ogni sorte de Cantore, & per gli Organisti di Lodovico Viadana Opera Duodecima. In Venetia Appresso Giacomo Vincenti* MDCII.

Only fifty-nine compositions were included, the whole work being completed by the second book of *Concerti Ecclesiastici*, which appeared as Op. 17 in 1607, and the third book, which appeared as Op. 24 in 1609.

There were later reprints in Venice, and the work was published as a whole by Nicolaus Stein at Frankfurt in 1613 under the title of *Opera omnia concentuum 1, 2, 3, 4 vocum cum Basso continuo et generali Organo adplicato; novaque inventione pro omni genere et sorte Cantorum et Organistarum accomodata Auctore excellentiss: Musico Dn. Lodovico Viadana Italo, huius novae artis Musices inventore primo*, with the addition of Latin and German translations of Viadana's Italian preface to the original publication of 1602.

In this preface, which ends with the twelve famous rules, or recommendations, to be given in § 4, Viadana sets forth his reasons for composing and publishing the *Concerti*, which were as follows:[3]

---

[1] Some of Viadana's *concerti* were, however, as he himself tells us, composed and performed in Rome five or six years before their publication, and were, moreover, admired and imitated. It is therefore quite probable that Peri, and especially Caccini and Cavalieri, who lived at Rome, had the benefit of a previous acquaintance with his Basses when they published the works to be described in §§ 6–8.

[2] See, however, § 4, under Rule 8, *ad fin.*

[3] Viadana's preface, up to the beginning of the rules (see § 4, Appendix I), is as follows:

"A benigni Lettori Lodovico Viadana.

"Molti sono stati le cagioni (cortesi Lettori) che mi hanno indotto à comporre questa sorte di Concerti: fra le quali questa è stata una dei principali: il vedere, cioè che volendo alle volte qualche Cantori cantare in un' Organo ò con tre voci, ò con due, ò con una sola, erano astretti per mancamento di compositioni a proposito loro di appigliarsi ad una, ò due, ò tre parti di Motetti à cinque, à sei, à sette, & anche à otto le quali per l' unione che deuono havere con l' altre parti, come obligate alle fughe, alle cadenze, à contraponti, & altri modi di tutto il Canto, sono piene di pause

Organists were often placed in a difficult position by the absence of some of the singers necessary for the performance of a polyphonic composition.

longhe, e replicate, priue di cadenze, senz' arie, finalmente con pochissima & insipida sequenza: oltre gl' interrompimenti delle parole in parte taciute, & alle volte ancora con disconueneuoli interpositioni disposte, le quali rendeuano la maniera del canto, ò imperfetta, ò noiosa, od infetta, & poco grata à quelli che stauano ad udire: senza che vi era anco incommodo grandissimo de' Cantori in cantarle. La doue hauendo hauuto piu volte non poca consideratione sopra tali difficultà, mi sono affaticato assai per inuestigare il modo di supplire in qualche parte à cosi notabile mancamento, & credo la Dio merce d' hauerlo all' ultimo ritrouato, hauendo per questo effetto composti alcuni di questi miei Concerti con una voce sola per i Soprani, per gli Alti, per i Tenori, per i Bassi: & alcuni altri per l' istesse parti accompagnate diuersamente, con hauer riguardo à dare in esse sodisfattione ad ogni sorte di cantanti; accopiando insieme le parti con ogni sorte di varietà; di modo che chi vorrà un Soprano con un Tenore, un Tenore con un Alto, un Alto con un Canto, un Canto con un Basso, un Basso con un Alto: due Soprani, due Alti, due Tenori, due Bassi, tutti l' hauerà benissimo accomodati; & chi vorrà l' istesse parti diuersamente variate, pur anco le trouerà in questi Concerti, hora à tre, hora à quattro, talmente che non vi sarà cantante, che non si possa hauere quà dentro copia di Canti assai commodi, & seconda il gusto suo per farsi honore.

"Alcuni altri poi ne trouarete ch' io ho composti per li stromenti variatamente, onde piu compita resta l' inuentione, & piu accomodati & variati i Concerti.

"Oltre di cio ho usato diligenza particolare di non lasciare pausare in essi, se non quanto comporta il modo, e la dispositione del Canto.

"Ho procurato à tutto mio potere la dolcezza & gentilezza dell' arie in tutte le parti, facendo le cantar bene & seguentamente.

"Non ho mancato di apportare à tempo & à luogo alcuni passi e cadenze con altri luoghi accomodati per Accentuare, per Passeggiare, e per fare altre proue della dispositione e gratia dei Cantori, se bene, per il più, e per facilità, si è usato passaggi communi, che la natura istessa porta, ma piu fioriti.

"Mi sono affaticato, che le parole siano così ben disposte sotto alle note, che oltre al farle proferir bene, & tutte con intiera & continuata sequenza, possino essere chiaramente intese da gli Uditori, purche spiegatamente vengano proferite da i Cantori.

"L' altra causa men principale appresso alla predetta è stata quella che mi ha anco affrettato à porre in luce questa mia inventione, il vedere, cioè che alcuni di questi Concerti, che io composi cinque ò sei anni sono ritrouandomi in Roma, (essendomi souuenuto all' hora questo nouo modo) trouorno tanto fauore appresso à molti cantori, & musici, che non solamente furno fatti degni di essere spessissime volte cantati in molti lochi principalissimi; ma alcuni ancora hanno pigliata occasione di imitargli felicemente, & darne alla Stampa: Onde, & per questo, & per sodisfare à miei amici, da quali son stato piu volte instantissimamente richiesto, & persuaso à porre in luce quanto prima detti miei Concerti, mi sono finalmente risoluto dopo haver compito il designato numero di donargli alle stampe, come hora faccio, persuadendomi che questa opera non habbia ad essere in tutto disgrata à prudenti cantori, & musichi, che quando anco non vi fosse altro di buono, non sarà almeno mancato l' animo pronto, & efficace all' Opera, la quale, perche insieme con la nouità, apporta seco qualche straordinaria consideratione, potrete non isdignarui di leggere gl' infrascritti Auertimenti, che nella prattica vi apporteranno non poco giouamento."

(*Translation*)

Lodovico Viadana to his kind readers.

[Chief reason for composing the Concertos.]

There have been many reasons (courteous readers) which have induced me to compose concertos of this kind, among which the following is one of the most important: I saw that singers wishing to sing to the Organ, either with three voices, or two, or a single one by itself, were sometimes forced by the lack of compositions suitable to their purpose to take one, two, or three parts from Motets in five, six, seven, or even eight; these [i.e. the parts selected], owing to the fact that they ought to be heard in conjunction with the other parts, as being necessary for the imitations, closes, counterpoints, and other features of the composition as a whole, are full of

It might happen that, in a composition of six, seven, or eight parts, several of the parts remained unrepresented. In such a case the singers who were long and repeated pauses; closes are missing; there is a lack of melody, and, in short, very little continuity or meaning, quite apart from the interruptions of the words which are sometimes in part omitted, and sometimes separated by inconvenient breaks which rendered the style of performance either imperfect, or wearisome, or ugly, and far from pleasing to the listeners, not to mention the very great difficulty which the singers experienced in performance.

[Combinations of voices employed.]

Accordingly, having repeatedly given no little thought to these difficulties, I have tried very hard to find a way of remedying to some extent so notable a deficiency, and I believe, thank God, that I have at length found it, having, to this end, composed some of these concertos of mine for a single voice (Soprano, Alto, Tenor, Bass) and some others for the same parts in a variety of combinations, always making it my aim to give satisfaction thereby to singers of every description, combining the parts in every variety of ways, so that whoever wants a Soprano with a Tenor, a Tenor with an Alto, an Alto with a Cantus, a Cantus with a Bass, a Bass with an Alto, two Sopranos, two Altos, two Tenors, two Basses, will find them all, perfectly adapted to his requirements; and whoever wants other combinations of the same parts will also find them in these concertos, now for three, and now for four voices, so that there will be no singer who will not be able to find among them plenty of pieces, perfectly suited to his requirements and in accordance with his taste, wherewith to do himself credit.

[Inclusion of instrumental concertos.]

You will find some others which I have composed for instruments in various ways [i.e. for different instruments or combinations of instruments], which makes the invention more complete and gives the concertos greater adaptability and variety.

[General character of the work as a whole.]

Furthermore, I have taken particular care to avoid pauses in them, except so far as is necessitated by the character and scheme of the different pieces.

I have, to the very best of my ability, endeavoured to achieve an agreeable and graceful tunefulness in all the parts by giving them a good and well-sustained melodic progression.

I have not failed to introduce, where appropriate, certain figures and cadences, and other convenient opportunities for ornaments and passage-work and for giving other proofs of the aptitude and elegant style of the singers, although, for the most part, to facilitate matters, the stock passages have been used, such as nature itself provides, but more florid.

[The underlaying of the text.]

I have taken pains that the words should be so well disposed beneath the notes that, besides ensuring their proper delivery, all in complete and due sequence, it should be possible for them to be clearly understood by the hearers, provided that they are delivered distinctly by the singers.

[Reason for immediate publication.]

The other less important reason (in comparison with the one aforesaid) which has also made me hasten to publish this my invention is the following: I saw that some of these *Concerti*, which I composed five or six years ago when in Rome (happening then to bethink myself of this new fashion), found such favour with many singers and musicians that they were not only found worthy to be sung again and again in many of the leading places [of worship], but that some persons actually took occasion to imitate them very cleverly and to print some [of these imitations]; wherefore, both for the above reason and also to satisfy my friends, by whom I have frequently been most urgently requested and advised to publish my said concertos as soon as possible, I have at last made up my mind, after having completed the intended number, to print them, as I am now doing, being convinced that this work need not be altogether displeasing to discerning singers and musicians, and that, even though it possess no other merit, a willing and active spirit will, at least, not have been lacking, and since it provides, along with its novelty, more than ordinary food for thought, you cannot disdain to read the following instructions, which, in practice, will be of no slight assistance.

[For the sequel see § 4.]

present were liable to have rests in their parts, while cardinal elements in the composition (imitations, closes, counterpoints, and the like) were being omitted, owing to the absence of the singers in whose parts they occurred; thus very little was left. The only way to patch up the performance, though Viadana does not specially mention it, was for the Organist to fill the vocal gaps as best he could. Sometimes, in all probability, wind or stringed instruments were available to perform the parts of the absent singers, but, in any case, the continuity of the words, which Viadana evidently regarded as important, was lost.

By supplying compositions for a single voice (Soprano, Alto, Tenor, or Bass), thus introducing Monody into the music of the Church, or for any possible combination of two, three, or four voices, Viadana provided for every contingency, short of the absence of *all* the singers!

Those pieces which were set for *Cantus, Altus, Tenor, Bassus* are all marked *à voci pari*, a term which has been often misunderstood and taken to refer to four deep voices, as being more equal in pitch than the normal combination.

§ 2. *Diego Ortiz.*

That the practice of improvising an accompaniment over a given Bass was known nearly fifty years before the publication of the figured Basses of Peri, Caccini, and Cavalieri, or of the *Cento Concerti* of Viadana, is revealed by the *Tratado de glosas sopra clausulas y otros generos de puntos en la musica de violones* ("Treatise on the ornamentation of cadences and other kinds of notes in the music for the Bass-Viol") of the Spaniard Diego Ortiz, published at Rome in 1553, and reprinted, with a German translation, by Professor Max Schneider (Berlin, Liepmannssohn, 1913) from the sole extant copy, preserved in the Royal Library (now the State Library) in Berlin.

In the second of the two books into which the work is divided Ortiz enumerates three ways in which the Violone (by which he means the Viol da Gamba or Bass-Viol) can play with the Cembalo:

(1) Both players improvise.

(2) A melody is played in an ornate form upon the Viol, while the Cembalo provides an accompaniment (over a given Bass) consisting of chords and also counterpoints suitable to the melody in question (*acompañandole con consonançias y alcun contrapunto al proposito de la Reçercada que tañera el Violon*).

(3) A Madrigal or Motet or other piece for several voices (the examples given are in four parts) is put into 'short score' and played upon the Cembalo, while the Violist makes variations ('divisions') upon one or other of the parts, or even improvises a fifth part. The very significant recommendation is added that, if the Violist selects the Soprano part as the basis of his 'divisions', *this part is best omitted on the Cembalo.*

To illustrate the second of these three ways, which here alone concerns us, Ortiz gives, as Bass, a *canto llano* (plain chant), consisting entirely of breves (except the last note, which is a semibreve), over which he gives, in turn, six *Recercadas* for the Viol. The first of these begins as follows:

§ 3. *Early Organ Basses.*

The terms 'Thorough-Bass' (*Basso continuo, Bassus generalis*, &c.) and 'Figured Bass' (*Basso numerato*, &c.) have come to be regarded as synonymous, but, strictly speaking, they are not so. The figured Basses of Peri, Caccini, and Cavalieri, already referred to, which are probably the earliest extant instances of the use of figures as a method of indicating the harmony, are incidentally *Bassi continui*[1] in the sense that they constitute an unbroken accompaniment to the voice part; but a figured Bass is not necessarily a 'Continuo', any more than a 'Continuo' is necessarily figured.

The true *Bassus continuus*, the earliest examples of which were not yet known by that name, and were unfigured, undoubtedly had its origin, mainly, in the polyphonic music of the Church.

If we were to figure the vocal Bass of a composition for several voices, and to use it as the basis of an Organ accompaniment which would, therefore, cease whenever the vocal Bass was not in operation, it would be a 'figured Bass', but not a true 'Thorough-Bass' or 'Basso continuo'. On the other hand, if, during the pauses of the vocal Bass (and perhaps other parts as well), we either *supplied* a Bass on the Organ, or incorporated into our Organ part whichever voice part in the composition *happened at the moment to be the lowest*, and therefore *the real basis of the harmony*, the result would be a continuous part, pervading and supplying a foundation to the entire structure—in other words a *Bassus continuus*, or, to use the old English term in its original and correct sense, a 'Through-Bass' or 'Thorough-Bass'.

Before the term *Basso continuo* was introduced by Viadana,[2] that which it denoted was already in existence, in the shape of Organ Basses (*Basso per l' organo*), some time before the close of the sixteenth century.

These Organ Basses often served as the foundation of two, or even more, harmonic groups or choirs. In such case the Organ part—*Partitura* or *Spartitura*, so called because it was generally 'partitioned' or barred, while the vocal parts were unbarred—sometimes consisted of the vocal Basses, printed one above the other on separate staves, from which it behoved the Organist to extract a single Bass, as he went along, by always selecting the lowest note, as being the foundation of the aggregate harmony. In other cases this was done beforehand, and an extract from the vocal Basses—in fact a 'general Bass'—was presented on a single stave.

How they managed to play the right chords is another question (cf. note 4).

According to Kinkeldey (*Orgel und Klavier in der Musik des 16. Jahrhunderts*, Leipzig, Breitkopf & Härtel, 1910, pp. 196–7), who has made an exhaustive study of the material bearing on the question, the earliest printed examples of Organ Basses belong to a collection of 8-part Motets by Giovanni Croce: *Spartidura* [sic][3] *delli Motetti a otto voci da Giovanni Croce Chiozzotto. Novamente poste in luce Venezia* MDXCIV, and to Adriano Banchieri's

---

[1] Indeed Guidotti, the original editor of Cavalieri's *Rappresentatione di anima, e di corpo*, 1600, uses the term 'Basso continuato' in his *Avvertimenti* (cf. § 8).

[2] The term was first brought into general notice owing to the large and immediate circulation of Viadana's *Concerti*, 1602, though the term *Basso continuato* was used by Guidotti in 1600 (cf. note 1); but as Kinkeldey points out (*Orgel und Klavier in der Musik des 16. Jahrhunderts*, p. 204), the terms *Basso principale* and *Basso generale* occur earlier.

[3] The word *partire* (*spartire*) originally referred simply to the division of the stave by means of bar-lines. In many cases, however, the barring of individual parts was

'Concerti ecclesiastici a 8 voci', Venetia (Vincenti), 1595: *Spartitura per sonare nel organo accomodate al Primo Choro nei Concerti di D. Adriano Banchieri, &c.*

Both works are preserved in the library of the Lyceum at Bologna. The two Organ parts differ in the following particulars. The Motets of Croce, like the *Concerti* of Banchieri, are for two choirs, and in his *Spartidura* the two Basses are given, one above the other, with an occasional ♯ or ♭ over the notes (to denote that the Third of the chord is major or minor), but no figures. Banchieri's *Spartitura*, on the other hand, gives the Bass only of the *Primo Choro*, adding the *Cantus* part (also of the *Primo Choro*) on the stave above it, which was, of course, an enormous help to the Organist in determining the harmony. The words 'à 4', 'à 8' are occasionally added to indicate whether both choirs are singing, or only the *Primo Choro*. The omission of the Bass of the *Secondo Choro* was to be rectified, according to a note (apparently by the publisher) addressed *A gli sig. organisti*, by simply adding to those portions of the printed Organ part marked 'à 8' the highest and lowest part (*Cantus* and *Bassus*) of the *Secondo Choro*.

It is evident that, in playing from an unfigured Bass of this sort, the organist was chiefly dependent on his ear as a guide to the correct harmony, though his task was, of course, incomparably easier when the *Cantus* part

merely part of the process of arranging them one above another, or, in other words, of putting them into score. As the earliest example of such a score Kinkeldey (*Orgel und Klavier*, p. 194) quotes a collection of the 4-part madrigals of Cipriano di Rore, published at Venice, by Gardano, in 1577: *Tutti Madrigali di Cipriano da* [sic] *Rore a 4 voci spartiti et accommodati per sonar d' ogni sorte d' instrumento perfetto & per qualunque studioso di contrapunti.*

Here the word '*spartiti*', while primarily denoting 'barring', evidently connotes 'scoring'.

It was owing to the fact that the earlier Organ Basses were, in most instances, barred, while the voice parts were not, that the term *Partitura* (*Spartitura*), or its Latin equivalent *Partitio* (or *Sectio*) *gravium partium*, came to be applied to them. It continued, moreover, to be so applied even when the Organ Bass itself was unbarred. Kinkeldey (*Orgel und Klavier*, p. 204) writes: "G. M. Asula's *Organicus Hymnodiae Vespertinae* (1602) is, however, an instance of an Organ part without regular bar-lines. In later years Organ Basses with very irregular barring, or with none at all, became more and more frequent. In many such cases the term *Partitura* is nevertheless retained."

In the two cases under discussion in the text (Croce and Banchieri) the *Spartitura* happens to be on two staves (giving, in the one instance, the vocal Basses of the two choirs, and, in the other, a single vocal Bass with the *Cantus* part on the stave above), and Kinkeldey (*Orgel und Klavier*, p. 201) mentions a collection of Masses by Mortaro (Milan, 1599) for three choirs, the three Basses being given, one above the other, in the Organ part; but the term *Partitura* (*Spartitura*) was applied equally to an Organ Bass on a single stave, as e.g. by Viadana in his 2nd, 6th, and 9th recommendations (cf. § 4).

On the other hand, in the case of Quintiani's Masses and Motets (to be mentioned presently), as well as in other cases, the *Partitura* includes full scores as well as Basses.

In 1607 we find Agazzari using the word *spartitura* in the sense of score (cf. § 10 *e*). In the sense of 'Organ part' the term was, by this time, beginning to be superseded by others—'*Basso continuo*', '*Basso generale*', '*Basso per l' organo*', &c., or their Latin equivalents—and was therefore more and more available in the sense of 'score'.

Kinkeldey, however, points out (*Orgel und Klavier*, p. 193) that as late as 1609 the word *partire* was used by Diruta ('*Il Transilvano*', *Seconda Parte*, Lib. I, p. 1) in the sense of 'barring'. About this period, therefore, it is only by the context that we can determine the exact sense.

was printed over the Bass.[4] As an alternative, he could, if he chose to take the trouble, prepare either a full score or an *Intavolatura* [5] for his own use.

In some cases the Organ part (*Partitura*) contained full scores alternating with Basses similar to those already described, the full vocal score being given for the most part only when the parts employed were not so numerous as to make it too complicated, as well as costly, to print. Kinkeldey (*Orgel und Klavier*, p. 198) describes, as follows, the Organ part to a collection of 8-part Masses and Motets by Quintiani: *Partitura de Bassi delle Messe et Motetti a otto voci di D. Lucretio Quintiani, Maestro di Capella di S. Ambrosio maggiore di Milano. Libro primo. In Milano appresso l' herede di Simon Tini, & Francesco Besozzi.* 1598.

"In it two staves (as in the work of Croce) are employed. When one of the two choirs begins alone, its highest vocal part is given on the upper stave till the entry of the second choir [when it makes way for the Bass of the latter]. The Crucifixus and Benedictus are mostly in four parts, and here the 4-part score is printed in full in the Organ part. The Mass 'Ego rogabam', the last of the three Masses which the work contains, is printed in full 8-part score. The Motets which follow are again restricted to the two Bass staves."

Kinkeldey describes at the same time another work, an Organ part to a collection of the Motets and instrumental Canzonas (as well as a Mass) of Joseph Gallus, prepared and edited by one Aurelius Ribrochus—according to his own description a 'nobleman of Tortona': *Totius libri primi sacri operis Musici alterius modulis concinendi Partitio seu quam praestantiss: Musici Partituram vocant. Auctore M. R. D. Josepho Gallo, Mediolanensi Religionis Somaschae. Studio tamen et labore R. D. Aurelii Ribrochi, Nobilis Derthonensis in gratiam Organistarum in lucem edita.[6] Mediolani apud haeredes Francisci & Simonis Tini.* 1598.

---

[4] Even in the absence of confirmatory evidence it is difficult to resist the conjecture that some Organists must occasionally have resorted to the device of putting in a few figures above the Bass with a pen (cf. § 9, note 2). The use of ♯ and ♭ *above* the Bass note (as in Croce's *Spartidura*), to denote the major and minor Third, involves the principle of using a sign above the Bass to denote an interval in the harmony, and the use of an actual figure is a very slight step. The most obvious necessity is to distinguish between Triads and first inversions, and we may therefore safely assume that the first figure to be employed was 6. It may be that no Basses with such MS. additions, dating from a period anterior to the appearance of the figured Basses of Peri, Caccini, and Cavalieri in 1600, have so far come to light, but, considering the extreme rarity of the works in question, this really goes for very little. It does not, on the face of it, seem likely that the three Monodists should have simultaneously blossomed out with figures, except as adopting a practice already tentatively in vogue. Had they done so, one would have expected some talk about the 'new invention', as in the title of Viadana's *Cento Concerti* (cf. § 1). Peri's *Dafne*, now lost, was performed in 1594, and, for all we know to the contrary, it may have had a figured Bass (cf. § 5), which, again, may have been Peri's own invention, while, on the other hand, it may have been based on an occasional practice already in existence, as suggested above.   [5] Cf. § 4, note 10.

[6] In a Latin preface, which Kinkeldey quotes *in extenso*, Ribrochus introduces his work with a great flourish of trumpets. He speaks of his method as a 'new industry' and dwells on the cacophony which results when Organists do not trouble to prepare an Organ part:

"Ecce novam industriam, novum studium, novum laborem: ecce sacri operis musici Libri primi Partitiones, sive quas Partituras vocatis: ecce allatam vobis facultatem omnia libentissime canendi, modulandique. Ars longa, vita brevis, aiebat ille. Sed

This *Partitura* includes several full scores, as well as Basses (the vocal Basses of the two choirs on separate staves as in Croce's *Spartidura*), and it presents the particularly interesting feature that Ribrochus has marked with a † all the notes in the upper parts which for the moment lie below the vocal Bass and, therefore, *temporarily assume the functions of the true Bass*.[7] This was a great step in the development of the *Basso continuo*.

Kinkeldey quotes several other Organ parts of a date anterior to the publication of Viadana's *Concerti* in 1602. Of these it will be enough to mention the '*Bassi per l' organo*' to Giovanni Bassano's Motets in 5–12 parts, published in 1598 by Tini and Besozzi of Milan, and a collection, published in 1599 by Vincenti of Venice, entitled *Motetti e Salmi a otto voci, composti da otto eccellentiss: Autori, con la parte de i Bassi, per poter sonarli nell' Organo.*

In both cases the Organ Bass is on a single stave, and therefore presents a true *Continuo* part which, in other cases, the Organist was obliged to construct for himself as he went along, by selecting the deepest notes from the Basses, given on separate staves, of two, or even three,[8] choirs.

§ 4. *Viadana's Rules.*

The term *Basso continuo* was, as has already been mentioned, first brought into general notice by Viadana, though it is evident that he cannot be regarded as the inventor of the thing itself. His Basses, however, differ in character from those described in § 3. In none of the cases there mentioned did the Organ Bass, though it supported and connected the whole structure, bring into it anything *that was not there before*. It was itself derived from the vocal Bass (or Basses), or any other part which happened at the moment to be the lowest, while the chords played by the Organist represented the vocal harmony. It served to keep the music together, but the music was, in itself, complete without it.

Viadana's *Basso continuo*, on the other hand, is, in many cases, an integral part of the whole, without which the rest of the composition would be incomplete.

The *Concerti* for a single voice, though differing in character from the Recitative of the Monodists, are comparable with it in their dependence on the Bass and the harmony founded thereon.[1]

In a proportionately lesser degree this is also the case with the *Concerti* for two and three voices. It is in those written '*à voci pari*' (*Cantus, Altus, Tenor, Bassus*), some of which could well be sung unaccompanied, that Viadana's *Basso continuo* comes nearest to the Organ Basses mentioned in § 3.

addimus nos: Multi adeo per multos jactantur labores, ut quandoque pluribus intenti seipsos destituant, quod optimum est relinquant, ac saepenumero ab instituto resiliant opere. Apertius loquar: multi subterfugiendi *l*aboris gratia, etiam quod aptum, quod conveniens, quod opportunum inimo, quod necessarium penitus esset turpiter negligunt, praetereunt, transmittunt: idque praecipue in arte Musica fieri conspicimus. Nonne plures, deficiente partitione, quae perjucunda, pergrataque animis ad audiendum forent, insuavia, inconvenientia, absona, & discrepantia modulantur? . . ."

[7] Ribrochus expressly states this in the following rule: ". . . *vos diligentissime monitos cupio. . . . Partem hoc signum crucis* † *sub se notatum habentem, vel bassum esse vel bassi parte functuram.*"

[8] As in the Masses of Mortaro mentioned in note 3.

[1] The *Concerti* for a Bass voice are in a class by themselves. In them the voice part is to a very large extent identical with the *Basso continuo* (or else reproduces it in a more ornate form), while at times it is completely independent.

But, even here, the *B. c.* is sometimes independent of the vocal Bass. Viadana was therefore unquestionably a pioneer, though his immediate object, as we have seen (cf. § 1), was not so much to introduce an innovation in the matter of accompaniment, as to provide a stock of pieces which could be adequately performed, however small the available vocal resources might be.

Of paramount interest are the twelve rules or recommendations which he formulated as a guide to the proper performance of his *Concerti*, and particularly of the *Basso continuo*.

Viadana tells his readers that they cannot "disdain to read the directions given below, which, in practice, will be of no small service".

They are as follows:

N.B.—The first and eleventh rules concern the singers only, but are too interesting to omit. The original Italian version is given at the end of the section (App. I).

(1) "Concertos of this kind must be sung with refinement (*gentilmente*), discretion, and elegance (*leggiadria*), using accents with reason [2] and embellishments (*passaggi*) with moderation and in their proper place: [3] above all,

[2] 'usando gli accenti con ragione'. As used by J. S. Bach the 'accent' was simply a long appoggiatura from above or below, as is shown by the Exx. which he himself prefixed to W. F. Bach's *Clavierbüchlein*. At an earlier period, however, it was treated with considerably more freedom. Praetorius (*Syntagma Musicum*, tomus iii, 1619, p. 233) gives the following Exx. under the heading 'Accenti':

[3] There seems, at first sight, to be a certain inconsistency in sanctioning the use of 'embellishments with moderation and in their proper place' (*passaggi con misura e à suoi lochi*) in view of the strong injunction, which follows, to 'add nothing beyond what is printed'. The '*passaggi*' in question must therefore have been of a kind sanctioned by tradition, so that a capable singer would know exactly how and when the composer expected them to be introduced. Their introduction was evidently an Italian characteristic, for the Latin and German versions of Viadana's Preface, in Stein's edition of 1613, respectively render the passage:

"necnon modulis Italices [*sic*] declaratis non ubique, non semper, sed loco et tempore, et cum moderatione judicioque usurpandis:"

"und dann die Italianische Modulos nicht allenthalben, noch immerdar, sondern an seinem rechten Ort . . . zu brauchen."

Praetorius, too (*Syntagma Musicum*, tomus iii, 1619, p. 240), uses the Italian word '*passaggi*', which he defines as follows:

'Passaggi'

"Sind geschwinde Läuffe, welche beydes *Gradatim* und auch *Saltuatim* durch alle

not adding anything beyond what is printed in them, inasmuch as there are sometimes certain singers, who, because they are favoured by nature with a certain agility of the throat (*un poco di gargante*), never sing the songs as they are written, not realizing that nowadays their like are not acceptable, but are, on the contrary, held in very low esteem indeed, particularly in Rome, where the true school of good singing flourishes.

(2) "The Organist is bound to play the Organ part (*Partitura* [4]) simply, and in particular with the left hand; if, however, he wants to execute some movement with the right hand, as by ornamenting the cadences, or by some appropriate embellishment (*passaggio*, cf. note 3), he must play in such a manner that the singer or singers are not covered or confused by too much movement."

N.B.—This rule contains in a nutshell one of the most essential principles of good accompaniment.

(3) "It will likewise be a good thing that the Organist should first cast an eye over the Concerto which is to be sung, since, by understanding the nature of the music, he will always execute the accompaniments better.

(4) "Let the Organist be warned always to make the cadences in their proper position (*à i lochi loro*): that is to say, if a Concerto for one Bass voice alone is being sung, to make a Bass cadence; if it be for a Tenor, to make a Tenor cadence; if an Alto or Soprano, to make it where they respectively make it (lit. 'in the place of the one or the other'), since it would always have a bad effect if, while the Soprano were making its cadence, the Organ were to make it in the Tenor, or if, while some one were singing the Tenor cadence, the Organ were to make it in the Soprano."

In the interpretation of this rule, which is a most important one, everything turns upon the exact sense to be attached to the words 'in their proper place' (*à i lochi loro*). Do they simply refer to pitch, i.e. to the Octave in which the 'cadence' (Tonic, leading note, Tonic) is to be played, or to the *part* of the harmony in which it is to appear?

The truth seems to be that Viadana, being perfectly clear as to his own meaning, did not trouble to be quite consistent in his expression of it.

It becomes apparent from Rule 12, where Viadana speaks of a 'cadence in the [lower] Octave', when a high voice is singing, not only as permissible, but as pleasing in its effect, that it was not exclusively to pitch that the words 'à i lochi loro' referred.

Intervalla, sowol *ascendendo* alss *descendendo*, über den Noten so etwas gelten, gesetzt und gemacht werden.

"Und sind zweyerley Art: Etliche sind einfeltige, so mit *Minimis* oder *Semi Minimis*, oder *Minimis* und *Semi Minimis* zugleich formirt werden: Etliche sind zerbrochene, so aus *Fusis* oder *Semifusis* zugleich gemacht werden."

("Die *Semi Minimae* werden von den *Italis Chromata*; die *Fusae* aber *Semichromata*: die *Semifusae, Bichromata* genennet.")

(" 'Passaggi' are quick runs, either by step or by leap, through all intervals, both rising and falling, which are written and performed over notes of any duration.

"And they are of two kinds. Some, which consist of minims or crotchets, or minims and crotchets at the same time, are simple; others, composed of quavers or semiquavers, or quavers and semiquavers at the same time, are broken.

"The semiminims (crotchets) are called by the Italians Chromata, the Fusae (quavers) Semichromata, and the Semifusae (semiquavers) Bichromata.")

Viadana's injunction to add nothing to the printed text evidently refers particularly to *trills*, as is shown by the use of the word *gargante*. 'Cantar di gargante' is equivalent to 'fioreggiare gorgheggiando', i.e. to ornament the melody with trills.

[4] Cf. § 3, note 3.

On the other hand, in the case of a Bass voice, as in Ex. 1 (from the Concerto 'Bone Jesu'), they cannot refer to anything else.

N.B.—In the original the voice part is unbarred, while the *Basso continuo* lacks the time-signature.

It is obvious that the cadence cannot be in the Bass *part* without inversion of the harmony:

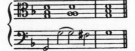

It therefore seems probable that Viadana's meaning was that, when a Bass was singing, the 'cadence' should be made in unison with the voice, and that, in the case of the other voices, it was to be in the *part of the harmony* corresponding to the voice in question. Generally speaking (except in the case of a high voice, as mentioned above), this would also imply identity of pitch.

Johann Staden, Organist of St. Sebaldus in Nuremberg, gives the following examples of cadences in the Tenor, Treble, and Alto respectively,[5] which (though given in a different connexion) serve to illustrate Viadana's rule:

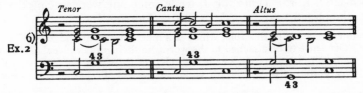

It will be noticed that the *Tenor* cadence is identical in *pitch* with the *Altus*, but in a different *part* of the harmony.

The following example, then, from Viadana's Concerto 'Peccavi super numerum', for either *Cantus* or *Tenor*, will have the accompaniment A, if sung by a Treble, and B, if sung, an Octave lower, by a Tenor.

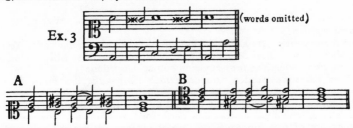

An important consequence of Viadana's rule is that, when any single voice *except a Soprano* is singing, the upper part of the accompaniment cannot, in the closes at

---

[5] *Kurzer und einfältiger Bericht für diejenigen so im Basso ad Organum unerfahren, was bei demselben zum Theil in Acht zu nehmen*, 1626: reprinted by Chrysander (*Allgemeine Musikalische Zeitung*, Jahrgang xii, 1877), p. 121; cf. § 16, Ex. 12.

[6] In the original the Exx. are given on a single 10-line stave, the clefs being shifted up or down to bring the music within the compass of the stave.

all events, be in unison (or octaves) with the voice. When the voice is a Soprano, on the other hand, the upper part of the accompaniment reduplicates it in the unison, or, upon occasion, in the lower Octave.

At a later period this reduplication came to be regarded as monotonous. Andreas Werckmeister (*Die nothwendigsten Anmerckungen und Regeln wie der Bassus continuus, oder General-Bass wohl könne tractiret werden &c.*, 1698, 2nd ed. 1715, § 69, p. 42) writes: "... one likes to see, especially when a Solo is performed, that the same part [i.e. the upper part, or melody, of the accompaniment] moves *in motu contrario* [7]; that is to say, when the voice part has, say, a Treble cadence, the Organist can use a Tenor one: and vice versâ" ('... man siehet gerne dass, insonderheit wenn ein Solo gemacht wird, mit derselben Stimme *in motu contrario* [7] moduliret werde, das ist, wenn die Vocal-Stimme etwa eine discantisirende Clausul hat, so kann der Organist eine tenorisirende gebrauchen: & vice versâ').

This means that if the voice part has , the upper part of the accompaniment should be . For it is important to note

that, by a 'Treble cadence' (*discantisirende Clausul*) and 'Tenor cadence' (*tenorisirende Clausul*), Werckmeister does not mean in the least the same thing as Viadana when he speaks of a 'cadenza del Tenore'. The latter term, if the explanation given above is correct, refers primarily to the *part* of the harmony in which the 'cadence' (Tonic, leading note, Tonic) occurs.

In German treatises, on the other hand, it is the progression peculiar to each individual part in the form of close known as *clausula principalis* [8] that is referred to.

Werckmeister (*Harmonologia Musica*, 1702, §§ 86-7, pp. 48-9) explains the matter as follows:

"These *Clausulae* derive their name from the 4 principal parts, namely Treble (Discant), Alto, Tenor, and Bass; wherefore they are called 'Discantisirend', 'Altisirend', 'Tenorisirend', and 'Bassirend'.

"As, quite simply:

"When, now, they are combined in harmony (*in die Harmonia gebracht*), one can invert these parts in divers ways, so that, now this, and now that part comes either on the top or at the bottom [i.e. immediately above the Bass], or in the middle; and it is at once recognized in the harmony when the Fourth resolves on the Third either in the Treble, Alto, or Tenor; as:

[7] Werckmeister explains elsewhere (*Harmonologia Musica*, 1702, § 31, p. 19) that he uses the term *motus contrarius* to include *progressus obliquus* (oblique motion), which is, of course, what is meant here.

[8] For note see page 14.

"In the first case the Treble ('discantizing') *Clausula* is on the top, and each part has its right position and progression; in the second case the Alto is in the top part, and, in the Third, the Tenor; so these three parts are capable of three inversions in the harmony."

When, therefore, Werckmeister speaks of the Organist "using a Tenor ('tenorizing') Clausula", he means (*a*) with the 'tenorizing Clausula' as the melody;[9] whereas, in

the sense of Viadana's rule, a 'Tenor cadence' (*cadenza di Tenore*) would be (*b*) with the 'cadence' (or what Werckmeister would call the 'discantizing *Clausula*') in the Tenor *part*.

If (*a*) be taken in extended harmony (*c*) the two are combined.

In the German version of Viadana's preface in Stein's edition of 1613 Rule 4 is quite correctly translated:

"Soll der Organist uffmercken, dass er die Cadentias in seinem Ort mache. Als zum Exempel: ist der Concentor oder Sänger ein Bass, so soll er die Cadentias *im Bass* auf der Orgel auslassen. Ist er ein Tenorist, *im Tenor*, &c."

But Winterfeld (*Joh. Gabrieli*, vol. ii, p. 59), followed by Chrysander (*Allgemeine Musikalische Zeitung*, Jahrgang xii, 1877, p. 87) and Haberl (*Kirchenmusikalisches Jahrbuch*, 1889, p. 52), translates: "also wenn eine einzelne Bassstimme singt, mache eine *bassirende* Cadenz; im Tenor eine *tenorisirende* &c." (the italics are the present writer's), which is quite misleading.

(5) "When a Concerto begins after the manner of a fugue, the Organist begins also with a single note (*con un Tasto solo*), and, on the entry of the several parts, it is at his discretion to accompany them as he pleases."

NOTE. In the figured Basses of a later period the absence of harmony was commonly indicated by the letters T. S. (*tasto solo*) which held good till the figuring began.

(6) "No tablature[10] has been made for these Concertos, not in order to

---

[9] It must be clearly understood that it is none the less a 'tenorizing Clausula' because it is used in the Octave above that in which it would appear as the Tenor *part*. In the following Ex. from Werckmeister the Bass is said to 'discantize' and to 'tenorize' in A and B respectively:

A   B

[10] The so-called Italian Organ Tablature (*Intavolatura d' Organo*) was not really a tablature at all. It was on two staves, in ordinary musical notation, the upper stave

Note 8, p. 13.

According to Werckmeister (*Harmonologia Musica*, 1702, § 111, p. 60) the *Clausulae Modi Ionici* (i.e. *C* major) were as follows:

Cl. principalis   Cl. affinalis   Cl. minus princ.   Cl. finalis

escape the trouble, but to make them easier for the Organist to play, since, as a matter of fact, not every one would play from a tablature at sight, and the majority would play from the Partitura [i.e. the Organ Bass] as being less trouble; I hope that the Organists will be able to make the said tablature at their own convenience, which, to tell the truth, is much better.

(7) "When passages in full harmony are played on the Organ,[11] they are to be played with hands and feet, but without the further addition of stops; because the character of these soft and delicate *concerti* does not bear the great noise of the full Organ, besides which, in miniature (*piccioli*) *concerti*, it has something pedantic about it.

(for the right hand) consisting of five or six lines, while the lower one had from six to eight. Unlike the German Organ Tablature (in which the letters of the alphabet were used to indicate the notes) the Italian Intavolatura failed to show the progression of individual parts. Thus, the crossing of parts, and the coincidence of two parts in the unison (except, occasionally, when one belonged to the upper, and the other to the lower stave) were entirely obliterated.

[11] *quando si farà i ripieni dell' Organo.* These words have been variously interpreted. The Latin translation of Viadana's preface in Stein's edition of 1613 has 'Cum pleno omnium tonorum concursu pulsandum erit Organum', and the German version is 'Wann man die Orgel völliglich mit allen *Tonis* zugleich schlagen müste'. Von Winterfeld (*Joh. Gabrieli*, vol. ii, p. 59) translates the passage: 'Die Füllstimmen können auf der Orgel mit Händen und Füssen gemacht werden', while Chrysander (*Allgemeine Musikalische Zeitung*, xii. Jahrgang, 1877, p. 87) alters 'die Füllstimmen' into 'die Tuttistellen'. This interpretation agrees with that of Praetorius (*Syntagma Musicum*, tom. 3, cap. vi), who paraphrases Viadana's rule as follows: 'Wenn in einem Gesang / oder solchem *Concert*, da etliche Stimmen zuvor allein in die Orgel gesungen haben / bissweilen alle Stimmen zugleich einfallen / welches [von] den Italiänern *Ripieni Concerti* genennet wird / &c.' ('When in a vocal composition, or a *Concerto* in which previously only a few voices have been singing with the Organ, all the voices enter together from time to time—what is known by the Italians as Ripieni Concerti—&c.')

This description applies exactly to some of Viadana's *Concerti*. In the majority of those written for four voices à *voci pari* (*Cantus, Altus, Tenor, Bassus*), as in the example 'O sacrum convivium' given at the end of the present section, the four-part harmony is more or less continuous—and in such cases Viadana would probably have approved the use of the pedals (at the discretion of the Organist) throughout—but, in other cases, sections in four-part harmony (*ripieni*) alternate with passages for a single voice. In the *concerto* 'Dic Maria' the words 'Dic Maria quid vidisti Contemplando crucem Christi, Lachrymosis oculis?' are sung by all four voices as a Chorus, which is sung five times in all, each repetition being preceded by a Solo for each of the four voices in succession, each Solo differing from the other in words and music. Thus the scheme of the *concerto* (A, b, A, c, A, d, A e, A) foreshadows that of the old Rondo. The *concerto* 'Diei solennia' consists of a Tenor solo, each phrase of which is repeated by the Chorus of four voices. In this single instance the alternation between Solo and Chorus is indicated below the *Bassus continuus* by the words (variously abbreviated) *Vodo* ('empty') and *Ripieno* ('full'). There are six strophes, and, in the last, a *Coda* is added in which the Soloist co-operates with the Quartet. The scheme of the *concerto* 'Congregati sunt inimici nostri' is almost the same as that of 'Dic Maria', the only difference being that the intervals between the Chorus and its repetition are not allotted to a single voice only.

These instances will suffice to make the meaning of Viadana's rule perfectly clear.

No directions are given for the use of the pedals in the *concerti* for a single voice, or those for two and three voices, but there is nothing in the rule under discussion to suggest that Viadana would have disapproved of their occasional employment when the occasion seemed to demand it, as, for instance, to enable the right hand to take its chords in a low position, if desired, without overlapping the Bass (as in the last bar of Ex. 14), or for some special effect.

(8) "Every care has been taken in assigning the accidentals ✗ ♮ ♭ where they occur, and the prudent Organist will therefore see that he observes them."

Viadana's use of the accidentals demands detailed consideration. It may first be mentioned incidentally that, although, in the above rule, he includes *B quadro* ♮ (which at that time was used only in connexion with the substitution of *B* natural for *B* flat), in actual practice—so far, at least, as the *Bassus continuus* is concerned— he almost (if not quite) invariably uses the *diesis* (or *signum cancellatum*) ✗ to con- tradict the ♭ in the key-signature, the only key-signatures (*chiavi* ='clefs') then in use being those *with a* ♭ (*per B molle*) and *without a* ♭ (*per B quadro*) respectively.

The use of the accidentals ✗ ♭ in a line with the note to which they apply (as they are used to-day) need not detain us. It is with those *above* the Bass that we are concerned.

In the first place, Viadana uses ✗ ♭ to indicate that the Third (or Tenth) above the Bass is accidentally sharpened or flattened, as the case may be. Instead of being placed above the stave, directly over the note, as in later Basses, and also in those of Peri, Caccini, and Cavalieri which appeared in 1600 (cf. §§ 5–8), the accidental was placed well to the *left* of the note (probably to give more room, as the *signum cancel- latum* was often of liberal dimensions) and *exactly a Third* (or, very rarely, a Tenth)

above it, as  . This position was the usual one in the

earlier Basses.

In Viadana's *concerti* misprints occur on almost every page. The accidental is often printed in a line with the note, instead of a Third above it, or otherwise mis- placed. Very frequently, too, it is omitted altogether.

It has hitherto been tacitly assumed that, in Viadana's *concerti*, the accidental above the Bass applied only to the Third (or Tenth). A careful examination, the results of which were given in letters to the *Musical Times* of July and September 1922, has, however, convinced the present writer that such is not the case.

In several instances a sharpened *Sixth* is undoubtedly indicated, as in the following examples, in which irrelevant voice parts are omitted:

'Sanctorum meritis' (*Cantus, Altus, Tenor, Bassus*), bar 13.

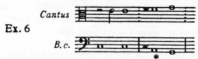

Ex. 4

'O dulcis amor Jesu' (2 *Cantus, Altus*, and *Bassus*), *ad init.*

Ex. 5

'Domine Jesu Christe' (*Cantus, Altus, Tenor, Bassus*), bars 6, 7.

Ex. 6

In none of these three Exx. (taken from Stein's edition of 1613) is the accidental exactly in the place in which we might expect to find it, namely, a Sixth above the note. In Exx. 4, 5 it is a Fifth, and in Ex. 6 a Third above the Bass. Nevertheless Viadana's intention seems fairly evident.

· Adriano Banchieri, in his *L'Organo suonarino*, 1605, and Galeazzo Sabbatini, in his *Regola facile, &c.*, 1628 (cf. § 17, III g 9), both mention the practice of using ✗ and ♭ to indicate an accidentally sharpened or flattened Sixth; but, according to them, the accidental is, in such a case, to be placed on the left of the bass note, *a Third below it*—obviously as the inversion of the Sixth (or Thirteenth) above. Sabbatini mentions this usage as being already (1628) nearly obsolete: 'but now this rule is observed by practically no one (*quasi da niuno*), and no distinction is made between accidentals beside the notes and those below them'.

Banchieri's rules for the use of the accidentals, given in the form of an introductory note (*Avvertimenti alle Guide del Basso tra l' Organo et Choro*) 'for such Organists as have not much knowledge of the middle parts', are as follows:

'Prima, quando saranno antecedenti alla nota seguente nell' istesso luoco, seruono alla detta nota.

'Secõda, q̃do saraño antecedẽti alla nota seguẽte una terza sopra, seruono alle terze, ouero Decime.

'Terza, q̃do saraño antecedẽte alla nota seguẽte una terza sotto, seruono alle seste, o Terzedecime.'

('Firstly, when they precede the following note on a level with it [lit. "in the same position"], they apply to the said note.

'Secondly, when they precede the following note a Third above it, they apply to the Thirds or Tenths.

'Thirdly, when they precede the following note a Third below it, they apply to the Sixths or Thirteenths.')

'Alla nota'   'Alla 3. ouero 10.'   'Alla Sesta o 13.'

Banchieri does not, however, always adhere to the notation prescribed in the third of the above rules.

In the second (considerably enlarged) edition of *L' Organo suonarino* (*Venetia, Amadino*, 1611) the author includes a *Dialogo musicale*, an imaginary conversation with a friend who craves enlightenment on the subject of playing from a *Basso continuo*. In it Banchieri gives an example (cf. § 13, Ex. 13) in which two accidentally altered Sixths † † occur:

Ex. 7

It will be observed that the accidental is placed, contrary to his own rule, *above* the bass note, as in the examples from Viadana, and, moreover, that it is placed a Third (instead of a Sixth) above, as in Ex. 6.

No example seems to occur in Viadana's *Concerti* of a ♭ indicating an accidentally flattened Sixth.

On the other hand, a ♭ is there used in a manner which, so far as the present writer has been able to ascertain, is unique, namely, to indicate a diatonic Sixth, *major* as well as minor, as at * in the following examples, in which it will be observed that the harmony indicated is sometimes $\frac{6}{3}$ and sometimes $\frac{6}{4}$, also that the usual position of the ♭ is a *Third* above (and to the left of) the bass note. Irrelevant voice parts are omitted.

Exx. 8, 9 also show ✗ as the indication of a sharpened Sixth † †. In Ex. 8 the ✗ is level with the bass note, and in Ex. 9 a Third above it.

'Peccaui super numerum' (*Cantus solus vel Tenor*), bars 26 and 27.

Cantus

Ex. 8

B.c.

'Verbum iniquum' (*Altus* and *Bassus*). 11 bars from end.

'Congratulamini' (*Tenor solus*), bar 6 sq.

'Montes Gelboae' (*Cantus* and *Bassus*), bars 22 and 23.

'Montes Gelboae' (*Cantus* and *Bassus*), *ad fin.*

'Ave hostia salutaris' (*Tenor solus*), bars 9 sq.

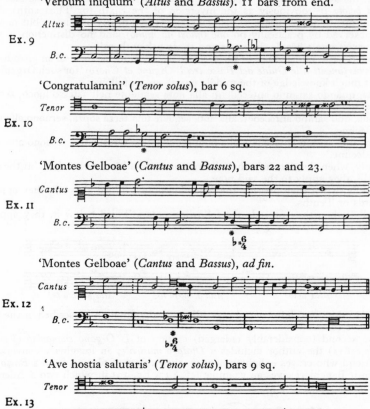

The question now arises, how this apparently irrational usage is to be explained. It would not be unreasonable to use a ♭ to indicate a *minor* Sixth, even though diatonic, but it seems *prima facie* impossible that it should have been deliberately used (as in Exx. 8, 9, 10) to indicate a *major* Sixth. And yet there can be no manner of doubt as to the connexion between the ♭ and the Sixth!

The most probable explanation seems to be that *what Viadana wrote was not ♭, but the figure* 6, which, on account of its rare occurrence, the printer mistook for ♭.

At that time ♭ was often, as e.g. in Cavalieri's *Rappresentatione* (cf. § 8), rounded at the bottom, and so hardly distinguishable from the letter *b* from which it took its origin. This would considerably facilitate confusion with the figure 6.

It is abundantly evident that little or no trouble was taken with the correction of proofs, so that it is not particularly surprising that the error should not have been discovered.

What is really remarkable is that Viadana should have chosen to indicate a Sixth in a few isolated instances, and not in others; for, besides the instances of ♭ = 6 given above, only three more have so far come to light in the *Cento concerti*, making twelve in all. But the fact remains!

(9) "The Organ part (*Partitura*) is never under any obligation to avoid two Fifths or two Octaves, but those parts which are sung by the voices are."

A rule of similar purport is to be found in Guidotti's introduction to Cavalieri's *Rappresentatione* (cf. § 8, 1). Instances of the practice indicated will be found in the penultimate bar of the example in § 10 *c*, also in § 11, Ex. 3 (cf. ibid., note 10); see also § 13, note 4, and § 15, *sub* Ex. 3 *a*, N.B. (4).

In spite of Viadana's reservation in favour of the voice parts, consecutives are to be found. The following example (in which the irrelevant voice parts are omitted) exhibits Octaves between the *Cantus* and *Bassus continuus* and Fifths between the latter and the *Altus*:

'Exultate iusti', *à voci pari* (bar 9 of the section in ₵ time).

(10) "If any one should want to sing this kind of music without Organ or Clavier (*Manacordo* [12]), the effect will never be good; on the contrary, for the most part, dissonances will be heard.

(11) "In these Concertos Falsettos will have a better effect than natural Sopranos; because boys, for the most part, sing carelessly, and with little grace, likewise because we have reckoned on distance to give greater charm; there is, however, no doubt that no money can pay a good natural Soprano; but there are few of them.

(12) "When one wants to sing a Concerto written in the four usual parts (*à voci pari* [13]), the Organist must never play high up, and, vice versâ, when one wants to sing a Concerto of high pitch (*all' alta*), the Organist must never play low down, unless it be in cadences in the Octave; because it then gives charm."

Of those who have quoted and commented on the above rules no one seems to have called attention to what, at first sight, looks like a contradiction between Rules 4 and 12. In the former Viadana expressly enjoins that the 'cadence' (Tonic, leading note, Tonic) in the accompaniment should be 'in its proper place', namely, in the same 'place' as in the voice part. In Rule 12 he speaks of a cadence 'in the [lower] Octave' as 'giving charm'. From this we must infer (unless we are to assume that Viadana contradicted himself) that Rule 4 refers primarily (except in the case of a Bass) not so much to the *pitch* of the notes in question as to their *position* in the chord (cf. note on Rule 4), for we gather from Rule 12 that Viadana would not object to, but would rather commend, such an accompaniment as the following, in which the 'cadence' in the Organ part is an Octave below the voice (or Cornetto), but is *in the Cantus part*, and, therefore, 'in its proper position'. The following Ex. forms the conclusion of the Concerto 'Accipite et manducate': [14]

Ex. 14

hoc fa - ci - te in me - am commemora - ti - o - - - - - - - - - nem.

---

[12] The word *manacordo* is apparently a corruption of *monocordo*, altered in conformity with an imaginary derivation from the Latin *manus*. The French equivalent is *manicordion*.

[13] The term *à voci pari* is applied by Viadana only to the Concertos for *Cantus, Altus, Tenor, Bassus* (cf. § 1, *ad fin.*).

[14] In the original the Cantus part (unbarred as always) is given as above; the

Most of the eighteenth-century treatises on figured Bass mention *e* or *f* (only one or two at the latter end of the century go as far as $\sharp f$ or even *g*) as the upward limit of the compass of the accompaniment, except when a C-clef is used in the Bass, and it seems as though Viadana's approval of a cadence an Octave below a high voice were based on a similar practice.

We shall see later (cf. § 10 *b*) that Viadana's views on the treatment of the accompaniment, when a high voice was singing, were not shared by all his contemporaries.

Appended is the original Italian version of Viadana's Twelve Rules, followed by six specimens of his *Concerti*. The latter are taken from Stein's reprint of 1613 (Brit. Mus., D. 212. c). One or two obvious misprints have been corrected, but, by the kindness of Professor Francesco Vatielli, Librarian of the *Liceo Musicale* at Bologna, all doubtful readings have been collated with the 4th impression (Vincenti, Venice, 1605) of Op. 12.

App. I

"Et prima, che questa sorte di Concerti deve cantarsi gentilmête con discretione, & leggiadria, usando gli accenti con ragione, & passaggi con misura, & a' suoi lochi: soura tutto non aggiungendo alcuna cosa piu di quello che in loro se ritrova stampato, percioche vi sono tal hora certi Cantanti, i quali, perche si trovano favoriti dalla natura d' un poco di gargante, mai cantano nella maniera che stanno i Canti, non si accorgendo essi, che hoggidi questi tali non sono grati, anzi sono pochissimo stimati, particolarmente in Roma, dove fiorisce la vera professione del cantar bene.

"Secondo, che l' Organista sia in obligo di sonar semplicemente la Partitura, & in particolare con la mano di sotto; & se pure vuol far qualche movimento dalla mano di sopra, come fiorire le cadenze, ò qualche Passaggio à proposito, ha da sonare in maniera tale, che il cantore, ò cantori non vengano coperti, ò confusi dal troppo movimento.

"Terzo, Sarà se non bene, che l' Organista habbia prima data un' occhiata à quel Concerto, che si ha da cantare, perche intendendo la natura di quella Musica, farà sempre meglio gli accompagnamenti.

"Quarto, Sia auuertito l' Organista di far sempre le cadenze à i lochi loro, come sarebbe à dire, se si cantarà un Concerto in voce sola di Basso, far la cadenza di Basso, se sarà di Tenore, far la cadenza di Tenore: se di Alto, ò Canto à i lochi dell' uno, e dell' altro, perche farebbe sempre cattivo effetto, se facendo il Soprano la sua cadenza, l' Organo la facesse nel Tenore, overo cantando uno la cadenza del Tenore, l' Organo la sonasse nel Soprano.

"Quinto, che quando si trovarà un Concerto, che incominci à modo di fuga, l' Organista anch' egli cominci con un Tasto solo, e nell' entrar che faranno le parti, sia in suo arbitrio l' accompagnarle come le piacerà.

"Sesto, che non si è fatta l' Intavolatura à questi Concerti, per fuggir la fatica, ma per rendere piu facile il sonargli à gli Organisti, stando che non tutti sonarebbero all' improviso la Intavolatura, e la maggior parte sonaranno la Partitura per essere piu spedita; però potranno gli Organisti à sua posta farsi detta Intavolatura, che à dirne vero parla molto meglio.

"Settimo, che quando si farà i ripieni dell' Organo, faransi con mani, e pièdi, ma senza aggiunta d' altri registri; perche la natura di questi deboli & delicati Concerti, non sopportano quel tanto romore dell' Organo aperto: oltre che ne i piccioli Concerti hà del Pedantesco.

Bassus continuus is given a Fourth lower, in D minor, with the note: 'Quod si cantatur hic Concertus cum Cornetto Organista per quartam superiorem ludat.' The whole is here given at the higher pitch (as though played on a 'Cornettus' instead of sung) as better illustrating the point at issue. In the last bar the first chord of the accompaniment goes below the Bass, but it will be remembered that Rule 7 prescribes the use of the pedals and, therefore, of 16-ft. tone in the Bass. Bianciardi, in his *Breve Regola,* 1607 (cf. § 11), tells us 'to play the Octaves below the Bass in the cadences' (*nelle cadenze toccar l' ottave sotto il Basso*).

"Ottavo, che si è usata ogni diligenza nell' assegnar tutti gli accidĕti ⚹ ♯ ♭ ove vanno, & che però doverà il prudente Organista haver riguardo à fargli.

"Nono, che non sarà mai in obligo la Partitura guardarsi da due quinte, nè da due ottaue, ma si bene le parti, che si cantano con le voci.

"Decimo, che chi volesse cantare questa sorte di Musica senza Organo, ò Manacordo, non farà buon effetto, anzi per lo piu se ne sentiranno dissonanze.

"Undecimo, che in questi Concerti faranno miglior effetto i Falsetti, che i Soprani naturali; si perche per lo piu i Putti cantano trascuratamente, e con poca gratia, come anco perche si è atteso alla lontananza, per render piu vaghezza; no vi e però dubbio, che non si puo pagare con denari un buon Soprano naturale: ma se ne trovano pochi.

"Duodecimo, che quando si vorrà cantare un Concerto à voci pari, non sonarà mai l' Organista nell' acuto, & all' incontro quando si vorrà cantare un Concerto all' alta, l' Organista non sonarà mai nel graue, se non alle cadenze per ottaua; perche all' hora rende vaghezza."

App. II

I. *Beatae Mariae Magdalenae* (*Voce sola. Bassus*).

** The reading of the Italian edition of 1605 (as also of Stein's reprint) is:

There can be little doubt that the misprint is in the vocal Bass.

II. *Peccaui super numerum (Cantus solus vel tenor).*

[1] The consecutive Fifths between the voice and the *B. c.* are in direct contravention of Viadana's 9th Rule; it is impossible to say whether they are intentional or due to a misprint (see under Rule 9), but the latter is much more probable.

[2] The ✕ should, of course, be in the space above the bass note. In other cases it will be noticed that the accidental denoting the sharpened Third (present in the voice part) is omitted altogether.

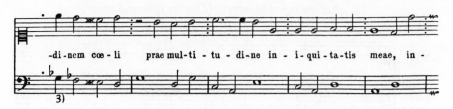

-di -ncm cœ - li   prae mul-ti - tu - di -ne in - i -qui-ta-tis   meae, in -

- i-qui-ta-tis   me -   ae   quo - ·ni-am ir - ri - ta-

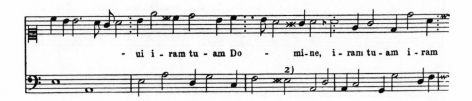

- ui i - ram tu - am Do - mi-ne, i - ram tu - am i - ram

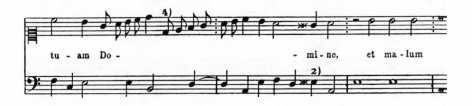

tu - am Do -   - mi - ne,   et ma -lum

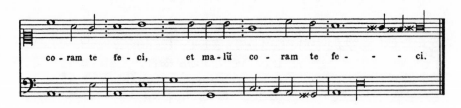

co - ram te   fe - ci,   et ma -lũ   co - ram te fe -   -   ci.

[2] See note 2 on p. 23.
[3] For the use of ♭ = 6 and ✕ = ♯ 6, see under Rule 8.

[4] The reading in the edition of 1605 (and Stein) is   ![notation] &c. , &c.,

with a superfluous quaver ✕.

III. *Sub tuum praesidium* (*A 2 voc. Cantus & Altus*).

* For the ♭ =6 ($^6_4$), see under Rule 8, Ex. 11.

IV. *Laetare Hierusalem (2 Cant. vel 2 Tenor).*

cum laeti - ti-a, laeti-ti - a, qui in tri-sti-ti-a,qui in tri-sti-ti - a fu - i -

- a   ij   qui in tri-sti-ti-a,qui in tri-sti-ti - a fui -

-stis ut   exul-te - tis   et sati - e-mi-ni ab u-be-ri-bus con-so-la-ti-o-nis ue -

- stis ut exul-te - tis   et satie - mi-ni ab u-be-ri-bus con-so-la-ti-o-nis ue -

-strae,ut ex-ul-te - tis ut exul-te - tis   et sature-mi-ni   ij

- strae   ut ex-ul-te - tis ut ex-ul-te - tis   et sature-mi-ni,et sa - tu -

---

[1] In Stein's edition of 1613 the accidental is, by a misprint, placed on the right

of the note:

[2] Almost without a doubt   is here intended, though

it must not always be assumed that the Third is to be sharpened when the Bass rises
a Fourth or falls a Fifth (cf. § 13, Ex. 10).

In similar cases of an ornamentally resolved 4 ♯ 3 suspension Viadana's usual

practice is to place an accidental before the long note only, as

except when the time is slow, as in the last bar of 'Peccaui super numerum' (II).

V. *Fili mi Absalom (A 3 Voc. 2 Cant. & Tenor).*

[3] Probably a misprint (both in the 1605 edition and Stein's reprint of 1613) for

, the accidental being misplaced as mentioned in note 1.

In the case of a repeated note Viadana sometimes repeated the accidental

, and sometimes not.

VI. *O sacrum conuiuium* (*A voci pari*).

§ 5. *The use of figures by the Monodists.*

Mention has already been made (cf. § 1) of the use of figures by Peri, Caccini, and Cavalieri at a date anterior to the publication of the first instalment of Viadana's *Concerti* in 1602, of which the *Basso continuo* is unfigured.

In spite of this priority, however, it is very possible that the composers in question were really followers in the footsteps of Viadana, improving upon their model by the use of figures.

For we learn from Viadana's Preface that some of his *Concerti* were known in Rome some years before their publication in 1602, and that they there found admirers and imitators.

After giving the reason for issuing the work referred to in § 1, Viadana proceeds: "The other, less important, reason . . . which has also made me hasten to publish this my invention is the following: I saw that some of these *Concerti*, which I composed five or six years ago when in Rome (happening then to bethink myself of this new fashion), found such favour with many singers and musicians that they were not only found worthy to be sung again and again . . . , but that some persons actually took occasion to imitate them very cleverly and to print some [of these imitations]." According to this statement Viadana's 'invention' was given to the musical world in 1596–7, and must have been known to Peri, Caccini, and Cavalieri. The question of their possible indebtedness to Viadana would be nearer a solution if we knew what form of accompaniment was provided in Peri's *Dafne*, performed at Florence in 1594 and now, most unfortunately, lost. Be this as it may: in one particular, apart from the use of figures, they certainly consulted the convenience of the accompanist more than Viadana, and that was in printing the voice part over the Bass, thus following the example of Banchieri in his *Spartitura* of 1595, mentioned in § 3.

This practice became very common in Italy. In the case of solos and duets the voice parts were frequently printed over the Bass, which, in such cases, was often left unfigured; where the vocal parts were more numerous, the highest alone was given.[1]

It is probably this form of Bass to which Joh. Staden (cf. § 16, III [5]) refers as follows: "for this purpose [i.e. the proper accommodation of the accompaniment to the pitch of the voices] the scores (*Partituren*) are not ill adapted which are coming into very general use in Italy, in which the vocal parts are given above the Basses, which gives good guidance."

The economy of time and trouble effected by the use of a *Basso continuo* as the basis of the accompaniment must have been far greater in the case of Peri, Caccini, and Cavalieri than in that of Viadana. In the case of the latter, it is true, the Organist, who alone was responsible for the accompaniment, was advised to make an *Intavolatura* for his own use (cf. § 4, Viadana's 6th recommendation). In the case of the *Concerti* for single voices, therefore, he would simply copy out the voice part over the Bass and regulate his harmony accordingly. But Peri and Cavalieri both mention several instruments which took part in the accompaniment, concealed from the audience; and, though Caccini mentions only the Chitarrone as the instrument best adapted for supporting the voice, it is not improbable that he, too, availed himself of similar resources.

If, therefore, the accompaniment were written out for, say, the Cembalo,[2] it would hamper the Chitarrone, on which the chords would be shaped quite differently, whereas a bare indication of the harmony by means of figures, supplemented by the voice part printed above the Bass, leaves either instrument free to shape its accompaniment in accordance with its own peculiar technique.

The figuring of the three Monodists differs from that in use at a somewhat later date, e.g. by Praetorius in 1619 (cf. § 15, Ex. 2 a), in the important particular that compound intervals are denoted in the figuring.[3] The figure

---

[1] Cf. Kinkeldey, *Orgel und Klavier*, p. 205: "After Viadana such Basses occur more frequently, often with a reference in the title to this peculiarity, as e.g. in Girol. Calestani's *Sacrati Fiori musicali à 8 . . . con il Basso continuato, & Soprano ove è stato necessario per maggior commodità de' Sig. Organisti*, Op. 2, Parma (*Viotti*), 1603, or *Cantus et bassus divisio pro organi pulsatore* (Massaini, 1607), *gravis et acutus ad organum* (Dom. Brunetti, 1609)."

[2] Kinkeldey (pp. 157–8) describes a collection of Madrigals for 1, 2, and 3 Sopranos by Luzzasco Luzzaschi with a fully written out accompaniment for a keyed instrument. The collection was published in 1601, but must, as K. proves, have been composed, at latest, in 1597. The two specimens, a madrigal for a single voice and another for two voices, which K. gives in his musical Appendix (pp. 286–95), are full of interest. (Cf. Grove's *Dict. of Music*, 3rd ed., vol. v, p. 82.)

[3] In Caccini's case, however, it was only in the *Nuove Musiche* (1602) that the

3, for instance, always denotes an actual Third from the Bass; if it is to be taken in the Octave above, it is figured 10. The differences in detail between the three composers will be mentioned in the following sections (§§ 6–8). Cavalieri's figuring is singularly mature in comparison with that of his two contemporaries. He freely uses one figure above another (e.g. $\frac{6}{4}$ with its variants $\frac{13}{4}$ $\frac{11}{6}$ $\frac{13}{11}$, &c.), and, in one instance at least, triple figures $\left(\begin{smallmatrix}10\\6\\ \times 4\end{smallmatrix}\right)$. He also occasionally figures passing notes to be included in the accompaniment.

Peri and Caccini, on the other hand, never use one figure above another, or above ♯ or ♭.

This economy of figuring often leaves the accompanist in doubt as to the composer's intention (cf. § 6).

There is, however, one point in which the practice of Peri, Caccini, and Cavalieri, and of Caccini in the *Nuove Musiche*, in particular, deserved to be imitated. Where the harmony changes over a sustained Bass, the latter always indicates the duration of each chord by breaking up the note in question into its component time values, uniting the whole with a slur, which latter is, however, often accidentally omitted.

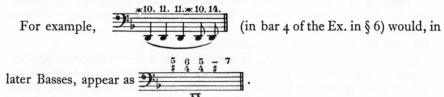

For example, (in bar 4 of the Ex. in § 6) would, in later Basses, appear as .

It is true that, in this particular instance, there could be no doubt as to the composer's intention, but there are many cases [4] where Caccini's method might well have been adopted.

figuring of compound intervals was adopted. In Caccini's *Euridice* (1600), of which only a modern reprint by Ricordi has been available for reference, the highest number in use appears to be 7.

[4] For example: when three figures occurred in succession over a note of duple value, it became an accepted convention that half of that value belonged to the first figure  .

Similarly, when two figures occurred over a note of triple value, two-thirds of that value normally belonged to the first figure .

If the composer desired something different, he could either put a small stroke (very liable to omission or obliteration) after the figure the duration of which was to be prolonged ; or, in the case of three successive figures, he could

place the last figure at a distance from the first two , in which case he was even more at the mercy of copyist and printer (cf. Ph. Em. Bach, *Versuch &c.*, Pt. 2, Ch. I, §§ 47–8, from whom these Exx. are taken). In such cases

The three following works all appeared in 1600:

> Peri. 'Le Musiche di Jacopo Peri nobil Fiorentino sopra l' Euridice del Sig. Ott. Rinuccini rappresentato nel Sponsalizio della Christianissima Maria Medici Regina di Francia e di Navarra. Fiorenza, 1600. G. Marescotti' (2nd ed. Venetia Raverii, 1608. Brit. Mus. K. 1. i. 4).

> Caccini. 'L' Euridice composta in musica in stile rappresentativo da Giulio Caccini detto Romano in Firenze appresso Giorgio Marescotti MDC.'

> Cavalieri. 'Rappresentatione di Anima e di Corpo.[5] Nuovamente posta in Musica del Sig. Emilio del Caualliere,[6] per recitar Cantando. Data in luce da Alessandro Guidotti Bolognese. In Roma Appresso Nicolo Mutij l' Anno del Jubileo MDC.'

In 1602 there appeared 'Le Nuove Musiche di Giulio Gaccini detto Romano &c. in Venetia appresso Alessandro Raverii MDCII'.[7]

§ 6. *Peri.*

Peri has himself left us a record of the instruments used for the execution of his figured Bass. In speaking of the performance of his *Euridice* he says in his Preface *A Lettori*: "Il Signor Jacopo Corsi, che tanto spesso hò nominato, sonò un gravicembalo; & il Signor Don Grazìa Montalvo, un Chitarrone; Messer Giouanbattista dal Violino,[1] una Lira grande; e Messer Giovanni Lapi, un Liuto grosso."

He adds the following *Avvertimento*:

'Sopra la parte del basso, il diesis congiunto del 6 dimostra sesta maggiore, e la minore senza diesis; Il quale quando è solo, è contrassegno della terza, ò della decima maggiore: Et il ♭ molle, della terza ò decima minore; e non si ponga mai, se non à quella sola nota, dove è segnato,[2] quantunque piu ne fussero in una medesima corda.'

("Over the Bass a sharp in conjunction with 6 denotes a major Sixth, and, without a sharp [i.e. 6 without a sharp], a minor one. The which [i.e. ♯], when it stands alone, is the sign of the major Third or Tenth: and the ♭, of the minor Third or Tenth; and it [i.e. the ♯ or ♭] is never to be put [i.e. played] save on that note alone on which it is marked,[2] although there may be several of them [i.e. notes] of the same denomination.")

Peri's figuring agrees in the main with that of Caccini and Cavalieri. He Caccini's method would have avoided all possibility of misunderstanding, as follows:

---

[5] Although this work is here mentioned last, it was, in point of fact, performed in February 1600, while Peri's *Euridice* was not performed till December.

[6] According to his own signature, prefixed in facsimile to Mantica's reprint of the work, his name was de' Cavalieri.

[7] The copy of this work in the British Museum (K. 8. h. 14) bears on the colophon the date 1607 and is therefore a reprint with the title-page left unaltered.

[1] Earlier in the Preface Peri speaks of "Messer Giouanbattista Giacomelli, che in tutte le parti della musica eccellentissimo, hà quasi cambiato il suo cognome col Violino, in cui egli è mirabile".

[2] In spite of this rule, in accordance with which an accidental over the Bass, when not repeated, is automatically contradicted, Peri sometimes thinks contradiction necessary, as e.g. on the first note (*g*) of bar 2 of Ex. 3, on which he puts ♭ to contradict ♯ in the previous bar. Similarly, he prefixes ♭ to the first bass note (♭ *b*) in bar 3 of Ex. 2 to contradict ♯ over *g* in bar 1.

does not, however, go beyond 11, whereas in Caccini's *Nuove Musiche* the cadence 11 ♯ 10 14 occurs almost *ad nauseam*, while Cavalieri goes as far as 18.

The following extract, Ex. 1, shows Peri at his best, besides affording a characteristic specimen of his figuring and notation.[3]

Peri's figuring, as will be seen from the following Ex., is often ambiguous owing to the fact that he never uses one figure above another, or above a ♯ or ♭.

Thus, in bars 14 and 15, the dominant Seventh is present in the voice

From Peri's 'Euridice'.

---

[3] In accordance with the custom of his time Peri uses ♯ to contradict ♭, and ♭ to contradict ♯ (cf. Ch. xxiv, 'Varieties of notation', § 2). In the suggested accompaniments, however, ♮ (B *quadratum*) is used in accordance with modern notation.

Euridice, 2nd ed., 1608, pp. 33-4.

part, but, not being specified in the figuring, it is impossible to say whether its inclusion in the accompaniment was intended or not.

This case is of frequent occurrence, as at * in the following Exx. 2–5:

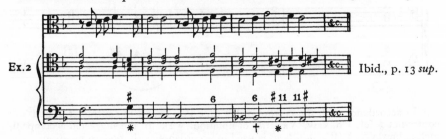

Ibid., p. 13 *sup.*

N.B.—The 6 on ♮ *b* (the 2nd minim † in bar 3) could be taken as $^6_4{}_3$, the 4 being present in the voice part. At a later period it was an accepted convention that 6 on the flat Submediant, falling a semitone to a Triad (or Seventh) on the Dominant, could be taken as $^6_4{}_3$ (cf. Ch. xxi, 'Incomplete figuring', II, § 2).

Ex. 3

Ibid., p. 16 *sup.*

N.B.—The ♮ over *g* † in bar 2 is unnecessary according to Peri's own rule that one never plays an accidental 'except on that note alone on which it is marked'.

Ex. 4

Ibid., p. 16 *sup.*

N.B.—The close, in the suggested accompaniment, a Third above the voice part would, at a later period, not have been considered good, but see § 7, note 3.

Ex. 5

Ibid., p. 17 *sup.*

In all the above Exx. the Seventh in the voice part would, at a later period (when two or more figures, one above the other, were freely used), almost certainly have been included in the figuring, though it would have been at the discretion of the accompanist to omit a discord present in the solo part, even though figured.[4]

[4] A. Werckmeister (*Die nothwendigsten Anmerckungen und Regeln wie der Bassus continuus, oder General-Bass wohl könne tractiret werden &c.* [1st ed., 1698], 2nd ed., 1715, § 70, p. 42) writes:
"Nor is it advisable that one should always blindly play together with the vocalists or instruments the dissonances which are indicated in the Thorough-Bass, and duplicate them. For, when the singer is expressing pleasing sentiment (*einen anmuthigen affectum*) by the dissonance written, a thoughtless accompanist (*General-Bassiste*), if he walk not warily, may spoil the whole pleasing effect with the same

The chief ambiguity of Peri's figuring occurs, however, in the case of 4 3 (with its variants 4 ♯3, 4 ♯, 11 10, 11 ♯10, 11 ♯), and 3 4 4 3 (10 11 11 10) with its variants ♯ 4 4 ♯, &c.

According to later usage, when double (i.e. superimposed) or even triple figures were in common use, 4 3 could only mean $\frac{5\;-}{4\;3}$, and one is therefore predisposed so to interpret Peri's 4 3 (11 10), as e.g. in the last bar of Ex. 5. But it may equally well stand for $\frac{6\;5}{4\;3}$. In the absence of guidance from the voice part personal taste alone must decide.

The common formula 3 4 4 3 (10 11 11 3) is also ambiguous. Normally it stands for $\frac{5\;6\;5\;-}{3\;4\;4\;3}$ (as in bar 15 of Ex. 1, in the last bar of Ex. 2, and in Ex. 4 where the 6 of the $\frac{6}{4}$, occurring in the voice part, makes the progression clear), and, at a later period, it was commonly expressed by three figures only, 3 4 3, &c. (cf. Ch. xxi, 'Incomplete figuring', v, § 1).

As used by Peri, however, there can be little doubt that it is sometimes (e.g. in the 14th and, perhaps, the 4th and 10th bars of Ex. 1) to be interpreted as $\frac{5\;----}{3\;4\;4\;3}$, a weak progression which, so far as the writer is aware, is not recognized in any treatise on figured Bass, but which frequently occurs at an earlier period, as e.g. in the works of the Elizabethan Composers in England.[5]

---

dissonance; therefore the figures (*Signaturen*) and dissonances are not always put in in order that one should just blindly play them (so *crasse mitmache*), but one who understands composition can see by them what the author's idea is, and avoid countering them with anything whereby the harmony would be impaired."

This rule, which is a most important one, has in no subsequent treatise been more clearly or concisely expressed. Niedt gives a more general rule (cf. § 25, III. 6, Reg. 8).

[5] The progression was used by Cavalieri (cf. § 8). The following examples from other composers are taken from the musical Appendix to Kinkeldey's *Orgel und Klavier in der Musik des 16. Jahrhunderts*, pp. 282 and 306–12:

Felice Anerio, 'Jesu mi dulcissime', *Canzonette a tre et quattro voci composte da diversi ecc^{mi} Musici Raccolta da Simone Verovio &c.*, Roma, 1586.

(words omitted)

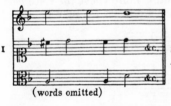

Antonio Arčhilei, *Intermedio* (voice part omitted).

Ibid.

N.B.—Four other examples occur in the same piece:

Luca Marenzio, *Intermedio*, Sinfonia à 5 (given in score in the original).

N.B.—The last three Exx. are from *Intermedii e concerti fatti per la Commedia rappresentata in Firenze nelle Nozze del Serenissimo Don Fernando Medici, e Madama Christiana da Loreno, Gran Duchi di Toscana*, Venetia (Vincenti), 1591.

Two points of especial interest in Ex. 1 are:

(1) The dominant minor Ninth (♭ *b*), on the first crotchet of bar 4, which does not resolve but leaps to another interval of the chord.

(2) The clash, on the fifth crotchet of bar 10, between ♮ *f* in the voice part and *e* in the accompaniment.

If the accompaniment in bar 4 be played in four parts, there is also a clash between the minor Ninth (♭ *b*) and the note of resolution (*a*) which would be present in the accompaniment at the same time.

Whether Peri approved this clash, and that in bar 10, or whether he intended them to be avoided by a (temporarily) 3-part accompaniment (Ex. 6 **)

it is impossible to say with certainty, but the former alternative seems the more probable.[6] It was an age of experiment and revolt against established rules.

Indeed, even if the ♯ 11 11 ♯ were, in both cases, taken as $^5_♯{^6_4}{^5_-}{^-_♯}$, the resulting clash between the *e* in the voice part

and the *f* in the $^6_4$ chord would have a parallel in the following example from Monteverde:[7]

[6] The following is another characteristic example of a clash between the voice and the accompaniment, which proceeds to a new harmony, while the voice, as in bar 10, lingers on a note * belonging to the preceding one.

o.c., p. 21, 2nd line.

[7] *Lamento d'Arianna*, arranged by the composer as a 5-part Madrigal (*Sixth Book of Madrigals*, Venice, 1614, Amadino) from his original setting of Rinuccini's *Arianna* (now, unfortunately, lost except for the *Lamento*, which is preserved in an anonymous collection, *Il maggio fiorito*, Orvieto, 1623) and quoted in part by Sir Hubert Parry in vol. iii of the *Oxford History of Music* (p. 47).

The resulting discord, $\frac{6}{5}$, is the same in both cases, the difference being that, in Monteverde's case, the *e* is held on from a harmony in which it is concordant, instead of being taken unprepared.

The same discord is used by Cavalieri (§ 8, Ex. 14, bar 8) in exactly the same way as by Monteverde.

§ 7. *Caccini.*

Caccini's *Euridice* has not been available for reference, but some slight evidence bearing on his method of accompaniment is to be found in the *Nuove Musiche*.

The instrument which he preferred for the performance of the figured Bass was, evidently, the Chitarrone, a form of bass Lute. In the Preface 'Ai Lettori' he speaks of 'il Basso per lo Chitarrone', and, again, of a person 'chi fa professione di cantar solo sopra l'armonia di Chitarrone, ò di altro strumento di corde', while, in the following extract, with which he concludes his Preface, he speaks of the Chitarrone as 'best suited to accompany the voice, and particularly the Tenor voice'.

"Conciosiache io habbio costumato in tutte mie musiche, che son fuori in penna di dinotare per i numeri sopra la parte del Basso le terze, e le seste maggiori ove è segnato il diesis, e minori il b molle, e similmente che le settime, ò altre dissonanze siano per accompagnamento delle parte di mezzo, resta ora il dire, che le legature nella parte del Basso in questa maniera sono state usate da me, perche doppo la consonanza si ripercuota solo la corda segnata, essendo ella la piu necessaria (se io non erro) nella propria posta del Chitarrone, e la piu facile da usarsi, e da farsi pratica in essa, essendo questo strumento piu atto ad accompagnare la voce, e particolarmente quella del Tenore, che qualunque altro; lasciando nel rimanente in arbitrio di che piu intende, il ripercuotere con il Basso quelle corde, che possono essere di migliore intendimento loro, ò che piu accompagnaranno la parte, che canta sola, non si potendo fuori della intavolatura per quanto io conosco descriverlo con piu facilità."

("Inasmuch as I have been accustomed, in all my musical works which have appeared, to indicate by figures over the Bass part the major Thirds and Sixths where a sharp is marked, and the minor ones where there is a flat, and, in the same way, [to indicate] that Sevenths and other discords should be included in the accompaniment (lit. 'should be in the intermediate parts [i.e. the parts between the voice and the Bass] as accompaniment'), it now remains to be said that the ties in the Bass part have been used by me, because, after the consonance [i.e. the chord on the first of the tied notes in the Bass, whether consonant or dissonant] only the note figured is to be

struck again, it being (if I mistake not) the most necessary one on the Chitarrone in the particular capacity of the latter, and the easiest to use and put
into effect, that instrument being more fitted to accompany the voice, and
particularly the Tenor voice, than any other; for the rest, I leave it to the
discretion of the more intelligent to strike afresh, together with the Bass,
such notes as may accord with their better judgment, or as shall more
adequately accompany the solo voice part, as one cannot, so far as I know,
give any clearer directions, except by the use of Tablature.")

Caccini's figuring exhibits the same disadvantages as that of Peri, owing
to the fact that he never used one figure above another, or above ♯ or ♭.
Thus, in the penultimate bar of the following Ex., 11 stands for $\frac{6}{4}$, and, in
the last bar, for $\frac{5}{4}$. Similarly, though 7 (14) is present in the voice part on
the first beat of the penultimate bar, it is impossible to know whether Caccini
desired its inclusion in the accompaniment, as it would have involved the
figuring $_{\sharp}\,^{14}_{10}$:

-seria in-au-di - ta Non poter dir à voi mo - ro mia vi - ta

O   mi-seria in - au - di - - - ta

Non po-ter dir à   voi mo-ro mia, vi - ta, Non   po-ter dir à voi   mo -

- - ro mia vi - - ta,   mo - ro

mia   vi - - - - - - ta

‡10 11   ‡10   11   11 ‡10 14

Nuove Musiche (reprint 1607), p. 23.

N.B.—For the false relations in the suggested accompaniment (in bars 2–3, 16–17, and 18) compare the following Exx. from Staden's *Kurzer und einfältiger Bericht &c.*, 1626 (cf. § 16, Ex. 3 *b ad fin.*).

It will be noticed that, in the Bass, Staden uses ♮ to contradict ♭, but ♭ to contradict ♯ (cf. § 6, note 3, and § 17, III *g* (2)).

In the foregoing Ex. there are several interesting points to be noticed:

(1) The use of suspended discords apparently unprepared.

On the first beat of bar 14 (and in the parallel passage in bar 20) the suspended *g* in the accompaniment, 11 in the 11 ‡10 ($= \frac{5}{4} \frac{}{{}^{\sharp}3}$) suspension, is taken unprepared as a changing (i.e. accented passing) note or appoggiatura.

Ph. Em. Bach (*Versuch &c.*, Pt. 2, ch. 21, § 7) gives similar examples

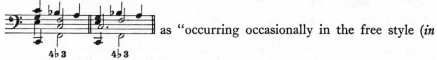

4♭3   4♭3

as "occurring occasionally in the free style (*in der galanten Schreibart*)"; but that was more than 150 years later.

It is, of course, possible that Caccini intended the 11 in question to be prepared by taking the preceding 6 on ♯*c* as $\frac{6}{5}$. He does not seem ever to use the figuring ♭5 (or 5♭) which, at a later period, stood regularly for $\frac{6}{5}$ with diminished Fifth, nor does he ever use one figure above another; in cases like the present, therefore, his intentions must remain a matter for conjecture.

On the third crotchet of bar 11 we find a Seventh (7 ♯6 on *e*) taken without preparation, an instance to which it would be difficult to find a parallel in any of the authoritative treatises on Figured Bass of the eighteenth century. Here, again, it is possible that the preceding Bass note *d**, instead of being taken as a passing note, was intended to bear a $\substack{\natural 6 \\ 4}$ chord, thus preparing the 7 on *e*.

6        $\begin{bmatrix} \natural 6 \\ 4 \end{bmatrix}$ 7   ♯6

Caccini would, as in other cases, presumably have figured such a $^{\natural 6}_4$ chord 4 or 11 (in the present instance 11), and the omissions in his figuring are so frequent [1] that the absence of the figure, in itself, counts for little; yet, on the whole, it seems more probable that he intended the 7 on *e* to be taken unprepared.

(2) Caccini showed great freedom in the clashes which sometimes occur between the voice part and the accompaniment.

In bar 4 the clash between *e* in the voice part 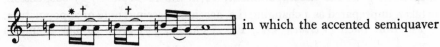 and *f* in

the $^6_4$ chord in the suggested accompaniment can, of course, be avoided by taking the $\sharp$10 11 on *a*, not as $^{5\,6}_{\sharp\,4}$, but as $^{5\,-}_{\sharp\,4}$, as was tentatively done in the suggested accompaniment in bars 4 and 10 of Ex. 1 in § 6. In the present case, however, it seems even less probable that this was intended.

In bar 17 the clash between *c* in the voice part and $\natural$ *b* in the Bass (on the 6th crotchet of the bar) is exactly parallel with that in the Ex. from Peri's *Euridice* quoted in § 6, note 6.

Bar 16 is of especial interest. The $\natural$ *b* in the voice part shows that the $7\,\sharp\,6$ suspension on *e* is, not $^7_3\,^{\sharp\,6}_-$, but $^7_3\,^7_5$ resolving on $^{\sharp\,6}_5$, the first inversion of $^7_5$ on the temporary leading note $\sharp$ *c* (cf. Ch. xi, 'Sevenths', III, § 2, and Ch. xii, '$^6_5$ chords', § 4).

The $^{\sharp\,6}_{\natural\,5}$ on *e* resolves directly on the Triad of *d*, the consecutive 5ths $^{\natural b\;a}_{e\;d}$ being escaped by the ornamental resolution in the voice part, $\natural$ *b g a*.

The chief interest, however, is in the boldness of the voice part

in which the accented semiquaver

c* is entirely alien to the harmony, while *a* ††, on which the voice dwells so insistently, is an anticipation of the final resolution of $\natural$ *b*.

(3) In the full closes in bars 4–5, 14, 20–1, and 23 the accompaniment, in each case, closes, in accordance with Caccini's figuring, a Third above the voice part.

At a later period this would not have been considered good. Ph. Em. Bach (*Versuch &c.*, Pt. 2, ch. 2, § 36) gives the following rule:

"In closes the Fifth must never be in the upper part.[2] The Octave is the best interval for the purpose, if it can be managed, and, next to it, the

---

[1] As often as not Caccini omits the 6 over a leading note (as in bars 1 and 12, &c.) as well as in the case of the first inversion of the tonic Triad (as on the third crotchet of bar 13). This omission is a regular feature of most of the earlier Italian figured Basses (cf. Ch. xxi, 'Incomplete figuring', III, § 4). He also constantly omits $\sharp$ over the Bass where it is given in the voice part (as on the first and last notes of bar 15).

[2] In the earlier part of the eighteenth century this had not become an established rule. G. Ph. Telemann in his *Singe-, Spiel- und General-Bass-Übungen*, Hamburg, 1733 (reprinted 1914, Berlin, Liepmannssohn), expressly permits full closes in the accompaniment with the Fifth in the upper part (No. 16 *c*, cf. No. 12 *ad fin.*). On the other hand, twelve years earlier, J. Mattheson, who, in 1721, edited a second edition of Niedt's *Handleitung zur Variation, wie man den General-Bass und darüber gesetzte Zahlen variiren, artige Inventiones machen und aus einem schlechten General-Bass Preludia, Ciaconen, Sarabanden, Menueten, Giguen und dergleichen leichtlich verfertigen könne &c.* (1st ed., Hamburg, 1706), finds it necessary, as he explains in a note, to correct Exx. in which Niedt has used the ending in question.

Third; but the final note of the principal part must not be lower than this Third." [3]

§ 8. *Cavalieri.*

(1) Cavalieri's *Rappresentatione di Anima e di Corpo*, edited, in token of gratitude for favours received, by his admirer Alessandro Guidotti of Bologna, has fortunately been reproduced in facsimile and re-edited by Francesco Mantica, with an introductory essay by Domenico Alaleona (Rome, casa editrice Claudio Monteverdi, 1912).

In the original preface Guidotti enumerates the instruments to be used for the accompaniment: "una Lira doppia, un Clavicembalo, un Chitarone, ò Tiorba che si dica, insieme fanno buonissimo effetto: come ancora un Organo suave con un Chitarone.[1] El il Signor Emilio laudarebbe mutare stromenti conforme all'affetto del recitante." The last sentence is particularly interesting as showing how much was left to the discretion and taste of the accompanists. "Signor Emilio [Cavalieri] would commend a change of instruments in conformity with the sentiment of the person reciting", but the details are left to the players.

An interesting fact regarding the accompaniment was brought to light through the discovery by Domenico Alaleona of an original copy of the *Rappresentatione* in addition to the two which were previously known to be in existence—the one in the Biblioteca di Santa Cecilia in Rome, and the other in the University Library at Urbino.

The copy in question was found (catalogued under the name of Guidotti) in the library of the Vallicella, where the first performance of the work took place in February 1600.

The word '*Tiorba*' inscribed on the first page shows that the said copy was appropriated to that instrument, and the word '*Tace*', prefixed to all the solo numbers, proves that the latter was employed only when several voices were singing, and, of course, in the 'Symphonies' and *Ritornelli*.

Cavalieri did not, therefore, agree with Caccini in regarding the Theorbo or Chitarrone as the most fitting accompaniment for a voice, "and particularly the Tenor voice" (cf. § 7).

(2) In the directions (*Avvertimenti*) which follow the Preface Guidotti mentions that 'the Symphonies and *Ritornelli* can be played with a great number of instruments', and also that 'a Violin playing the upper part note for note (*per l'apunto*) will have an excellent effect'.

He further explains the letters g, m, t, z, sometimes prefixed to notes in the voice parts, by the following example:

It will be noticed that the *groppolo* differs from the *trillo* in finishing with

---

[3] G. Ph. Telemann, in the work referred to in note 2, frequently has closes in the accompaniment with the Third in the upper part, above the voice.

[1] Cf. § 10 *a*, note 3.

a turn, and that both differ from the normal German shake of the eighteenth century, in beginning with the main note.

After warning both singers and players that *fa* must never be changed to *mi*, or *mi* to *fa*,[2] without express indication, and that the *diesis* ✕ raises only the note to which it is actually prefixed, even if other notes of the same denomination follow,[3] Guidotti gives the following brief rules for the interpretation of the figures, &c.:

[1] "Li numeri piccoli posti sopra le note del Basso continuato per suonare, significano la Consonanza, ò Dissonanza di tal numero: come il 3 terza: il 4 quarta: & cosi di mano in mano.

[2] "Quando il diesis ✕ è posto avanti, overo sotto [4] di un numero, tal consonanza sarà sostentata: & in tal modo il b molle fa il suo effetto proprio.

[3] "Quando il diesis posto sopra le dette note non è accompagnato con numero, sempre significa Decima [5] maggiore.

[4] "Alcune dissonanze, & duo quinte sono fatte à posta.[6]

[5] "Il segno ℥ significa incoronata, la qual serve per pigliar fiato, & dar' un poco di tempo à fare qualche motivo."

([1] "The small figures, placed over the notes of the Thorough-Bass to be played, indicate the concord or discord of the figure in question: as 3, a Third, 4, a Fourth, and so on.

[2] "When a sharp ✕ is placed in front of, or underneath [4] a figure, the interval in question will be raised: and, similarly, a flat has the effect belonging to it.

[3] "When a sharp, placed over the said notes, is not accompanied by a figure, it always signifies a major Tenth.[5]

[4] "Some discords, and two Fifths [i.e. consecutive], are taken as occasion demands.[6]

[5] "The sign ℥ indicates the *incoronata*, which is to serve for taking breath and to give time for making some gestures.")

[2] *Fa*, as the fourth note of the *Hexachordum molle*, = ♭ b; *mi*, as the third note of the *Hexachordum durum*, = ♮ b.

[3] Peri gives the same rule (cf. § 6), which it is most important to bear in mind.

[4] It is only in the case of 7⅝ (over the same bass note) that Cavalieri places the *signum cancellatum* ✕ (which represented the sharp till well on in the eighteenth century) *below* the figure to which it applies. This practice, which is evidently due to economy of lateral space, is quite contrary to the usage which became firmly established at a very early date, in accordance with which a sharp in a similar position always denotes the major Third (Tenth or Seventeenth) from the Bass :

[5] This rule appears to be peculiar to Cavalieri; in Peri's and Caccini's Basses ✕, unaccompanied by a figure, sometimes evidently indicates a Third rather than a Tenth. Guidotti gives no corresponding rule for a ♭ unaccompanied by a figure, but the same principle holds good; Cavalieri generally uses the full figuring ♭10, but when ♭ stands alone over the Bass it always represents ♭10, never ♭3.

[6] The expression 'Alcune dissonanze' ('Some discords') probably refers chiefly to the dominant Seventh, which, according to the later established practice, might always be added in a full close, even though not indicated in the figuring (cf. Ch. xxi, 'Incomplete figuring', II, § 5). With regard to the 'duo quinte' ('two [consecutive] Fifths') compare Viadana's 9th recommendation in § 4.

(3) It has already been mentioned (cf. § 5) that, in his figuring, Cavalieri is far in advance of his contemporaries, Peri and Caccini, chiefly by reason of his use of double (and, in one instance, triple) figures.

But, even so, a good deal of ambiguity would remain, were it not for the part-writing, which affords important clues to the interpretation of Cavalieri's own figuring, while it incidentally sheds valuable light on the ambiguities of Peri and Caccini already alluded to (cf. §§ 6, 7).

Choruses in five and six parts occur, it is true, in Peri's *Euridice* and Caccini's *Nuove Musiche* respectively, but they are *unaccompanied*. The *Rappresentatione*, on the other hand, contains choruses in from four to eight parts, besides instrumental 'symphonies' and *Ritornelli* in four or five parts, all with a figured Bass.

A wider range between the extreme parts of the accompaniment is thus involved, and, whereas the highest figure in Peri's *Euridice* is 11, and, in Caccini's *Nuove Musiche*, 14, Cavalieri goes as far as 18, so that a 4 3 suspension may appear either as 4. 3 (4. ✕3), or 11.. 10 (11. ✕10 or 11. ✕), or 18. 17 (18. ✕17), while a $\frac{6}{4}$ chord appears in no less than five forms, $\frac{6}{4}$, $\frac{13}{4}$, $\frac{11}{6}$, $\frac{13}{11}$, and (in one instance) $\frac{18}{13}$. Curiously enough, the figuring $\frac{6}{5}$ never occurs, though $\frac{12}{6}$ and $\frac{13}{12}$ are common.

In attempting to reconstruct the accompaniments it must be remembered that, as we are entitled to infer from the copy of the *Rappresentatione* discovered by Alaleona, each player had all the parts, printed above the figured Bass, before him. In the choruses and 'symphonies' he could, therefore, if he pleased, disregard the figures and play from the score. In any case he would be enabled to shape his upper part with due consideration for the voice or voices.

(4) It will be remembered that, in Ex. 1 from Peri's *Euridice* (cf. § 6), the figures ✕. 4. 4. ✕ (✕. 11. 11. ✕) were found to be capable of two interpretations, namely, $\frac{5}{\sharp}\frac{6}{4}\frac{5}{4}\frac{-}{\sharp}$, which we will call *Formula* A, and $\frac{5}{\sharp}\overline{\frac{-}{4}\frac{-}{4}}\frac{-}{\sharp}$, which we will call *Formula* B, and, moreover, that it was not always certain which of the two interpretations was the right one.

In Cavalieri's *Rappresentatione* we find, not only A (as in Exx. 1–4) and B (as in Exx. 5 and 6), but a third variant $\frac{5}{\sharp}\frac{4}{4}\frac{5}{-}\frac{-}{\sharp}$ (as in Exx. 7–10), which we will call *Formula* C.

In some cases (as in Exx. 11 and 12) both figuring and score leave us in doubt as to the accompaniment. Ex. 13 presents a variant intermediate between B and C.

In Ex. 14, which is in five parts, we find B combined with C, and also A combined with B with remarkable boldness, exactly as in the example from Monteverde quoted in connexion with Peri (§ 6 *ad fin.*).

Besides those mentioned above, other variants occur, as e. g. in Ex. 15, where Formula B is modified by an ornamental note in the Bass.

Examples may seem to have been unnecessarily multiplied, but a study of their *minutiae* cannot but throw light on the accompaniments to be supplied in the case of Peri and Caccini, in whose Basses there is so much less to guide us to the composer's intentions; and, in such cases, no detail, however trifling it may seem, is unimportant.

Rappresentatione &c., p. xxx, No. 71 *ad fin.*

In bars 4–7 it will be noticed that the third and fourth Sopranos move in Octaves with the instrumental Bass, and that the consecutive Fifths between the extreme parts are very thinly veiled.   *Rappresentatione &c.*, p. v, No. 6.

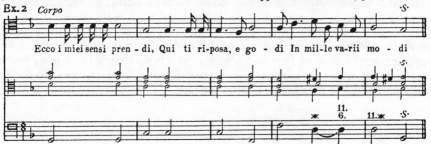

Ex. 3

ibid., p. xvii, No. 28.

Note the slurs in the
figuring 4 4 in bars 2,
4–5, and 7.

Ex. 4

ibid., p. xiv, No. 21.

ibid., p. xii, No. 18 *ad fin.*

Ex. 5

N.B.—In bars 3 and 6 the 13 on ♯ *c* is taken in the suggested accompaniment as though figured $^{13}_6$, the 6 being, in both cases, present in the voice parts. When such is the case, it may be assumed that we are at liberty to treat 13 as $^{13}_6$, for Cavalieri's figuring throughout the entire work points to a close adherence (within certain limits) of the accompaniment to the progression of the principal parts in the choruses and 'symphonies'. In the Soprano solos, too, it is evident that the upper part of the accompaniment is intended to follow the salient points of the voice part, though without, necessarily, always moving in unison with it.

It is in the Tenor Recitatives that the accompaniment is freest. Just as 13 may, upon occasion, be taken as $^{13}_6$, so the converse is sometimes the case. But when the figuring is 6, the 13 must never be added in such a way as to discount the progression of the upper principal part, as in bars 3 and 6 of Ex. 9, or, indeed, unless it is present in the principal parts.

Curiously enough, the figuring $^{13}_6$ occurs only once in the course of the entire work, as follows:

ibid., p. xvii *ad fin.*

ibid., p. xxi, No. 46 *ad fin.*

N.B.—In bar 5 of the 'Basso continuato' (as Guidotti styles it) the first note *d* ✳ is derived from the vocal Tenor, as being, for the moment, the lowest part (cf. § 3).

In bars 5 and 6 the accompaniment might, without any departure from the figuring, be taken as follows:

It may be assumed that the Clavicembalo, 'Organo suave', and Chitarrone (or Theorbo) co-operated in some, if not all, of the Choruses, and, in all probability, they shaped their accompaniment in different ways, so far as the figuring permitted. Viadana's (sixth) recommendation to the Organist to make an *Intavolatura* (cf. § 4)

points, it is true, to a close adherence to the voice parts; on the other hand, Agazzari concludes his treatise on the performance of a *Basso continuo* with a reminder to the Organist that there is no necessity to reproduce the voice parts exactly (cf. § 10 *e ad fin.*).

ibid., p. iiii, No. 2 *ad fin.* (words omitted).

N.B.—The $^{\sharp}_{4}^{9}$ on *e* * in bar 3, indicating passing notes, must not be confused with the suspended $\frac{9}{4} \left(= \frac{9}{5} \atop 4 \right)$ resolving on $\frac{8}{3} \left(= \frac{8}{5} \atop 3 \right)$ (cf. Ch. xvii, § 4).

In later Basses the progression shown in the present Ex. would generally be figured

The figure 9 would not be used, unless it fell a degree to 8, as:

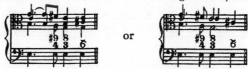

or unless, in rare instances, it was preceded and followed by 10.

It will be noticed that the figuring ⚹. 11. ⚹. in the last bar leaves the accompanist in ignorance, but for the score, as to whether Formula A, B, or C is intended. In the following Ex., as in most other instances in which it occurs, Formula C is clearly indicated.

p. xvi, No. 24, bars 4-5 (words omitted).

Ex. 8

N.B.—The figuring $^{12}_{6}$ may have been intended on $\sharp c$ *, the 12 being present in the Soprano.

ibid., p. xxviii, No. 60.

N.B.—On the last bass note in bar 7 a change is made in the position of the chord ✱ in the suggested accompaniment, in order to gain the position prescribed by the figuring in bar 8. It is, however, doubtful whether Cavalieri would have objected to

the consecutives with the Bass if the accompaniment were as follows :

though Guidotti's sanction of consecutive Fifths does not, like Viadana's, expressly include Octaves.

ibid., p. xx, No. 39.

ibid., p. ix, bar 8 (Sinfonia).   ibid., p. xvii, bar 12 (words omitted).

N.B.—In both of the foregoing Exx. the figuring and the score alike leave us in doubt as to how the second chord is to be taken.

In both cases the 6 of the $\frac{6}{4}$ ($\frac{11}{6}$) which characterizes Formula A is present in the principal parts, if only as a passing note ✱.

On the other hand, in Ex. 11, 4 † and 11 are present simultaneously, which suggests Formula C, and it seems, on the whole, probable that this is what was intended, as it obscures the progression of the first Alto part less than would A.

In Ex. 12 C is equally suitable, though B (as well as A) is possible.

ibid., p. xiii, bar 9.   Ex. 13

N.B.—In Ex. 13, in which the progression of 5 to 4 follows in the wake of that of ♯10 to 11, we have a variant intermediate between the Formulae B and C.

It occurs several times in the course of the number (No. 19), a trio sung by 'Piacere con doi cõpagni' (Pleasure with two companions).

The accompaniment probably followed the voice parts exactly. In default of this, Formula B would be more suitable than C (cf. bar 4 of the next Ex.).

To express the progression as it stands it would have been necessary to figure it as

follows:

ibid., p. ix (Sinfonia) *ad fin.*

N.B.—Ex. 14 contains three interesting features.

In bar 4 we find a combination of the Formulae B and C, B being represented by the three upper parts, and C by the two upper parts and the Tenor; there is, however, no indication in the figuring that the progression of the Tenor is to be represented in the accompaniment.

Similarly, in bar 8, A and B are combined, exactly as in the Ex. from Monteverde quoted at the end of § 6. In accordance with the figuring, A alone is represented in the accompaniment.

In bars 2 and 6 we find a progression which Cavalieri uses very freely, and which is closely analogous to Formula B, the discordant interval, in both cases, rising a semitone from the concord on which it subsequently resolves, with no other change in the harmony.

ibid., Sinfonia, bar 1 sq.

N.B.—In bars 3 and 6 of the above Ex. we have Formula B modified by an ornamental note * in the Bass.

It will be noticed that *f* in the Bass of bar 5 is figured 6, though 13 is present in the score, and 6 *is not*. In the first half of the example the figuring ✕13 on *e* in bar 2 makes it clear that the upper part of the accompaniment is intended to follow the upper instrumental part. If the second half of the Ex. is to follow the same pattern (and no reason is apparent why it should not do so), the 6 on *f* in bar 5 must be taken as $^{13}_{6}$ (cf. note on Ex. 5) as follows:

(5) *Unprepared discords.*

Cavalieri shows remarkable freedom in his use of unprepared discords. Apart from the use of the dominant Seventh, as in the penultimate bar of Ex. 16, either as a passing note (as in the suggested accompaniment) or rising a Third from the Supertonic (as in the voice part), and of its first inversion ($^6_5$ on the leading note) with the diminished Fifth taken unprepared, either by step, as in Ex. 17, or by leap, as in Ex. 18, we find $^6_5$ ($^{13}_{12}$ or $^{12}_6$) on the Subdominant with the 5 (12) unprepared, as in Ex. 19.

The use of the dominant Thirteenth in Ex. 20 is strangely modern.

Like Caccini, Cavalieri sometimes treats the 4 in a 4 3 (11 10) suspension as a free appoggiatura, as at * in Ex. 21.

N.B.—The penultimate bar of Ex. 16 is of special interest as an instance in which the composer has definitely indicated that a dissonance should be taken in a different Octave in the accompaniment from that in which it appears in a principal part. The importance of this point will become apparent later on (cf. Ch. iii, 'The general character of a Figured-Bass accompaniment', § 5, B III *a*). It is, of course, only Cavalieri's practice of indicating compound intervals in the figuring that gives us this important clue to his idea of accompaniment. In later Basses there is nothing to show whether 7 or 14 is intended.

It will be noticed that the 7 in the accompaniment, besides being in a different Octave, does not synchronize with, but follows, the 14 (*c*) in the voice part. This is one of many instances in which the accompaniment of the solo numbers is far more independent than when several principal parts are in operation. In the latter case the figuring follows the score closely.

ibid., p. xv, No. 23, bar 5 sq.

Ex. 16

Tut - te le vos - tre co - se, Che pai-on di - let-to - se, Al fin son tutte a-ma-re;

ibid., p. xiv, No. 20 *ad fin.* (words omitted).

Ex. 17

ibid., p. iii, last line, Ritornello *ad fin.*

Ex. 18

N.B.—The 5 (12) of the $\frac{6}{5}$ ($\frac{13}{12}$) is taken by leap in the Alto part ✳, as well as in the accompaniment.

The progression is a remarkable one in other respects (cf. Ch. xi, 'Sevenths', v, § 4, Ex. 5).

ibid., p. x, No. 17, bar 12 sq. (words omitted).

Ex. 19

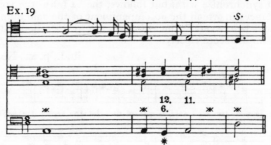

Ex. 20

ibid., p. xxi, No. 43.

Vita Mondana

Oi - - - me che non vor - re - i

N.B.—The arrangement of the figures, ✳X$_{13}$, on *e* is probably due to a misprint. One would expect the ✕ (= ✕10) to be *below* the ✕13.

The stricter accompaniment would, no doubt, be

but it would seriously discount the dramatic effect, and there can be little doubt that Cavalieri intended the chords to follow the voice.

ibid., p. xxxix, No. 89, bar 10 sq.

Ex. 21

Da ter - ra al - - z'a le stel - le.

(6) *Figuring of passing notes.*

In certain cases, ✕ over a note in the Bass indicates, not the major Tenth of a Triad, but a passing note, as in Exx. 22 and 23.

Cavalieri frequently indicates, in the figuring, notes extraneous to the harmony which occur in the principal part or parts, whether in the form of an appoggiatura, as in bar 2 of Ex. 25, or of an unaccented note, as in the following bar of the same Ex.

In Ex. 26 the passing notes indicated in the figuring are independent of the voice.

ibid., p. xxvii, l. 3, last bar sq. (*Sinfonia*).

Ex. 22

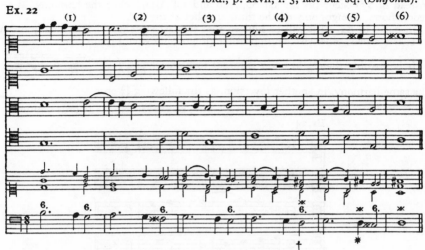

† figured ⚹6. in the original, by an obvious misprint.

N.B.—From the fact that *d* ⚹ in bar 6 is figured ⚹, denoting a passing note, it is probable that in the preceding bars, too, passing notes, following the Bass in Thirds, are meant to be included.

Otherwise, the accompaniment might be

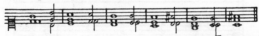

At a later period passing notes like the above were generally left to the discretion

of the accompanist, but such figuring as   is some-

times found.

ibid., p. xix, No. 33.

Ex. 23

N.B.—As in the preceding Ex., ⚹ over *d* ⚹ in bar 2 indicates a passing note and seems to suggest that the accompaniment, as well as the voice, should follow the Bass in Thirds.

Where there are two quick minim beats to the bar, and the Bass moves by step in crotchets, the second and fourth crotchets, if unfigured, 'pass'; that is to say, the preceding harmony remains unaltered (save, possibly, for such passing notes as those above mentioned) and no fresh chord is struck.

In the present case, though the time is obviously slow, there can be little doubt that this is what was intended.

A reference to Ex. 24 will make this clear. The Bass, as far as it goes, is identical with that in the present example, and, in bar 2, the same passing notes (with $\natural f$ instead of $\sharp f$) occur (in the 1st Soprano and 1st Alto), while the harmony, as the score shows, changes only on the third crotchet of the bar.

In bar 6 of Ex. 23 it will be noticed that the last crotchet f † is evidently meant to bear a Triad; otherwise, an impossible progression would result.

It is possible that $^{11}_{\ 6}$ in bar 7 is meant to be taken as $^{6}_{4}\ \left(^{11}_{10}\right)$
$\ _3\ \ \ _6$

the same harmony, in another inversion, as the following $^{13}_{12}$ on *c*.

ibid., p. xxxviii, No. 88 (words omitted).

Ex. 24

N.B.—In bar 2, if desired, passing notes, moving in Thirds with the Bass, could, of course, be included in the accompaniment, as in Ex. 23.

ibid., p. xxi, No. 43.

Ex. 25 *Corpo*

Met-ti giù que-sta spo - glia   C'hò di ve-der-ti vo - glia

N.B.—At * the 9 is a changing (accented passing) note, accompanying the appoggiatura in the voice part.

It may be that 4 on *d* † was intended to be taken as $^{11}_{\ 4}$, as in Exx. 7-10.

ibid., p. x, No. 17 *ad fin.* (words omitted).

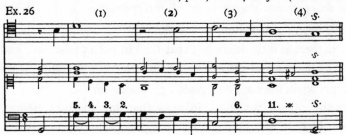

N.B.—The passing notes in the suggested accompaniment, moving in Thirds with the Bass, in bar 2 are, of course, arbitrary.

Those indicated in the figuring in bar 1 occur in the following similar example (ibid., p. v, No. 13 *ad fin.*), which deserves quoting on account of the interesting progression of the Bass.

The omission of *c* after *d* ✳ in bar 2 produces a form of *Transitus ad quartam*,

for , which came later to be recognized as a licence peculiar to the true Allabreve style (cf. Heinichen, *General-Bass in der Composition*, 1728, Pt. 1, cap. 4, §43, p. 338), Ch. xviii, §1 *m*, Ex. 14, note 11. In the present instance it serves to keep the Octaves between extreme parts 'hidden'.

(7) *Special points in Cavalieri's figuring.*

A salient characteristic of Cavalieri's figuring is the care with which it is adjusted to the texture of the vocal (or instrumental) harmony. Ex. 27 is a good instance. Whatever its drawbacks may have been, the practice of indicating compound intervals undoubtedly gave the composer a control over details of the accompaniment, as regards both its compass and the distribution of the harmony, which was afterwards lost. It not unfrequently called for the employment of what Ph. Em. Bach called a 'divided accompaniment' (i.e. 'extended harmony'), as in the penultimate bar of Ex. 3 and in Ex. 14. This could, in some cases, be avoided by awkward skips, which were, however, evidently not intended.

Certain figurings call for special notice.

In Ex. 28 we have the single instance in which Cavalieri uses triple figures, $\begin{smallmatrix}10\\6,\\✕4\end{smallmatrix}$[7] and it seems strange that, having done so once, he did not employ them oftener.

---

[7] At a later period the chord would have been figured $\sharp^4_3$ $\left(\begin{smallmatrix}4!\\3\end{smallmatrix}\right)$, omitting the 6 (cf. Ch. xiii, '$\begin{smallmatrix}6\\4\\3\end{smallmatrix}$ chords', § 1).

In Ex. 29 $^6_4$, over a stationary Bass (Tonic pedal), is quite misleading. Only the score shows that it is to be interpreted as $^9_6$. In later Basses it would have been figured thus, or, less correctly, $^6_2$.

In Ex. 30 there is little doubt but that the $^6_4$ in bar 15 (also over a stationary Bass) is to be taken as $^6_2$, so as to include the interval present in the voice part.

In Ex. 31, again over a Tonic pedal, $\widehat{^7_{4.4.}}$ stands for $^{6\ 7}_{4\ -}_{2\ -}$.

Besides these cases, we find $^6_4$, in more than one instance, doing duty for $^6_4{}_3 \left(^{10}_{\ 6}_{\ 4}\right)$, as in Exx. 32 and 33.

In Ex. 34 there is still greater economy, $\times\!\!\!\times$ 6 . 11 . representing the progression $^{10\ 11}_{10\ -}$.

In bar 2 of the same Ex. may be noted, incidentally, the treatment of a $7\sharp6$ suspension, as compared with the somewhat exceptional treatment of the same progression in Ex. 35.

Ex. 27   ibid., p. xl, l. 2, bar 3 sq.

N.B.—The figuring $\flat$ 3. $\flat$ 10. is evidently designed to prevent the false relation between the Soprano ($\natural$ b) and the Tenor ($\flat$ b) from being covered up by the accompaniment, as would be the case if the latter were

ibid., p. xxix, No. 69, bar 6 sq. (words omitted).

Ex. 28

N.B.—Cavalieri does not trouble to figure the ♯*f* ($\begin{smallmatrix}11.\\ ✕5\end{smallmatrix}$ ✕·) in the last bar †, thus foreshadowing the practice, which for a long time was very general, of assuming a Fifth to be perfect unless the contrary was indicated (cf. Ch. xxiii, 'Varieties of figuring', § 5).

He uses the figuring ✕5 only where there is a possibility of doubt, as in the

following instance:  ibid., p. xxvii, l. 2, bar 3.

ibid., p. xv, No. 22, *Ritornello.*

Ex. 29

N.B.—The voices end on the first half of bar 1.

ibid., p. xxxi, No. 74.

Ex. 30

Anime dãnate una soia

Eter - na, eterna mor-te Ahi ciè toccata in sorte Mor-

- te che mai non mo-re Sepolta nel do-lo-re Aspra penosa, e for - te.

N.B.—The above Recitative has been quoted *in exenso* as being one of the most successful of Cavalieri's attempts at dramatic effect.

Besides the $\frac{6}{4}\left(=\frac{6}{4}\atop{2}\right)$ over a Tonic Pedal (in the temporary key of *c* major) in bar 15, there are several minor points to be noted:

(1) In bar 6, the change of key-signature, from which the ♭ disappears.

(2) In bar 12, in spite of Peri's rule that an accidental, if not repeated, is to be regarded as contradicted, Cavalieri uses the figuring ⨯3 to contradict the flat in the previous bar (cf. § 6, note 2).

(3) In bars 10 and 13 we see $\frac{6}{⨯}$ = ⨯6 (cf. Guidotti's rules).

It will be noticed that, from bar 7 onwards, the Tenor part of the suggested accompaniment closely follows the voice.

Ex.31

ibid., p. xvii, No. 27.

Corpo

Non so s'e stato bene Lasciar tanto piacer, che'l mõdo tie - ne

ibid., p. iii *ad fin.* (the vocal Bass, being identical with the *B. c.*, and the words are omitted).

Ex. 32

N.B.—In Basses of a later period the progression shown in bar 2 would be little likely to occur on account of the thinly veiled consecutive Fifths $\frac{d\,b}{g\,e}$. Should it do so the most correct figuring would be $\begin{smallmatrix}6\,5\\4\,3\\3\,-\end{smallmatrix}$, $\left(\begin{smallmatrix}3\,-\\6\,5\\4\,3\end{smallmatrix}\right)$ or $\begin{smallmatrix}4\,5\\3\,3\end{smallmatrix}$.

ibid., p. x, l. 3, bar 5 sq. (words omitted).

Ex.33

N.B.—Even in later Basses the progression shown in bar 2 is sometimes figured $\begin{smallmatrix}6\,-\\3\,4\end{smallmatrix}$, which, however, is misleading. Either $\begin{smallmatrix}6\,-\\3\,4\\3\,-\end{smallmatrix}$ $\left(\begin{smallmatrix}3\,-\\6\,-\\3\,4\end{smallmatrix}\right)$ or 6 $\frac{4}{3}$ is required for clearness.

ibid., p. xxxiv, l. 2, bar 7 sq. (words omitted).

N.B.—In fully figured later Basses the progression at ✳ would appear as $\begin{smallmatrix}6-\\3\ 4\\3\ -\end{smallmatrix}\left(\begin{smallmatrix}3-\\6-\\3\ 4\end{smallmatrix}\right)$
or $6\,\begin{smallmatrix}4\\3\end{smallmatrix}$, though the insufficient figuring $\begin{smallmatrix}6-\\3\ 4\end{smallmatrix}$ is also found.

The 7 ♯6 suspension † in bar 2 is resolved in accordance with A. Scarlatti's rule that the 4 should be added when (i.e. not before) the 7 resolves. In the present instance it is added *after* the resolution of the 7, as the position of the 11 (slightly to the right of the 6) is no doubt intentional. Compare the different treatment of the progression in the next Ex.

Note that the last two notes of the 'turn' which forms the conclusion of the *groppolo* (g) ǂ in bar 2 are written out in full, no doubt in order to make sure of ♯*f* (instead of ♮*f*) being sung (cf. Guidotti's list of 'ornaments').

Ex.35   ibid., p. v, No. 11.

N.B.—The full figuring of the progression at ✳ would, in later Basses, be $\begin{smallmatrix}7\ 6\\4\ -\\3\ -\end{smallmatrix}$, to ensure the inclusion of the 4 with the 7. Note the 5ths and 8ves by contrary motion at †† in the suggested accompaniment.

One point in which Cavalieri's figuring differs from that which became established in Basses of a later period is that, in the latter, a Triad which follows some other harmony over another bass note of the same denomination (whether in the same Octave or not) is nearly always figured, the figuring varying in accordance with the progression of the intervals in the preceding

chord, as

In similar cases, as e.g. in the penultimate bar of Ex. 32, Cavalieri and his contemporaries leave the Triad unfigured.

§ 9. *Figures not universally adopted.*

It seems strange that Viadana should not have generally availed himself of a device of such obvious convenience as the use of figures to denote the harmony, since it is impossible to imagine that he was ignorant of their employment by Peri, Caccini, and Cavalieri, and, more particularly, since it seems not improbable that he himself made occasional use of the figure 6 (cf. § 4 under Rule 8). His sixth rule shows that he realized that an unfigured Bass was an insufficient guide to the harmony, but that he favoured the practice of playing from an *Intavolatura*, prepared by the Organist for his own use.

Agazzari, writing five years after the publication of the first instalment of Viadana's *Concerti*, emphasized the impossibility of divining the harmonies intended by the composer without the aid of figures (cf. § 10 *a*), and Praetorius, in his *Syntagma Musicum*, does the same (cf. § 15).

Nevertheless, it is certain that a number of Viadana's contemporaries not only did not figure their Organ Basses, but were definitely opposed to the practice.

Kinkeldey (*Orgel und Klavier &c.*, Appendix II, pp. 222–6) quotes extracts from the prefaces to a number of works, published between 1603 and 1625, in which many of the writers express themselves against the use of figures, which some of them regard as more likely to confuse than to help the player, whose best guide they consider to be his musical knowledge and ear.[1]

Kinkeldey points out (p. 208) that there were also typographical difficulties to consider,[2] and, undoubtedly, the addition of the figures, &c., must have considerably increased the cost of publication.

Even apart from works in which the principal part or parts were printed over the Bass, and in which the figures were therefore less necessary, unfigured Basses were to be found at a period long after that at present under consideration. For not only do Agazzari, in 1607, and Praetorius, in 1619, think it necessary to emphasize the necessity of figures, but much later writers as well.

Andreas Werckmeister (*Harmonologia Musica*, 1702, § 120, p. 65) writes: "Those, too, who say that the 'signatures'[3] over the notes in a Thorough-Bass are quite useless and unnecessary, display no slight ignorance and folly; for it is clearly impossible for even an adept, who understands the natural course of harmony and composition, to play everything correctly in accordance with the idea of another, for the progressions and resolutions may take place in many different ways."

Francesco Gasparini (Lucchese), whose treatise *L'Armonico pratico al*

---

[1] Giovanni Piccioni, in the preface to his *Concerti ecclesiastici à 1—8 voci con il suo Basso seguito. Venetia (Vincenti)*, 1610, quoted by Kinkeldey (pp. 224–5), says that "in this sort of concerto I have not chosen to put any sort of accidentals, such as sharps, flats, and figures, over the notes, as many do, because, to such Organists as are not expert, they are a source of confusion rather than otherwise, while to those who know, and to competent men, such accidentals are not necessary, since they play them correctly by ear and by art".

[2] In the preface to the *Bassus ad Organum & Musica Instrumenta . . . Sacrarum Laudum . . .*, Lib. II. *Venetiis (Amadinus)*, 1608 (1st ed. 1603), quoted by Kinkeldey (p. 224), Agostino Agazzari, himself a strong advocate of the use of figures (cf. § 10 *a*), explains that he has been unable, owing to shortage of type, to print sharps and flats over the notes (to denote major and minor Thirds) or figures 'in conformity with the requirements' of the players, and he recommends them to listen carefully to the singers and to follow the harmony (*tessitura*), 'unless they care to put them [i.e. the figures, &c.] in with a pen'.

[3] The German word 'Signaturen' includes both the figures themselves and ♯ ♭ ♮ *above* the Bass.

cimbalo (Venice, 1708, Antonio Bortoli) enjoyed a wide circulation and went through several editions, gives elaborate rules for dealing with an unfigured Bass.

Heinichen (*Der General-Bass in der Composition*, 1728, Pt. 2, Ch. I, § 2, p. 585) distinguishes carefully between the cases in which the principal part, or parts, are printed over the Bass and those in which they are not, as follows:

"Whereas the Thorough-Basses in Church Music, Sonatas (and all other cases where no vocal or instrumental part is given above the Bass) always ought to be, and usually are, properly figured: in the Chamber and Theatrical style, on the other hand, the case is quite different. For there Arias, Cantatas, Operas, Instrumental Solos, Duets, &c., are placed before us, in which, ordinarily, no figures are to be found over the Bass; instead, one is obliged to seek them out *ex tempore* from the score, nay, generally, from a single part written above, and, as it were, divine the rest by dint of art and ear."

The following chapter (pp. 725–68), "Von dem General-Bass ohne Signaturen, und wie diese in Cameral- und Theatralischen Sachen zu erfinden", is devoted to rules for dealing with unfigured Basses, and, in Ch. 4 (pp. 797–836), the author takes us, bar by bar, through an entire Cantata for a soprano voice, which he uses to illustrate the rules in question.

Lastly, Ph. Em. Bach (*Versuch &c.*, Pt. 2, 1762, Ch. 35) devotes an entire chapter to the 'Necessity of figuring'. He tells us that, from time to time, he had himself attempted to formulate rules for dealing with unfigured Basses, but that he became convinced of the inadequacy of any such method.

He expresses himself very strongly on the subject: "May unfigured Basses, too," he writes, "become gradually rarer, and Clavier players show less readiness to do whatever is asked of them! Every other Ripienist is entitled to complain if an incorrectly written part is put before him, while the accompanist, on the other hand, has to be content if his part is either not figured at all, or so scantily that the few figures perchance to be found are generally put where they could easily be guessed."

And, farther on: "The figures (*Signaturen*) are there; let people, therefore, avail themselves of this useful invention, and torment neither themselves with the excogitation of inadequate rules, nor their pupils with the acquisition of the latter. If any one is too indolent, or too ignorant, to figure his own Basses, *as a good rendering demands*, let him get it done by a skilled accompanist."

§ 10 *Agazzari.*

(*a*). In 1607 a work appeared which demands especial notice. This was a short treatise by Agostino Agazzari,[1] *Del suonare sopra il basso con tutti stromenti & uso loro nel conserto* (Siena, Dom. Falcini), reprinted in the same composer's *Sacrae Cantiones quae Binis, Ternis, Quaternisque vocibus concinendae, Liber II, Opus V, Motectorum, Venetiis apud Ricciardum Amadinum*, 1609,

---

[1] Agazzari was a native of Siena, in the Academy of which town he enjoyed the title of '*Armonico intronato*'. He was *Maestro di Capella* at the *Collegium Germanicum*, then located at St. Apollinare in Rome. He must have made the acquaintance of Viadana when the latter visited Rome about 1597 (cf. § 5), and his admiration for him is proved by the number of Viadana's works which were acquired, as soon as published, for the choir of St. Apollinare, and which were afterwards purchased from the *Collegium Germanicum* by Haberl (cf. *Kirchenmusikalisches Jahrbuch*, 1889, p. 61).

as a preface to the *Bassus ad organum*, and given *in extenso* by Kinkeldey (*Orgel und Klavier &c.*, App. I, pp. 216–31).

The accompaniment contemplated by Agazzari is a far more complicated matter than that which Viadana's rules suggest.

Besides the instruments which play the Bass itself, together with the chords indicated by the figuring, Agazzari reckons on others whose function it was to execute extemporized counterpoints, and ornaments of various kinds.[2]

He divides the instruments which play from the *Bassus ad Organum* into two classes: 'instruments of foundation' and 'instruments of ornamentation'.

"As foundation", he writes, "there are those which guide and sustain the entire body of the voices and instruments of the said Concerto, such as the Organ, Gravicembalo, &c., and, similarly, in the case of few or single voices, the Lute, Theorbo, Harp, &c.

"As ornamentation there are those which disport themselves (*scherzando*), and play counterpoints (*contrapontegiando*), and thus make the harmony more agreeable and sonorous; such are the Lute, Theorbo, Harp, Lirone, Cither, Spinet, Chitarrina, Violin, Pandora, and the like."

What Agazzari describes is, in fact, a small orchestra which improvises its accompaniment from a figured Bass, while the Organ, or Harpsichord, or both together, supply the harmonic background.

It will be observed that some of the instruments enumerated (the Lute, Theorbo, and Harp) may be used as instruments either of foundation or of ornamentation, and the question suggests itself whether the *Chitarrone* (Theorbo) and *Liuto grosso* mentioned by Peri (cf. § 6), as well as the *Lira doppia* and *Chitarone [sic]*[3] mentioned by Guidotti (cf. § 8, 1), were perhaps employed in the latter capacity.

With regard to the necessity for figuring the Bass Agazzari is very definite indeed. "But, to come to practical questions," he writes, "I conclude that it is not possible to give a fixed rule for playing works where there are no signs of any sort, because it is necessary to obey the mind of the composer, which is free, and can, at his discretion, put a Fifth or a Sixth on the first half of a note, and vice versâ, and that [i.e. the Sixth] major or minor, as seems the more appropriate, or is necessitated by regard for the words. And even though a certain writer, who treats of counterpoint, has defined the order of progression from one harmony (*consonanza*) to another, just as though one could not do differently, it is no good; he will pardon me, for he shows that he has failed to understand that the chords (*consonanze*) and the entire harmony are subjected and subordinated to the words, and not the other way about; and this position we will defend with all the reasons, if occasion should arise. It is quite true that in simple music (*semplicamente*), and for the most part, it would be possible to give a definite rule for progression, but where there are words, it is necessary to clothe them with suitable harmony calculated to awaken or illustrate the sentiment (*che faccia ò dimostri quello affetto*).

---

[2] Hence the title 'Bassus ad Organum *& Musica Instrumenta*' (cf. § 9, note 2).

[3] Guidotti mentions the 'Chitarone' *twice*, and his second mention of it in close connexion with the Organ (*un Organo suave con un Chitarone*) seems to suggest that, while the *Organo suave* played sustained harmony, the *Chitarone* may have been employed to execute a freer accompaniment such as that which Agazzari describes (cf. § 10 d).

"Not being possible to give a definite rule, it is unavoidably necessary for the player to use his ear and follow the work and its progressions (*movimenti*); but if you wish to find an easy method of escaping these difficulties, use the following method; that is to say, indicate with figures,[4] above the notes of the Bass, the consonances or dissonances which are used by the composer, as, for instance, if, on the first half of the note, there is a Fifth or a Sixth, or vice versâ; or a Fourth and then a Third, as in the example:

"You are to know, furthermore, that all consonances are either natural to the key in question, or accidental; when they are natural, one puts no sign at all; as, for instance, with no ♭♭ in the key, the Third on G, which is ♭♭ or ♮♭, is naturally a major Third (*come per be quadro la terza sopra G solreut, che è befabemi, viene terza maggiore naturalmente*); but, if one wants to make it minor, it is necessary to put a flat over the note G, and then it is accidentally minor. And so, too, vice versâ, if there is ♭♭ in the key (*se si canta per Bemolle*), if one wants to make it [i.e. the Third] major, one must put a sharp above; and I say the same about the Sixths, bearing in mind that the sign [♯ or ♭] which is below, or close to the note, refers to the note in question, while that which is above it refers to the consonance which it has to indicate, as in the following example."

* obviously a misprint for

"All cadences, whether medial or final, demand the major Third; some people, therefore, do not indicate it, but, for greater safety, I advise putting the sign,[6] especially in medial cadences."

(b). *Instruments of foundation. General principles.*

There is one point in which Agazzari differs somewhat from Viadana. It will be remembered that, in his 12th Rule (cf. § 4), the latter prescribed that, when a high voice was singing, the accompaniment should not, with a certain exception, be low.

Agazzari, on the contrary, in laying down certain general principles for the

[4] This suggests that the Organist is likely to have to figure the Bass for himself (cf. § 9, note 2).

[5] Over the fourth note (*c*) it will be observed that the ♭, denoting the minor Third is placed over, instead of under, the other figures, contrary to the later custom, in accordance with which the higher figure was always (in the absence of a special reason to the contrary) placed above the lower.

[6] It will be observed that Agazzari does not follow his own advice, as he omits the ♯ over the penultimate note of both Exx.; also he does not think it necessary to put a 6 over a leading note (♯*f* in Ex. 1, and ♯*c* and ♯*f* in Ex. 2). Both omissions were very general in the earlier Italian figured Basses (cf. Ch. xxi, 'Incomplete figuring', I, § 3, and III, § 4, 1).

players of instruments of foundation, says that, in delicate passages, when only a few voices are singing, the accompanist should *avoid the territory of the upper voices*, and should be careful to avoid, as far as he possibly can, *playing the same notes as the Soprano is singing*.

The passage, which deserves quoting in its entirety, is as follows:

"Since, then, the instruments are divided into two classes, it follows that they have a different function and operate differently; accordingly, when one plays an instrument which serves as foundation, one must play with great judgement, keeping one's attention on the body of voices; for, if they are many, one must play full harmonies and use more stops, but, if they are few, reduce them [i.e. the stops] and use few consonances [i.e. play in a few parts only], playing the work as simply and correctly as possible, and not with many florid passages or runs;[1] but, on the other hand, supporting the voices by occasionally doubling the Bass in the lower Octave,[2] and constantly avoiding the high registers while the voices, especially the Sopranos and Falsettos, are occupying them; one must then be careful to avoid, as far as possible, the same note which the Soprano is singing, and not to make diminutions[3] on it, so as not to double the voice part and obscure the goodness of the said voice, or the passage [i.e. the extemporized 'diminution'] which the good singer is executing above; therefore it is good to play within quite a small compass and low down."[4]

The above refers, of course, especially to the Organ. Agazzari continues: "I say the same of the Lute, Harp, Theorbo, Harpsichord (*Arpicordo*), &c., when they serve as foundation while one or more voices are singing; for, in such a case, they must keep the harmony firm, sonorous, and unbroken, so as to support the voice: playing now softly, and now loud, according to the quality and quantity of the voices, of the place, and of the work: avoiding too frequent repercussions while the voice executes its passage, and expresses some kind of emotion,[5] so as not to interrupt it."

Michael Praetorius and Johann Staden, of whom anon (cf. §§ 15, 16), both comment on the difference of opinion between Viadana and Agazzari.

Staden says: "I, for my part, am not too much inclined to differ from Agazzari when he requires that one should give way on the Clavier to the high voices (that is to say, that one should avoid touching the note sung by the Soprano), *but, in practice, it is not always feasible. . . .*"

(*c*).   *Rules for the Organ.*

Agazzari concludes his directions to the players of instruments of foundation with the following excellent rules.[1]

[1] 'suonando l' opera piu pura, e giusta, che sia possibile, non passegiando ò rompendo molto.'

[2] 'ma si bene aiutandole con qualche contrabasso.'

[3] i.e. break up long notes into short ones, as, e.g.:

as written   diminutio

[4] 'assai stretto e grave', i.e. making the chords as *compact* as possible.

[5] "non ribattendo troppo le corde, mentre la voce fa il passaggio, e qualche affetto ..."

[1] Praetorius quotes these rules *in extenso*; instead, however, of giving them, as Agazzari does, in a single sentence, he numbers them, and also the portions of the example which illustrate the rule in question. His example has here been followed.

He presupposes in the pupil a knowledge of certain elementary principles of harmony. "Whoever does not know them", he writes, "must learn them. We will now give directions for the conduct of the hand on the Organ.

"The Bass proceeds in many different ways: namely, either by step, or by leap, or in quick notes moving by step (*con tirata continovata*), or with black disjunct notes.

1. "When it rises by step, the right hand must move downwards, either by step or by leap.

2. "And, vice versâ, when the left hand rises or falls by leap of a Third, a Fourth, or a Fifth, then the right hand must proceed by step, for it is not good for both to rise or fall together, which is ugly to look at and to hear, and there is no sort of variety in it; instead, there would be nothing but Octaves and Fifths.

3. "If the Bass rises by step with quick notes (*se il Basso va insu con tirata*), the right hand remains stationary.

4. "If the motion is disjunct, with black notes, one must give each note its own accompaniment.

"Here is an example of the whole." [2]

It will be noticed that the consecutive Fifths $\substack{g\,a\\c\,d}$, and the barely hidden Octaves $\substack{b\,d\\b\,d}$ in the penultimate bar are in accordance with Viadana's 9th Rule.

(*d*). *Instruments of ornamentation.*

Agazzari next proceeds to give directions to the players of instruments of ornamentation.

"The instruments which mingle with the voices in various ways, mingle with them, I think, for no other reason but to adorn and beautify, and, indeed, to season (*condire*) the said concerto."

The player of an instrument of foundation had a far less difficult and delicate task than the player of an instrument of ornamentation. "For", writes Agazzari, "as the former has to play the Bass before him as it stands, it is not necessary that he should have a great knowledge of counterpoint,

---

[2] In the first chord ✳ of the fifth bar either the Bass should be *c*, or the Alto *a*. It is odd that Praetorius has copied this misprint, apparently, without noticing it.

but the latter needs it, since he has to compose new parts, and new and varied passages and counterpoints over that same Bass.

"Therefore, whoever plays the Lute, which is the noblest instrument among them all, must play nobly, with much invention and variety, and not, as some do who, because they have a facile hand, do nothing but play runs and diminutions (cf. *b*, note 3) from beginning to end, especially in the company of other instruments which do the same, when nothing is heard but chaos (*zuppa*) and confusion, displeasing and offensive to the listener.

"Chords are sometimes to be struck, with gentle repercussions; sometimes passages, slow or quick, are to be played, as well as imitations at different pitches and at various points (*le medesime fughe in diverse corde, e lochi*), also ornaments in the shape of *gruppi*,[1] and trills,[1] and appoggiaturas (*accenti* [2]).

"And what we say about the Lute, as the principal instrument, we wish understood of the others according to their kind, as it would be a long business to go into detail about each.

"But, since every instrument has its own particular limits, the player must observe them, and regulate himself accordingly, to be successful. For example: bowed instruments have a different style from those sounded by a quill [like the harpsichord], or a finger [like the harp]. Therefore, whoever plays the Lirone [Lira da gamba] must draw long bows, clear and sonorous, bringing out the middle parts well, and paying attention to the Thirds and Sixths, major and minor: a difficult matter, and one of importance for this instrument."

Then follow hints for the various other instruments. Graceful passages, imitations, and ornaments are appropriate to the Violin. The Violone [3] is to "proceed gravely, sustaining with its mellow (*dolce*) resonance the harmony of the other parts, keeping as much as possible to the thick strings, and often touching the Octave below the Bass".[4]

The Theorbo, the Arpa doppia, "an instrument which is serviceable throughout, as much in the Soprano as in the Bass", and the Cither (*Cetera*), both the ordinary one and the *Ceterone*, are also mentioned, and their part in the accompaniment briefly described.

"But everything", Agazzari continues, "must be used prudently; for if the instruments are alone in the Concerto, they must do everything and lead the Concerto; if they are in company, they must have regard, one to the other, giving way to, and not interfering with each other; if there are many of them, they must each bide their own time and not do like the sparrows, all playing at once, and each trying to make the most noise."

(*e*). *Agazzari's account of the origin of accompaniment from a Bass.*

Agazzari concludes his little treatise with a short dissertation on the origin of the practice of accompanying from a Bass.

[1] Cf. § 8 (2).   [2] Cf. § 4, note 2.
[3] The Violone, the largest of the Viols, was fretted. In its completest form it had

six strings tuned

[4] It is probably on account of this latter function (of playing an Octave lower than the notes written) that Agazzari includes the Violone among the instruments of ornamentation.

"Having hitherto treated of how to play on a Bass, it has seemed good to me to say something about the latter in itself; for I know that it is disparaged by sundry who either do not understand its purpose, or who lack the soul (*anima*) to play it. It is for three reasons, then, that this method was first put into use: first on account of the modern style of singing and composing recitative; secondly for convenience; thirdly on account of the quantity and variety of the works which are necessary for the Concerto."

It is in reference to the first of the three reasons given that Agazzari's reflections are especially interesting, as illustrating the complete revolution in musical taste which had taken place.

He writes as follows: "With regard to the first [reason], since the true style of expressing the words has at last been found, namely, by reproducing the same thought (*imitando lo stesso ragionare*) in the best manner possible, which succeeds best with a single voice, or only a few, as in the modern airs of sundry able men, and as is the constant practice at Rome in Concertos, I say that it is not necessary to make a score (*spartitura* [1]) or tablature (*intavolatura* [2]); a Bass, with its signs [i.e. figures and ♯ ♭ ♮ *above* the Bass], as we said above, is enough. But if some one were to tell me that, for playing the old works, full of fugues and counterpoints, a Bass is not enough, my answer is that vocal works (*cantilene*) of this kind are no longer in use, on account of the confusion and chaos (*zuppa*) of the words arising from the long and intricate fugues, and also because they have no charm, since, being sung by all the voices, one hears no period or sense, it being interrupted and covered up (*inter[r]otto e sopraposto*) by the fugues; in fact each voice is singing different words from the other at the same moment, which, to men of intelligence and judgement, is displeasing; and, for this very reason, Music was within a very little of being banished from Holy Church by a certain Chief Pontiff, had not a remedy been found by Giovan Palestrino [*sic*], by showing that the defect and mistake lay with the composers and not with Music; and, in confirmation of this, he composed the Mass entitled *Missa Papae Marcelli*. Wherefore, although such compositions are good according to the rules of counterpoint, nevertheless, according to the rules of true and good music, they are faulty; and this arises from a disregard of the object, and function, and good precepts of the latter; for such men want to take their stand solely on the observance of fugue and imitation, and of the notes, and not the feeling and portrayal of the words (*e non dell' affetto, e somiglianza delle parole*); indeed, many composers wrote the music first, and then added the words. And this is enough for the present, as it is not to the purpose here to discuss such a subject at length."

The second of Agazzari's reasons refers to the saving of trouble by "being free from the *Intavolatura*, a difficult and tiresome thing to many, and indeed a frequent source of mistakes (*anzi molto soggietta à gl' errori*) on account of the eye and mind being entirely taken up with following so many parts, especially when occasion arises for making music on the spur of the moment".

It will be remembered that Viadana also spoke of the difficulty of playing at sight from an *Intavolatura* (cf. § 4, Rule 6).

Agazzari's third reason refers to the saving of space by the absence of scores or 'tablatures', as, otherwise, "the Organist would need a larger library than a Doctor of Laws".

---

[1] Cf. § 3, note 3.   [2] Cf. § 4, note 10.

He adds: "Wherefore there is abundant reason for the introduction of such a Bass, after the fashion described above; and, in conclusion, there is no necessity for the player to cause the parts to be heard as they stand, as long as he is playing to accompany singing (*mentre si suona per cantarvisi*), and not in order to play the work as it stands, which is a matter apart from my subject."

The treatise then ends with the following modest words: "And let this which has been said suffice in place of the much which might be said; for I want briefly to satisfy your courteous demands (inasmuch as you have several times urged me), rather than my own bent (*genio*), which is more in the direction of learning from others than of instructing. Accept it, then, such as it is, and excuse me on account of the shortness of the time [at my disposal]."

§ 11. *Francesco Bianciardi.*

I. In the September of 1607, the year in which Agazzari's treatise appeared, there was published, after the author's death, a little work by Francesco Bianciardi entitled *Breve regola per imparar a sonare sopra il Basso con ogni sorte d' Instrumento* ('A short guide for learning to play on a Bass with every kind of instrument').

A copy is fortunately preserved in the library of the *Liceo Musicale* at Bologna, to the courteous librarian of which institution, Professor Francesco Vatielli, the present writer is indebted for a transcript and description.

The entire work is printed on a single giant folio, or broadsheet, ornamented at the top with a picture showing various musical instruments—a small Organ in the centre, flanked by a Spinet, a Harp, and sundry Viols (including two Violones, a Viol da gamba, and a smaller member of the tribe), as well as a Chitarrone or Theorbo, and three various Lutes.

The work is dedicated by the publisher, Domenico Falcini, to Alessandro Petrucci, Bishop of Massa, who appears to have been an enthusiastic patron of Art and Literature, and the terms of the dedication testify to the high esteem in which Bianciardi was held, both as a man and as a musician.

The dedication runs as follows:

"Al Molto Ill^re e Rev^mo Sig^r e Proñ mio Osserv^mo il Signor Alessandro Petrucci merit^mo Vescovo di Massa.

"A V. S. Rev^ma che amò con tanto affetto il singolare valore, e merito dell' Ecc^te Musico, gia con tanto cordoglio pianto da questa citta, Sr Francesco Bianciardi, dedico questa carta, così aspettata da tutti quelli, che di musicalmente sonare intendono, sendo ella da tant' huomo fabricata, valevole non meno ne gli stromenti musici di quello, che nel armonia vocale habbia valuto al mondo. Ella che vivendo l' onorò (solito di così fare tutti i letterati e virtuosi) hora morto, in questa carta l' accolga, e me nel numero riponga di quelli, che vivamente l' onorano e servono.

"Di Siena, il di 21 Settembre 1607.
       "Di V. S. molto Ill^re e Rev^ma Serv^re div^mo
                                   "Domenico Falcini."

('To the most Illustrious and Reverend Signor, and my most revered Patron, Signor Alessandro Petrucci, most worthy Bishop of Massa.

'To your most Reverend Lordship, who so warmly loved the singular worth and merit of that excellent Musician, now so deeply mourned by this

City, Signor Francesco Bianciardi, I dedicate this sheet (*carta*), so much looked forward to by all who understand musical playing, as being the work of such a man, no less valuable to the world in connexion with musical instruments than with vocal harmony. May you who honoured him when alive (being accustomed so to do with all men of letters and artists) welcome him, now that he is dead, in this broadsheet (*carta*), and count me among those who sincerely honour and serve him.

'Siena, the 21ˢᵗ day of Septʳ 1607

'Your Illustrious and most Reverend Lordship's most devoted Servant,
Domenico Falcini.')

II. Bianciardi's little treatise consists, mainly, of rules for playing from an unfigured Bass; indeed, there is only a single reference to the use of figures (to be quoted later), which reference, however, clearly indicates that he recognized that, in certain cases at least, they were indispensable to a correct performance (cf. note 15).

He gives, however, certain rules of taste, and also a general example (Ex. 3), which is particularly instructive, and àlso serves as an admirable illustration of Viadana's 9th Rule concerning the liberty to use consecutive Fifths and Octaves in the accompaniment.

III. It is not necessary to follow Bianciardi through his introductory explanations concerning the preliminary knowledge of music to be possessed before attempting to 'play on the Bass', the perfect and imperfect consonances, &c.

His definition of the Bass is, however, worth quoting: "Note that, for the Bass, one takes the lowest note of the music, because, when the Bass pauses, there enters in its place the Tenor, or the Alto, and whichever part is below the others is always called the Bass."

The rules which follow are founded on ten possible progressions of the Bass, which may either rise or fall (*a*) a degree, (*b*) a Third, (*c*) a Fourth, (*d*) a Fifth, (*e*) a Sixth, as shown below:

Ex. 1

'rises a degree 'a 3ʳᵈ' 'a 4ᵗʰ' 'a 5ᵗʰ' 'a 6ᵗʰ' 'falls a degree' 'a 3ʳᵈ' 'a 4ᵗʰ' 'a 5ᵗʰ' 'a 6ᵗʰ'
(*per grado*)

"The rise or fall of an Octave makes no difference. The progression (*movimento*) of a Seventh is not used."

"Perfect harmony", we are told, "consists in the union of three notes of different denominations (*la musica ha l' armonia perfetta in tre termini, cioè in tre corde di diversa spetie insieme unite*), of which one is the Fifth above the Bass, and the other, the Third—the one a perfect, and the other an imperfect consonance. And this is to be observed in the case of all the notes of the Bass which can have such consonances."

Bianciardi goes on to explain that those notes which have no perfect Fifth above them, as B, when there is no ♭ appended to the clef (*quando si canta per Bequadro*), and E, when there *is* a ♭ (*quando si canta per B molle*), and also all Bass notes accidentally sharpened, take a *minor Sixth instead of a Fifth*.

IV. Then follow rules[1] for the use of the imperfect consonances (the Third and the Sixth) in the various progressions of the Bass shown in Ex. 1. These rules, which, though of little value in themselves, are of great interest as representing the earliest extant attempt to formulate directions for assigning the right harmonies to an unfigured Bass, run as follows:

"The greatest difficulty to be found in playing consists in the use of the imperfect consonances in their proper place and time. We will therefore speak first of the Third, and observe the following order, in accordance with the above-mentioned progressions of the Bass.

[1] "When the Bass rises a degree [2] (*per grado*), or a Third, we give it the natural Third. [Ex. 2 *a, b.*]

[2] "When it rises a Fourth, we give it the major Third, and, if it is not naturally major, it is made so by adding the *Diesis* [i.e. by sharpening the note], because it is by this progression (*movimento*) that the close (*cadenza*) is made. [Ex. 2 *c.*]

[3] "When it rises a Fifth, we give it the natural Third [Ex. 2 *d*]; but in many cases (*in molti luoghi*) one gives it the minor Third [Ex. 2 *e*], and particularly in proceeding to a close.

[4] "When it rises a Sixth, one gives it the natural Third [no example].

[5] "The rise of an Octave makes no difference.

[6] "Next, when it falls a degree (*per grado*), or a Third, we give it the natural Third. [Ex. 2 *f, g.*]

[7] "When it falls a Fourth, we do the same as when it rises a Fifth. [Ex. 2 *h, i.*]

[8] "When it falls a Fifth, we give it the major Third, as when it rises a Fourth. [Ex. 2 *k.*]

[9] "When it falls a Sixth, or an Octave, the natural Thirds [no example]; and, in the final closes, one always ends with the major Third."

"We will now speak of the Sixth, from which the best effects in music arise. In accordance, therefore, with the same progressions of the Bass, we will observe the following order.

[10] "When the Bass rises a degree (*per grado*), or a Third, if there is occasion to use the Sixth (*occorrendo usar la sesta*), we give the natural one. [Ex. 2 *l, m.*]

[11] "When it rises a Fourth, the Sixth is not used. [See, however, Rule 14.]

[12] "When it rises a Fifth, we give it the major Sixth." [Ex. 2 *n.*]

[No rule is given for a Bass rising a Sixth.]

[13] "Next, when it falls a degree [3] (*per grado*), we always give it the major Sixth." [Ex. 2 *o.*]

[No rule is given for the Bass falling a Third, or a Fourth, as Ex. 2 *p.*]

[14] "When it falls a Fifth, the Sixth will not do (*non ci va la sesta*), except

---

[1] In the original the text, throughout, runs continuously in long paragraphs. The examples are not numbered, and the rules are separated only by a semicolon. For the sake of greater clearness, and to facilitate reference, the rules and examples have here been numbered, and the subdivisions in the latter indicated by numbers or letters.

[2] The Italian expression *per grado* applies equally to a progression of a single degree and to one of several notes moving 'by step'. In the example illustrating the above rule the Bass happens to rise *two* degrees, whereas Rule 13 applies only to a progression of a single degree.

[3] i.e. a whole tone (as in the example), in which case the Third must be minor

that one sometimes uses the minor Sixth [4] on the first part of the note, in order to arrive at the Fifth. [Ex. 2 *q*.]

[15] "Furthermore, when the Bass falls a degree, or a Fourth,[5] one can use the Seventh resolving on the major Sixth; and when it falls a Fifth, or rises a Fourth, one can use the Fourth resolving on the major Third in making a close (*in atto di cadenza*), as in the example." [Ex. 3, bar 13.]

V. There now follow some directions and suggestions, partly illustrated by a general example, which give us considerable insight into Bianciardi's actual practice in the treatment of the accompaniment and therefore constitute by far the most interesting portion of his little treatise:

(1) "And, although compositions are written in 4, 5, 6, 8, and more parts, they have the same harmony, consisting of the three parts [Bass, Third, and Fifth] above mentioned, since, if one wants to add other consonances to these, one can only add Octaves to one of them, so that the parts are doubled, while the harmony remains the same; for the Octave corresponds to the unison, and the player will satisfy the requirements of the composition by using the three notes aforesaid. It is quite true that, by using compound intervals (*consonanze composte e replicate*), we shall make the harmony more varied: that is, if, instead of the Third, we take the 10th or 17th, and, instead of the 5th, the 12th or 19th, and so on. But, because the harmony would be too poor if we only put in the three parts, it is very useful to add Octaves to the Bass and to the other parts, in order to enrich it, and to give the opportunity of passing from one consonance to another more smoothly,[6] with more elegance (*leggiadria*), and with greater convenience to the hand.

---

[4] i.e. $\frac{6}{4}$.

[5] It is difficult to understand why Bianciardi should have selected a Bass falling a Fourth as a typical seat of a suspended Seventh, 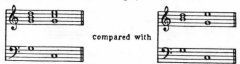 and also whether he had in mind a major Seventh as suggested by his example (Ex. 2 *p*) of a major Sixth on a Bass falling a Fourth, or a minor Seventh

[6] *piu continuatamente*, i.e. with fewer skips, as in

compared with

(2) "Oftentimes, too, the words necessitate recourse to full harmony, and, in exclamations, the support of the highest notes.[7]

(3) "When the subject is cheerful, keep, as much as possible, to the higher registers, and, when it is mournful, to the lower ones.[8]

(4) "In full closes (*nelle cadenze*) play Octaves below the Bass; avoiding Thirds and Fifths in the very low registers, because they make the harmony too congested [9] and offend the ear.

(5) "And, above all, since harmony arises from diversity of sounds arranged by contrary motion (*perchè l' armonia nasce de diversità di suoni ordinati per contrari movimenti*), one must see to it (*osservare*) that, when the Bass rises, another part falls, and that, when it falls, another part rises [Ex. 3, bars 1 and 6]. And more especially must this be observed in the case of the extreme parts, avoiding the progression from one perfect consonance to another of the same species,[10] using contrary motion, or proceeding by

---

[7] *Anzi che molte volte per necessità delle parole si ricerca pienezza di voci, e nell' esclamationi aiuto con le corde estreme.*

[8] *nelle materie allegre star nell' acuto, più che si puo, nelle meste star nel grave.*

[9] *fanno troppo borda l' armonia*; cf. Matthew Locke's 9th rule (§ 21).

[10] *fuggendo il procedere per consonanze perfette della medesima spetie.* It is evident from Ex. 3 that Bianciardi's own observance of this rule was not strict. He did not object to consecutive Fifths arising from a passing note, such as occur between the

Tenor and Bass in the last bar:  He also regarded consecutives as

avoided by an intervening passing note as in bar 9:  The Octaves

in bar 3 are, no doubt, to be regarded as a mere doubling of the Bass in the lower Octave, the harmony being:

The worst consecutives in the example are the Octaves (doubled leading note and Tonic) between Tenor and Bass in bar 6. It may, however, very well be that they are due to a misprint, and that the following was intended:

In bar 4 (apart from the bad progression of the Tenor) there are unmistakable Octaves, which extend to the first chord of bar 5, between Alto and Bass, and in bar 10 there are both Fifths and Octaves between the last two chords.

It is very possible that Bianciardi would have explained the Octaves in bar 4 by the assumption that the Alto and Tenor crossed as follows:

Adriano Banchieri gives two examples for practice on the Organ or Harpsichord (§ 13, Exx. 5, 6), which, being printed on four staves, show the progression of the

Thirds,[11] which, in the higher registers (*nell' acuto*), produce an excellent effect.

(6) "When the Bass moves in diminished notes [i.e. crotchets or quavers], or runs (*tirate*), one takes the harmony (*consonanza*) on the first note of the beat, so that one note of the run is good [12] and the other bad. [Ex. 3, bars 6 and 7.]

(7) "Thus, when there is a dotted minim followed by a crotchet, the chord (*consonanza*) falls upon the dot, and the note which follows is treated as a passing note (*passa per cattiva*). [Ex. 3, bar 5.]

(8) "But when the Bass leaps more than a Third, one must give a chord to every note [Ex. 3, bar 11]; and when it falls by step with diminution [i.e. in crotchets], a Fifth is played upon the first note, and a Sixth upon the second, accompanied by a Tenth in the upper part. [Ex. 3, bar 9.]

"Example in illustration of as much as has been said": [13]

Ex. 3

individual parts; these cross as freely as in a vocal composition, and each example contains a progression which, on a keyed instrument, would produce the impression of consecutive Fifths, though, as vocal writing, it is perfectly correct. It was Heinichen (*General-Bass &c.*, 1728, Pt. I, ch. 2, § 32, note e) who was the first to enunciate the principle that no progression which, on a keyed instrument, strikes the ear as faulty can be justified by a nominal crossing of the parts.

[11] It is not quite clear whether, by this, Bianciardi means Thirds between the two upper parts (in parallel motion with the Bass), as in bars 4 and 5 of the example, or Tenths with the Bass, as in bar 9.

[12] i.e. an accented note, whereas a passing note is said *passare per cattiva* ('to pass as bad').

[13] The unequal staves—the upper of five, and the lower of six or more lines—are characteristic of the Italian *Intavolatura d' Organo*. The C clef (in addition to the F clef) on the lower stave is a convenient guide to the eye when the number of lines exceeds five.

With regard to the example itself, besides the points of interest mentioned in notes 10 and 11, it will be observed that considerable freedom is exercised in the number of parts employed. In the second half of bar 13 a fifth part is added at the

(9) "Many other directions might be given, but, because they are difficult to describe briefly, we will omit them, having by now mentioned the most necessary existing rules.

"Therefore, in place of further rules, let us exhort the player to practise himself with a quick ear in the consonances (*exercitarsi nelle consonanze coll' udito presto*), in recognizing Fifths, Sixths, and Thirds, major and minor; availing himself of the information already given to gain the knowledge in question (*valendosi delle cose sopradette à pigliar tal notitia*); taking note that, though we have written these little rules in accordance with the style in which vocal works (*canti*) of every sort are ordinarily composed, there nevertheless remains to the composer the liberty to use the consonances according to his own fancy; that is to say, to use a Sixth in place of a Fifth, and minor Thirds in place of major,[14] interspersing (*mescolando*) divers sorts of dissonances, for which a fixed rule cannot possibly be given (*delle quale il darne sicuro ordine è impossibile*). And it is therefore necessary to make a distinction between compositions, not all of which can be conveniently played from a Bass; not, for instance, ancient fugal compositions, much less, however, certain modern ones, which we find adorned with new inventions (*che si veggono comparire vaghe di nuove inventioni*); in such instances, unless the intervals to be used are noted above the Basses,[15] and unless the player has the art of counterpoint, or a most highly trained ear (*grandissima prattica dell' udito*), he will easily ruin the composition instead of assisting."

Bianciardi then concludes his work with a simple example of transposition, which it is not necessary to reproduce here, in the shape of a series of Triads on the notes *d, e, f, g, a, c*, transposed a tone, a minor Third, and a perfect Fourth downwards, as well as a tone, a minor Third, a major Third, and a Fourth upwards.

After this follows the publisher's dedication already given.

§ 12. *Opponents of Basso continuo.*

The *Basso continuo* was by this time fairly launched upon the musical world, and was not long in spreading from Italy to other countries. But while, on the one hand, it was welcomed and recommended, as by Agazzari, it was also brought into a certain disrepute by incompetent musicians, who were incapable of reading from a full score, and who played, as best they could, from the *Basso continuo*, in order to save themselves the trouble of preparing an *Intavolatura*, or short score on two staves, as Viadana expressly recommended Organists to do (cf. § 4, Rule 6).

Agazzari, on the other hand, recommended the use of figures (cf. § 10 *a*) and considered it unnecessary to use either score or *Intavolatura* (§ 10 *e*). In default of printed figures, he recommended accompanists to listen carefully to the singers and follow the harmony, unless they cared to put in the figures with a pen (cf. § 9, note 2). It must often have happened that an Organist had no time either to prepare an *Intavolatura* or to figure an unfigured Bass, and

top; on the last chord of bar 5, too, and in the second half of bars 7 and 12, a fifth part is added and afterwards dropped again, while bar 9 is in three parts only.

[14] Cf. Banchieri's example illustrating 'The free mind of the composer in sometimes avoiding a full close' (§ 13, Ex. 10).

[15] This is the only reference to figures which occurs in Bianciardi's treatise.

was therefore obliged to rely on his ear. We can well imagine that the result, in such cases, was often highly unsatisfactory, and contemporary references prove this to have been the case.

Kinkeldey (*Orgel und Klavier*, p. 211) quotes Diruta, and also Banchieri, who was himself one of the first to print Organ Basses (cf. § 3). He writes as follows: "Sometimes the practice of playing from a Thorough-Bass is mentioned in the more important theoretical works at the beginning of the seventeenth century, and, moreover, not in a friendly spirit. Diruta, for instance, in the second part of his *Transilvano* (1609, Lib. 4, p. 16) counsels his pupil to study thoroughly as many Ricercares, Masses, Canzonas, Motets, and Madrigals as possible, in order to attain the highest perfection in playing the Organ. Each type, he says, has its special advantage for musical education. The pupil must not do as many do, who are content with playing defective four-part harmony, with no foundation whatever, and with playing on a Thorough-Bass. By so doing they disparage the competent player and discredit the good rules, imagining, as they do, that they can attain great knowledge with little study. With regard to the proper playing of a Thorough-Bass he cannot, he says, give any definite rules, because, from a Thorough-Bass alone, one cannot divine the intervals in the remaining parts. The figuring is supposed to get over this difficulty, but one cannot tell from the figuring in which part the consonance or dissonance in question occurs.* The advocates of the Thorough-Bass (*Bassisten*) maintain that one must practise oneself in it and listen very attentively. Diruta answers that, when the singers stand close by the Organist, one certainly can distinguish the individual parts, but that, if they were at a distance, the Organist could not possibly play faultlessly. He advises the pupil to *score the pieces and play all the parts.*"

Kinkeldey continues: "The contrasts which arose with the new musical practice are most sharply and appositely characterized by an author whose acquaintance we made as one of the first composers who made their appearance with printed Organ Basses. It is Adriano Banchieri (*Conclusioni del suono del Organo*, Bologna, 1609) who says about the *Basso continuo*:

'because it is easy to play it, many Organists nowadays are highly successful in concerted playing; but, in their great vanity on the score of their sureness in playing with others, they give little thought to exerting themselves in improvisation (*Fantasia*) and playing from score, whereas it is in this very domain that many a good man has made himself immortal. So that, in short, we shall soon have two classes of players: on the one hand Organists, that is to say, such as practise good playing from Score and improvisation, and, on the other hand, Bassists who, overcome by sheer laziness, are content with simply playing the Bass [i.e. playing from the *Basso continuo* as opposed to playing from the score]. . . . I do not mean to say that playing from a Thorough-Bass is not useful, and is not easy, but I do say that every Organist ought to seek to play the Thorough-Bass in accordance with sound rules.'

"We see, therefore, that the introduction of the Thorough-Bass was not effected quite without opposition."

---

* Diruta's conception of the ideal accompaniment is, evidently, that it should exactly reproduce the texture of the vocal harmony. Cavalieri to a very large extent ensured this by the practice of indicating compound intervals (cf. § 8, 7 *ad init.*). Agazzari had attained a much freer conception of the accompaniment, for he expressly warns the Organist that it is not necessary that the vocal parts should be reproduced "as they stand" (cf. § 10 *e ad fin.*).

§ 13. *Adriano Banchieri's 'Dialogo Musicale'.*

(a) In 1611 there appeared a second edition of *L' Organo suonarino opera ventesima quinta del R. P. D. Adriano Banchieri Monaco Olivetano*, printed at Venice by Amadino (Brit. Mus. K. 4. i. 2).

The first edition, which appeared in 1605, contains the rules for the use of accidentals already quoted (cf. § 4 under Rule 8), but nothing further concerning the treatment of a *Basso continuo*. In the second edition, however, there is an important addition (pp. 59–65) entitled: *Dialogo musicale del R. P. D. Adriano Banchieri Bolognese con un amico suo, che desidera suonare sicuramente sopra un Basso continuo in tutte le maniere* ('Musical dialogue between the Reverend Father Master Adriano Banchieri of Bologna and a friend of his who desires to play with security from a Thorough-Bass on the Organ in all styles').

Banchieri does not claim to be an authority on the subject, professing, as he says in his concluding discourse, to be 'a composer (for my recreation) rather than an Organist', but the dialogue is, nevertheless, well worth recording, and it is interesting to note that Banchieri expresses himself strongly in favour of the practice of using figures.

(b) The dialogue is introduced as follows:

A friend reminds Banchieri how he had met him coming out of church, 'S. Fedele here in Milan', a few days before, and had asked him to give a few general rules for playing in concert from a *Basso continuo*, and how Banchieri had asked for from four to six days' grace. He further reminds Banchieri that yesterday was the sixth day and that 'a promise is a debt'.

Banchieri modestly answers that, though he does not know the subject sufficiently to treat it adequately, he will keep his promise as best he can, and, after his friend has made a suitable reply, he proceeds:

'BANCHIERI'. "You must know that, among modern composers, Lodovico Viadana, Francesco Bianciardi, Agostino Agazzari, and perhaps others of whom I am not cognizant, have discovered and briefly touched upon certain short rules (*regolette*) on the subject of playing in concert from the *Bassi continui* attached to their compositions; however, in view of differences between them (*vedendosi diversita*), it would be well to treat of them all separately." [1]

'FRIEND'. The friend then says that he has remarked four points in which composers differ:

"Firstly, some bar (*partiscono*) the Bass, others do not bar it.

"Secondly, some place the accidentals ⚹ and ♭ above or below the notes, and others do not so place them.

"Thirdly, some put arithmetical numbers (*numeri aritmetici*) below the notes, namely, 3, 10, 6, and 13, and others do not use them.

"Lastly, some put figures consonant and dissonant (*sonori* and *dissonanti*) 4. 3, 11. 10, 7. 6, 14 and 13 ; why such variety?"

(c) 'BANCHIERI'. "It is not good (as the farmers say) to 'put the cart before the oxen', but if you want to know the method which must be followed in playing a *Basso continuo* with full mastery (*con ogni sicuro possesso*), it would be well to practise and master first the necessary rules, and then to under-

---

[1] Unfortunately, Banchieri does not carry out the intention here indicated, as no further mention is made of the composers in question by name.

stand in actual practice, by the examples, the diversity which you mention in these Basses, which, although they may seem like different methods, are not really so, but increased subtleties (*sottigliezze augmentate*) which have nowadays made (*ridotto*) a safe model representing the score of the whole Concerto; so that praise is due, not only to him who was its inventor, but equally to him who made it so easy and sure of acquirement (*chi l' ha ridotto in cosi facile e sicuro possesso*) owing to the accidentals ✕ and ♭, and afterwards the figures consonant and dissonant, and likewise barred it.''

(*d*) Banchieri then goes on to say that the incipient Organist who desires to play on a *Basso continuo* must possess certain preliminary knowledge, and that he must be able "to read and sing with certainty the Bass clefs of F *fa ut*, both with *b molle* and ♮ *quadro*, with their mutations, both ascending and descending, and, retaining this practical knowledge, to practise first of all with his fingers from key to key, and accompany his own voice with harmony quite simply''.

'FRIEND'. The friend then asks him to explain 'the twofold Clef of *b molle* and ♮ *quadro* with the mutations which you mention', which he does by giving the following examples: [2]

'BANCHIERI'. 'Pratica nella Chiave di F *fa ut* per *b* molle.'

'Pratica nella Chiave di F *fa ut* per ♮ quadro.'

(*e*) Banchieri continues: "After having practised from key to key with fingers and voice, one can then take a *Basso continuo* printed with whole notes, broken notes, notes moving by step, and notes moving by leap (*note intiere, spezzate, pausate, continue & saltante*), and practise the said Bass with fingers and voice, and, with the right foot, practise the highly necessary beating of time (*battuta*), . . . so that, when this simple practice is thoroughly mastered (*assicurato perfettamente in tal pratica semplice*), the simple accompaniments can presently be practised, first in two parts, and afterwards in three and four, in complete harmony."

'FRIEND'. "And what is meant by these accompaniments?"

'BANCHIERI'. "You must know that, on each note of the *Basso continuo* to be played in concert, two Consonances are sought, the one perfect, which will be the Fifth, and the other imperfect, which will be the Third, or their

[2] The black lozenge-shaped notes indicate the mutations where the one Hexachord passes into the next.

compounds, the Twelfth and Tenth, adding the Octave, or its compound the Fifteenth, by way of accompaniment and reinforcement (*riempitura* = 'filling-up'); let us now see such accompaniments in two, three,[3] and four parts, to be practised in due order" [Exx. 3–6].

'Accompagnamenti à dui voci per *b* molle'

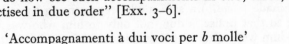
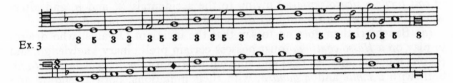

Ex. 3

'Accompagnamenti à dui voci per ♮ quadro'

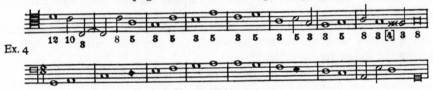

Ex. 4

'Accompagnamenti à tre voci per *b* molle.
Et aggiuntoui l' Ottaua per quarta parte & riempimento.'

Ex. 5

† 8 in the original.   ‡ 5 in the original.

'Accompagnamenti à Tre Voci alla Chiaue F per ♮ quadro.
Et aggiuntoui l' Ottaua per riempimento.'

Ex. 6

† 8 in the original.   [3] See note 3 opposite.

"This is the *Basso continuo* of which I am speaking, with the accompaniments of Fifth, Third, and Octave, or their duplicates and triplicates [i.e. compounds], which must be practised by degrees, first the Bass alone, then with the Tenor, in two parts, adding the Alto and Soprano, and let them serve as an example and criterion for whoever practises them (*& seruino per esempio & giudicio di chi pratica*)." [4]

(*f*) The friend points out to Banchieri that, in the Bass of the above examples, he omitted the note E *la* in the example with a flat (*per b molle*), and the note ♮ (i.e. B natural) in that without one (*per ♮ quadro*). Banchieri points out that the notes in question have not got a perfect Fifth, "wherefore, since their Fifth is false (as it is vulgarly called), or a Diminished Fifth (as expert musicians call it), on the said two notes or keys (*corde ò tasti*), E and [B] ♮, in *molle* and *quadro* respectively, in place of the Fifth, the Sixth is required, of which the accompaniments [i.e. the parts above the Bass] will be the Third, Sixth, and Octave, or (as has been said) their Duplicates and Triplicates."

[3] No example in three parts is given, but it will be noticed that the examples in four parts are headed '*a tre voci*'.

[4] It is evident at a glance that the two last examples, with the parts continually crossing, are vocal writing pure and simple: that is to say, they are conceived entirely from the point of view of the progression of the individual part, and not in the least as a succession of chords. A clearer idea of their effect on a keyed instrument will be gained by noting them on two staves, as follows:

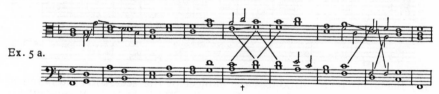

Ex. 5 a.

† Apparent Fifths between Alto and Bass.

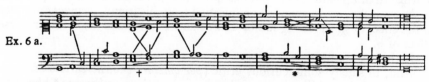

Ex. 6 a.

† Apparent Fifths, and * Octaves, between Alto and Bass.

In both examples we get, at †, the effect of consecutive Fifths between Alto and Bass, though, on paper, they are avoided by the crossing of the parts. At a later period the effect upon the ear was held to be the decisive factor, and, although crossing of the parts was not in itself forbidden, it was not admitted in justification of a progression which produced the impression of consecutive Fifths or Octaves.

At the beginning of the seventeenth century, however, in accompanying vocal compositions in which several Triads are liable to occur in succession on a Bass moving by step, such progressions as those shown above are practically inevitable—hence Viadana's 9th rule permitting Fifths and Octaves in the accompaniment (cf. § 4). The only alternative would be to maintain contrary motion between the Bass and upper parts at all costs.

An example follows showing the chord in question, on the bass notes E
and B, in its three positions, $\frac{8}{6}$, $\frac{10}{8}$, $\frac{13}{10}$.
$\frac{8}{3}$ $\frac{10}{6}$ $\frac{13}{8}$

(*g*) Banchieri next proceeds to explain the effect of the accidentals ✕ and
♭ on the bass note,[5] continuing: "and here we should take it as a general
rule that all notes in the Bass with the accidental ✕ always demand the
Sixth in place of the Fifth in the accompaniments; I will not omit to mention
that, with the said notes, one never takes the Octave (playing, of course, as
expert Organists do), but, in place of the sharpened (*accidentata*) Octave,
one will take the Third, Sixth, and Tenth;[6] further, in the case of accidental
flats (*accidenti di b molle*), one will take the Fifth when it is 'natural'
(*hauendola Naturale*), and the Sixth at pleasure, according to the taste of the
Composer[7] (*e piacendo la Sesta à gusto del Compositore*)."

'Accompaniments to accidentally altered notes in the F clef, both with
and without a flat' (*Accompagnamenti alle note accidentate, nelle Chiaui di F
si per b molle, come ♮ quadro*).

Ex. 7

(*h*) Banchieri then introduces the subject of the accidental alteration of
notes in the upper parts when the *Bass falls a Fifth or rises a Fourth.* There
are three 'positions' (i.e. points in the scale), he tells us, in which the said
downward or upward leap of the Bass gives rise to the accidentals in question,
as shown in Ex. 9. In answer to a question from his friend, he gives examples
of the effect of ✕ in raising minor Thirds and Tenths, and also of the reverse
effect of ♭.

He then continues:

"And, to satisfy some curious critic (*per quietare qualche curioso censore*),
know that such accidentals cause the same alterations in Sixths;[8] however,
in a *concerto* for two or three voices, even though the vocal Bass make a Sixth
with the upper part, modern Organists and composers alike (the intelligent

---

[5] Banchieri does not mention the raising or lowering of the note, but merely the
change from a white to a black key, except in the case of the change from B flat to
natural. He uses both ✕ and ♮ to contradict the flat in the signature (Ex. 7 *b*).

[6] Cf. § 17, III, *g*, 14, where Galeazzo Sabbatini says that, in such a case, either the
Third or the Sixth may be doubled, but that *the Third is better.* It will be observed
that, in the example, Banchieri doubles the Sixth as well as the Third, both in the
Octave (Ex. 7 *a*, *c*, *f*, *h*) and in the unison (Ex. 7 *e*).

[7] In Ex. 7 *d* the Fifth is followed by a Sixth, and in *g* the Sixth only is taken.

[8] Cf. Banchieri's *Avertimenti* concerning the threefold function of accidentals in
the *Basso continuo* quoted in § 4 under Rule 8.

ones for the most part), in such an event, insert in the *Basso continuo* a Fifth below the vocal Bass, in which case cognizance is taken only of the Tenth between the instrumental Bass and the vocal Soprano; the vocal Bass will be a middle part, and no cognizance is therefore taken of altered Sixths."

'Example of how to avoid Sixths in the *Basso continuo*' (*Esempio di sfuggire le Seste nel Basso continuo*).

† Almost certainly a misprint for *g*.

"The middle part makes a Sixth with the Soprano, and, as the two vocal parts have below them the Fifth in the *Basso continuo*, cognizance of the Tenth suffices for the Organist, and not that of the Sixth likewise,[9] a rule of much importance, conducive to facility and useful in practice (*auertimento di molta consideratione, & di facilita, & utilita alla pratica*)."

'FRIEND'. "I have understood splendidly (*stupendamente*), and I think that it is a rule of the greatest importance for whoever composes these *Bassi continui* to make everything easy for the inexperienced Organist; now I desire you to show me when the Organist ought to alter [i.e. sharpen] the parts above the *Basso continuo* in the leaps which you mentioned to me, of which there are three falling a Fifth, and three rising a Fourth."

'BANCHIERI'. "Here they are, distinctly in all the positions,[10] and arranged in order; noting that, when there is a flat in the key (*nella Chiaue di b molle*), there are two more of them, one falling a Fifth, and one rising a Fourth, but the effect is the reverse, the change being from a black key to a white."

'Example of the three leaps of a Fifth and Fourth, and two more in *b molle*.'

[9] This in a great measure accounts for the fact that the practice of indicating a sharpened Sixth by ✕ a Third below (or a Sixth above) the bass note (cf. § 4 under Rule 8) never became firmly established.

[10] It will be noticed that Banchieri ignores the progression $^{\#d\ e}_{b\ e}$, although it occurs in Viadana's *Concerti*.

(*i*) 'FRIEND'. "So, if one observes these leaps of a Fifth and Fourth, it would be superfluous to put in (*segnar*) the accidentals and the figures which many modern composers and Organists put below the *Bassi continui*."

'BANCHIERI'. "You would be making a great mistake to believe that, since, on the contrary, these accidentals and figures are put in with very good reason (*ottimamente posti*); in the first place, because, by putting in the figures 3 and 10, two Octaves are avoided [11] which might otherwise occur between the voice and the note played (*il Tasto*); in the next place, because the composer of to-day is free in his composition to suit the words, to the end that people may sing with feeling in modern fashion, by sometimes avoiding a full close; so that, in executing a *Basso continuo* without accidentals, a practical Organist, though well grounded in his playing (*sonando con gli buoni fondamenti*), might occasion discord; [12] it is therefore necessary (whenever occasion arises) to put in ♭, 𝕏, 3, and 10, and when the above-mentioned leaps of a Fifth and Fourth have neither accidental nor figure, the Organist can avoid disaster (*il cattiuo incontro*), and, by using his ear, cause the *concerto* to pass off in a satisfactory manner. And, although certain modern composers have published the opinion that accidentals in *Bassi continui* seem superfluous, presupposing that the Organists understand their business, they are to know that they are, nevertheless, in error, both for the reasons adduced, and also because the majority of Organists at the present day live up to (*osseruano*) the common proverb 'It is not every cock that knows a bean'. And, to conclude, here is an example of the freedom of the composer's mind in avoiding the accidental in leaps of a Fourth and Fifth."

'The free mind of the composer in sometimes avoiding a full close.' [13]

Ex. 10

"And this is as much as I can briefly tell you on the subject of playing a *Basso continuo* in concert on the Organ."

(*k*) 'FRIEND'. "I am infinitely consoled; I only want you to tell me, in order, the four differences between *Bassi continui* already mentioned at the outset, which I will repeat for the sake of greater clearness.

1. "Some bar the *Basso continuo*, and others do not bar it.
2. "Some put in accidentals, and others do not put them in.
3. "Some put in the consonant figures 3, 6, 10, and 13, others do not use them.
4. "Finally, the consonant and dissonant figures are put in together, how about this?"

---

[11] Banchieri was evidently in complete agreement with Viadana's 4th Rule. It cannot be denied that there is much to be said in favour of the short-lived practice of differentiating in the figuring between the simple and the compound intervals.

[12] i.e. by assuming that the Third is to be sharpened when the Bass falls a Fifth or rises a Fourth. Some composers went so far as to put a ♭ over the bass note as a warning against a full close.

[13] Compare Joh. Staden's example, § 16, III [2], Rule 2 *ad fin.*

'BANCHIERI'. "With regard to these four varieties, about which you inquire, I will briefly give you complete satisfaction.

1. "Those who bar the Bass operate in so doing with much judgement, because, not seeing the words, and hearing (for the most part) difference in the agreement of the vocal parts (*concerto differente dalle parte cantabili*),[14] the Organist, even though experienced, may easily lose the beat (*smarrire la battuta*), besides which the said barred Bass gives much light in the closes, and success is more certain than when it is unbarred.

2. "The flats and sharps are put in with very good reason (*stanno benissimo*), and are necessary, and whoever was the inventor of them deserves no little praise for the reasons and practical examples given above.

3. "Still greater praise is deserved, in the next place, by whoever added to the ✕ and ♭ the figures 3 and 10.

4. "The greatest praise, and that beyond all comparison, is due to whoever added to the consonant figures the dissonant ones. Thus, having treated the matter sufficiently above, all that you wanted is here summed up (*eccoui epilogato ogni vostro desiderio*), and this is that *Basso continuo* which, when all these conditions are fulfilled, represents a true epitome of the entire score (*un sicuro compendio di tutta la spartitura*); and, since examples make a greater impression than words, here is an example for the sake of greater clearness:

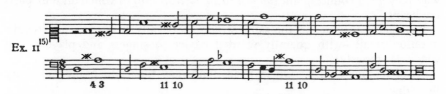

Ex. 11[15]

"The lower line (*quel di sotto*) is the *Basso continuo*, and the part above shows the two effects of the accidentals ♭ and ✕ with figures consonant and dissonant, so you must be satisfied when you have seen a similar example in the key with a flat (*nella chiaue di b molle*) with different accidentals:

Ex. 12[15]

(*l*) "And, for greater clearness, in leaving a subject of importance, it remains for me to say that some modern composers, for the sake of greater safety (*per maggior sicurezza*), figure the Fifths and Sixths, Sevenths and Sixths, and suchlike, which follow each other in harsh and syncopated passages (*nelle durezze e legature*), as here:

---

[14] i.e. different singers singing different words, and also, perhaps, *cross-accents*.
[15] Banchieri has not yet reached the stage (reached by Peri, Caccini, and Cavalieri in 1600) of prefixing the accidentals to the figure (as ✕10); he also differs from them in placing the figures below, instead of above the Bass.

Ex. 13 [16)]

56 76   76   76   65 43   [43] 3 6   4 3   4 3

(*m*) 'FRIEND'. "I thank Your Reverence very much indeed and beg you to tell me, as the final cadence of our discourse, some short method which, after having acquired the said foundations, must be adhered to in putting them into practice."

'BANCHIERI'. "You are asking too much in making this last request, nor do I consider myself competent [to answer you], as I profess to be a Composer (for my recreation) rather than an Organist; however, I will tell you in discursive fashion my own opinion. As for this new fashion of playing on a *Basso continuo*, I do not condemn it, but I do not praise it, because the new-fashioned Organists omit to study the Ricercatas in four parts and improvisations (*fantasie*) of illustrious men in the profession, seeing that nowadays many consider themselves adept (*sicuri*) Organists on the strength of a few stretches of the hand (*con quatro sparpagliate di mano*) and playing on a *Basso continuo*; but it is not true, seeing that adept Organists are those who play good counterpoint (*un ben tirato Cõtraponto*) in which all four parts are heard."

Banchieri continues in the same strain—not really answering his friend's question at all—with quaintly worded advice to singers and players, and concludes piously:

"And let this suffice. Go in peace, and may the Lord grant you every blessing."

§ 14. *The addition of an Organ Bass to earlier works. Rapid spread of the 'Basso continuo' from Italy.*

I. We have seen that the *Basso continuo* had its opponents (cf. § 12). Some musicians, on the other hand, so much appreciated its advantages that even the works of earlier composers seemed to them incomplete without it.

In Italy the re-publication of some of the works of Palestrina, with the addition of a figured or unfigured *Basso continuo* for the Organ, began within a very few years of the first appearance of Viadana's *Concerti*, as will be seen from the list given below.[1] One such publication, which included three selected Masses of Palestrina and one by Anerio, appeared in 1619, and was

---

[16] We were told in Banchieri's *Avertimenti alle guide del Basso* (cf. § 4 under Rule 8) that the accidental indicating a sharpened or flattened Sixth should be placed a Third *below* the bass note; in the above example it is placed a Third *above*.

[1] The following instances are recorded in Eitner's *Quellenlexicon*:

    (1) *Missarum cum 4 et 5 vocibus Lib. 4* (original ed. Venice, 1582), 1610, *Basso principale* [figured] *co'l Soprano* (cf. § 5, note 1). *Milano, Tini & Lomazzo.*

    (2) *Motettorum quinque vocibus Lib. 4* (original ed. Venice, 1587), 1611 (Venice, Gardanus), with Bassus ad Org. [unfigured] (R. C. of Music).

    The same, 1613, Venice, Aere B. Magni (Bassus ad Org. in Brit. Mus.).

    (3) *Messe à 4 voci: Le tre prime del Palestrina* cioé, *Iste Confessor, Sine Nomine, & di Papa Marcello, ridotta à quattro di Giov. Franc. Anerio, & la quarta*

reprinted no less than three times (in 1635, 1639, and 1689), which shows that there was a considerable demand.

We have an instance of the same procedure in Germany, at an equally early period, in the case of the *Promptuarium Musicum*, a collection of ecclesiastical works by different composers, of which three parts appeared in 1611, 1612, and 1613 respectively, compiled by Abraham Schadaeus, Organist (presumably of the Cathedral) at Speyer. To this work one Caspar Vincentius,[2] who became Organist at Speyer in 1611, two years before Schadaeus left that town, added a figured Bass in a separate volume entitled:

> *Promptuarii Musici . . . Pars Prima. Collectore Abrahamo Schadaeo, Senfftenbergensi Scholae Spirensium Rectore. Cui Basin vulgo generalem dictam & ad Organa musicaque instrumenta accomodatam addidit Caspar Vincentius ejusdem civitatis Musicus Organicus. Argentinae* [Strassburg], 1611. *Paul Ledertz.*

Pars Secunda followed in 1612, and Pars Tertia in 1613, with a preface by Vincentius to the figured Bass part. In 1617 Vincentius, then Organist at Worms, to whom Schadaeus appears to have entrusted his manuscripts, issued a fourth part, likewise with the addition of a figured Bass.

Kinkeldey (*Orgel und Klavier*, p. 214) describes the work as follows: "Vincentius's Bass is plentifully figured, but for the most part without bar-lines. For pieces in 5–7 parts it is single, for the 8-part pieces [3] it is double, and here bar-lines are frequently used at long intervals, especially at the points where the change between the choirs takes place. In the preface to the Thorough-Bass of the second part (1612) Vincentius gives sundry theoretical directions which are based on Viadana's rules. Vincentius also quotes the authority of Viadana, and, without more ado, styles him the inventor of this kind of 'Partitur'. In the last part (1617) Vincentius writes a short preface addressed to the '*Organicis Zoilis*', for in Germany, too, the Thorough-Bass had its opponents, who met him with much the same arguments as the Italians. Vincentius advises the less experienced Organists to put the pieces into Italian, German, or French [4] Tablature."

In 1625 Vincentius prepared and published (at Würzburg) a figured Bass to Orlando di Lasso's *Magnum opus musicum*. It is in this work that he describes himself as 'Audomariensis Arthaesii', a native of St. Omer in the old province of Artois.

> della Battaglia dell' istesso G. F. Anerio. Con il Basso continuo per sonare, Roma, 1619, L. A. Soldi.
> The same, 1635, Roma, Masotti.
> The same, 1639, Roma, Andr. Fei (Brit. Mus.).
> The same, 1689 . . . con il Basso ad org. di novo diligentia corretti da Fr. Giannini. Roma.

(4) *Hymni totius anni, secundum Sanctae Romanae Ecclesiae consuetudinem 4 vocibus concinendi &c.* (original ed. Romae, 1589, Jac. Fornerius & Bern. Donangelus), 1625, *Roma.* Cum Basso ad Org.

[2] Caspar Vincentius, originally Gaspard Vincent, was a Frenchman by birth, a native of St. Omer.

[3] i.e. for two choirs, each with its own vocal Bass as in the Motets of Croce and Quintiani mentioned in § 3.

[4] The French so-called 'Tablature' for keyed instruments (cf. *Tablature pour le jeu d'orgues, espinettes et manicordions*, Paris, 1530, Attaignant) was, like the Italian 'Intavolatura d' organo' (cf. § 4, note 10), simply a condensed score on two staves in musical notation.

In the preface he castigates the organists through whose negligence so many admirable compositions fell into disuse, because, as he says, they put into Tablature only what they happened to fancy, and repeated it *ad nauseam*. "In my opinion", he writes, "the worthy and noble Master Lodovico da Viadana desired to punish the negligence of these fellows and quell their arrogance by inventing a new method of relieving Organists of the trouble of making Tablatures, and of, as it were, compelling those who are unversed in music to learn it better before they become practitioners (*ehe sie Hand anlegen*). He has been followed, not in Italy alone, but in Germany as well, by others, who set, not only their own vocal compositions (*Gesänge*), but those of others as well, in a similar manner and over a general Bass, just as I myself have issued four such books under the name of *Promptuarium Musicum*."

The procedure of Vincentius, and especially of those who added a *Basso continuo* to works of Palestrina, strikes one at the present day as unmitigated Vandalism, but, when the circumstances are taken into consideration, it is not so incomprehensible as it would appear at first sight.

As Viadana himself explained (cf. § 1), totally inadequate vocal resources often rendered the proper performance of polyphonic works impossible. Missing parts had to be supplied by the Organ, which also served to bolster up and connect the entire work, especially where two or more bodies of singers were in co-operation.

We saw that, in the last decade of the sixteenth century, composers found it advisable to provide their own works with a *Bassus ad Organum* (cf. § 3). The support of the Organ had come to be regarded as a necessity, and it is not, therefore, so much to be wondered at that the *Basso continuo*, which in Viadana's *Concerti* for the most part formed an integral and indispensable part of the whole (rather than the mere duplication of that which was already present in the vocal parts) should have been extended to cases in which, according to the original intention of the composer, it was wholly inappropriate.

II. We saw in the last section that the use of figured Thorough-Basses had spread from Italy to South Germany within a very short time of their first appearance in print in the former country; for it was as early as 1611 that the Frenchman Gaspard Vincent (Caspar Vincentius), then Organist of Speyer, published his figured Bass to the first part of the *Promptuarium Musicum* of Schadaeus.

It seems more than probable that the practice was imported into England direct from Italy.

The *Cantiones Sacrae* of Richard Deering, for five voices with a figured *Basso continuo* for the Organ, published at Antwerp by Peter Phalese in 1617, of which a copy is preserved in the library of Westminster Abbey, is probably one of the earliest English works of the kind, though further research is needed to confirm this supposition. Sir F. Bridge describes it in his most interesting account of Deering in *Twelve Good Musicians*, 1920 (pp. 56–60), where he disposes effectually of the widely circulated myth (which probably originated in a misprint) to the effect that Deering published a set of 5-part Motets at Antwerp in 1597.[5]

[5] Deering's 'Supplication' for the degree of Bachelor of Music at Oxford was made in April 1610, and in it he speaks of having 'spent ten years in the study and practice

When Deering published his Motets (*Cantiones Sacrae*) at Antwerp in 1617, he was Organist to the English nuns, in the monastery of the Blessed Virgin Mary, at Brussels, but, from a passage in the Latin 'Dedication', of which Sir F. Bridge gives a translation, it would appear that they had been awaiting publication for some time, and, moreover, that they were composed in Italy. The passage is as follows: "For long my Music has desired to come forward. She is not unpolished (for she was born in the first City of the World) but she is modest."

Sir F. Bridge quotes a statement of Antony à Wood to the effect that 'Deering was bred up in Italy, where he obtained the name of a most admirable musician'. He was also a Catholic. There is therefore little doubt that, by the 'first City of the World', he meant Rome.

Combined with Antony à Wood's statement, this leads to the inevitable conclusion that it was in Italy, and, almost certainly, at Rome, that he learned to equip his *Cantiones Sacrae* with a figured *Basso continuo*.

§ 15. *Praetorius.*

I. The sixth chapter in the third volume of the *Syntagma Musicum* of Michael Praetorius, published in 1619, is entitled *De Basso generali seu Continuo.*

In it the author sets forth how the *Bassus continuus* is to be treated, not only on the Organ, but on "Lutes, Harps, Chitarrone or Theorba", used either as instruments of foundation—in which case the rules given for the Organ apply equally to them—or as instruments of ornamentation (cf. § 10 *e*).

He speaks of it as in general use in Italy. "The *Bassus generalis seu continuus*", he says, "is so called because it continues from beginning to end, and, as a general part, contains in itself the whole music or *concerto*, as is the common practice in Italy, and has now in particular been brought to light and put into print by that excellent musician Lodov. Viadana, *novae inventionis primario*, when he invented the fashion of singing with one, two, three, or four voices to the accompaniment of an Organ, Regal, or other similar instrument of foundation, when there is need of such a *Bassus generalis* and *continuus pro Organoedo vel Cytharoedo tanquam fundamentum.*"

He explains that the *Bassus continuus* was not invented as a convenience for lazy organists who disliked the trouble of preparing a tablature, but rather in order that it might form the foundation of a score or tablature from which the Organist might construct his part. This is in perfect accordance with Viadana's sixth Rule, or rather recommendation. It also shows that Praetorius did not regard it as necessarily part of a composer's duty to provide a Bass figured ready for use.[1] We shall see presently that he regarded figures

---

of music', according to which statement his musical studies began in 1600. It is therefore *primâ facie* unlikely, as Sir F. Bridge, who unearthed these important facts, points out, that he published Motets in 1597, three years before beginning the study of Music!

[1] We find a suggestion of the same point of view, at a much later period, in Purcell's preface to his *Sonnatas* [sic] *of Three Parts*, 1683. The Sonatas are for two Violins and a figured Bass for the Organ, as well as a Violoncello part which, in some movements, reduplicates the Organ Bass, while, in others, it is more or less free.

In the preface Purcell mentions that he figured the Bass at the last moment, and as an afterthought.

It is not likely that he would expect the accompanist to supply the harmony by

as a necessity, and must therefore conclude that the score or tablature above mentioned was to be made, not in order that the accompanist might play from it, but merely as a preliminary to the figuring of the Bass.

II. Praetorius gives short directions as to how the *Bassus generalis* is to be extracted from the vocal Bass.

"It is further to be observed", he writes, "that, when one wants to make a general Bass from an actual Bass, one should write and put down the runs in black notes, not as one finds them, but just simply in Semibreves and Minims, in accordance, however, with what is suitable.[2] As, for example:"

Ex. I

He gives, among others, the following example to illustrate how the Organist is to figure his Bass:

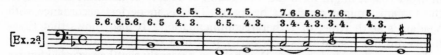

Ex. 2

"This", he writes, "is now noted as follows with the *signa* [i.e. ♯ ♭] and figures over the General Bass":

[Ex. 2ª]

N.B.—The ♯ over the bass notes, denoting the major Third, is placed as in Viadana's Basses (cf. § I, note 2), on its proper line of the stave. In the original the ♯ in the penultimate bar is placed too high, either by a misprint or from lack of space.

---

ear, still less to play the Bass without any chords at all. If, therefore, he had left the Bass unfigured, in accordance with his original intention, it must have been on the assumption that a score would be made, and the Bass figured accordingly.

[2] This proviso is illustrated in the fourth bar of the Ex. by 𝄢 instead of 𝄢

"Some people, who want to be very accurate in all details, indicate with their figures the actual distance of the intervals, when the notes [i.e. the Bass and upper part] are a Tenth, 11, 12, 13, &c., apart.[3] The Alto, in the present case, might accordingly have been noted as follows:

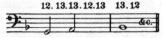

But as it is too complicated (*gar zu weitläufftig*), and only makes the work more difficult, it will be best to adhere to the simple *numeri*; for an Organist must himself take notice, with a good ear and great attention, whether it seems better to keep to the Third, Fourth, Fifth down below, or to use their upper Octaves, the 10, 11, 12, &c."

Praetorius quotes freely from the precepts of both Viadana and Agazzari, comparing their views and accompanying his quotations with comments headed M. P. C. (*meae propriae considerationes*).

He is most emphatic on the necessity of using figures to indicate the harmony. After quoting Agazzari on the subject (cf. § 10 *a*) he adds:

M. P. C. "But it is impossible for even the best composer to know or guess at once what species of concords or discords the author or composer has used.

"It is therefore in the highest degree necessary, not only for the tyro, but for practical and experienced Organists and players of foundation instruments, to indicate the *signa* [♯ ♭] and figures over the notes."

In further confirmation of his view he adds a long quotation from the preface to the third book of Bernhardus Strozzi's *Affettuosi Concerti Ecclesiastici*, of which the following is a part:

"As, however, some of them observed and realized that one heard much discord (*viel dissonantien*) when such a Bass [i.e. an unfigured *Basso continuo*] was played just simply as it stood (*also schlecht und 'simpliciter'*), because everybody applies the musical rules after his own fashion, caprice, inclination, and pleasure, it was highly necessary to invent means by which one could play it quite correctly, and in such fashion that no mistakes were heard, and treat it as much as possible in accordance with the intentions of the composer. And this could not be brought about otherwise, or more easily, than by this device of numbers or figures, by means of which any little boy, even, if only he has familiarized himself with them a little, will play the music (*den Gesang*) just as correctly and without discord as if he were playing from a complete Tablature [i.e. the Italian 'Intavolatura', cf. § 4, note 10]. And indeed I have heard sundry persons, and found by actual experience (*Wie ich denn etliche gehört, auch 'in effectu' probiret*) that, by the aid and employment of the figures in question, they treated and played the Motets of Palestrina [4] (which, as every one well knows, are admirably constructed in accordance with the rules, filled with imitations [*fugiret*], and, in short, interwoven and complicated with beautiful ties and syncopations) in such a manner that it seemed to the hearers quite as though they had all been set out in complete Tablature, since they heard nothing that sounded amiss (*keine dissonantien*) in the playing."

III. Praetorius begins his directions for the actual performance of a figured Bass with Agazzari's four rules, already given in § 10 *c*.

---

[3] As in the case of Peri, Caccini, and Cavalieri (cf. §§ 5-8). It will be noticed that, in the last bar of Ex. 2 *a*, Praetorius places the ♯, not a Third, but a Tenth above the final note. [4] Cf. § 14.

He makes an interesting comment on the treatment of what were afterwards known as 'Bassetti', i.e. those portions of the Tenor, or Alto (or any
upper part) which, during the silence of the actual Bass, became the temporary foundation of the harmony, and were incorporated, *with their appropriate clefs*, in the *Basso continuo*. It was an accepted rule in the eighteenth
century that the Bass might be played in 8ves on the Harpsichord, or with
the pedals on the Organ, at the discretion of the performer, except in the
case of 'Bassetti', as indicated by the change from an F- to a C-clef in the
figured Bass.

Praetorius (in 1619) makes the following comment:

M. P. C. "In sundry General-Basses, as in the *Dialogicis Concentibus* of
A. Agazzari and others, I find that, although high Alto or Tenor voices are
the foundation [of the harmony], the Octave below is given to be played
on the Organ; the which is disapproved by some, but does not seem to me
so very wrong or unreasonable, inasmuch as, on Organs, and especially
Positive Organs, one cannot always have pipes (*Stimmen*, lit. 'voices') which
are of 8-foot tone and of equal pitch with the human voice, but must sometimes use the small pipes, which are an Octave higher, with only 4-foot tone.
Sometimes, too, one has 'Regals' of 16-foot tone which, in themselves, sound
an Octave below the human voice. In which case the effect, as compared
with the human voice, is an Octave lower, even though the vocal part is
played as high as it is written. And, in this matter, I find that Adrianus
Banchieri, in his *Cartella*, is quite of my opinion."

This explanation, though interesting, is not very convincing: it seems
almost incredible that, in a published work, the composer should have noted
the *Basso continuo* on the assumption that it would be performed on an
Organ with only 4-foot tone.

The following passage from Viadana's *Concerto* 'Sanctorum meritis' will
serve to illustrate the practice to which Praetorius alludes:

In accordance with the established practice of a later period the *Bassus
continuus*, instead of reduplicating the *Altus* in the lower Octave, would have
appeared as follows:

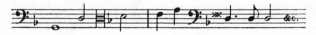

IV. The section of the chapter on General Bass in which Praetorius deals with the Organ concludes with the following Appendix:

"As I have found with those Organists who were previously unaccustomed to the style in which only two or three parts are composed over a General Bass, that they put into Tablature (*absetzen*) and play the General Bass and the one or two parts, just as they are written, and as it would sound very bad and bare if no additional middle parts were played upon the Organ, or some other instrument of foundation, I have been obliged to explain here somewhat more clearly (since an unpractised person might not comprehend it from the account hitherto given) how a tyro and beginner is to address himself (*sich schicken*) to a General Bass and learn to play from it.

(1) "When any one is confronted with a General Bass, he must be careful to take with his left hand, with each fundamental note that occurs in the General Bass, a Fifth, either by itself, or with the Third as well: or again, a whole Octave, either by itself, or with the Fifth; but, with the right hand, the Octave of the Bass, alone, or with its Third (the Tenth as compared with the Bass), or again, this Tenth and Twelfth together: and so on right through (*und diss also durch und durch*). The *signa* ♯ ♭ above the Bass, and the figures 3, 4, 5, 6, 7, &c., denoting *Tertias & Sextas majores & minores* [&c.] . . . must, however, be carefully attended to. And, accordingly, it is not necessary that the Organist should have regard, in playing, to the vocal parts as they are sung,[5] but merely that he should, on his own account, play the harmony appropriate to the Bass (*die Concordantien zum Fundament greiffe*).

"Wherefore I have chosen to include, *melioris intellectus & declarationis gratia*, the following example from the second part of my 'Wir glauben', which is to be found in *Polyhymnia Caduceatrice seu Pacis nuncia*." [6]

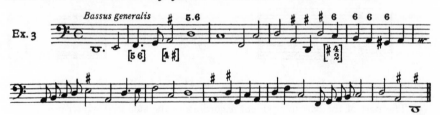

N.B.—The figures in brackets, below the Bass, are supplied from the *Resolutio*.

[5] It will be remembered that Agazzari, too, warned the accompanist against attempting to reproduce the vocal score (cf. § 10 e *ad fin.*). To organists whose idea of accompaniment was based on the use of either an Italian 'Intavolatura' (cf. § 4, note 10) or a German Organ Tablature, or a full score, this warning was not unnecessary (cf. § 12, note).

[6] Brit. Mus. G. 131. Several of the part books are unfortunately missing; it is therefore impossible to give the full vocal and instrumental score for comparison with the accompaniment as set out by the composer (Ex. 3 a).

N.B.—(1) The irregular barring of the *Bassus generalis* is corrected (from bar 5 onwards) in the *Resolutio*.

(2) The small notes in brackets in bars 3, 6, 8 are omitted in the original, obviously by inadvertence.

(3) In bar 5, on the second crotchet †, the original has *e* in the Tenor by a misprint for *f*.

(4) The consecutive Octaves in bar 5, and the thinly veiled Fifths and Octaves in

bar 6, are in perfect accordance with Viadana's 9th rule (cf. § 4), as are also the Octaves $^{c\ d}_{e\ d}$ between Alto and Bass in bar 9. At a later period they would, of course, have been condemned in a 4-part accompaniment.

It was only when the accompaniment was 'full', i.e. with as many concordant intervals of each chord doubled as the fingers could conveniently manage, that consecutives arising from such duplication were allowed, provided that the thumbs were close enough together for them to be covered up (cf. Ch. III, § 3 II).

Thus      would not be good, but

is quite permissible. It was, of course, on the Harpsichord (rather than the Organ) that this style of accompaniment was mainly used.

(5) The part of the example which, according to the standard which prevailed at a somewhat later date, is especially open to criticism is the first half of bar 5, on account of the wide gap between the upper part and the close chords in the left hand. This seems to have been a common fault in the early seventeenth century. Werckmeister (*Harmonologia Musica*, 1702, § 11) writes:

"Thus the best musicians of the present day nearly all treat the General Bass in this manner [i.e. with the Bass only in the left hand and the chords in the right], which their predecessors did not do, but played most of the chords in the left hand, the result of which was a rumble (*Gemurre*) and must have been far from pleasing."

(2) "Attention must constantly be paid to the variety and change of clefs

𝄢 𝄡 at the beginning of the stave and in the middle; otherwise, mistakes may easily be made."

(3) "When a Treble alone, or two together, sing to the accompaniment of a General Bass, it is, in my opinion, better that one should keep in the upper registers,[7]

---

[7] "oben in den kleinen Stimmen und Claviren", lit. "among the small voices and keys". The word 'small' refers to the size of the pipes which produce high notes.

but that when Tenors, Altos, or Basses sing, one should keep down in the lower registers." [8]

(4) "When few voices sing, one should also use few notes (*Clavire*), such as c g ē, d a f, c c̄ ē, &c.,[9] in order that the voices may be heard clearly and distinctly above the Organ; but when more voices begin to sing, one should use more notes (*Claves*) and fuller harmony."

N.B.—(5) "It is also particularly to be observed, when 2 or 3 voices sing to the accompaniment of the General Bass which the Organist or Lutenist has before him and plays from, that it is very good, indeed almost necessary, to have the same General Bass played, in addition, by some bass instrument, such as a Bassoon (*Fagott*), Dolcian (also = Bassoon), or Trombone, or, what is best of all, on a Violone. I have therefore exhorted several singers (*Cantores*), that a number of them should (as would be very praiseworthy) practise playing the Bass Viol (*Bassgeige* = Violone) in the chorus, which is a very easy matter, and is an admirable adornment to the foundation,[10] and helps to strengthen it, since one cannot, in every school, always have good Bass singers.

"Or one can also have the General Bass sung, to which end I have added the words, as well as they could be adapted, in those *Cantiones* in which the words are not already to be found in the instrumental Basses."

V. Praetorius concludes his chapter on the *Bassus continuus* with a section entitled: *Vom Lauttenisten, Harffenisten, &c.* ('On the Lutenist, Harpist,&c.'). In this he gives a translation of Agazzari's rules for the treatment of the 'Instruments of Ornamentation', of which a brief summary has already been given (cf. § 10 *d*), adding his own approving comments, headed M. P. C. (= *Meae propriae considerationes*).

Then follows a translation of Agazzari's account of the reasons which led to the introduction of the *Bassus continuus* (cf. § 10 *e*).

In this rule, as in the next, Praetorius uses the word 'Clavir', not = 'manual', but = Clavis (key), which latter word is also used in both rules.

It will be observed that Praetorius agrees with Viadana's 12th Rule (cf. § 4) as opposed to Agazzari's recommendation (cf. § 10 *b*).

[8] "unten in den groben und tiefen *Clavibus*", lit. "among the coarse and deep notes". The word 'grob' evidently refers to the size of the pipe rather than to coarseness of tone.

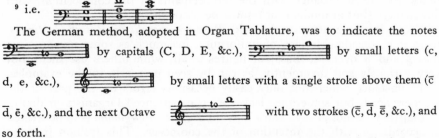

The German method, adopted in Organ Tablature, was to indicate the notes by capitals (C, D, E, &c.), by small letters (c, d, e, &c.), by small letters with a single stroke above them (c̄ d̄, ē, &c.), and the next Octave with two strokes (c̿, d̿, ē̄, &c.), and so forth.

Later on the stroke was usually made by the side of the letter (c', d', e', &c.), as in German treatises of the present day, in which the Octaves in question are referred to as the 'large Octave' (*die grosse Octave*), the 'small Octave' (*die kleine Octave*), and the 'Octave with one stroke' (*die einmal gestrichene Octave*), &c., respectively.

[10] The Violone, thus used, was included by Agazzari among the instruments of ornamentation (cf. § 10 *d*).

The chapter ends with some quaintly worded advice to Organists, as to how they may best arrange their prelude to any large performance, in Church or Chamber, especially in the matter of assisting the tuning of the various instruments. The notes required—G, which, as we are told, the Lutenists and Violists generally tune first, then D, A, E, C, and F—are to be given, first in Octaves with both hands, then with the left hand, while the right hand executes "elegant runs and other *Diminutiones* such as are used in Toccatas". The tuning accomplished, "a little Fugue, a pleasing (*lieblich*) Fantasia or Toccata" may be played. The Organist is then to "break off short" before modulating "neatly (*fein seuberlich*) and gradually" into the key of the music to be performed.

In conclusion, Praetorius complains of the interruption to the Organist's prelude caused by the Bassoons, Trombones, or Cornets (*Zincken*), and suggests that the players of the two latter might reasonably be expected to do their tuning and try their mouthpieces in their own lodging (*Losament*)!

§ 16. *Johann Staden.*

I. In 1626 there appeared a treatise, which deserves more than a passing mention, by Johann Staden, Organist of St. Sebaldus in Nuremberg. It was entitled *Kurzer und einfältiger Bericht für diejenigen, so im Basso ad Organum unerfahren, was bey demselben zum Theil in Acht zu nehmen* ('Short and simple account, for those who are inexperienced in the Bassus ad Org., of some of the necessary precautions therein'), and was appended to the Bassus ad Org. of the author's *Kirchenmusic, Ander Theil, Geistlicher Gesäng und Psalmen auf die fürnembsten Fest im Jahr und sonsten zu gebrauchen; von 1, 2, 3, 4, 5, 6 und 7 Stimmen: Dabei etliche auf Violen und andern Instrumenten gericht: mit einem Basso ad Organum* ('Church Music, Second Part, consisting of Sacred Songs and Psalms to be used on the chief Festivals of the year, and at other times . . . : also sundry ones adapted to Viols and other instruments: with a Bassus ad Organum'), 4to, printed at Nuremberg by Simon Halbmayer.

The treatise in question has been reprinted by Chrysander[1] in the *Allgemeine Musikalische Zeitung*, Jahrgang xii, 1877, pp. 99–103 and 119–23.

II. Staden begins as follows:

"*Bassus Generalis* or *Bassus Continuus ad Organum* is, it is true, commonly indicated with only a single part; but more parts, with consonances, sometimes, too, in accordance with the requirements of the composition, with dissonances (but in moderation), must be used with it.

"Now, in the matter of the said *Bassus Generalis* or *Bassus Continuus*, there is a considerable lack of uniformity, inasmuch as some use no *signa* [i.e. ♯ and ♭ over the Bass] or figures at all, while others use them, but very variously and divergently, as can be seen presently in the examples, a circumstance which not only easily occasions errors on the part of the inexperienced, but sometimes leaves even experienced Organists in doubt, so that they cannot always know how the *Bassus ad Organum* is to be treated in accordance with the intention of the composer. This fashion [i.e. the *Bassus continuus*] first came into vogue in Italy, the invention in question

---

[1] Chrysander gives the examples in modern notation. In the original they are given (he tells us) on a 10-line stave, the clefs (presumably an F clef below a C clef) being moved higher or lower as occasion requires. The old form of sharp, the *signum cancellatum* or 'latticed sign' ✕, would, of course, be used.

being ascribed to Ludovico Viadana, inasmuch as he, of set purpose, adapted to it sundry *opera* in 1, 2, 3, 4 and more parts, in which he paid more attention to the voices of good singers than to the Organist, and this method is now being practised by others likewise, so that it now promises to become common in Germany as well.

"I have never, it is true, regarded it as a matter of necessity to provide this same Bassus ad Organum, except in Viadana's fashion above mentioned, when it is not to be dispensed with;[2] I am still of the same opinion, but I leave every one free to add one wherever he pleases.

"But the said Bassus Generalis or Bassus Continuus ad Organum requires a person to whom the musical rules and the keyboard (*Clavier*) are familiar, who is experienced in putting into score or tablature (*Partirn*[3] *oder Aussetzen*[4]), and who knows how the concords and discords are to be used in relation to the Bass, and can make the *Clausulae*.[5]

"As, however, some lack the means to attain to this, and yet would fain set to work to learn, I therefore hope that my account will not be unserviceable to them for the purpose, but will help them somewhat, and give them occasion for further thought."

III. After the above introduction the treatise is divided into the following headings:

[1] 'Account of the *signa* [i.e. ♯, ♭ above the Bass] in use, and the distinction between them [i.e. their respective application]' ('Erzählung von den gebräuchlichen Signis sammt derselben Unterschied').

Staden mentions that ♯ and ♭ (denoting the major and minor Thirds respectively) are sometimes placed a Third above the actual bass note (cf. § 1, note 1), and sometimes above the stave, in accordance with the practice which soon became universal. He adds that a major Third is sometimes indicated by ♯ prefixed to the bass note ![notation], as though that note itself were to be raised a semitone. This, he says, may be merely a mistake on the part of the amanuensis or compositor. He reminds his readers that the intervals in question (major and minor Thirds) are not necessarily to be reckoned from the Bass itself, but that a Tenth or Seventeenth may be used instead of a Third, and that the same principle applies to the other intervals such as Fourths, Fifths, Sixths, and Sevenths, &c. He adds the following Ex., in which the black notes represent the Thirds indicated by the *signa* ♯ and ♭:

[Ex. 1]

[2] 'Account of the *numeri* or figures in use and the distinction between them' ('Erzählung von den gebräuchlichen Numeris oder Zahlen, sammt derselben Unterschied').

---

[2] In writing this Staden was no doubt thinking of Vincentius, whose figured Bass to the *Magnum opus musicum* of Orlando di Lasso had appeared at Würzburg the year before, in 1625 (cf. § 14).

[3] i.e. 'partiren' (spartiren) = Ital. 'partire' (spartire); cf. § 3, note 3.

[4] The word 'aussetzen', which came to be used in the sense of 'setting out' a figured Bass, is here synonymous with '*absetzen*' (= to put into Organ tablature).

[5] Cf. § 4, note 8.

Staden begins with some general directions and advice:

"As concerns the *numeri* or figures, they have hitherto been put in, for the most part, on account of dissonances, such as Seconds, Fourths, Sevenths, and Ninths, &c., and also the Thirds and Sixths, as imperfect consonances, to show that the Organist is not to touch any dissonances where they are not indicated, but is to keep to his consonances and concords. Not, it is true, that he is to allow the perfect consonances, like Octaves or Fifths, to follow each other, either by step or by leap, but he must alternate, as much as possible, between the perfect and imperfect consonances.

"This is easily revealed by the scores or the putting into tablature of good writers . . . ('Wie denn solches leichtlich entdecket die Partitura oder das Aussetzen in die Tabulatur guter Authorum, als *Orlandi, Lucae Marentii, Claudii Merulae, Petri Aloysii Praenestini* [Pierluigi Palestrina], *Andreae* und *Johannis Gabrielii, Horatii Vechii, Joh. Pauli Cimae, Johan. Leo. Hasleri, Gregorii Aichinger, Christiani Erbach, Augustini Agazzarii, Flaminii Comanedi* &c.'), especially in their four-part writing, from whom a tyro can best learn how the harmony is to be adapted to the Bassus ad Org. (*wie hernach zum Basso ad Org. der Concentus zu führen*). For, if any one were to take up the present elegant, vocal style (*sich auf die jetzige zierliche singerische Art legen*) and apply it to the keyboard (*Clavier*) without first knowing what is in accordance with the musical rules, he would assuredly not learn from the said new style to recognize what is bad or good, on the contrary, he would run quite counter to it (*vielmehr aber würde er derselben gar zuwider handeln*), inasmuch as it constantly demands a quite different form of harmony (*Concentum*) from that which the actual parts give. This I wanted to mention in passing."

These words show that Staden clearly recognized the function of a figured Bass accompaniment, namely, to provide an harmonic background to the whole, without attempting to reproduce the vocal or instrumental parts, especially when the latter are of a florid character.

He next proceeds to describe the practice of Italian composers (and his own) in the figuring of 4 3 and 7 6 suspensions when the Third and Sixth, respectively, are accidentally major.

"In the matter of the *numeri* and the accompanying *signa* I have hitherto found a threefold distinction in the Italian *cantiones*.

   1. "By the figuring 4 ♯, they intend 4 to indicate the Fourth, and ♯, the

major Third: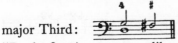

   2. "By the figuring 4 3, some likewise wish 4 to be understood as indicating the Fourth, and 3 (without ♯) the major Third. This idea they some-

times extend to 7 6 as well: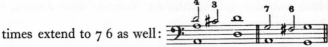

"Note. A practised Organist knows well that the manner of indication in question [i.e. with ♯ omitted before the 3 and 6] demands the cadences [i.e. Tonic, leading note, Tonic] by reason of the fact that the Bass moves a Fifth downwards, or a Fourth upwards. Similarly, he recognizes by the bass note which falls a Second, where the major Sixth is necessary in view of the Octave which follows. Nevertheless, this is certainly not a sure rule, and a composer may sometimes avoid the cadences in the case of the Third or Tenth, as also in that of the Sixth (reckoned, that is to say, from the Bass).

3. "Some put 4 ♯3 and 7 ♯6, &c., side by side (among them, in Italy, S. Petro del Negro) as a proper indication of the major Third and Sixth, which major Sixth, even when not preceded by another figure, is indicated thus: ♯6.

"I also find in the works of this same composer, and others, the ♯ over the 3 and 6, as follows: ♯♯, which is intended to have the same meaning.[6]

"But I have myself thought fit to use this ♯ before 3 (with another figure preceding), and ♯ before 6 (with or without another figure preceding), in accordance with the requirements of the Bass, since there are, after all, two kinds of Thirds and Sixths [i.e. major and minor]. But, nevertheless, with a distinction:

"When ♯ or ♭ is found, without being followed by a figure, this notation, without figures over the notes in question, simply indicates, ♯, a major Third, and ♭, a minor Third (as mentioned before). But if ♯ is followed by a figure, 3 or 6, I understand thereby that, in the case of the Third or Sixth, the Semitonium is required [i.e. that they should rise a semitone to a Triad]. Just as, in the contrary case, when there is merely 3 or 6, without ♯, the Semitonium is excluded."

Staden's rule for the use of the figuring ♯ 6 does not take into account the possibility

of an accidentally major Sixth *not* rising a semitone, as  though,

in such a case, the ♯ is, of course, absolutely necessary.

Staden then proceeds: "The aforesaid *signa* and *numeri* are sometimes placed one above the other, whereof the following examples and their explanation:

Then follow two "*Exempla* showing how the ordinary *signa* and *numeri* are

---

[6] In Cavalieri's *Rappresentatione, &c.*, the ♯ is sometimes put *below* the 6 (cf. § 8, note 4).

to be put into practice over a Bassus ad Org. with the admixture of other consonances":

[N.B.—The black notes in Exx. 3 *a* and *b* indicate the interval to which the figure or accidental refers.]

[Ex. 3a]

* The first note in the upper part of the last bar appears in Chrysander's reprint as *b*, without a prefixed ♭, which would be required if ♭ *b* were intended. It seems almost certain that this is due to a misprint (either in the original or the reprint) and that *g* was intended, as above.

It will be observed that, in the above Ex., Staden does not use the figuring ♯3, even when the Third is cadential.

[Ex.3*b*]

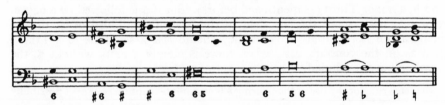

N.B.—In the last bar ♮ (B *quadratum*) is used instead of ♯ to indicate ♮ *b*. The false relations in changing the position of the chord in the last two bars is characteristic.

Staden evidently did not disapprove of the practice of denoting compound intervals (as in the Basses of Peri, Caccini, and Cavalieri), for he adds in conclusion: "And, although not only the *numeri* or figures hitherto employed, but 10, 11, &c., as well, might reasonably be used in the figuring, nevertheless, as it has not been done by others, I have not thought fit to say anything about it either."

[3] 'Concerning the slurs above and below the notes and figures' ('Von den Bögen über und unter den Noten und Zahlen').

No example is given, but the practice indicated is the same as that of the Monodists (cf. § 5) described by Caccini at the end of the extract from his preface to the *Nuove Musiche* given in § 7. Staden's rule is as follows:

"When, in the case of the notes of the Bassus ad Org., as also in that of the figures above it, slurs like the following ⌣ are found, it is an indication that the notes or the figures are subdivided as far as the allotment of the time is concerned, but are to be regarded as whole and undivided."

An instance of the use of slurs in the figuring will be found in § 8, Ex. 3.

[4] 'Concerning the dots next the *numeri* or figures' ('Von den Punkten neben den *Numeris* oder Zahlen').

"The dots next the *numeri* or figures are not put for nothing,[7] but give an indication of the time-value (*Mensur*) of the minims and crotchets, &c., according to what note they stand over.

"Now, when a dot is found at the end of a figure,[8] it is an indication that the figure in question has nothing to do with the following one. But if, over a $\circ$, there is a dot after the first figure, and two figures follow, it means that the first figure is $\downarrow$, and the other two $\downarrow\downarrow$. It is to be understood in the same way when a little dot follows the first two figures: the latter are then to be regarded as two $\downarrow\downarrow$, and the last figure as a $\downarrow$, and the same principle is to be applied to the *fusae* [quavers].

"*Exempla:*

It is evident that this employment of dots to indicate the time-values of figures over a sustained Bass is merely an alternative to the use of slurs as described above. Exx. 3 *a* and *b* could equally well be noted as follows:

Before proceeding to the next heading, Staden touches upon a point which he omitted to mention under [2].

Some composers, he tells us, do not think it necessary to put the figure 6 over *e* or $\natural$ *b* when there is a $\flat$ in the signature, and also omit it over other Bass notes which, as a matter of course, require a minor Sixth instead of an imperfect (diminished) Triad.[9]

This, he considers, is sound in principle (*Welche Meinung zwar gut*), but unsatisfactory in practice, because, as he says,

"experience teaches us that in the composition of the present day there is sometimes an interchange between keys with $\flat$ *b* and those with $\natural$ *b*, so that, in a key with $\flat$ *b*, *e* sometimes requires its [perfect] Fifth $\natural$ *b* (and not the Sixth), and, in keys with $\natural$ *b*, similar semitonic [i.e. with one or both intervals

---

[7] As, e.g., in Cavalieri's figuring (see Exx. in § 8).

[8] i.e. after the last figure in a bar (as in bar 1 of Ex. 4 *a*), or the last figure over the same Bass note (as after the third figure in Ex. 4 *b*).

[9] In playing from an unfigured Bass it was a rule that the seventh degree of the scale, or *Semitonium Modi* (as *e* in the key of F), or any other degree accidentally sharpened, either rising a semitone to a Triad, and thus becoming a temporary leading note (as $\natural$ *b* in the same key), or rising a whole tone to a Sixth (as $\natural$ *b* in the ascending

scale of D minor ), should bear a minor Sixth.

These are the cases which Staden has in mind, and in them, as he says, the 6 was often omitted in the earlier figured Basses, especially those of Italian origin (cf. Ch. xxi, 'Incomplete figuring', III, § 4).

raised by a semitone] Fifths are necessary, as , which
is approved chiefly on account of the words [10] and a change of ear (*Aenderung des Gehörs*).[11] And, for this reason, in my own Bassus ad Org., I have, for the sake of the inexperienced, generally put in the *signa* and *numeri* in abundance, where necessary."

[5] 'There now follow directions for the treatment of the dissonances, in the shape of Seconds, Fourths, Sevenths, and Ninths, in accordance with the musical rules' ('Folgt nun ferner, wie die Dissonantien, als die Secunden, Quarten, Septimen, Nonen, vermög der musikalischen Regeln zu gebrauchen').

"The dissonances are, it is true, indicated by the *numeri*, which, to an experienced Organist, is a sufficient indication, but on the other hand he who does not know how to treat them with discretion (*Bescheidenheit*) will cause wrong chords to be heard, wherefore it must be well noted what the dissonances demand."

Staden begins by giving examples, in two parts only, of the discords in question. The Sevenths of which he treats are, except in one instance (Ex. 9 II), suspensions, resolving on 6 over the same Bass.

In the case of the Second, he fails to explain that it is not the Second itself, but the Bass which is dissonant, and therefore requires preparation, though the examples make this plain. The examples being in two parts, and only single figures used, no account is taken of the other intervals with which the Second is associated in four-part harmony, or what, in many German treatises of the following century, were known as 'Füllstimmen', i.e. the intervals which 'filled up' the chord to its proper complement. Moreover, in his third example (Ex. 5 c), the only one in more than two parts, the Second is calculated, not from the Bass, but from the middle part. This example remains unfigured.

The rules, which chiefly concern the preparation of the discords, are as follows:

"The Second, before being touched, must be preceded by a consonance, such as the Third, Fifth, or Sixth, and resolves on the Third or Sixth, sometimes also on the Fifth:

"It is wrong to use the Fourths, Sevenths, and Ninths as follows:

[10] It will be remembered that Agazzari, in emphasizing the impossibility of giving rules which should enable the player to dispense with figures, mentions that this is especially the case where there are words, since the latter demand 'suitable harmony, calculated to awaken and illustrate the sentiment' (cf. § 10 *a*).

[11] By this expression Staden evidently means a change in the attitude of the ear to the impressions which it receives; in other words, a change of *taste*.

"Therefore the striking of the consonances before the dissonances is of no little importance, and it is not enough just to use the dissonances without discretion (*Ist derwegen nicht wenig an den Anschlägen der Consonantien vor den Dissonantien gelegen, und nicht genug allein die Dissonantien mit Unbescheidenheit führen*), for the dissonances are generally introduced in syncopation, as is here to be seen in the case of the Fourth, which is used in many different ways and resolves on a Third.

[N.B.—II is an example, not of a suspended Fourth, but of an essential Seventh.]

"Concerning the Seventh. The Seventh, too, can be used [i.e. prepared] in various ways, and resolve on the Sixth."

[In IV the words 'vel 10' stand for '3 vel 10', indicating that the two lower notes are alternatives, and that 7 may be prepared by either 3 or 10.]

"Concerning the Ninth. The resolution of the Ninth is intended to take place on the Octave (*ist auf die Octav angesehen*), and it is generally used in harmony of several parts."

Staden then continues: "What has here been presented in two parts is not meant to convey the idea that this is how one has to treat the Bassus ad Org.; on the contrary, one can sometimes use one or two consonances in addition, according to the circumstances. For, as was mentioned at the outset, the idea is not that one should always reckon the Thirds, Fourths, Fifths, Sixths, and Sevenths from the Bass itself, but the figuring is often to be understood as applying to a middle part, sometimes, too, to an upper part, as is shown by the above examples [12] of how the ordinary *signa* and *numeri* are to be put into practice over the Bassus ad Org. with the admixture of other consonances.

"To make the matter clearer there follow sundry examples, in several parts, of 4 3, 7 6, and 9 8 severally:

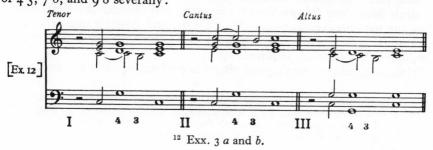

[12] Exx. 3 *a* and *b*.

"From these it is now plain how the *signa* and *numeri* quite frequently demand a different interpretation from that which, at first sight, they appear to have,[13] wherefore it is reasonable that an Organist should adapt himself according to whether a Treble or a Tenor is singing;[14] but for this purpose the scores are not ill adapted, which are coming into very general use in Italy, in which the singers' parts are given over the Bassus ad Org., which gives capital guidance.[15]

"For better information, some persons note in the Bassus ad Org. what parts, and how many of them, are in operation with it, which is a good plan. I myself employ this method. For, with only a few parts, one must not let the Organ or Regal be heard too much, but must vary the registration according to whether there are many or few singers.

"It is also necessary, in view of the present style, that one should keep a slow time (on which point some directions are to be found accompanying the Bassus ad Org. in the first part of my Church Music), in order that the words and the bravura passages (*Coloraturen*) of the singer (for which purpose, especially, good, practical voices are needed) should be distinctly heard; for, with hurry and an ill-regulated voice, there will not be much that is agreeable to be heard.

"And since the Bassus Generalis, or Bassus ad Org., is not intended for the deep Bass alone (as one sometimes varies and changes the clefs, which often alternate between Soprano, Alto, Tenor, and Bass), it must therefore be carefully remembered that, when the clef (*clavis signata*) is Soprano or Alto, only a few parts are required.

"Moreover, when a single good singer is performing, it is not necessary,

---

[13] Inasmuch, namely, as they denote either a simple or a compound interval (a Third, Tenth, or Seventeenth, &c.), which may, at the discretion of the player, be above, or below, or between other intervals not specified in the figuring.

[14] As prescribed by Viadana in his 4th recommendation (cf. § 4).

[15] Cf. § 5, note 1.

when the Bassus ad Org. has ♩ and ♪, to play a chord to each one (*jede insonderheit mit Consonantien zu berühren*).[16]

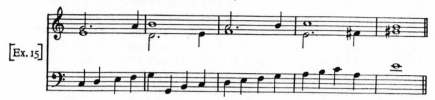

[Ex. 15]

"And Viadana is not ill advised in exhorting those who are inexperienced in the matter, and in regarding it as a matter of necessity, that they should look through the often-mentioned Bassus generalis or Bassus ad Organum diligently and thoroughly beforehand, previous to a performance;[17] for all concertos will not admit of its being used *ex tempore*.

"In conclusion, in playing from a Bassus ad Org., one must give way, possess a good ear and judgment, and, indeed, it is not the least important point that one should make way for the singers as regards their part (*den Singern in ihrer Stimm weiche*), a matter on which Lud. Viadana, Augustinus Agazzarius,[18] and others are not agreed (as may be seen in the *Syntagma Musicum* of Michael Praetorius, tomus tertius de Basso generali seu continuo).

"For my part, I am not overmuch opposed to the view of Augustinus Agazzarius when he wishes that one should make way (*weichen*) on the Clavier for the high voices (that is to say, that one should not touch the part which the Soprano is singing). But, in point of fact, it cannot always be so, and frequently, too, the practice in question (lit. 'the making way') gives rise to Fifths and Octaves (as musical blemishes), which, it is true, are not always felt by the ear in the course of the music and the alternations of harmony (*im Fortgehen, da man abwechselt*), and of which Viadana himself does not take such great account, as may be seen in his account of the Bassus generalis.[19] And a distinguished musician, on the occasion of having composed sundry Misereres, writes the following words at the end of his Bassus ad Org.: that he had treated it after Viadana's fashion and that things did not always turn out according to rule (*er habe es auf die Viadanische Art dirigirt, und gehe nicht allzeit 'regulariter' zu*). I will say no more.

"And herewith I conclude my simple but well-meant account, which (in accordance with its title) is intended only for those who are inexperienced in the Bassus ad Org., and have no knowledge of it, as I have had no intention of instructing experienced Organists and practised musicians, who themselves well know what they ought to do and leave undone. And I hope that an intelligent mind will find no occasion to cavil at it."

'End'.

[16] The evanescent tone of the Harpsichord necessitated the repercussion of the harmony over passing, or repeated, notes in the Bass, the numbers of the repercussions varying in accordance with the *tempo* (cf. Ch. ii, § 9, *c.* 3 and Ch. xviii, § 4), but on the Organ no such necessity exists.

[17] Cf. § 4, Viadana's 3rd recommendation.

[18] Cf. § 10 *b ad init.*

[19] Cf. § 4, Viadana's 9th recommendation.

§ 17. *Galeazzo Sabbatini.*

I. In 1628, two years later than Johann Staden's essay (cf. § 16), there was published in Venice by Salvatori (reprinted there in 1644 by Vincenti, and again in 1669 at Rome by Paolo Moneta) the first part of a treatise entitled: *Regola facile e breve per sonare sopra il Basso continuo nell' Organo, Manacordo, ò altro Simile Stromento. Composta da Galeazzo Sabbatini. Dalla quale in questa Prima Parte ciascuno da stesso potrà imparare da i primi principij quello che sarà necessario per simil effetto* ('A short and easy Guide for playing a Thorough-Bass on the Organ, Clavichord, or any similar instrument. Composed by Galeazzo Sabbatini. From which, in this first part, any one can, by himself, learn from the very beginning whatever is necessary to the end in question').

The Second Part, which unfortunately never appeared, or, at all events, is not now extant, was intended to meet the requirements of those who had made some progress in the art, as we learn from the words with which the author concludes the First Part: "*Molti altri auertimenti si douriano dare; mà per hora basteranno questi per non confonder tanto il principiante poiche col aiuto di Dio nell' altra parte si tratera più a pieno con qualche gusto per auuentura anco de gli Intendenti*" ('Many other directions might be given, but for the present the above will suffice, in order not to confuse the beginner too much, since the matter will, with God's help, be treated more fully in the other part, with some satisfaction, perchance, even to the initiated').

II. In the First Part Sabbatini deals with no harmony but Triads and Sixths: the latter only on the seventh degree of the scale, and on any other degree accidentally sharpened.

In Cavalieri's *Rappresentatione*, 1600 (cf. § 8), we saw that the three upper parts of the accompaniment could, for the most part, be conveniently played by the right hand, though the figuring not unfrequently made it necessary to divide the harmony equally between the two hands. At a somewhat later period, again, than the one which we are at present considering, it came to be assumed that the normal manner of treating a figured Bass (except when full chords were played in both hands, a form of accompaniment more appropriate to the Harpsichord than to the Organ) was for the left hand to play the Bass (often in Octaves), and for the right hand to supply the harmony, though Ph. Em. Bach (*Versuch &c.*, Pt. 2, 1762) emphasizes the desirability of mastering the 'divided accompaniment', and of occasionally using it, both as a means of avoiding consecutives and also for the sake of variety. Sabbatini, on the contrary, presupposes that the chords are to be divided between the two hands—sometimes he assigns three parts to the left hand and only one to the right—and the greater part of his little treatise is devoted to explaining in minute detail what intervals are to be played by the *left* hand.

It is to these alone that the figures over the examples, of which only the

Bass is given, refer, as: [Ex. I]

The only definite directions for the conduct of the right hand are embodied in a rule quoted *in extenso* later (III *c.* 4).

III. The work, which consists of thirty small quarto pages, is divided into twenty chapters.

(*a*) In the first, which is without any heading, Sabbatini sets forth his intentions as follows:

"To play the Thorough-Bass on the Organ, Clavichord (*manacordo*), or any other similar instrument, with certainty (*con regola sicura*), and to carry the hands well, both by step and by leap; to know also, in a short time, without looking at the keyboard, whether the note in question is to be played by the left hand alone (*col tasto solo*), or with the Third, or with the Fifth, or with another consonance, and what is the function of the right hand,—information which, so far as I have been able to see, has hitherto been revealed by no one, though, perhaps, much desired by every beginner—to have knowledge, in short, of all the above-mentioned matters, the following rules must be observed, which serve for the Bass notes in the following clef of F. *fa*, *ut* on the fourth line  with the ordinary chords (*accompagnamenti*), since the extraordinary ones, as also the way to play notes in other clefs, will be treated of in the second part."

The remainder of the chapter defines the preliminary knowledge which the pupil must possess.

He must know the names and alphabetical order of the notes:

A. la mi re	E. la mi
B ♭. fa, B ♯ mi	F. fa ut
C. sol fa ut	G. sol re ut
D. la sol re	

and have a practical knowledge of their time-values.

He must also know the consonances, Third, Fifth, Sixth, and Octave, and recognize their identity with the compounds formed by adding the number seven, or its multiple, to any one of the above simple intervals.

The author thinks it necessary to explain how any consonant interval may be found by counting the notes in their alphabetical order from the Bass upwards, and he adds that the same principle may be applied to the dissonant intervals, the Second, Fourth, Seventh, and their compounds.

(*b*) The second and third chapters, entitled '*Della cognitione, & Dichiaratione della Tastatura*', and '*Della dichiaratione della Tastatura*', respectively, contain minute instructions for finding any note or interval on the keyboard.

Sabbatini explains that the normal keyboard has the 'short Octave' in the Bass: that is to say, the first white key, E, sounds , while the black keys, ♯ F and ♯ G, sound D and E, so that the sounding notes ♯ C, ♯ F, ♯ G are lacking.

(*c*) In the fourth chapter, '*Delle Precognitioni della Regola*', which contains some instruction of a purely elementary character, only the following points need be noticed:

(1) All Bass notes not preceded by ✕, except B *quadro* or B *mi* (i.e. ♮ B), as well as those preceded by ♭, are to be accompanied by the Third, Fifth, and Octave.

N.B.—Sabbatini does not mention the possibility of doubling the Third, or the Fifth, instead of the Bass.

(2) B *quadro* or B *mi*, as well as any Bass note preceded by ✕, as

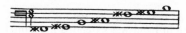

is to be accompanied by the Third, Sixth, and Octave, even though not figured (*benche non habbia segno alcuno*).

N.B.—The mention of the Octave in connexion with bass notes accidentally sharpened is a slip on the author's part (which he repeats in Ch. 17), for later on, in Ch. 18, he expressly tells us that, in such a case, the Bass, according to strict rule, must *not* be doubled, but, instead of it, either the Third or the Sixth, preferably the former.[1]

(3) Sabbatini defines the function of the left hand as follows:

"Secondly it must be noted that the whole foundation of playing on a Bass rests with the left hand, which must proceed regularly, playing the Bass note either alone (*col tasto solo*), or accompanied by a single [2] consonance, such as either the Octave, or the Fifth, or the Sixth, or the Third."

It is evident that the manner of distribution of the intervals of a chord is to some extent determined by the depth, or the reverse, of the Bass. For example, if the Bass is very low, it would clearly be unadvisable for its Third, or even Fifth, to be played by the left hand, whereas, if it is very high, the Octave must be avoided, as, otherwise, the right hand would be driven too far up the keyboard.[3]

Sabbatini therefore divides the Bass into five divisions, each of which he treats separately in the subsequent chapters, adding numbers to the alphabetical names of the notes to distinguish the different Octaves.

[1] Cf. III *g* (14).

[2] This is inaccurately expressed, for Sabbatini explains in his 14th chapter (cf. III *f* of the present §) that the Octave and Fifth played by the left hand may be either 'empty' (*vota*) or 'full' (*piena*), in which latter case they include, respectively, the Fifth and the Third, as:

Ottava vota Ottava piena Quinta vota Quinta piena

[3] We may assume that the upward compass of the chords played over a Thorough-Bass (except when a C clef was used) was strictly limited from the beginning.

No actual rule is to be found in the earliest treatises of all, but Cavalieri's practice of figuring compound intervals (see the Exx. in § 8 of the present chapter) enables us to form a fair idea of the compass of his intended accompaniments, and an occasional hint may be found elsewhere. For example, Sabbatini tells us, in the seventh chapter

of the treatise under discussion, that the Octave of the bass notes ![notes] must not be played in the left hand, "because, otherwise, in giving the remainder of the chord with the right hand, one would get too high up " (*perche nel dare il restante de gli accompagnamenti con la destra si verrebbe troppo ne gli acuti*).

If   was 'too high up , we must infer that Sabbatini's usual upward

limit—though not necessarily a hard-and-fast one—was ♭ *b*. Werckmeister (*Die nothwendigsten Anmerckungen &c.*, 1698) says that, with rare exceptions, the right

hand should not go above $\bar{\bar{c}}$ (= ![notes]). This may possibly be a misprint for $\bar{\bar{e}}$,

though no alteration is made in the later edition of 1715. Niedt, in his *Musicalische Handleitung &c.*, 1700, gives $\bar{\bar{e}}$ or $\bar{\bar{f}}$ as the upward limit. It was only late in the eighteenth century that *g* was sanctioned in a text-book, unless the Bass itself was exceptionally high (cf. Marpurg, *Die Kunst das Clavier zu spielen*, Pt. 2, 1761, *Hauptstück* ii, Cap. II, § 24, and G. M. Telemann, *Unterricht im Generalbass-Spielen*, 1773, Abschnitt III, § 1, p. 98).

In the case of '*Bassetti*' (i.e. when the Bass was in any one of the C clefs) the upward compass of the right hand was extended indefinitely.

"And in order", he says, "that one may know when the left hand is to touch each of the said consonances, let the following divisions in the Bass be observed. . . ."

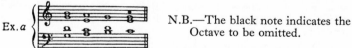

Prima Divisione. Seconda Divisione.   3 *Divis.*   4 *Divis.*   5 *Di.*

[Ex.2]

C1 D1 E1 F1 | G1 A1 B1 C2 D2 | E2 F2 G2 | A2 B2 | C3 D3

(4) The function of the right hand is defined as follows:

"Thirdly it must be observed that those consonances which the [Bass] note must have, and which are not played by the left hand, must be supplied by the right hand, being careful, however, from G 2 to B 3 inclusive, to keep the hands as close, the one to the other, as possible, because, from the said G 2 to B 3, the missing intervals can sometimes be supplied on more keys than one (*poiche dal detto G2 sin al B3 alle volte in piu tasti si potranno supplire le consonanze che mancano*); for example, if the left hand plays G 1, giving it, by way of accompaniment, the Octave, which is G 2, the right hand must play the intervals which are lacking, namely the Third, which is B, and the Fifth, which is D 3; but as the Third can be played on two different keys, namely either B 2 or B 3, it will be better, or rather one will be bound, to play B 2 as being closer to the left hand; let this advice be well noted in order to know how to dispose the intervals correctly in the right hand."

(5) When the Bass moves by leap, we are told that the left hand must not take two consecutive Octaves, Fifths, Sixths, or Thirds, except in the case of the first division (cf. Ex. 2), as is set forth in Sabbatini's fifth chapter (cf. III *d*). When, however, the Bass moves by step, it is allowed for the duration of two consecutive notes, rising or falling (*quando poi caminera il Basso di grado all' hora quando occorrera per ispatio di due note ascendenti, ò discendenti, cio sara lecito*), i.e. one may take two Octaves, &c., in succession, but not more.

(6) Sabbatini writes: "Seventhly it must be noted that, when the Bass note alone is struck by the left hand, if it is not convenient for the right hand to play its full complement of consonances by including the Octave (*se con la destra non tornasse commodo dar per compimento delle consonanze debite l' ottaua*), it will not only suffice for it to strike the Third and Fifth, but, for the space of half a beat or less (*per spatio di mezza battuta ò meno*), it can strike the Third only." [4]

---

[4] The cases which Sabbatini probably has in mind are: (*a*) when the Bass is so high that the inclusion of the Octave by the right hand would cause the latter to exceed its due compass (cf. note 3) perhaps with the additional disadvantage of hidden Octaves, as:

Ex. *a*

N.B.—The black note indicates the Octave to be omitted.

(*b*) When consecutive Fifths between extreme parts would result from the inclusion of the Fifth, which is therefore to be omitted 'for the space of half a beat, or less', as:

Ex. *b*

(*d*) The fifth chapter, '*Delle regole da osservarsi nelle note che deuono haver per accompagnamento Terza, Quinta, & Ottaua nella prima Diuisione*' ('Rules to be observed in the case of the notes in the first Division which must have as their accompaniment the Third, Fifth, and Octave'), runs as follows:

"In the case of the notes belonging to the first division, given above in the preceding chapter, both when the Bass rises, and when it falls, either by step or by leap, the left hand will strike either the Octaves or the Bass notes alone, whichever is most convenient to the hand. Example:

Note, however, that, in this division alone, Octaves by leap are permitted, because, apart from the fact that such low notes rarely occur, a mistake is also less dangerous." [5]

(*e*) Chapters vi–xiii [6] contain Sabbatini's rules for the intervals to be taken by the left hand in the second, third, fourth, and fifth divisions of the Bass, ascending or descending, either by step or by leap.

[5] '*perche oltreche di rado si formano le note nelle corde cosi basse, è anco meno pericoloso il fallire*'.

What Sabbatini probably means by saying that 'a mistake is less dangerous' is that, when consecutive Octaves are played so low down, it is more likely to produce the impression of *three*-part harmony with the Bass doubled in the *lower* Octave (as when played on the pedals of an Organ). Thus, if the above example were played as follows:

the last bar would give the impression of three-part harmony on a Bass

N.B.—The Fifths by contrary motion between extreme parts at * * are necessary as, otherwise, the last chord would either lack the Fifth, which Sabbatini does not appear to regard as permissible when Octaves are played by the left hand (cf. III *f*, 1 and 2), or else it would quite exceed the upward limit of the compass contemplated

(cf. note 3): The chords cannot, moreover, be taken

in a lower position to start with, as since, in the

first division of the Bass, the Fifth from the Bass may not be taken by the left hand (and therefore, presumably, not by the right hand either), because the whole chord would thereby be carried too far downwards.

[6] Cap. vi. Della seconda diuisione mentre il Basso ascende.
Cap. vii. Della terza Diuisione mentre si ascende.
Cap. viii. Della quarta diuisione ascendendosi.
Cap. ix. Della quinta diuisione.
Cap. x. Della quarta diuisione mentre il Basso discende.
Cap. xi. Della Terza Diuisione discendendosi.
Cap. xii. Della Seconda Diuisione discendendosi.
Cap. xiii. D' alcuni altri auertimenti generali.

It must here suffice to indicate the main principles on which these rules are based.

(1) In accordance with the principle of keeping the accompaniment within the proper compass—neither going too high with the right hand when the Bass is high, nor following the latter into the depths—a larger interval may be taken by the left hand in the lower divisions of the Bass than in the higher.

In the first division, as we learnt from Sabbatini's fifth chapter (cf. III *d*), any smaller interval than an Octave is excluded.

In the second division, [music], either the Octave, Fifth, or Third may be taken, and, as we shall learn from Sabbatini's fourteenth chapter (cf. III *f*), these intervals may be either *vota* or *piena*. The meaning of these terms, as applied to the Octave and Fifth, has already been explained (cf. note 2); Sabbatini calls the Third *vota* when the right hand supplies only the Fifth, and *piena*, when the right hand strikes the Fifth and Octave of the Bass, though he adds that, in the case of the Third, as well as of the *tasto solo*, the terms are inappropriate.

In the third division, [music], the left hand may take either the Fifth, or Third, or the Bass note alone (*tasto solo*).

In the fourth division, [music], only the Third, or the Bass note alone, may be taken, and in the fifth division, [music], only the latter.

(2) In the case of a rising Bass the first note is, generally speaking, to be taken by the left hand with the largest interval permitted in the division of the Bass within which the note in question occurs. Thus, in the second division, the first note is taken with the Octave: [Ex.4] [music]

in the third division, with the Fifth: [Ex.5] [music] and in the fourth division, with the Third: [Ex.6] [music]

(3) In the case of a falling Bass the converse is the case: the left hand takes the first note with the smallest interval permitted in the division in question. Thus, in the second division, the first note is taken with the Third:

[Ex.7] [music] in the third division, *tasto solo* (i.e. the left hand strikes the Bass note alone), except where there are not more than two falling notes, in which case the Third may be included: [Ex.8] [music]

in the fourth division, *tasto solo*: [Ex.9] [music]

(4) In certain cases the left hand takes two Octaves, and also two Fifths, in succession.

Thus, the first two notes of the second division are taken with the Octave:

[Ex. 10] (and so, also, with a falling Bass, as in Ex. 23).

In such cases it is evident from Ex. 25 that real consecutives were not intended, but that the lower of the two Octaves was *vota* (cf. note 2), and the higher, *piena*, as: r.h. l.h.

In passing, however, from the lowest note of the first division to that of the second, *three* Octaves are found in succession:

[Ex. 11] (Cf. Ex. 21.)

In this case it may well be that the two lowest Octaves were intended by Sabbatini to be consecutive on the ground that, in the case of such low notes, "a mistake is less dangerous" (cf. III *d ad fin.*), in which case the Ex. would be played as follows:

In each of the following Exx. we find two Fifths in succession:

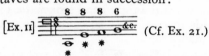

[Ex. 12] [7] [Ex. 13] [8]

[7] Ex. 12 occurs in Sabbatini's sixth chapter (cf. note 6), and illustrates the following rule: "The Fifth is struck [i.e. in the left hand] when the Octave has been struck on the preceding note, but one must notice whether, after the Fifth has been struck, the Bass rises several degrees or not, because, if it does, the Octave will again be struck

after the Fifth: If, again, after the Fifth has been struck, the Bass

does not rise several degrees, then, after the Fifth, one can strike another." Then follows Ex. 12.

[8] Ex. 13, which occurs in Sabbatini's eighth chapter (cf. note 6), illustrates the following '*Regola generale per ascendere*': "Let it be noted here, as a general rule, that the last of a succession of rising notes (*l' ultima nota ascesa*), in the third or fourth division of the left hand [cf. Ex. 2], must be taken either with the Third, or by itself (*col tasto solo*); and, in order that this rule may be observed, it is permitted to the left hand (that is to say, while the Bass moves by step) to strike two Octaves, or two Fifths, or two Thirds, one after the other, or to strike whatever consonance is most convenient to it, to the end that the last of the rising notes may be struck with the Third, or by itself, as has been said." Then follows Ex. 13.

Sabbatini then continues, under the heading '*Ordine che si deve tenere nel ascender del Basso*': "Meanwhile one must be careful to aim, so far as possible, at the following order, while the Bass rises, namely, that the lowest note should be struck with the Octave, next the Fifth, and, finally, either with the Third, or by itself, as follows:

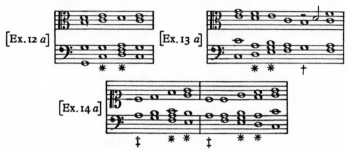

It would seem probable that, in each case, the Fifth on the lower of the two Bass notes in question was intended to be '*vota*', and that on the higher, '*piena*', as follows: [10]

(5) After giving the rules (in Ch. vi) that, with a rising Bass, a Fifth is struck in the left hand, when the preceding note has been taken with the Octave (except, of course, in the cases mentioned above, Exx. 10 and 11), as follows: [11] [Ex. 15] and that, when the Bass leaps more than a Fifth, the lower note should be taken with the Octave,[12] and the higher

---

[9] Ex. 14, which occurs in Sabbatini's twelfth chapter (cf. note 6), illustrates the following '*Regola generale per descendere*': "It must here be noted, as a general rule, that, when the Bass falls several degrees, the last note of the series (*l' ultima discesa*) must be struck by the left hand, either with the Fifth, or with the Octave, according to what division it is in (*conforme che saranno le diuisioni*), and, to observe this, it is permitted to strike consecutively, either two Thirds, or two Fifths, or two Octaves, on two notes falling by step, to the end that the last of the series may be struck with the Fifth, or the Octave, as has been said." Then follows Ex. 14.

Sabbatini then proceeds to describe '*L' ordine che si tiene nel descendere*' as follows: "Meanwhile one must be careful to aim, so far as possible, at the following order while the Bass falls, namely, that on the highest note the Bass note alone should be struck, then the Third, and finally, in the third division, the Fifth, and in the second division, the Octave: ."

[10] The treatment of the penultimate note † of Ex. 13 *a*, with the Fifth added on the second half of the note, is in accordance with Sabbatini's directions (cf. note 4, Ex. *b*). It could, however, also be taken (like the first and fifth notes of Ex. 14 *a*) with the Third only, in which case the following chord would lack the Octave.

With regard to the incomplete harmony on the first and fifth notes ‡ ‡ in Ex. 14 *a*, Sabbatini explains that a '*tasto solo*' (i.e. a bass note unaccompanied, *in the left hand*, by any other interval) may be either '*voto*' or '*pieno*', though he observes that the terms are, in this instance, not appropriate (cf. III *f*, 8 and 9). In the former case, only the Third is added by the right hand (as in Ex. 14 *a* ‡ ‡), and in the latter, the Third and Fifth.

[11] For the rule in full see note 7.

[12] Sabbatini does not tell us how such a leap should be dealt with if the lower note should happen to be in a higher division of the Bass than the second (in which case the Octave cannot be included in the left hand), as

with the Third, or by itself (*tasto solo*), as follows: [Ex. 16] ,

Sabbatini proceeds to deal with the difficulty which arises when one upward

leap is followed by another, as , owing to the fact that (by the

above rules) the middle note demands the Fifth in regard to the preceding note, and in regard to the one which follows, the Octave.

"In this, and other similar cases," he writes, "the note where the difficulty is—that is to say, the one which, in regard to the preceding and following notes, must be played differently—must be divided into two parts: the first to be treated in conformity with what the preceding note demands, and the

second, in conformity with the following one, thus: [Ex. 17]

Thus, too, if there are two or more notes in the same space, or on the same line, one must treat one of the said notes as the preceding one demands, and the other as the following one, just as one does when the note is itself

divided, as has been said: [Ex. 18]

Furthermore, every time that more than two Bass notes rise, and that the greater number of them rise by leap, then the note which is of the greater

value must be divided, thus: [Ex. 19] ; if, again, all the

notes are of the same value, and such as can be divided, then whichever one is most convenient will be divided. But, in playing the note of difficulty, when it is of such small value that it cannot conveniently be divided, then it must be treated in conformity with the preceding note, and the following one can be played in three ways. Firstly, in the lower Octave, if one chooses, or, if one wishes to play it in its proper Octave, the said following

note can be taken by itself (*col tasto solo*), thus: [Ex. 20]

And, thirdly, one can play it with the right hand, giving it as accompaniment the Third only, and also, if it should be convenient, the Fifth, and meanwhile one will prepare the left hand for the note which follows."

(6) In Ch. xiii, containing 'Certain general directions', Sabbatini gives the sound rule that, when the Bass rises by leap, the left hand must not take

a smaller interval with the lower note than with the higher, as

and that, conversely, when the Bass falls, the first note must be taken with

the smaller interval, as

"The contrary must not be done, as mistakes are easily made."

(7) Sabbatini gives the following general examples, first of a rising Bass, then of a Bass both rising and falling, by step and by leap, in all the divisions:

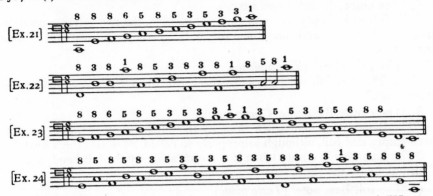

(f) Sabbatini's fourteenth chapter, '*Del modo di sonar osservato*' ('How to play in correct style'), is exceedingly ·important for the understanding of earlier portions of his treatise (cf. note 2), and for the correct interpretation of his examples (cf. Exx. 10–14); it is, therefore, here given *in extenso*:

"Since it was conceded above (in Ch. iv, No. 10) that two Octaves, two Fifths, and two Thirds might be struck, one after the other, by the left hand, by step only [cf. III *c.* 5], I therefore thought it worth while, for the benefit of intending players, to make—along with the universal and good, but difficult, rule, namely that, while one hand ascends, the other should descend, and vice versâ—certain observations, in virtue of which, even though the said two Octaves, &c., are struck, as above mentioned, there will, because they are struck with a certain difference, be no breach, but rather observance, of the said rule. I did not insert this observation earlier, because I found some difficulty in disposing the method of playing the figures and the accidentals, which will be treated in their proper place in the second part."

1. 'Empty and full consonances' (*consonanze vote e piene*).

"In the first place, then, it must be noted that two kinds of Octaves, Fifths, and Thirds are struck, namely, the one empty (*vota*), and the other full (*piena*)."

2. 'The empty Octave' (*Ottaua vota*).

"The Octave is empty when, of any eight white keys, the two extreme ones are struck by the left hand: for example, if G 1 and G 2 [13] are struck by the left hand, and B 2 and D 3 by the right."

3. 'The full Octave' (*Ottaua piena*).

"The Octave is full when, besides the aforesaid two extreme keys, the fifth key is struck (beginning to count the keys from left to right), and the other hand supplies the consonances which are lacking: for example, if G 1 and G 2, together with D 2, are struck by the left hand, and B 2 by the right."

4. 'The empty Fifth' (*Quinta vota*).

"The Fifth is empty when, of five white keys, the two extreme ones are struck by the left hand, and the remaining consonances are supplied by the right."

5. 'The full Fifth' (*Quinta piena*).

"The Fifth is full, when, besides the two aforesaid extreme keys, the third one, which lies between them, is also struck, and the other consonance, which is lacking, is supplied by the right hand."

[13] Cf. Ex. 2.

6. 'The empty Third' (*Terza vota*).

"The Third is empty when, of three white keys, the two extreme ones are struck by the left hand, and the Fifth only by the right, without adding the Octave."

7. 'The full Third' (*Terza piena*).

"The Third is full when, besides the Fifth, the Octave is added by the right hand."

8. 'The empty Bass note' (*Tasto voto*).

"The Bass note, when struck alone by the left hand (*Il tasto solo*), occurs both empty and full, although improperly so called, as is also the Third."

"The Bass note is empty when it is struck alone by the left hand, and the Third alone by the right."

9. 'The full Bass note' (*Tasto pieno*).

"It is full when, to the Third, the Fifth also is added by the right hand."

10. 'In ascending, the first consonance must be empty, and the other full' (*Ascendendosi la prima consonanza deue esser vota e l' altera piena*).

"Having well mastered the above-mentioned terms, it must be noted that, when taking the two Octaves, the two Fifths, the two Thirds, or the two Bass notes alone (*i due tasti soli*) in ascending, the first Octave, Fifth, Third, or Bass note, as the case may be, must be empty, and the other full."

11. 'In descending vice versâ' (*Discendendosi il contrario*).

"Further, when striking the said consonances in descending, the reverse will be the case: that is to say, the first must be full, and the other empty.

"By observing all that has been said, any one will come to play almost as though the harmonies were written out in full (*quasi come fosse il Basso intauolato*), and whoever cares to avail himself of this little guide,[14] if only he adheres to what has been said above, cannot do otherwise than well, and will be praised by any one who sees him play." 'Examples':

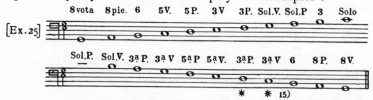

[14] '*questa poca regola*', referring to the title of Sabbatini's treatise, 'Regola facile &c.'

[15] The figures over the notes marked * are so blurred in the original that it is impossible to decipher them. They have been figured 3 (*Terza piena* and *Terza vota*) in the above, for the following reasons:

(1) The figure is certainly the same over both notes, because the whole example is an illustration of intervals taken in pairs, 'empty' and 'full'.

(2) That figure cannot be 5, because the two preceding ones are 5, and successive Octaves, Fifths, &c., are taken in the left hand 'for the duration of two notes' only (*per ispatio di due note*), cf. III c, 5.

(3) If the figure were 8, real consecutive Fifths, and also Octaves, would arise between the chord on *e* (with the empty Fifth) and that on *d* (with the full Octave):

Notwithstanding Viadana's permission to disregard consecutive 5ths and 8ths in the Organ part, it seems hardly likely that anything quite so crass was intended.

By following Sabbatini's directions, we obtain the following solution of the example:

Nothing more crude can well be imagined. It will be noticed that, where successive Thirds occur in the left hand (*vota* followed by *piena* ∗ ∗ in ascending, and *piena* by *vota* † † in descending), the chord with the *terza vota* must be regarded as in four parts, with one or other of the two lower intervals doubled in the unison, as though it is not probable that any such technical defence of the progression occurred to Sabbatini's mind. It was probably enough for him that, by taking the chord in question in three parts, the Fifths, , were in some degree veiled, and Octaves avoided.

Clumsy skips in the upper part, so detested by Ph. Em. Bach, did not trouble him at all.

(*g*) Chapters xv–xix [16] deal chiefly with the use of the *Diesis* 𝕏 (sometimes known as *signum cancellatum* = the 'latticed' sign), B *quadro* (B *quadratum*, in early English treatises B sharp) ♮, and B *molle* ♭.

It will be enough to give a brief summary of their contents. Some of Sabbatini's rules, based on the hexachordal names of the notes (C *fa ut*, D *la sol re*, E *la mi*, &c.), sound quaint to-day.

(1) 'Major' and 'minor' notes (Cap. xv).

He divides all the notes (or 'letters', as he calls them), A, B, C, D, E, F, G, into 'major' and 'minor': all those into the name of which the syllable *Mi* enters (i.e. A *la mi re*, B *mi*, and E *la mi*)—in other words those with a major Third below them on the white keys—being 'major', and the others 'minor'.

(2) The effect of accidentals before notes depends on the nature of the note (ibid.).

A 'minor' note, he tells us, cannot be further flattened, nor a 'major' one sharpened; therefore ♭ before *c* "has no more effect than if it were not there". The same applies to 𝕏 before a 'major' note.

Both 𝕏 and ♭ always indicate a black note, except in the case of B, when the presence of 𝕏 indicates the use of a white key: "in the case of the said letter one ought, it is true, instead of 𝕏 to put ♮, which is its proper sign (there being some difference between them) but, as 𝕏 is commonly used, I will not for the present gainsay it."

[16] Cap. xv. *Del Diesis, del B quadro, e del B molle.* Cap. xvi. *Delle Terze, e Seste maggiori, e minori.* Cap. xvii. *De i siti de gli accidenti.* Cap. xviii. *De gli accompagnamenti del 𝕏 per tutte le Diuisioni.* Cap. xix *Della differenza che è tra sonare per B quadro & per B molle.*

The difference between ♮ and 𝕏, according to Sabbatini, is that the former "serves only for the letter B, and that 𝕏 is common to all". E flat would therefore be contradicted by 𝕏, and B flat by ♮.

(3) Use of one accidental to contradict another (ibid.).

Sabbatini's explanation of the use of ♭ to contradict 𝕏, and vice versâ, is based on the above-mentioned axiom that ♭ does not affect a 'minor' note, nor 𝕏 a 'major' one. "Here be it noted", he writes, "that, when wishing to cause the note to return to its own nature, one puts the sign which does not alter it; for example here: [musical notation] , in the case of *c*, altered by the 𝕏, I put the ♭, which serves no other purpose but to cause *c* to become 'minor' again, as it would be by its own nature; and 𝕏 has the same effect in the case of a 'major' note, altered by the B *molle*: [musical notation] ."

(4) Rule for major and minor Sixths (Cap. xvi).

In order to know how to recognize and form Sixths, major and minor, the pupil is instructed to notice "whether, or not, one, at least, of these two syllables, Mi or La, occurs in the letter [i.e. the name of the note] which forms the Sixth; because, if it does, the Sixth will be major, and, if not, it will be minor; for example, if we form a Sixth on F, . . . so that D forms the Sixth, the syllable La occurs in the said letter D [D la sol re], consequently the Sixth will be major."

(5) Position of the accidentals (Cap. xvii).

The accidentals, Sabbatini tells us, may occupy three positions: above, beside, or below the Bass note.

The more important part of his rules for the use of accidentals beside (i.e. before) a note has already been given (cf. 2 and 3 above).

(6) Accidentals above Bass. (7) Omission of 𝕏 in full closes (ibid.).

In describing the familiar use of 𝕏 and ♭ above a Bass note, to indicate a major and minor Third, respectively, Sabbatini adds the rule that, when the Bass rises a Fourth, or falls a Fifth, as [musical notation] , it usually indicates a full close (*cadenza*), and the first of the two notes must be taken with the major Third *without further indication*.

(8) Use of ♭ as a warning against a full close (ibid.).

If a full close is *not* desired, a ♭ is often found above the note in question, to indicate that the Third is to be minor, whether naturally or accidentally.

(9) Accidentals below Bass (ibid.).

Sabbatini's rule for the use of accidentals below the Bass is as follows: "The accidentals, finally, which are below the notes indicate the Sixth, in accordance with the quality of the accidental [i.e. 𝕏 and ♭, below the Bass, indicate a major and minor Sixth,[17] respectively], but now this rule is observed by practically no one (*quasi da niuno*), and no distinction is made between accidentals beside the notes and those beneath them."

(10) Effect of 'short Octave' (Cap. xviii).

In explaining how Bass notes to which 𝕏 is prefixed are to be accompanied, Sabbatini alludes to the prevalence of the 'short Octave' (cf. III *b*), which

---

[17] Cf. § 4 under Rule 8.

makes it necessary to take sharpened notes in the first division (cf. Ex. 2) an

Octave higher, as  &c.

N.B.— does not belong to the first division, but is evidently included here as being the only note in the second division affected by the 'short Octave'.

By striking the following keys r.h. , he explains, the following

l.h.

sounds are obtained.

(11) Sharpened notes and ♮ B in the second division (ibid.).

Sharpened notes in the second division are to be played with the Sixth, and if desired, the Third also, in the left hand, the Third being doubled in the right hand, and the Octave of the Bass added only when full chords are played (*solamente aggiungendo ui l' ottaua ne i ripieni*).[18]

In the same division ♮ B is to be played with the Third, Sixth, and Octave (cf. III *c*. 2).

(12) In the third division (ibid.).

In the third division the Sixth on sharpened notes is to be taken in which-ever hand the Fifth would otherwise have been taken (cf. III *e*. 1 *ad fin.*).

(13) In the fourth and fifth divisions (ibid.).

In the fourth and fifth divisions the sharpened Bass note alone is to be taken in the left hand, the Third and Sixth being added in the right hand.

(14) The Octave of a sharpened Bass note must not be added (ibid.).

Sabbatini concludes the chapter with the following:

"Be it noted, finally, that notes with a sharp beside them must not, in accordance with strict rule (*conforme la regola buona*), be accompanied by the Octave as well as the Third and Sixth: instead, either the Third or the Sixth should be doubled, though the Third is better."

(15) Apparent contradictions between Sabbatini's rules.

The above rule is to be found, in substance, in most of the later text-books, though without the rider to the effect that it is better to double the Third than the Sixth.

Sabbatini, like many later writers, fails to point out the distinction between the instances where a note, accidentally sharpened, becomes a temporary leading note (as at * below), and may therefore not be doubled, and those in which this is not the case (as at †):

---

[18] Cf. § 20 (*o*), p. 153 (15 and 16).

It may have been his failure to envisage this distinction which led him, earlier in the same treatise,[19] twice to make the statement that a Bass note to which a sharp is prefixed should have as its accompaniment the Third, Sixth, and *Octave*.

Be the explanation what it may, Sabbatini contradicts himself in a remarkable manner.

It is also remarkable that, in Cap. xviii, as also in Cap. iv (cf. III *c*. 2), he should lay down the rule that ♮ B, in the Bass, should be accompanied by the Third, Sixth, and *Octave*; for, in Cap. iv, he explicitly associates ♮ B with notes sharpened by 𝕏.

In this case, too, the explanation may be the one suggested above.

(16) 'The difference in playing according to whether there is a flat in the key-signature or not' (Cap. xix).

Sabbatini recognizes *only two key-signatures*, that without ♭, and that with it. Like other Italians of the time he speaks of 'playing with B natural' (*sonare per B quadro*), and 'playing with B flat' (*sonare per B molle*). He defines the matter as follows: "One plays with B natural when, at the beginning, before the time-signature, there is no sign indicating a flat, thus:

One plays with B flat when, at the beginning, before the time-signature, the ♭ is placed, thus: ."

(17) Change of signature (ibid.).

He then proceeds to warn his readers that, when there is a change of signature at the beginning of a stave, the change should also be made at the end of the preceding one by the repetition of the clef, with or without the ♭,[20] as the case may be: , otherwise, he tells us, the change of signature at the beginning of the new stave should be disregarded, as the absence or presence of a ♭ may be due to an error.

As a matter of fact this rule was not always observed: in Cavalieri's *Rappresentatione &c.* (cf. § 8), for example, there is at least one instance of a genuine change of signature at the beginning of a stave with no indication whatsoever at the end of the preceding one.

(18) Treatment of E when there is a flat in the signature (ibid.).

Sabbatini concludes Cap. xix with the rule that, when there is a ♭ in the signature (*quando si sona per B molle*), E, in whatever division it may occur, is to be accompanied by the Third, Sixth, and Octave,[21] even though it has the cadential progression (*se bene facesse il moto di cadenza*), i.e. rises a Fourth or falls a Fifth (cf. III *g*, 7, 'Omission of 𝕏 in full closes'), unless

---

[19] The first occasion (in Cap. iv) has already been referred to (cf. III *c*, 2). In Cap. xvii he says: "The said note with 𝕏 beside it must have, as its accompaniment, the Third, Sixth, and Octave, as will be mentioned in the following chapter", quite unconscious, apparently, that, in that same following chapter, he was about to state the exact opposite.

[20] It was only later that the contradiction of ♭ by ♮ became general. So far as the present writer is aware, the first to prescribe the use of ♮, in contradiction of either 𝕏 or ♭, was Michel de Saint-Lambert, whose *Traité de l'accompagnement &c.* appeared in 1680, and his *Nouveau traité &c.* in 1707 (cf. § 23).

[21] The inclusion of the Octave in this instance is to be regarded in the same light as in the case of ♮ B (cf. III *g*, 15, 'Apparent contradictions, &c.').

there is a ✗ over it, in which case it is to be treated as though there were no flat in the signature, and accompanied by the major Third, Fifth, and Octave.

(*h*) Sabbatini's twentieth, and last, chapter, '*Del sonar le Note nere*', deals with the treatment of black notes in the Bass, in so far as they may either bear a harmony of their own, or be treated as passing notes. This subject was treated exhaustively, nearly a century later by Heinichen, in his *Neu erfundene und gründliche Anweisung &c.*, 1711, and again in his *General-Bass in der Composition*, 1728; but, in the page and a half which he devotes to it, Sabbatini seizes some of the most important points.

His rules are as follows:

(1) "In order to know how to play black notes, it must be noted that a black note cannot stand alone, but must have a companion in the shape either of another similar note, or of its equivalent time-value, preceding or

following it, as [music] [music]."

(2) "It must be noted which of any two crotchets, or their equivalent values, is first and which is second [i.e. which is on the stronger beat, and which on the weaker].

(3) "It must be noted that the first of any such two crotchets is accompanied as though it were a white note [i.e. as one of the main beats of the bar].

(4) "Further it must be noted whether the second crotchet of the pair is either preceded or followed by a leap, because, if so, it also has its own

accompaniment, as though it were a white note: [music]

"If, on the other hand, it proceeds, from the preceding, and to the following note, by step, then the second crotchet in question is treated as a passing note [*passa per cattiua*, lit. 'passes as a bad note'], that is to say, it passes under the harmony of the preceding note, with this difference, that, in striking the first crotchet, the whole chord is struck with it, whereas the second one is struck alone (*col tasto solo*), while the chord belonging to the first is held

down: ."

N.B.—It is, of course, assumed that the last note of the example is not followed by a leap, in which case it would bear an independent harmony.

(5) "Further, when all the parts are heard to be moving simultaneously in crotchets, or even shorter notes, then they must all count as good notes [i.e. each must bear its own harmony], and, in such a case, it will be a good thing if the said black notes, or some of them, are struck alone (*col tasto solo*) by the left hand, while the greater part of the accompanying consonances (whichever prove most convenient) are struck by the right.

(6) "Finally it must be noted that, in the case of any four [22] black notes moving by step, the accompanying harmony may be struck on the first of them, while the others, being struck alone [cf. Rule 4], may be treated as

[22] This does not agree with the example given under Rule 4, in which the third (as well as the first) of a series of four crotchets bears a harmony of its own. By 'any four black notes', therefore, Sabbatini probably meant quavers, to which he himself says that the rule especially applies, or else he had a quicker time in mind, in which the crotchets were on a par with the quavers in a slower measure.

passing notes, and this is usual, especially, in the case of quavers, two of which, moving by step after the first crotchet, or its equivalent time-value,

may be treated as passing notes, thus :

and struck alone."

The last note of the above example would appear, at first sight, to be a misprint for *c*, and it may well be that it is so. On the other hand it is quite possible that it is what Sabbatini intended, and that he forgot to explain

the irregularity. If so, ♮ must be regarded as standing

for

After giving the example in question Sabbatini concludes his little treatise with the simple and earnest words already quoted (cf. 1 *ad fin.*).

The work is of very great interest from the point of view of the antiquarian, but of little practical value, partly because the second (and by far the more important) part was either never written, or has disappeared, but also because the examples, dealing as they do with strings of Triads, rarely represent anything likely to be encountered in actual practice.

§ 18. *Heinrich Albert.*

In 1640 Heinrich Albert (born 1604), Organist of the Cathedral at Königsberg, and a nephew of the great Heinrich Schütz, whose pupil he had for

---

[23] A somewhat similar instance occurs in the accompaniment (bar 3) of John Dowland's song, 'Think'st thou then by thy feigning?'—*First Booke of Songes or Ayres, 1597*, edited by Dr. E. H. Fellowes (London, Stainer & Bell, 1920) :

At a later period, this skip of a Third, due to the omission of a passing note, came to be regarded as a licence peculiar to the strict *Allabreve* style, in which, as Heinichen tells us (*General-Bass &c.*, 1728, Pt. I, Ch. 4, § 43, p. 339),

instead of , came to be regarded as a privileged form of the *transitus ad quartam* (i.e. passing notes bridging the interval of a Fourth), the object being to avoid the use of quavers, which, except in certain stereotyped *formulae*, such as , were disallowed in this style. (Cf. Ch. xviii, § 1, note 11, p. 725).

a short time been, published a set of nine rules for the treatment of a
Thorough-Bass for the benefit of beginners, having, as he explains, been
requested to do so.

They are incorporated, like those of Viadana, in the preface to one of his
works, namely the second part, dedicated to his uncle, Heinrich Schütz, of
his sacred and secular 'Airs',[1] of which the first part appeared at Königsberg
(Segebads Erben) in 1638, and the eighth and last, in 1650.

The rules, which, in the present instance, are taken from the second edition
of the work in question (Königsberg, Paschen Mense, 1643, Brit. Mus. G. 61),
are as follows:

(1) "Assume that all Musical Harmony, even though it were conveyed in
a hundred parts at once, consists only of *Three Sounds*, and that the fourth,
and all other parts, must of necessity coincide, in the Octave, with one of
these three.

(2) "Thus the Thorough-Bass ('General-Bass') is the lowest sound of
every piece of Music, to which one must adapt and play its consonances in
accordance with the indication of the composer.

(3) "Everywhere, therefore, where no figures or *signa* [i.e. ♯, ♭] appear
above it, the Fifth and Third are to be taken and played in accordance with
the key in which a piece is written. In so doing, take heed always to keep
such consonances close together, and to cultivate the practice of varying them
nicely (*euch einer feinen Abwechselung derselben befleissiget*), in suchwise that,
when the Bass is high, the Third is, for the most part, nearest to it, and
when it is low, the Fifth. By which observance you can also guard against
many Fifths and Octaves being heard in succession and perchance causing
displeasure."

N.B.—This rule embodies the principle, stated in every complete treatise on the
manipulation of a Thorough-Bass, that contrary motion is the surest way of avoiding
consecutives.

(4) "In addition to the three sounds (*Sonis*) you can play another part,
or, occasionally, several; and the best one is, first, the Octave of the Bass,
and, next, that of the Fifth.

(5) "Since, however, in all well-written pieces, the consonances are
mingled, in a certain fashion, with the dissonances, and, so to speak, interwoven with them, which combinations are known as bindings [2] or *Syncopationes*, these must, consequently, always be indicated, where necessary, by
the composer, in the said Bass, by figures, to which you must adhere diligently
and pay close attention. Therefore, the tied 2nds, 4ths, 7ths, &c., must

---

[1] "Ander Theil der Arien etlicher theils geistlicher, theils weltlicher, zur Andacht,
guten Sitten, keuscher Liebe und Ehren-Lust dienender Reime, zum singen und
spielen gesetzet und dem Fürtrefflichen und Welt-berümbten Hn. Heinrich Schützen
. . . als seinem hochgeEhrten Herrn Oheim Ao: 1640 zugeschrieben von Heinrich
Alberten."

('Second part of the Airs to sundry rhymes, partly sacred and partly secular,
serving for devotion, good morals, chaste love, and devotion to honour, set for
singing and playing, and inscribed to the excellent and world-renowned Master
Heinrich Schütz [here follow titles], his revered Uncle, in the year 1640, by Heinrich
Albert.')

[2] The term 'binding', as the equivalent of the Germ. 'Bindung', is now obsolete,
though it was formerly used, as e.g. by Matthew Locke, *Melothesia*, Rule 3 *ad fin.*
(cf. § 21). A 'Bindung' was more than a mere syncopation, as it implied a discord,

actually *be* tied on a Flute-work or Choir Organ (*Positiv*), and, accordingly, sustained on the keyboard. (Thus it is also good to retain, in like manner, such notes as are common to successive chords,[3] and not to take them up.) But on an 'Instrument'[4] or Harpsichord (as also on a Lute or Bandora), since the sound of a string, when touched, soon wanes and becomes weak, it is necessary that the fingers should be raised, and that both the tied notes (*Bindungen*) and the consonances should be frequently repeated and struck, so that, now the upper part, now one of the middle ones, and now the lowest part, moves and does its duty.[5]

whether essential or suspended, prepared on the weak beat of the bar, so as to produce syncopation in the part in which it occurs, as in the following examples:

In (*a*) the discord ∗ is essential, and in (*b*), suspended.

Syncopations which were purely melodic (but not those of stationary notes, as ), were called in German 'Rückungen', a term which corresponds closely to the old-fashioned English term 'driving notes'. The following is an example:

The terms 'Bindung' and 'Rückung' were often loosely used, as though synonymous, but Schröter (*Deutliche Anweisung zum General-Bass*, 1772, § 292, p. 167) clearly defines the difference, as follows: "It must here be specially noted that 'Bindung' differs markedly from 'Rückung' (*Syncope*), inasmuch as 'Rückung' can also take place with concords on all the accented notes without regard to *Thesis* and *Arsis*, and is moreover concerned with the melody; whereas 'Bindung', on the other hand, aims, with one or more discords, † at the harmony. Assuredly a great difference!"

It will be clear from the above that every 'Bindung' is also a 'Rückung', but that a 'Rückung' is not necessarily a 'Bindung'. *Majus continet minus.*

[3] 'diejenigen Accorde, so von einer zur andern Note sich schicken': lit. 'such chords as belong from one note to another'.

[4] The Harpsichord or Spinet was frequently spoken of as an 'Instrument'.

[5] Albert seems to have had in mind a sequence, such as 4 3 on a Bass alternately falling a Fourth and rising a Fifth, or 7 6 (or $\frac{9}{7}\frac{8}{6}$) on a Bass rising by step (cf. Ex. in note 2), in which the discord appears in each of the three upper parts successively. He expresses himself inaccurately, since the suspended discord would 'move and do

† As in the following example from Schröter (ibid., § 248 *e*, p. 137):

(6) "Where a Fugue begins with a single part, one waits with the consonances till the second and more parts enter.

(7) "To move up or down the keyboard with both hands at once is not at all good. It is generally regarded as the most elegant way to play from a Thorough-Bass if, when it [the Bass] rises, one moves in the opposite direction with the consonances, moving upwards by step when it falls, but in such a way that the hands do not get too far apart.

(8) "When the Bass rises with quick notes in succession, retain for every four the concords which are appropriate to the first note of the four in question.[6] But if it falls by step, then one must always play fresh concords to every two, and it is then only every second note that does not count (*und fällt nicht mehr als nur die andere Note hinweg*).[7] But if notes, even quick ones, stand apart from each other [i.e. do not move by step], then they must each severally be given their own concords."

its duty' (*sich rühre und ihre Gebühr thue*) in an equal degree, whether played as on the Organ (*a*), or as on the Harpsichord (*b*).

[6] Albert omits to mention the important fact that the harmony appropriate to the first of a group of four quick notes rising by step cannot be retained if the *fourth note is followed by a leap*. In such a case the *transitus irregularis* takes place; that is to say, the third of the group of quick notes (quavers or semiquavers, according as the time-unit is a minim or a crotchet) is treated as a 'changing' or accented passing note, and bears the harmony appropriate to the unaccented note which follows, as at * * in the following, taken from an example of Heinichen (*Der General-Bass &c.*, 1728, Pt. I, Ch. 4, § 15, p. 169):

[7] The distinction which Albert makes between rising and falling notes, moving by step, in the Bass is a remarkable one, and does not seem to occur elsewhere. Heinichen, whose rules on the treatment of quick notes in the Bass occupy the whole of a chapter of 122 pages, and are by far the most detailed extant (cf. Ch. xviii of the present work), makes no such distinction, as the first bar of the example of which two bars are given in note 6 shows:

But, as a matter of fact, Albert evidently based his rule, as so often happens, upon particular instances which he had in mind, without due consideration of other possibilities, as the following examples from his own works (*Arien &c.*, Pt. 2, No. 20, Symphonia à 5, bar 5 sq., and Pt. 6, No. 15, bars 3, 4), given here in condensed score, show. It will be seen that, in the case of the groups of four quavers falling by step, marked * (in both examples), the harmony remains unchanged, contrary to

(9) "As a particularly useful distinction between the Thirds, to show whether *Tertia Major* or *Minor* is to be played, I have used the figure 3 and the *signum chromaticum* ✗,[8] so that one can make no mistake on this point.

Albert's rule, while, in those marked †, the harmony changes on the third quaver, in accordance with it.

N.B.—The rule given in note 6 does not apply to the upward leap of a Seventh (as between the second and third group of quavers in the above Ex.) when the downward motion of the preceding notes is continued, or vice versâ.

The above Exx. provide an admirable illustration of the deficiencies of the figuring in the seventeenth century. At a somewhat later period than that now under consideration slurs (*liaison*) over the notes were used in France (cf. § 23, note 11) to denote the continuance of the harmony, and later still dashes took their place. Thus the quavers in Exx. (*a*) and (*b*) would have been figured as follows:

Or, if the pace and character of the composition were such as to justify the assumption that four quavers, rising or falling by step (and not followed by a leap), would, in default of an indication to the contrary, go to a single chord, a change of harmony on the third quaver of such a group would be indicated by a figure:

Some composers would have used the dash over the first group as well.

In Ex. (*b*) the quaver *e* ♮, on the fourth beat of the first bar, is a 'changing' note (*transitus irregularis*), and bears the harmony—a Sixth—appropriate to the following quaver *d*.

At a later period the figuring would have been:

$$\begin{smallmatrix}5\\2\end{smallmatrix} \quad \text{or} \quad \text{—}6$$

(cf. Ch. xix, 'The figuring of transitional notes', §§ 4, 5).

As *d* is the Supertonic, the Sixth may, at pleasure, be taken as $\begin{smallmatrix}6\\4\\3\end{smallmatrix}$ (cf. Ch. xxi, 'Incomplete figuring', II, § 1).

[8] Albert does not mention the use of ♭ above the Bass to indicate the minor Third, though he regularly used it, as e.g. ⸝⸝⸝⸝⸝ 6 ♭ ✗ (*Arien &c.*, Pt. I, No. 1 *ad fin.*).

I should have been glad if the type had been available to indicate the difference between the Sixths: as it is, I must leave the matter to your acute ear and good intelligence. So much for the Thorough-Bass."

§ 19. *Wolfgang Ebner.*

(*a*) A set of fifteen rules for the treatment of a Thorough-Bass, somewhat more complete than those of Heinrich Albert, was compiled in Latin by one Wolfgang Ebner, who became Organist of the Church of St. Stephen at Vienna in 1634, and in 1663 attained to the position of Director of Music (*Capellmeister*) in the same city.

These rules were apparently never printed in their original form, but were translated into German by Johann Andreas Herbst (b. 1588 at Nuremberg, and afterwards Director of Music at Frankfurt), and appended, *corollarii loco*, to his *Arte prattica et poetica* (Frankfurt, 1653) under the following title: 'A short instruction and guide to Thorough-Bass (*General-Bass*): previously written in Latin by Wolff Ebner, Court Organist to his Imp: Maj: Ferdinand III, but now translated into the German language for the benefit of all lovers of this Art by J. A. H.'

The rules contain little that we have not already encountered in earlier treatises. It will be enough to give some extracts which cast a light on Ebner's method of accompaniment.

N.B.—In the original all the Exx. are given in lozenge-shaped notes.

(*b*) After giving the following example of a Sixth and a Third delayed by suspension (7 6 and 4 3):   [Ex. 1]

Ebner adds (Rule 5): "Fifthly it is to be observed that, though it is beautiful and artistic (*künstlich*) to play continuously or invariably in four parts, nevertheless, because this is very difficult, it is sufficient to play sometimes in three parts, after the manner just shown."

(*c*) As instances of the figurings which must be 'very carefully attended to' (Rule 6) Ebner gives 7 6, 4 3, 9 8, 5 6, 3 4 3,[1] together with ✕, the sign of the Diesis.

(*d*) In giving the rule for a full close (Rule 8) when the Bass falls a Fifth or rises a Fourth, as: [Ex. 2]

Ebner adds: "But when it is a final cadence (*ein[e] vollkömmliche Cadentia*), the last note must always be taken with the *signo Diœseos* ✕." That is to say, the last chord (in a final cadence) is to be major (*Tierce de Picardie*), even though the preceding music is minor. Friderich Erhard Niedt (*Handleitung*, Pt. 1, 1700) gives the same rule (Reg. 6) with great explicitness, adding that it is not in accordance with the French custom (cf. § 25 III, 8 *b*).

(*e*) Ebner's ninth rule, like H. Albert's (cf. § 18), forcibly illustrates the prevalent incompleteness of figuring, and especially the typographical economy in the matter of accidentals:

"Ninthly it is to be noted that every note may have either a sharp (*Diœsin*)

---

[1] For the interpretation of the condensed formula 3 4 3 see Matthew Locke's 'Examples in yᵉ 3ᵈ Rule' (§ 21), where, however, the fuller figuring ⁷₃ ⁶₄ ⁵₃ is used.

𝕏 or a flat (*b-moll*). When, therefore, the Organist is in doubt what he is to play, he must wait a little for the singer to come out with a Third or Sixth, and then he can follow him; thus, if he sings it without 𝕏, he can do likewise, &c."

(*f*) Ebner's eleventh rule is of especial interest and deserves to be quoted in full:

"In the eleventh place it is to be noted that, when there are four voices, as *Cantus, Altus, Tenor, Bassus*, one must never go above the Treble with the right hand: on the contrary, it will sound better if all the parts [of the accompaniment] are kept below it; for, when opposites (*widerwertige Dinge*) are contrasted with each other, they will always appear to better advantage: thus, by way of illustration, when the lower parts are played, the higher vocal parts can be the better heard. This rule is to be well observed and attended to."

We see that, in this important matter, Ebner was in complete agreement with Agazzari (cf. § 10*b*). It has always remained an accepted rule that, in playing from a Thorough-Bass, the accompaniment should not, in a general way, go above the principal vocal or instrumental part,[2] except when the latter (as frequently happens in the case of e.g. a Violin) indulges in a downward leap, which the accompaniment is not allowed to imitate.

(*g*) The example illustrating the twelfth rule (concerning the use of contrary motion as a means of avoiding consecutive Octaves and Fifths) shows that Ebner sometimes divided the harmony between the hands (like Sabbatini), and sometimes not:

[Ex. 3]

N.B.—In the original most of the middle parts are indicated by black dots.

(*h*)

[Ex. 4]

N.B.—The Sixth on the second crotchet of the example was probably intended to be ♯*f*, as in Ex. 6 on the same Bass.

[Ex. 5]

N.B.—In both the above examples the figuring $\frac{6}{3}$, instead of the usual 6, is gratuitous, as Ebner has already explained (Rule 3) that where 6 is figured the Third also is to be taken.

[2] A Bass voice or instrument (Violoncello or Bassoon) constitutes a special case, with regard to which there was a difference of opinion concerning the pitch of the accompaniment (cf. Ch. iii, 'The general character, &c.', § 5 B).

In giving the above examples of Sixths on an ascending and descending Bass (Rule 13) Ebner makes a rather curious comment: "In the thirteenth place, it is to be noted that there is a *modus* and way in which one can both ascend and descend in three parts. Although the manner in question is far from agreeable, I nevertheless include it as the result of considerable experience, because it is nowadays much in vogue among sundry Musicians of standing, &c."

Ebner's feeling with regard to this simple progression seems to have been to some extent shared by Michel de Saint-Lambert, who, however, deals with it only in four-part harmony (cf. § 23, Exx. 29–31).

(*i*) The fourteenth rule is to the effect that 5 6 on a rising Bass is often found. The example (on the same Bass as Ex. 4) is marked 'à Giov. Valentino'.

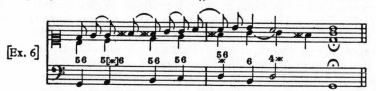

[Ex. 6]

Ebner adds that 'this example is not used in descending', by which he probably means, not 5 6, but 6 5 on a descending Bass (cf. § 21, note 5).

(*k*) In the fifteenth (and final) rule we are told that there is yet another way (i.e. than that illustrated in Ex. 5) of descending by step, namely, by Sevenths and Sixths, as in the following example:

[Ex. 7]

N.B.—The four last examples (Exx. 4–7) are given in a twofold form, first, 'Exempel mit Zahlen', or figured Bass only, and next, 'Exempel mit Einstimmung', on two staves with the figures replaced by musical notation, the middle part being indicated by dots only.

(*l*) It will have been noticed that the only difficulty which arises in connexion with any of the progressions included in the above rules, that of playing them correctly in four parts, is carefully avoided. Nevertheless, more information is given than in H. Albert's rules, and the examples, which render it easy of comprehension, must have been welcome to many a beginner.

§ 20. *Lorenzo Penna.*

(*a*) A work of extraordinary interest is a treatise bearing the following title and description:

LI PRIMI ALBORI / MVSICALI / Per li Principianti della Musica Figurata; / DISTINTI IN TRE LIBRI / Dal Primo spuntano li Principj del CANTO FIGVRATO; / Dal Secondo spiccano le Regole del CONTRAPVNTO; / Dal Terzo appariscono li Fondamenti per suonare l' ORGANO / ò CLAVICEMBALO sopra la Parte; / Del P[adre] F[rà] LORENZO PENNA / DA BOLOGNA / Carmelitano della Cong. di Mantoua, Maestro di / S. Teologia, Dottore Colleg. frà li Accademici / Filaschisi, Filarmonichi, e Risoluti, l' Indefesso / al Reueren-

dissimo Padre / CLEMENTE MARIA / FELINA / Maestro e Dottore di Sacra
Teologia, Lettore Publico / Viceuicario, Diffinitore perpetuo, e Priore / di
S. Martino di Bologna. /

In Bologna, per Pier Giacomo Monti. 1672 Con Licenza de' Superiori. /

According to Eitner, Penna was born in Bologna in 1613 and died on the
20th October 1693. Reprints of *Li Primi Albori* appeared in 1674, 1679,
1684, 1696, and, of the Second Book alone, in 1678.

(*b*) With the exception of some instructions for supplying the *Basso continuo* to an (otherwise) completed composition, which are given in the penultimate chapter of the Second Book of Penna's treatise, and will be referred to
later on (cf. *n*, note 51), it is with the Third Book alone that we are here
concerned. According to its heading, it professes to give the rules for playing
the *Organ* from a Thorough-Bass (*per suonare l' Organo sopra la Parte*), and
the omission of the word *Clavicembalo*, which appeared in the title (given
above) of the entire work, as well as Penna's close association with the Church,
and also his frequent mention of the *Organist*, shows that it was, after all, the
Organ and not the Harpsichord which he had chiefly in mind.

(*c*) The contents of the Third Book are as follows:

Introduction; Ch. 1, "On the rules in general"; Ch. 2, "On a Bass rising
or falling by step"; Ch. 3, "On leaps of a Third downwards and a Third
upwards"; Ch. 4, "On leaps of a Fourth downwards and a Fifth upwards";
Ch. 5, "On leaps of a Fifth downwards and a Fourth upwards"; Ch. 6, "On
the interruption of long notes"; Ch. 7, "On a Bass moving in small notes";
Ch. 8, "On the numbers (i.e. figures) most used in a Thorough-Bass"; Ch. 9,
"On cadences"; Ch. 10, "On cadences of the first order"; Ch. 11, "On
cadences of the second order"; Ch. 12, "On cadences of the third order";
Ch. 13, "On cadences of the fourth order"; Ch. 14, "On the accompaniment
of compositions for a single voice"; Ch. 15, "On playing [i.e. accompanying]
fugal polyphonic compositions (*Del suonar fugato à Capella*)"; Ch. 16, "On
transposition (*Del suonar trasportato*)"; Ch. 17, "On transposition to the
Fourth below"; Ch. 18, "On transposition to the Fifth below"; Ch. 19, "On
playing one, two, three, or four, &c., notes lower, or one, two, three, four,
&c., notes higher"; Ch. 20, "Some instructions as to what to do, and others
as to what to avoid, in playing the Organ from a Thorough-Bass".

(*d*) The chief interest attaches, undoubtedly, to the last chapter, in which a
very clear idea is given of the accompaniment suitable to compositions of different kinds, and also to the fourteenth, in which directions are given with regard
to certain important details relating to the accompaniment of single voices.

Apart from these, a very striking feature in the Third Book is the great
importance attached to the use of the *shake*.

At a later period, as we learn chiefly from Heinichen (*General-Bass &c.*,
1728), the shake was one of the various forms of embellishment the employment of which was regarded as admissible only under certain circumstances,
namely, when the attention of the listener was legitimately claimed by the
accompanist, as during a prolonged silence of the principal part or parts, or
while the latter were occupied with sustained notes or some figure devoid
of melodic interest, &c.[1]

Penna, on the contrary, evidently regarded a shake, sometimes a shake in
each hand, as the proper adjunct of *every form of cadence*, and it is therefore

[1] Cf. Ch. iii, § 8 *a*.

not surprising that he laid stress, as we shall see later, on the cultivation of manual dexterity.[2]

(*e*) A few words must be said about Penna's practice in certain particulars:

(1) He follows the nomenclature of the Hexachords (which he explains in detail in his First Book, together with the celebrated Hand of Guido d'Arezzo): thus *a* is 'A, *la, mi, re*', &c.

(2) Though he alludes to the practice, on the part of "modern composers", of using as many as three sharps or flats in the key-signature, a practice which, he tells us, is not altogether modern, "as can be seen from my *Prima Opera*, printed at Milan in the year 1656",[3] he distinguishes, as a rule, only between signatures *without* a flat (*Chiaui per* ♮ *quadro*) and those *with* one (*Chiaui per* ♭ *molle*). No allusion is made to the distinction between major and minor, except incidentally, as when we are told that, in transposing one or more notes downwards or upwards, to suit the convenience of singers, the first thing to be noted is "whether the composition is of a nature to proceed by the Lesser Third, *Re, fa, la*, or whether, in accordance with its nature, it progresses with the Greater Third, *Ut, mi, sol*".[4]

(3) He adheres, in his examples, to the old practice of figuring compound intervals, 10, 11, 12, &c., going, in one instance, as far as 22 (cf. *f*, Ex. 1), but is far from consistent, often using 4 for 11, 7 for 14, &c., and vice versâ.

(4) Most of the examples are noted in three, only a few in four, parts, each on a separate stave,[5] but apparently always with the understanding that, if desirable, the harmony may be reinforced with the appropriate consonances (*con le consonanze della Nota scritta*).[6]

(*f*) Of the twelve rules which form the first chapter of the Third Book the more important are, in substance,[7] as follows:

1. (Rule 1) "The harmony is to be replete with consonances (*Che il suonare sia pieno di Consonanze armoniose*), namely, the Prime, Third, Fifth, or Sixth, Octave, and their compounds." [8]

[Ex. 1][9]

<hr/>

[2] Cf. *o*, Rule 18. [3] o.c. First Book, Ch. 8. [4] o.c. Third Book, Ch. 19.

[5] With few exceptions the examples will here be given on two staves, generally with *the Bass only* on the lower stave, but it will be understood from the above that the fact of a note being printed on the upper stave must not be taken to indicate that it was necessarily meant to be played with the *right hand*.

[6] Apart from the rule given by Penna that, save under special circumstances, there should always be at least four sounding parts (cf. *f*. 2), the fact that an essential interval of a chord, as the 3 of a Triad is not unfrequently omitted in his three-part examples (cf. *f*, last chord of Ex. 5; also *g*, Ex. 11 (*c*) and (*d*)) is proof enough that they are to be regarded as skeleton harmony.

[7] Where the contrary is not indicated by inverted commas, the author's text has been (more or less freely) paraphrased, rather than translated. As will be seen, the order in which Penna gives the rules has not been adhered to.

[8] The circumstances under which full harmony, or the reverse, is to be employed are defined in Rules 13–16 of Penna's last chapter (cf. *o*).

[9] The notes on the upper stave of (*a*) represent the lowest part played by the right

2. (Rule 6) "There should always be at least four sounding parts (*Che suonino sempre almeno quattro tasti* [Ex. 2 (*a*)], except the Bass go very high, in which case three will suffice [(*b*)]." [10]

3. (Rule 10) "Two consecutive Octaves are to be avoided, and two Fifths,[11] and their compounds, either by step or by leap; which Rule applies principally to the extreme parts." [12]

4. (Rule 8) Contrary motion should be employed as much as possible.

[Penna gives examples, in which the Bass rises and falls by step.]

5. (Rule 9) When that is impossible,[13] the right hand should move by step in Tenths with the Bass:

hand; the figures above them are counted (as Penna explains) from the Bass. The effect can be seen at a glance in (*b*), which has been added for clearness' sake.

[10] Penna tells us later on (cf. note 8) that in accompanying a single voice the number of parts should rarely exceed three.

[11] In his Second Book (Ch. 2, Rule 5) Penna tells us that a perfect Fifth may always be *followed* by a false (i.e. diminished) one, as at (*a*), and that the progression shown

at (*b*) is also possible:  The latter progression

may be seen (between the upper and a middle part) at the end of Ex. 1 (*b*), above.

[12] Penna's four examples, which it is unnecessary to quote here, all show consecutives *between extreme parts only*. In Ex. 2 (*a*) above we see consecutive Octaves between Treble and Tenor, and in a later example (o.c. Ch. 8, Rule 2, bar 5 of example) we find consecutive Fifths of a similar character:

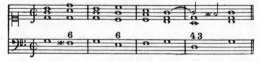

[Penna doubtless intended the harmony to be fuller than as noted in the above example (cf. note 6).]

In filled-in harmony, as shown in Ex. 1 above, it is obvious that, except between extreme parts, consecutives cannot be avoided.

[13] It will be observed that, in point of fact, the Bass of Penna's example presents no obstacles whatever to an accompaniment in contrary motion, as:

and that, in this respect, the example is ill chosen. It is nevertheless characteristic, and therefore interesting. The minims in the middle part, rising from the 5, or 6, of

6. (Rule 2) "Every bass note is to be accompanied by Thirds and Fifths, or their compounds, excepting the *mi*'s, which ordinarily take Thirds and Sixths, or their compounds; but it is rarely that the Octave [of the Bass] is taken with *mi*; [14] if anything different is to be done, it will be indicated by a figure. Be it remarked that the notes *mi* in the keys without a flat are B and E [Ex. 4 (*a*)]; and in the keys with a flat, A and D [15] [Ex. 4 (*b*)]."

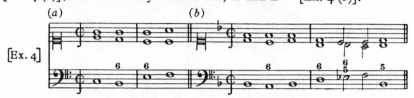

[Ex. 4]

7. (Rule 3) "When the bass note is accidentally sharpened (*quando la parte inferiore haura il* ✕), it is, for the most part, to be accompanied by the Third and Sixth."

[Ex. 5]

8. (Rule 5) "Care must be taken to proceed with hands [16] and fingers close together (*Che si procuri di andar unito con le mani, e dita*)."

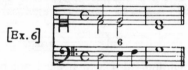

[Ex. 6]

each chord to the Octave of the Bass, present an appearance quite different from that with which one is familiar in the examples given in most of the text-books of the eighteenth century. In the third bar they serve, incidentally, to save consecutive Fifths with the Bass, but Penna's chief object was, undoubtedly, to break the monotony of the semibreves (cf. *h*). This was a matter to which Geminiani, more than a century later, attached the greatest importance, though from a somewhat different point of view, since he was considering the evanescent tones of the Harpsichord, and not (like Penna) the sustained notes of the Organ (cf. Ch. iv, § 4 *a*).

[14] Although he does not trouble to mention it here, Penna assumes that the *Octave of the Bass*, as well as the Third and Fifth, is to be taken with the other notes of the scale (cf. Ex. 1). In Ex. 4 (*b*) (at the beginning of the second bar) it will be seen that the *Octave*, as well as the Sixth, is taken with *mi*. (For the omission of the 3 see note 6.) So also in Ex. 6. In neither case is the *mi* in question a *leading note*.

[15] The *mi* of the *Hexachordum durum* (G, A, B, C, D, E) is B (B *mi*), that of the *Hexachordum naturale* (C, D, E, F, G, A), E (E, *la*, *mi*), and it is in these two hexachords that the *Chiaui per* ♮ *quadro* (the keys without a flat) are comprised. The *mi* of the *Hexachordum molle* (F, G, A, ♭B, C, D) is A (A, *la*, *mi*, *re*), and it is in this and the *Hexachordum naturale* that the *Chiaui per* ♭ *molle* (the keys *with* a flat) are comprised. It is plain, therefore, that E (E, *la*, *mi*) is a *mi* common to the *Chiaui per* ♮ *quadro* and the *Chiaui per* ♭ *molle*. If, however, the latter are transposed by the introduction of ♭E (whether actually included in the signature, or not) as in Ex. 4 (*b*), then the *mi*'s will be, not E and A, but, as Penna says, A and D. His tacit assumption of the said transposition is probably due to the practice, which originated in the employment of the Dorian, Lydian, and Mixolydian Modes in a transposed form, and which survived until well on in the eighteenth century, of putting a ♭ (or a ♯) too few in the signature.

[16] The closeness of the hands is not very apparent at the beginning of the example,

9. (Rule 11) "Shakes are to be made with the main note (whether written or figured) and the note above it, closing on the main note.[17] In the left hand the middle and index fingers are generally used, and in the right, the ring finger and middle finger."

[Ex. 7]

"Execution with the left hand"

[Ex. 7a]

"Execution with the right hand"

[Ex. 7b]

10. Of the three remaining rules, which need not be given here, Rule 4 explains and illustrates the resolution of suspended discords, Rule 11 the effect of the accidentals ✗ and ♭, (1) by the side of (and level with) the bass note, and (2) above it,[18] while Rule 7 deals with a detail of fingering (cf. *o*, note 52).

(*g*) The second, third, fourth, and fifth chapters consist of rules framed as though for dealing with an *unfigured* Bass. We are told what harmonies are usually associated with the progressions of the Bass enumerated in the Table of Contents quoted above (*c*). Among these rules the two following call for special attention on account of Penna's striking way of dealing with the progressions in question, especially in the matter of the shakes which he prescribes:

1. Ch. 4 deals with a Bass leaping a Fourth downwards, or a Fifth upwards,

but we may assume that a fourth (Tenor) part, ending in unison with the Bass: is to be supplied (cf. note 6).

[17] It will be noticed that, at the close of the final shake in both examples (Ex. 7 *a* and *b*), the note below the main note is touched, as in the turn which can be seen in Ex. 12 A (in the Tenor). A remarkable feature in these shakes is the rapid repercussion (of the main note) which follows upon the alternation between main note and auxiliary.

[18] Like Viadana and other earlier writers, Penna places the accidentals denoting a major or minor Third exactly a Third above the bass note and slightly to the left of it.

both to a major Triad (as in a half-close on the Dominant), and also to a minor one (as from the Subdominant to the Tonic of a minor key). The rules are as follows:

"First Rule.

"When the Bass falls a Fourth [Ex. 8 (*a*)], or rises a Fifth [(*b*)], the minor Triad is to be given [i.e. to the first bass note], although in some cases the major Triad can be given [(*c*), (*d*)]; one must conform to the nature of the composition."

"Second Rule.

"When the note which falls a Fourth, or rises a Fifth, is of the value of a semibreve (*una battuta*) [Ex. 9 (*a*) (*c*)], or of a minim (*mezza battuta*), in the *tempo minore* [Ex. 9 (*b*) (*d*)],[19] the accompaniment, since there is plenty of time, may be as follows: First take the minor Third with the Fifth, but never the major Third (unless it is indicated); afterwards the major [i.e. augmented] Fourth and major Sixth, making one shake with the Octave and Ninth, and another shake with the Fourth and Fifth; and on the last note another shake is to be made with the Fourth and major Third, afterwards falling a Second and finishing on the major or minor [20] Third and the Fifth."

"Execution with the plain notes"

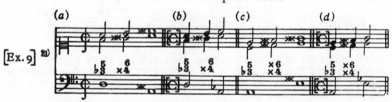

[19] In the *tempo maggiore* (or *alla breve*), of which the signature was ₵, the actual value of the notes was half of what it was in the *tempo minore*, of which the signature was C. That is why the term *battuta*, though in the *tempo maggiore* it actually had the duration of a breve, was commonly used (as above) to denote a semibreve. Penna's description of the *battuta* (given in Ch. 15 of his First Book) is worth quoting: "The *Battuta* has four parts. . . . With black notes [i.e. crotchets] these four parts come out admirably, because the first [crotchet] comes with the actual beat (*nel percuotere*), the second with the lifting of the hand with a slight undulating movement (*nel leuare un poco ondeggiando la mano*), the third with the rise (*nell' alzata*), and the fourth with the pause on high (*nel fermare in su*)." The first half of the *battuta* (the *thesis*) was commonly called in Italian the *battere di mano*, and the second half (the *arsis*), the *levare di mano*. In the various forms of *Tripola*, or triple time, the division of the *battuta* was, of course, different from that described above.

[20] Penna gives no example in which the final shake closes on the minor Third; it is therefore impossible to determine whether, as seems more probable, the rule is carelessly given, or whether he really intended the shake to be made with the major Third and to close on the minor.

[21] Compare Michel de Saint-Lambert's treatment of similar progressions of the Bass (§ 23 *h*. 3). It will be seen that he avoids the progression of an augmented Second, to which Penna apparently does not object.

"Execution with shakes"

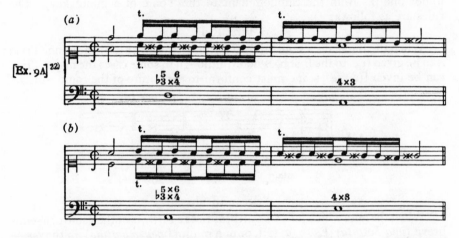

"But if the note which leaps is of the value of a quarter, or an eighth, of a semibreve (*battuta*), the above-mentioned minor Third with the Fifth will suffice [Ex. 10 (*a*), (*b*)]; although it may sometimes happen that the [augmented] Fourth and Sixth are added afterwards [Ex. 10 (*c*)]."

[22] Several points are to be noted in connexion with the above example:

(1) In the original the first note in the upper part of (*a*) is *A*, a Fourth lower. This is almost certainly due to inadvertence, the *A* being taken from the example "with the plain notes" (Ex. 9 (*a*)).

(2) It will be seen that the augmented Second between the first two notes of the middle part in Ex. 9 (*a*) and (*b*) is considerably mitigated by the shakes in Ex. 9 A.

(3) The figuring (4 × 3) in the second bar of (*a*) and (*b*) takes the shake in the upper part into account just as though it were an *appoggiatura* (a suspended Fourth).

(4) The execution prescribed by Penna calls for the use of the *pedals*, as it is quite out of the question that he should have intended both the shakes in the first bar of (*a*) and (*b*) to be played with the same hand. On the Harpsichord, therefore, the Bass would have to be taken an Octave higher.

(5) If the shakes are to be fingered as directed by Penna in his first chapter (cf. *f*. 9), the fourth part, necessary to complete the harmony, will be best taken by the right hand; the upper parts of (*a*) will therefore appear as follows:

[If the progression of the $_{\times 4}^{6}$ (on the second minim of bar 1) to the following chord is to be the same as in Ex. 9, we must, of course, assume a wholesale crossing of parts.]

2. Ch. 5 deals with a Bass falling a Fifth, or rising a Fourth. The rules are as follows:

"First Rule.

"The major Third is always to be given [23] [Ex. 11 (*a*), (*b*)], because, if it happens that the minor Third is to be given, it will be figured [*e, d*]."

[Ex. 11]

"Second Rule.

"When the note which leaps is of the value of a semibreve (*battuta*), and one has time, the accompaniment must be as follows: first the major Third must be taken with the Fifth; then the Fourth and the Sixth, major or minor in accordance with the nature of the composition, which Sixth can make a shake with the Seventh; then the Fourth and Fifth, with a shake of the Fifth and Sixth; [24] and finally the major Third with the Fifth, making a shake with the Fourth and major Third in the left hand, and taking the minor Seventh,[25] and minor Ninth [26] with the right hand; and, on the last note, a shake with the Fourth and major Third." [27]

"Execution with the plain notes"

[Ex. 12] [28)]

---

[23] i.e. whether figured or not. This is a most important rule to remember in dealing with some of the older Basses.

[24] If Penna's description is compared with Ex. 12 A, it will be seen that there is also a shake on the Fourth, but *with the major Third, instead of the Fifth, as auxiliary note*, in other words, not really a shake at all, but a prolonged *mordent*, the effect being exactly the same as though the figuring were $\times_3^5$ instead of $^5_4\times^5_3$. A parallel instance will be met with later on (Ex. 25 (*b*), cf. note 40).

[25] It will be seen from the example that the Seventh is to be taken *ex abrupto*, and not as a passing note following the Octave.

[26] It is to be noted that the Ninth is to be minor, *irrespective* of the "nature of the composition".

[27] Even if the Sixth in the $^6_4$ chord on the preceding note (the Dominant) is minor, the Third on the Tonic is always to be major (the so-called *Tierce de Picardie*).

[28] Penna gives four examples: two major (one with a falling, and the other with a rising Bass), and two minor; one of the latter must suffice here.

"Execution with shakes"

[Ex. 12*a*] 29)

(*h*) Ch. 6 deals with the "interruption" of long notes in the Bass. We have already had an instance of it in Ex. 3 (cf. *f*, note 13). The rules are as follows:

"First Rule.

"When the Bass is a semibreve this note must always be interrupted by one of the other parts with at least two notes of half its value (*Quando il Basso è di una battuta, si deve interrompere quella Nota da una delle altri parti, con due note di mezza battuta l' una almeno*)."

"Example"

[Ex. 13]

"Execution"

[Ex 13*a*] 30)

[29] It seemed best to give this example in score, as in the original. The question arises how Penna intended the ♭ 9 to be introduced. There are two possibilities: a fifth part, *d* rising to ♭ *e*, can be taken, either (1) above the present upper part, or (2) below the present Alto, and beginning in unison with the Tenor. The former alternative will result in an ugly progression of a diminished Fifth falling to a perfect

one: 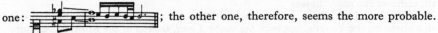 ; the other one, therefore, seems the more probable.

If it be adopted, the execution will be as follows, the Bass being, of course, relegated to the pedals, and the upper parts being distributed in such a way that the double shake on the third crotchet is divided between the two hands:

In whatever way it is taken, the example remains a very remarkable one, and the writer is not aware of any similar instance of the employment of the minor Ninth as a regular constituent of an ordinary compound cadence.

[30] It will be observed that this example (like Exx. 8–12 *a*) serves chiefly to illustrate the treatment of an unfigured Bass (as seen in Ex. 13).

"Second Rule.

"When the Bass has a dotted note, this dot must be interrupted in a similar manner by at least one part with another note."

[Ex. 14]

(*i*) Ch. 7 deals with the treatment of quick notes (*note minute*) in the Bass. The rules are as follows:

"First Rule.

"If the Bass moves in minims, the other parts must not move in notes of the same value (*con le istesse Figure*), but each minim must be interrupted by one of the other parts with two crotchets, or else one part must be held for a semibreve to every two minims [in the Bass]."

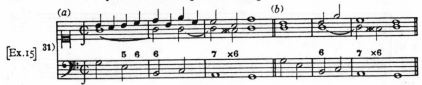

[Ex. 15]

"Second Rule.

"When the Bass, falling by step, has a minim followed by two crotchets, the harmony belonging to the second crotchet will be struck [Ex. 16 (*a*)],[32] making a shake on the first, if desired [(*b*)]."

[Ex. 16]

"Third Rule.

"If the Bass has many crotchets, the less the right hand moves, the better, provided that consonant harmony results (*purche si facci consonanza*), and thus a single harmony can be taken with every four crotchets (*ad ogni quattro nere si potrà fare consonanze*), namely, on the first note [Ex. 17 (*a*)]; if a single one cannot serve for all four, one harmony must be given to every two, namely, on the first and third note [(*b*)]; and if this, too, is not possible, a chord (*consonanza*) must be given to each crotchet [(*c*)]; and this occurs when the crotchets move by leap, and a single harmony will not serve."

[31] In (*a*) the minims in the Bass are treated not as 'short notes', but as 'long notes' (*note grosse*), to be interrupted by notes of half their value, as prescribed in Penna's previous chapter. In (*b*), though the process is reversed, the principle is the same: in both cases the object is to give fluency to the harmonic progression by minimizing the line of cleavage between the perpendicular blocks.

[32] *Si fa la consonanza con la seconda Semiminima*: in other words, the first crotchet is to be treated as a changing (i.e. accented passing) note (*nota cambiata*, Germ. *Wechselnote*). This was known as *transitus irregularis*, as opposed to the *transitus regularis* of unaccented passing notes (cf. Ch. xviii, § 3 *n*, Exx. 57–9).

[Ex. 17] 33)

"Fourth Rule.

"When the Bass has quavers, rising or falling by step, it is well to be careful to take eight with one harmony [Ex. 18 (a)]; or, if eight are not possible, let four be taken [(b)]; and, if it is possible to adjust the harmony (*accomodar la consonanza*) with a single finger of the right [34] hand, without putting down the others of the same hand [(c)], it would be a very good thing; but if the quavers move by leap, in such a way that a number of quavers cannot be suited with a single harmony, each quaver must be given its own chord." [35]

[Ex. 18]

(k) In Ch. 8 Penna professes to present the figurings most commonly to be met with. These are embodied in two long groups of examples, the one containing 'cadences' and the other 'ligatures', the latter embracing, not only suspensions, but changes of harmony (as 5 6, 6 5) on the same bass note, &c. The following are of special interest:

1. In Exx. 19 and 20 we see condensed *formulae*, of three successive figures, denoting the four steps of the cadences in question ($\begin{smallmatrix}7&6&5&-\\\sharp&4&-&\sharp\end{smallmatrix}$, $\begin{smallmatrix}5&6&5&-\\\sharp&4&-&\sharp\end{smallmatrix}$): [36]

[Ex. 19]   [Ex. 20]

2. In the following example, 4 (instead of 2 or $\frac{4}{2}$) is used to denote a $\begin{smallmatrix}6\\4\\2\end{smallmatrix}$ chord:

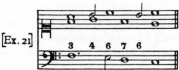

[Ex. 21]

[33] The 6, supplied in square brackets over the bass note *B* in all three examples, would not be regarded by Penna as necessary, since a *Sixth* (together with the Third, and possibly the Octave) is to be assumed, in the absence of any indication to the contrary, as the natural accompaniment of a *mi* (cf. *f*. 6).

[34] By an obvious error the original has *sinistra* (left).

[35] The example given is identical with Ex. 17 (c), except that the notes are of half the value.   [36] Cf. Ch. xxi, 'Incomplete figuring', v, § 1.

(*l*) Chapters 9–13 are devoted to cadences. These Penna divides into four classes or 'orders':

1. In the first, the Bass falls a Fifth, or rises a Fourth.

Besides the form which this takes when the Bass is in semibreves, already fully described (cf. *g*, Exx. 12 and 12 *a*), Penna illustrates the varieties, as being those of most common occurrence, when the cadence occupies four crotchets. Shakes are to be introduced into each one, as indicated by the letter t. They are as follows:

2. In the 'cadence of the second order', which, Penna tells us, is not, properly speaking, a cadence at all, but is classed as such on account of "a sort of resemblance" (*una tale quale somiglianza*), the Bass falls a Fourth, or rises a Fifth. This has already been fully described (cf. *g*, Exx. 9 and 9 A).

3. In the third order the Bass falls a degree. Penna's rule is as follows: "This cadence is accompanied by giving the penultimate note the Seventh, and then the major Sixth with a shake, afterwards striking the Fifth and then the Sixth,[37] and finally closing on the Octave, that is to say, when the cadence is in semibreves [Ex. 25], or minims in the *tempo minore* [38]; but when it is in crotchets, one will either proceed as described [Ex. 26 (*a*)], or give only the major Sixth [(*b*)]."

"Accompany the Seventh and Sixth with the consonances of the written note, namely, with the Octave, Tenth, and Twelfth,[39] and their compounds, and this will produce an excellent effect."

---

[37] The Fifth, followed by the Sixth, serves to conclude the shake with a turn. Penna's alternative treatment, as we have seen, was the repercussion of the main note after striking the note below (cf. Ex. 7 *a*, *b ad fin.*).

[38] Cf. note 19.

[39] There is nothing extraordinary in the inclusion of the perfect Fifth (or Twelfth) in a suspended Seventh (cf. Ch. xi, 'Sevenths', IV, §§ 2, 3), but that the Fifth should be retained when the Seventh resolves (thus producing a ⁶₅ chord) is indeed remarkable. Yet there can be no doubt that this is what Penna intended. In his Second Book (Ch. 22) he gives an example of this same cadence, for four choirs, in sixteen parts, and in the Tenor of the fourth choir the Fifth (*e*) is retained throughout the full duration of the bass note *a*, after which it rises four degrees to *b*, the 3 of the Tonic chord.

We shall see later on that Penna did not hesitate to include the Third (as one of the *Consonanze della nota scritta*) in a $\frac{5}{4}$ chord (cf. note 41).

"Example with plain notes"

4. In Penna's "cadence of the fourth order" the "ligature" is in the Bass. The following examples speak for themselves:

To the rule in which these examples—(1) in long notes, with shakes, and (2) in short ones, without—are described Penna adds the following: "Here, too, the dissonances can be accompanied (if desired) with the consonances of the written note,[41] and the Seventh, minor or major [i.e. diminished or

---

[40] It will be observed that the lower of the two shakes in Ex. 25 (*b*) is exactly as though the Bass were figured × 6 instead of 7 × 6, and that the distinction between the Seventh and its resolution is obliterated in exactly the same way as that between the suspended Fourth and its resolution in Ex. 12 *a* (cf. note 24). Assuming the plain notes to be *g ♯f*, in accordance with the figuring, the ornament begins as a prolonged *mordent* and ends as a shake. The only alternative, however, would be to omit the ornament on the *g* altogether, making a shake on the *♯f* only, as it is plain that a double shake in Fourths, $\frac{d\ c\ d\ c}{a\ g\ a\ g}$, &c., would be almost as ugly as one in Seconds, $\frac{bb\ a\ bb\ a}{a\ g\ a\ g}$, would have been in Ex 12 *a*.

[41] These are the Octave, Fifth, and Third, and their compounds. That the 5 should be associated with the $\frac{4}{2}$ on *d*, as figured in Ex. 27 (*a*), is in no way remarkable, though,

minor] according to the nature of the composition,[42] added to the false Fifth."

Penna evidently attached considerable importance to the acquisition of perfect familiarity with the different cadences in all keys, for each of the chapters devoted to the four 'orders' just described concludes with a *Circolo, ò Ruota delle Cadenze*, an extended example in which a passage is made through twelve keys, both 'ordinary' (*ordinarie*) and 'remote' (*extrauaganti*), back to the starting-point; and to each such series are appended the cadences

at a somewhat later period, the Sixth (major or minor in accordance with the mode) was usually employed in the progression in question. But that the Octave of the Bass (which is itself the discordant note of the harmony), and even the *Third* (which has *no place in it at all*), should be included seems, at first sight, almost incredible. That Penna regarded their inclusion as admissible (in a filled-in accompaniment) cannot, however, be doubted. In the example for four choirs already alluded to (cf. note 39) our cadence is given in sixteen parts, and, in the fourth choir, the 3 (or rather the 10) and the 8 are actually included in the $\frac{4}{2}$ on *d* (the 2 itself is omitted, being supplied by the second and third choirs). The Octave (Fifteenth) is also present in the upper part of the first choir. The harmony of the fourth choir is as follows; the 3 (10) is seen in the upper part *, and the 8 in the Tenor *:

(The downward leap of an augmented Fifth, with which the Soprano opens, is an example of the "difficult leaps" which Penna tells us are permitted here, "especially by reason of being for four choirs".)

The dissonant effect produced by the clash between the 3 (10), an interval *foreign to the harmony*, in the Soprano, and the 4 (11), in the Alto, is akin to (but much more extreme than) that of the *acciaccatura* so beloved by the Italian Harpsichordists, the main difference being that the *acciaccatura* is no sooner touched than it is again released (cf. Ch. iv, § 3, 11 *f*). That Penna attached considerable importance to the employment of such effects is clear from the following words with which he concludes the fourteenth chapter of his Third Book: "With regard to the completion of the accompaniment of [bass] notes bearing dissonances to be resolved on consonances (*Per compimento dell' accompagnare le Note, che sono con Dissonanze da risoluersi con le Consonanze*), let the pupil be informed that it is a universal rule that one can, or rather ought to, add to the dissonances the Thirds, Fifths, Octaves, and their compounds, of the written note, sounding them all together (*facendo suonare ogni cosa insieme*), more especially when the composition is for several voices, that is to say, for five or more voices, for two choirs, for three choirs, for four choirs, &c., because even the composer writes them [the 3, 8, 5, &c.] with the dissonances, as may be seen in my Second Book, Chapter Twenty-second."

[42] It will be observed that the inclusion of the "minor" (i.e. diminished) Seventh, instead of the Sixth, in the chord on the leading note, ♯ *c*, is exactly parallel with that of the minor Ninth in a perfect cadence (see Ex. 12 *a* and note 29). There is, however, this remarkable difference, that, whereas the Ninth remains minor, irrespective of the mode, the Seventh, according to Penna, is to vary.

enharmonically identical, and so common to the flat and sharp keys, as:
♭E ♭A, ♯D ♯G; ♭A ♭D, ♯G ♯C; &c.

(*m*) Ch. 14, "On the accompaniment of compositions for a single voice", is
of especial interest on account, *inter alia*, of important details which it contains
concerning the relation of the upper part of the accompaniment to the voice part.

The latter, Penna tells us, is usually to be found above the Organist's
part, and it is upon this assumption that his instructions are based.

Nothing is said about the accompaniment of voices of low pitch (Tenor
or Bass), though mention is made of this in the final chapter (Rules 11 and 12).

In accompanying a Soprano or Alto, the upper part of the accompaniment
is to *coincide with the voice part*, or, at least, *follow its general outline*, the
presumption evidently being that the singer is likely to be in need of such
support, for we are told that the Organist must be careful "to be quick in
touching the key, in order to give the note to the singer".

The procedure when the voice part is *not* to be followed exactly is best
described in Penna's own words:

"If unable to accompany all the sung notes, let him [the Organist] take
only the consonances or, at least, the first and last notes of the down-beat
(*del battere*),[43] and the first and last notes of the up-beat (*del leuar di mano*),
disregarding the others, as in the example [44] . . . ."

[Ex.29]

Penna goes on to tell us that "in the *Ritornelli*, or the pauses designed to
rest the singer, the Organist should play something after his own fancy
(*alquanto di Capriccio*), imitating the *Arietta*, or other gay piece (*ò altro
allegro*), just sung".

The remainder of the chapter describes the treatment, in the "Recitative
style", of certain dissonances expressive of emotion (*affetti dissonanti*), of
which the following, we are told, are the most usual:

(1) the (major) Ninth, major Seventh, minor Sixth, and Fourth, or their
compounds, on a stationary Bass; [45]

(2) the major Sixth, major (i.e. augmented) Fourth, minor Third (Tenth),
and Octave [46] (following upon a minor Triad) on a Bass falling a Fourth, or
rising a Fifth;

[43] i.e. the first half of the *battuta*, equivalent, in the *tempo minore*, to a minim
(cf. note 19).

[44] Penna gives separate examples: (1) the voice part and the Bass, (2) the upper
part of the accompaniment and the Bass (leaving the chords to be supplied). Here
the two have been combined.

[45] i.e. the diminished Seventh on the leading note of a minor key, used as a passing
chord over the Tonic, as Bass.

[46] This progression (but without any mention of the inclusion of the *Octave*) was
given, as the "Cadence of the second order" in Penna's eleventh chapter, where the
reader is referred, for the method of execution (shakes, &c.), to the rules and examples

(3) a minor Seventh (with major Third) on a Bass falling a Fifth, or rising a Fourth;

(4) and (5) the progressions the treatment of which is described in Penna's twelfth and thirteenth chapters, to which he now refers us (cf. Exx. 25, 26, 27, and 28).

The characteristic feature in the prescribed treatment of (1) is the employment of what was sometimes known as *superjectio*,[47] as seen in Ex. 30.

Penna's directions, supposing the Bass to consist of a breve or a semibreve (*di una, ò mezza battuta*), or of repeated notes of the same pitch, are as follows; after enumerating the intervals of the discord, he proceeds: "play them all together with the right hand, either falling [from the preceding chord] or rising; and, before proceeding to the concord, touch the Tenth or Twelfth [the *superjectio*], whichever is most convenient."

[N.B.—It seemed best to give this example and the two following in score, exactly as in the original.]

In the following example, illustrating (2), we have a *superjectio* of a somewhat different type, rising by leap of a Fourth, instead of by step: [49]

in the fourth chapter (cf. *g.* 1). In the latter no mention is made of the *Third* (Tenth), but the inclusion or omission of the latter would never have struck Penna as making a vital difference to the character of the harmony in question, since, in accordance with what he terms a "universal rule", *every* discord may, when the harmony is full, include the "consonances of the written note", the Third, Fifth, and Octave (cf. note 41 *ad fin.*).

[47] This arises in passing from one harmony to another, and consists in briefly touching a note foreign to the first harmony and above (generally a degree above) the preceding note, and then falling to the next harmony, of which *it is itself an anticipation.* A glance at Penna's examples will make this clear.

[48] It seems probable that the figure 13 in Ex. 30 (*a*) is due to inadvertence, and that 6 was intended, as it would, otherwise, have to be *above* the present upper part, and the *superjectio* would lose much of its effect.

[49] This is, of course, due to the fact that the harmony note, ♯*f*, *rises* to the major Third of the following chord (to which the *superjectio* has to fall), whereas in Ex. 30 ((*a*) and (*b*)) the progression from the second to the third chord is *downwards.*

[50] The figure 10 in Ex. 31 (*a*) (above the upper stave) should almost certainly be 3

The point of the next example, which illustrates (3), seems to be this, that the Seventh, instead of being struck together with its Bass, is to follow it, the rhythmical effect of which procedure is comparable with that of the *superjectio* in the last two examples:

[Ex. 32]

The chapter concludes with instructions, which were quoted *in extenso* at the end of note 41, for the filling in of the harmony. These, as well as the figuring of Exx. 30 and 31, make it abundantly clear that what Penna says in his last chapter, about accompanying a single voice in three, or, at most, four, parts (cf. *o*, Rule 13), does *not* apply to the "Recitative style".

(*n*) Chapters 15–20 need not detain us. In Ch. 15, on the accompaniment of fugal compositions, we are merely told that, whether the first entry is in the upper part or in the Bass, the accompanist should play, first with one finger, then with two, and so on, the actual notes of the principal parts, as they enter one by one, till all have entered.[51]

The contents of Chapters 16–20, on transposition, are not relevant to the purpose of the present treatise.

(*o*) Penna's twentieth, and last, chapter is headed "Alcuni auertimenti da farsi, & altri da fuggirsi nel suonare l' Organo sopra la parte", and is well worth quoting *in extenso*, the rules for the accompaniment of individual singers, or of two, three, or four voices, on the one hand (Rules 10–15), and of large bodies of voices, on the other (Rule 16), and, again, of instrumental polyphony (Rule 17), being of special interest. The rules are as follows:

(cf. note 48). The figuring in Penna's examples is often very careless. For instance, in Ex. 31 (*b*) the 3 × 4 (below the middle stave) should obviously be 10 × 11, while the × 13 in the same example appears in the original as 12, and is also misplaced.

[51] The twenty-third (penultimate) chapter of Penna's Second Book contains instructions for the equipment (by the composer) of a completed composition with a Thorough-Bass. Those relating to a fugal entry are worth recording, in the present connexion, on account of the alternative treatment prescribed. After directing that each part, as it enters, should appear in the Thorough-Bass with its appropriate clef, as:

1 *Esempio*

he continues: "although one can (if one pleases) make a new Bass, and therewith accompany the parts until the entry of the Bass", as:

2 *Esempio*

"1. Be careful, as soon as you have the part from which to play, to understand its character, in order to be able to accompany it suitably.

"2. When the right hand ascends, let the fingers move one after the other, first the middle finger, next the ring-finger, and then the middle finger, and thus they are to proceed in turn, as long, that is to say, as the fingers are not playing together; but, in descending, they are to change: [first] the middle finger, then the index finger after the middle finger, &c.; but when the left hand ascends, the process is to be reversed: that is to say, first the middle finger, afterwards the index finger, &c., and, in descending, the middle finger, then the ring-finger, &c.[52]

"3. Neither the left hand nor the right hand must be low down, and the fingers high up, but they, both hands and fingers, must be outspread (*distese*) so as to make a pretty hand (*che formino bella mano*).[53]

"4. To play from a Bass (*sopra la parte*) one must, at least, know the consonances, namely, the Unison, Third, Fifth, Sixth, Octave, Tenth, Twelfth, Thirteenth, Fifteenth, and their compounds. So, too, the dissonances and their resolutions, namely, the Second, Fourth, false [i.e. diminished] Fifth, Seventh, Ninth, Eleventh, Fourteenth, and their compounds; among which the Second resolves on the Unison, Third, Fifth,[54] and Sixth; the Fourth on

[52] It will be noticed that in every case the *middle* finger is to begin. Earlier in the work (Third Book, Ch. 1, Rule 7) Penna mentioned an exception to this rule. When the number of notes, rising or falling by step, is *uneven*, as:

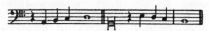

the ring-finger, or (when more convenient) the index finger, is to begin, after which the procedure will be as above described. It will, of course, be when the left hand descends, and the right hand ascends, that the index finger will naturally be used. The chief point to be noted is that the *middle* finger is associated with an *accented* note, and that, in this particular, Penna's practice coincides with that of the English Harpsichordists rather than that of his fellow countrymen or of the Germans (cf. Dolmetsch, *The Interpretation of the Music of the Seventeenth and Eighteenth Centuries*, Novello & Co., ch. vi, p. 365).

[53] The meaning of this obviously is that the hand is not to hang below the keyboard, thus cramping the fingers, but is to be in an easy position allowing full play (and stretch) to the fingers.

[54] The inclusion here of the Fifth among the resolutions of the Second is evidently due to inadvertence. The resolutions mentioned by Penna in his Second Book, which deals with Counterpoint (Ch. 6, Rule 1, "On the tied Second"), are the Unison, the Third, minor or major, and the Sixth, minor or major. He gives the following examples:

It will be observed that the Second in Penna's first example, though actually at the distance of a Second from the Bass, is really the equivalent of a Ninth, as is shown by its downward resolution, whereas in the subsequent examples the discord and its resolution are in the Bass, and the Seconds are genuine ones. Penna explains that the resolution of the discord in the last example requires to be followed by other notes, which he adds in the Bass only the Third, false Fifth, Sixth, Octave, and Tenth; [55] the false Fifth on the Third; the Seventh on the Third, false Fifth, perfect Fifth, Sixth, Octave, Twelfth, and Thirteenth; [56] and the Ninth on the Octave and on the Tenth; [57] the Eleventh on the Tenth, &c.; the Fourteenth on the Thirteenth, &c.; examples of all of which are in the Second Book, Sixth Chapter, and in this Third Book, Eighth Chapter; I refer the student to the one and to the other.

"5. One must further know that over every bass note (*Nota di fondo*) there are required the Third, Fifth, and Octave; and, if the Fifth is impossible, the Sixth must be taken, but never the Fifth and Sixth together, save when there is a tie (*se non in ligatura*),[58] or unless the composer has figured them together.

"6. On a [bass] note on which there is to be a Sixth,[59] the Sixth can be by itself, without the Octave, and it will be better so.

[55] Penna's so-called resolution of the (perfect) Fourth on the false Fifth, or Sixth, is again due to a resolution in the Bass, as:

No example is given of any sort of resolution of the Fourth on the Octave.

[56] In neither of the chapters to which Penna refers at the end of Rule 4, nor elsewhere, is any example given of a Seventh resolving either on the diminished Fifth, or on the Octave. In Ch. 8 of the Second Book, besides genuine resolutions on the Sixth (major and minor), Penna gives the following examples in which a suspended minor Seventh "resolves" (*si scoglie*) on the Fifth and on the Third. But it will be seen that it is not a resolution in the usual sense of the term:

A genuine resolution of a Dominant Seventh on the 3 of the Tonic chord may be seen in Ex. 12 *a*.

[57] Penna gives the following example of the resolution of the Ninth (Book II, Ch. 6, Rule 5):

It will be observed that the second example is identical except in key, and in the fact that the upper and lower parts are an Octave further apart, with the second example in note 54, and that Penna's 'Ninth' is here really a Second.

[58] i.e. when the 5 is prepared, as:

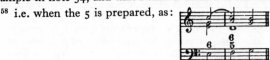

[59] i.e. primarily, on a leading note, either diatonic or accidentally sharpened (cf. *f*, Exx. 4, 5).

"7. It is at all times a very good thing to play *legato*, in order not to interfere with the vocal part (*che non si molesti la parte Cantante*).

"8. In resolving the discords, be ready to give the consonances, namely, the major or minor Third, and the major or minor Sixth, and do not come in with the one in place of the other [i.e. the minor Third or Sixth in place of the major, or vice versâ], and this applies to the other dissonances.

"9. All the numbers [i.e. figures] which are above the Octave must be taken with the right hand in accompanying concerted music (*nell' accompagnare in Concerto*).

"10. In playing with a Soprano or Contralto one must not play above the vocal part, or make 'divisions' (*diminuire*).

"11. With a Tenor, one may go above, and remain above, but not play in the Octave the notes which he is singing, nor make 'divisions'.

"12. With a Bass, one may indulge in some little movement, but if the Bass has passages, it is not good to move at the same time.

"13. In accompanying a single voice one must not sound more than three or (and that but rarely) four keys [at a time], and it is not good to put the Octave [of the Bass] in the upper part (*e non è bene vi ponga l' ottaua di sopra*).[60]

"14. With two voices, likewise, few shakes must be used, and the Octave [of the Bass] avoided.

"15. With three or four voices the harmony may be somewhat fuller (*si può empire un poco più*), but the Bass must rarely be doubled when it is a leading note, or is accidentally sharpened (*quando è su li mi ò ✕*).

"16. With eight voices [i.e. a double choir], with three choirs, and four choirs, &c., the harmony is to be full (*si empia*), and the duplicate intervals[61] and accidentally sharpened notes are to be doubled (*e radoppi pure le repliche, li ✕ ✕*), and this is desirable because it sounds well with such a variety of harmony.

"17. In accompanying instruments which are playing, it is better to avoid movement (*non è bene far mouimenti*),[62] in order that the listeners may be able to hear the *ensemble* (*il loro concerto*), the imitations, the mutual calls and answers (*le chiamate, le risposte fra loro*), &c.

"18. Play a great deal, seeking to practise yourself in rapidity and shakes with the right hand and left alike, for thus the hand is loosened and a practical acquaintance with the keyboard gained (*perchè così si rompe la mano, e si fa prattico della tastatura*).

---

[60] At a much later period we find, in certain text-books, the same warning, namely, that, in chords which include the Octave of the Bass, the position in which that Octave would appear in the upper part is, generally speaking, to be avoided. Ph. Em. Bach gives this rule in connexion with chords of the Sixth (*Versuch &c.*, Part II, 1762, Ch. 3, I, § 12), and Türk goes so far as to apply the same rule to the perfect Triad, saying that the position in question is best avoided as far as possible *except in closes* (*Kurze Anweisung &c.*, 1791, § 86, p. 109).

[61] By the 'duplicate intervals' (*repliche*) Penna here clearly means the intervals which, even in a less full accompaniment, might be supposed to be doubled, and which, under the conditions now described, may be even trebled, as the Third of the second chord in the following example, in which we also see the duplication of the accidentally sharpened leading note:

[62] i.e. 'divisions', &c. (cf. Rules 11 and 12).

"19. Be careful to spread the chords (*arpeggiare*), in order not to leave a void in the instrument (*per non lasciare vuoto l' Instrumento*).[63]

"20. Go frequently to musical gatherings and performances (*alle Accademie e Musiche*), noting well the procedure (*gli andamenti*) of whoever plays this instrument [i.e. the Organ], in order to put it into practice."

§ 21. *Matthew Locke.*

In 1673 there appeared the first extant English treatise upon the art of playing from a figured Bass.

The full title is as follows:

MELOTHESIA

OR

Certain General RULES for Playing

UPON A

CONTINUED-BASS

WITH

A choice Collection of Lessons for the *Harpsichord* and *Organ* of all Sorts: *Never before published.*

All carefully revised by M. LOCKE, Composer in Ordinary to His Majesty, and Organist of Her Majesties Chappel.

THE FIRST PART

LONDON, Printed for *J. Carr*, and to be sold at his shop in the Middle Temple Gate, 1673.

In the 'Advertisements to the Reader' which precede the Rules, Locke explains the notation of a figured Bass as follows:

'A Flat or Sharp set a little above or before a *Note*, belongs to the Third which is to be played upon that Note.

'A Figure set on the same manner, signifieth, that such a Degree or kind of Descant belongeth to the said *Note*.

'A Flat or Sharp set by any Figure over a *Note*, belongeth to the Descant signified by the Figure; which accordingly is to be Flat or Sharp.'

Then follow:

'General Rules for Playing on a Continued Bass.[1]

(1) "After having perfectly observed the *Tone* or *Key* you are to Play on, (which is ever known by the last *Note* of the *Bass*) with what *Notes* are

---

[63] This rule seems to refer to the Harpsichord rather than to the Organ. The intervals of silence which, on a quilled instrument, must ensue between chords of which all the notes are struck simultaneously are what Penna refers to as 'leaving a void'.

[1] In the British Museum (Add. 4910, f. 43) there is a manuscript copy of these rules, followed by the examples, with a superscription in faded ink: 'Rules for playing from a Basso Continuo By Mr. Matthew Locke Composer in Ordinary to the King given to mee Silas Domvil aіs Taylor.' Whether this manuscript is Locke's autograph or not it is difficult to determine. But, in any case, it looks as if the rules were in

properly Flat and Sharp therein, play Thirds, Fifts,[2] Eights or their Compounds on all *Notes* where the following Rules direct not otherwise or the
contrary be not Figured, beginning the account on the *Note* you Play on
and reckoning upward; and making the Third either *Major* or *Minor*,
according to the nature of the *Tone*, and Flats or Sharps set by your *Cliff*:
But (for prevention of glutting or offending the Ear) never ascend or descend
with two Fifts, or two Eights together between the *Treble* and *Bass*, nor Play
your Thirds, Fifts or Eights, one Flat and another Sharp at the same time.

(2) "On the *half-Note* below the *Tone* you play in, on the Third and Sixt
Major above the *Tone*, on B *sharp* (when E is not the *Tone*)[3] and on all
sharp Notes out of the *Tone*, Play a *Sixth Minor* except the rule of *Cadences*[4]
take place. *For Example*: If G be the *Tone*, F sharp, B, and E, are proper
Notes to Play Sixes on. If A be the *Tone*, then G sharp, C sharp, and F sharp,
are proper for Sixes, &c.

(3) "A *Cadence* is a Fall or Binding, wherein after the taking of a *Discord*
or *Discords*, there is a meeting or Closure of Concords, as is to be seen in the
two *last Notes* of all Strains of *Pavans* or any other grave *Musick*, Vocal or
Instrumental, the last of which two *Notes* generally riseth Four, or falleth
five *Notes* from the former; by which it is known (for the most part) to be

existence prior to the publication of the *Melothesia*. Of Domvil als Taylor the
Dictionary of National Biography says: "From his father Taylor inherited a fine taste
for music and was intimate with the Playfords, the elder Purcell, and Matthew Lock",
so that it may well be that Locke gave him a copy of the rules.

[2] 'Fift' is the older form, and etymologically more correct than 'Fifth'; Locke,
however, as we see, uses both forms indifferently. Similarly, in Rule 2, he writes
the correct form 'Sixt', and elsewhere 'Sixth'; but he always adheres to the older
form 'Eight' rather than 'Eighth'.

[3] This part of the Rule is a little obscure. B 'sharp' is, of course, B natural. In
view of the words 'when E is not the Tone', it must be remembered: (1) that Locke
did not take account of keys with more than four sharps, and (2) that the signature
commonly contained a sharp too few, a practice which, probably dating, in the first
instance, from the transposition of the Mixolydian Mode, survived till Handel's time,
as e.g. in the 'Harmonious Blacksmith', which is in E major with a signature of three
sharps. In A major, if there were only two sharps in the signature, B would therefore bear a *minor* Sixth unless the contrary were specified, or unless, in Locke's own
words, 'the rule of Cadences take place'.

[4] i.e. when the Bass rises a Fourth, or falls a Fifth, either *to* or *from* the note in
question. A seventeenth-century manuscript (Brit. Mus. Add. 4910, f. 61) from Silas
Domvil als Taylor's collection (cf. note 1) gives the following example to illustrate the
rule in question, which is there given in a slightly less complete form than by Locke,
as the 'Sixt Major above the Tone' is inadvertently not mentioned:

The exceptions due to the 'Rule of Cadences' are illustrated, in the case of the 'half-
Note below the Tone', at * (in bar 9); in the case of the 'Third and Sixt Major above
the Tone', at ♮ ♮ (in bars 5 and 10), and at † † (in bars 6 and 12–13), respectively.
The remaining cases at ‡ ‡ (in bar 8) in which the 'Third and Sixt Major above the
Tone' do not bear a minor Sixth (though, in the second of the two, a 'Neapolitan'
Sixth is possible) are not provided for in Locke's Rule.

a *Cadence.* Upon the first *Note* therefore of all such *Cadences,* Play either a
Fourth and Third with a Fifth against them, or a Third, Fourth, and Third,
with a Seventh, Sixth, and Fifth (or a Sixth and Fifth) against them, making
the Fourth as long as both the Thirds, and the Fifth as long as the Seventh
and Sixth. *See the Examples of the Third Rule.* Where you must observe
that the Thirds are *Thirds Major,* and so are to be Play'd on all Bindings,
and generally on all such *Notes* as the following *Notes* riseth four or falleth
five *Notes.*

(4) "Where a Seventh and Sixth are figur'd, Play the Sixth a *Sixth Major*;
and if the *Note* following descend half a *Note,* let the Third be a *Third
Major* against it; if a whole *Note,* a *Third Minor,* which is generally to be
observed in all passing Closes, and all long *Notes* so descending, though not
figur'd. *See the Examples of the Fourth Rule.*

(5) "Omit a Third when a Fourth is figur'd; a Fifth, when a Sixth is
figured; and a Sixth when a Seventh is figur'd.

(6) "If many *Notes* of the same length immediately ascend one after
another, the common *Descant* is a Fifth and Sixth upon every one, or most
of them: And if many descend in the like manner, the *Descant* is to be a Sixth
and Fifth,[5] or a Seventh and Sixth, on each of them. *See the Examples of
the Sixth Rule.* But which of these two last are to be used, cannot be set
down by any Rule, but must be left to your own Ear, as also the inclination
or change of the *Ayr,* or *Descant* from one key to another, which you must
be careful to listen after, and follow, applying the Sixes in every Introduction,
as if you were really in the *Key,* you are going to.[6]

(7) "When a *Bass* moves by Thirds, the common *Descant* is a Sixth on
every other Note. *See the Examples of the Seventh Rule.*[7]

[5] This progression, which is also given by Dr. Blow in his manuscript treatise
described in § 22, was disallowed at a later date. Marpurg (*Handbuch bey dem
Generalbasse und der Composition,* Part I, 2nd ed. 1762, Abschnitt II, p. 95) writes:
"Wenn bey vorangehender Sexte die Fortschreitung der beyden Stimmen stuffen-
weise geschicht, so kann solche nur mit aufsteigenden Noten, wie bey Fig. 4, nicht
aber bequem bey herabsteigenden Noten geschehen, weswegen die nachschlagenden
Quintengänge bey Fig. 5 als pure fehlerhafte Quintengänge betrachtet werden."

("When the progression of the two parts takes place by step, with the Sixth coming
first, it can only take place with rising notes, as in Fig. 4, but not comfortably with
falling notes, wherefore the series of trailing * Fifths in Fig. 5 is regarded simply as
a faulty progression of Fifths.")

* We seem to have no exact equivalent for the Germ. 'nachschlagend' ('eine
nachschlagende Septime', &c.) in the sense of struck after the main note, and so
'trailing' or 'lagging' behind it.

[6] This points, on the one hand, to the frequent occurrence of unfigured, or very
sparsely figured Basses, and, on the other, to the lack of differentiation between
major and minor Sixths by means of ♯ ♭ prefixed to the figure (cf. Heinrich Albert's
9th rule, § 18 *ad fin.*).

[7] It will be observed that the first bar of the second example, which Locke has
left unfigured, is not on all fours with the following bar, inasmuch as the first note
of the bar bears a Triad instead of a Sixth. In the manuscript copy of Locke's Rules

(8) "When a *Bass* hath many swift Notes running one after another, 'tis sufficient, either to set the Right hand true to the first Note of the Measure, and there rest till you come to the middle thereof, and then place it true to the first Note of that part, and so keep it till the next Measure; or else to Play Thirds and Tenths only, during such motions. *See the Examples of the Eighth Rule.* But for the *Theorbo* &c. it is sufficient to Play single Notes.

(9) "When the *Bass* is below C *fa ut* [Tenor C], it is better to make your account from the Octave above the *Bass* than otherwise; for the Playing of Thirds and Fifts so low will produce rather a confused than Harmonious sound.

(10) "For the prevention of successive Fifts and Eights in the Extream Parts (prohibited in the First Rule) the certainest way for the beginner is to move his Hands by contraries: That is, when one Hand ascends, let the other descend. *See the Examples of the Tenth Rule.*

'Conclusion.

"By these Directions the Ingenious Practical Student, who has a through [*sic*] knowledge of the *Scale of Musick*, and Hands fitly prepar'd for the Instrument he aims at, may in a short time attain to his desired end of accompanying either Voyces or Instruments; and may with much ease arrive at the first Rudiments of *Musick*. Wherein, that he may be fortunate, I have annexed (*see the Examples of the Conclusion*) an Example or two by way of Transition, or passing from one Key to another; which being truly understood and applyed, will (in my Opinion) acquaint him with *All that's Teachable*, as to matter of *Ayr*; the rest intirely depending on his own Ingenuity, Observation, and Study, whate'er our New Air-Mongers pretend. For to teach Number and Distance [i.e. time and intervals] only, which is all that hitherto has been produced, (and the last, God wot, so weak, that 'tis a shame to mention it) is a down-right Cheat, and may with as much reason be applyed to a Carryers Trotting-Horse, or a *Jocky's* Hand-Galloper, as to any that has been only so instructed; and indeed, in some sense with more: For these Laborious Animals *know*, when they come to their *Inn* or *Post*, and with Joy cry, *Clink in the Close* [8] (as a Learned Essayer [9] would

already alluded to (cf. note 1) only the Bass of this particular example is given, but the bar in question is figured ♪ , in exact agreement with the harmony of the printed version; there is therefore no question of a misprint.

[8] The origin and exact meaning of this expression is obscure. In the passage referred to in the *New English Dictionary* (s.v. 'clink') from W. Cartwright's *Royall Slave*, Act I, Sc. i, where the slaves sing:

    'Then drinke we a round in despight of our Foes,
    And make our hard Irons cry clinke in the Close'

the whole phrase seems to mean little more than 'ring'.

In Locke's use of the phrase there seems to be a distinct allusion to the musical sense of the word 'close'.

The horses, having hammered out a tune with their hoofs on the road, shake their harness and jingle their bits when they reach their journey's end.

[9] As Locke was a friend and admirer of Christopher Simpson, in whose *Division Violist* a eulogistic poem by him appears, it was natural to look for the passage referred to, either in the above-mentioned work, or in Simpson's *Compendium of Practical Musick*; but Simpson does not appear to have been the 'Learned Essayer' referred to.

once have had it for the *Viol*). But these Deluded Mortals, after all their Labour and Expence, remain as Compleatly Ignorant of what they've done, that when they come to hear any of their own Conceptions, they cunningly whisper their dear Pedagogue, *Master is this Mine?* After which, having received a gracious *affirmative Nod*, they patiently retire; but with what content, I believe 'tis not hard to guess; they being thereby assured, they were as wise the first day they began, as at that instant.

"But leaving them and their Way.

"If this Publication prove acceptable, (it being the first of its kind yet produc'd) 'twill be an encouragement for presenting a SECOND PART, wherein I intend to Collect something of every kind of *Musick*, both Vocal and Instrumental, now in use of the best Authors; and withall, a *brief Discourse* with Examples on the subject of *Musick in Parts, by Fuge and Canon.*"

'M. L.'

'The Examples[10] of Precepts in the Rules for Playing on a Continued Basse.'

The Examples in the 3ᵈ Rule

* In the original, by an obvious misprint, the first note in the upper part of the second bar of the second example in the third rule is *d*.

Examples in the 4ᵗʰ Rule

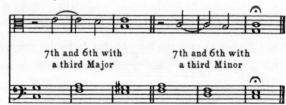

Examples in yᵉ 6ᵗʰ Rule

[10] The examples are on a six-line stave, both clefs being, in every case, on the third line from the top of the stave.

Examples in yᵉ 7th Rule

Examples in yᵉ 8th Rule   Examples in yᵉ 10th Rule

Examples of Transition Mention'd in yᵉ Conclusion

N.B.—Locke places ✕ and ♭ either before, or after, or above, or below the figures which they qualify. It will be observed that, in the cases where the accidental is *beside* the figure, it is placed *before* the first, and *after* the last note of a group, as ✕ 3 4 3 ♭, thus avoiding ambiguity.

Thus ends Locke's admirable little treatise, which gives his readers all the information that could possibly be contained in so small a space. The examples of 'Transition', i.e. modulation, well illustrate the economy of accidentals in the figuring of the period.

Two points will be noticed: (1) When the minor Seventh in a cadence is prepared by the accidentally flattened Third of the previous chord (as on the breve C at the beginning of the fourth bar of the first example, and on the (sixth) breve F in the second example), the 7 itself is *never accompanied by* ♭, as it would, quite unnecessarily, be at a later period. (2) In the cadences, the 4 (in the $\frac{6}{4}$) is always assumed to be perfect. At a later period the sixth and seventh breves (F and ♭ B) in the second example would have been figured $\flat7\,\flat\frac{6}{3}\,\frac{6}{4}$, &c.

If we set out the examples, they will be found instructive in other ways as well.

At * * * (in bars 3, 4, 7) are seen instances of the way in which, in playing from a figured Bass, a higher position was gained for the right hand when the hands got too close together. An extra part (which, of course, had to be a consonance) was taken in at the top; the lowest part being dropped directly afterwards, as indicated above by the minim rests.[11]

[11] The fact that, in the above instances, the part to be dropped happens to coincide in the unison with another part (or parts) is purely accidental and does not affect the principle, which can be better illustrated by taking the last bass note in the lower Octave and thus giving the Tenor room to go down to *d* (though it is below the usual compass of the right hand).

It is important to bear in mind, in this connexion, that the entry of a fresh part does not produce consecutives (cf. Marpurg, *Handbuch &c.*, 1755, p. 65, *Tab.* viii, *Fig.* 17; 2nd ed. 1762, p. 97, *Tab.* vi, *Fig.* 17); the change of position could therefore be effected on the second beat of the bar by taking ♯*f* * as a new part:

To gain a lower position, the process could, presumably, be reversed. The limited compass of the accompaniment (cf. Ch. iii, 'General character', &c., § 5A), on the one hand, and, on the other, the rule that the hands should, in general, be kept as close together as possible, oblige the player not infrequently to avail himself of this device when the presence of a dissonance makes the repetition of the whole chord, in a higher or lower position, as the case may be, impossible.

In the above setting-out of Locke's example some progressions have purposely been introduced which would not pass muster in a modern harmony exercise :

(1) The progression at † in bar 4, with its rising Seventh instead of

, is never found in the stricter treatises of the eighteenth

century, such as Marpurg's *Handbuch bey dem Generalbasse &c.*, Pt. 1, 1755, or Ph. Em. Bach's *Versuch &c.*, Pt. 2, 1762, but similar ones occur regularly in the older treatises; [12] in fact, the rising of the Seventh in a full close, when the chord was in that particular position $\left(\begin{smallmatrix}3\\7\\5\end{smallmatrix}\right)$, seems to have been as fully recognized a licence as the falling of the leading-note to the 5 of the Tonic

[12] e.g. in Dr. Blow's manuscript treatise, presently to be described, where we find:

(cf. § 22, Ex. 12), in Michel de Saint-Lambert's *Nouveau traité de l'accompagnement*, where the progression occurs repeatedly (cf. § 23, Ex. 8), and, at a later period, in Mattheson's *Kleine General-Bass-Schule*, 1735, &c. That Locke himself used the progression is shown by the final cadence of one of the Organ pieces of his composition given at the end of the *Melothesia* (p. 78):

In the following example from another of Locke's Organ pieces (*Melothesia*, p. 80) we have a clear case of transference of the resolution (to the Bass *), while the Seventh (in the top part) rises † :

and this must be the explanation of the rising Seventh in the two preceding examples, since the assumption that there is a crossing of the parts (Alto and Tenor) would involve consecutive Fifths between Tenor and Bass.

chord, in another position:  At a later period, however, in

cases like the above, a common device, which combined strictness of progression with fullness of harmony, was the temporary adoption of a fifth part, which vanished when its purpose was served, as:

(2) The false relation at ‡ in bar 4. Similar instances occur in Johann Staden's treatise, already described (cf. § 16, Ex. 3 (*b*)). Others may be found, at a later date, in Mattheson's *Kleine General-Bass-Schule*, 1735.

(3) The progression at ‡ in bar 7, whereby the Tenor part proceeds to d,[13] the lower Octave of the resolution of the suspended Seventh. This progression, though not approved to-day, was freely used by Ph. Em. Bach, the most fastidious of all the eighteenth-century writers on Figured Bass (cf. Ch. xi, 'Sevenths', IV, § 6, Ex. 2 (*a*), (*b*)).

[13] The right hand was, generally speaking, not supposed to go below g or f, but in an example like the above such restrictions may be disregarded. Locke himself evidently regarded e (or ♭e) as the downward limit, as is to be inferred from Rule 9.

In Locke's second example of 'Transition', set out above, a point deserving to be noted is the $\sharp 6$ (at the end of the chord-groups on the 8th and 9th breves), which, by briefly anticipating the 5 of the following chord, was regarded as sufficient to veil the consecutives.   The $\frac{7}{3}\frac{6}{4}$ on the 1st, 3rd, 5th, 7th, and 9th breves has been treated as Locke himself would assuredly have treated it (cf. note 12).

§ 22. *Dr. John Blow.*

In the British Museum there is a small treatise (Add. 34072, ff. 1–5), containing directions for playing from a 'Through'-Bass, by no less a person than Dr. John Blow, Henry Purcell's predecessor, and also successor, as Organist of Westminster Abbey.   It would seem, from a comparison with assured autographs, to be in the handwriting of its author—and in the catalogue it is described as 'autograph'—but it is difficult to determine with certainty.

It is also impossible to say whether it was written before or after the publication of Locke's *Melothesia*, of which an account has just been given.

Many of the examples are practically identical with what we have already encountered in the *Melothesia* and in Ebner's rules (cf. § 19), while others, again, are thoroughly characteristic of Blow himself, whose originality so offended Dr. Burney that he made a collection of excerpts entitled 'The Beastialities of Dr. Blow' (Brit. Mus. Add. 11586, ff. 46–8, and Add. 11587, ff. 96, 147, 167, 213).   In any case, the interest attaching to its author is sufficient to warrant the reproduction *in extenso* of Blow's manuscript.

To avoid explanatory notes, certain quite obvious clerical errors have been corrected, and some punctuation has been added, but Blow's spelling (and occasional grammatical eccentricities) remain unaltered.

In the original the examples are given on a six-line stave, with a G clef on the second line from the bottom of the upper stave, and the F clef on the second line from the top of the lower one:

'Rules for playing of a Through Bass upon Organ & Harpsicon.

[1] 'Music consists in Concords & Discords.   The concords that are is [*sic*] a 3rd, 5th, 6th, & 8th.   Perfect cords [i.e. concords] is a 5th & 8th.   Imperfect is a 3rd & 6th.   Discords are the 2nd, 4th, 7th, & 9th.   The 9th is the same as the 2nd, only it is other ways accompanied.

[2] 'To all Counterpoint notes being a Samibreif, Minom, or Chrochet (unless a 6th) you must play, with your Right hand, an 8th, 5th, & 3rd, as shall happen most convenient to your hand.   Not playing two 8ths or 5ths ascending, or descending together.   It is a general rule, when your Bass ascends, to avoid playing 5ths & 8ths in Counterpoint, [that] your treble must descend towards your Bass.

'But you may play as many 3ds or Sixes, ascending or descending together, as you please, they being imperfect Cords.

'As for example:

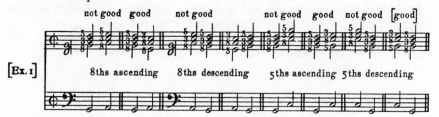

[Ex. 1]

[3] 'Scale of Comon Cords is a[s follows:] $\begin{smallmatrix} 8 & 3 & 5 \\ 5 & 8 & 3 \\ 3 & 5 & 8 \end{smallmatrix}$.

'The several ways of playing Comon cords to one note:

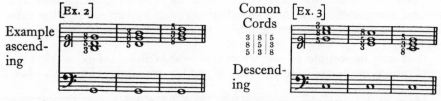

Example
ascend-
ing

Comon
Cords $\begin{smallmatrix} 3 & 8 & 5 \\ 8 & 5 & 3 \\ 5 & 3 & 8 \end{smallmatrix}$

Descend-
ing

[4] 'Whenever you find your Bass figured with a 6 you must accompany
it with a 3rd:

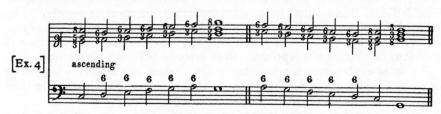

[Ex. 4]   ascending

[5] 'Example of Comon Corde ascending, the Bass moving:

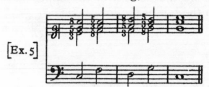

[Ex. 5]

'Example of Comon Corde descending, the Bass moving:

[Ex. 6]

[6] 'When you see a flat mark'd thus ♭, or a sharp thus ♯, above or under
a note, you must play a ♭ or ♯ third to the Bass.

'When a ♯ or a ♭ is mark'd by any figure, that signifies you must play the
Figure ♯ or ♭.

[7] 'Discords must be prepared by Concords, & resolv'd into Concords:

'Example :   'Example of 7th & 6th :

[Ex. 7]   [Ex. 8]

'Example of 7th & 6th, the Bass descending:

[Ex. 9]

'Example of $\frac{9}{7}$ & $\frac{8}{6}$, the Bass ascending; the 9th & 7th, the 4th & 9th resolving into the 8th & 6th, 3rd & 8th: [1]

[Ex. 10]

[8] 'Example of 5th & 6th ascending gradually:

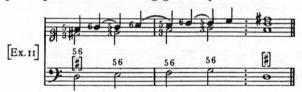

[Ex. 11]

[9] 'Note that in a Cadence y'e 4th always descends half a note into the sharp 3rd, & the 8th descends into the flat 7th.'

'Example of y'e Cadence taken different ways, according to the scale of figgures: [2]

[Ex. 12]

---

[1] Blow apparently forgot to give an example of $\frac{9}{4}$ resolving on $\frac{8}{3}$. The omission of a fourth part in the first bar of the example (*g* on the first minim, *e* on the second) is probably accidental and due to the fact that Blow was chiefly concerned with the suspended discords and their resolution.

[2] This example shows that, in the case of the figuring $\frac{5}{4}\frac{7}{3}$, the 7 was ordinarily struck after, and not with, the 3 (cf. § 20, Ex. 32).

[10]   'How to know the close or Cadence in a ♭ key.

'The principal key is where yᵉ Song or Lesson begins.

'The 5th above yᵉ key, or 4th below yᵉ key, & the 3rd above the key, or 6th below the key: the first in gamut, yᵉ 2nd in *D sol re*, yᵉ 3d in B mo[lle]: [3]

'Example in the ♭ 3rd:

[Ex.13]

'But if yᵉ key be sharp 3rd, there are 4 proper closes: yᵉ key, the 4th [above the key, the 5th above the key, the 3rd above the key]:

'The 5th & 6th [i.e. ⁶₅ as in the 1st and 4th Exx.]

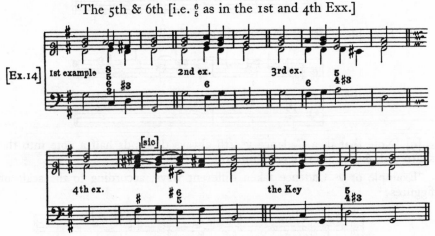

[Ex.14]

[11] 'If your Bass move by Quavers or Semiquavers, you need not play wᵗʰ your right hand more than once to four quavers, or once to two quavers, being the same as if your Bass had been Minums or Crochets:

---

[3] This somewhat obscurely worded sentence indicates that in a flat (i.e. minor) key, closes, besides that on the Tonic (which in the example begins and ends the series), may be made on the Dominant (minor) and the Mediant—in G minor, therefore, on G, D, ♭B. This defines what was known in the earlier German treatises (e.g. Heinichen's *General-Bass &c.*, 1728) as the *ambitus modi*, in its widest sense, namely, the harmony natural to the key itself and its 'attendants'.

[Ex.15]

[12] 'To all discords figur'd over the Bass is required, to accompany them, a 3d & 5th [4] (unless it be to a 2d), and to y^t must I have a 4th & 6th, according as it is figur'd ♯4 or ♭4.[5]

[4] Blow was evidently thinking mainly of a Seventh $\frac{7}{5}$ and Ninth $\frac{9}{5}$; the rule does
not apply, save in exceptional cases, to $\frac{9}{7}$, or, in any case, to $\frac{9}{4}$.

[5] See Ex. 29.

[13] 'Throughbass 5th & 6th ascending: [6]

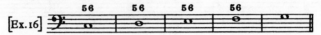

'6th & 5th descending: [7]

'$^6_4\,^5_3$ descending: [8]

[14] 'One may observe generally y^t when 2 notes ascend or decend, one of y^m requires a 6th:

[15] 'A rule of playing in 4 or 5 parts, 3 with y^e right hand & 2 wth y^e left, y^e Bass ascending by graduall notes, 5th & 6th; the treble by 7 & 8 ascending,'[9] $^{7\,8}_{6\,5}$:

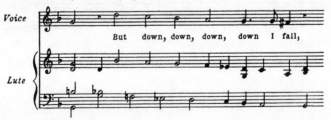

---

[6] An example had already been given (cf. Ex. 11).

[7] cf. § 21, note 5.

[8] This progression, which is subject to the same theoretical objections as the preceding one, is used with wonderful effect by Dowland, in 'Sorrow, stay' (bar 22) in the *Second Book of Airs*, 1600 (see *The English School of Lutenist Song-writers*, ed. Dr. E. H. Fellowes, Stainer & Bell, London, 1920):

[9] When Blow speaks of the treble ascending 7 8, it is clear that he is thinking only of the *apparent* progression, as heard on a keyed instrument, the *real* progression 7 6 (indicated by the way in which the stems of the notes are turned in the second bar)

[Example of $\begin{smallmatrix}7\\5\end{smallmatrix}\begin{smallmatrix}6\\4\end{smallmatrix}\begin{smallmatrix}\\3\end{smallmatrix}$ descending]

being obscured by the crossing and recrossing (in bars 3, 4) of two of the parts. If we transfer the lowest of the right-hand parts to the bottom stave (noting that the fifth part enters at *), the progression will become clear:

The example is a particularly instructive one, as illustrating the contemporary attitude towards consecutive Octaves, whether real or apparent. They were regarded as sufficiently veiled by a retardation. Henry Purcell did not hesitate to prepare a Ninth by the Octave (a progression strictly forbidden by Marpurg and Ph. Em. Bach) as is shown by the following example (*Sonatas in Four Parts*, 1697, Son. III, Canzona, antepenult. bar) in which the 9, though not figured, is present in the 2nd Violin part:

Even at a considerably later period we find such an example as the following (Mattheson, *Kleine General-Bass-Schule*, 1735, 'Höhere Classe', 5te Aufgabe ['Higher Class', Lesson 5], § 7, bar 10 sq.), in which the retardation is in the Bass. The chords are here filled in in accordance with Mattheson's directions, each example being given twice, (1) with the ordinary figuring (as here given below the stave), (2) with all three upper parts figured in the order in which they are to be taken (as here above the stave):

It is therefore clear that, save for the apparently rising Sevenths, Blow's progression did not need to be excused by the crossing of the parts. At a later period it would in no case have passed muster, for it is emphatically stated by Heinichen (*General-Bass &c.*, 1728, Pt. 1, Ch. 2, § 32, note *e*, p. 132) that a crossing of parts which the ear cannot apprehend is no justification of a progression which, in its effect, is faulty —a view from which no later writer was found to dissent.

[16] 'The half Cadence divided by 4 Crochets, ♭ 6, 5th, [4th], & 3 :[10]

[Ex. 22]

'The comon Cadence divided by 4 crochets, 3, 9th, & 8th, & 7th:

[Ex. 23]

'The comon Cadence divided by moving from the ♭ 9th & 3d to yᵉ 3d :[11]

[Ex. 24]

[17] 'There are severall ways of playing the half Cadence in ♭ 3d [i.e. minor] keys, (that is) the plain note falling a 4th or rising a 5th, [either by] the Treble moving by 5th & 6th,[12] or else the Bass moving gradually 4 & 3d down:[13]

---

[10] This beautiful form of cadence—which Dr. Burney would doubtless have condemned along with the two following Exx. (see p. 163)—was commonly used by Byrd and other sixteenth-century composers.

[11] i.e. from $\frac{9}{6}$ on ♭ *b* to $\frac{5}{3}$ on *g*. The expression '♭ 9th' (for '9 on a flattened Bass') is simply a slip on Blow's part. His figuring would be quite incomprehensible if

the upper parts were not given. The figuring required is

The $\frac{5}{4}$ *under* the Bass is simply a reminder that the whole progression is a sophisticated form of $\frac{5}{4 \, 3}$ on *g*.

[12] This apparently refers to the 5 6 in the '3d Example divided' (Ex. 27).

[13] This somewhat enigmatic description probably refers to the second versions of the 1st and 3rd Examples (Exx. 25 and 27), in both of which the Bass moves three degrees down, and also to the second version, 'divided', of the 2nd Example (Ex. 26). In the latter the first bar is merely introductory to the Tonic-Dominant half-close, which alone is in question, and in which the Bass 'moves gradually a 3d down' from *f* to *d*.

It will be noticed that in the '3d Example divided' (Ex. 27) the initial chord is the relative major of the '3d minor key' illustrated (cf. Ex. 13), taken in its first inversion.

N.B.—The last example is added (as in Exx. 13, 14) to establish the key of the whole series, which, in Blow's manuscript, is *continuous*; hence the ♭ at the beginning of the 3rd Example (Ex. 27) in contradiction of ♯ *c* at the end of the preceding one.

[18] 'A 4th & 2nd accompanied with a 6th must be prepared by concords,[14] & must be resolv'd into a 6th:

N.B.—The ⌄ in the last bar of Ex. (*a*) evidently represents a temporary fifth part, added in order that the chord may include its Fifth. The small notes without stems supply the other parts omitted in Blow's manuscript.

[14] Blow's rule is, as usual, less clear than his examples, since it is, of course, the *Bass* of a $\frac{6}{4}$ chord which is discordant and requires preparation.

[19] 'Observe an exstream ♭ 7th [i.e. diminished 7th] is no more than a ♯ Sixth. If the ♭ 5th and exstream ♭ 7th happen before a Cadence your 3d before is most comonly ♯, unless figur'd to the contrary:

[Ex.30]

N.B.—The small notes without stems represent parts omitted.

[20] 'A scale of flat 3ds & sharp 3ds belonging to every key as follows:

[Ex.31]

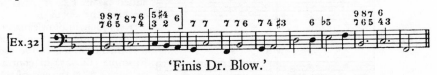

'Observe in plaing yᵉ Cords to this Scale you beging your Treble from the Octave, ascending gradually 8th, 3d & 5th.'[15]

[The following, final example is added without comment.]

[Ex.32]

'Finis Dr. Blow.'

Thus ends Dr. Blow's little treatise, doubtless compiled for teaching purposes, and, with all its many faults of arrangement and expression, it must be admitted that it gives more information than any of its predecessors and, above all, that it casts considerable light on Dr. Blow's own method of treating a figured Bass.

§ 23. *Michel de Saint-Lambert.*

a. In 1680 Michel de Saint-Lambert, about whom very little besides is known, published a treatise entitled *Traité de l'accompagnement du clavecin, de l'orgue et de quelques autres instruments* (Paris, Ballard), but, unless it is to

[15] as follows :

It will be observed that the continuity of the 'scale' is thrice broken : between [♭] B ♯3d and [♭] E ♯3rd, between F ♭3d and D ♯3d, and, immediately after, between B ♭3d and E ♯3d.

be found in private hands, this work does not appear to have survived except in a manuscript Italian translation of Chapters V–IX preserved in the library of the *Liceo Musicale* at Bologna.

We can, however, form an idea of its contents from the same author's (extremely rare) *Nouveau traité de l'accompagnement*, &c. (Paris, 1707, Ballard, reprinted at Amsterdam by Estienne Roger), of which an Italian translation also exists at Bologna, as well as Roger's reprint of the original, which latter is also in the British Museum.

The *Nouveau traité* is evidently not a distinct work, but merely a revised and enlarged second edition of the earlier work.

The titles of the five extant chapters of the latter, in the above-mentioned Italian translation, correspond exactly (as Professor Francesco Vatielli, the courteous librarian of the *Liceo Musicale*, has kindly informed the writer) with those of the same chapters of the *Nouveau traité*.

Regarding Roger's reprint of this latter work the catalogue of the library of the *Liceo Musicale* has the following note appended: "La prima edizione è di Parigi (Ballard 1680) in 4° oblongo. Nel 1707 lo stesso tipographo ne fece una ristampa in 4° obl. Questa sarà senza dubbio una terza edizione che non vedendosi citata del Fétis conviene credere che gli fosse ignota." ('The first edition is of Paris (Ballard, 1680). In 1707 the same printer [Ballard] reprinted it. This [i.e. Roger's reprint] is doubtless a third edition, and, not being mentioned by Fétis, we must conclude that it was unknown to him.')

There seems, therefore, to be ample justification for including so interesting a work as the *Nouveau traité* in a chapter dealing with the period 1600–1700.

The work contains 134 pages, and is divided into the following chapters:

Chapitre I. *Définition de l'accompagnement* (p. 1).
    II. *Des Intervalles* (p. 5).
   III. *De la pratique de l'Accompagnement* (p. 19).
   IV. *Des Tons, des Modes, & de la Transposition* (p. 51).
    V. *Du mouvement des Mains* (p. 65).
   VI. *Du choix des Accords* (p. 71).
  VII. *Règles pour deviner les Chiffres, quand les Basses-Continuës ne sont pas Chiffrées* (p. 90).
 VIII. *Des Licences qu'on peut prendre en accompagnant* (p. 118).
  IX. *Du goût de l'Accompagnement* (p. 128).

This is far more comprehensive than any of the works already noticed. The information is given clearly and concisely, and the arrangement of the work is admirable. Indeed, it may be said to be the first attempt that we have met with so far, to give a complete and systematic account of the treatment of a Thorough-Bass. Sabbatini's work (cf. § 17) was, so far as we know, never completed, and Locke's *Melothesia* (cf. § 21), admirable as it is for its compass, does no more than set the feet of the beginner upon the path which he has to travel.

Saint-Lambert's treatise was evidently well known among musicians of other countries than his own, as we can gather from the existence of the Italian translations at Bologna, and also from the fact that Heinichen twice alludes to it.[1] He refers with satisfaction to the fact that authors of three

---

[1] *General-Bass &c.*, 1728, p. 93 note, and p. 133 note.

different nationalities, namely, Saint-Lambert, Francesco Gasparini,[2] and himself, have compiled rules for the treatment of an unfigured Bass, and he also quotes with approval Saint-Lambert's dictum: *Comme la Musique n'est faite que pour l'oreille, une faute qui ne l'offense point n'est une faute* (cf. *i.* 5).

It will be sufficient to note points of especial interest as they occur in successive chapters.

b. (Ch. I). In his first chapter Saint-Lambert defines accompaniment as follows: "Accompaniment is the art of playing the Thorough-Bass on the harpsichord, or any other instrument. It is called 'Accompaniment' because, in playing the Bass, one has to unite other parts with it to form chords and harmony. These parts are added in accordance with certain principles and certain rules, the explanation of which will form the material of this treatise on Accompaniment."

The remainder of the chapter is occupied with purely elementary information, upon which it is unnecessary to enter here.

c. (Ch. II). The second chapter deals in great detail with the various musical intervals.

The compound intervals ('double', 'triple', or 'quadruple', according to the number of Octaves added) are to be regarded, we are told, as exactly on a par, so far as the accompaniment is concerned, with the absolute intervals, save only in the case of the Ninth, which, as a true Ninth, is liable to quite a different accompaniment from that which it receives as the compound equivalent of a Second.[3]

d. (Ch. III).

1. The third chapter deals mainly with the interpretation of the figures, and, after a short introduction including a list of the figures used, is divided into six sections, as follows:

    I. Rules for the accompaniment of notes figured with a single figure only.

    II. Rules for the accompaniment of notes figured with two figures.

    III. Concerning notes figured with a triple figure.

    IV. Concerning notes which bear several figures, the one beside the other.

    V. The reduction of figured chords to common chords.

    VI. Concerning the cadence.

---

[2] *L'Armonico pratico al cimbalo, Di Francesco Gasparini Lucchese. In Venetia* MDCCVIII *appresso Antonio Bortoli.*

[3] Saint-Lambert does not mention the fact, which is sometimes overlooked, that, just as the actual interval of a Ninth may be, in reality, a compound Second, so also the actual interval of a Second may, so far as its treatment is concerned, be the equivalent of a Ninth. As Ph. Em. Bach puts it (*Versuch &c.*, Part 2, 1762, Ch. 17, II, § 1): "The Ninth is and remains a Ninth, even though it be taken next the Bass note." The following example (cf. ibid., Ch. 17, I, § 8) will illustrate this:

2. In the introduction the rule is given that the Bass should be played with the left hand and the chords with the right. No allusion is anywhere made to any other form of accompaniment.

The principal interest attaching to Saint-Lambert's list of figures, including ♭ ✕ ♮ *over* the bass note (the *signa* of the German treatises), lies in the fact that here, for the first time, we find the use of ♮ prescribed, to contradict, not only a flat other than B flat (cf. § 17, pp. 121, 122), but a sharp as well: "Le ♮ marque la tierce mineure quand on joue en grand B quarré, & la tierce majeure quand on joue en B mol; ou pour mieux dire, il rend la tierce naturelle, le ♮ servant à ôter le ✕ s'il y en a, & à ôter le B mol s'il s'y en trouve accidentellement, ou après le Clef."

It would be interesting to know whether this passage was included in the original *Traité* of 1680.

The only other details to be noticed are the following:

(*α*) ♭ and ✕ above the Bass (and presumably ♮ also) may, or may not, be accompanied by the figure 3;

(*β*) The accidental qualifying a figure is placed after, as well as before it: thus 4✕ or ✕4 denotes the Tritone; and

(*γ*) ⚏ (the predecessor of the ♯ which later became almost universal) is also used for the same purpose.

3. In Section I (pp. 22–34), dealing with the accompaniment of notes with a single figure, as also in the subsequent ones, the only points that need here be noticed are the cases in which Saint-Lambert's usage diverges, on the one hand, from what we have encountered in earlier treatises, and, on the other, from that which became established later.

His use of a single figure differed from the later practice in the following points:

(*α*) At a later period, 2 was always accepted as the equivalent of $\frac{6}{2}$, whereas Saint-Lambert never appears to use it so, but only as the equivalent of:

(1) $\frac{5}{2}$, as:

(2) $\frac{5}{4}{}_{2}$, as:

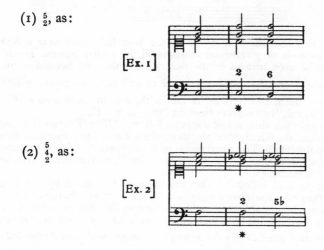

(*β*) According to the stricter usage of a later period ♯4 (♯⚏ ♮ 4) was used only as the equivalent of $\sharp\frac{6}{4}{}_{2}$.

Saint-Lambert uses 4✕, not only in this sense,[4] but also as the equivalent of:

(1) ♯4 6 (6 4 ♮4 6) = 8 6 ♯4, as:[5]

[Ex. 3]

N.B.—The last chord in each bar illustrates a remarkable rule given by Saint-Lambert in his seventh chapter (cf. *h.* 3).

and (2) ✕4 6 3, as:[6]

[Ex. 4]

(γ) In every other treatise known to the present writer 3 is regarded as the *normal* accompaniment of a suspended 7 (resolving on 6 over the same Bass), a fourth part being obtained by doubling either the 3 or the Bass, though the 5 *may* also be included (cf. Ch. xi, 'Sevenths', iv, § 2).   Saint-

---

[4] He gives the rule that the Tritone should be accompanied by the Second and Sixth when the Bass falls a tone or a semitone, as:

but he omits to mention that the note to which the Bass falls must bear a Sixth, neither does he figure it—a very common omission in the earlier Basses. He adds that the Octave may be used instead of the Second, but that the Second is more usual.   The progression 8 6 4 on a Bass falling a degree to a Sixth is not given by either Heinichen or Ph. Em. Bach, but it is to be met with, e.g. in Geminiani's *Art of Accompaniment* (cf. Ch. xxi, 'Incomplete figuring', iv, § 4, Ex. 8).

[5] Saint-Lambert's rule for this use of 4✕ is as follows: "The Tritone is accompanied by the Octave and the Sixth when the Bass falls a Fourth to a common chord upon the first beat of the bar."   The progression of a diminished, rising to a perfect Fifth, as at the beginning of Ex. 3, was freely used in Saint-Lambert's time and recurs constantly in his examples.

[6] The rule here given is as follows: "The Tritone is accompanied by the Third and Sixth when the Bass falls a semitone to a major Triad."   It will therefore be seen that the only instances where ambiguity could arise are in the case of major Triads which do *not* require to be indicated by ✕ above the Bass. Thus, for example, owing to the omission to figure the 6 after 4✕ = 6 4 2 (cf. note 4), the accompaniment demanded by

Lambert, on the other hand, regards the 5 as a *normal* constituent of the chord, and its omission as excusable only by necessity. His rule is as follows:

"The Seventh, whether major or minor, is accompanied by the Third and the Fifth:

"Or one can accompany it with the Third and the Octave:

"The Seventh is less well accompanied by the Third and Octave than by the Third and Fifth. It is a kind of licence to include the Octave instead of the Fifth: one must never do so except when one is forced to. We shall mention in the chapter on the choice of chords what the necessity is that forces one [to include it]." [9]

[7] Compare Ph. Em. Bach's method of accompanying a 7 6 sequence on a rising Bass (Ch. xi, 'Sevenths', IV, § 7, Ex. 1). It is remarkable that Saint-Lambert gives no example of the infinitely commoner progression 7 6 on a falling Bass.

[8] It will be noticed that the essential Seventh on *g* (in the second bar) has an ornamental resolution, so that Saint-Lambert manages to bring in the 5 after all.

[9] The necessity alluded to is that of avoiding (1) consecutive Fifths with the Bass, when the Seventh follows a common chord on a Bass a degree below that of the Seventh itself (as in Exx. 6 and 7), and (2) the bad progression of an augmented Second in one of the parts. Saint-Lambert gives the following examples (*Nouveau traité*, Ch. VI, Rule 16, pp. 79 and 83):

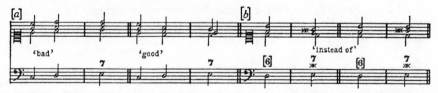

He explains, however, that, in the first case (Ex. [*a*]), the 5 may still be included by the device of crossing the parts: "One could, nevertheless, here accompany the Seventh with the Third and Fifth by allowing all the parts of the third chord to

fall, as follows · 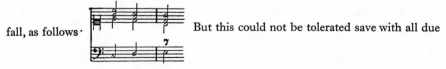 But this could not be tolerated save with all due

strictness (*à toute rigueur*); for regularity of composition demands that the note which

"The Seventh is accompanied by the doubled Third when the preceding note is a semitone or a tone lower than that which bears the Seventh, having as accompaniment a major common chord, that is to say, a common chord in which the Third is major:

"This manner of accompanying the Seventh is not practicable except after a major chord in which the Third was the highest of the three parts, as in the example above."

(δ) Saint-Lambert gives the following remarkable rule concerning the accompaniment of the figure 9:

"The Ninth, when it is major, is accompanied by the Third and Fifth; and, when it is minor, by the Third and Seventh:

"The figure does not indicate whether the Ninth is major or minor; the accompanist must judge for himself."

This rule is evidently meant as a general direction for the interpretation of the sparsely figured Basses common at the time—it will be noticed that in the above example (as also in Ex. 6) Saint-Lambert does not trouble to figure the resolutions of the discords resolving over the same Bass, or the cadence—and is not meant to suggest that a major Ninth *cannot* be accompanied by a Seventh, or that a minor Ninth *must necessarily* be so. In the section dealing with double figures an example of $\frac{9\,8}{7\,6}$ is given which includes major Ninths (cf. Ex. 13). Moreover, a Seventh, as a discord requiring pre-

forms the Seventh against the Bass should not do so, except it keep to the same part which it occupied in the previous chord, which would not be the case if one allowed all the parts to fall, except on the supposition that, while the lowest note remained in the same part, the middle part jumped over it so as to get below it. This is what is termed crossing the parts, and it is a licence really permitted, but one of which only a sparing use should be made."

[10] Observe the crossing of the parts in the penultimate bar of Ex. 7:
(cf. note 9).

[11] The slur over the two crotchets *e f* in the Bass denotes, as Saint-Lambert explains in connexion with another example, the retention of the harmony belonging to the first one, and may be regarded as the predecessor of the dash which was afterwards used for the same purpose.

paration, obviously cannot be associated with a Ninth, either major or minor, unless it was present in the previous chord. In such a case, therefore, as:

Saint-Lambert's rule could, obviously, never have been applied.

(ε) The rising Seventh in a full close (when taken in the position shown at the end of Ex. 8) has already been noticed (cf. § 21, note 12).

4. In Section II (pp. 34–41), dealing with double figures (one above the other), the points to be noticed are:

(α) Saint-Lambert's ambiguous use of the figures $\frac{4}{2}$, which, according to later and stricter usage, represent $\frac{6}{4}$ only [12] (cf. 3 (a) above).

Saint-Lambert's rule is as follows: "$\frac{4}{2}$ The double figure, two and four, is accompanied by the Fifth, or, if desired, by the Sixth, but the Fifth is better:

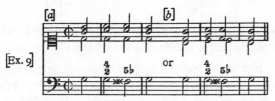

[Ex. 9]

"$\frac{4}{2}$✕ The double figure, two and tritone, is accompanied by the Sixth" (Example given).

N.B.—In Ex. 9 [a] the figuring $\frac{5}{4}$ is absolutely demanded: Saint-Lambert's rule is a striking example of how little figuring was as yet standardized.

(β) The remarkable distinction which Saint-Lambert makes between the double figuring $\frac{6}{3}$ and a single 6. His rule is: "$\frac{6}{3}$ The double figure, three and six, is accompanied by the Octave. It is the simple chord of the Sixth." He had explained, in the previous section, that the single figure 6 might be treated either as $\frac{8}{6}$ (*l'accord simple*) or as either $\frac{3}{6}$ or $\frac{6}{3}$ (*l'accord doublé*). The present rule would therefore appear to indicate that Saint-Lambert intends the figuring $\frac{6}{3}$ to exclude the doubling of either Sixth or Third (*l'accord doublé*).

(γ) The ambiguous use of $\frac{7}{4}$, when not occurring in a cadence.

Saint-Lambert's rule is: "$\frac{7♭}{4}$ The double figure, Fourth and minor Seventh, in a cadence, is accompanied by the Fifth or the Octave. Otherwise than in a cadence, it is accompanied by the Octave or the Ninth: [13]

---

[12] Except when resolving on $\frac{5}{3}$ over a stationary Bass, $\frac{3\ 4\ 5}{1\ 2\ 3}$ (cf. Ch. xiv, '$\frac{6}{4}$ chords', § 7, Ex. 5).

[13] According to the stricter usage of a later period, the inclusion of the Ninth would demand the figuring $\frac{9}{7}$

'Example in a cadence'

'Example without cadence'

(δ) A similar ambiguity in the case of the figuring $^9_4$, which ordinarily stands for $^9_5$ (representing a common chord with Octave and Third delayed by suspension), but which Saint-Lambert allows to stand for $^9_7$, resolving on $^6_3$ over the same Bass. His rule and example are as follows: "$^9_4$ The double figure, four and nine, is accompanied by the Seventh or the Fifth:

'Example'

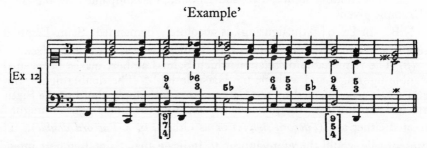

In connexion with the above rule, Saint-Lambert mentions that Marc-Antoine Charpentier, in his opera *Médée*, 1693, uses the figuring $^{11}_{9}$ $^{10}_{8}$ for $^9_4$ $^8_3$. This is in accordance with the practice of figuring compound intervals adopted by Peri, Caccini, and Cavalieri (cf. §§ 6–8), as an indication of the composer's wish that the interval in question should be used in the higher Octave.

Saint-Lambert, however, condemns the practice on the ground that it needlessly embarrasses the accompanist with figures to which he is unaccustomed.

[The reference to Charpentier's *Médée*, as the date shows, was obviously not to be found in the *Traité* of 1680.]

(ε) A similar licence in the case of the figuring $^9_7$ (indicating a chord of the

Sixth $\frac{8}{6}$ with the 8 and 6 delayed by suspension), which is ordinarily taken as $\frac{9}{7}$, but in which, in place of the 3, Saint-Lambert allows another interval (4 or 5) [14] to be retained, at pleasure, from the preceding chord. His rule is as follows:

"$\frac{9}{7}$ The double figure, seven and nine, is accompanied by the Third:

'Example'

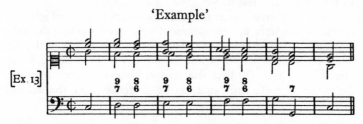

[Ex. 13]

"Instead of accompanying seven and nine by the Third, one can give the note bearing these figures the same chord as the preceding note. This is more convenient, and sometimes more agreeable to the ear:

'Example'

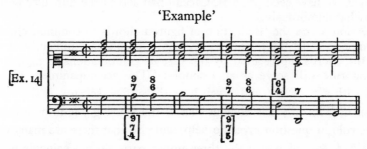

[Ex. 14]

5. Section III, dealing with triple figures (one above another), tells us little. Saint-Lambert merely says: "The only rule to be observed in regard to such notes is to give them, as accompaniment, the three intervals indicated by the three figures which they bear, without adding anything else."

The only triple figuring which he gives in his example is $\frac{6}{4}$ on the Subdominant, where 4× (4♯) would have done as well, or better.

6. Section IV, "Concerning notes which bear several figures, the one beside the other", deals with the time-values to be assigned to the several figures standing consecutively above a single note. Saint-Lambert gives some general rules, but the gist of what he says is that, unless the accompanist has the principal parts before him, he must rely mainly on his ear and instinct. He expresses regret that the carelessness and ignorance of copyists

[14] The 5 is often included, *as a fifth part*, in a $\frac{9}{7}$ chord, without being indicated in the figuring, when its presence is necessary for the preparation of a subsequent discord, as, for example:

Instances of the kind are particularly frequent in the figured Basses of Jean-Marie Leclair (cf. Ch. iii, § 4 III, Exx. 19, 20).

prevent the arrangement of the figures at exactly proportionate distances from each other, so as to make the time-values clear to the eye, an arrangement, he says, which ought to be as much an essential rule of musical notation as the correct indication of the notes themselves. He adds: "but I much doubt whether musicians will trouble about it, for I see several other things, of even greater importance than this, needing to be established or reformed in Music, to which no one has as yet given a thought."

There is only one small point in Saint-Lambert's rules which needs comment. When two figures appear consecutively over a single dotted note, he says that *either the first or the second* may occupy two-thirds of the time-value of the note. At a later period it was held (cf. Ph. Em. Bach, *Versuch &c.*, Pt. 2, 1762, Ch. 1, §§ 47–8) that the greater time-value fell to the *first* note unless the contrary were indicated, as by a stroke after the second figure:

Ph. Em. Bach, like Saint-Lambert, deplores the lack of adequate notation, though, as we have seen (cf. § 7), Caccini had solved the difficulty perfectly, if somewhat cumbrously.

7. Section V, on the 'Reduction of figured chords to common chords', is an attempt to assist the learner to overcome the primary difficulty of recognizing the chords represented by the various combinations of figures. The following rule will serve as an example: "The accompaniment of a note figured with a 7, or five and seven $\frac{7}{5}$, or three, five, seven $\frac{7}{3}$, is the common chord of its Third." It is obvious that, if the figuring 7 is to be interpreted as $\frac{8}{7}$, the rule in question gives no help, and also that there are many chords, such as $\frac{6}{5}$, $\frac{4}{3}$, &c., of which the three upper parts do not coincide with any Triad, and to which, therefore, no such rule can be applied.[15]

---

[15] Nevertheless we find Ph. Em. Bach giving similar directions. Of the $\frac{3}{2}$ $\left(\frac{5}{3}\atop 2\right)$ chord, which is simply a $\frac{4}{3}$ $\left(\frac{6}{4}\atop 3\right)$ chord modified by the suspension of the Bass (*a*), or on a 'changing', i.e. accented, passing note (*b*), as:

he says (*Versuch &c.*, Pt. 2, 1762, Ch. 12, § 4): "If one takes the Triad with the Second instead of the Octave, one has the $\frac{3}{2}$ chord (*Secundterzaccord*) in one's hand." It would have been scarcely more confusing if he had said that the chord was identical with the chord of the Ninth $\left(\frac{9}{5}\atop 3\right)$, but with different preparation and resolution!

Thus, too, Mattheson ('Organisten-Probe', 1719, *Mittel-Classe, Prob. Stück* 18, *Erläuterung*, § 4) tells us that the Low Bass clef (𝄢 on the top line of the stave) may be learned by reading it as the Treble clef 𝄞 two Octaves lower, and that, vice versâ, the French Violin clef (𝄞 on the bottom line of the stave) may be read as the Bass

It is when dealing with the ambiguous figurings already mentioned that Saint-Lambert's directions become worse than useless. Thus, his first rule is: "The accompaniment of a note which bears four and seven $\frac{7}{4}$, or four and nine $\frac{9}{4}$, or seven and nine $\frac{9}{7}$, or four, seven, nine $\frac{9}{7}$, is the common chord of a note a tone lower."

8. In Section VI, 'Concerning the Cadence', there is little to detain us. The more elaborate form of cadence, $\frac{7}{3}\frac{6}{4}\frac{5}{3}$ (sometimes known as the 'Grand Cadence'), given in Locke's *Melothesia*, is not mentioned.

The normal cadence, Saint-Lambert tells us, consists of three notes, the Dominant, its lower Octave, and the Tonic, of which the first two, *whether figured or not*, are to bear the 4 (not necessarily prepared) and the 7 respectively, as:

[Ex. 15]

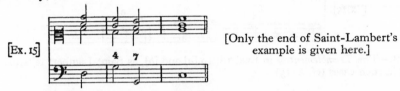

[Only the end of Saint-Lambert's example is given here.]

N.B.—The rising Seventh has already been mentioned (*d.* 3, ε).

The Dominant may, however, not be repeated in the lower Octave, in which case, if a long note, it is treated as above, but, if short, bears only a Triad (without the Seventh), as:

'Example'

[Ex. 16]

'Cadence'   'Cadence'

Besides the Perfect Cadence, the Interrupted Cadence is also given, in which it will be observed that the leading note is made to fall to the Octave, instead of rising to the Third of the following chord:

'Example'

[Ex. 17]

There are three forms, we are told, of Imperfect Cadence, of which a description is promised in subsequent chapters. The following examples are

clef two Octaves above its proper pitch, while Schröter (*Deutliche Anweisung zum General-Bass*, 1772, § 134) gives detailed directions for modulation into all keys by means of imaginary changes of clef (to be read if necessary in a different Octave), and alterations of key-signature.

given, in Ch. VI, Rule 15 (at the end of an example), Ch. VII, Rule 20, and Ch. IX, Rule 15, respectively:

N.B.—The *Tremblement* ⌁ in Exx. 18, 19 [*a*] and [*b*], as Saint-Lambert tells us, is usual in such cases (cf. *k*. 15).

e (Ch. IV). The fourth chapter, on the Tones (i.e. keys), and Modes (major and minor), and Transposition, is purely elementary.

One point, however, deserves mention, as concerning an important detail in the practice of figuring, as it then obtained:

If a note of which the Fourth above it is a *Tritone* (as *f* in the key of *C* major) is figured 4, instead of 4✕ (4͜), the *perfect*, and not the augmented Fourth, Saint-Lambert tells us, is assumed to be intended.

Some musicians, however, use a simple 4 (without the added ✕ or stroke through the tail) to denote an augmented Fourth (Tritone), when the latter is in accordance with the key-signature.

In such cases, Saint-Lambert tells us, the *accompanist must be ready to divine the intention of the composer*.[16]

He goes on to say that he, personally, prefers this system of figuring (then an innovation), by which a ✕ or ♭ is never attached to a figure except

---

[16] For example, if *f*, in a key without a flat in the signature, were figured $\frac{4}{2}$, and were followed by 6 on *e*, the Tritone would be intended, *unless the context demanded b flat*, whereas, if the figuring were $\frac{6}{4}\frac{5}{3}$, the perfect Fourth would be indicated. The obvious criticism of this method of figuring is that a composer who abandons the use of 4✕ (4͜) when the augmented Fourth is diatonic, ought to use the figuring ♭4 (4♭) when the perfect Fourth is accidental. The reason against doing so was probably the fear that 4♭ might be taken to indicate a *diminished* Fourth, just as some composers actually used ₆ as the indication of a diminished *Seventh*, because ♭7 was regarded as appropriated exclusively to the *minor* Seventh (cf. Ch. xxiii, 'Varieties of figuring', § 17, Ex. 1).

to denote an interval at variance with the key-signature [or, of course, to restore a 𝄪 or ♭ previously contradicted].

As an aid to transposition he recommends imaginary changes of clef and key-signature (cf. note 15 *ad fin.*).

f (Ch. V). Saint-Lambert's fifth chapter, 'On the Movement of the Hands', embodies the following principles:

(1) Contrary motion between the Bass and upper parts, as a means of avoiding consecutives.

(2) The right hand must take each chord in the position nearest to the preceding one, progressing by the smallest possible intervals, and retaining, if possible, any interval of the preceding chord which may be common to the two.

[N.B.—This rule, which we have not met with in any of the treatises already discussed, has always held good.]

(3) The upper part must not go above *e″* or, at most, *f″*, except when the Bass becomes 'Haut-contre' [i.e. when it is written with a C clef, indicating that the true Bass is silent], in which case it may go very high.

(4) When the Bass rises or falls by leap of a large interval (that is, a Fourth or Fifth, or any larger interval, the 'small intervals' being the Second and Third), the hands may move by similar motion.[17]

(5) So also in taking or quitting an *accord doublé* (the chord of the Sixth with either Sixth or Third doubled instead of the Bass):

'Example'

[Ex. 21]

(6) In the penultimate chord of a [perfect] cadence, the Third [the leading note] must rise *if in the upper part.*

(7) When the two hands are so close together that the right hand cannot take three parts without moving upwards together with the left hand, two parts only are to be taken, the Octave of the Bass being dropped.[18]

---

[17] Because, in such case, if the upper parts move by step, there is no danger of consecutives.

[18] Saint-Lambert explains later (Ch. VI, Rule 19), with regard to the progressions:

that, in such cases, there is no real dropping of a part, but rather the *coincidence of two parts in the unison.* This applies equally to Ex. 22. It will be observed, moreover, that the part 'dropped' in the penultimate chord cannot be the 'Octave of the Bass' (in accordance with the wording of Saint-Lambert's rule), since the latter, being the leading note, could, in no case, be doubled, though Saint-Lambert gives no rule on this point, or, indeed, concerning any of the intervals which may not be doubled in a four-part accompaniment.

'Example'

[Ex. 22]

(8) The Fourth, the diminished Fifth, the Seventh, and the Ninth must fall:

'Example'

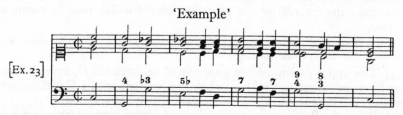

[Ex. 23]

(9) The Tritone 4✗, the augmented Fifth 5✗, the major Sixth, figured 6✗ [i.e. the major Sixth with *minor* Third, on the Supertonic, or temporary Supertonic], and the major Seventh 7✗ [i.e. $\frac{7}{4}$ resolving on the same Bass] must rise:

'Example' [19]

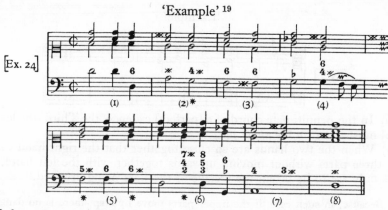

[Ex. 24]

If the augmented Fifth is not in the upper part, it falls a Third instead of rising a semitone: [20]

[19] The last chord in bar 1 illustrates a very curious rule given by Saint-Lambert in his chapter on the treatment of an unfigured Bass (cf. *h*, Exx. 36, 37). But, whereas in the example there given (Ex. 36), the 6 *rises*, as a passing note, to the 3 of the following chord, in the present example it *falls* back a degree to the 8.

For the slur in bar 4 see note 11. Note also the 'Tremblement' ⌁ (cf. note 37). The 5✗ in bar 5 affords another instance of the inadequate figuring of the period (cf. *d*. 3, 4). Saint-Lambert's treatment of the chord demands the figuring $\frac{9}{7}$ or $\frac{7}{5}$✗, whereas 5✗ denotes the augmented Triad, to be taken, either with the Octave of the Bass, or with doubled Third, or in three parts only, according to the circumstances.

[20] This rule must be taken to apply only to the chord $\left(\frac{9}{7} \text{ or } \frac{7}{5}✗ \right)$ as given in the example: the 5✗ in the augmented Triad (cf. note 19) must rise. It will be

'Example'

g (Ch. VI). In the sixth chapter, 'On the Choice of Chords', there are several points of interest.

The first directions which Saint-Lambert gives really belong more properly to Ch. VIII, 'On the Licences which may be taken in accompanying'.

He tells us that:

(1) The harmony on a long Bass note may be varied by a succession of two or three chords, where only one is figured, provided that they harmonize (*quadreront*) with the voice part.

(2) Sometimes, on the contrary, some of the chords prescribed may be dispensed with, if the Bass seems too copiously figured.

1. "On peut sur une note de Basse, d'une valeur un peu considerable, faire deux ou trois accords differens [*sic*] l'un après l'autre, quoique le livre n'en demande qu'un, pourvu qu'on sente que ces accords quadreront avec la partie chantante.

2. "On peut au contraire se dispenser de faire tous les accords marquez dans le livre, quand on trouve que les notes en sont trop chargées."

By the latter rule Saint-Lambert probably means that the harmony should be lightened, rather than that certain chords should be omitted bodily.

Rule 7 is to the effect that, if a Triad is followed by a Fourth and a Sixth, or a Sixth alone [i.e. $\frac{6}{3}$], on the same Bass, the Sixth must be of the same kind (major or minor, as the case may be) as the Third in the preceding chord, as in the example overleaf:

observed that, in the second complete bar of the second section of the example, the 5✕, though in reality a retarded 6, is taken unprepared in a very unusual manner. Heinichen gives examples of the same chord in the two positions shown in Saint-Lambert's example (*General-Bass &c.*, 1728, Part I, Ch. 3, § 89, 2, p. 247).

In the first case the 5✕ (5⟊) is allowed to fall, but in the second 3 is added to the chord as a fifth part, thus enabling the 5✕ to rise to a unison with the 7 of the previous chord:

N.B.—In the original, by an obvious misprint, the resolution of the chord in the first example is figured $\frac{8}{6}$ instead of $\frac{8}{6}$.

Note the false relation ♭*b* ♮*b* in the first complete bar of the second section of Ex. 25.

Note also that Saint-Lambert, as in Ex. 24 and several other of his examples, and as was very commonly done, takes the final chord in five parts, thus securing the downward resolution of the Seventh, which, in other cases, he allows to rise (cf. *d.* 3, ε).

'Example'

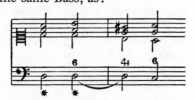

No account is taken of, for instance, a *major* Sixth following a Triad with a *minor* Third upon the same Bass, as:

Rules 12 and 13 mark the definite abandonment of the older practice, according to which ♭ or ✕ over a bass note is regarded as automatically contradicted unless renewed over every repetition of the same note (cf. § 6). According to Saint-Lambert the accidental holds good when the note on which it first occurred is repeated, or even when it recurs after a short interruption.

'Example'

Rule 14, which must be carefully borne in mind in playing from the earlier figured Basses, relates to a particular economy in figuring which remained in vogue till well into the eighteenth century.

The rule is to the effect that, when a note, accidentally sharpened or flattened *in the Bass*, occurs (either immediately before, or immediately after)

---

[21] The omission of ✕ over *a* (at the beginning of the second complete bar of Ex. 27) is probably unintentional, as, in the corresponding bar of the previous example

(not quoted here) the ♭ is repeated:

In the same bar it will be noticed that Saint-Lambert adheres instinctively to the old practice of contradicting a ✕ with a ♭, though, in his third chapter, he prescribed the use of ♮ for this purpose (cf. *d.* 2).

The 6✕ on *e* at the beginning of the penultimate bar of the example affords yet another instance of inadequate figuring (cf. *d.* 4, *a*, *γ*, *δ*, *ε*). The chord, as taken above, demands the figuring $^{6✕}_{5♭}$, in default of which it would most naturally be taken as $^{6✕}_{4}$:
$_{3}$

, called by Saint-Lambert 'le petit accord' (cf. Ex. 30), as opposed to 'la grande Sixte', Rameau's 'chord of the added Sixth'.

in an upper part, it is subject to the same accidental alteration, though not indicated in the figuring, as at * * and † in the example:

'Example'

[Ex.28]

At a later period the figuring at * would, as a rule, have been ✕, and 7_b; at †, where a Triad follows immediately *after* its first inversion, the accidental would frequently have been omitted.

In Rule 16 (forbidding consecutive Octaves and perfect Fifths with the Bass) the device of crossing the parts is introduced, as has already been mentioned (cf. note 9).

In Rule 17 (forbidding the progression of an augmented Second or Fourth) Saint-Lambert makes the interesting observation that there is reason to believe that the Italians are not sensitive to such progressions, since they often use them in the subjects of their pieces. "One finds them", he says, "in the Sonatas of the famous Corelli, now so celebrated in Europe, and, for some years past, so much in vogue amongst ourselves. You will not, therefore, be doing a very great wrong if you allow yourself some bad progressions in the parts of your accompaniment, provided that you do not affect them, and that you do not use them except by a kind of necessity. I should, however, prefer them not to be used at all, unless it be in certain very extraordinary cases, where one feels that similar negligences are better than a more exact regularity."

[Corelli's *Opera prima* (*Sonate a trè, doi Violini e Violone ò Arcileuto col Basso per l'Organo, Roma, Gio. Angelo Mutij*) appeared in 1681 (2nd violin part Brit. Mus. d. 73 f.)—not, as is commonly stated, 1683; this reference to his works cannot, therefore, have been contained in the original *Traité* of 1680, and is, strictly speaking, out of place in a survey of the period 1600–1700, but is too interesting to omit.]

In Rule 19 Saint-Lambert explains that the dropping of a part, recommended in that and in the previous rule as a means of avoiding (1) consecutive Octaves or Fifths with the Bass, and (2) the bad progression of an augmented interval in an upper part, is really *a coincidence of two parts in the unison* (see note 18).[22]

Rule 20 deserves to be quoted in full, on account of the interest attaching to a practical hint founded on the long experience of an exponent of the Art of Accompaniment:

"When the Bass rises, by step or by leap, if the second note bears two or

---

[22] Many years later Ph. Em. Bach (*Versuch &c.*, Part 2, 1762) frequently emphasized the desirability of employing this device as a means of avoiding consecutives, and also the inelegant progressions used by an older school who insisted on the employment of four sounding parts throughout, as e.g. in the accompaniments given in G. P. Telemann's *Singe-, Spiel- und Generalbass-Übungen*, 1735 (reprinted Berlin, 1914), of which an account will be found in Ch. ii, § 8.

more figures, whatever they may be, one can retain, on this second note, the chord belonging to the first.

"Observe that I say that one *can*, not that one *must* retain it; for although it nearly always answers, yet it may sometimes not answer; nevertheless it answers so ordinarily that I would willingly make it a general Rule, it being very rarely that defects arise (*qu'il s'y trouve de la defectuosité*); and, should it occur, they would be remedied so naturally by the chord of the following note, that I should not scruple to retain it [i.e. the first chord].[23]

Rules 24–6 deal with the treatment of a succession of two or more Sixths on a rising or falling Bass.

The three-part accompaniment given by Ebner (with some disapproval), and by Locke and Blow (cf. §§ 19, 21, 22), is not mentioned.

Saint-Lambert first directs that the *accord simple*, i.e. $\frac{8}{6}{3}$, which, of course, necessitates contrary motion, should be used with each Bass note:

'Example'

[Ex. 29]

At a later period, the awkward progression between the third and fourth chords of the example (with the leading note falling a Third in the upper part) would not have commended itself.

If the use of the *accord simple* on two successive notes is impossible [as when one of them is a leading note], or if it is not desired, we are directed to use two different kinds of chords, either the *accord doublé* $\left(\begin{smallmatrix}6\\3\\6\end{smallmatrix}\text{ or }\begin{smallmatrix}3\\6\\3\end{smallmatrix}\right)$ alter-

---

[23] This rule is not as absurd as would appear at first sight. Saint-Lambert was evidently thinking of the Harpsichord, rather than of the Organ (though the latter is included in the title of the work now under discussion), and, when in doubt, it is clearly better, on an instrument of so evanescent a tone, to retain a chord than to risk striking a wrong note.

In the second place, the rule was probably framed with a view to double, or even triple, suspensions, which, even if fully figured, are liable to present some of the most puzzling combinations likely to be encountered in playing at sight from a figured Bass, and we have seen (*d.* 4, δ and ε) that, in such cases, Saint-Lambert's figuring was highly ambiguous. The interpretation of the figures there advocated (Exx. 12 and 14) is entirely in accordance with the present rule.

By the expression 'the chord of the following note', used at the end of the rule, we are probably meant to understand (though, if so, it must be admitted that the expression is misleading), not only the chord on a *third* Bass note, but also the resolution, *over the same Bass*, of the discords indicated by the troublesome figures, as in the following examples:

(taken from Schröter's *Deutliche Anweisung, &c.*, 1772, §§ 256–7).

nating with the *accord simple* (in which case the former is to be on the higher of the two bass notes), or the *accord simple* alternating with the *petit accord*, $^6_4$ [with major Sixth and minor Third, on the Supertonic (cf. Ch. xxi, 'Incomplete figuring', II, § 1)]. It is remarkable that Saint-Lambert should not here mention the combination of the *accord doublé* with the *petit accord*, and that, instead of the natural and smooth progression:[24]

he should give only:

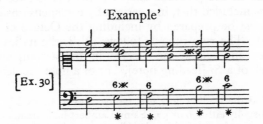

It will already have become abundantly evident how far the *Traité* is in advance of any work hitherto noticed, both in completeness and in the attempt at systematic arrangement; but a weak point in Saint-Lambert's rules is that they are sometimes unconsciously framed so as to apply only to a particular case which he had in mind, or to a particular example given. Thus, of two Sixths on a rising Bass, he tells us that, *if the Bass rises a semitone*, the first note should bear the *petit accord*, and the second, the *accord simple*:

'Example'

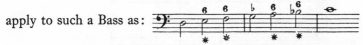

[Ex. 30]

He does not add that, in such case, the Sixth on the first of the two notes must be major (and the Third minor), forgetting that his rule would not

apply to such a Bass as:

The final example of the chapter is interesting only as illustrating a traditional licence in the interpretation of the figures: "Finally," we are told, "when the two Sixths are minor, and when, after them, the Bass further rises a semitone, one can take, on the first note, the *accord simple* or the *accord doublé*,[25] and, on the second, the diminished Fifth (*fausse quinte*)."

[24] He gives it, however, as an alternative to (*b*), in the following chapter on the treatment of an unfigured Bass (Ch. VII, Rule 24).
[25] Ph. Em. Bach infinitely preferred the former, on account of the skip in the two upper parts involved by the use of the latter (*Versuch &c.*, Part 2, 1762, Ch. 3, II, § 3).

'Example'

Thus, in the progression described, the leading note, though figured 6, may be treated, at pleasure, as though figured 5♭.[26]

h (Ch. VII). Saint-Lambert's seventh chapter contains rules for the treatment of an unfigured Bass.

They are naturally founded on experience of the harmonies most commonly associated with certain progressions of the Bass, and, equally naturally, fail to meet exceptional cases.

Similar attempts were made, notably by Francesco Gasparini (*L' armonico pratico al cimbalo*, 1708), and by Heinichen (*General-Bass in der Composition*, 1728), but later writers, as Mattheson (*Kleine General-Bass-Schule*, 1735) and Ph. Em. Bach (*Versuch &c.*, Part 2, 1762), recognized the impossibility of framing rules to meet all cases, though, of course, the difficulty is greatly diminished when (as, generally, in the case of vocal or instrumental Solos) the principal part is written or printed above the Bass.

Saint-Lambert's rules are, however, not even what they profess to be, since, in some cases, they presuppose a Bass, at all events, partially figured. A single instance will suffice. In Rule 2, which would have been more properly in place in the previous chapter, 'On the Choice of Chords', the important rule is included that, in a series of 7 6 suspensions on a *rising* Bass, each Seventh must be prepared by including the Octave of the Bass in the preceding chord. The rule runs as follows (N.B. the italics are the present writer's): "One can include the Octave in the accompaniment of a *Mi* [Mediant major], of a *Si* [leading note],[27] or of a note accidentally sharpened

---

[26] At that period the leading note was rarely, if ever, figured $\frac{6}{5}$. If figured at all, the figuring was usually either 6 or 5♭. Saint-Lambert had already explained that the *fausse-Quinte* 5♭ "is accompanied by the 6", except where the Bass falls or rises by leap, as:

At a later period, only the second of these two examples (in which the 5♭ is on the Supertonic of a minor key) would have held good. In the first example, the 5♭ (on the leading note) would ordinarily have been treated as $\frac{6}{5}$:

[27] It will be noticed that *Si* does not occur in the example: *b* (in the first complete bar) bears an imperfect Triad as the Supertonic in A minor.

(*Dieze*),[28] when the Bass falls a major Third, or rises or falls by a considerable interval. One is bound to include it when the Bass rises a tone or a semitone to a note *figured with a Seventh*":

'Example'

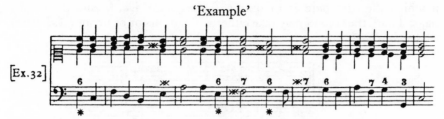

[Ex.32]

It will, therefore, suffice to notice certain points of interest which present themselves, without entering into further details:

(1) In the examples illustrating Rules 7 and 18 Saint-Lambert is entirely at variance with the practice of a later period, and indeed with his own rule (Rule 1 of the chapter under consideration; cf. note 28).

The rules are as follows:

(Rule 7) "When the Bass falls a minor Third, if the first note bears a minor Triad, the second must have the diminished Fifth in its chord, in place of the perfect Fifth:

'Example'

[Ex.33]

[N.B.—The notes marked * demand the *fausse-quinte* $\frac{6}{5\flat}$ (*not* the imperfect Triad), or the *accord doublé*.]

(Rule 18) "If the Bass has three notes in succession, the first falling a minor Third and then rising a semitone to the first beat of a bar, the first note should have the major Triad, the second the *accord simple* $\left[\begin{smallmatrix}8\\6\\3\end{smallmatrix}\right]$ or the *accord doublé* $\left[\begin{smallmatrix}3\\6\end{smallmatrix} \text{ or } \begin{smallmatrix}3\\6\\3\end{smallmatrix}\right]$ of the minor Sixth, and the third the major Triad":

'Example'

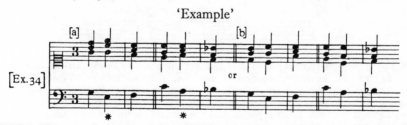

[Ex.34]

[N.B.—The notes marked * demand the *accord doublé* as shown in the alternative example.]

[28] The preceding rule (Rule 1) was to the effect that *Mi*, *Si*, and a *Dieze* (a note accidentally sharpened) are *always assumed to be figured 6*, and take the *accord doublé*, $\begin{smallmatrix}6\\3\end{smallmatrix}$ or $\begin{smallmatrix}3\\6\end{smallmatrix}$, when the Bass rises a semitone to a common chord.

(2) Rule 20 is to the effect that, in the progression:

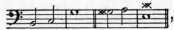

in which the first note is to bear a *fausse-quinte*, i. e. $^6_{5b}$, and the third a major Triad, the second may take either a Triad, major or minor (cf. Ex. 20), or a *major Sixth*:

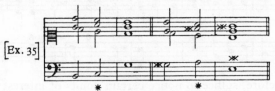

[Ex. 35]

(3) Rules 21 and 22 make a very remarkable distinction between the ways in which a repeated Bass note is to be treated: *according to whether it rises a Fifth, or falls a Fourth,* to the first beat of a bar.

In the first case, when the Bass *rises* from one Triad to another, major or minor,[29] according to the key (as Saint-Lambert carefully explains), the repeated note takes a major *Sixth* (with major or minor Third as the case may be):

'Example'

[Ex. 36]

but, when the Bass *falls*, if the first Triad is *major*, the repeated note takes the major Sixth *with the Tritone* $^8_{6}_{4 \times}$: [30]

'Example'

[Ex. 37]

[29] The examples (Ex. 36, *a, b*) do not meet all possible cases. In the first bar of Exx. 24, 27, 28, however, we find (unlike Ex. 36) the first Triad minor, and the second major. In these three examples the Sixth, instead of forming a passing note to the 3 of the following chord (as in Ex. 36), falls to its Octave. For the common case in which the first Triad is major and the second minor see note 30.

[30] In a previous example of Saint-Lambert (not quoted in the present work) we

find the progression: 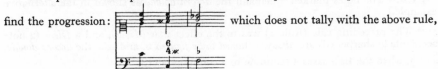 which does not tally with the above rule,

(4) The following examples, illustrating Rules 23 and 29, afford instances of the crossing of parts:

In Ex. 38 the progression would not pass muster according to the stricter standards of Heinichen and Ph. Em. Bach, on account of the impression of consecutive Fifths conveyed to the ear on a keyed instrument. The former states explicitly (in speaking of consecutives between extreme parts) that faulty-sounding progressions are not excused by crossing (*General-Bass &c.*, Part I, Ch. 2, § 32, note *e*, p. 132).

i (Ch. VIII). Saint-Lambert's eighth chapter, 'On the Licences which may be taken in accompanying', regarded in conjunction with his final chapter, 'On Taste in the Accompaniment', gives a good idea of the freedom which had been attained in certain respects since the days when the ideal accompaniment was that which most nearly reproduced a sedate vocal or instrumental score, and also of Saint-Lambert's high conception of the duties of the accompanist.

according to which the note repeated in the lower Octave (as in Ex. 24) should bear a $^6_3$ chord, not $^6_{4\times}$, because the Bass *rises* (instead of falling) to the following Triad. It seems probable (as we have already seen that the accurate framing of rules was not Saint-Lambert's strong point) that his actual practice was to use the $^6_{4\times}$ chord on the repeated note *when the first Triad was major and the second minor, whether the Bass fell a Fourth or rose a Fifth*, the progression of the 6 (rising to the 3, or falling to the 8 of the following chord) depending on the position in which the chords were taken:

In the position last given, the 6 could also rise:

(cf. *d*. 3, Ex. 3), since the progression of a diminished Fifth rising to a perfect one was not objected to, and occurs repeatedly in Saint-Lambert's examples.

After giving the usual rules for quick notes in the Bass (cf. § 10 *c*, Rules 3 and 4; § 11, v, Rules 6–8; § 17, III *h*; § 18, Rule 8; § 21, Rule 8; § 22, Rule 11) —to which he adds the rule that, in quick $\frac{3}{4}$ time, only one chord goes to the bar, provided the Bass moves by step and is not figured to the contrary— he enumerates the following points:

N.B.—Inverted commas mark Saint-Lambert's own words.

(1) Certain liberties may be taken with the Bass itself:

(*a*) If the Bass moves too quickly for the convenience of the player, he need play (and accompany with the right hand) only the first note of the bar, leaving the rest to the Gamba or Violone [the use of which, as a support to the Bass of the instrument on which the chords are played, is assumed by Saint-Lambert]. Or he can modify (*reformer*) the rapidity of the passages by striking only the principal notes, namely, those which fall on the principal beats of the bar. "Great pace is quite inappropriate (*les grandes vitesses ne conviennent point*) to the instruments which accompany."

(*b*) "Conversely, if the Bass has too few notes, and drags too much for the liking of the Accompanist, he may add other notes to embellish it (*pour figurer d'avantage*),[31] provided that he is assured that this will be no detriment to the air, and, above all, to the voice which is singing. For the purpose of the accompaniment is to second the voice, and not to smother or disfigure it by an ugly jingle (*mauvais carillon*). There are some Accompanists who have such a good opinion of themselves that, believing themselves alone to be of more importance than the rest of the performers, they insist upon shining above them all. They load the Continued Basses with passages, they embellish the accompaniments [i.e. the harmonies played by the right hand], and do a hundred other things which are, perhaps, very pretty in themselves, but which, under the circumstances, are extremely injurious to the general effect (*Concert*), and only serve to exhibit the clever vanity of the Musician who produces them. Whoever takes part in a joint performance (*Concert*) must play for the credit and perfection of the whole, and not for his own particular credit. It is no longer a joint performance when each plays only for himself."

(*c*) He may take an upward Fifth instead of a downward Fourth and vice versâ, or even *play the entire Bass, for several bars together, in a higher or lower Octave than it is written,* if his hands are too far apart or too close together. In a cadence, instead of: he may,

at pleasure, play:

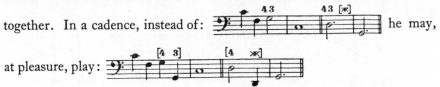

(2) The rules previously given, to the effect that, when the Bass moves by small intervals of less than a Fourth, contrary motion should be employed, and that the right hand should, in all cases, progress by the smallest possible intervals from one chord to another, retaining any note common to the two, may, upon occasion, *be entirely disregarded*:

(*a*) When the hands have got too close together, instead of dropping a part

[31] i.e. by making 'divisions', e.g.   for

(i.e. doubling an interval of the chord in the unison) as in Ex. 22, the right hand may leap to the following chord by similar motion with the Bass:

'Example'

N.B.—At a later period the final Tonic chord in the accompaniment was not allowed to be taken, as above, with the 5 in the upper part (cf. § 25, III, 8 *c ad fin.*).

(*b*) On a long note, a higher or lower position may be gained for the right hand by the repetition of the chord in the desired position:

'Example'

N.B.—Ph. Em. Bach more than once mentions the repetition of the harmony in a higher position over the same Bass as a means of escape when the hands have got too close together (*Versuch &c.*, Part 2, 1762, Introd. § 37, Ch. 29, § 25, Ch. 34, § 2), but whether he would have approved the leap of an Octave, as in the above example (where so large a leap is quite unnecessary), is another question.

(3) Consecutive Fifths or Octaves in the accompaniment may be disregarded in accompanying a large body of voices or instruments. "But when one accompanies a single voice, one cannot adhere too rigidly to correctness, especially if one is accompanying alone [i.e. without the support of a Gamba or Violone]; for then everything is apparent, and it is there that the Critics let nothing pass."

(4) A false (i.e. diminished) Fifth followed by a perfect one is allowed in the upper parts [as at the beginning of Ex. 3], but not between the Bass and an upper part.

A perfect Fifth may be followed by a false or superfluous (i.e. augmented) one between the Bass and any upper part without its being regarded as a licence:

'Example'

N.B.—Saint-Lambert gives no instance, in any part of his work, of a diminished

Fifth *falling* to a perfect one in the upper parts, or of a perfect Fifth *falling* to an augmented one, though his rule does not exclude such cases.

His views agree closely with those of Marpurg (cf. *Handbuch bey dem Generalbasse &c.*, Part I, 1755, 2nd ed. 1762, Section II, 'On the harmonious progression of the intervals', IX. *a*, 2nd ed., p. 99), who says:

"This sequence of Fifths [diminished followed by perfect] is forbidden in two-part writing, and allowed only where there are several [i.e. at least three] parts, but only in the middle parts, or between an extreme [is this meant to include the Bass, unlike Saint-Lambert's rule?] and a middle part. On the other hand, whatever the writing (*Satz*) [i.e. whatever the number of parts], and between whatever parts, one can always pass from a perfect to an imperfect [i.e. diminished] or an augmented Fifth, because the reason of the prohibition, namely the hidden perfect Fifth, is absent. But it is better to rise from the perfect to the augmented than to fall, and to use the latter progression only in polyphony, between the middle parts."

Ph. Em. Bach, on the other hand, does not approve the progression of a perfect Fifth rising to a diminished one *between the Bass and another part* (cf. *Versuch &c.*, Part 2, 1762, Ch. 2, § 23). He says: "The upward progression of a perfect Fifth to a false one is better than that of a false to a perfect, *because the false Fifth by nature inclines downwards.* Both progressions are in place *only in the middle parts*" [the italics are not Bach's]. By the latter expression he probably means all parts but the Bass,

otherwise such a progression as, e.g.,  would stand condemned.

For the unprepared augmented Fifth in Ex. 42 see note 20.

(5) A concession is made, which, taken in connexion with the reservations in (3), is somewhat surprising:

"Finally, it would be but a trifling (*légère*) licence for one part to make even a perfect Fifth twice running with another part. I know that the *greatest* regularity would not admit of it; but since this fault (if it be one) is not at all apparent, I hold that one can boldly commit it. For, since Music is only made for the ear, a fault which does not offend it at all is not a fault:"

'Example'

[Ex. 43]

k (Ch. IX). The sixteen recommendations which constitute Saint-Lambert's ninth chapter, 'On Taste in the Accompaniment', would seem to be the first extant attempt at a systematic exposition of those modifications of the accompaniment which depend not so much on the observance of the rules of harmony as on the good taste of the performer, and it will therefore be well to give a condensed summary, Saint-Lambert's own words, where used, being indicated, as before, by inverted commas:

(1) Taste is exhibited, primarily, in the perfect adjustment of the accompaniment to the principal part or parts, which must be adequately supported without being overpowered. This is to be achieved on the Harpsichord by striking the keys smartly or lightly, as the case may be, and by the judicious use of the stops.

(2) For very delicate voices the tone can be reduced by means of the stops, or the accompaniment can also be played in three parts only, the part to be dropped being, where possible, the Octave of the Bass.

(3) When the voices are strong, the left hand may double one, or even all, of the parts played by the right hand. If one part only is doubled, it should be the Octave; if two, the Fifth; if three, they should be the same as those taken by the right hand.

(4) When thus 'filling in', however, so far from one's being obliged to take the same notes in the left hand as in the right, it is more elegant to choose others.[32] It is, at most, in the case of Triads that they ought to be the same.

Above all, one must never double dissonances,[33] except the Second.[34]

Thus, in a chord containing a dissonance, only the consonances may be doubled. For example, in the case of a Seventh, the Third and Fifth, "its natural accompaniment", may be doubled, and, "since the Seventh in a chord takes the place of the Octave", the Octave of the Bass * may be, not only included, but doubled as well.

as:

It is not, however, permissible in the case of any dissonance other than the Seventh for the consonance, of which that dissonance takes the place, to be included in the accompaniment.[35]

[32] "Bien loin pourtant qu'en remplissant ainsi l'on soit obligé de mettre de la main gauche les mêmes notes que de la main droite, il y a au contraire d'élégance à en choisir d'autres "; e.g. (a) (b) are better than (c) (d).

(a)   (b)   (c)   (d)

[33] In this, though he makes little mention of the subject of 'filling-in', Ph. Em. Bach (*Versuch &c.*, Part 2, 1762) seems to agree with Saint-Lambert. Heinichen, on the contrary, who treats the matter in great detail (*General-Bass &c.*, 1728), allows discords to be doubled freely in the left hand, *provided they are properly prepared and resolved in the right hand.* When so doubled, they may either (1) resolve in Octaves with the right hand, or (2) rise a degree, or (3) leap to an interval in the next chord.

[34] It is, of course, not the Second itself but the Bass which is the dissonant note.

[35] For instance, in the case of a suspended Fourth, the Third may not be included, nor, in the case of a suspended Ninth, the Octave. What Saint-Lambert says of the Seventh (as taking the place of the Octave) can only apply, with any degree of correctness, to the Seventh as an *essential discord*, since the Octave could always be sub-

stituted for it, as:  for:

whereas a suspended Seventh takes the place, not of the Octave, but of the Sixth.

We have already seen (cf. *d.* 3 γ) that, like other musicians of his time, Saint-Lambert took no account of the radical distinction between the two.

With regard to the rule itself, it may be noted here that Heinichen (*General-Bass &c.*, 1728, Part I, Ch. 3, § 54, 3, p. 206 sq.) permitted the resolution of a suspended

(5) "When a note rising a tone [to a note bearing a Triad or Seventh] bears a Sixth instead of a common chord, one can take, besides this Sixth, and double by way of filling-in, all the notes which compose the common chord."[36]

(6) The repercussion of chords is desirable, when possible without impairing the rhythm or spoiling the effect of the melody. It is almost invariably practised in accompanying a Chorus.

(7) The accompaniment may be 'filled in' even in accompanying a single voice, but, in such case, the notes are not struck simultaneously, but one after the other, with judgement. This is called *harpéger les accords*.

(8) The chord may be thus broken, even when the parts are not doubled. The same chord may be repeated several times, now with an upward, now with a downward break. "But this repetition, which requires great judgement (*qui veut être bien ménagée*), cannot be taught in a book: one must see some one practise it."

Broken chords are appropriate only in Recitative, where there is no fixed rhythm. [It must be carefully noted that Saint-Lambert is speaking of chords broken *ad libitum* (each note being held down as struck), and not of the arpeggio which fits as well into a fixed rhythm as do any other quick notes.]

In other cases (*dans les Airs de mouvement*) the chords must be struck simultaneously with the Bass, except that, in $\frac{3}{4}$ (and also in $\frac{2}{4}$) time, when the Bass moves in crotchets, a single note of the chord is delayed, so that it comes between two beats:

[Ex.44]

9, 7, and 4 to be anticipated in the left hand, in a 'filled-in' accompaniment, while the discord was duly resolved in the right, as:

[36] The following example would seem to present the kind of case that Saint-Lambert had in mind:

Compare G. P. Telemann's permission to treat 6 on the Subdominant (in a cadence) as though figured $\frac{6}{5}$ (Ch. xxi, 'Incomplete figuring', II, § 6). It will be noted that in framing the above rule Saint-Lambert takes no account of the discordant nature of the 5 in a $\frac{6}{5}$ chord, since he permits it to be doubled (contrary to his own express prohibition); neither does he make any provision for its preparation.

(9) In accompanying Recitative it is sometimes good, when the Bass permits, to dwell a long time on a single chord [of which the sound, on a Harpsichord, would, of course, soon die away] and to let the voice sing several notes unsupported before striking another chord.

(10) "At other times, after striking a full chord, and dwelling on it some time, one strikes one or other of the notes of the chord quite by itself, but so judiciously (*avec tant de ménagement*) that it seems as though the Harpsichord did it of itself, without the consent of the accompanist.

(11) "At other times, doubling the parts, one strikes all the notes again, one after another, with a continuous repetition, producing on the Harpsichord a crackling (*pétillement*) almost like musketry fire; but, after having made this agreeable *charivari* for three or four bars, one stops quite short on some great Harmonic chord (that is to say, without a dissonance) as though to recover from the exertion of making such a noise."

(12) In accompanying a single voice in an air (*Air de mouvement*) which lends itself to such treatment, like the Italian airs, one can introduce imitations on the Harpsichord (*on peut imiter . . . le Sujet & les Fugues de l'air*), making the parts enter one after the other. "But this demands consummate science, and, to be a success, must be of the first order."

(13) The greatest manifestation of taste that can be given depends on the power of adapting the accompaniment to the character of the voices and of the airs sung, and of entering fully into the spirit of the words.

(14) On the Organ, repercussion of chords is not practised, nor are broken chords [cf. Rule 8] ever used. A legato style is to be cultivated, and the parts are rarely doubled. The sustaining power of the instrument renders unnecessary the devices resorted to on the Harpsichord to supplement its thin and evanescent tone (*pour suppléer à la sécheresse de l'Instrument*).

(15) Both on the Organ and on the Harpsichord a trill (*tremblement*),[37] or other embellishment, may occasionally be introduced where appropriate, either in the Bass itself or in another part. A trill (*tremblement*) is *always* made:

(1) on a bass note of considerable duration bearing an *accord doublé* $\left(\begin{smallmatrix}6\\3\\6\end{smallmatrix} \text{ or } \begin{smallmatrix}3\\6\\3\end{smallmatrix}\right)$;

[37] Couperin (*L'Art de toucher le Clavecin*, 1717, p. 24) defines the *tremblement* as follows: "Les tremblements d'une valeur un peu considérable renferment trois objets, qui dans l'exécution ne paroissent que même chose. 1° L'appuy [long *appoggiatura*] qui se doit former sur la note au-dessus de l'essentièle. 2° Les battemens. 3° Le point-d'arèst:

Example

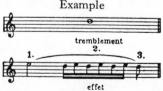

"A l'égard des autres tremblements ils sont arbitraires. Il y en a d'appuyés; d'autres si courts qu'ils n'ont ny appuy ny point d'arrest. On en peut faire même d'aspirés."

The *tremblement* may therefore be anything from a shake, preceded by a long *appoggiatura* and ending as in Couperin's example, to a form of 'inverted mordent', according to the length of the note to be embellished.

It is interesting to note that Mattheson recommends a shake in the cases exemplified in Ex. 45 (cf. Ch. IV, § 2 *e*, Ex. 9 to the end).

(2) on the penultimate note of an imperfect cadence (half close); and
(3) on the penultimate note of those cadences in which the Bass moves to
the close by step and not by leap, as:

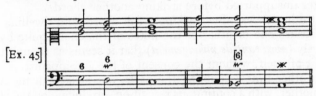

[Ex. 45]

"In these two kinds of cadence, instead of making the trill on the Bass
note, as marked above, one can make it on the note which forms a Sixth
from the Bass; but sometimes the position of the hand does not allow of it,
and besides, it produces a better effect in the Bass than in the other parts.
One might make it in the Bass and the other parts at the same time; but
I should not like it done with either of these two kinds of cadence. It would
be too affected."

(16) To connect the chords, and prevent them from appearing too abrupt,
an interval of a Third may sometimes be bridged by a passing note, as:

[Ex. 46]

"Just as one is not obliged always to include three different parts [besides
the Bass] in a chord, being at liberty to double some of them at pleasure
[as $\frac{3}{7}$ for $\frac{7}{5}$], or even to drop one of the three when it seems necessary, so
also one can sometimes add a fourth part to the chords prescribed by the
ordinary Rules, either in order to soften the harshness of a dissonance, or,
on the contrary, to make the latter more *piquant*, so as to enhance the enjoyment of the consonance on which it resolves. To say what interval from the
Bass this fourth note ought to represent would demand too great detail: it
would be necessary to examine afresh all the tones and, particularly, all the
chords. Let your ear decide when occasion arises, and, if you cannot decide,
do not put it in."

Thus, with a few words added in conclusion, ends Saint-Lambert's
interesting and eminently practical treatise.

§ 24. *Andreas Werckmeister* (b. 1645, d. 1706).

I. In 1698 there appeared a little treatise by Andreas Werckmeister, Court
Organist at Quedlinburg (1675), and afterwards (from 1696) Organist of
St. Martin's Church at Halberstadt and Inspector of all Organs built in that
principality, entitled:

Die nothwendigsten Anmerckungen und Regeln wie der Bassus continuus *oder*
General-Bass wohl könne tractiret werden, und ein jeder, so nur wenig Wissen-
schaft von der Music und Clavier hat, denselben vor sich erlernen könne, &c.
('The most necessary notes and rules as to how a *Bassus continuus*, or

Thorough-Bass, may be treated, and how any one who has but little knowledge of Music and keyed instruments may learn it for himself', &c.), and published by Gottlob Ernst Strunze at Aschersleben.

There is also an *undated* edition [Brit. Mus. 7895, aaa. 26 (2)], issued by the same publisher, which was reprinted in 1715, after the author's death.

It is on this undated edition (and the reprint of 1715, in the present writer's possession) that the account given in this section is based. The reprint of 1715 is styled 'Andere Auflage' ('*Second* edition'), thus ignoring one or other of the two previous issues.

The undated edition *cannot*, as Eitner suggests (*Quellenlexicon*, vol. 10, p. 229), be the original, and that of 1698 the second edition, since the former is described on the title-page as *aniezzo mercklich vermehret* ('now considerably enlarged').[1]

II. Werckmeister explains in his preface that his little treatise was compiled for teaching purposes, but that, owing to the misleading mistakes which were liable to arise in transcription ("weil aber durch das viele Abschreiben ein solch Werk sehr verfälschet, und ein *Incipiente* dadurch verführet wird"), he had resolved to print it.

III. The work does not remotely compare with that of de Saint-Lambert (cf. § 23), either in completeness or methodical arrangement, or even with that of Niedt (cf. § 25), while, on the other hand, it lacks the conciseness of Locke's *Melothesia* (cf. § 21). There are no chapters, but only short paragraphs (§§), the main divisions of the work being indicated by the two headings: *Von den Sätzen* ('On the chords'), at the beginning, and *Hierauf folget nun von den Progressionen, wie man von einem Sazze, oder Griffe zum andern schreiten kan* ('Here follows concerning the Progressions, how one can proceed from one harmony or chord to another'), which latter comes in the middle of a paragraph!

The examples (except a few illustrating the use of accidentals) are not given in musical notation but in *letters*, in fact—but for the omission of barlines and of the signs used to indicate the time-values of notes—in the old

German Organ-Tablature, in which the 'Large Octave' is given

in large letters, the 'Small Octave' in small letters, while the

one above is indicated by a stroke above (or beside) a small

letter, $\bar{c}$ or c', and is known as the 'Octave with one stroke' (*die einmal gestrichene Octave*), a stroke being added for each succeeding Octave. Thus

---

[1] The edition of 1698 has, unfortunately, not been available for comparison, but the *wrong references* given in the undated one (and uncorrected in the reprint of 1715) give a clue to the extent of the enlargement. At the end of his treatise Werckmeister gives a short summary, consisting of eight rules, of what has been said earlier in the work (cf. VI). In this summary the references to previous sections are evidently taken, unaltered, from the earlier edition. A reference (in Rule 5 of the summary) to § 12 is *correct*, but a reference (in Rule 6) to § 31 really applies to § 41. *Ten* sections between §§ 12 and 41 have, therefore, *been added*. Again, references (in Rules 7 and 8) to §§ 39 and 43 apply to §§ 50 and 54 respectively; *one* more section has, therefore, been added between §§ 41 and 50.

the scale runs as follows: *C, D,* &c., *B; c, d,* &c., *b; c̄* (or *c′*), *d̄* (or *d′*), &c., *b̿* (or *b′*); *c̿* (or *c″*), &c., and so on.

The simplicity of Werckmeister's examples renders bar-lines and the indication of time-values superfluous.

The following one (in which consecutive Fifths between the Alto and Bass of the first two chords have been allowed to pass) will serve as an illustration:

$$
\begin{array}{cccccc}
\overline{\overline{d}} - \overline{\overline{d\,c}} & \overline{h} & \overline{a} \;[-]\; \overline{a\,gis} & \overline{a} \\
\overline{a} & \overline{h\,a} \;[-]\; \overline{a\,g} - \overline{g\,f} - \overline{f\,e} & \overline{e} \\
\overline{fis} & \overline{gis\,e} & \overline{f\,e} - \overline{e\,d} & h & \overline{c} \\
& \begin{smallmatrix}7&6\\5&4\end{smallmatrix} & \begin{smallmatrix}6&5\\5&3\end{smallmatrix} & \begin{smallmatrix}6&5\\5&3\end{smallmatrix} & \begin{smallmatrix}6&5\\5&\end{smallmatrix}\!\!\times \\
[\times] & [\times] & & & \\
d & e & d\;e & c\;d & d\;e & A
\end{array}
$$

The horizontal dashes occurring between two consecutive notes of the same denomination (supplied in square brackets where the omission was clearly unintentional) are meant to indicate the retention of the first note, thus taking the place of ties in musical notation. We may, accordingly, interpret the example as follows:

IV. Considerable space is devoted by Werckmeister to the advocacy of a tempered scale [2] whereby the necessity for more than twelve keys to the Octave may be avoided.

[2] The temperament which he advocates, as explained in an Appendix: 'Kurzer Unterricht und Zugabe, wie man ein Clavier stimmen und wohl temperiren könne' ('Short Instruction and Supplement, as to how a Clavier may be tuned and tempered'), is a form of unequal temperament in which *all* the major Thirds are slightly sharp (especially ♯ *g* and ♯ *d*), while *most* of the Fifths are slightly flat. The exceptions are best described in Werckmeister's own words: "with this *c* sharp the Fifth, *g* sharp, can be tuned almost true [i.e. infinitesimally flat]; the test for the *g* sharp is *e*; this Third is usually a little too much on the sharp side (*diese Tertia pfleget wohl ein wenig scharf zu fallen*), but if one contemplates using the ♯ *g* in the place of ♭ *a*, as *f ♭a c̄*, it cannot be helped. With the ♯ *g* the Fifth ♯ *d* is tuned. The ♯ *d* may be just a little sharp in relation to the ♯ *g*, in order that it may be tolerably consonant as major Third to *b* and as major Third to *ḡ* [i.e. when used as ♭ *ē*]. With this ♯ *d* the Octave ♯ *d* is again made true; with this ♯ *d* the Fifth ♭ *b* may be tuned, which may also be slightly sharp, in order that the *d̄* may be tolerable as its appropriate Third.

"With ♭ *b* the Fifth *f̄* may be tuned, again slightly sharp, or quite true, according to how the *f̄* sounds in relation to the *ē*, as the last *Terminus,** or, again, to the last test-note *ā*, as a major Third *f̄–ā*." †

* A 'leading note' (in the wider sense of the term) was called *terminus acutus* or *terminus gravis,* according as the resolution was upward or downward. Thus the upper notes of an augmented Sixth or Fourth and the lower note of a diminished Fifth are *termini acuti,* while the opposite extremes are *termini graves.*

† The major Thirds are to be used throughout as tests: if their sharpness is excessive the Fifths must be flattened.

Werckmeister's whole scheme (given in accordance with his own minute instructions) is as follows; the round black notes represent the standard notes, and the white

He shows by an example, in which the German names of the corresponding notes in the *tempered* scale are given below the stave,[3] that without temperament it is impossible to return by a series of upward or downward alternate major and minor Thirds (or Sixths, as their inversions) to the original starting-point.

It is interesting to note that he approves of correct musical *notation* (including the use of ×× or × and ♭♭), and condemns such monstrosities as:

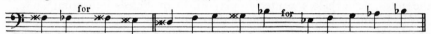

in which the notation follows the *names* of the notes then in universal use in Germany, as shown in note 3), while, on the other hand, he expressly says that he regards it as "unnecessary to give two names to a single key on the Clavier, as *ais* [♯ *a*] to *b* [♭ *b*], *es* [♭ *e*] to *dis* [♯ *d*],[4] and so on".

V. Werckmeister's directions for the treatment of a figured Bass are of a purely elementary character.

He begins by explaining that the normal accompaniment to any bass note is the Third, Fifth, and Octave (generally to be played by the right hand only, in order to leave the left hand free to deal with any passages that may occur), and that the three possible arrangements (i.e. in close harmony) of these intervals, namely:

$$\begin{array}{ccc} 3\ \bar{e} & 5\ \bar{g} & 8\ \bar{c} \\ 8\ \bar{c} & 3\ \bar{e} & 5\ \bar{g} \\ 5\ g & 8\ \bar{c} & 3\ \bar{e} \\ \hline 1\ c & 1\ c & 1\ c \end{array}$$

constitute the three 'ordinary'[5]

chords (*Ordinar-Griffe oder Säze*).

3)

[4] In view of the rare occurrence (at that time) of *d* sharp, as compared with *e* flat, it is remarkable that, in Germany, *e* flat should, till well on in the eighteenth century, have been universally known as *dis* (*d* sharp).

[5] Werckmeister explains the term as follows: "They are called *ordinary* chords,

notes those which are tuned to them, while the diamond-shaped black notes are the tests:

"The ordinary chords", writes Werckmeister, "are changed by the figures to be found over the notes in the Thorough-Bass: for all figures to be found over the notes are nothing but *Exceptiones*, or, as the Italian musician Galeazo [*sic*] Sabbatini expresses it, *Accidentia* to the above-mentioned ordinary chords."

It need not, perhaps, greatly surprise us when we read later on: "I have, moreover, had pupils who, although Seconds and Fourths were figured over the notes, nevertheless wanted to play Fifths or Thirds indiscriminately."

VI. It will be sufficient to quote the eight rules with which Werckmeister concludes his treatise (§§ 122–4 of the undated edition and the reprint of 1715), and in which he summarizes his instructions for the treatment of a Thorough-Bass:

N.B.—The examples here quoted in the footnotes are translated into staff-notation; it must therefore be remembered that the time-values and the barring are arbitrary.

1. "With every note in the Thorough-Bass an Octave, Fifth, and Third is ordinarily (*ordinarie*) taken.

2. "On the other hand, the figures above the notes alter the ordinary harmonies or chords (*Ordinar-Säze oder Griffe*); thus,

3. "When there is a 6 or 7 over the note, one is wont to leave out the ordinary Fifth.[6]

4. "But when there is a 2 or 4, the ordinary Third is left out.[7]

because they are in such *order* as God and Nature itself established and ordained: thus, *c. g. c̄. ē* correspond to the proportions of 2. 3. 4. 5; *c. c̄. ē. ḡ* [to those] of 2. 4. 5. 6; and *c. e. g. c̄* [to those] of 4. 5. 6. 8."

This explanation suggests the idea that our English term, 'common' chord, may have originated in a misunderstanding (and consequent mistranslation) of the Latin *ordinarius* (or the French *ordinaire*), as used (in Werckmeister's sense) in this particular connexion.

It may be mentioned here that, in some German treatises of the early eighteenth century, the three positions of the Triad (with the 8, the 3, and the 5 in the upper part, respectively) were also known as 'the three chief chords' (*die drey Hauptaccorde*), while *all chords that required figuring*, i.e. all chords *other than Triads*, were styled 'extraordinary chords' (*Extrordinar-*, or *Extrordinair-, Accorde* or *Sätze*).

[6] The following example in illustration of this rule is given earlier in the work (§ 10 of the undated edition and, presumably, also of the original edition of 1698; see note 1):

and so on in various ways."

[7] The following Exx. (continued opposite) are given in § 8 of the undated edition:

5. "If there is a 6, 4, or 2 over a note, the Fifth and Third, and probably (*wohl*) the Octave, are not taken with it. *Vid. Exempl.* § 12.[8]

6. "In the progression [of the parts] *Motus Contrarius* is observed as far as possible: or, at least, [it must be observed] that, when the Bass leaps, the other parts should some of them remain stationary, or only rise and fall by step with the leaping Bass. *Vid. Exempl.* § 31.[9]

"Or:  and so on in various ways."

The following points are noticeable in the above examples:

(1) At the beginning, and also in the second half of the first example, 2 stands (contrary to the later practice) for $\frac{5}{2}$ [cf. § 23, *d*. 3 (*a*)].

(2) In the second example the relative position of the figures $\frac{3}{6}$ is unusual: ordinarily, the lower number is never placed above the higher, except as an indication that the interval in question is to be taken in the upper part, which, in the present instance, is obviously not the case.

[8] The example here referred to is the following:

In giving the example Werckmeister remarks that, in the [suspended] Seventh at †, the Fifth, if included, "is very hard" (cf. Ch. xi, 'Sevenths', IV, § 2).

[9] The reference to § 31 (given, as above, in the undated edition and the reprint of 1715) was evidently taken from the original edition of 1698 and allowed to remain unaltered (cf. note 1). It is in § 41 of the two former that the examples in question occur, none of which illustrate the *latter* part of the above rule:

Werckmeister also adds (in § 44 of the undated and 1715 editions) an example of *motus rectus* between the extreme parts moving by step:

Of this he says: "Here the two extreme parts, Treble and Bass, move, it is true, *motu recto*, but the Third *f* is doubled, which is contrary to the natural order of the proportional numbers. These progressions, too, can be employed, and are not to be censured, but they are not so natural as the ordinary progressions [i.e. Third, Fifth, and Octave]."

The original statement (§ 45 of the undated and 1715 editions) of Rule 6 differs slightly from that given in the summary, and runs as follows: "*Motus rectus* can,

7. "When two notes in the Thorough-Bass represent a progression of a *Semitonium*, whether it be upwards or downwards, a 6 is taken with the lowest, unless a 5 *quinta* is expressly marked over it. *Vid. Exempl.* § 39 [§ 50 of the undated and 1715 editions].[10]

8. "When the notes move quickly by step ("*gradatim* fortlauffen"), the chord which was assigned to the first note is usually held. *Vid. Exempl.* § 43 [§ 54 of the undated and 1715 editions].[11]

"These, then, are the chief rules briefly repeated: where the major and minor Thirds come in is shown by the *Systema* [i.e. the stave and key-signature], even in the most unusual transpositions." [12]

Werckmeister does not include in the above summary any mention of the cadences (*Formal-Clausulen*), of which he treats at considerable length earlier

however, be employed when one extreme part moves *gradatim* and the other *saltuatim*, as:

"Although the last [example] is not much good, it will, nevertheless, pass at a pinch, and is sanctioned by some."

In such cases, in the older (especially the Italian) figured Basses, the 6 was commonly taken for granted, and the figure omitted; Werckmeister, therefore, wisely

insists that 5 must be figured when 6 is not intended, as:

"Now if the composer had written a Fifth, and the Organist played a Sixth, . . . the harmony would be spoilt, therefore the figures must always be put in, as is done by all sensible composers. . . ."

Werckmeister points out (§ 44 of the undated and 1715 editions) that the rule, given by some, to the effect that Sixths (even though not figured) must be taken with ♯f, ♯c, ♯g, is not of universal application: "for if a piece of music were written in A [major], ♯C, or ♯F, and a Sixth were always taken with ♯f, an insufferable dissonance would often be caused."

[11] The original statement of this rule is somewhat more explicit: "When quavers or semiquavers [in the Bass] move by step, the chord demanded by the first note is generally held; this may also apply to crotchets, as:

"But one's action in the matter of this rule must depend on whether the time be fast or slow; the figures (*Signaturen*), too, are generally an indication."

N.B.—The rule, as given, presupposes, of course, that the notes to be treated as passing notes are *unfigured*.

[12] i.e. keys with many accidentals: the Modes with flats or sharps in the signature were known as *Modi ficti* or transposed Modes.

in the work (§§ 58–64 of the undated and 1715 editions). It is evident that they were a stumbling-block to the imperfectly initiated, for he introduces the subject as follows: "As the cadences are often much mutilated and confounded (*verstümmelt und verwirrt*), I have now been minded to say a little about them."

In his preface, too, in speaking of Organists, he says: "Many do not know how to make a correct cadence (*Formal-Clausul*), either in a Chorale or in their preludes (*Praeambulis*)."

His explanations, as given in the *Harmonologia Musica*, 1702 (§ 111, p. 60), corresponding closely to those given in the work now under discussion, are quoted *in extenso* in § 4 in connexion with Viadana's fourth rule.

VII. It will already have become abundantly evident that, as a practical introduction to the art of playing from a Thorough-Bass, Werckmeister's treatise leaves much to be desired, and certain early allusions to it indicate that it was not regarded as having fulfilled its purpose.

So, for instance, Niedt's reference (quoted at the end of § 25) to the lack (in 1700) of any serviceable elementary treatise on the subject, in making which he must, almost certainly, have had Werckmeister in mind. At a later date, Schröter (*Deutliche Anweisung &c.*, 1772, Preface IV, p. viii), in mentioning the first appearance of Heinichen's splendid work, *General-Bass &c.*, 1728, speaks of "Organisten die sich bey Werckmeister's Anmerckungen über den General-Bass von 1700 [13] grau studirt hatten" ('Organists who had turned grey over the study of Werckmeister's Remarks on Thorough-Bass of 1700'[13]).

Of far more interest than his actual rules are some of Werckmeister's reflections on the function and scope of the accompaniment founded on a Thorough-Bass, on the value of the latter as a means of educating the ear, and on other subjects.

(1) With regard to the first he says (§§ 65–6 of the undated and 1715 editions):

(*a*) "Because the Thorough-Bass must be nothing else but an agreeable murmur (*ein liebliches Sausen*), and a foundation in a piece of music upon which the whole structure rests, it must be treated without much in the way of runs and intricacies (*ohne viel Lauffwerk und Gewirrle*): for if the vocalists and instrumentalists are executing their runs or passages, as the composer wrote them, and the Organist were to put in his own embellishments (*colores*) in the upper parts [of the accompaniment], the harmony would be spoiled. However, even the simple chords must not be taken too full, especially when there are weak singers or instruments.

"An expert may, doubtless, occasionally treat a Thorough-Bass with embellishments in the shape of broken chords and suchlike (*durch gebrochene Manieren*): in short, a musical intellect (*ein Musicalischer Kopff*) and judgement are needed. For if 1,000 rules were given to one who had no natural turn for Music, and illustrated by 10,000 examples, the object would, after all, not be attained. But whoever possesses a natural gift, industry, and inclination can learn much by means of these few rules."

(*b*) A little later (§§ 69, 70 of the undated and 1715 editions) Werckmeister gives some further important hints regarding the relation which the accompaniment should bear to the principal part or parts:

[13] It is impossible to determine whether the date 1700 is a mistake (for 1698), or whether, perhaps, this was actually the year in which the undated edition appeared.

"And, even though all the figures, &c., were [correctly] rendered (*Und da nun alle Signaturen möchten angebracht werden*), one must, nevertheless, be careful to avoid continually moving in Octaves [14] with the vocalists and instrumentalists [15]: one likes to see, especially when a Solo is performed, that the same part [i.e. the upper part, or melody, of the accompaniment] moves *motu contrario* [16]: that is to say, when the voice part has, say, a Treble cadence, the Organist can use a Tenor one, and vice versâ.[17]

"It is also not advisable that one should always just blindly play, together with the vocalists and instrumentalists, the dissonances which are indicated in the Thorough-Bass, and double them: for when the singer expresses a pleasing emotion by means of the dissonance written, a thoughtless accompanist may, if he walk not warily, spoil all the beauty with the same dissonance: therefore the figures and dissonances are not always put in in order that one should just blindly join in with them; but one who understands composition can see by them what the composer's intention is, and how to avoid countering them with anything whereby the harmony might be injured." [18]

This latter paragraph (which is reproduced almost *verbatim* in Werckmeister's *Harmonologia Musica*, 1702) embodies a most important principle, nowhere else so clearly and explicitly stated. According to it, the figuring of discords is, *under certain circumstances*, to be regarded merely as an indication of what is going on in the principal part or parts (especially valuable when the latter are not printed above the Bass), and as a warning to the accompanist to avoid anything that might clash with the discord in question: thus, if the latter is a Ninth (9 8), or a Fourth (4 3), the Octave or the Third, as the case may be, must not be included till the moment of resolution.

If this principle is important when the dissonance in the principal part falls within the compass permitted to the accompaniment, it is doubly so when it is above it, so that, if reproduced in the accompaniment, it would have to be in the lower Octave.

Generally speaking, this reproduction is no more offensive to the ear than the use of a 16-foot stop on the Organ, but in some cases the reduplication in the lower Octave (more especially in the upper part of the accompaniment) of a discord in the principal part serves only, as Werckmeister expresses it, to "spoil all the beauty". The only guide in this matter is the good taste of the accompanist.

[14] The term 'Octaves' is here loosely used to include the *unison*.

[15] i.e. the upper part of the accompaniment must not continually reproduce the upper principal part. Werckmeister's point of view is the opposite of that of Viadana, whose injunction to the Organist to prepare an *intavolatura* (§ 4, Rule 6) implies a desire that the accompaniment should reproduce, as closely as possible, the vocal score.

[16] Werckmeister, as he himself explains, uses the term *motus contrarius* to include *motus obliquus* (cf. § 4, note 7). The latter is obviously what is here meant.

[17] The above passage is fully explained in § 4 under Rule 4.

[18] "Es ist auch nicht rathsam, dass man allemahl die Dissonantien, so im General-Bass angedeutet werden, mit den Vocalisten und Instrumenten so *crasse* hinmache und verdoppele: Denn wenn durch die gesezte Dissonanz der Sänger einen anmuthigen *affectum* exprimiret: so kann ein unbesonnener General-Bassiste, wenn er nicht behutsam gehet, alle Lieblichkeit verderben: darum sind die Signaturen und Dissonantien nicht allemahl gesezet dass man sie so *crasse* mitmache, sondern ein Composition-Verständiger kan sehen, was des *Autoris* Meynung sey, und wie er nichts dagegen bringe, wodurch die *Harmonia* verlezet werde."

Werckmeister, however, gives a very useful hint in the words: "wenn durch die gesezte Dissonanz der Sänger einen lieblichen *affectum* exprimiret" ('when the singer expresses a pleasing emotion by means of the dissonance written')—the more *emotional* the discord, the less does it bear reproduction (least of all in a different Octave) in the accompaniment.

(2) Werckmeister's observations (§§ 71–3 of the undated and 1715 editions) on the educational value of the study of Thorough-Bass deserve to be quoted: "Experience teaches what is gained by proper tuition in Thorough-Bass: for, in the first place, the *Discipuli* are directed to the foundation of composition; in the next place, it impresses upon their minds the sound of the notes in their relation to one another ('darnach bringet sie die *Claves* in den Verstand wie einer mit dem andern klinge'), so that they learn to make cadences on their own account and to develop a theme (*dass sie vor sich clausuliren, und ein Thema führen lernen*); further, they are drilled into keeping correct time, without which no harmony has life.

"Those, on the other hand, who adhere only to Tablature [i.e. German Organ-Tablature] sometimes make it a mere matter of habit [19] (*Die aber hingegen bloss an der Tabulatur hangen, machen bissweilen eine Gewohnheit daraus*): when they play their chords they do not impress them on their memories as regards the sound of one note in relation to another; but one who has to seek the harmony to suit the foundation-note (*Fundament-Clave*) is more apt to learn how one note (*Sonus*) sounds in relation to another.

"Sometimes, too, the Tablaturists keep very unequal time—one bar quick and another slow, without their being themselves aware of it—because they have got into the habit of so doing; but when several persons are making music together, the one is constantly driving the other, so that the time remains even and correct—I do not, it is true, mean by this that I despise those who have accustomed themselves to Tablature—on the contrary, I have a high opinion of it—I am merely reminding them that here, too, one should accustom oneself to keep correct time and practise thoroughly."

These comments of Werckmeister are remarkably interesting: they make it clear why the excessive use of Tablature exercised—as it undoubtedly did —such a bad influence upon the musicianship of German Organists,[20] while, on the other hand, the value of the study of Thorough-Bass as a means of gaining an insight into the principles of harmony, and, more especially, as a means of learning to hear mentally the sounds depicted by notes and figures —to 'hear with the eye', one might almost say—can be doubted by no one who has had the chance of judging by experience.

(3) Werckmeister, as a Church musician, regarded a knowledge of the Modes as still necessary to the equipment of a competent Organist.

The melodies of many of the German Chorales are modal in their origin, and he rightly held that the prelude or *Praeambulum* should be in character. Some of the most beautiful of J. S. Bach's Chorale-preludes for the Organ bear witness, however free their treatment, to a perfect knowledge and appreciation of the Modes in which the melodies were originally conceived.

It is as the sequel to his reflections (already quoted) on the use of the German Organ Tablature that Werckmeister introduces the subject (§§ 75–6 of the undated and 1715 editions):

"But musicians of the right sort ('rechtschaffene *Musici*') think more of

[19] i.e. play purely mechanically.   [20] Cf. § 25, II.

any one who can perform well on the keyboard *ex tempore*, instead of sticking too closely to Tablature.

"But whoever wants to extemporize well ('*ex tempore* vor sich etwas gutes spielen') and to play a proper prelude (*Praeambulum*) from the Thorough-Bass (*vor dem General-Bass*) must needs understand the Modes (*Modos Musices*), in order that he may know how to distinguish the correct answer in imitations ('die richtige *Repercussion* in den Fugen'), the correct cadences (*clausulae formales*), and the correct scope (*ambitus*) [21] of each Mode; also that he may see how far, and with what justification (*Raison*), he can digress from the Modes [22] ('von den *Modis* abweichen'), so that the result may not be a muddle (*damit nicht ein Mischmasch daraus werde*)."

Then follows an enumeration of the six *Modi principales*, or *authentici*, and the corresponding *minus principales* or *plagales*; also a table of the former, showing the position of the semitones in the *Pentachord* (Quinta) and *Tetrachord* (Quarta), respectively, by means of which the modes can be transposed, and the transposed Modes (*Modi ficti*) verified by comparison with the untransposed (*Modi regulares*) given in the table.

The transposition of the Modes is the origin, as Werckmeister points out, of the *Claves signatae* or Key-signatures. "In the composition of to-day", he tells us (§ 92 of the undated and 1715 editions), "one could get on very well with [only] two Modes", i.e. major and minor.

He gives the *Clausulae formales* in the Ionic and Dorian Modes (on *c, e, g* and *d, a, f* respectively, as follows:

I   II   III

c cb c | *g g♯f g* | *e ed e* | or: *e e♯d e*
c g   c | *g d   g* | *e f   e* | *e b   e*

I   II   III

d d♯c d | *a a♯g a* | *f fe f*
d a   d | *a e   a* | *f c   f*

[21] In the strictest sense of the term the *ambitus modi* denoted simply the scale represented by each Mode or Key (e.g. in the Ionic Mode, or *C* major, *c. d. e. f. g. a. b. c*; in the Aeolian Mode, or *A* minor, *a. b. c. d. e. f. g. a*, &c.), and the harmony appropriate to it. In a wider sense, however, the term came to be applied to the harmony of attendant Modes or Keys (*Digressiones*), whose Triads were composed of notes belonging to the main key. Thus a close in *G* major, or even *D* minor, though involving the use of accidentals, could be regarded, in the wider sense, as within the *ambitus modi* of *C* major; but one in *G minor* or *D major* could not be so regarded, because the Thirds of the respective Triads, *g. ♭b. d, d. ♯f. a*, are notes extraneous to the key in question (cf. Heinichen, *General-Bass &c.*, 1728, Part II, Ch. 2, §§ 20–2, p. 760 sq.; ibid., *Supplementa ad Cap. 2, Sect.* II, § 2, p. 957).

[22] i.e. from one Mode to another. Werckmeister explains the matter as follows (§ 96 of the undated and 1715 editions): "A digression (*Abweichung*) of this sort must, however, be made on sound principles ('mit guter *Raison*'): thus, if one proceeds from *C* major *c. e. g* to *A* minor *a. c. e*, it is a good change; for the Mode *A* minor *a. c. e* has two cadences (*Formal-Clausulen*) [i.e. in common with *C* major], namely on *c* and *e*: consequently there is a close relationship between the two Modes. And many such good *Digressiones* can be found and admitted."

He goes on to say that he has heard Organists—presumably in the extemporaneous prelude to the Chorale—pass from *a. c. e* to *f. a. c*, thence to ♭*b. d. f*, with full closes on ♭*e* and *f* minor, and "back again to the regular *c. e. g* or *a. c. e*, with the result that some of the singers got quite bewildered, and it was well-nigh disgraceful to listen to".

the first of the three *Clausulae* (that on the Tonic) being known as *Clausula principalis et finalis* or *primaria*, the second (on the Dominant) as *minus principalis* or *secundaria*, and the third (on the Mediant) as *affinalis* or *tertiaria*.

Closes made on other notes—a tone or semitone above one of the three notes of the Triad—were known as *clausulae assumptae* and *peregrinae*; in the use of these, Werckmeister tells us, great caution is necessary. He goes on to say (§ 101 of the undated and 1715 editions): "To light upon a rare chord by means of an unusual leap or progression is pleasant, for the ear is soon delighted by the *Resolutiones*; therefore one must introduce suchlike strange embellishments (*Maniren*) on sound principles ('mit guter *Raison*). . . .

"Of new inventions and new figures (*Maniren*) there will, doubtless, never be an end in practical music (*Musica practica*) as long as the world lasts, but the foundations (*Fundamenta*) must not be destroyed."

Again, a little later (§§ 109–10 of the undated and 1715 editions): "And although one can get on, after the musical fashion of the day, with two Modes, the ancient Modes can, nevertheless, not be entirely discarded, since our Church-song (*Kirchen-Gesänge*) is written in accordance with them, in order that no muddle (*Mischmasch*) or disorder may be occasioned in Church.

"However, the two Modes in vogue to-day must maintain correctness in their *ambitus*,[23] repercussion,[24] *clausulae formales*, &c., that no disorder may creep in, as aforesaid."

Considerations of space forbid us to follow Werckmeister through all his reflections on the decadence of some of the younger generation of his contemporaries; we will take leave of him by quoting words (§ 117 of the undated and 1715 editions) so applicable to the present day that it is difficult to realize that over two centuries have passed since they were penned:

"In a word, just as everything is at present in confusion in the world, so it is at the present time with Music: that which sounds elegant and agreeable (*was fein und wol lautet*) is discarded, and that which sounds wrong and ugly (*was falsch und übel klinget*) is prized. Confused minds love confused Music, and make the minds of their hearers wild and confused, as various clever and learned men prove."

§ 25. *Friderich Erhard Niedt.*

I. In 1700, exactly a century after the appearance of the figured Basses of Peri, Caccini, and Cavalieri, there was published a little treatise of quite exceptional interest, namely, the First Part [1] of Niedt's *Musicalische Handleitung* (Musical Guide), dealing with the practical treatment of a Thorough-Bass—now, unfortunately, extremely rare.

---

[23] See note 21.

[24] i.e. the answer to a fugal subject or point of imitation.

[1] Of the remaining three parts only the second (*Handleitung zur Variation &c.*) concerns us. It was published at Hamburg (B. Schiller) in 1706 at the author's expense, and sets forth 'How the Thorough-Bass and the figures over it may be varied, elegant Inventions made, and how, from a simple Thorough-Bass, Preludes, Ciaconas . . . Gigues and the like may be constructed, &c.' Thus, in scope and intention, the work is in some degree comparable with Christopher Sympson's *Division Violist*. It was republished, with comments and other additions, in 1721 by no less a person than Johann Mattheson.

The full title of the work (a small oblong 4°, unpaged) is:

Friderich Erhard Niedtens /
Jenensis, Not. Publ. Caes.
Musicalische Handleitung
oder
Gründlicher Unterricht.

Vermittelst welchen ein Liebhaber der Edlen Music in kurzer Zeit sich so weit
perfectioniren kan / dass er nicht allein den General-Bass nach denen gesetzten
deutlichen und wenigen Regeln fertig spielen / sondern auch folglich allerley
Sachen selbst Componiren und ein rechtschaffener Organiste und Musicus
heissen könne.

Erster = Theil
Handelt vom General-Bass, denselben schlechtweg zu spielen.
Hamburg,
Gedruckt bey Nicolaus Spieringk /
Anno 1700.

('Frederick Erhard Niedt of Jena, Imperial Notary Public, his Musical
Guide or Fundamental Instruction, by means of which a lover of the Noble
[Art of] Music can in a short time so far perfect himself as to be able, not
only readily to play a Thorough-Bass in accordance with the few clear rules
laid down, but also, in consequence, to compose all manner of things himself
and to be styled a proper Organist and Musician.

'First Part, treating of the Thorough-Bass, how just simply to play it.
Hamburg, printed at Nicholas Spieringk's, A.D. 1700.')

We see from this title that Niedt held an official position entirely uncon-
nected with Music.

Strong testimony to the esteem in which the little treatise now under discussion was, nevertheless, held among musicians lies in the fact that J. S.
Bach himself (who was fifteen years of age at the time of its publication) did
not disdain to borrow from it in compiling rules for the benefit of his own
pupils.[2]

---

[2] The compilation in question has survived in the form of a manuscript, formerly
in the possession of Professor Wagener of Marburg, now in the library of the *Con-*
servatoire at Brussels, published by Spitta in an Appendix to his *Life of Bach* (vol. iii
of the English translation, App. B, pp. 315–47). The title, in the handwriting of
Bach's pupil, Johann Peter Kellner (which, as Spitta tells us, is also noticeable further
on, in corrections and additions), runs as follows: 'Des Königlichen Hoff-*Compositeurs*
und Capellmeisters ingleichen *Directoris Musices* wie auch *Cantoris* der Thomas-
Schule Herrn *Johann Sebastian Bach* zu *Leipzig* Vorschriften und Grundsätze zum
vierstimmigen Spielen des *General-Bass* oder *Accompagnement,* für seine *Scholaren*
in der Music. 1738.' ('Instructions and rules for the playing of a Thorough-Bass in
four parts, or Accompaniment, by Master John Sebastian Bach, Royal Court Composer . . . , for the use of his scholars in Music. 1738.')

The recurring mis-spelling 'mo*dus*' for '*motus* contrarius' (which exhibits the Saxon
characteristic of failing to distinguish between *d* and *t*, *b* and *p*, &c.) seems to indicate
that the manuscript in question was either taken down from dictation, or (far more
probably) copied from one so taken down. The contents appear under four headings:

(1) 'Short Rules for what is called Thorough-Bass.'
(2) 'Fundamental Instruction (*Gründlicher Unterricht*) in Thorough-Bass', consisting of ten chapters, of which the first seven are taken almost verbatim from Niedt,

The chief interest of the *Handleitung* (Part I) lies, however, not so much in the actual rules and examples, which (though clearly and systematically arranged) contain little that we have not already met with, as in the extra-ordinarily vivid picture, contained in the Introduction, of the conditions under which the less fortunate among contemporary German Organists acquired and practised their art, and of the deadening influence of the German Organ Tablature already alluded to (cf. § 24, VII, 2).

II. *Niedt's Introduction.*

This Introduction, divided into twenty-four paragraphs (§§), and occupying twelve closely printed folios (as against the eighteen occupied by the treatise itself), is assuredly one of the quaintest ever written.

a (§§ I–IX in the original).

The author tells us how, on a certain beautiful day, when 'Flora had already clothed the fields with a many-coloured garment, and Pomona had already adorned the bare tree-tops afresh', he set forth into the country to revel in the beauties of Nature. In a valley, through which flowed a babbling brook, he lay down to rest, when he was startled by a deep sound, proceeding at intervals from a wood on his right, which at first he took to be the booming of a bittern.

The sound, however, seemed to grow nearer and louder, and, fearing that it might be a Satyr blowing his horn, he prepared to flee, when, lo and behold! two horsemen hove in sight, one of whom accosted him politely, saying: 'My good friend, if you are one of our company, follow us to the appointed place.'

They were on their way, it seemed, to a musical gathering (*Collegium Musicum*) to be held in a palace in the wood, and our author (whose flute they saw peeping out of his pocket, and who confessed to being a lover of Music, though not sufficiently accomplished to join in an impromptu per-formance, in spite of the fact that his 'apprentice years [*Lehr-Jahre*] were long past') gladly accepted their cordial invitation to join the party.

The mysterious sounds which had so terrified him proceeded, it appeared, not from either a bittern or a Satyr, but from a Positive Organ which their host, Florimon by name, had caused to be conveyed to the scene of the music-making, and which he was trying, in order to ascertain that it had taken no harm on the way.

though (in Cap. 6) there are certain omissions to be noticed in due course (cf. III, 6, note 10).

(3) 'Rules for playing *en quatre*', i.e. in groups of four notes, as:

(4) 'The most usual *clausulae finales*.'

The second of these four sections is followed by a number of additional examples. In these (as also in some of the examples given under the several rules) the setting-out of the figured Basses, which were apparently given by Bach to his pupils as exercises to be worked out by themselves, is (in many cases at least) glaringly incorrect, and is evidently the work of a not very intelligent beginner; there are also mistakes in the Basses themselves, and in the figuring; these may have been made when the Basses were taken down in the first instance, or, more probably, when the original manuscript was transcribed.

One of the two horsemen proved to be one Tacitus, Director of Music (*Capellmeister*) at 'Klingewoll', the story of whose life, presently to be related to the assembled company, is designed to prove that a sound knowledge of music can be best and most quickly attained by means of the study of Thorough-Bass.

This autobiographical monologue on the part of Tacitus is ingeniously led up to.

The scene of the musical gathering is 'a rather desolate palace' in a wood, 'and, in it, a great paved hall', in which Florimon was permitted by favour of the 'Landes-Obrigkeit' (presumably a petty prince) to hold his meeting, and to which he had caused his numerous paraphernalia to be conveyed.

Besides himself, twelve musicians were already assembled when our author with his two newly made friends came upon the scene.

When they had been duly welcomed, the music began. First, compositions of Florimon, who played the Thorough-Bass on his Positive Organ.

The performance seems to have been, at best, a rough-and-ready one, but 'all ended without particularly great confusion, so that one might say: *In fine videbitur cuius toni*'. Florimon concealed his chagrin at the faulty rendering of his compositions and hospitably caused 'a good-sized glass of wine to be poured out for each person'. The music then proceeded after an exchange of instruments, 'so that the person who had previously played the Violin now had to take the *Violabranio* [i.e. *Viola di braccio* or Tenor] and vice versâ', while Florimon took the *viola di gamba*, begging Tacitus to play the Thorough-Bass on the Organ, in which he was supported by one Mopsus (of whom more anon) on the *Violone*. 'A pause of some 100 bars (*ganze Schläge*) was made between all the pieces' to give time for a glass of wine, and our author remarks dryly that 'instrumentalists, too, know how to benefit by the adage: *Cantores amant humores*'.

At sundown the music was abandoned in favour of an excellent cold meal, to the delight of our author, who, as he explains, had tasted nothing since sunrise. 'There was also', he tells us, 'a good drink of wine, and likewise delicious Ceres-juice [i.e. beer] which we finally chose in preference to the wine.'

When the liquor had loosened the tongues of the company, trouble began.

Mopsus, 'who had just now been the worst music-spoiler', began to boast of how 'he had been for a full eight years under the tuition of a world-renowned Master, and, with great and untiring industry, had at last achieved such skill that he could not only himself put anything into the German Letter-Tablature, but could also play it straight off, after merely glancing through it'.

His neighbour, Fidelio, an Organist, ventured to remark that 'he had heard that there was a famous Master who thought nothing at all of the laborious German Tablature,[3] and could, nevertheless, in a short time teach a sensible person Music so thoroughly that he need not be ashamed to be heard by any one'. At this Mopsus 'nearly jumped out of his skin'. His friend, Coridon, told Fidelio that he, too, had heard this Master's praises sung, but

---

[3] It may be mentioned here that J. S. Bach was familiar with the German Organ Tablature, which he used in the last few bars of the Organ Chorale 'Der Tag, der ist so freudenreich', in the *Orgelbüchlein*, in order to save space and avoid encroaching on a fresh page.

that, in his opinion, if what he heard was true, 'forbidden supernatural arts must be employed'. Negligentius, who had been Organist in the same little town for fifty-six years, expressed himself in favour of 'keeping to the old ways'.

The discussion became general, and from words the excited company would soon have come to blows, had not Florimon had satellites, armed with old-fashioned partisans, within call.

During the lull which ensued, Florimon addressed Tacitus: 'Sir, I commend the modesty with which, though, in my opinion, you understand more about Art than all the rest of us, you have, nevertheless, listened with patience to so many absurdities.'

Tacitus made a dignified reply (in the course of which his quotation of Proverbs xxvi. 4, 'Answer not a fool according to his folly', provoked an outburst from Coridon, quickly quelled by the threatened intervention of the satellites with their partisans) ending with the words: 'I know by personal experience that, when as yet I knew next to nothing about Music, I was in my own opinion the most excellent Master, but, since my eyes were opened by my last preceptor, I have been ashamed of myself.'

'Asking your pardon, Sir, for interrupting,' said Florimon, 'I know that you had two preceptors who, in different and contrary ways, professed to teach you the principles (*Fundamenta*) of Music; some say that it was the first, others, that it was the last of the two whom you have most to thank for your knowledge; I beg you to be kind enough to give us your candid opinion on the subject.'

Tacitus replied that this would involve relating his whole career, which, at Florimon's earnest request, he consented to do; 'but this', he said, 'I must stipulate beforehand, that, even though I have to relate my own follies, no one shall laugh in his sleeve who has, perhaps, been a greater fool in his time than I have been, if he is not so at this very hour.'

His narrative, exaggerated as it may be, presents a vivid picture of contemporary musical conditions in the smaller towns and country districts of Germany, and of the baneful effects of a reactionary adherence to the Organ Tablature tradition.

In outline, shorn of many of its picturesque (and often comical) details, the story is as follows.

The Narrative of Tacitus

b (§§ X–XII).   His first apprenticeship.

When barely twelve years old, Tacitus, whose education from his sixth year (besides the reading, writing, and arithmetic learnt at school) had included singing and fiddling, for which he had great inclination, was placed by his father under the tuition of one Orbilius of 'Poltersheim', who enjoyed the reputation of being the best Organist in the neighbourhood.

The first few years were spent in learning the notes on the keyboard, the letters, &c., of the German Organ Tablature, 'including the crows'-feet which are intended to mark the time' (though the unfortunate pupil often wished that he were allowed to play from the notation with which he was already familiar), in learning to play a so-called 'Bergamasco' (which was, in reality, a popular song in Low-German dialect, 'Ripen garsten wille wi meyen' ['We will mow ripe barley'], 'sung by all the boys in the street'), a few Sarabandes,

&c., and a Chorale, and, finally, in attempting to learn by heart 'cruelly long Preludes, Toccatas, Chaconnes, Fugues, and other monstrosities'.

Orbilius, who encouraged his pupil's efforts by continually boxing his ears, slapping him on the mouth, filliping his nose, pulling his ears and hair, as well as with occasional doses of the strap, &c., assured him that, unless he mastered these compositions, he would never, as long as he lived, learn the *Basso Continuo*.[4]

Poor Tacitus did not realize that he was alluding to the Thorough-Bass (*General-Bass*), of which he had heard in connexion with his singing, and wondered 'what sort of a creature the *Basso Continuo* might be'.

Seven years had passed before he was able to play five Preludes, and 'the Chorales, or German Psalms, in two parts'.

At this point of the story Florimon considerably interrupted the narrator to administer a, doubtless, welcome glass of wine, bidding the rest of the company pledge him.

After this refreshment Tacitus proceeded with his narrative.

He was at length to receive instruction in Thorough-Bass, a prospect which filled him with the liveliest apprehension, for he had noticed that, when his master and the Cantor (or Choirmaster) rehearsed together, they constantly fell out on this very subject.

His experiences are best described in his own words: 'In teaching, my Preceptor adhered to the following plan: he showed me neither rules nor figures; the figures above the Bass were little better than Greek (*Böhmische Dörfer*) to him; he first played it [i.e. the figured Bass] to me once or twice, saying: "You must play it in such and such a way; that is how I learnt it." When I could not get on, you should have seen how keen my teacher was, and what excellent devices (*Inventiones*) he had for instilling the art into me. I caught the Sixth on the right, behind the ear, the Fourth on the left, the Seventh on my cheeks, the Ninth in my hair, the false [i.e. diminished] Fifth on my nose, the Second on my back, *Tertia minor* on my fingers, *Tertia major* and Fifth on the shins; *Decima* and *Undecima* were special kinds of boxes on the ear. It was by the place where the blow or push caught me that I was to know what I had to play, but the best of it was that the knocks on my shins made my feet beautifully nimble on the pedals (which I was at that time also beginning to learn). He also showed me how to put the Thorough-Bass into Tablature, whenever it was possible to procure the entire piece; but at times there was such stuff in it that, as it stood, neither my Preceptor nor I could play it.'

The end, however, soon came. Orbilius attempted to throw his pupil downstairs, but the latter caught him by the legs, with the result that they both landed in the street together.

Tacitus, whose parents had fortunately met the pecuniary claims of Orbilius previous to their death, which occurred a short time before the events just recorded, wisely betook himself to the house of a kind neighbour, and, having forced Orbilius by threats of legal action to hand over his effects, decided to seek his fortune.

---

[4] It may be noted that, up to a point, Orbilius was right. Ph. Em. Bach himself lays stress on the importance of learning 'Handsachen' (i.e. independent pieces, as opposed to anything played from a figured Bass) as a means of cultivating a good style in the treatment of a figured Bass (cf. *Versuch &c.*, Pt. 2, 1762, Introd. § 12).

With a little money, the legacy of his parents, in his pockets, he set forth into the world at the age of twenty-one, with a good conceit of himself and full of confidence that his nine years' apprenticeship with Orbilius had fully qualified him to earn his living as an Organist. He was soon to be undeceived!

(*The Narrative of Tacitus continued*)

c (§§ XIII–XIX). His experiences as Organist.

Having at length reached the province of 'Marcolphia', he happened, one Sunday, to enter a village church where Divine Service was in progress.

Every time the Organist made a cadence, he used his nose to get down an extra note, explaining afterwards that, had he recognized his visitor as a colleague, he would not have permitted him to witness this 'secret artistic device'. After the sermon, Tacitus (who carried a selection of music in his pocket), having asked permission to exhibit his skill, and obtained a some-what reluctant consent, performed one of his best Manual Preludes, and afterwards, as a final voluntary, a 'Tonata'. [It may here be remarked parenthetically that our author, Niedt, is much addicted to playfully coined or distorted words, as 'Tonata', suggested by 'Toccata' and 'Sonata', &c.; cf. notes 5 and 7.]

Orbilius seems at least to have imparted some technical skill to his unfor-tunate pupil, for his performance so impressed a nobleman who happened to be present, that he sent for him after the Service and promised to use his influence to procure him the post of Organist (which had recently fallen vacant) in a town near his own seat, the sole condition being that Tacitus should espouse his wife's maid. This offer was gratefully accepted, and Tacitus was there and then conveyed to the nobleman's seat.

He does not seem to have been daunted by the appearance of his pro-spective bride, Cornaria, who, we are told, 'had all the hues of beauty about her . . . only that the white and the red were not in the right place', for the red was in her rheumy eyes and the white in her hair, though the latter defect was not immediately noticeable 'because, like the crow in the fable, she had decked herself with borrowed plumes'.

Meanwhile, the day approached on which Tacitus was to give a public exhibition of his skill preparatory to his appointment as Organist; for this condition the authorities refused to waive, though it was promised that all due weight should be attached to his noble patron's recommendation. How-ever, all went well. 'Happily for me', he tells us, 'there was an old Cantor in this place, who had not forgotten much about Music, because he had never been very well versed therein, so that it was a case of "birds of a feather", as the proverb says, and I did not have to submit to being worried with Thorough-Bass (which I dreaded like the hangman).'

Tacitus was duly appointed and congratulated, and the annual audit of the Church accounts, to which he was bidden that very evening, afforded him an opportunity to meet both the ecclesiastical and civic authorities, an oppor-tunity which he used to boast of his own skill, and to disparage every one else.

The conceit which he displayed on this occasion was doubly unfortunate in view of subsequent events. 'One pastor', he tells us, 'praised a certain Organist of his acquaintance, from whom he had, for some months, had lessons on the Clavier; I was just wise enough not to contradict him publicly, but the praise of another caused me much inward mortification, and I at

once thought that my own authority was somewhat impaired thereby. . . .
I wrote an account of everything to my sweetheart, Cornaria, and, in particular, that I had got to a place where there were people who understood
music well, and regarded me as the most famous Master in the world, whereas,
to tell the honest truth, I was, in fact, a wretched bungler and could not
play anything worth hearing, beyond what was written in my book.'

The Organist alluded to above was one Prudentius, of whom we shall hear
presently.

Tacitus was now installed in his new office, but his good fortune was
destined to be shortlived.

Not only did he learn that his noble and influential patron had died suddenly, but, worse still, the old Cantor (of whom we have heard) died also,
and it fell to Tacitus to conduct the public trial of his successor and to set
the test-pieces.

The lame excuse 'that his things had not yet arrived' was promptly met
by the new Cantor with the suggestion that he should 'devote a few hours
to composing something new', a suggestion which was acclaimed by every
one except Tacitus himself.

To admit that he could not compose was out of the question, and the trial
was to take place on the following day!

While debating whether to stand his ground or run away, he had an
inspiration! He looked through all his fugues, and succeeded in finding one
which fitted the words *Laudate Dominum omnes gentes*, and so arranged it
that, when the subject was in the pedal part, the Cantor should sing in
unison with it.

The latter had brought a couple of instrumentalists with him, who offered
to assist with Violins or Cornets (*Zincken*), but Tacitus explained that it was
'vocal and not instrumental music that was contemplated for the trial, and that,
in the newly composed piece, he had, therefore, omitted the instruments.'

After a prelude on the full Organ the performance began, the full power
of the Organ being maintained 'in order that it might sound the more joyful'.
The Cantor 'sang full-throated' (as well he might!), and the two instrumentalists were bursting with laughter. Tacitus thought that it was the
Cantor who was the object of their ridicule, and it was only when the latter
exchanged glances with them and joined in their laughter that he was undeceived. The shock of this discovery was almost too much for him!

When the performance was over, the Cantor produced from his pocket
some vocal and instrumental pieces and begged Tacitus to play the Thorough-Bass. 'There I stood', he tells us, 'like butter in the sun.' He explained
that he would have been delighted to oblige, if he had been given the music
on the previous day, in order that he might have put it into Tablature, or,
at least, looked through it a few times, but that he could not undertake to
play so thickly figured a Bass at sight.

His services were easily dispensed with! One of the instrumentalists played
the Thorough-Bass upon the Organ, and the other played the Violin, while
the Cantor fiddled and sang at the same time, and the three of them seem to
have made delightful music and to have enchanted their audience.

There was nothing for it but for Tacitus to ask to be relieved of his office
and disappear from the scene.

The Cantor was appointed, as also were his two friends, of whom the one was to fill the post (and enjoy the salary) of Organist, while both were to act as 'Town-Musicians' at weddings and other festivities, dividing between them the money thus earned.

Fortunately for Tacitus, the loss of his appointment gave him a welcome excuse for ending his engagement to Cornaria.

(*The Narrative of Tacitus continued*)

d (§ XX). He makes a fresh start.

Completely humbled, he wisely resolved 'to wipe out his disgrace and enter an apprenticeship once more, under Prudentius'. This was the Organist concerning whom he had heard (on the occasion already alluded to), 'that he was also a Composer of outstanding excellence. Although he lived at "Schönhall", over 60 miles [i.e. over 200 English miles] away,' Tacitus told the company, 'I was willing to take the long journey rather than remain an ignoramus and a failure (*verdorbener Mensch*) all my days.'

Prudentius received him kindly, and, after questioning him closely as to the instruction which he had already received, addressed him as follows:

'My friend, since I perceive in you so earnest a desire to become a sound musician, I cannot find it in my heart, though, as it is, I have a full day's work, to let you return hence disappointed. Provided that you have the money to stay in this town for a year, I will, during that time, impart to you the fundamental principles both of the Organist's art and of Composition, so that, from being a bungler, you shall become an Organist,[5] and I do not ask a single farthing for my trouble, but if you will promise to be diligent, and to use your art to the glory of God, I will instruct you gratuitously every day for an hour, from 7 to 8 in the morning, and, besides, you can come to my house whenever you like and practise by yourself in a room where there are several Claviers.'

Prudentius at once began to instruct his pupil in Thorough-Bass, for 'in this', said he, 'is comprised the entire foundation of practical Music (*Musica practica*) and Composition, and it is with this that I start with all my pupils; from it they derive this benefit, that they do not need to trouble their heads about that precious (*verdienlich*) Tablature, and, after many years' study, remain Paper-Organists after all, but that they become, in a short time, good sound Musicians (*Fundamental-Musici*).'

At the end of a year Prudentius dismissed his pupil with the following valediction: 'Well, my dear Tacitus, I have so far grounded you in Music that you need no longer bear the name of a blunderer (*eines Argenisten*), but of a proper Organist, Musician, and Composer. Go hence, and use it to the glory of your God, and, if you find any one who is anxious to learn the art, impart it to him for nothing, just as you have received it from me without recompense, and as I have, at your request, faithfully dictated it to you.'

Tacitus took leave of his kind teacher with tears and many expressions of gratitude, and returned to his native parts, where he subsequently attained the honourable position in which we first found him.[6]

And so ends his narrative. 'To do the bidding of Master Florimon', he concluded, 'I have been obliged to tell you all this at such length; if I have thereby displeased any one among this company, I will gladly ask his pardon.'

---

[5] *dass ihr aus einem Argenisten ein Organiste werden sollet*: the coined word 'Argenist' (from *arg* = 'bad') and the pun are alike untranslatable.   [6] See p. 216 *sup.*

e (§§ XXI–XXIV). Conclusion.

After expressing his thanks—and after the company had duly quenched their thirst—Florimon proceeded to point the moral of the narrative to which they had just listened. 'I must admit', he said, 'that Master Prudentius adopted the right course with Tacitus; I know the man, moreover, and know that he starts his pupils in Thorough-Bass at once, in which, if they know their notes and can count twenty, they so perfect themselves in a year that it is a pleasure to witness. I know, too, that in so teaching them he shows them how to make a Fugue and the like *ex tempore*, and that, when they can play fairly well from a Thorough-Bass, he sometimes, by way of recreation, lets them play Allemandes, Courantes, &c., or the like, from the notes [i.e. full musical notation as opposed to a figured Bass], in order that they may be able to imitate the graces (*Manieren*) in them; they find that much easier than learning the German Tablature; and I do not heed what some say to the contrary, to the effect that one should keep to the old ways. The old Germans deserve all respect, and, in their time, attained a very high standard with the Tablature: 60 years ago, or a little more, one hardly ever saw a German Organist who played from a Thorough-Bass or from notes. But, since a better and truer, and an easy way has been found, why should not the old humdrum (*die alte Leyer*) be abandoned? The Italians have never used any German Tablature, but, for untold years, nothing but notes, and this very fact is the real reason why they have, for so long, undoubtedly borne the palm above us Germans.'

This provoked a patriotic protest from the veteran Negligentius, and Florimon continued: 'Yes, I know well that many German Organists are now not far behind the foreigners in their art, if they do not, in certain matters, excel them; but the fact remains that the reason of it is that they have accustomed themselves to play from a Thorough-Bass so much earlier than used to be the case, whereas, according to the doctrine of Prudentius (who can never be praised highly enough), this should come at the very beginning; for then one would notice the splendid effect on pupils, and, finally, no one would any longer be able to say shamelessly that people who had not been learning for nine or ten years, but had acquired their art in a short time, must have been to school with a magician.'

The speech ends with an appropriate allusion to the judgement of Midas.

Our author then tells us how the company continued their discussions and music-making (and doubtless their potations) till night-fall, and how he sought the tuition of Tacitus, who taught him faithfully, just as he himself had been taught by Prudentius, and: 'Just as my preceptor faithfully taught me,' Niedt concludes, 'so will I, too, in the following First Part of my Musical Guide, or Instruction in Thorough-Bass (as also in the subsequent Second Part), faithfully impart everything to Music-lovers and those eager for information, and, moreover, in the first place, the proper way to learn to play from a Thorough-Bass, in the hope that I may, thereby, be doing many people a signal service which Christian love, too, demands of me, not heeding what some contrary-minded persons may think [7] about it.'

III. The treatise itself comprises twelve short chapters which we will now briefly consider:

[7] *kuhdiciren*: a playful alteration of the word *judiciren*, suggesting a reference to *Kuh* = 'cow'.

1. 'Cap. I. Von der *Etymologiâ* des *General-Basses* oder woher Er also genen-
    net wird.' ('On the etymology of the *Bassus generalis* and why it is
    so called.')

Niedt tells us that the word *Bassus* is derived by some from the Greek
noun *basis* (= 'foundation'), by others from the Latin adjective *bassus*
(= 'deep'), and that the *Bassus generalis* (Germ. *General-Bass*) is so called
because "all, or nearly all the other parts of the music are comprised *genera-
liter*, that is to say in common (*insgemein*), in this single part".

He adds: "It is also called *Bassus Continuus*, or, with the Italian termina-
tion, *Basso Continuo*, because it plays on continuously, whereas the other
parts occasionally pause the while. But nowadays this Bass, too, frequently
pauses, especially in Operas and ingeniously (*künstlich*) composed secular
pieces; moreover, any Violone-Bass might be styled a *Bassus Continuus*;[8] therefore the name *Bassus Generalis* (*General-Bass*) seems more convenient here."

2. 'Cap. II. Von der *Definition* oder Beschreibung des *General-Basses*.' ('On
    the definition or description of the Thorough-Bass.')

"The Thorough-Bass (*General-Bass*) is the completest foundation of the
music, and is played on a keyboard (*Clavier*) with both hands, in such a way
that the left hand plays the prescribed (*vorgeschrieben*) notes, while the right
hand strikes the appropriate consonances and dissonances, so that an agreeable
harmony may be produced, to the glory of God and for the permissible
gladdening of the heart (*Ergetzung des Gemühts*)."

Niedt goes on to comment at some length on this definition, explaining
that he uses the word 'completest' to distinguish the 'general' Bass from that
played on the Violone, Bassoon, &c., instruments which produce only a single
note at a time.

He further explains that when a large body of from ten or twenty to thirty
voices is employed, an expert Organist may play the 'fundamental notes' on
the pedals and 'exhibit his skill at pleasure'.

No mention is made of occasionally dividing the harmony between the
two hands.

Then follows a classification of the consonances and dissonances:

Perfect consonances (which cannot be altered, and yet remain concordant),
the Fifth and Octave.

Imperfect consonances (which may be either major or minor), the Third
and Sixth.

Perfect dissonances, the Fourth, false [i.e. diminished] Fifth, and Eleventh.

Imperfect dissonances, the Second, Seventh, and Ninth.

Niedt gives the following curious and obscure explanation of the term
'perfect dissonances': "The reason is that they arise from the Perfect Consonances, for the Fourth comes from the Octave or Fifth, the false Fifth
from the Octave, and the Eleventh, in every case, from the Fifth."

No mention is made of the augmented Fourth, though the interval itself
(with its figuring) occurs later in the work, in the examples (cf. 8 c).

The conclusion of the chapter deserves to be quoted in full:

"Finally, the end or final cause of all Music, and, therefore, of the *Bassus*

---

[8] J. S. Bach applied the term *Continuo* to the unfigured part used by the Bass
instruments (both strings and wind) playing in unison with, and supporting the
Organ, as well as to the figured Organ-part. According to Niedt's definition, the term
'*General-Bass*' applies only to the Bass *plus* the harmony indicated by the figures.

generalis (*General-Bass*) as well, must be nothing but just the glory of God and the recreation of the mind (*Recreation des Gemühts*); if this be not kept in mind, there is no real Music, and those who misuse this noble and divine Art as tinder, to kindle lust and carnal desires, are Devil's musicians, for Satan delights in hearing such shameful things; for him such Music is good enough, but in the ears of God it is a shameful din (*ein schändliches Geplär*). Whoever, then, along with his musical profession, wants to enjoy the grace of God and a good conscience, let him not dishonour this noble gift of God by misusing it for disreputable purposes."

3. 'Cap. III. Von denen *Clavibus signatis* die im *General-Bass* vorkommen.' ('On the clefs which occur in a Thorough-Bass.')

The nine clefs in common use are given in the following order:

(1) French Violin clef 𝄞 ; (2) German Violin clef 𝄞 ; (3) Treble

(*Discant*), or *Cantus* 𝄡 ; (4) High Alto, or Low Treble [9] 𝄡 ;

(5) Ordinary Alto 𝄡 ; (6) Tenor 𝄡 ; (7) Ordinary Bass 𝄢 ;

(8) High Bass [9] 𝄢 ; (9) Low Bass 𝄢 .

Niedt adds: "The High Bass clef on the middle line is commonly called a *Bassetto* (*Basset*); all the other high clefs, when they occur in a Thorough-Bass, are called *Little Bassetti* (*Bassetgen*)."

In later German treatises of the eighteenth century the terms *Basset* and *Bassetgen* were applied indifferently (as by Niedt himself in his Cap. X) to *C* and *G* clefs used in the Thorough-Bass.

Niedt also makes the following observation: "Although I have no opinion of German Tablature, as far as learning to play from it is concerned, I, nevertheless, find one good point about it, namely, that the *claves* or notes, in their sequence on the keyboard, can be conveniently named in accordance with it, as: the large [or capital] *E*, the large *D*, and so on; the *c*, *d*, *e*, &c., with two strokes; the *f*, *g*, *h*, &c., with one stroke; the *d*, *e*, *f*, &c., without a stroke; which method will, therefore, be observed by me in this treatise" (cf. § 24, III *ad init.*).

4. 'Cap. IV. Von dem *Tact* oder *Mensur*' ('On Time or Measure').

No details are given, on the ground that the student of Thorough-Bass is supposed to know the intervals and, also, the differences of time.

Niedt adds: "This a learner must note, that, nowadays, common time (*ein schlechter Tact*) is indicated in two ways, as: ₵ 2 . The second way is used by the French in such pieces as are to be played briskly and quickly. The Italians and Germans, however, in sacred Church Music, generally adhere to the first way, and keep a slow and solemn (*gravitätisch*) time; if it is to go quickly the Composer expressly puts *allegro* or *presto* underneath. . . ."

---

[9] Niedt mentions that the High Alto (sometimes known as *Mezzo Soprano*), as also the High Bass (sometimes known as Barytone) clefs are much used by French composers. It may also be mentioned here that the French Violin clef (No. 1) is to be found in English publications for the Violin in the eighteenth century, as e.g. in Michael Christian Festing's *Opera Prima* (London, William Smith), Sonata vi, Allegro.

5. 'Cap. V. Von der TRIADE HARMONICA' ('On the harmonic Triad').
The *Trias Harmonica*, or combination of Third and Fifth,

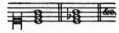

may appear, we are told, in three forms:

(1) "*Radix simplex*, that is to say, the simple and properly so called Triad, consists of only three notes as shown in the above example."

(2) "*Radix aucta*, that is to say, the increased Triad, has as its companion the Octave, that the harmony may be varied and more complete; for example:

(3) "*Radix diffusa*, that is to say, the scattered Triad, is scattered over different Octaves; e.g.

In connexion with the latter, Niedt adds the rule: "The closer the notes are together, the better the harmony (*Symphonie*)."

6. 'Cap. VI. Etliche allgemeine Regeln beym Spielen des General-Basses zu observiren' ('Some general rules to be observed in playing a Thorough-Bass').

These rules contain little that we have not already met with elsewhere, but they are worth quoting owing to the fact that J. S. Bach used some of them in teaching his own pupils.[10]

'Reg[ula] 1'. "The prescribed Thorough-Bass is played with the left hand alone, the other parts (whether indicated by figures or not) with the right hand."

'Reg. 2'. "The right hand inclines to keep (*Mit der rechten Hand bleibt man gerne*) within the 2-foot Octave ⟦♪⟧, and does not go higher than $\bar{\bar{e}}$ with two strokes, or, at most, $\bar{\bar{f}}$, and not farther down than *a, g*, without a stroke."

'Reg. 3'. "As many Sixths and Thirds as one pleases may be taken in succession,[11] unless a figure over the Bass forbids."

'Reg. 4'. "The Third is taken with all figures, unless the Second or Fourth prevent."

'Reg. 5'. "Two Fifths and two Octaves must not follow one upon the other, for that is a fault (*vitium*) and sounds bad. To avoid it, there is an old rule that the hands should always move in opposite directions: that, when the left hand ascends, the right should descend; and, conversely, that, when the left hand descends, the right hand should ascend in the Treble."

'Reg. 6'. "To avoid two Octaves and two Fifths, the best plan is to invoke the aid of the Sixth and use it in alternation" (*Zwo Quinten und zwo Octaven*

[10] In the manuscript described in note 2 (q.v.) only four of Niedt's nine rules are given, Reg. 2, 3, 7, 8, 9 being omitted.

[11] The procedure here indicated is fully illustrated by Ph. Em. Bach (cf. Ch. iv, § 5, *c, d, e*).

zu vermeiden | ist diss der beste Vortheil dass man die Sexte mit zu Hülffe nimmt | und damit umwechselung hält).[12]

'Reg. 7'. "When the Bass or Little *Bassetto (Bassetgen,* cf. 3, p. 224) goes high up, one must follow it with the right hand, and the consonances and dissonances are played in the same Octave [13] as that in which the Little *Bassetto* is *(und werden die Con- und Dissonantien dazu gespielet in eben derselben Octave in der das Bassetgen steht)."*

[12] This rule would seem to apply to composition rather than to playing from a figured Bass. It is not, however, among those omitted by J. S. Bach (cf. note 10).

The rule, as it stands, seems to suggest that, instead of employing the contrary motion prescribed in Reg. 5, such Fifths and Octaves as:

should be avoided by the interposition of a Sixth (not indicated in the figuring, and irrespective of the vocal or instrumental principal parts) as:

And yet, it seems hardly possible that this was meant. In the case of (c), it is true,

the $\frac{6}{5}$ chord: , resulting from the Fifth (which we may presume to

be present) in the principal parts and the Sixth in the accompaniment, would have its proper resolution; but not so in the case of (d).

Marpurg, who, in a general way, disallows the justification of consecutive Octaves by the interposition of an imperfect consonance (*Handbuch bey dem Generalbasse,* Pt. 1, 1755, Section [*Abschnitt*] II [2nd ed., 1762, p. 90]), gives the following example (Tab. IV, Fig. 8) as permissible "in compositions in several parts (*mehrstimmigen Sachen*) if the movement be not too quick":

[13] The meaning evidently is that the accompaniment should be kept within the compass of an Octave above the Bass notes to which a C (or G) clef is prefixed. It is, however, clear that this is sometimes impossible, as e.g. in the following passage, in which the preparation and resolution of the Seventh (B flat) at * necessitate the interval of a Tenth between the extreme parts at † †:

Heinichen's rule for the accompaniment of *Bassetti (General-Bass &c.,* 1728, Pt. I,

'Reg. 8'. "If the Singer or Instrumentalist sings or plays the intervals figured above the Thorough-Bass (*Wann der Sänger oder Instrumentist die Zahlen welche über dem General-Bass gesetzt sind | singet oder spielet*), it is not necessary that the Organist should play them: instead, he can just play Thirds [cf. Reg. 4], according as seems fitting; or, if he prefers to do something more elaborate (*etwas künstlichers*), it is at his own discretion." [14]

'Reg. 9'. "The figures which appear one above another over the Bass are struck simultaneously, but those which are placed one after the other are played one after the other, in due order."

7. 'Cap. VII. Wie man einen schlechten General-Bass, der keine Zahlen vonnöthen hat, spielen solle' ('How to play a simple Thorough-Bass which needs no figures').

Niedt takes a simple Bass:  and shows the

three positions:  in which the chords

(Triads) may be played over it.

He further shows how either the upper parts (*a*), or the Bass itself (*b*) may be varied by playing them *arpeggio*:

This latter part of the chapter is omitted by J. S. Bach (cf. note 2), and it is evident, as far as the variation of the Bass itself is concerned, that Niedt was thinking, not so much about an ordinary accompaniment, as about the free extemporizations on a figured Bass (in which even the rhythm of the Bass is subject to variation, triple time being substituted for quadruple, &c.) which forms the subject of the Second Part of the *Handleitung* (cf. note 1).

The chapter ends with examples of consecutive Fifths and Octaves, showing how they may be avoided by employing contrary motion, where necessary.

8. 'Cap. VIII. Von den [*sic*] bezifferten General-Bass' ('Concerning a figured Thorough-Bass').

This chapter consists of twelve rules illustrated by examples. It will be enough to mention certain points connected with them:

(*a*) With regard to the Sixth ($\frac{6}{3}$), Niedt does not mention the possibility of either the 6 or the 3 being doubled, still less of the possibility of either interval being doubled in the unison; he also expressly forbids the doubling of the Bass, in all of which respects he is far behind Saint-Lambert (cf. §23, Exx. 29–31).

He tells us (Reg. 2) that: "Where a Sixth is figured over the Bass note,

Ch. 5, § 18, p. 516) is far clearer: "The harmony over the *Bassetto* may be played with both hands—but with a discreet regard to whether there are many or few instrumental and ˙vocal parts co-operating (*jedoch nach Discretion der vielen oder wenigen dazu spielenden und singenden Stimmen*)—in as many parts *as the available space in the upper Octaves of the keyboard permits.*" [The italics are the present writer's.] It must be remembered, of course, that the compass that Heinichen had in mind was that of the Organs and Harpsichords, &c., of the early eighteenth century.

[14] It will be remembered that Werckmeister gives a less general rule, to the effect that a *dissonance*, occurring in the Solo part, *may* (even though figured) be best omitted in the accompaniment (cf. § 24, VII, 1 *b*).

one takes no more than the Third in addition; the Octave must be omitted both in composing and playing."

He also tells us that Sixths (whether indicated in the figuring or not) are to be played: (1) on any bass note accidentally sharpened (Reg. 1), and (2) on A, B, and E, "when A is followed by B flat, E by F, B by C", and vice versâ (Reg. 5),—in other words, on the lower of the two notes when the Bass rises or falls a semitone.

We saw that, in such cases, Werckmeister wisely insisted on the note in question being figured 5, if a Sixth were not intended (cf. § 24, VI, 7).

(*b*) In giving the rule (Reg. 6) that the final chord must always be taken with the *major* Third, irrespective of what precedes it, as:

[Ex. 1]

Niedt adds: "I know very well, it is true, that French composers do the opposite, but everything is not good just because it comes from France, or derives its name from there. . . ."

(*c*) Niedt gives the following details regarding the actual use of figures:

(1) In Reg. 4 he gives ⟂, ⟂, ⟂, ⟂, ⟂ as the alternatives of 2✕, ✕4, 5✕, 6✕, 7✕,[15] which alone were in use in the earlier Basses, but, in the example which follows (but which it is unnecessary to quote here), he uses the still later forms 6̶, 4̷.

(2) Reg. 7 runs as follows:

"Where there are full closes (*Cadenz-Clausuln*), as $^{7\,6\,5}_{3\,4\,4\,3}$, or, also, $^{5\,6\,5}_{✕\,4\,4}$✕, they are called *Syncopationes*, because they are as it were bound together and entangled (*weil sie sich gleichsam verbinden und verwickeln*); sometimes, too, they are indicated by single figures (*einfach gesetzt*), but are, nevertheless, played in full, just as though they were fully (*ausdrücklich*) figured as above mentioned. In the case of entire beats [*ganze Schläge*, i.e. semibreves] the cadences are also composed (*gesetzt*) as follows: $^{5\,6\,5\,6}_{3\,4\,3\,4}$ $^{7\,6\,5\,6}_{2\,3\,4\,3\,4}$ $^{5}_{4}$✕ [$=^{5}_{4\,3}$✕]; in such case, no intervals are held over from the previous chord (*alsdann lieget nichts*) till the end:

[Ex. 2]

[1]   [2]   [3]   [4]   [5]   [6]

[7]   [8]   [9]   [10]   [11]   [12]

---

[15] The position of ✕ or ♭, before or after the figure to which it applies, is quite arbitrary, and depends largely on individual habit: thus, Ph. Em. Bach (in Pt. 2 of his *Versuch*) always has ♭7, but 5♭; Niedt has ✕4 and 4✕ at random.

N.B.—In the above example some obvious errors in notation (omission of stems of notes), probably due to misprints, have been corrected.

In bar 4 it is impossible to tell whether  or  (com-

pare bar 8) was intended: in his examples Niedt sometimes uses black stemless notes (in the inner parts) as *minims* (cf. Ex. 3ª), while, on the other hand, the stems of many crotchets are inadvertently omitted; in the original the bar in question appears as

follows: ; the ambiguity is obvious.

The above example shows awkward and unnecessary alternations between 3- and 4-part harmony. It also exhibits the close (with the Fifth of the Tonic in the upper part) which at a later period was forbidden in accompaniment. Mattheson, in his edition of the Second Part of Niedt's *Handleitung* (cf. note 1), takes occasion to correct this supposed fault.

(*d*) Reg. 8 is worth quoting in full because of the glimpse which it gives of Niedt's method of treating a figured Bass during a prolonged pause of the principal part or parts, when something more interesting than plain chords is to be expected of the accompanist:

"When there are quick notes or notes with tails [*geschwänzte Noten*, i.e. quavers or semiquavers] in the Thorough-Bass, one must not take the Third and Fifth with each note, nor play all the figures (when there are many of them over the Bass),[16] but only [strike a chord] with the first note [i.e. quaver or semiquaver] of a half-bar [i.e. minim] or crotchet: the other notes are called passing-notes (*Durchläufer*), because they, as it were, steal by un-noticed, e.g.:

"Supposing a Bass were first written quite simply:

[Ex. 3]

"and were then varied:

[Ex. 3ª]

[N.B.—The black stemless notes on the upper stave, of course, have the value of minims.]

[16] It is difficult to understand why Niedt should, in this case, have instructed the accompanist to disregard the intentions of the composer as expressed by the figures If, for instance, the above Bass were figured as follows:

and if the harmony represented by these figures were present in the vocal or instrumental parts, the chords shown in Ex. 3ª would (especially on the Organ) clash disagreeably with the said harmony. Niedt must, in framing his rule, have had some case in mind where no such clash would be produced.

It may be noted here, in passing, that, in giving rules for the treatment of quick

"It is after such fashion that the Treble is played with all quick Basses. But if it happened that a Solo occurred in the Thorough-Bass, the Organist must then play more elaborately (*manierlicher*) than when music is going on *vocaliter* and *instrumentaliter* at the same time. Supposing that the above Bass occurred in the course of a musical performance as a Solo (as it is called), that is, if it had to be played alone; the Treble is then played in the following fashion, and, for the most part, in Thirds [with the Bass], because they make a pleasant harmony:

[Ex.3ᵇ]

(*e*) Reg. 9–12, illustrated by examples, deal with the intervals requiring preparation. They are, in substance, as follows:

(1) When a bass note is figured 4 3 or $\frac{5}{4}$ ✕, the 4 must be retained from the previous chord (*in den Fingern schon zuvor liegen*).

(2) When a note is figured $\frac{4}{2}$ or $\frac{6}{4}{}_{2}$, there is no preparation (*so liegt nichts*): "it is a chord of simple percussion (*ein gemeiner Schlag*)."

N.B.—Niedt omits to mention that the Bass itself, as the discordant note, requires preparation.

(3) When a note is figured $\frac{6}{5}$, the Fifth must be retained from the previous chord.

(4) When a note is figured 5 6, the Fifth must always be prepared (*so muss die Quinta erst allezeit liegen*), but when the Sixth precedes the Fifth (6 5), no preparation is needed.

The following example is given, in which the difficulties arising in the case of a 5 6 sequence when played in four-part harmony, treated in great detail by Ph. Em. Bach (cf. *Versuch &c.*, Pt. 2, 1762, Ch. 3, I, § 16), are entirely ignored:

[Ex. 4]   56 56   56 56   56 65   ♮ 65   6 5   5 4 ✕

The awkwardness of the progression between bars 3 and 4 will be noticed, as also the *Tierce de Picardie* (not indicated in the figuring) at the end (cf. *b*).

(5) "When the false [i.e. diminished] Fifth 5♭ is figured, it must always

notes in the Bass, Niedt (like Locke and Blow, and others) is less precise than Bianciardi and Sabbatini, both of whom carefully distinguish between notes moving by step and those interspersed with leaps (cf. § 11, v. 6–8, and § 17, III *h*. 4). As already mentioned, Heinichen was the first to treat the matter exhaustively, first in his *Neu erfundene und gründliche Anweisung &c.*, 1711, and afterwards in his monumental *General-Bass &c.*, 1728.

be prepared (*liegen*); the Sixth and Third are played with it $\left(\begin{smallmatrix}6\\ \flat 5\\ 3\end{smallmatrix}\right)$ whether they are figured or not."

N.B.—Although Niedt requires the diminished Fifth (in a $\begin{smallmatrix}6\\5\end{smallmatrix}$ chord on the leading note) to be prepared, it will be noticed that, in his next chapter (Cap. IX), he allows the Dominant Seventh itself to be taken unprepared. Marpurg, an enthusiastic follower of Rameau, was probably the first German writer to bring the three inversions of the Dominant Seventh into line with the parent chord, in his *Handbuch bey dem Generalbasse*, Part I, 1755.

9. 'Cap. IX. Einige Anmerckungen von der *Septima, Nona, Undecima, und andern neben folgenden Zahlen*' ('Some remarks on the Seventh, Ninth, Eleventh, and other figures which follow next them').

The examples given in this chapter exhibit the same alternation between three- and four-part harmony as those already quoted. All Sixths (and suspended Sevenths resolving on Sixths) are taken in three parts as a matter of course (cf. 8, *a*), as well as some other chords, as will be seen.

The Dominant Seventh—though not alluded to by that name—is taken in four parts, so as to include the Fifth, and is figured in full $\begin{smallmatrix}7\\5\\3\end{smallmatrix}$. It has the same irregular resolution (rising a degree to the Fifth of the Tonic chord) as we saw in the examples of Locke, Blow, and Saint-Lambert. It is also worthy of note that Niedt allows it to be taken unprepared, although in the case of its first inversion, the 'false Fifth', he insists on preparation (cf. 8, *e*. 5).

The rules and examples are as follows:

(1) "Where the Seventh is figured, it must always be prepared (*in den Fingern liegen*), and no more than the Third is struck with it; where it is suitable, one can take the Fifth in addition." 7^{17}

(2) "Where the Seventh and Sixth are figured side by side, the Seventh must always be prepared (*zuvor liegen*); the Sixth is struck afterwards, and the Third taken with them." 7 6

(3) "Where the Seventh, Fifth, and Third are figured one above another, nothing is prepared: it is a chord of simple percussion (*ein gemeiner Schlag*)." $\begin{smallmatrix}7\\5\\3\end{smallmatrix}$

(4) "When the Seventh, Fifth, Fourth, and Third are figured thus, above and beside one another, the Fourth must, as above mentioned, be prepared (*liegen*). The Seventh and Fifth are struck together, while, meantime, the Fourth is held (*lieget*), and straightway resolves on the Third." $\begin{smallmatrix}7\\5\\4\ 3\end{smallmatrix}$

N.B.—The numbers in brackets below the examples refer to the above rules.

[Ex. 5]

---

[17] In the original, by an obvious misprint, 7 6 is printed opposite this rule.

[Ex. 6]

(3)

(4)

(5) "Where the Ninth and Octave are figured, the Ninth must always be prepared (*zuvor liegen*); the Octave is struck afterwards; the Fifth and Third can be taken with the Ninth and the Octave."

9 8

(6) "Or, again, when the Ninth and Seventh, Octave and Sixth are figured thus, $\frac{9\ 8}{7\ 6}$, the $\frac{9}{7}$ is first prepared, and the $\frac{8}{6}$ is struck afterwards."

9 8
7 6

(7) "At times, too, the following figures, Eleventh and Ninth, Tenth and Octave, occur one above another, thus, $\frac{11\ 10}{9\ 8}$; then the $\frac{11}{9}$ is first prepared, and the $\frac{10}{8}$ struck afterwards."

11 10
9 8

[Ex. 7]

(5)

(6)

(7)

10. 'Cap. X. Von denen Bassetgen und Fugen im General-Bass' ('On the Little *Bassetti* [18] and Fugues in a Thorough-Bass').

"It is not always the Bass down below in the two deep Octaves [C to c'] which

[18] i.e. C or G clefs (cf. III. 3 of the present §, also Ch. iii, § 6).

is the lowest part: the Ordinary and the Low Treble  ,

likewise the Alto and Tenor, may serve as Bass (*den Bass führen*). A high
foundation-part (*Fundament-Stimme*) of this kind is called a *Bassetto* or Little
Bassetto: [19]

[Ex. 8]

N.B.—The stemless black notes, which, in the above example, Niedt uses more

[19] In Cap. III Niedt applied the term 'Bassetto' (*Basset*) to the F clef on the
middle line, and 'Little Bassetto' (*Bassetgen*) to the C and G clefs. The ordinary
practice of German writers of the eighteenth century was, however, to apply the terms
Basset and *Bassetgen* indifferently to the C (or G) clefs occurring in a Thorough-Bass.

[20] In the above example the following points demand notice:

(1) In the first half of bar 1, where three quavers, bearing the same harmony, are
preceded by a quaver rest, the usual practice would have been to strike the chord *on
the rest* (to mark the time for the other performers), or on the second quaver (cf.
Ph. Em. Bach, *Versuch &c.*, Pt. 2, 1762, Ch. 37, Ex. *a*).

(2) In bar 4 the harmony is taken in two parts only, a matter which was at the
discretion of the accompanist (cf. the extract from Heinichen given in note 13). In
the case of a *Bassetto*, the accompanist would be more than usually careful not to
exceed the upward compass of the principal vocal or instrumental part or parts, and
thus obscure their effect. In the present case, moreover, a better upper part is secured
than if the harmony had been taken in three or four parts, either with a skip of
a Ninth in the upper part from the third beat of bar 3, as:

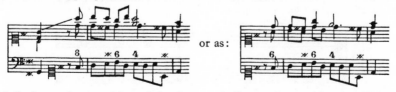

or as:

(3) In bar 5 the repetition of the figure 3 indicates that nothing but Thirds are
required.

(4) In the last bar, the figuring $\frac{6}{5}$ on C is an obvious misprint. The harmony shown

abundantly than usual, have not been here reproduced; in the original, the last bar appears as follows:

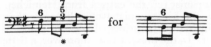

One or two obvious omissions have also been rectified.

"When Fugues [21] occur in a Thorough-Bass, it is to be noted that a Fugue consists of no more than two parts, and yet a Fugue can be written and composed with from three, four, ten, to twenty parts. In a Fugue, sometimes the left hand, and sometimes the right begins first alone. The first two parts are generally written one above the other,[22] so that it may easily be seen how it is to be played:

[Ex. 9]

[Left Hand]

[Right Hand]

N.B.—In bars 7, 13, 25 of the original, the figures 76, and in the last bar 43, are placed together (perhaps intentionally) over the first quaver (the dominating note) of the group. The interpretation is as indicated above.

in the upper parts demands, strictly speaking, the figuring $\frac{7}{5}_2$, but Niedt probably intended $\frac{7}{5}$ only: in those days ambiguous figurings abounded, as we have seen in connexion with Saint-Lambert (cf. § 23, *d*, Exx. 1, 2, 4, 9). The formula was common enough, and is a good example of *anticipatio transitus per ellipsin* (cf. Ch. xxii, § 7):

When the time was quick the chord in question was often not figured at all, as in the following two examples from Heinichen (*General-Bass &c.*, Part 1, Ch. IV, § 20 *ad fin.*, p. 282; § 33 *ad fin.*, p. 324):

[21] The term *Fugue* here includes any form of imitation.
[22] These 'cues' were played exactly as written, no chords being added till indicated by the presence of figures.

"If God will, the kind Music-lover shall be given proper instruction in the other Parts for treating Fugues *ex tempore*. For the present we have only had to do with Thorough-Bass. The whole art of playing it is contained in the above few rules and remarks."

11. 'Cap. XI. Wie man manierlich aus einem Thon in den andern fallen sol' ('How to get elegantly from one key to another').

In this chapter Niedt presents three ways of modulating:

(*a*) By a circle of keys descending by alternate major and minor Thirds: C major, A minor, F major, &c. The circle, however, is broken: after passing from B flat major to G minor, instead of proceeding to E♭ major, a close is made on the *major* chord of G, and the transition is to E minor, and so back to C:

[Ex. 10]

(*b*) By taking a Sixth on the leading note (accidentally sharpened if necessary) of the new key, as:

[Ex. 11]   D [minor]   to   E [minor]

(*c*) By a circle of keys *ascending* by alternate major and minor Thirds: C major, E minor, G major, &c. Here again there is a break in the circle, the transition made from B minor to D *minor*:

[Ex. 12]   B [minor]   to   D [minor]

After this, F major and A minor follow in due course, and C major is reached again.

A far greater sense of key-relationship (as well as ingenuity) was displayed, only a few years later, by Johann David Heinichen in the 'musical circle', which will be mentioned in its proper place.

12. 'Cap. XII'.

Niedt's twelfth and last chapter (the only one without a heading) contains nothing but a list of sixteen key-signatures (C, D, E, F, G, A, B flat, B, both major and minor) and need not detain us, save to note the inconsistency with which, in certain cases, the author gives alternative signatures (D minor with or without a flat, G minor with or without E♭, A major with or without G sharp), while, in others, only the full complement of flats or sharps is given. The omission of a flat in the signature of a minor key, and that of a sharp in a major one, is, of course, a relic of the Doric and Mixolydian modes, respectively.

The chapter ends with a valedictory Conclusion (*Beschluss*), from which the following modest words deserve to be quoted: "I admit that there are many excellent Masters in the world, who could have carried out the instruction in Thorough-Bass far better than I have done; but since, so far as I know, there has been no one who has written anything fundamental (*gründlich*) on this subject, and most of the descriptions of Thorough-Bass which are already in print and accessible [23] are not for beginners and pupils, but only for those who can play a Thorough-Bass almost perfectly, and are very difficult of comprehension for beginners, I have, therefore, made the venture in God's name, and know, at least, that no mistakes have crept in for which an honest Musician ought to blame me.''

§ 26. *Summary*.

After following in great detail the history of the *Bassus continuus*, or Thorough-Bass, through the whole of the seventeenth century, it will be well to pass in brief review some of the salient points.

I. The first point of importance is that Viadana's 'new invention', claimed as such by himself, and apparently conceded without dispute by his contemporaries and successors, really only consisted in the application to monody of the principle already in operation in the earlier Organ-Basses (cf. § 3).

We saw that works by Peri, Caccini, and Cavalieri, furnished with Thorough-Basses, and, moreover, with *figures*, were published two years before the first instalment of Viadana's *Cento concerti* appeared in 1602, and also that the term *Basso continuato* was used by Guidotti in the first of the Rules which he prefixed to his edition of Cavalieri's *Rappresentatione* in 1600; but we also saw that Viadana's *concerti* were known, and *imitated*, five or six years before their actual publication (cf. § 1, note 1).

Nor must it be forgotten that the accompaniment of a melody with chords and 'counterpoints', played *ex tempore* over a plain Bass, was mentioned by the Spaniard Diego Ortiz as early as 1553 (cf. § 2).

II. (*a*) With regard to the character of the earliest accompaniments founded on the *Bassus continuus*, we may probably infer from the fact that Viadana expected the Organist to prepare an *Intavolatura* for his own use (§ 4, Rule 6), and also from Cavalieri's use of double figures (10, 11, &c., up to 18) to denote compound intervals in the accompaniment, corresponding to those in the principal parts, that the accompaniment (in the cases where several principal parts were employed) was intended to be, as far as possible, an exact *replica* of the score, as far as the relative position of the intervals in the chords was concerned.[1]

A natural consequence of this was the rule given by Viadana to the effect that consecutive Fifths and Octaves might be disregarded in the accompaniment (§ 4, Rule 9), and a similar rule given by Guidotti with regard to Fifths (§ 8, 2, Rule 4).

In the vocal score, especially where Triad followed upon Triad (as so commonly occurs in Viadana's four-part writing), *consecutives were avoided by the crossing of the parts*, but with the same harmonies, as played on a keyed

---

[23] It would be of the greatest interest to know what works are here alluded to. It seems probable that he was thinking chiefly of Werckmeister, whose work, described in § 24, gives but little practical assistance to the beginner.

[1] As an exception to this, we must not forget Agazzari's injunction to avoid, in the accompaniment, the region of the high voices, and not to repeat (and on no account to embellish) the notes sung by the Soprano (cf. § 10 *b*).

instrument, this was not the case. At a later period, the accompanist would have avoided such consecutives by the employment of contrary motion between the upper parts and the Bass, and the harmonic texture of the accompaniment would no longer have been identical with that of the vocal score.

(*b*) With regard to the figuring we saw:

(1) That Viadana used no figures except, perhaps, an occasional 6, which, being of such rare occurrence, was mistaken by the printers for a ♭ (cf. § 4 under Rule 8).

(2) That the use of ✕, a Third below (or, in Viadana's case, a Sixth above) the Bass, as the indication of an accidentally sharpened Sixth (cf. § 4 under Rule 8), rapidly became obsolete.

(3) That the non-employment of double figures (one above the other) by Peri and Caccini—especially in the formula 10. 11. 11. 10—gave rise to great uncertainty as to the exact form of cadence desired, an uncertainty which Cavalieri sometimes avoided by the use of two figures (cf. § 8, 4).

The fact that, in the case of Peri and Caccini, there was never more than a single voice to be accompanied, and that the details of the accompanying harmony were therefore of comparatively small importance, must be borne in mind in estimating this divergence between the practice of Cavalieri and that of his two contemporaries.

(4) At a considerably later period in the seventeenth century, we also saw that ambiguity arose owing to the use of two figures only (one above another) instead of three (cf. § 23, *d.* 4), not to mention the confusion arising from the lack of uniformity in certain details (cf. § 23, *e*, note 16).

III. The 'instruments of ornamentation', concerning which certain details are given by Agazzari (cf. § 10 *d*), and afterwards by Praetorius, who gives a complete translation (accompanied by approving comments of his own) of the precepts supplied by the Italian musician, would seem, since no subsequent mention is made of them, to have fallen rapidly into disuse. This is not a matter for surprise, when we consider the difficulty of securing unanimity of intention, in an accompaniment improvised over a Bass, by several individuals, on Violins, Lutes, &c., even assuming unusual musical endowment and mutual adaptability on the part of the performers.

On the other hand, the use of the Violone, Viola da gamba, &c., as 'instruments of foundation', supporting the Bass of the Harpsichord (or whatever instrument was used to supply the harmony), seems to have survived till the time when Ph. Em. Bach laid it down as an axiom that "The most complete accompaniment to a Solo, to which nobody can take any exception, is a keyed instrument (*Clavierinstrument*) in conjunction with the Violoncello" (*Versuch &c.*, Pt. 2, 1762, Introd., § 9). There is, it is true, no special mention of the practice by any of the authors treated of in the present chapter, after Praetorius (cf. § 15 *ad fin.*), till we come to Saint-Lambert; but the latter speaks of the Gamba or Violone, as an adjunct to the Harpsichord, as though it was quite a matter of course that it should be so used (cf. § 23, *i.* 1 *a*).

IV. We saw that the use of figures over the Bass was not, at first, adopted as unanimously as might have been expected, partly on account of the extra expense involved, and partly, no doubt, from conservative prejudice on the part of those who had accustomed themselves to the use of the older unfigured Organ-Basses (cf. § 9).

We saw, too, that the *Bassus continuus* itself was regarded in some quarters as a doubtful boon, not so much on account of any inherent demerits, as because the younger school of Organists seem to have considered that, by acquiring the art of using it, they were absolved from the necessity of cultivating other important branches of the Organist's equipment, such as the art of improvisation, playing from score, and a solid knowledge of counterpoint (cf. § 12).[2]

On the other hand, the indubitable advantages of the 'new invention', which caused it to spread rapidly from the land of its origin, led to what cannot be regarded otherwise than as an abuse, in the shape of 'putting old wine into new bottles', by adding a *Bassus continuus* for the Organ to the works, not only of minor composers, but even of Palestrina himself (cf. § 14).

V. As the century advanced, certain changes in the manner and character of the accompaniment took place.

These changes, no doubt, arose partly as a consequence of the gradual alteration in the character of the compositions themselves (fewer Triads in succession, &c.); but, however that may be, the accompaniment gradually acquired the character of an harmonic background to the polyphony of the principal parts, without any attempt at arranging the intervals of the chords in the same order as that in which they appeared in the latter.

This we gather: (1) from the rapid disappearance of the double figures 10, 11, &c., with which Peri, Caccini, and Cavalieri were wont to indicate the compound intervals to be used in the accompaniment, and without the use of which (save in the case of an almost superhuman ear) no approximation of the harmonic texture of the accompaniment to that of the vocal score would be possible, and (2) from the fact that, after Sabbatini (cf. § 17) and Ebner (cf. § 19, Ex. 3), we hear nothing more of the distribution of the accompaniment between the two hands. All subsequent authors recorded in the present chapter (Locke, Blow, Saint-Lambert, Werckmeister, Niedt) either expressly state, or indicate by their examples, that, in a general way,[3] *the Bass is to be played with the left hand, and the chords with the right.*[4]

This would not have been possible in the case of an accompaniment on the lines of the *intavolatura*, prepared from the vocal score, which Viadana suggests for the use of the Organist (cf. § 4, Rule 6). At the end of the century, moreover, we have the clear testimony of Werckmeister, who expressly warns the accompanist against "continually moving in Octaves [i.e. unison] with the vocalists and instrumentalists" (cf. § 24, VII, 1, *b*).

In other ways, too, the accompaniment became more free, especially, no

---

[2] A consideration of another sort was founded on the assumption that the accompaniment ought to reproduce, exactly, the harmonic texture of the vocal score (cf. II, *a*).

Of such a nature was Diruta's objection, to the effect that, even if the Bass were figured, one could not tell, from the figuring, *in which part the consonance or dissonance in question occurred* (cf. § 12, note).

[3] Subject to such occasional exceptions as § 19, Ex. 3 *b*, § 22, Exx. 20 and 21, and some of Locke's examples in three parts in § 21, in which, however, the two upper parts *can* be played with the right hand.

[4] At a much later period, it is true, Ph. Em. Bach (*Versuch &c.*, Part 2, 1762) realized and laid stress on the desirability of occasionally playing a four-part accompaniment in extended harmony, divided between the two hands, either in order to avoid consecutives, or for the sake of obtaining variety in a repeated passage, or for some special reason. But this is quite another matter.

doubt, on the Harpsichord as opposed to the Organ, the upholder and symbol of ecclesiastical tradition.

Saint-Lambert (who writes as though he had derived his experience, to a large extent, from the Opera) is the first of our authors to make mention of a 'filled-in' accompaniment (the *vollstimmige Begleitung* of later German treatises), which was chiefly used to supplement the limitations of the Harpsichord tribe in the matter of gradation of tone,[5] and in which (as Heinichen explained later) consecutives, except those between the extreme parts, were entirely disregarded, provided that they were covered by keeping the thumbs of the two hands close together.

Saint-Lambert also enumerates in detail various means by which the effect of the performance, especially in the case of a Solo, could be enhanced.

One significant change had taken place, since the early part of the century, which caused the term *Bassus continuus* (or its Italian equivalent, *Basso continuo*) to be no longer entirely appropriate: it was, in fact, no longer 'continuous', but, as Niedt observed, often paused, "especially in Operas and elaborate secular pieces", which was partly the reason why he gave the preference to the alternative term *Bassus generalis*, or its German equivalent, *General-Bass* (cf. § 25, III, 1).

VI. It remains only to recall the effect produced in Germany by the obstinate adherence of Organists to the old German Organ-Tablature, to the total or partial exclusion of the study of Thorough-Bass.

The Narrative of 'Tacitus' (cf. § 25, II) presents a picture to which nothing need be added, and makes it clear why Saint-Lambert's treatise is so disproportionately in advance of those of his German contemporaries, Werckmeister and Niedt.

---

[5] On a large Harpsichord, with two manuals and stops, a wide gradation of tone is, of course, possible; but on smaller and less complete instruments, and Spinets, the only way to distinguish between loud and soft (apart from the comparatively slight difference produced by striking the key smartly or the reverse) is by increasing or diminishing the number of sounding parts.

CHAPTER II

THE PRINCIPAL TREATISES OF THE EIGHTEENTH CENTURY ON ACCOMPANIMENT FROM A THOROUGH-BASS

THE PRINCIPAL TREATISES OF THE EIGHTEENTH CENTURY ON ACCOMPANIMENT FROM A THOROUGH-BASS

§ 1. *Introductory*.

It will not be necessary to give more than a brief survey of some of the better-known treatises on Thorough-Bass of the eighteenth century, many of which will be so freely quoted in the course of the present work as to render a detailed preliminary description almost unnecessary.

They are, as might be expected, of widely different character, ranging by degrees from those, on the one hand, which are purely theoretical and which do not profess to deal with the practical details of accompaniment, to those, on the other, which deal with their subject from a purely practical point of view.

To the former class belong such works as Marpurg's *Handbuch bey dem Generalbasse*, 1755, the First Part of Kirnberger's *Kunst des reinen Satzes*, 1771, and Sorge's *Vorgemach*, 1745-7.

With these, important as they are, we need not concern ourselves here, though frequent reference will be made in subsequent chapters to the two first named.

To the latter class belong Mattheson's *Organisten-Probe*, 1719 (in spite of the so-called *Theoretische Vorbereitung* or Theoretical Preparation with which it opens), and Geminiani's *Art of Accompaniament* [sic], 1755.

Concerning these two works enough will be said in a subsequent chapter [1] to render it unnecessary to describe them here.

Towards the middle of the century and later, there is a further distinction to be drawn between those writers who base their classification of the chords (more particularly the Dominant discords) on Rameau's principle of inversion and those who do not. Among the former are Marpurg, Kirnberger, and Schröter [2] (whose work, though not published till 1772, was completed, except for the introduction, in 1754); conspicuous among the latter is Ph. Em. Bach, who begins his account of the discords with the $\frac{6}{3}$ chord, after which follow the $\frac{6}{5}, \frac{6}{4}, \frac{4}{2}$, and, after three intervening chapters, the Seventh.

The section of the *Versuch einer Anweisung die Flöte traversiere zu spielen*, by Johann Joachim Quantz (1697–1773), which deals with the duties of the accompanist on the Clavier, and of which G. M. Telemann says that it "deserves to be learnt by heart by every budding accompanist",[3] is so abundantly quoted in the following chapter, "On the general character of a figured Bass accompaniment",[4] that no further mention of it need be made here.

---

[1] Ch. iv, 'On certain niceties', &c., §§ 1, 2, 4.

[2] As we shall see presently (cf. § 10) Schröter adopts the classification of the $\frac{6}{5}, \frac{4}{3}, \frac{6}{4}, \frac{4}{2}$ chords as derivatives from the Seventh only as a concession to prevailing opinion.

[3] Cf. § 9 *a ad fin.*, where Telemann is quoted at length.

[4] See Ch. iii, § 3, VI, § 5 B, and § 11.

§ 2. *Johann Philipp Treiber* (1675-1727).

(*a*) In 1704 there appeared a manual (it can hardly be called a treatise) bearing the following title and description:

"Der Accurate Organist / Im General-Bass / Das ist: / Neue, deutliche und vollständige / Anweisung / zum / General-Bass, / Worinne, statt der Exempel, / Nur zweene Geistliche General-Bässe / nemlich die von denen Choralen: / Was GOTT thut, das ist wohlgethan &c / und / Wer nur den lieben GOTT läst walten &c / durch alle Tone und Accorde / dergestalt durchgeführt sind, / dass in denenselben zweyen Exempeln / alle Griffe, mithin die Signaturen aller Clavium, / anbey / die bequemsten Vorthel zur Faust, / gewiesen werden. /

"Jena, in Verlegung Caspar Junghanszens, Kupferstechers. / MDCCIV. / "Arnstadt / druckts Nicolaus Bachmann. / "

('The Accurate Organist in Thorough-Bass, that is: a new, clear, and complete Guide to Thorough-Bass, in which, instead of examples, only two Sacred Thorough-Basses, namely those of the Chorales: "Was Gott thut, das ist wohlgethan", and "Wer nur den lieben Gott läst walten", are carried through all keys and chords in such a way that, in those two examples, all the chords, and consequently the signatures of all the notes, and, incidentally, the most convenient devices for the hand, are shown.

'Published at Jena by Caspar Junghans, copper engraver. MDCCIV.

'Printed at Arnstadt by Nicolaus Bachmann.')

The dedication is to Christian Friedrich Witt, "world-renowned artist on the Clavier " and "Capell-Director" to the Prince of Saxe-Gotha.

Only a very few exemplars of this work are still in existence.

A second edition of the year 1716 is recorded by Eitner.

(*b*) The author, whose name does not appear on the title-page, was Johann Philipp Treiber, born in 1675 at Arnstadt, where his father was Rector of the Lyceum or school. His master in composition was Adam Drese, *Capellmeister* in the same town. He was evidently a man of an unsettled disposition. After studying Philosophy, Theology, Medicine, and afterwards Law, at Jena, he seems to have led a wandering life. Finally he became a Roman Catholic, and achieved some distinction as Professor of Jurisprudence at Erfurt, where he died in 1727.

As a musician, therefore, he was, like Niedt [1] and Kellner,[2] an amateur.

Christopher Gottlieb Schröter makes grateful mention of Treiber as his "first preceptor", inasmuch as he received the *Accurate Organist* as a New Year's gift from his father, four years after its publication, when himself in his ninth year.[3]

(*c*) The main value of the work, to a beginner, lay in the practice afforded by the Basses of two well-known Chorales, carried through all the major keys except ♯ F, ♯ C, and ♭ G, and their relative minors, respectively, with slight variation of the harmony and of the Basses themselves.

The last two examples, xxiii and xxiv, are designed to help the learner to recognize which notes in a Bass are to be allowed to pass without alteration of the preceding harmony. For this purpose the Bass of the Chorale: "Was Gott thut, das ist wohlgethan" (which had hitherto appeared in minims, with a harmony to each note) is now given in a florid form, first in crotchets and then in quavers, in the key of G major.

---

[1] Cf. Ch. i, § 25.   [2] Cf. § 6 (of the present chapter).   [3] Cf. § 10 *c*, p. 298.

In none of the examples is the melody of the Chorale in question given above the Bass, as perfect familiarity with it is assumed.

(*d*) The instructions which precede the examples are clear and good as far as they go, but are quite elementary, a great deal of space being devoted to the explanation of the function of sharps and flats: (1) in the signature, (2) by the side of a note, (3) over a note, (4) by the side of a figure.

Every rule is illustrated by reference to the examples.

The arrangement of the material is at first difficult to follow owing to the repeated subdivision of the headings; no aid is given to the eye by the use of Roman and Arabic numerals, capital and small letters of the alphabet, &c., all headings and sub-headings being numbered, alike, with small Arabic numerals, as may be seen from the "Schatten-Riss", or Outline, which serves as a Table of Contents, and of which a translation is here appended:

"Outline of the entire Guide to Thorough-Bass.

"The Guide to Thorough-Bass consists of such rules as teach how to take the chords correctly, and these rules treat of:

1. that which is to be observed before the beginning of a Thorough-Bass, or before the commencement of its notes, which rules concern
    1. crosslets,[4] and therefore, alternatively,
        1. the absence of crosslets before the beginning of a song,
        2. the presence of crosslets;
    2. B's,[5] and therefore, alternatively,
        1. the absence of B's before the beginning of the Thorough-Bass,
        2. the presence of B's;
2. that which is to be observed in the Thorough-Bass itself, as regards the notes, and these rules concern

1. the absence of signatures over the notes, and teach what is to be played when there is no signature over a note,
2. the presence of signatures, and show

1. the note (*Clavem*) which the signatures indicate, when such signatures
    1. stand side by side, and are
        1. letters, namely B's, which B's have a different meaning when they
            1. appertain to the notes, and have different meanings when they are
                1. by the side of the note,
                2. over a note;
            2. appertain to the figures;
        2. not letters, but
            1. crosslets, which have a different meaning when they are placed
                1. by the side of a note,
                2. over a note;
            2. figures;
    2. stand one above another;
2. the complement [6] to the note indicated by the signatures; and these rules show
    1. the complement to each note individually,
    2. the proper complement to several notes at a time [i.e. consecutively]."

---

[4] For notes 4, 5, and 6 see opposite page.

(*e*) The text which follows this outline, or summary, is entitled: "Erweiterung des vorhergehenden Schatten-Risses" (*Amplification of the foregoing Outline*).

The divisions and subdivisions correspond exactly to those in the 'Outline' (except that some further subdivisions are introduced), and are numbered in the same way, with Arabic numerals of uniform size, thus forming a labyrinth to which the only clue is to be found in the perpendicular lines at the side of the page, connecting one numeral with another, as in the 'Outline'. In the latter, these lines, of which none exceeds the limits of a single page, can be followed with ease, but in the main text it sometimes happens that one, two, or even three lines are continued from page to page; in such cases, the lines are labelled with small italics, *a*, *b*, *c*, *d*, at the top and bottom of the pages in question, in order to enable the reader to identify them. In one instance the figures 1 and 2 are connected by a line extending from p. 7 to p. 15! Apart, however, from the initial difficulty of mastering this complex arrangement, Treiber's simple instructions are given clearly and well.

(*f*) As has been said, the chief value of his work lies in the practice afforded by the examples. In these the author has evidently made it his aim to accustom the student to the various methods of figuring to be met with in actual practice, especially as regards the accidentals (or strokes representing accidentals) attached to the figures. Some figurists made it their aim to indicate the dimension of the interval in question, *independently of the key-signature*, and would use, e.g. ♭ 7 to denote a minor Seventh, and 6̄ (or ✕ 6) to denote a major Sixth, even when these intervals were diatonic.

It was in accordance with this method that 4⌉ and 5♭ were so very commonly used to denote $\frac{6}{4}{}_{2}$ on the Subdominant and $\frac{6}{5}$ on the leading note, respectively, even though the augmented Fourth and diminished Fifth were already indicated by the key-signature. With this usage no fault can be found, but in some instances the use of superfluous accidentals (or their equivalents) in the figuring is productive of great confusion. Thus, in the flat keys, Treiber constantly places a ♮ over the bass note [7] to indicate that the Third is major, quite irrespective of the key-signature.

Similarly, in both sharp and flat keys, he frequently uses an equally superfluous ♭ to indicate that the Third is minor, sometimes, too, a crossed figure, 5⫫, to indicate a perfect Fifth, already sufficiently indicated by the key-signature.

(*g*) Into what strange inconsistencies a figurist may be betrayed, who adheres to the principle of associating a certain figuring with an interval of

---

[4] *Kreutzgen*, i.e. the *signum cancellatum*, ✕, the predecessor of the later ♯. The translation 'sharp' is here deliberately avoided, because the sign was used by Treiber (alternatively with ♮) to contradict a flat as well as to sharpen a natural.

[5] In the letterpress Treiber uses B and b, indifferently, to denote ♭. The translation 'flat' is here avoided, because the sign was used by Treiber to contradict a sharp as well as to flatten a natural.

[6] *Zugriff*, i.e. the interval or intervals necessary to complete the harmony indicated by the figuring, but not actually expressed in it: thus, in a $\frac{6}{5}$ chord the *Zugriff* is 3 (or possibly 3˙and 8), in a $\frac{4}{3}$, 6 (or possibly 6 and 8), &c. In other German treatises of the early eighteenth century the terms: *Füll-Stimmen, Hülfs-Stimmen, Neben-Stimmen*, are used in the same sense; *Zugriff* seems to be peculiar to Treiber.

[7] In the music, i.e. *before* a bass note, Treiber generally uses ✕ (rarely ♮) to contradict a flat.

a definite dimension, *irrespective of the key-signature*, may be seen from Treiber's use of 6̄ to indicate a *diminished Seventh*, in spite of the fact that 6̄ (especially when associated with 5♭) suggests an upward and not a downward resolution. Treiber argues (o.c., p. 14 *inf.*) that ♭7 indicates a *minor* Seventh and that, therefore, ♭7 on *C* sharp should indicate *B* natural and not *B* flat. "Consequently", he proceeds, "when *B* flat is to be taken on *C* sharp, and *C* on *D* sharp, the signatures should not be written thus: $\frac{7}{5}_3$, but must be written thus: $\frac{6}{5}_3$ or $\frac{♭6}{♭5}_{♭3}$."

(*h*) Treiber employs no sign to indicate a double sharp in the Bass itself; for *F* double sharp he writes *G*, and for *C* double sharp, *D*. In the figuring the doubly sharpened major Third is indicated by 𝕏 over the Bass note.

The above-mentioned peculiarities are illustrated in the two following examples (o.c. No. xix and No. xii): [8]

"Was Gott thut, das ist wohlgethan"

"Wer nur den lieben Gott läst walten"

[8] For clearness' sake, the melody of the two Chorales, not given in the original, has been added. In the melody of Ex. 2 the double sharp and its contradiction are given in modern notation. The bars are numbered for reference.

[9] In bar 6 of Ex. 1 the ♭ before the 7 on the second minim is due to an obvious misprint in the original. Treiber intended either a simple 7 or, more probably, the crossed figure 7̸ which he constantly uses, irrespective of the key-signature, to denote a major Seventh, as in bar 14.

In bar 13 the figure 6 on the first crotchet is due to a misprint in the original for 6̄, as there can be no doubt that *D natural* was intended. Strictly speaking, the figuring on the second crotchet should be 7̸𝕏 or 7♮, but the crossed 6̄ on the preceding one would render a further indication of the natural superfluous.

[10] In bar 7 of Ex. 2 the 5+ on the crotchet, *A* sharp, is due to a misprint in the original: either 5 or, more probably, ♭5 was, no doubt, intended. In bar 8 of the same example, on the crotchet *G* natural (= *F* double sharp), a ♭, omitted in the original, is required before (or after) the 6, as shown in bar 1.

(i) If the above examples are examined carefully, abundant instances of superfluous accidentals in the figuring, and of figures unnecessarily crossed, will be found. In Ex. 1 *every single* ♮ over the Bass is unnecessary. In the same example, the only bass notes bearing a minor Sixth, without a super-fluous ♭ being prefixed to the figure, are the second minim in bar 1 and the first note in bar 13. Again, it is only on the final crotchet of bars 1 and 8 in Ex. 2 (*G* natural = *F* double sharp), and on the first quaver of bar 4 in the same example (where the foregoing double sharp is to be con-tradicted), that a ♮ over the Bass, as the indication of a minor Third, is required.

In Ex. 1 the ♭ prefixed to the 4 in bars 3 and 7 is unnecessary, as also is the stroke through the tail of the 5 in bars 2, 7 (*ad fin.*), 9, and 13 of Ex. 2.

The figuring 6̸ (accompanied by an unnecessary ♭ 3), as the indication of a diminished Seventh, is seen in bar 15 of Ex. 2, over *D* natural = *C* double sharp. This figuring is used in all the remaining ten examples of the same Chorale.

(k) With regard to the superfluous use of accidentals and crossed figures, it must not be supposed that all Treiber's examples are alike: his object was evidently to accustom the learner to the vagaries that he was liable to encounter, and the two Basses given above have been purposely selected as extreme cases.

Attention may be called to the very weak Ninth, prepared on a stronger beat than that on which it occurs, in bar 11 of Ex. 2. Curiously enough, the same harmonization is used in all the other examples of the same Chorale. The augmented Second between bars 14 and 15 will also be noticed.

But, whatever its faults, Treiber's work must have afforded very welcome help to incipient Organists, especially to such as were largely thrown upon their own resources in the acquirement of their art.

§ 3. *Godfrey Keller* (d. before 1707).

A considerable circulation was attained in England by a little treatise of which the full title is as follows: *A Compleat Method for Attaining to Play a Thorough Bass upon either Organ or Harpsichord or Theorbo Lute by the late famous Godfrey Keller.*

It first appeared in 1707, after the author's death, as an engraved folio, pub-lished by John Cullen, and was afterwards reproduced by Walsh (undated).

It reappeared in 1731, in the form of an appendix to a treatise on Har-mony by William Holder, D.D., "Printed by W. Pearson, *over against Wright's Coffee-House in Aldersgate-street*; for J. Wilcox in *Little Britain*; and T. Osborne in *Gray's Inn*".

The original publication is very rare, and Walsh's reproduction is not easy to obtain, but Pearson's reprint appears not infrequently in the catalogues of second-hand dealers.

It professes to contain "Several new Examples, which before were wanting, the better to explain some Passages in the former Impressions. The whole being Revis'd, and Corrected from many gross Mistakes committed in the first Publication of these Rules." Some of the examples, indeed, have been altered, but, with regard to the correction of the 'gross Mistakes', it cannot be said that any great improvement is noticeable, as the work teems with misprints, and many obscure (and sometimes misleading) statements in the rules themselves remain as they were.

Pearson has, however, added an Index which greatly facilitates the perusal of the work. The contents are as follows:

[1] *Of Concords and Discords.*

[2] *Of Common Chords differently taken* [i.e. in different positions].

[3] *Of Common Chords and Sixes differently taken.*[1]

[4] *Of Cadences.*

[5] *Of the Several Discords and Manner of playing them.*

[6] *How to move the Hands when the Bass ascends or descends.*

[7] *Of Dividing upon Notes in Common Time.*[2]

[8] *Of Dividing in Triple Time.*

[9] *Of Natural Sixes, and Proper Cadences in a sharp* [i.e. major] *Key.*

[10] *Of Natural Sixes, &c., in a flat* [i.e. minor] *Key.*

[11] *Rules how Sixes may be used in Composing.*

[12] *Rules about Sevenths and Ninths.*

[13] *Several Ways of Accompanying when the Bass Ascends and Descends by Degrees.*

[14] *Of playing all Sorts of Discords in a flat Key.*

[15] *Of playing Discords in a sharp Key.*

[16] *Of making Chords easy to the Memory.*

[17] *Of playing some Notes the same way, which have a different appearance in Writing.*[3]

[18] *Of Transposition.*

[19] *Of Discords, how prepar'd and resolv'd.*

[20] *Some Examples for playing a Thorow-Bass.*

[21] *Short Lessons by way of Fugeing.*

[22] *Rules for Tuning an Harpsichord, &c.*

Some of the above headings refer merely to an example, not preceded by any rule.

It will be noticed that information on the important subject of discords is to be sought under scattered headings [5, 12, 14, 15, 19], and that there is, altogether, very little attempt at arrangement; it is, however, only fair to remember that the author did not live to prepare his work for publication and that, had he done so, many faults would possibly have been remedied.

---

[1] Keller gives the three forms of the Sixth: $\frac{6}{3}$ and $\frac{3}{6}$ (the *accord doublé* of Saint-Lambert), and $\frac{8}{6}{\scriptstyle 3}$ (the *accord simple* of Saint-Lambert) in its three different positions.

[2] i.e. breaking up a simple Bass into shorter notes (Ital. *diminuire*).

[3] e.g. a diminished 5th $^{\flat b}_{e}$, and augmented 4th $^{\sharp a}_{e}$.

The 'Examples for playing a Thorow-Bass' (which in Keller's text are entitled 'Some Lessons where the F and the C Cleffs Interfere one with the other') are by no means without value to the student. They consist of a dozen figured Basses, averaging about twenty bars each, in which the Alto clef alternates freely with the Bass clef, and they afford excellent practice. The same may be said of the nine 'Short Lessons by way of Fugeing' which follow. These begin with a short fugal exposition, after which the student is left to introduce the Subject or Answer in an upper part over the figured Bass at appropriate points indicated for his benefit. The opening bars of the fifth 'Lesson' will serve as an illustration:

The only information that Keller gives with regard to consecutives is contained in the following rule: "In common *Chords* which are the 3rd, 5th, and 8th avoid the taking two 5ths or two 8ths together, not being allow'd either in Playing or Composition; and the best way to do it in playing is to move the Hands contrary one to the other."

Apart from the special case referred to in the above rule, i.e. that of two Triads in succession, Keller shows himself careless in the matter of consecutives, as may be seen from the following examples (Exx. 2, 3): [4]

In Ex. 2, besides the consecutive 5ths between Treble and Tenor we here see the forbidden interval of an augmented 2nd as well.

[4] These examples occur, respectively, on folios 3 and 10 of the original edition, and on pp. 163 and 190 of Pearson's reprint.

[5] Keller's use of $\frac{4}{3}$ to indicate $\frac{7}{4}{3}$, as in the above example, is contrary to the practice which came to be generally accepted, in accordance with which $\frac{4}{3}$ stands for $\frac{6}{4}{3}$. Keller's rule (original ed., fol. 2; Pearson's reprint, p. 163) is as follows:

"When the 3rd and 4th are mark'd above one another $\begin{array}{c|c|c} 7 & 3 & 4 \\ 4 & 7 & 3 \\ 3 & 4 & 7 \end{array}$ here, instead of the 7th, *sharp 6th* may be used, but then it ought to be mark'd."

A curious feature in Keller's harmony is the regular omission of the Third (instead of the Fifth) when a suspended Ninth is taken in three parts, as in the following example: [6]

Ex. 4

In only two cases in the entire work is a suspended Ninth taken in four parts $\frac{9}{5}$, and in every other case the 3 is omitted.

§ 4. *Francesco Gasparini* (1668–1727).

(a) A work of a very different character from that of the one last described was the following: L'ARMONICO PRATICO / AL CIMBALO / Regole, Osservazioni, ed Avvertimenti per ben / suonare il Basso, e accompagnare sopra il / Cimbalo, Spinetta, ed Organo / DI / FRANCESCO GASPARINI / LUCCHESE / *Maestro di Coro del Pio Ospedale della Pietà in* / *Venezia, ed Accademico Filarmonico* / DEDICATO / *All' Illustrissimo, ed Eccellentissimo Signore* GIROLAMO ASCANIO / GIUSTINIANI / Nobile Veneto / IN VENEZIA, MDCCVIII / Appresso Antonio Bortoli.

It was reprinted several times, the sixth and last occasion being as late as 1802, nearly a century after its first appearance.

Gasparini was a pupil of the celebrated Bernardo Pasquini in Rome, as well as of Corelli, and it was no doubt upon the teaching of the former that his treatise was founded. He pays his master the following grateful and eloquent tribute (o.c. Cap. viii *ad fin.*):

"Chi averà ottenuta la sorte di praticare, o studiare sotto la scuola del famosissimo Sig. Bernardo Pasquini in Roma, o chi almeno l' avrà inteso o veduto suonare, avrà potuto conoscere la più vera, bella, e nobile maniera di suonare e di accompagnare; e con questo modo così pieno avrà sentita dal suo Cembalo una perfezione di Armonia maravigliosa.

  . . . .

"Ed io, che ebbi la fortuna lungo tempo di praticarlo, non devo, nè posso tacere, (e mi si conceda pure il dirlo), che tanta virtù fu sempre sì bene accoppiata all' eccellenza de' costumi, che si potrà giustamente dire tra i nostri Professori:

> *Quo justior alter*
> *Nec virtute fuit, modulis nec major, & arte."*

('Any one to whose lot it has fallen to associate with, or study under the tuition of, the renowned Sig. Bernardo Pasquini in Rome, or who has at least heard or seen him play, will have been able to become acquainted with the truest, most beautiful, and noblest manner of playing and accompanying; and, together with this richness of style, will have heard from his Harpsichord a marvellous perfection of Harmony.

  . . . .

'And I, who for a long while had the good fortune to associate with him, must not, and cannot, conceal (and I may surely be allowed to say) that all this great skill

---

[6] Cf. original ed., fol. 9; Pearson's reprint, p. 189.

was ever coupled so happily with excellence of character that, amongst our Professors, he may justly be said to be one:

> *Quo justior alter*
> *Nec virtute fuit, modulis nec major, & arte.')*

(b) Gasparini's work consists of twelve short chapters headed as follows:
Cap. I. *De' Nomi, e Posizioni de' Tasti.*
  II. *Del modo di formar l' Armonia con le Consonanze.*
  III. *Degli Accidenti Musicali.*
  IV. *Osservazioni sopra i moti per salire, e prima di grado.*
  V. *Osservazioni per discender di grado, e di salto.*
  VI. *Per far le Cadenze d'ogni specie.*
  VII. *Delle Dissonanze, Legature, Note sincopate, e modo di risolverle.*
  VIII. *Osservazioni per meglio impossessarsi degli Accompagnamenti per ogni Tuono, per ben modulare, prevedere, e passar con proprietà da un Tuono all' altro.*
  IX. *Delle false dei Recitativi, e del modo di far Acciaccature.*
  X. *Del diminuire, abbellire, e rifiorire gli Accompagnamenti.*
  XI. *Del diminuire, o rifiorire il Fondamento.*
  XII. *Modo di trasportar per ogni Tuono.*

The author's object is apparently not so much to instruct the reader in the different ways of treating a given figuring, and the best progression from one harmony to another, as to teach him to deal with an *unfigured Bass*. The examples, therefore, consist almost entirely in short figured Basses, designed to show what harmonies may normally be expected with certain progressions of the Bass, and the reader is for the most part left to interpret the figuring as best he may.

(c) The parts of Gasparini's treatise which have the greatest value for us, insomuch as they are those which throw the most light on contemporary Italian practice, are perhaps that portion of Ch. IX which deals with the *Acciaccatura*,[1] and Ch. X, which deals with the embellishment of the accompaniment by means of passages of a melodious or brilliant character, shakes, broken harmony, &c., in the right hand. In this latter chapter the examples are given with the right-hand part in full, and it is explained that the left hand is responsible for the completion of the harmony.

The second of Gasparini's fourteen examples will serve here as an illustration:

Gasparini adds a salutary warning to the Accompanist against trespassing upon the domain of the Soloist by using any figure or embellishment which the latter might himself wish to introduce. "Similarly", he concludes, "one must never play note for note the same as the voice part or any other upper part composed for the Violin, &c., since it suffices that the consonance or

---

[1] Heinichen's account of the *Acciaccatura* (*General-Bass &c.*, 1728, Part I, Ch. VI §§ 16–25) is avowedly based on that of Gasparini (cf. Ch. iv of the present work "On Certain niceties of the Accompaniment", § 3, II, *f*).

dissonance which is composed [i.e. in the Solo part], or required by the Bass, should be found in the body of the harmony [i.e. not in the highest part] in conformity with the Rules of Accompaniment."

(d) It is worth mentioning here that our author begins the following chapter, "On the division and embellishment of the Bass", by stating roundly that he does not approve of the practice: "because one may easily depart from or abandon the intention of the Composer, the good taste of the Composition, and fall foul of (*offender*) the Singer." He adds, however, that, "in order to indulge a fanciful taste" (*per dare nel genio a qualche umor bizarro*), some examples shall be given of a procedure which, when used with judgement, may be introduced without detriment to the intentions of the composer.

In all the examples he introduces a quicker movement than that of the actual Bass by some form of "divisions". The following quotations will suffice:

Gasparini gives 'absolute licence', he tells us, to use such divisions of the Bass in *Ritornelli*, and when the principal part is silent, apart from which cases the accompanist must use his judgement and discretion. He is well aware, however, that opinions differ, and that many of the most competent judges would condemn his examples as childish and absurd; "and", he adds modestly, "I cannot condemn the view of such men. But whoever is willing and able to use it [i.e. the above-mentioned treatment of the Bass] at the right time, and with discretion, can hold himself independent (*licenziarsi*) of such opinions. And I protest that I acted thus [i.e. in giving the examples] in order to bring some relief and enjoyment into the labours (*applicazione*) of the Students of Harmony of to-day." The above quotation throws a pleasant light upon the human side of Gasparini's character as a teacher.

(e) Gasparini gives the usual rule against the use of consecutive Octaves or Fifths by similar motion, but he tells us expressly that, when the accompaniment is filled in by the reduplication of consonances in the left hand, the rule need not be so strictly observed, so far as consecutives "in the middle" (i.e. between middle parts or even between a middle and an extreme part [2]) are concerned, because they can be regarded as *saved by crossing of the parts*, as in compositions for 5, 6, or 8 voices (o.c. Ch. viii *ad fin.*).

In support of this view Gasparini continues: "And this opinion I derive from the famous Ruettino of sainted memory, Organist at the *Ducale* of St. Mark's in Venice, having seen it in a letter of his, written to two *Virtuosi*, between whom a similar question arose, concerning the possibility of allowing more Fifths and Octaves in the middle of the accompaniment [cf. note 2]; and it was brilliantly settled by that same letter with the very reasons adduced by myself."

(*f*) There are two further points on which Gasparini's views are worth recording:

(1) He lays down the rule (o.c. Ch. vii) that a diminished Fifth, which he tells us may be associated with the Third alone, or with a Sixth or prepared Seventh as well, "cannot be resolved after the manner of the other discords, because it would then fall to a Fourth, but must, by the movement of the Bass, fall to a Third". As a consequence of this (as is made clear by the examples, though no further rule is given) *no Seventh may include the diminished Fifth, except where the Bass rises a semitone,*[3] as in the following example (given later in the same chapter), in which the downward resolution of the *terminus gravis* (5) happens to be delayed by suspension:

The *perfect* Fifth, on the other hand, may be freely included in *either a suspended or an essential Seventh*, as the following examples show:

'*Qui può star la Quinta*'   '*qui nò*'   '*qui nò*'   '*qui si*'
(*Here the 5th may stand*) (*Here, no*)   (*Here, yes*)

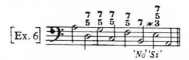

'*Nò* '*Si*'

[2] That the term 'in the middle' (*nel mezzo*) is intended to include consecutives occurring between *a middle part and the Bass* is clear from the following example from Gasparini's second chapter, one of the few in the entire work in which the chords are given in full:

[3] It is, no doubt, the same fastidiousness in the use of a diminished Fifth (even *between two upper parts*) that leads Gasparini to give the rule (later in the same chapter) that, in a 9 8 suspension, a *minor* Ninth should not include the [perfect] Fifth, except in a sequence on a rising Bass, in which case the 5 is to move to 6 [i.e. rise a *semitone* to a minor Sixth, though this is not expressly stated] simultaneously with the resolution of the 9, whereby the diminished Fifth $^{\flat 9}_{5}$ acquires its proper resolution on the Third $_{\flat 6}^{8}$.

(2) An interesting detail of the practice of Italian Harpsichordists of the early eighteenth century is recorded in the following passage which treats of the resolution of a $\frac{6}{4}$ chord on $\frac{5}{3}$ in a cadence: "Alle volte il radoppiare la Quarta e Sesta con la mano sinistra fa buonissimo effetto, ma nel resolvere non si deve far sentire la Terza maggiore, e nel Cembalo lasciando la Quarta unita con la Quinta, mentre la destra risolve con la Terza maggiore, si riceve un' Armonia assai grata, ed è una specie (come molti Suonatori dicono) di Acciaccatura, di che ne faremo il suo Trattato. Questo però non fa bene in Organo, se non in Compositioni piene."

('Sometimes the reduplication of the Fourth and Sixth in the left hand has an excellent effect; but, in resolving, one must not let the major Third be heard, and, on the Harpsichord, by leaving the Fourth joined with the Fifth, while the right hand resolves it on the major Third, a very pleasing harmony is obtained, and it is (as many players aver) a species of Acciaccatura, concerning which we shall treat specially. This is not, however, suitable on the Organ, save in full Compositions.')

(*g*) This rule is in exact accordance with a number of examples given in a manuscript bearing the name of Alessandro Scarlatti [4] (Brit. Mus. Additional MSS. 14244) in which 4 (either in $\frac{5}{34}$ or $\frac{65}{43}$) is resolved in the right hand but remains unresolved (with or without repercussion) in the left. The following examples will serve as an illustration:

[Ex. 7]   (o. c., f. 47 b.)

[Ex. 8]   (o. c., f. 48.)

[Ex. 9]   (o. c., f. 51 b.)

[4] This manuscript (which does not appear to be a "made-up" volume as the same watermarks are continued throughout) contains a number of rules and examples, evidently compiled for the instruction of pupils in Thorough-Bass, as well as exercises for the Harpsichord (some of them elaborately fingered) and other *miscellanea*. In the opinion of Mr. Augustus Hughes-Hughes, part of the manuscript is in the writing of Scarlatti himself, besides which three other hands are to be distinguished, one of them being that of Nicola Fago, a Neapolitan and probably a pupil of Scarlatti. The examples about to be quoted are taken from a series of short preludes entitled: *Varie Introduttioni per sonare, e mettersi in tono delle Compositioni* (o. c., ff. 46 b–52 a).

[Ex. 10]   (o. c., f. 52.)

(h) Before taking leave of Gasparini, it may be mentioned that Heinichen (who, as he tells us, chanced upon his treatise when in Italy) frequently quotes him and speaks of him with great respect, although, as he remarks, he rarely agrees with him "either *quoad principia* or *quoad methodum*" (cf. *General-Bass &c.*, 1728, Preface, note t, pp. 91 sqq.). It has already been mentioned above that Heinichen's account of the *Acciaccatura* is based on that of Gasparini (cf. note 1).

§ 5. *Johann David Heinichen* (1683–1729).

I. In 1711 Heinichen published a work of modest proportions entitled: "Neu erfundene / und / Gründliche / Anweisung / wie / ein Music-liebender auff gewisse vortheil⸗/hafftige Arth könne / zu vollkommener Erlernung des / General-Basses, / entweder / Durch eigenen Fleiss selbst gelangen / oder durch andere / kurz und glücklich dahin angeführt werden/ / dergestalt/ / Dass er sowohl die Kirchen- als Theatrali⸗/schen Sachen / insonderheit auch das Accompagnement / des Recitativs-Styli wohl verstehe / und geschickt / zu tractiren wisse. / Woeben zugleich auch andere schöne Vortheil in der Music / an die Hand gegeben/ / Und alles / Mit vielfachen Exempeln, und hierzu mit Fleiss auserlesenen / nützlichen Composition-Regeln erläutert worden. / Nebst einer / Ausführlichen Vorrede. / Herausgegeben / von / Johann David Heinichen. /

"Hamburg in Verlegung Benjamin Schiller's im Dohm / 1711."

This little work was, however, so completely dwarfed and superseded by a second edition which appeared seventeen years later, in 1728 (a year before the premature death of the author), that we need not further concern ourselves with it.

The framework of the two is the same, as far as the division into two Parts and the headings of the chapters are concerned, except that, in the later version, the first chapter of each of the two Parts is an addition. But the later publication, which runs to 960 pages (exclusive of Preface, list of *Errata*, and Index), so far exceeds the earlier one in scope as to acquire the character of an independent work.

It appeared under the following title: "Der / GENERAL-BASS / in der / COMPOSITION, / Oder: / Neue und gründliche / ANWEISUNG / Wie / Ein Music-Liebender mit besonderm Vortheil, durch die *Principia* der Composition, nicht allein den General-Bass / im Kirchen⸗ Cammer⸗ und Theatralischen *Stylô* vollkommen, & *in altiori* / *Gradu* erlernen, sondern auch zu gleicher Zeit in der Composition selbst, wichtige / *Profectus* machen könne. /

"NEBST EINER EINLEITUNG / oder / Musicalischen *Raisonnement* / von der Music überhaupt, und vielen besondern / Materien der heutigen *Praxeos*. / Herausgegeben / von / JOHANN DAVID HEINICHEN / Königl. Pohln. und Churfl. Sächs. Capellmeister.

"In Dressden bey dem *Autore* zu finden 1728."

The Introduction, which embraces 94 pages, is, in effect, a treatise on musical expression, illustrated by copious and voluminous examples in the form of short *Arias*, showing different ways of treating the same words, according as one or other idea contained in the latter be taken as giving the key to the sentiment.

The main work is divided into two Parts, of which the contents are as follows:

ERSTE ABTHEILUNG / von / Denen *Principiis* des General-Basses. /
(*First Part, on the first principles of Thorough-Bass.*)

Cap. I

"Von Musicalischen Intervallen und deren Eintheilung" (*On the musical intervals and their classification*), p. 95.

Cap. II

"Von denen ordentlichen Accorden, und wie selbige denen *Incipienten* nutzbar beyzubringen" (*On the common chords, and how they may profitably be taught to beginners*), p. 119.

Cap. III

"Von denen Signaturen des General-Basses, und wie selbige ordentlich und gründlich zu tractiren" (*On the signatures of the Thorough-Bass* [i.e. the figures and ♯ ♭ ♮ placed over (or under) the Bass], *and how they are to be properly and thoroughly treated*), p. 138.

Cap. IV

"Von geschwinden Noten und mancherley Tacten" (*On quick notes and various measures*),[1] p. 257.

Cap. V

"Von der Application der Accorde, Signaturen und geschwinden Noten in allen übrigen Tonen" (*On the application of the chords, signatures, and quick notes in all other keys*), p. 379.

Cap. VI

"Vom manierlichen General-Bass, und fernern *Exercitio* eines *Incipienten*" (*On the embellishment of a Thorough-Bass and the further practice of a beginner*),[2] p. 521.

ANDERE ABTHEILUNG / von / Der vollkommenen Wissenschaft des General-Basses. /
(*Second Part, concerning the complete science of Thorough-Bass.*)

Cap. I

"Von theatralischen *Resolutionibus* der Dissonantien" (*On the resolutions of dissonances found in operatic works*), p. 585.

Cap. II

"Von dem General-Bass ohne Signaturen, und wie diese in Cammer- und Theatralischen Sachen zu erfinden" (*Concerning a Thorough-Bass without signatures, and how the latter are to be divined in chamber- and operatic music*), p. 725.

---

[1] The substance of this chapter is given in Ch. xviii of the present work.
[2] The substance of this chapter is given in Ch. iv, § 3, of the present work.

Cap. III

"Vom Accompagnement des Recitativs insonderheit" (*On the accompaniment of Recitative in particular*), p. 769.

Cap. IV

"Von der Application der gegebenen Regeln, welche nebst einigen *Observationibus practicis*, in einer gantzen *Cantata* deutlich und nutzbar gezeiget wird" (*On the application of the rules given, which, together with sundry practical observations, is illustrated clearly and usefully in an entire Cantata*), p. 797.

Cap. V

"Von einem Musicalischen Circul, aus welchem man die natürliche Ordnung, Verwandschafft und Ausschweiffung aller *Modorum Musicorum* gründlich erkennen, und sich dessen sowohl im Clavier, als in der Composition mit trefflichem Nutzen bedienen kan" (*Concerning a Musical Circle, from which the natural order, relationship, and modulations of all the keys can be thoroughly learnt, and of which use can most profitably be made, both on the keyboard and in composition*), p. 837.

Cap. VI

"Von einem nützlichen *Exercitio practico* und einigen *Conciliis*, wie man sich selbst weiter helffen, und die Perfection im General-Basse suchen müsse" (*Concerning a useful practical exercise, and certain hints as to how to aid one's own progress and seek perfection in Thorough-Bass*), p. 917.

II. The point in regard to which Heinichen stands apart from other authors of works dealing with the same subject is his prodigality of examples, for which those who are trying to re-establish the tradition of accompaniment from a figured Bass cannot be grateful enough. Heinichen never contents himself with giving a figured Bass and leaving the reader to construct the harmony in accordance with the rules supplied. Every rule is supplemented by examples on two staves illustrating the chord or chords in question, but far more valuable to us are the General Examples (*General-Exempel*) appended to each main group dealt with in Ch. III of the First Part (Sixths, Sevenths, Ninths, &c.) in which we encounter the chords in question in their natural context and not as isolated specimens. These examples are first given in four-part harmony (with an occasional fifth part where necessary or desirable), but not only does Heinichen give them *in triplicate*, the three different versions beginning, respectively, with the three different *Hauptaccorde*, i.e. the three different positions in which the upper parts of the opening chord, whether a Triad or its first inversion, may appear: he repeats the example, again in triplicate, with 'filled in' harmony (*vollstimmig*).[3] Nor does he trouble to give only that which looks well on paper: the examples contain many an irregularity which would be severely censured in a modern harmony exercise, and we feel that Heinichen has set down what he himself would have played when seated at his Harpsichord in the Opera House. The value of this treatment cannot possibly be over-estimated: from the triplicate

---

[3] The substance of Heinichen's rules for the filling-in of the accompaniment is given in Ch. iii of the present work, § 3, II, III.

versions the student learns how the less favourable positions of certain chords may be dealt with, and from the dual treatment, in four-part and in full harmony, he gains a practical acquaintance with the style of accompaniment suitable on the Organ (or a modern Grand Pianoforte), on the one hand, and on an Harpsichord (or old-fashioned, thin-toned Pianoforte) on the other.

Not content with this wealth of illustration of individual chords and groups of chords, Heinichen devotes the fifth chapter of Part I to a General Example summarizing the teaching of the two preceding chapters. This example, which embodies different measures, C, $\frac{3}{2}$, C (Adagio), $\frac{3}{2}$ (Allegro leading to Adagio), C (Adagio), is given (both in four-part and filled-in harmony) in *seven keys*, C (major), F, G, $\flat B$, D, $\flat E$, A, and *also with changes of measure*, ₵ (Presto) being substituted for C, and $\frac{3}{4}$ $(\frac{6}{4})$ and $\frac{3}{8}$ $(\frac{6}{8} \frac{9}{8} \frac{12}{8})$ for $\frac{3}{2}$, thus illustrating the difference of treatment in accordance with the speed of the Bass. For the sake of still greater variety a different Bass has been substituted in the penultimate section, $(\frac{6}{8}, \frac{9}{8}, \frac{12}{8})$, of the versions in G, $\flat E$, and A.

This chapter of Heinichen's deserves to be printed in characters of gold.

III. Something must be said concerning Ch. III in Part I, in which Heinichen presents "the most commonly used signatures [4] of a Thorough-Bass".

(*a*) The consonant Triad having been disposed of in the preceding chapter, he next deals with its first inversion, *as well as that of the diminished Triad*.

The full harmony of a Sixth (*Die Harmonie einer vollstimmigen Sexte*) $\left[\text{i.e. } \begin{smallmatrix} 6 \\ 3 \end{smallmatrix}, \begin{smallmatrix} 8 \\ 6 \\ 3 \end{smallmatrix}, \begin{smallmatrix} 6 \\ 3 \end{smallmatrix}, \begin{smallmatrix} 3 \\ 6 \\ 3 \end{smallmatrix}\right]$, he tells us (l. c., § 2), is, besides the common chord, "the only other possible combination of a number of free and unbound consonances (*ungebundener Consonantien*)".[5]

The second inversion of the consonant Triad is relegated to a place among the discords on account of its Fourth with the Bass, which Heinichen uncompromisingly classes as a dissonance.

On the other hand, in accordance with what was evidently a widespread tradition (cf. Ch. xxi, 'Incomplete figuring', II, §§ 1, 2), two undoubted discords are treated as mere optional variants of what are in reality entirely distinct harmonies.[6]

(1) A major Sixth with a *minor* Third [on the Supertonic (actual or temporary) of either a major or minor key, falling to the Tonic or rising to its first inversion], though figured with a simple 6 (6), may, under certain circumstances, by the addition of a perfect Fourth, be treated as $\frac{6}{4}$ $\left(\frac{6}{4}\right)$ [i.e. as the second inversion of a Dominant Seventh] as in the following Exx.:

---

[4] In first introducing the subject of dissonances Heinichen writes characteristically: "Their *Combinationes*, or different combinations and inversions, are, so to speak, innumerable, and can still be daily varied and refined by good practicioners" (l. c., § 13, p. 159).

[5] Heinichen explains this term as including the 3rd, 5th, 6th, 8ve, "as long as, in accordance with their nature, they are neither syncopated nor resolved". E.g. the 5 in a $\frac{6}{5}$ chord, though consonant with the Bass, is "syncopated" by the Sixth, the 3 in a $\frac{6}{4}$ chord by the Fourth, &c., and the interval in question has a downward resolution.

[6] In the second of the two instances to be mentioned it will be seen that the harmony for which the discord is arbitrarily substituted is purely concordant.

[Ex. I] (l. c., § 7.)

[Heinichen gives two further similar examples with the alternative figuring $\frac{4}{3}$, $\frac{6}{4}$.]

(2) Similarly, by the addition of an augmented Fourth, a major Sixth with a *major* Third [on the Submediant of a minor key falling a semitone to the Dominant] may be treated as $\frac{6}{4}$ $\left(\frac{6}{4}\right)$ [i.e. as the second inversion of a Seventh on the Supertonic] (cf. Ch. xxi, 'Incomplete figuring', II, § 2, Ex. I).

The conditions, as defined by Heinichen, under which this Fourth (perfect or augmented, as the case may be) may be added, though not included in the figuring, are that it should have been present, in the same part, in the preceding chord and should be retained in the following one. So far, however, was he from a correct apprehension of the resulting harmonies, that it was *the Fourth* (known in this connexion as *4ta irregularis* or *la quarta irregolare*, on account of its remaining without resolution[7]), *and not the Third*, which he regarded as the dissonant note.

Heinichen was acquainted with Rameau's *Traité de l'Harmonie réduite à ses principes naturels* (Paris, 1722), which he mentions more than once, and his failure to recognize the 3 of a $\frac{6}{4}$ chord as an inverted 7, and therefore *as the dissonant note of the chord*, is the more remarkable, since he recognizes the principle of inversion, though, as will be seen, he does not apply it with complete accuracy. Thus, in giving the rule that an accidentally sharpened Bass note, bearing a Sixth, must not be doubled, *unless the Sixth itself is accidentally sharpened as well*, he adds the following explanation:[8]

"If such a Bass note, with a prefixed ✕ or ♮, at the same time bears over it an accidentally sharpened ♭ 6 ♮, it is nothing else but an inverted 5th (*eine superstruirte 5te*), and can, therefore, always be unhesitatingly doubled in accordance with the nature of all (perfect) 5ths. *Probetur*: In the two chords: ♯♯♯♭♭♯♮ let the 5th be taken as the Bass and the two other parts be left in their place; one will then obtain the Bass notes in question, with prefixed ✕ and ♮, and bearing over them the *6ta maj. accidentalis*:

"If, however, such a Bass note bears over it a *6ta min. naturalis* (combined in the ordinary way with a *3a min.*), it cannot well be doubled, because, in

---

[7] Cf. Ch. xxi, 'Incomplete figuring', II, §§ 1, 2.

[8] l. c., § 6, note f, pp. 147 sqq.

[9] It is hardly necessary to remark that $\frac{6}{4}$ is the second inversion, not of $\frac{5}{✕}$, as Heinichen's examples would seem to indicate, but of $\frac{7}{5}$.
$✕$

its origin, it is an inverted accidentally sharpened major Third (*eine super-struirte 3a maj. accid.*) which has lost nothing of its hardness through the

inversion of the parts. For if, for example, in the chords:

the accidental 3*a maj.* be taken as the Bass, and the other two parts be left in their place, we obtain a Bass note with a prefixed $\times$ or ♮, and bearing

over it a 6*ta min. naturalis*: ...."

It is noteworthy that neither Heinichen, nor, at a later date, Ph. Em. Bach, make any mention of the seventh degree (or leading note) of a scale, as an interval which may not be doubled, but only of an *accidentally sharpened*

major Third, i.e. when not associated with a major Sixth, as:

in which case, as Heinichen explains (l. c., § 4, note c, p. 142), the accidentally sharpened major 3rd is really the 5th of the fundamental note (*Fundamental-Clavis*), and can therefore be doubled at pleasure.

This insistence on the accidental nature of a major Third, as the all-important factor militating against the duplication of the interval in question, betokens a point of view entirely at variance with that of later harmonists, who would as little think of doubling the leading note in the key of *D* major, in which ♯ *C* is in accordance with the key-signature, as they would in the key of *D* minor, in which the note in question is accidentally sharpened.

Heinichen is, however, very explicit on the subject. After explaining why an accidentally sharpened major Third may be doubled when associated with a major Sixth, he continues (in the footnote referred to above) as follows:

"But as regards the duplication (*Vermehrung*) of the other *Tertiae majores*, not included in a chord of the Sixth, an important distinction is certainly to be made, as to whether they are *naturales* or *accidentales*. The 3*ae maj. naturales* can be doubled without hesitation (and regardless of all delusions generally entertained on the subject) not only in a *Quatro* [i.e. in 4-part writing], but in a *Trio* as well, when a suitable opportunity offers, because the ear has already been prepared for it by a regular striking of these essential tones belonging to the key, as the daily practice of the most famous composers shows, without need for further proof. On the other hand, the 3*ae maj. accidental.* (when a strange $\times$ or sharpening ♮, external to the key, is introduced, and doubled in addition) assuredly have a much harsher effect upon the ear (*fallen . . . dem Gehöre viel härter aus*). This distinction can easily be tested. For instance, let the 3*a maj. nat.* in the two following chords, in the key of *D* major, be doubled in any way that one pleases:

; even with only a few parts an unprejudiced ear will take

no exception to such duplication. On the other hand, let the 3*a maj. accidental.* be doubled in the very same chords, in the key of *D* minor, after the ear has

already become preoccupied by the *ambitus* of *D* minor:

,

and discomfort will be experienced, the more intense, the longer one of the doubled notes in question is sustained. Nay, the further and the more unexpectedly a *3a maj. accident.* departs from the regular limits of the original key, the more intolerable to the ear will its duplication prove when there are only a few parts. . . ."

The same applies *mutatis mutandis* to the duplication of a major Sixth with a minor Third, and of a bass note bearing a minor Sixth (and minor Third). In *D major*, Heinichen tells us (l. c., § 6, note f, p. 149), it is possible to double ♯ *C* as major Sixth on the Bass *e*, or the bass notes ♯ *c* and ♯ *f* when figured 6, without offence to the ear; but not in *D minor*, in which the notes in question are accidentally sharpened.

(*b*) In treating of the discords Heinichen arranges them in their numerical order: the Second, the Fourth, the diminished Fifth, the Seventh, and the Ninth.

In this way it comes about that harmonies of a widely differing nature are treated together. Thus, under the heading of the "Syncopating 2nd" (l. c., § 15) are included the following harmonies: (1) $\frac{6}{4}$ = the third inversion of a Seventh; (2) $\frac{5}{4}$ = $\frac{6}{5}$, the first inversion of a Seventh, with retarded Bass; (3) $\frac{5}{2}$ = $\frac{6}{3}$, the first inversion of a Triad, with retarded Bass.

A further result of Heinichen's arrangement is that harmonies *of which the dissonance is not with the Bass* have no real place in the scheme, and have to be, as it were, smuggled into it in the wake of an "invited guest".

Thus, of the $\frac{6}{4}$ chord in which the 3 is prepared (unlike those shown in Ex. 1) Heinichen writes (l. c., § 16): "Kindred to the *2da syncopata* is the *3a syncopata* which, together with the Bass, is tied, and, at the same time, is syncopated [10] by the *4ta (maj. or min.)* and subsequently resolves a semitone or a whole tone downwards.[11] The Bass, which resolves [12] at the same

---

[10] See note 5.

[11] Heinichen here appends the following footnote: "i.e. it allows itself to be treated just like a dissonance, and surrenders itself voluntarily into the very same slavery as also the *5ta perfecta* does in the case of the 6th."

The latter allusion is to a $\frac{6}{5}$ chord with a perfect Fifth, which, on account of the consonance of the said Fifth with the Bass, does not find its natural place in Heinichen's scheme any more than the $\frac{6}{4}$ chord just discussed. Of it our author writes (l. c., § 34):

"The *5ta perfecta* is frequently used as a dissonance and *5ta syncopata*, namely, when it is syncopated by the 6th and treated in all other respects just like the *5ta min.* [i.e. the diminished or 'false' 5th]. There is only this difference, that it requires to be tied [i.e. prepared] in the regular way (*Nur dieses hat sie voraus, dass sie gern vorhero legaliter bindet*)." Heinichen here appends the following note:

"The following example, in a cadence, might perhaps be excused:

"But, for my part, I would sooner use the *5ta min.*, thus:

[12] It would seem from this that Heinichen regarded the Bass as participating in the dissonant nature of the 3 (cf. note 11 *ad init.*).

time, can here, as in the case of the *2da syncopata*, likewise bear the chords: $6 \mid {}^{6}_{5\flat} \mid {}^{6}_{5} \mid {}^{5}_{\times} \mid$ over it, as is clear from the following examples: [13]

(*c*) After dealing with the harmonies which include the intervals from the Bass enumerated above (2, 4, 5♭, 7, 9), as well as the augmented Fourth (4♯) and the diminished Seventh (♭7), Heinichen devotes the remainder of the chapter to the *Falsae*, which he defines as those intervals which contain a *semitonium minus* [i.e. the difference between, e.g., *c* and ♯*c*, *e* and ♭ *e*] too much or too little, namely, (1) the augmented Second, Fourth, Fifth, and Sixth, and (2) the diminished Third, Fourth, Fifth, and Seventh. Of these, the augmented Fourth, and the diminished Fifth and Seventh, having already been dealt with, are now excluded from the list; there remain, therefore, (1) the augmented Second, Fifth, and Sixth, and (2) the diminished Third [14] and Fourth.

Heinichen points out that *Falsae* may arise either (1) between the Bass and another part, as in the case of the augmented Sixth, or (2) between two upper parts, as in the case of a major Third with a minor Sixth, from which

---

[13] Heinichen here appends the following footnote: "This harmony $\left({}^{6}_{4}_{3}\right)$ has nothing in common with the harmony mentioned above in § 7 [cf. Ex. 1] beyond the external characteristic of the figures, inasmuch as both harmonies can be indicated by ${}^{6}_{4}_{3}$." This is, indeed, a remarkable statement.

[14] No example is given, however, of the diminished Third, an interval which Heinichen regarded as too harsh to be tolerated, even between two upper parts, let alone between an upper part and the Bass. In giving the following examples of ${}^{6\flat}_{4\!\!\!/}_{2}$ and ${}^{6\flat}_{4\!\!\!/}_{3}$ (the first inversions of the 'French' and 'German' Sixths, respectively):

he writes (l. c., § 83): "In expressing harsh feeling (*bey harten Expressionibus*), certain learned and distinguished composers are wont to associate the *6ta min.*, as an auxiliary part (*Nebenstimme*), with the *4ta maj.* (${}^{6\flat}_{4\!\!\!/}$). Now if this 6♭ is struck at the top, and the 4♯ below, there results between the two parts an intolerable *Falsa*, namely, the *3a min. deficiens*, which, it is true, claims to be excused on the ground that it is only in relation to a middle part that it arises, and not in relation to the Bass or *Fundamental-Clavis* (for on that, surely, no conscientious composer has as yet ventured). But it is a bad excuse, for if the *3a min. deficiens* is intolerable and impracticable in relation to the Bass, it is so in relation to all the other parts likewise. On the other hand, I should be more inclined to sanction this harsh harmony (${}^{6\flat}_{4\!\!\!/}$) if, in composition, the 4♯ is sounded above, and the 6♭ below it, because in this way a *6ta maj. superflua* arises between the two parts, instead of the previous intolerable 3rd, and because the previously existing harshness seems to disappear (*evanesciren*) to some extent owing to the greater distance. . . ."

there results either a diminished Fourth or an augmented Fifth, according to the position in which the chord is taken.

Space does not permit us to follow our author through the resulting harmonies which he illustrates individually, and also collectively in general examples, given both in four parts and with filled-in harmony.

(*d*) At the end of the chapter, in which, as Heinichen tells us, all the signatures most generally in use are treated of, a Table of Signatures is added "for the benefit of beginners". It is in parallel columns (thirty-two in number), with three horizontal divisions. In the uppermost of these are given the figurings generally used to indicate the chords in question, while in the two lower ones there are added the remaining intervals belonging to the harmony, but not usually expressed in the figuring. The idea is that, by "looking out" any particular figuring in the uppermost division (as in a dictionary), the student may be enabled to see at a glance how the harmony is to be completed. The table is as follows:

Group braces (top): **2** | **3** | **4** | **5** | **6**

	2	3 / 2♭	✕	♭	4 / 2	4+	4 / 3	4	43	5♭	5+	6	6 / 4	6 5 / 4 3	6♭ / 4+	6 / 5	6 / 54
Common signatures of a Thorough-Bass	2	3 / 2♭	✕	♭	4 / 2	4+	4 / 3	4	43	5♭	5+	6	6 / 4	6 5 / 4 3	6♭ / 4+	6 / 5	6 / 54
The parts which go with them	6 / 4	5	5 / 8	5 / 8	6 / 2	6	6 / 8	5	5 / 8	6 / 3 / *8	3 / 8	3 / *8	8	8	2 / *8	3	8

Group braces (top): **7** | **9**

	7	7 6	7 / 2	7 / 4 / 2	7 / 4	7 6 / 5+6	♭7 / 5♭	♭7 / 6 5	9	9 8	9 / 4	9 / 6	9 / 7	9 / 7 / 4	9 8 / 7 6 / 5 6
Common signatures of a Thorough-Bass	7	7 6	7 / 2	7 / 4 / 2	7 / 4	7 6 / 5+6	♭7 / 5♭	♭7 / 6 5	9	9 8	9 / 4	9 / 6	9 / 7	9 / 7 / 4	9 8 / 7 6 / 5 6
The parts which go with them	5 / 3 / *8	3 / 5	4 / *5	*5	5 / *8	3 / *8	3 / *8	3 / *8	5 / 3	5 / 3	5	3	3 / 3†	5	3

N.B.—The 3† at the bottom of the antepenultimate column is evidently intended for 5.

Some signatures showing accidental alteration (as 2♭ | ♭6/✕ | 4+/2+ | ♭7/♭3 | &c.) have been omitted, Heinichen tells us, from the upper divisions of the table. In such cases the complementary parts are to be sought under the same signatures without accidental alteration (2 | 6/3 | 4/2 | 7/3 | &c.). The asterisk * appended to certain figures indicates that they can be omitted in a 4-part accompaniment "unless they fall into the hand comfortably and, as it were, of their own accord".

IV. A short account of the contents of the Second Part of Heinichen's great work must suffice.

(*a*) The first chapter (which is a treatise in itself) deals exhaustively with all the irregularities in the resolution of discords found in the free [15] (and, in particular, the *theatrical*) style.

[15] The term *der galante Styl*, so much used by Ph. Em. Bach, is not employed by

The accompanist, Heinichen tells us (l. c., § 2), is constantly liable to be confronted with "Arias, Cantatas, Operas, instrumental Solos, Duets, &c.", in which *the Bass is not figured*, and he is consequently obliged to infer the correct harmony either from the score, or, more commonly, from *a single Solo part* given above the Bass.

It is, therefore, as a preparation for these demands upon his skill that Heinichen proposes to familiarize the student with the free progressions and resolutions characteristic of the style in question. He distinguishes carefully between legitimate and illegitimate freedom: every discord, he tells us (l. c., § 5), must be followed by its proper resolution (*legale Resolution*), whether in the same part or in a different one.

Under certain circumstances, indeed, it may not even be *in the same Octave*, as in the following example (l. c., § 52), in which there is an exchange between the principal part and the Bass in the resolution of the $^6_{5b}$ chord: the downward resolution of the ♭ *b* in the principal part is transferred to the Bass *, an 8ve and a semitone below the discord, while the upward resolution of *e* in the Bass is transferred to the principal part *, two 8ves and a semitone above:

[Ex. 3]

Of the following example, on the other hand, and other similar ones, in which the resolution is entirely omitted:

[Ex. 4]

Heinichen writes (l. c., § 13): "Now all these examples can be defended neither on the score of inversion of the parts nor in any other way, consequently they are and remain wrong."

The permissible irregularities of the 'theatrical' style in the resolution of discords are treated by Heinichen under eight headings:

(1) Ornamental resolutions (either in the Bass itself or in a principal part, as the case may be).

(2) Discords of such kind as ordinarily require preparation, including even suspensions, taken by leap in a principal part.

(This is justified on the ground that the discord in question has been prepared in another part, i.e. in the accompaniment.)

A special case arises when the discord in a principal part, thus taken by leap, is immediately *followed by another leap in the opposite direction*, thus leaving the resolution, as well as the preparation, of the discord to the accompaniment.

Heinichen. He speaks of the *Stylus Theatralis* in contradistinction to the *Stylus Gravis*, and sometimes, too, of the 'Cammer-*Stylus*' (chamber style) in contradistinction to the 'Kirchen-*Stylus*' or *Stylus Ecclesiasticus*.

(3) The transference of the discord to another part before resolution.[16]
(4) The transference of the resolution to another part.[17]
(5) The anticipation of a passing note (*Anticipatio transitus*) in the Bass.[18]
(6) Retardation and anticipation in the upper (principal) parts.
(7) The resolution of discords following an enharmonic change.
(8) Certain obscure and doubtful cases in the practice of the time.

The latter are all taken from Recitatives, "because", as Heinichen tells us, "it is just in this style that the greatest abuses of the principles of dramatic composition (*der Theatralischen Fundamenta*) occur".

After explaining them, in doing which it must be admitted that, despite his ingenuity, our author is hard put to it to reconcile some of the passages in question with his axiom that every discord must have its resolution, he adds: "While it is not my idea that any one should accustom himself to suchlike free progressions (*Sätze*), and seek to imitate them without discrimination; at the same time there accrues to students of Music at least this advantage, that, in them, they exercise their *Judicium practicum*, and learn to distinguish black from white, I mean the degrees of a good, passable, bad, better, and worse theatrical progression."

To the above warning against indiscriminate imitation Heinichen appends the following very characteristic footnote: "Although I do not deny that, before now (*sonst*), I have myself imitated the liberties of foreigners (lit. "free foreigners") in this matter, in which, after a thorough investigation of the subject, I shall, to be sure, take a goodish step backwards."

(*b*) After thus elucidating the principles of dramatic composition, so far as the treatment of discords is concerned, from a theoretical point of view, Heinichen devotes the next three chapters to the practical question of accompaniment from an unfigured Bass, above which, however, the *concertante* part is given, in accordance with the general practice of the operatic composers of the day.

In Ch. II the student is taught to divine the required harmony by the aid of:
(1) The vocal or instrumental part given above the Bass.
(2) Eight general rules based on the interval between the bass notes in question (irrespective of their place in the scale).
(3) Eight special rules based on the *ambitus modi* (and therefore on the position in the scale of the bass notes in question).

It is on the first six of these latter (and also on one of the general rules, in accordance with which a bass note bearing a major Triad, and then falling a whole tone, bears a $^6_4{}_2$ chord) that Heinichen bases the following schemes (which he subsequently transposes into the remaining twenty-two keys):

[16] Cf. Ch. xxii of the present work, "Inversion, transference of the discord", &c., § 2.
[17] Cf. ibid., § 3.   [18] Cf. ibid., § 7.

The 5 and 6 over the second and sixth degrees of the major scale, Heinichen explains (l. c., § 15), are *not to be taken consecutively*, as would ordinarily be the case, but as *alternatives*.

With the above schemes Heinichen compares the following ones from Rameau's *Traité de l'Harmonie réduite à ses principes naturels* (Paris, 1722), p. 384:

[Ex. 7]

[Ex. 8]

He also quotes Gasparini's schemes of the major and minor mode. The chief difference between these and his own is (1) that, in *some* of the scales, *both major and minor*,[19] Gasparini (like Rameau) figures the fourth degree of the ascending scale $^6_5$, while in others, again, he figures it 6; and (2) that he sharpens the Sixth on the sixth degree of the descending major scale *as an alternative* to the natural Sixth.

As compared with the schemes of Gasparini and Rameau, Heinichen claims the following advantages for his own:

(1) That, by placing the *Semitonium modi* (leading note) at the beginning of the scale, the irregular progression from the flat Sixth to the sharp Seventh of the minor mode is avoided,[20] and the whole made clearer to beginners.

(2) That, by omitting certain figures [particularly, no doubt, the $^6_5$ on the fourth degree of the ascending scale], and also by giving 5 and 6 as alternative figurings on the second and sixth degrees of the major scale, the schemes are made more universal in their application and the right harmony can be found *irrespective of the order in which the bass notes are arranged*.[21]

(3) That, by not sharpening the Sixth on the sixth degree of the descending major scale, he has kept more closely within the limits of the mode. "For", he writes (l. c., § 24), "if, for instance, in *G* major, our composers figure the notes descending from the 8ve to the 5th as follows: $_g$ $^6_{\sharp f}$ $^5_{ed}$, it is practically (*schon*) a half-close and an excursion into *D* major, with which *G* major has nothing to do. Not to mention that, even if it were allowed to pass as in

---

[19] This point would appear to have escaped Heinichen, who quotes the scale of *G major*, in which the fourth degree of the ascending scale is figured $^6_5$, and that of *G minor*, in which it bears a Triad, thereby conveying the impression that Gasparini made this distinction between the major and minor modes. An example of Gasparini's scales, *D* minor and major (in one of which the fourth degree is figured 6), is given in § 7 *h*, note 20.

[20] Heinichen explains (l. c., § 13) that the "two special progressions" (*ausserordentliche Gänge*) of the Bass, shown in Ex. 5 b, are thus given separately "because they alter the *Claves* of the usual *ambitus modi*, and therefore do not properly speaking belong to the scheme".

[21] In Ch. V (§§ 24–33) Heinichen shows how his harmonic scheme of the major and minor modes may be made the basis of *ex tempore* preludes by combining the schemes of nearly related keys, and by introducing suspensions and other discords, and also by *varying the order of the bass notes*.

G major, it would, after all, be a special case which holds good only so long as the notes remain in just that order."

(*c*) Ch. III deals with the accompaniment of Recitative, which presents special difficulties because of the frequent and daring changes of key and also because there is usually *no key-signature*, the necessary accidentals being prefixed to each note as required. It is therefore necessary that the accompanist should be quick to recognize in what key the music is at the moment, and that he should be perfectly familiar with what Heinichen calls the *Species Octavae* (i.e. the notes of the scale) of the remotest keys.

(*d*) In Ch. IV the rules previously given are illustrated by an entire Solo Cantata for a Soprano voice with an unfigured Bass composed by no less a person than Alessandro Scarlatti. Heinichen selected this composer, he tells us, on account of his "extravagant and irregular treatment of harmony", and, in particular, his bold and frequent changes of key, similar to, and frequently harsher than, those in a Recitative. Heinichen is far from admiring his style. "We will, however," he writes (l. c., p. 798, footnote), "let our accompanist profit by these irregularities."

Every bass note that requires a figure bears, instead, a number referring to a footnote which explains what the harmony ought to be in accordance with the general and special rules given in Ch. II. Where the vocal part is a sufficient guide to the harmony, the bass note is marked with an *obelus* †. Among these footnotes are interspersed, in the course of the Cantata, twelve *Observationes practicae*, supplementing the rules previously given.

The chapter is an interesting and most instructive one.

(*e*) The connexion of the subject of Ch. V with the accompaniment of unfigured Basses (to the consideration of which the Second Part of Heinichen's work is avowedly devoted) is not at first apparent.

In it the author explains the merits of his 'Musical Circle', which, as he tells us, he invented for his own benefit, when a pupil of Kuhnau at Leipsic. Kuhnau had told him of Kircher's method of going through the keys by Fourths (*C*, *F*, ♭ *B*, &c.) or Fifths (*C*, *G*, *D*, &c.), but he found that this was of no assistance in getting from a *major* key to a remote *minor* one or vice versâ, since, by this method, one major or minor key (as the case might be) only led to another of the same description. The result of his experiments was the scheme on the following page.

He gives examples (figured Bass and upper part only):

(1) going through the entire circle from left to right;
(2) ditto from right to left;
(3) going through alternate degrees of the circle from left to right, starting with *C major*;
(4) ditto from right to left;
(5) going through *alternate* degrees from left to right, starting with *A minor*;
(6) ditto from right to left.

In the last four instances the method is identical with that of Kircher, mentioned above.

The examples are all in the strict *Allabreve* style, but, to illustrate the matter further, Heinichen gives an additional one (complete in two parts without further harmony) in common time (*Un poco allegro, mà cantabile*), starting in *A* minor, and completing the circle from left to right, omitting only the keys of *E* and *F* sharp major.

It is not practicable, he tells us, to go through the circle skipping *two* keys each time: "For although the first skip over 2 *Modi* may be ventured upon successfully (no new thing to good practicians), a skip of this kind cannot

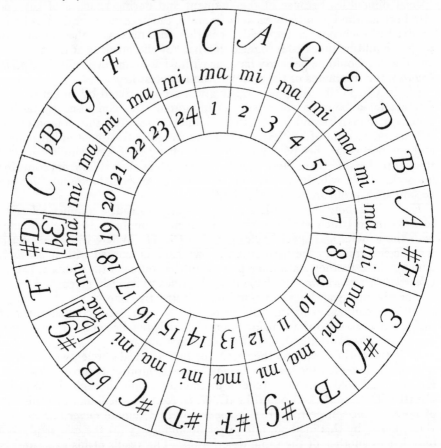

well be repeated over the next two *Modi* without jarring unpleasantly on the ear. If one were actually to make a third skip, over 2 other *Modi*, it would be quite intolerable to the ear. . . ." (l. c., § 17).

The Musical Circle is useful, Heinichen tells us, (1) in composition, (2) in accompanying from an unfigured Bass, (3) in playing *extempore* preludes on keyed instruments,[22] and (4) as tending to the total abolition of the ancient Modes.

With regard to its bearing on accompaniment, which is what chiefly concerns us here, Heinichen points out, truly enough, that, in accompanying from an unfigured Bass, especially when (as in Recitatives) there are abrupt changes of key, a thorough knowledge of key-relationship and of modulation is essential. "If", he writes (l. c., § 23), "one wishes to learn to grasp these changes quickly and thoroughly, and to acquire dexterity in Accompaniment, one must, above all things, acquire a thorough understanding of the connexion between, and the usual divagations of, all the keys (*so muss man vor*

[22] See note 21.

allen Dingen die Connection *und gewöhnlichen* Digressiones *aller* Modorum *aus dem Fundamente verstehen*).''

(*f*) In the sixth and last chapter of the Second Part the rules given in Ch. II are applied to an unfigured Bass of twenty-eight bars *without any Solo part printed over it*. It is given in full in the keys of *C*, *G*, and *F* major, and the student is left to transpose it for himself into the remaining major keys.

And thus we take leave of Heinichen. Whatever the defects of his work may be, it would be difficult to name one which bears witness to greater endeavour and sincerity on the part of its author.

§ 6. *David Kellner.*

A book which had as wide a circulation in Germany as Gasparini's work had in Italy was David Kellner's *Treulicher Unterricht im General-Bass &c.*, Hamburg (Kissner), 1732. In the first edition only the initials of the author appear on the title-page, but in later editions his full name is given, and he is, moreover, described as 'Captain' (*Capitain*). According to Eitner he was in the service of the town of Hamburg, though Schröter speaks of him as a "Swedish captain" (see below). According to an author quoted by Fétis (Jonas Oedman, *De Musica Sacra*, Lundini Gothorum, 1745) he was Director of Music in the German Church at Stockholm, and there published his treatise in Swedish (cf. Eitner, *Quellenlexicon*), but this does not seem very probable, as the German work above mentioned was translated *into Swedish* by one Jonas Londec in 1739 (Stockholm), as well as into Dutch by Gerh. Havingha in 1741 (Amsterdam).

The second edition, issued by the original publishers in 1737, contained a preface by Telemann, and the third edition (Hamburg, Christian Herold, 1743), one by Daniel Solander, Professor of Jurisprudence at Upsala. The sixth, and apparently last, edition appeared in 1782. All this shows that the work was held in considerable esteem.

It is of modest dimensions, containing only 98 quarto pages, exclusive of preface and index, and it is therefore not surprising that it hardly comes up to the author's description of it on the title-page, to the effect that "all diffuseness is avoided, and, nevertheless, many newly-invented devices (*Vortheile* [1]) are fully and clearly given, by means of which any one can in a short time fully master everything that pertains to this science".

Schröter (*Deutliche Anweisung &c.*, 1772, Preface, vii) writes of it as follows: "The 'Instruction in Thorough-Bass' by the well-known Swedish captain, Mr. David Keller [*sic*], which, on account of its low price, is in great demand, and has consequently been reprinted several times, contains, in spite of its shortness, much that is good. People have complained that the author in question has neither observed order nor given adequate examples; to which others have answered: This martial soul has accomplished more than one could have expected of him."

And again (ibid., lvi):

"No one will deny that Keller's [*sic*] Instruction, like other similar Methods, can advance a beginner in Thorough-Bass far enough to play his part *taliter qualiter* in easy *Arias*, as also in Sonatas and Concertos with a drumming

---

[1] This word, which in modern German signifies 'advantage', is constantly used in the musical treatises of the eighteenth century in the sense of the *most advantageous way of doing a particular thing*, and so a device, plan, or "dodge".

Bass. But it is also known that such disciples of Keller (*Kellerianer*) have stumbled lamentably over the works e.g. of Telemann and other composers whose harmony is rich, since they cannot possibly have learnt all diatonic progressions (*Wendungen*) from their instructor's two Tables. . . ."

Kellner's work contains seven chapters, given in the table of contents [2] as follows:

- I. "Von den Intervallen, Accorden, Regulirung der Stimmen, und unterschiedlichen andern Vorfällen" (*On the intervals, chords, regulation of the parts, and divers other matters*).
- II. "Vom Gebrauche der Signaturen" (*On the use of the signatures*).
- III. "Von der Töne natürlichen *Ambitu* und Accompagnement" (*On the natural scope and accompaniment of the several keys*).
- IV. "Von den extraordinairen Sätzen, so von den natürlichen abgehen" (*Extraordinary progressions, which differ from the natural ones*).
- V. "Von den Ausweichungen der Töne" (*On the digressions of the several keys*).
- VI. "Von der Beschaffenheit der Consonantien" (*On the nature of the consonances*).
- VII. "Von der *Praxi* der Dissonantien" (*On the use of the dissonances*).

Besides a Table of thirty signatures, given at the end of Ch. II, Kellner also gives two Tables (in Ch. VII) showing on what degree of the major and minor modes, respectively, the various dissonances most commonly occur, and also whether on a rising or falling Bass, or without regard to the progression of the Bass. Thus, e.g. $\frac{6}{3}$ is given only on the 2nd and 6th degrees of the major scale: on the 2nd degree on either a rising or falling Bass, and on the 6th degree (as an alternative to $\frac{6}{3}$) on a falling Bass only.

The author remarks with great satisfaction that nothing of the kind is to be found in any previous treatise on Thorough-Bass.

It is very remarkable that, although Kellner actually gives a Table showing $\frac{6}{5}$, $\frac{6}{4}$, and $\frac{6}{2}$ chords as inversions of the Seventh, he nevertheless, in giving examples of $\frac{6}{3}$, tells us that in every case the *Fourth* remains without resolution, as though that were the dissonant note.

He more than once takes occasion to criticize Heinichen, of whose Musical Circle he does not approve. He writes as follows (Ch. VI): "In Heinichen's new work, p. 837, we also find a musical Circle. But it occurred to the said author himself that a newer or better kind might be invented, when on p. 28 he speaks as follows: 'Perhaps some day a different kind of musical Circle from that given farther on, in Part II, Ch. 5, will appear, or at least a new way of using it.'"

Nevertheless, in perusing Kellner's work one finds it difficult to resist the impression that its author gleaned a good deal from Heinichen.

§ 7. *Johann Mattheson* (1681–1764).

(*a*) Although Mattheson bestowed upon the second edition (1731) of his *Organisten-Probe* (1719) the title of 'Grosse General-Bass-Schule' (*Great Thorough-Bass School*), it can hardly be said (important, and indeed indis-

---

[2] The headings of the chapters themselves are, in some cases, slightly different.

pensable, as this work is to the student) that the new title is appropriate, inasmuch as no information whatever is given about the chords to be employed or the progression of the intervals.

It was to remedy this deficiency that the 'Kleine General-Bass-Schule' (*Little Thorough-Bass School*) was written. It must have been begun before the publication of the larger work in 1731, as the dedication is dated 'New Year 1735', and the author mentions incidentally (*Vorbericht* [Preface] xxxiii) that the book had "been waiting for the press" for five years.

The author's purpose is clearly set forth in the following words (*Der untersten Classe oder Einleitung Erste Anzeige* [First Announcement of the Lowest Class or Introduction], § 2). After mentioning that he had assumed that "whoever desired to embark upon the said Great Thorough-Bass School would be sure to have already learned the first rules from some good book or other, or from the oral tuition of an intelligent teacher", he proceeds: "Since, however, it turns out that my assumption has not always proved correct, but that there still are, from time to time, many persons eager for information who, from ignorance of the elements in question, are unable to make use of the Great Thorough-Bass School as they would wish, for whose needs, however, provision must be made, it has therefore been decided, in response to many requests, to arrange the present small, it is true, but nevertheless correct, proper, and genuine (*reine, rechte und ächte*) Thorough-Bass School, in which even the smallest details are taught, for the benefit of beginners, so clearly, simply, and completely, that nothing further could well be desired."

The full title of the work is as follows:

JOHANN MATTHESON's, / Hoch-Fürstl. Schleswig-Holsteinischen Capell-Meisters, und Königl.-Gross-Britan-/nischen Gesandten-Secretars im Nieder-Sächsischen Kreise, / KLEINE / GENERAL-BASS-SCHULE. / Worin / Nicht nur LERNENDE, sondern vornehmlich LEHRENDE, / Aus / Den allerersten Gründen des Clavier-Spielens, / überhaupt und besonders, / Durch / VERSCHIEDENE CLASSEN u. ORDNUNGEN DER ACCORDE, / Stuffen-weise, / Mittelst / GEWISSER LECTIONEN ODER STÜNDLICHER AUFGABEN, / Zu / Mehrer Vollkommenheit in dieser Wissenschaft, / Richtig, getreulich, und auf die deutlichste Lehr-Art / kürtzlich angeführet werden. / *Utilia, non subtilia.* / Hamburg, bey Joh. Christoph Kiszner. 1735.[1]

(*b*) The work (which Mattheson tells us in the dedication ought to occupy the pupil seven or eight months) is divided into four 'Classes': (1) the 'Lowest Class or Introduction', (2) The Ascending (*aufsteigend*) Class, (3) The Higher Class, (4) The Upper Class.

Each Class is again divided into seven 'Tasks' (*Aufgaben*) which, in the Lowest and Ascending Classes, are again preceded by four introductory sections, which, in the former case, are styled *Anzeigen* (Announcements), and, in the latter, *Nachrichten* (Notices).

In some instances the 'Tasks' are divided into sections (*Abtheilungen*).

The four 'Announcements' which precede the 'Lowest Class' deal with: (1) "The question: What Thorough-Bass is?" (2) "The method of instruction generally", (3) "The teacher", (4) "Pieces (*Handsachen*) generally".

---

[1] A second impression appeared in the same year with *different pagination*. The earlier impression is at once recognizable by the red printing (alternating with black) on the title-page.

Concerning these, it must suffice to say that Mattheson (like Ph. Em. Bach) attaches great importance to a thorough study and *technical mastery* of pieces written for the Clavier (*Handsachen*) as a necessary preliminary to the study of Thorough-Bass. He also suggests that the teacher should take this opportunity of acquainting the pupil "incidentally and conversationally" with the principles of harmony.

The seven 'Tasks' of the 'Lowest Class' deal with such matters as (1) the Keyboard; (2) and (3) the different *G*, *C*, and *F* clefs [2] (which, as Mattheson very wisely insists, are to be mastered *at once* [3]) and their application; (4) the signs ✕, ♭, and ♮; (5) time; (6) the notes, rests, and dots; and (7) the intervals and keys.

With all this we are not here concerned, and may therefore pass on, after mentioning one small point which deserves notice: Mattheson classifies the dissonance between *C* and *C* sharp as the "smallest *Second* (*allerkleinste Secunde*)", and *figures it as such* in a subsequent example (*Ober-Classe, 1ste Aufgabe*, § 3). The example is as follows: [4]

Ex. 1

Concerning it Mattheson writes (l. c., § 4): "The most extraordinary part of it is that this smallest Second cannot be indicated by any other sign than the very same ♭ with which the diminished [5] Second [i.e. the interval between

[2] i.e. two *G* clefs (the 'French clef' on the lowest line, and the ordinary Treble clef, which Mattheson calls the "German clef"), four *C* clefs (Soprano, high Alto or Mezzo-soprano, Alto, and Tenor), and three *F* clefs (the ordinary Bass clef, the high Bass on the middle line, and the low Bass on the top line).

[3] He writes (*Unterster Classe, 2te Aufgabe*, § 23): "Many a person will here think that all this might be learnt by degrees, and that one must not muddle a pupil's brains with it (*einem Untergebenen . . . den Kopff damit warm machen*) at the wrong time. To this I say: no. It is not at the wrong time, but at the right time, for this reason: If any one does not acquire at the very beginning a fundamental conception of the whole matter (*von dem gantzen Wesen*), detailed information, and abundant light, i.e. not merely concerning the *signs*, but the *things* themselves, he will for ever be groping in the dark. For the pot always tastes of the first soup [that was in it]. . . ."

[4] The chords in small print have been added, for clearness' sake, in accordance with the figures (here placed *under* the Bass) with which Mattheson, as will be explained later (*c, ad init.*), indicates the desired interpretation of the *normal* figuring (as shown here *above* the Bass), and especially the *position* in which the chords are to be taken.

[5] Mattheson is driven to apply the term 'diminished' to the interval in question, because he applies the term *small* Second to the interval of a minor tone (as between *d* and *e* in the untempered scale of *C* major) to distinguish it from a *major* tone (or the interval between *C* and *D* in the same scale) which he calls a *great* Second. It is worth noting in this connexion that Mattheson did *not* regard the other major scales as mere transpositions of *C* major, but as distinct modes characterized by the different relative position of the major and minor tones. Thus (according to his view), the interval *d–e*, which, as the second interval in the scale of *C* major, is a *minor* tone, *remains so, as the first interval in the scale of D major* (cf. *Organisten-Probe*, 1719, 'Theoretische Vorbereitung' [Theoretical preparation], § cxciii, p. 107).

C and D flat, or a major semitone] is figured. On the *Clavier*, it is true, there is no difference between them, and a practiced player will also easily infer from the key that it must be ✕*c* and not ♭*d*; however, it is just the ignorance of former days which is to blame for this defect,[6] and there is perforce nothing more to be said about it for the present (*und wir können nicht umhin, es fürs erste so dabey bewenden zu lassen*)."

The author here appends a characteristic note: "If, instead, the sign ✕1 were to be used, it might thereby be indicated that the unison, *unisonus*, had to be raised at its upper extremity, and the required smallest Second thus produced; but it would not do to introduce an *unisonus superfluus*[7] with Mr. Rameau, for this reason, that there is a contradiction inherent in it; nor must we make an interval of the unison itself, as he nevertheless does, against and contrary to his own principles, on p. 167 of his *Traité de l'Harmonie*, where, likewise (p. 165), an augmented Third ♭E–✕G and a diminished Sixth ✕D–♭B and other monstrosities see the light of the world. Altogether, we find in the works of this Clermont Organist some thousand hundredweight of indefatigable work and deliberate hair-splitting (*Klauberei*); five hundred stone of tiresome fads and eccentricities (*Sonderlings-Fratzen*); some three pounds of personal experience, not counting hear-say; two ounces of sound judgement; and barely a drachm (*Quintlein*) of good taste."

(*c*) The remaining three 'Classes', each with its seven 'Tasks', are devoted to the illustration of the chords of which the figurings appear in the 'Table of Signatures' to be mentioned presently.

Before proceeding further it is necessary to describe briefly Mattheson's method of instruction and the order which he observes.

Rules, in the ordinary sense of the word, are hardly ever given, except with regard to the necessary preparation of certain discords. We are never told, for example, that this or that discord resolves a degree downwards or a semitone upwards, or that this or that interval may not be doubled. Such things as these Mattheson leaves to be imparted orally by a teacher, or to be inferred from the examples.

The latter are abundant and of ample length. Each example, moreover, is given in duplicate: first, a Bass figured in what Mattheson regarded as the

---

[6] A somewhat parallel case is the use by some of the older figurists, e. g. Daniel Treiber (cf. § 2), of ♭ or ✕6 to indicate the diminished Seventh.

[7] A good example of the interval in question occurs in G. P. Telemann's *Singe-, Spiel- und General-Bass-Übungen* (cf. § 8) and also of its compound, the augmented 8ᵛᵉ (o. c., No. 29, 1st section, bar 5; and 2nd section, bar 8). The examples (omitting the voice part) are as follows:

Concerning (*a*) (where, by a curious oversight, the crossed figure ✗ = ♯1 is omitted in the original) Telemann writes (on the following page): "This indication of the augmented unison (✗) is, generally speaking, uncommon, and 8 is usually chosen in its stead, as at (*b*) on the other page; but we wanted to show here that such an unison really does exist, which others call the diminished [Mattheson's 'smallest'] Second."

normal way, and, secondly, the same Bass with each one of the three (or sometimes four) upper parts figured, *not in the usual order* (with the highest figure on the top), but *in the order which they are to be played*, thus forming a sort of tablature,[8] and, in the earlier examples, the name of the note is given opposite to each figure.

With regard to the order observed, it cannot be said that there is any attempt at *classification* of the chords, since Mattheson (as he explains in the 3rd 'Notice' preceding the 'Ascending Class') bases his arrangement solely on the *frequency with which the chords in question occur*. It will be remembered that Heinichen followed this principle only to the extent of placing the *Falsae* (i.e. diminished or augmented intervals), with the exception of the augmented 4th and diminished 7th (on account of their frequent occurrence), in a group by themselves at the end of all the other chords.

Some of the details of Mattheson's arrangement are certainly surprising. For instance, $\frac{6}{4}\frac{}{3}$ on the Supertonic (the second inversion of the Dominant Seventh), one of the most frequent harmonies, appears in the 'Upper Class' as one of "Three fairly rare chords of the Fourth"; as a matter of fact, this chord had already been used in two examples of the 'Ascending Class' (3rd 'Task', Second Section (*Abtheilung*), § 9, bars 19, 23; 7th 'Task', § 12, bar 2)![9]

---

[8] In only one instance (*Aufsteigender Classe, 6te Aufgabe, Erste Abtheilung* [1st section], § 2), an example illustrating the progression $\frac{5}{3}\frac{6}{4}\frac{5}{3}$ over the same Bass, does he content himself with prefixing the letters *o, m, u* (*oben, mitten, unten*) to the upper figure to show its position in the chord: 'above', 'in the middle', or 'below'.

[9] Mattheson makes a sharp distinction between the use of this chord when its use s indicated by the figuring $\frac{4}{3}$ or $\frac{\overset{6}{4}}{3}$, and when it is arbitrarily used at the discretion of the player in the manner described by Heinichen (cf. § 5, III, Ex. 1). This is in complete accordance with the tacit assumption prevalent in the earlier part of the eighteenth century, and especially marked in the case of Mattheson, that the complementary parts (*Füll-Stimmen*), namely those parts not usually indicated in the figuring (and shown in the lower half of Heinichen's and Mattheson's 'Tables of Signatures'), are actually of less importance than the interval or intervals (*Haupt-Stimmen* = main parts) represented by the figures actually used (*Haupt-Signatur* = main signature). There can be little doubt that, in some cases, this point of view tended to blind those by whom it was entertained to the real nature of the harmony. Thus, we see how $\frac{6}{4}\frac{}{2}$ and $\frac{5}{4}\frac{}{2}$, which represent totally different harmonies, were lumped together by Heinichen (cf. § 5, III *b*), and Mattheson (cf. note 19, below), and also G. P. Telemann (cf. § 8 *c, sub* Ex. 8), simply because the loose system of figuring prevalent in their day permitted the two harmonies to be represented by the figure 2 alone, thus reducing the accompanying $\frac{6}{4}$ or $\frac{5}{4}$, as the case might be, to the rank of mere *Füll-Stimmen*.

Concerning the figurings 6 (6̅) and $\frac{4}{3}$ $\left(\frac{\overset{6}{4}}{3}\right)$ on the Supertonic Mattheson writes as follows ('Upper Class', 2nd 'Task', §§ 2 and 6):

"Furthermore it is not at all the question here, what permissible liberties a clever and experienced player knows how to take and therewith adorn his accompaniment; it is certainly the case that practiced masters are accustomed, it is true, in the case of the ordinary chord of the major Sixth [with minor Third], almost invariably to include a Fourth, if the latter has already been in the hand and subsequently changes into a consonant interval in the next harmony, which chord the French . . . call *la petite Sixte*; but a pupil who wishes to imitate this, and carry it out further, must necessarily be shown how far he is justified, and how distinct these things are."

"It is here to be noted that, when $\frac{4}{3}$ is employed as signature, the appropriate Sixth should always be included (*mitgegriffen*) and heard as a complementary part; but that,

The diminished Seventh, too, appears in the 'Upper Class' (4th Task) as one of "Two rare chords of the Seventh".

(d) The 'Ascending Class' deals professedly with *consonances*. This Class, it says in the Table of Contents at the beginning of the volume, "consists of four Notices and seven Tasks on the consonances"; and in the third Notice, "On the three orders of chords in general" (§ 3), Mattheson writes: "As far, then, as this first order is concerned, the seven Tasks of this Class are to be devoted to the following purpose, namely, that, from them, any one should learn to know and to use the consonant (*wol-lautend*) chords of *most frequent occurrence....*" Among these 'consonances', however, we find the diminished Triad, the augmented Triad, $^6_5$ chords (both on the leading note and the Subdominant, as well as $^6_{5b}$ on the Supertonic of a minor key), and the augmented Sixth (not only the 'Italian' Sixth, with the major Third only, but the 'French' Sixth, with the major Third and augmented Fourth, as well).

Mattheson's views on the consonant nature of the diminished Fifth are highly interesting. Agreeably with the character of his work, he makes no preliminary distinction between the use of this interval on the leading note and on the Supertonic of a minor key, but writes as follows (l.c., 7th 'Task', §§ 2, 3): "Its employment is of several kinds. Firstly, without the Sixth, with the Third and Octave, like a Triad (*Haupt-Accord*). Secondly, together with the ordinary [i.e. minor] Sixth, in which case the Third and Octave may also be sounded. Thirdly, struck together with the sharpened [Sixth]. And fourthly, following the [minor] Sixth and struck after it [i.e. as a passing note]."

"Its regular complementary parts (*Neben-Stimmen*) are therefore by no means the Sixth and Third, but rather the Third and Octave: so then there is no question whatever of preparation (*da weiss sie von keiner Bindung nichts*), and it resolves just like a Sixth [presumably a Sixth on the leading note, falling to 3 on the Tonic], and has all the characteristics of a consonance. Its signatures are ♭5 . ♭$^6_5$. ♭$^{\overline{5}}_5$. 6♭5."

Two examples must suffice.[10] From the first of these it will be seen that Mattheson went further than Heinichen in his treatment of a leading note, inasmuch as he doubles it just as freely when accidentally sharpened as when diatonic (cf. § 5, III a):

'The Chord of the diminished Fifth without the Sixth' (l. c., § 4)

[Ex. 1]

when only the Sixth is figured over the note, it is not always necessary to strike the Third and Fourth in question, which, in such case, are there only for the sake of ornament and fulness (*Zierraths- und Vollstimmigkeit halber*): not but what many a mistake is thereby avoided."

N.B.—Mattheson does not, of course, mean by this that the *Third* should ever be omitted.

[10] See note 4. The black notes in the Bass are those which bear the chord in question.

In the following example the doubled leading note is seen in the ninth and eleventh bars:

"The chord of the diminished Fifth struck simultaneously with the ordinary Sixth" (ibid., § 5)

[Ex. 2]

N.B.—The first eleven bars of the example are here omitted.

In view of this treatment of the leading note it is perhaps not surprising that Mattheson should permit the doubling of the Bass of an augmented Sixth, though he gives no example of it. He writes ('Ascending Class', 3rd 'Task', Second Section, § 6): "A chord of the augmented Sixth (which has 9 keys to show between its two extremities, and is really a minor Seventh) sounds very hard and piercing (*schneidend*); but not necessarily bad or dissonant. The Third and Octave are, in its case, two consonant (*wolklingend*) complementary parts (*Füll-Stimmen*), and agreeable sounds: many people also take, now the augmented Fourth with the Third, now the perfect [11] Fifth; but the latter must then be prepared, for which reason we omit it here." [12]

Mattheson indicates the augmented Sixth by *two* strokes through the figure (6̄), to distinguish it from 6̄, which merely indicates that the Sixth (whether major or augmented) is accidentally sharpened. It is, of course, only when figures are quoted *apart from the actual Bass* (as in a 'Table of Signatures') that this distinction is of any practical importance.

(*e*) In the *Grosse General-Bass-Schule* (*1731*) our author wrote in the most complimentary terms of Heinichen's *General-Bass &c.* (cf. Ch. III, § 6 *c*, note 11 and the text above), and he mentions it with due respect in the work now under discussion ('Lowest Class', 1st 'Announcement', § 3); but to Mattheson an opportunity of boasting, especially at the expense of any one whom he regarded as a rival, was like a brandy-bottle at the elbow of a drunkard, and such an opportunity presented itself in the first 'Notice' (*Nachricht*) of the 'Ascending Class', 'On Key-relationships', and also in the second 'Notice', 'On Figuring'. In the former he presents a 'Musical Circle' designed to supersede that given by Heinichen (cf. § 5, IV *e*), and, in the latter a 'Table of Signatures', of which presently. In both cases he purposely refrains from mentioning Heinichen's name.

With regard to the 'Circle', after telling us (l. c., § 3) that it is out of place (1) towards the *end* of a treatise, (2) in an *advanced* treatise, and that "all the trouble which has till now been spent on Circles has not only failed, as we shall presently prove, but been applied in the wrong place", he proceeds (l. c., § 4): "That which some one, with his SUPPOSED NEW *Methodus* (per-

[11] By obvious inadvertence Mattheson writes "die *kleine* Quinte" (the *diminished* Fifth).

[12] Presumably on the ground that preparation implies dissonance, whereas the 'Ascending Class' professes to include consonances only.

sonally I regard it as of feminine gender [13]) has failed to achieve, and has moreover introduced far too late, thus putting the cart before the horse, we will attempt and be at pains to achieve more successfully; but not to make such a long business of it, nor derive our proofs from the bare sharps and ♭♭, as that great man seems to have done,[14] thinking the while that nothing better than his Circle could ever be invented as long as Music remained Music."

Mattheson's Circle is as follows:

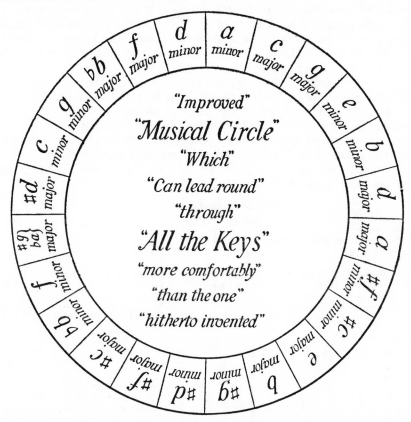

"It only remains", he writes in conclusion (l. c., § 13), "to answer briefly one objection, namely, that, in our Circle, one cannot go backwards as well as forwards. I say: if I begin e.g. in D minor, and go down on the right hand, do I not at once go up again and indeed get back to my D, or just as far as I wish? What need have I, then, to fish with Peter on the left-hand side and to begin walking like a crab? Enough! I run around my Circle and get to whatever key I wish with all comfort and with the greatest approval of the ear: what more can one want? Or is the circle described by the sun defective because it goes from East to West rather than from West to East, like the Danube, as well?"

[13] This sneer is directed at Heinichen's certainly abundant use of foreign words. In German *methodus* changes its gender and becomes *die Methode*.

[14] As a proof of the relationship of the keys Heinichen mentions that the signature of every two adjacent keys in the Circle is identical and that, in going round to the right, it is increased by a single sharp and, in going round to the left, by a flat (*General-Bass &c.*, p. 843).

(f) Mattheson's criticism of Heinichen's 'Table of Signatures' (in the second 'Notice' of the 'Ascending Class') is in much the same style as in the case of the 'Musical Circle'. First, he finds fault with the fact that it is placed at the *end*, instead of the beginning, of the chapter. "This puts me in mind", he writes (l. c., § 2), "of a school-master who should say to a young child: read me what is written here, with all the notes, quite distinctly; afterwards I will show you the letters in their order, and teach you how they must be combined." [15]

Next he blames the author for tabulating only the *common* signatures of a Thorough-Bass. "What", he writes (l. c., § 3), "would a little boy learning spelling (*ein Fibel-Knabe*) say, if, instead of 24 and more letters, he were to find in the German ABC-book only 20 or 21, and nothing at all of x, y, and z, because they are not as common as a, e, i, o, u?"

"And it is no excuse", he continues (l. c., § 5), "that the signatures with 𝕏, ♮, and ♭ prefixed, or with a stroke through them, are omitted because they have the same complementary parts as the unaltered figures: for, if everything in the shape of accidentals is to be left out, why are 2♭, ♭, 𝕏, 4♮, 5♭, 5+, ♭7 taken into account? Otherwise, those 32 signatures [the number in Heinichen's Table] would, perforce, lack another eleven."

"Therefore", he concludes (l. c., § 7 *ad fin.*), "a proper list of all the signatures must appear as follows:

"Table of Signatures" [16]

	"Seconds".			"Thirds".			"Fourths".							
"All the signatures of a Thorough-Bass"	♭2	2	2+	3 / ♭2	♭	♯	4/2	4/3	♭4/3	4+/6	4+/2+	4+/3	4/5	4 3
"The complementary parts (*Füll-Stimmen*) that go with them"	6/4	6/4	6/4 4+	5	5/8	5/8	6	6	6	3	6	6	8	5/8
	[1]	[2]	[3]	[4]	[5]	[6]	[7]	[8]	[9]	[10]	[11]	[12]	[13]	[14]

	"Fifths".						"Sixths".							
	5♭	5♭	5+	5♭/6	5 6	5 6̄	6	6	6	6/4	6̄	6̄/4	6̄	6/4/2	6/5
	3/8	6/3/8	3/8	3	3/8	3/8	3/8	3/6	3/8/6	8	8	3/8	3/8	8	3/8
	[15]	[16]	[17]	[18]	[19]	[20]	[21]	[22]	[23]	[24]	[25]	[26]	[27]	[28]	[29]

[15] It seems almost incredible that any sane person should advocate the study of a Table of Signatures before the pupil has become practically acquainted with the meaning of a single one of them. Yet such was Mattheson's idea. In the 2nd 'Announcement' of the 'Lowest Class' ('On the method of instruction generally') he writes (l. c., § 14): "If everything has gone well so far [i.e. the study of Clavier-pieces (*Handsachen*), accompanied, if possible, by the teacher on any convenient instrument, or with the voice], it is then time, and not before, to bring in the fundamental rules of Thorough-Bass. First of all (not last), let a Table be made of all (not some of) the figurings or so-called signatures, in order that the pupil may, at a single glance, nay! at first sight, know beforehand each and every sign that occurs over a Thorough-Bass, before he gets at grips with them. Whoever does differently, teaches the manner and use of a thing before he has taught or demonstrated the thing itself. And that is, alas! what they almost all do, even the greatest; and brag and boast, into the bargain, about what they imagine to be their splendid method of tuition."

[16] The signatures have here been numbered to facilitate reference

"Sixths".										"Sevenths".				
6 5♭	6 5	6 ♭5	6 5 4 3	♭6 ♯	6♭ 4+	6 5 4	6̄ 5	6̄ ♭5	6 4+	7 2	7	7 6	7 6̄	7 6̌
3	3 8	3	8	8	2	8	3	3	3	4 5	5 3 8	3 8	3 8	3 8
[30]	[31]	[32]	[33]	[34]	[35]	[36]	[37]	[38]	[39]	[40]	[41]	[42]	[43]	[44]

"Sevenths".														
7 4	7̸ ♭6	7 4 2	7̸ 4 2	7̸ 5	7 5	♭7 ♭5	7 5 2	7 5♭	7 4	7̸ 4 2	7̸ 5 4	7 6 5+6	♭7 5♭	♭7 6 5
5 8	3	5	5	3 8	3	3	8	3	5 8	8	2	3	3 8	3 8
[45]	[46]	[47]	[48]	[49]	[50]	[51]	[52]	[53]	[54]	[55]	[56]	[57]	[58]	[59]

"Octaves".		"Ninths".								
8 7	8 ♭7	9	9 8	9 6	9 7	9 7 4	9 8 7 6 5+6	♭9 6 5 3	9 3 8 5	9 8 7 6 5 6
5 3	5 3	5 3	5 3	3	3	5	3	3 8	3 8	3
[60]	[61]	[62]	[63]	[64]	[65]	[66]	[67]	[68]	[69]	[70]

"Meanwhile", Mattheson concludes (l. c., § 8), "the little word *all* is not meant to imply that even more than these 70 signatures could not be evolved and combined: for who can impose limits in this matter? Only, this time, ALL THE KNOWN ONES, UNCOMMON AS WELL AS COMMON, have been brought in."

Let us see how far Mattheson's confidence is justified.

His Table contains 44 signatures [17] not given in that of Heinichen, besides the 26 which are common to both.

Heinichen, on the other hand, has six signatures omitted by Mattheson: $\frac{4+}{6}_{2}$, $\frac{4}{5}_{8}$ (which occurs whenever the suspended 4 resolves over a different Bass), $\frac{7\,6}{3}_{5}$, 18)$\frac{5+6}{3}_{8}$, $\frac{9\,[8]}{4\,[3]}_{5}$, $\frac{7\,[8]}{6\,[6]}_{5}$.

Of these all but the third and fourth occur in the lists of signatures prefixed by Mattheson to each Task, as well as in the subsequent examples, but are *omitted in the Table* through carelessness.

Similar omissions are $\frac{7}{✕}_{5}$ and $\frac{9\,8}{✕}_{5}$, two of the commonest and most necessary signatures, as well as $\frac{✕6}{4}_{3}$ (the 'French' variety of the augmented Sixth), and

---

[17] It will be noticed that Nos. 45 and 54 are identical, but it may be assumed that in the latter case an accidental is omitted and that $\frac{♭7}{4}_{8}$ was intended, as $\frac{♭7}{4\,3}{5}_{8}$ occurs in a subsequent example (Upper Cl., Task 5, § 12, bar 5).

[18] For the inclusion of the Fifth in a 7 6 suspension, see Ch. xi, 'Sevenths', IV, §§ 2–5.

$\frac{5}{4}$ (= $\frac{6}{5}$ with retarded Bass) which Mattheson seems to regard as a mere variety (and an inferior one) of $\frac{6}{4}$.[19]

Not a very creditable achievement on the part of one so severe in his criticism of others!

(*g*) Considerations of space do not permit a detailed review of the twenty-one 'Tasks' of the three 'Classes' ('Ascending', 'Higher', and 'Upper') devoted to the illustration of the different chords.

It may be mentioned incidentally that, in at least two instances, Mattheson has included the same chord (and progression) in both the 'Higher' and 'Upper Classes', i.e. $\frac{7}{4}$ on a Bass falling a tone to a Triad ('Higher Class', 5th 'Task', § 7, and 'Upper Class', 5th 'Task', § 9), and $\frac{7}{4}$ $\left(\begin{smallmatrix}7\\5\\4\\2\end{smallmatrix}\right)$ resolving on a Triad over a stationary Bass (in § 11 of the same two 'Tasks').

(*h*) The 'Upper Class' is followed by an Appendix (*Zugabe*), in which six scales (D, ♯F, ♭B, major and minor) are figured so as to show the harmony normally appertaining to each degree, somewhat after the manner of Gasparini, Rameau, and Heinichen, the only difference being that Mattheson's scales ascend and descend without a break from Tonic to Tonic.[20]

This method came to be known as the *Règle de l'Octave* or *Regola del-l'Ottava*, as in the *Traité d'Accompagnement & de Composition selon la Règle des Octaves de Musique*, published in 1716 by one Campion, a French Theorbist, to whom it was imparted (as he himself tells us) as a valuable secret by a friend named Maltot.

"Rousseau (*Dictionnaire de Musique*, 1768) attributes the first publication of the formula to Delaire [Delair], in 1700.

Mattheson's scales, like his other examples, are given in duplicate: (1) with

---

[19] Prefixed to the 1st 'Task' of the 'Ascending Class' Mattheson gives the signature $\frac{2}{5}$ *enclosed in square brackets.* He writes (l. c., § 4): "We shall, therefore, here speak of small and great Seconds [cf. note 5], how each of them, even though figured quite alone over the Bass notes, has the Sixth and Fourth as companions; although, occasionally, they are also accompanied by the Fifth instead of the Sixth, in the manner shown above in square brackets (*Haaken*): as it sounds somewhat empty the Fifth can be doubled at pleasure." (cf. § 8 *c*, *sub* Ex. 8, for G. P. Telemann's rule for the interpretation of 2.)

[20] Gasparini carries the ascending scale only as far as the sixth degree, but in descending he goes *beyond* the Tonic, as far as the Dominant; thus the sharpened sixth and seventh degrees of the minor mode do not appear at all. His scales of D minor and major appear as follows:

For Rameau's and Heinichen's scales, see § 5, IV *b*, Exx. 5–8, and, for Gasparini's different figurings of the fourth degree (Triad, $\frac{6}{5}$, 6), ibid., note 19.

N.B.—The asterisks under the Submediant of the major scale denote, as Gasparini explains, that the Sixth may either be major (as above) or minor.

the ordinary figuring, and (2) with each interval figured in such a way as to show the position in which the chords are to be taken, as explained above (*c*).

He starts the scales in different positions: D (major and minor) with the 5 in the upper part, ♯F with the 3, ♭B with the 8, but the harmonization is the same in all three cases, and is identical with that of Rameau.

(*i*) Before closing this account of the *Kleine General-Bass-Schule*, mention must be made of some of the extraordinarily slovenly and incorrect progressions which the author occasionally permits himself in the examples.

Some of these he would fain excuse on the ground of a crossing of the parts. In the second of the 'Neben-Erinnerungen' (*Incidental Memoranda*) which follow the Table of Contents he writes in his characteristic contemptuous style:

"Should some Octave-Hunter perhaps think to rout out (*aufstäubern*) his favourite quarry in the four- and five-part chords, e.g. p. 229 ['Upper Class', 2nd 'Task', § 15], stave 3, bar 2, and elsewhere, he must allow himself to be informed what sort of a thing the inversion or exchange (*Vertauschung oder Verwechselung*) of parts is; any one, however, who has too strict a conscience in this matter also,[21] need only omit a part, as, for example, *the Octave*, p. 250 [Appendix (*Zugabe*), § 3], stave 2, 8th note."

The two progressions to which Mattheson alludes (8ves between the highest and lowest of four upper parts, and an upward progression of the Dominant Seventh in its first inversion) are as follows:

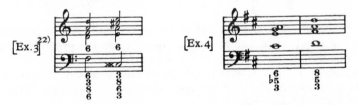

In suggesting the omission of the 8 in the last chord of the second example Mattheson, of course, assumes that the Tenor will then be in unison with the Bass.

The following are characteristic instances of the faulty progression to be found in our author's examples:

(1) Consecutive 5ths.

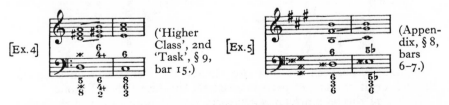

('Higher Class', 2nd 'Task', § 9, bar 15.)

(Appendix, § 8, bars 6–7.)

---

[21] It is accepted as an axiom by the best authorities that an hypothetical crossing of parts cannot be held to excuse an incorrect progression (notably consecutives) on a keyed instrument (on which the said crossing *is not appreciable to the ear*), except in a filled-in accompaniment, and, even then, not between extreme parts (cf. Ch. iii, § 9, 1).

[22] Cf. note 4, which also applies to all subsequent examples.

('Higher Class', 7th 'Task',
2nd section, § 5, (bars 1–2).

(ibid., § 9, bars 8–11.)

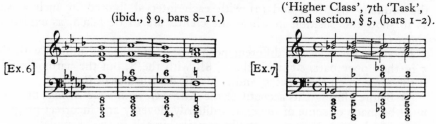

The progression shown in Ex. 4 is actually one of the 'Six dangerous progressions' (*Die sechs gefährlichen Gänge*) enumerated by some later writers, e.g. W. A. Mozart in the small *Generalbass-Schule* attributed to him (though his authorship has been doubted), and Albrechtsberger, while that shown in Ex. 5 is one against which beginners are especially warned.

(2) Consecutive 8ves.

('Ascending Class', 4th 'Task',   ('Higher Class', 4th 'Task',
§ 7, bars 7–8.)   § 4, bars 9, 10.)

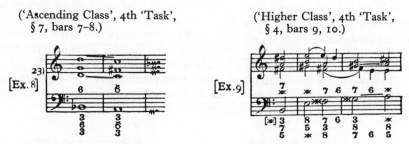

The consecutives in the last bar of Ex. 9 (arising through the doubling of the leading note) are as bad as any can be, nor can the progression be made a good one by any assumption of crossed parts.

This same assumption, with which Mattheson would doubtless excuse the upward progression of the 7 between the first two chords, involves consecutive 5ths with the Bass, ♯f b/b e.

(3) Other forbidden progressions.

('Upper Class', 4th 'Task',   ('Higher Class', 2nd 'Task',
§ 8, bars 6–7.)   § 9, bars 18–19.)

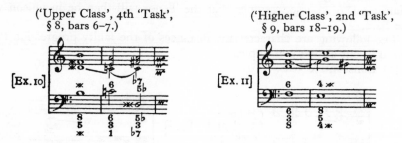

In Ex. 10, between the first two chords, the Tenor falls an augmented Second, or, if crossing of parts is assumed, the Alto falls a Tritone.

In Ex. 11 this assumption is necessary for the preparation of the 4 in the second bar, therefore the Tenor (in the first chord) rises a Tritone.

(4) The following example, in which the crossing of the parts is neces-

---

[23] This progression is used by Heinichen, but with the Bass *an* 8ve *higher*, so that the consecutives are somewhat less apparent (cf. Ch. iv, § 3, II *c*, Ex. 3, note 6).

sitated in a similar manner, but *without* involving any incorrect progression, may be given in conclusion:

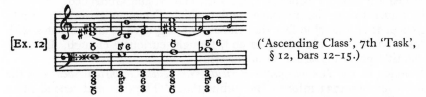

[Ex. 12]

('Ascending Class', 7th 'Task', § 12, bars 12–15.)

(*k*) The examples already given will, it is hoped, suffice to enable the reader to form an idea of Mattheson's attitude in the matter of dealing with a figured Bass.

The above examples show clearly what liberties he, a musician of acknowledged eminence and of immense learning, was prepared to take. He was only two years older than Heinichen, and it is, therefore, somewhat remarkable that his standard of correctness in the employment of 4-part harmony (a filled-in accompaniment is, of course, a different matter) should be so much lower.

If there were any means of gaining such knowledge, it would be of supreme interest to know how far his great contemporary and intimate friend, Handel, was in accord with him in this particular.

§ 8. *G. Ph. Telemann* (1681–1767).

(*a*) A work of extraordinary interest has been preserved to us in the "Singe-, Spiel- und Generalbass-Übungen" of G. Ph. Telemann, which appeared at Hamburg in instalments dating from the 20th November 1733 to the 17th January 1735, on which day the complete work was offered for sale for the price of 4 *Gulden* 8 *gute Groschen* (about 15*s*. 6*d*.). Four copies remain in existence, two in the Royal Library in Berlin, one in the University Library at Königsberg, and one in that of the Brussels Conservatorium.

Most fortunately the work has been re-edited by Professor Max Seiffert among the publications of the International Music Society (Berlin, 1914, Leo Liepmannssohn), and it is to his interesting Introduction that the present writer is indebted for the following particulars with regard to its genesis, and also the high esteem in which it was held, inasmuch as Mizler wrote of it that: "all beginners ought by rights to have this work in their hands".[1]

It must first be mentioned that Telemann's "Übungen" consist of forty-eight songs (presumably of his own composition) with a fully figured Bass, and also an upper stave with the accompaniment set out in accordance with the figures. Each song occupies a single page (except a single one entitled 'Toback' which occupies two pages and is accordingly headed Nos. 39, 40), and at the bottom of each page are footnotes referring to and explaining every detail in the interpretation of the figures which might otherwise be obscure to a beginner.

The verses thus set to music, many of which are of an humorous character, were chosen with evident care from the best contemporary poets. In some

---

[1] *Neueröffnete musikalische Bibliothek*, vol. ii, Part I, p. 144 (1743).

cases, abbreviations of their names are given, in others, only an initial. Of these initials some are still unidentified. Among the names which have been identified are those of Brockes, Hagedorn, Haller, and Gottsched.

To return to the circumstances under which Telemann's work came into existence: it is a notable fact that the author engraved it on tin plates with his own hand from beginning to end, though, curiously enough, his name on the title-page was added in manuscript.

A notice in the *Hamburgische Berichte von neuen Gelehrten Sachen* of the 20th November 1733 informs the public that: "The first and second piece of the 'Exercises in Singing, Playing, and Thorough-Bass' which our Capellmeister Telemann has undertaken to issue weekly, namely every Thursday, like a periodical, is now really out". That some Thursdays were missed is clear from the fact that the 48 folios were not complete till January 1735.

This method of publication explains the fact that in two of the extant copies the *verso* of each *folio* is blank, while in another (one of those in the Royal Library at Berlin) both sides are utilized. In the latter case copies were evidently struck off after the forty-eight plates were complete, while in the two former the sheets which had been struck off week by week were bound together.[2]

(*b*) The purpose of the work, namely, to initiate a beginner into the principles of a plain chordal accompaniment—what was known in the German of the eighteenth century as *ein simples* (as opposed to *manierliches*) *Accompagnement*—is best explained in the author's own prefatory words: "As the intention is to give guidance to Thorough-Bass by means of the examples in this work, it is presumed that whoever practises himself in them must already know the elements: what is major or minor, what a chord is, a con- or dissonance, a Second, Third, &c. Here it will only be shown, in particular, how the chords (*Griffe*) are to be taken correctly (*rein*) and comfortably. With regard to the notes, no systematic arrangement will be adhered to, but, just as the songs (*Arien*) are written in a free style, so, too, only a chance mention will be made of whatever the harmonies (*Sätze*) suggest as they occur. . . ."

The notes are, indeed, most excellent, and no one who peruses them carefully from the beginning can fail to be struck by the amount of information compressed into so small a space, as well as by its admirable clearness.

Telemann's valedictory note is worth quoting: "Herewith we conclude these exercises and wish that the object in view, namely, to be of use and to entertain (*belustigen*), may have been fulfilled. We confess that there is much still remaining which pertains to the doctrine of Thorough-Bass. But, nevertheless, the greater part will have been touched upon in the notes given, and whoever has duly pondered them cannot find it difficult to understand whatever else may present itself. With a view to their further use the following index has been added. For the rest, our critics must be kind enough to note, in common with ourselves, the purport of the above song."

This last is a sly touch of humour. The title and words of the song in question (by Stoppe) are as follows:

---

[2] The above information, as Professor Seiffert explains, is derived from Dr. Max Schneider's preface to vol. xxviii of the *Denkmäler Deutscher Tonkunst*, first series.

"Jeder sein eigner Richter"	(*Every man his own judge*)
"Ich will vor meiner thüre kehren;	('I will sweep in front of my own door;
ich habe gnug für mich zu thun;	I have enough to do for myself;
ich kenne mich, ich bin kein engel;	I know myself, I am no angel;
ein jeder mensch hat seine mängel,	Every human being has his defects,
wer diese tilgen will,	Whoever wants to remedy them
darf lebenslang nicht ruhn."	Must not rest as long as he lives.')

(*c*) Before taking leave of Telemann certain points of interest must be briefly noticed:

(1) Telemann belonged to that older school, to which Ph. Em. Bach alludes in his *Versuch*, who, in a 4-part accompaniment, insisted on four *sounding* parts and therefore avoided unisons, which on a keyed instrument are not distinguishable from a single note.

After giving examples of consonances resulting from the resolution of dissonances (p. 9), he writes: "To the unison, which is also a consonance, we have not given a place, because, through it, one of the 4 parts, which we are

using here, would be lost: ⨎ ."

As a means of avoiding a unison, an interval not indicated in the figuring may sometimes be taken. In connexion with the following bar, No. 12, bar 5 (voice part omitted):

[Ex. 1]

he writes: "It is indeed a useful property of the small [i.e. diminished] 5, that one can put it in on all sorts of occasions. At (*a*) it is not figured, but nevertheless it goes well with the 6 (*wird doch aber von der 6 gern geduldet*); and without it we should have to strike only three parts, or, in spite of all artificial treatment of the

notes of this bar, introduce 8ves or 5ths:

'3 parts'   '5ths'   '8ves'

(2) Telemann gives the same rule as Heinichen for the use of the *Quarta irregularis*,[3] although he does not use this name.

He writes (p. 2) as follows: "It is here to be noted: that, as often as the Bass, after a 6, falls a half or a whole tone to a chord [i.e. a common chord], one can always take the 4 as well as the 3 with the 6 in question."

And again (p. 6): "The unfigured 4, of which mention is made in connexion with Nos. 1 and 2, also occurs with a 6 when the Bass rises immediately afterwards a half or a whole tone to another 6."

The two cases, (*a*) a major Sixth with a *minor* Third, to which may be added a perfect Fourth, and (*b*) a major Sixth with a *major* Third, to which may be added an *augmented* Fourth, are not so clearly distinguished as by Heinichen, nor does Telemann (or, for the matter of that, Heinichen) tell us that, in the second case, the Bass must fall to a *major* Triad (i.e. the

---

[3] Cf. § 5, III, immediately before and after Ex. 1.

Dominant of a minor key); but the examples which occur in the course of the work suffice to put an intelligent student in possession of the facts.

(3) Telemann was sensitive where strictness of progression was concerned. In connexion with the second of the following chords:

[Ex. 2]

he tells us that the Bass, rather than the 6, has been doubled to avoid *hidden Fifths*.

(4) On the other hand, in the case of 5ths arising between a principal part and the accompaniment, *which cannot possibly be guarded against, unless the accompanist has the score before him,* Telemann is lenient.[4]

The two following examples occur:

[Ex. 3]

[Ex. 4]

(a)   (b)

Of the first of these (No. 17, antepenult. bar) Telemann writes: "The voice part has *g ♯f* with *d ♯c* above it; these are two perfect (*grosse*) and forbidden 5ths; they may pass (*durchwischen*), because the ♯*f* is to be regarded as only a grace-note, and it is really the following *e* which counts."

Of the second (No. 23, second half of antepenult. bar) he writes: "Here the upper notes at (*a*) (*b*) form two perfect (*grosse*) Fifths with the

voice-part: 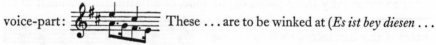 These … are to be winked at (*Es ist bey diesen …*

---

[4] Ph. Em. Bach, too, sensitive as he was in the matter of Fifths, does not demand the impossible. In enumerating cases where the chord of the Seventh is to be taken with the Octave of the Bass $\frac{8}{3}$, instead of the Fifth $\frac{7}{3}$, he gives the following example (*Versuch &c.*, 1762, Part II, Ch. 13, II, § 2, Ex. b):

[given on a single stave in the original and in the lower 8ve (cf. Ch. iii, § 3, v, notes 29 and 30). The second example has been added for clearness' sake.]

Of this he writes: "… by means of the Octave we avoid the forbidden Fifths which may occur between the principal part and the accompaniment, $\frac{a}{d}\frac{g}{c}$, if the former does not lie below the latter. This remark seems, it is true, somewhat too far fetched: but with a slow Tempo and delicate execution such Fifths can very well be heard, and therefore one is also bound to avoid them, IF THE PRINCIPAL PART APPEARS OVER THE BASS."

durch die finger zu sehen).   For if the player were guided by the figures alone, without the score, he would play these very notes, and yet not be culpable (*strafbar*)."

(5) It is noteworthy that Telemann constantly takes the accompaniment above the voice part, although this was, as we shall see,[5] against the general rule.

The following will serve as an example (No. 16, 2nd section):

(6) It is also noteworthy that Telemann had no objection to a full close with the 5 of the Tonic chord in the upper part, contrary to the doctrine of Ph. Em. Bach[6] and other later authorities, and even of his own contemporary, Mattheson.[7]

Apropos of such a close (No. 16, 1st section, *ad fin.*) he writes: "Some would have it that one should not conclude with the 5 on the top, because it is incomplete; but so it is in the middle and at the bottom [i.e. of the three upper parts] as well: so take it where you please."

(7) The following quaint note with reference to the progression of an augmented 2nd in a middle part (No. 19, 4 bars from end) is worth quoting:

"Here a *mi contra fa*, which an older generation (*die Alten*) called the Satan in Music, has been purposely introduced; it consists in the occurrence of unnatural and unvocal (*dem Gesange zuwiedere*) progressions, as:

Now, they are the composers' favourites. But I do make a concession to the old people (*Ich thue aber auch den alten was zu gefallen*) and seldom use them, especially as one can generally avoid them."

(8) Two characteristic instances of the arbitrary interpretation of the inadequate figurings so common in the earlier Basses (apart from the universally accepted interpretation of 6 as $\frac{6}{4}$ under the circumstances mentioned above) occur in the course of Telemann's 'Exercises'.

---

[5] cf. Ch. iii, § 5 B.

[6] *Versuch &c.*, Part II, 1762, Ch. 2, I, § 36.

[7] In re-editing the Second Part of Niedt's *Handleitung* (cf. Ch. i, § 25, I, note 1) Mattheson took upon himself to correct this supposed fault in the author's examples.

In the first of these (No. 11, bar 12) it is true that the full figuring is given:

[Ex. 7]

N.B.—In Seiffert's edition the first ♭B is erroneously figured $\frac{7}{5}$, whatever may be the case in the original.

Telemann, however, writes as follows: "The 5♭ is not always written, but it is always in place with ♭ when the movement is upward to a minor interval [(*in einen weichen Ton*) i.e. the Third of a minor key] and when the composer has not introduced the 4 (likewise unfigured) at the point in question [i.e. in the principal part or parts]; a good ear, that listens for what is coming, is needed. A 3 accompanies it."

It will be noticed incidentally that, in the case of the chord in question, Telemann does not follow the ordinary rule which prescribes that it should be taken in the position nearest to that of the preceding one.

The second instance, we are bound to admit, requires more explanation (for beginners, at all events) than Telemann gives.

[Ex. 8]

Of the above progressions (from No. 44, 1st, 2nd, and final sections) Telemann writes as follows: "When 2 stands by itself, namely, on a tied note, which subsequently falls a semitone (*b*), or a whole tone (*a*) (*c*), it requires $\frac{6}{4}$ or $\frac{5}{4}$ (*d*); but if it is not tied, only $\frac{6}{4}$ is in place (*e*).[8] In order to be safe in the first case [i.e. when the bass note is tied], let only 3 parts be taken:

N.B.—In Seiffert's edition the upper note is given as ♭♭: the author cannot, however, have meant this, for, if the difficulty consists in choosing between $\frac{6}{4}$ and $\frac{5}{4}$, the parts which may safely be taken are obviously those which are common to both, i.e. $\frac{4}{2}$.

---

[8] It would have made the matter easier to a beginner to explain that $\frac{5}{4}$ represents a $\frac{6}{5}$ chord with a retarded Bass, and that it is therefore necessary, before deciding to interpret 2 as $\frac{5}{4}$, to see whether the Bass, after falling a degree (to a $\frac{6}{5}$ chord), rises again to a Triad (as above in Ex. 8 b), or else proceeds in some other way compatible

(9) There occur several instances, in *full closes*, of apparent discrepancy between the voice part and the harmony actually played. These are characteristic of the musical notation of the seventeenth and early eighteenth centuries, and are to be explained by the contemporary tradition, in accordance with which, in the cases in question, a long *appoggiatura* (followed by a shake), *even though not indicated*, was taken for granted.

In no instance does Telemann *indicate* a shake, since it was as much a matter of course as the preceding long *appoggiatura*. That one was *intended* in such cases is pretty clear from the author's explanation of the following example (No. 5, 1st section, penultimate bar), where the *tr.* in brackets has presumably been added by Professor Seiffert in accordance therewith:

[Ex 9]

Here Telemann writes: "At (*r*) . . . the $\frac{6}{4}$ are taken as grace-notes (*für maniren*), as, of course, the singer emphasizes the *g*, namely the 4, before the shake begins (*weil doch der sänger das g, als die 4, stark hören läst, ehe das tr. kömt*)."

In such cases the figuring of the Basses of the eighteenth century is extraordinarily irregular: sometimes, as in Ex. 9, it agrees with the *notation* of the principal part; sometimes, as in the following example (No. 36, bar 4), with the actual harmony:

[Ex. 10]

In Exx. 9 and 10 the strict contemporary notation of the voice part (apart

with a preceding $\frac{6}{5}$, e.g. leaping to another inversion of the same harmony (a), or remaining stationary as the Bass of a $\frac{6}{4}$ chord (b):
                                                                   2

(a)   (b)

In a word, it is not merely the falling of a tied Bass one degree, but the *further progression of the Bass*, that has to be considered.

from the shake) would be:[9] [musical notation] and the notes

sung:[10] [musical notation]

The *appoggiatura*, as Telemann reminds us, was always played *louder than the main note.*

(*d*) In taking leave of Telemann, it may be said that no one acquainted with the rudiments of harmony, and desiring to learn to play from a figured Bass, could be more pleasantly and efficiently initiated than by our author's 'Exercises'.

§ 9. *Carl Philipp Emanuel Bach* (1714–88).

(*a*) There is no single treatise on the art of accompaniment from a figured Bass to which those who wish to recapture the tradition owe a deeper debt than to the Second Part of Ph. Em. Bach's celebrated work on the Clavier, first published in 1762, nine years after the appearance of the First Part. The latter deals with the Clavier [1] as a solo instrument, and does not, therefore, concern us here.

[9] According to a practice which, as Ph. Em. Bach tells us (*Versuch &c.*, Part I, Hauptstück [Section] II, Abtheilung [Subsection] II, § 5), was then gaining ground (i.e. about the middle of the eighteenth century), and which he himself employed, the *appoggiatura* was no longer uniformly indicated by a quaver, but by a note of its actual approximate value: thus the notation in Exx. 9, 10 would be:

[10] It must always be remembered that, in actual practice, the short note following a dot was generally curtailed to half its value (or, under certain circumstances, a quarter, or even an eighth), so that, roughly speaking, dotted notes in Bach and Handel (and still later composers) can be treated as *double-dotted*. There is, however, abundant scope for individual discretion in dealing with them, as cases are always liable to arise in which a too literal application of a supposed rule would entirely spoil the effect. The following words of Ph. Em. Bach (*Versuch &c.*, Part II, Ch. 29, § 15) deserve to be constantly borne in mind:

"In the notation of dotted notes generally there is still very often a lack of the needful exactness. With regard to the execution of such notes, therefore, the establishment of a certain main rule has been claimed, which is, however, subject to many exceptions. In accordance with this rule, the notes following a dot are to be disposed of as shortly as possible, and, for the most part, this precept is correct; but, now, the arrangement (*Eintheilung*) of certain notes in the different parts, by which they are to enter together at the same moment, makes a difference; now, again, an ingratiating sentiment (*ein flattirender Affect*), which is incompatible with the defiant character usually characteristic of these notes, is the reason why we linger a little less over the dot. If, therefore, we establish as a principle only a single way of executing these notes, we lose the other ways."

[1] This term is here used by Bach to include all keyboard-instruments with strings, and, in the Second Part, the Organ as well. This is clear from the following passages: "Besides many sorts of *Claviers*, some of which have remained unknown on account of their deficiencies, while others have not yet been introduced everywhere, we have principally two kinds, namely, Harpsichords (*Flügel*) and Clavichords, which have till now met with the most approval. The former are generally used for performances on a large scale (*zu starken Musiken*), the latter for solo playing. The more recent Pianofortes (*Fortepiano*), when they are durable and well made, have many advantages,

The Second Part, on the other hand, while giving adequate information on questions of theory (the progression of the various intervals, &c.), deals first and foremost with the practical problems of *accompaniment*.

The full title is as follows:

"CARL PHILIPP EMANUEL BACH's / VERSUCH / UBER DIE WAHRE ART / DAS CLAVIER ZU SPIELEN / ZWEITER THEIL, / IN WELCHEM DIE LEHRE VON DEM ACCOMPAGNEMENT / UND DER FREYEN FANTASIE / ABGEHANDELT WIRD. / Berlin, Winter, 1762."

('Carl Philipp Emanuel Bach's Essay on the true method of playing the Clavier. Second Part, in which the doctrine of Accompaniment and free extemporization is expounded.')

The character of the work cannot be better described than in the words of G. M. Telemann, a grandson of the well-known composer whose "Singe-, Spiel- und Generalbass-Übungen" were described in § 8. In the Preface to his *Unterricht im Generalbass-Spielen*, to be noticed presently, he writes as follows (pp. 10 sq., footnote):

"This admirable work . . . distinguishes itself from all other works of the same kind, quite apart from the concise order and accuracy which prevail in it, by exceptional clearness as well. The point, however, in which it especially differentiates itself is the fact that it does not aim (like other text-books) merely at the making of one who can play a plain accompaniment from a Thorough-Bass (*die Bildung eines simplen General-Spielers*), but endeavours, rather, to mould an accompanist adorned with taste, subtlety (*Feinheit*), and discretion; something more, in fact, than a mere everyday accompanist. The author wrote, it is true, from his own long experience in accompaniment, and at a place which is, so to speak, the seat of musical taste. But to collect all the individual instances, scattered as they are, to deduce rules from them, and to propound these in their proper order, without any pioneer in this field (*ohne hierinn vor sich gearbeitet zu sehen*): that was, indeed, no small achievement. This much is certain, that an accompanist who wishes to raise himself above the ruck (*Trosz*) of Thoroughbass-threshers, as miserable as they are numerous, cannot well dispense with this book, since it is unique of its kind, or study it enough. This work, however, admirable as it is in itself, is quite too learned for mere beginners; nor was such the intention of its famous author, inasmuch as it was the refinements of accompaniment (*das feine Accompagnement*) that he had in view. It is rather to be regarded as a school for many an accompanist who imagines himself perfect, from which he can learn what he still has to learn. For it is with good reason that Herr Quantz, in his incomparable 'Instruction in playing the German Flute' [*Anweisung die Flöte traversiere zu spielen*] (a work from which no practical musician ought by rights ever to be parted, since each can learn

---

although their treatment must be specially studied, and is not without difficulty. They answer well for solo playing, and for music in which too many performers are not engaged (*bey einer nicht zu stark besetzten Musik*); but I believe, nevertheless, that a good Clavichord, except for the fact that it has a weaker tone, shares all the beauties of the other, and, further, enjoys an advantage in the *vibrato* (*Bebung*) and the sustaining of the tone, because, after striking it, I can give each note a further pressure. The Clavichord is, therefore, the instrument on which one can form the most accurate judgement of a *Clavierist*" (Part I, Introd., § 11).

"The Organ, the Harpsichord, the Pianoforte, and the Clavichord are the *Clavier*-instruments most generally used for accompaniment" (Part II, Introd., § 1).

his duties from it; though this is not exactly to be gathered from the title), states in the vi[th] Subsection (*Abschnitt*) of the xvii[th] Section (*Hauptstück*), which deals with the duties of the *Clavierist* and deserves to be learnt by heart by the budding accompanist, at the very beginning of the said Subsection, that: NOT ALL WHO UNDERSTAND THOROUGHBASS ARE, ON THAT ACCOUNT, ALSO GOOD ACCOMPANISTS."

(*b*) The Second Part of the *Versuch* is quoted so freely, and in such detail, in subsequent chapters of the present work [2] that it will not be necessary to do much more than indicate the contents and general arrangement.

The contents are as follows: *Introduction*; Ch. i, "On the intervals and signatures"; Chs. ii–xxi, dealing with the various chords; Ch. xxii, "On the unison"; Ch. xxiii, "On one-part accompaniment with the left hand alone"; Ch. xxiv, "On the Pedal Point"; Chs. xxv–viii, dealing with modifications in the accompaniment necessitated by various ornaments in the principal part; Ch. xxix, "On style" (*Vom Vortrage*); Ch. xxx, "On final cadences"; Ch. xxxi, "On pauses" (*Von den Fermaten*); Ch. xxxii, "On certain niceties (*Zierlichkeiten*) of the accompaniment"; Ch. xxxiii, "On imitation"; Ch. xxxiv, "On certain precautions in accompanying"; Ch. xxxv, "On the necessity of figuring"; Ch. xxxvi, "On passing notes"; Ch. xxxvii, "On striking a chord beforehand [i.e. in anticipation of the Bass] with the right hand"; Ch. xxxviii, "On Recitative"; Ch. xxxix, "On changing [i.e. accented passing] notes"; Ch. xxxx, "On a theme in the Bass" (*Bassthema*); Ch. xxxxi, "On free extemporization".

(*c*) The following points demand brief notice:

(1) The author's views on the accompaniment of a Pedal Point are most interesting, and very comforting to an Organist confronted with masses of figures, in the most unfamiliar combinations, e.g. in the first chorus of J. S. Bach's St. John's Passion.

Philip Emanuel writes as follows (Ch. xxiv, §§ 4, 5):

"Pedal Points are not very likely to be figured (*man beziffert die Orgelpunkte nicht leicht*), but are disposed of *tasto solo*. Whoever figures them must put up with it, if they are, nevertheless, played *tasto solo*. For this, not merely a VERY NECESSARY desire to save trouble (*Bequemlichkeit*), but very often IMPOSSIBILITY is to blame: and granted that one were able to accompany all Pedal Points with the right hand, the credit for so doing would, after all, not be nearly as great as the anxiety and trouble which it costs many an individual so to do.

"With t.s. [*tasto solo*] throughout the Pedal Points, the eye does not have to take in so many figures, heaped one above another, and unaccustomed chords (*Aufgaben*). Often the disposal of the harmony is such that one part rises above (*übersteiget*) another, which is liable to occasion a crossing of parts in the Thorough-Bass, which is not allowed, for the reason that many faults could, otherwise, be excused thereby, without the ear being satisfied after all; in such a case, then, if the right hand is not to get too far down, it would be necessary, for the sake of correct preparation and resolution, to

[2] Of the forty-four sections of the Introduction, §§ 1–9 are quoted *in extenso* in Ch. iii, § 2, of the present work. Abstracts of the following chapters will be found as shown below: For Chs. xxii, iii see Ch. iii, § 12 of the present work.

„	Chs. xxv, viii „	Ch. iii, § 14	„	„
„	Ch. xxxii „	Ch. iv, § 5	„	„
„	Ch. xxxiii „	Ch. iii, § 8 *e*	„	„
„	Ch. xxxvii „	Ch. iii, § 13	„	„

play the entire Pedal Point in extended harmony, which cannot be demanded. Often the changes of harmony follow so quickly upon each other that it is almost impossible to bring them out, even if one wished to play them."

(2) In Ch. xxx, 'On final cadences', there occurs a characteristic instance in which the closing shake in the principal part, with its *accented auxiliary note*, involves a departure from the figuring. Somewhat similar instances were quoted from G. P. Telemann (cf. § 8 *c*, Exx. 9, 10). In the examples about to be given, however, another factor enters, that of *pace*: the treatment in a slow *tempo* is not the same as in a quick one; but *in neither case does it correspond with a figuring which is liable to occur.*

Our author writes as follows (l. c., § 9):

"In the following examples,[3] which sometimes occur,[4] a Triad is taken with the first note and, if the *tempo* be quick, sustained till the last note, and there, for the first time, a pause is made. The intermediate notes, regardless of the figures above them, are allowed to pass without accompaniment in the right hand (*a*). In a slow *tempo*, however, the figuring [i.e. the interpretation thereof] must be changed, the accompaniment being taken as in (*b*), and a pause being made on the *D*:

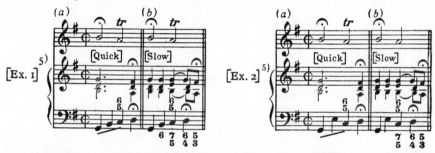

(3) In Ch. xxxvi, 'On passing notes' (§§ 7–11), our author gives singularly precise rules for the number of repercussions of the harmony in the right hand in the case of repeated notes in the Bass. It will, of course, be understood that these rules do not apply to the Organ, or (without considerable modification) to a modern Pianoforte. They are as follows:

"§ 7". "With regard to the treatment of a number of Bass notes WHICH REMAIN AT THE SAME PITCH, AND PASS [i.e. under the same harmony], we have

---

[3] The principal part (but not the Bass) is here given an 8ve higher than in the original (cf. Ch. iii, § 3, v, notes 29 and 30). For the sake of clearness, the figuring actually to be found is given *above* the Bass, while the oblique strokes and figures *below* the Bass indicate the treatment prescribed by Bach. The chords in small print have been added, and can, of course, be taken in any other position. The pauses over the last Bass note, prescribed by Bach, have also been added.

[4] "Sometimes" refers, of course, to the discrepancy in the figuring, not to the form of cadence.

[5] It will be remarked that, in these examples, there is no indication of the *appoggiatura* which is certainly to be assumed (even though not indicated) in those of Telemann. In Ph. Em. Bach's examples it is clear that no *appoggiatura* was intended, as his notation is very exact. Telemann belonged to an older generation. In the First Part of the *Versuch* (Hauptstück [Section] II, *Abtheilung* [Subsection] III, § 1) Ph. Em. Bach writes: "Formerly they [i.e. shakes] were hardly used except after an *appoggiatura*, or in repeating a preceding note; in the former case they are known as ATTACHED SHAKES (*angeschlossene Triller*); but nowadays they occur . . . in cadences . . . without a preceding *appoggiatura*, and also with one."

several remarks to make. These remarks are based on the *tempi* (*das Zeitmaas*) in vogue here,[6] in accordance with which the Adagios are executed far more slowly, and the Allegros far more rapidly, than is customary in other parts."

"§ 8". "From the SLOW TEMPO, DOWN TO THE LARGO, crotchets and still slower notes are struck with both hands, and sustained for their entire value (*ganz ausgehalten*). Quavers are likewise struck with both hands, but sustained for only half their value (*halb ausgehalten*). All the semiquavers are struck by the left hand, and sustained, if there are no marks indicating a *staccato* (*wenn keine Zeichen des Abstossens vorhanden sind*). With these semiquavers, and still quicker notes, the right hand strikes quavers sustained for half their value, as long as no special expression alters the case. When the Bass has continuous, or at all events a great many, demisemiquavers, or even quicker notes, then the accompanist, if he has a Bass-player [i.e. a string Bass], can let one or more notes pass in the left hand without striking them; but if he has no assistant, he must torture himself alone with this trembling movement. With quaver and semiquaver triplets, the right hand strikes only with the first note, as also in the case of any figure consisting of three quavers, or their equivalent, in $\frac{3}{8}$, $\frac{6}{8}$, $\frac{9}{8}$, and $\frac{12}{8}$ time."

"§ 9". "From LARGHETTO and ANDANTE onwards, to ALLEGRO, crotchets, sustained for their entire value, are struck in the right hand with the crotchets, quavers, and still quicker notes, in the Bass. The slow notes are sustained in both hands."

"§ 10". "In a SICILIANO, be it quick or slow, the crotchets, and still slower notes, are struck with both hands and sustained. The single quavers, which follow the crotchets, are likewise played in the right hand. Apart from that, be the figure in the Bass what it may, the right hand strikes only once to every equivalent of three quavers."

"§ 11". "From ALLEGRO ASSAI to PRESTISSIMO, either sustained minims, or crotchets sustained for half their value, are struck in the right hand with quavers in the Bass. Crotchets [i.e. in the Bass] are sustained in both hands for half, and still slower notes for the whole of their value. . . ."

(4) A quaint reference to J. S. Bach is worth recording. In Ch. i, 'On the intervals and signatures' (§ 5), Philip Emanuel writes: "One should let one's pupils diligently accompany pieces in which, on account of the chromatic harmony which occurs in them, the Basses are adequately, and therefore thickly, figured. With this in view, I have used the figured Basses of my late Father with much profit to the pupils and without endangering their lives. They do no harm to the fingers either."

§ 10. *Christoph Gottlieb Schröter* (1699–1782).

(*a*) A work of very exceptional interest, and abounding with information, is the following: "Deutliche Anweisung / zum / GENERAL-BASS, / in beständiger Veränderung / des uns angebohrnen / HARMONISCHEN DREYKLANGES, / mit zulänglichen Exempeln; / wobey / EIN UMSTÄND-LICHER VORBERICHT / der vornehmsten / vom General-Basse handelnden Schriften dieses Jahrhunderts; / von / CHRISTOPH GOTTLIEB SCHRÖTER, / Componist und Organist an der Hauptkirche in der kaiserl. freyen Reichsstadt / Nordhausen. / Halberstadt / bey Johann Heinrich Gross. / 1772."

('A clear Guide to Thorough-Bass, in its perpetual variation of the Triad,

---

[6] i.e. in Berlin.

our original heritage, with adequate examples; also a detailed preliminary notice of the chief writings, treating of Thorough-Bass, of this century; by Christoph Gottlieb Schröter, Composer and Organist at the Principal Church of the imperial free town of Nordhausen, &c.')

The date of publication, 1772, is misleading, for the date given at the end of the work (§ 387, p. 202) is 30 December, 1754. The first half of the *Vorbericht* or Preliminary Notice (i–xxxx), again, is dated 10 Nov. 1754, and the second half (xxxxi–lvii), 20 Dec. 1769, more than two years before the book actually appeared. Thus some eighteen years elapsed between the completion of all but the concluding sections of the *Vorbericht* and the date of publication, and the manuscript was ready for press eight years before the appearance of the Second Part of Ph. Em. Bach's *Versuch*.[1]

[1] The first inception of the work, as we learn from the author himself, may be said to date as far back as 1724, when Schröter was twenty-five years old. His account is full of interest, and parts of it must be recorded.

[*The numbers prefixed to the following quotations denote the sections of the 'Vorbericht', from which they are taken.*]

xiii. "In this century", he writes, "the number of harmonies (*der harmonischen Sätze*) has been greatly increased. It cannot, however, be maintained that this increase is the work of only one harmonist. Herr [Johann Nicolaus] Bach, a popular Organist at Jena, wanted to persuade me in 1724 that a Frenchman, Mr. Rameau by name, had contributed most towards it by taking the Seventh on *Chorda* V [i.e. the Dominant], 1, 3, 5, 7, as the origin of all the four-part chords $\left[\text{i.e. } \substack{6\\5\\3}, \substack{6\\4\\3}, \substack{6\\4\\2}\right]$. When I politely requested the said Herr Bach kindly to send me, for perusal, the treatise published by Mr. Rameau on the subject in question, I received the answer that the information, which he had given me by word of mouth, had been similarly imparted to him in writing. A vain hope for me!"

xiv. "This unexpected circumstance induced me to write down, at first only in notes and figures without any accompanying words, all THREE and FOUR-PART CHORDS, as ALTERATIONS OF THE HARMONIC TRIAD, in doing which I kept as closely as possible to the HARMONICAL ORDER OF THE INTERVALS (*die harmonicalische Rangordnung der Intervallen*). Through this endeavour (founded on the nature of sound) ONLY SEVEN PRINCIPAL CHORDS (*Hauptsätze*) were found (each, however, of a distinct nature and arrangement) in the two following main divisions:

Three three-part harmonics.			Four four-part harmonics.			
8	8	8	6	6	7	6
5	6	6	5	4	5	4
3	3	4	3	3	3	2
1	1	1	1	1	1	1

[Note especially the order in which Schröter arranges the discords.]

Although many subsidiary circumstances arose in connexion with these TWO FIRST MAIN DIVISIONS, nevertheless, each one fell into its proper place, and the dissonant harmonies arising through passing notes were awarded a special chapter. Finally, for the THIRD MAIN DIVISION, I took once more EACH OF THE SEVEN PRINCIPAL CHORDS, and showed, in notes and words, WHERE and HOW, either ONLY ONE, or TWO, or THREE UPPER PARTS, COULD BE RETARDED IN THE HARMONY (*sich harmonisch verzögern liessen*); after which, by the inversion of these same chords, the anticipations of the harmony were also revealed."

[N.B.—A retardation of the *Bass* was regarded by Schröter and other writers of his time as giving rise to *anticipation* in the three upper parts, as:

xv. "This scheme I submitted at the very beginning to all my pupils in Jena,

The reason of the delay is apparent from the following: "Could I guess", our author writes (*Vorbericht*, xxxxi), "that various legitimate reasons would hinder my publisher for so long in the fulfilment of his promise? But this unexpected delay is no detriment to our main purpose, but rather gives me the opportunity to express myself more clearly on certain matters, but, first of all, to continue the above incipient narrative concerning writings treating of Thorough-Bass, in course of which continuation many interesting pieces of information will occur."

Some of the latter will be noticed presently.

(*b*) Far worse things, however, had befallen poor Schröter than the delay which he accepted so cheerfully. The Seven Years' War, which intervened between the completion and publication of his work, had tragic consequences for him.

Besides the volume under discussion, he had completed (not later than the summer of 1761, as will be seen presently) a Second Part, in which, as we gather from various allusions,[2] he treated mainly of accompaniment in 5, 6, and more parts, and also from an unfigured Bass, as well as other matters. In one or two instances, indeed, he promises his readers (without giving an actual reference) that, in the Second Part, they will find the explanation of something hitherto left unclear.[3]

Besides this Second Part he had completed a History of Harmony (*Historie der Harmonie*), begun soon after drawing up the scheme described above (cf. section xiv of the extract given in note 1). Of this work he gives

Minden, and Nordhausen. Since 1747 I have acquainted them, not only with my own, but also with Herr SORGE's arrangement of the FOUR-PART CHORDS $\left[\text{i.e. } \frac{7}{3}, \frac{6}{3}, \frac{6}{3}, \frac{6}{2} \right]$ . . . ."

xxxvi. ". . . In 1725, while I was lodging with the celebrated bookseller Herr Bielken, at Jena, I was asked to compile a complete Guide to Thorough-Bass. . . . But man proposes, God disposes. For, early in the following year 1726, contrary to all expectation and without any initiative on my part, I was called to Minden as Composer and Organist at the principal Church. . . . There I found far more work in composition, which scarcely left me a few hours weekly for the perusal of periodicals, let alone for the elaboration of theoretical treatises."

xxxvii. "Not long afterwards, namely in 1732, I was called to the imperial free town of Nordhausen, likewise as Composer and Organist at the principal Church. Here I at last found more time and quiet . . . and, first of all, put my above-mentioned TRIPLE SCHEME into proper form for my pupils, with complete elucidations. I should wander from the point, were I now to relate how many, and what, musical articles I subsequently completed, mostly for my own edification. Meanwhile the popular bookseller here, Herr Johann Gross, had heard something of my untiring industry, probably from friends who visited him, and accordingly asked me in 1753 whether I would entrust the publication of my Guide to Thorough-Bass to him. He assured me at the same time that, of the various Guides of this century, almost all the copies were exhausted, and that, consequently, my work would find friends in plenty. This charming picture did not as yet avail to persuade me to appear as a public instructor in Thorough-Bass."

xxxviii."As, however, I received reminders, about the same time, from various patrons elsewhere, who knew of a promise which I had made at Jena, I found myself under a manifold obligation to make my treatise, which had long been lying in readiness, known to the public. I therefore enriched my old essay with this Preliminary Notice and the INTRODUCTION IN SEVEN CHAPTERS which follows, and thereupon concluded an agreement with the above-mentioned Herr Gross on conditions established between us, namely, that this work should go to press within the year at latest."

[2] Cf. o.c. § 40 *ad fin.*, p. 17; § 344, note, p. 187; § 384, p. 201.
[3] Cf. ibid., § 135 *ad fin.*, p. 72; § 284, p. 165.

us a brief abstract (*Vorbericht*, xvi–xxvi). In it he traced the development of harmony from the times when only Triads were used. The first innovation, according to him, was the acceptance of the chord of the Sixth: 1, 3, 6, 8, whereas the *status* of the $^6_4$ was not settled till 1738 "by Mizler's impartial pronouncement".

Next came the use of certain [suspended] discords *in Thesi Tactus*, whereas discords had previously occurred only *in Arsi*, as passing notes. First came $^{8}_{5\ 43\ 1}$ and $^{9\ 8}_{4\ 3\ 1}$, and later, "in the middle period", $^{7\ 6}_{3\ 8\ 1}$ and, likewise, $^{9\ 8}_{7\ 6\ 3\ 1}$. Then came—and this is the nucleus of Schröter's whole theory of harmony—the modification of the Triad by the *addition of the Sixth*, at first only on the

4th degree of the scale, as:

Afterwards the number of discords was increased (1) by the use of $^6_5$ on all degrees of the scale, and (2) by the generation, by inversion, of $^6_{4\ 3}$, $^7_{5\ 3}$, and $^6_{4\ 2}$. [4] The order of these inversions is determined by the degree of dissonance *with the Bass*: 4, 7, $^4_2$.

All subsequent discords arose through (1) the retardation, (2) the anticipation of one or more intervals of the seven principal chords enumerated above (cf. note 1).

Whether Schröter intended to publish his 'History of Harmony' it is impossible to say. Very possibly he wrote it, like those many articles on the subject dearest to his heart, "for his own edification" (cf. note 1, xxxvii), namely, as the best means of arriving at clearness in his own mind; but there can be no doubt that he intended the Second Part of his work on Thorough-Bass to appear in due time. The sad fate which befell these two works is best related in his own words (*Vorbericht*, lii, liii):

"Among many terrible days in the late war", he writes, "the 23rd August 1761 was one of the saddest. . . ."

After relating how his house was forcibly entered, in search of a supposed fugitive, he continues: "Although the assurance was given by me and mine, that the door of the house had remained locked the whole morning, as also in the night, all was in vain. They first plundered me and mine, then scoured the whole house, burst open all the doors, and finally reached the top room, in which was the best and largest part of my musical, mathematical, and philosophical books, cut them to pieces, tore up every single thing, and burnt the scraps. This misfortune befell also the above-mentioned HISTORY OF HARMONY, likewise the SECOND VOLUME, ON A FILLED-IN ACCOMPANIMENT AND UNFIGURED THOROUGH-BASS (*vom vollstimmigen und unbezifferten General-bass*), . . .

"When I related this occurrence, which had caused me such manifold loss, to certain (reputedly clever) persons, I received the following comfortless answer: 'Why! those were only papers. We, on the other hand, have had

---

[4] Schröter retained his belief in the priority of the $^6_5$ chord, but, in the *Deutliche Anweisung zum General-Bass*, for reasons which will appear presently, he adopted (as far as the *external* arrangement of that work is concerned) the prevalent classification: $^7_{5\ 3}$, $^6_{5\ 3}$, $^6_{4\ 3}$, $^6_{4\ 2}$.

the most valuable mugs, glasses, cups, and other crockery, smashed.' Very sound judgement from the Copper brandy-still!

"Should God, in His great mercy, grant me, now that old age is approaching, a few more years of health, I shall hope, in my few leisure hours, to work out afresh the SECOND VOLUME ON A FILLED-IN ACCOMPANIMENT AND UNFIGURED THOROUGHBASS. For it is easy to realize that the above-mentioned incidents of war cannot deprive me of the necessary material, for, as to that, I say, like Bias of old: ALL THAT PERTAINS TO IT I CARRY WITH ME."

(c) Schröter's *Vorbericht* is full of interesting, and sometimes amusing, reminiscences, which is not unnatural when we consider that he lived through a period of rapid development in the science of Harmony as well as in the art of accompaniment from a Thorough-Bass. Born a year before the publication of Niedt's *Handleitung* (cf. Ch. I, § 25), he records the successive appearance of the works of Heinichen, Mattheson, and Sorge; and, in the second part of the *Vorbericht*, of those of Marpurg, Quantz, and Ph. Em. Bach, though, curiously enough, at the time of writing (seven years after its appearance), he had been unable to procure a copy of the Second Part of the last-named author's *Versuch*.[5] His pleasant style, and the modest and amiable character which reveals itself, enlist the interest and sympathy of his readers. A few extracts only must suffice:

[The Roman numerals prefixed to the passages quoted refer to the sections of the *Vorbericht*.]

"ii". "No one who knows my character will expect me to pass over in silence my first preceptor in Thorough-Bass. By this I mean Dr. Treiber's ACCURATE ORGANIST IN THOROUGH-BASS, published at Arnstadt in 1704. This little *folio* I received from my late Father, . . . as a New Year's gift, in 1708, when I was no longer with my parents, but in Dresden. . . ."

"iii". "Afterwards, when Heinichen published his first treatise, in a small quarto volume, in 1711, there were already the following 12 signatures and indications of the altered harmonic Triad to be learned:

Signatures	6	4 3	7 6	7	9 8	9	$\frac{6}{5}$	$\frac{6\,5}{4\,3}$	♭7	$\frac{4}{3}$	4+	2
Complementary parts	$\frac{3}{8}$	$\frac{5}{8}$	$\frac{3}{8}$	$\frac{3}{5}$	$\frac{3}{5}$	$\frac{3}{5}$	3	8	$\frac{3}{5}$	6	$\frac{2}{6}$	$\frac{4}{6}$

"I still remember that an Organist, then well known in Dresden, was violently angry about the CHORD OF THE NINTH, which was unknown to him, and openly called it a fad (*Grille*), thereby showing that he had either never read his considerable store of musical writings, or else not understood them. A natural bent (*mein gutes Naturell*), and untiring diligence in the attentive perusal of the said HEINICHEN and the above-mentioned TREIBER, besides other works in manuscript, soon advanced me, WITHOUT ANY ORAL INSTRUCTION, far enough to be able, with the consent of the highly accomplished Director of Music at the Church of the Holy Cross (*Kreuzkirche*) at Dresden, Herr Grundig, to play the Thorough-Bass at the public rehearsals with general approval, besides which I always had first to tune the Harpsichord (*Clavierinstrument*) belonging to the school. . . ."

[5] He also mentions incidentally (*Vorbericht*, xxxxvi) that he had read the First Part only in a borrowed copy.

"iiii". "But when the aforesaid Heinichen . . . came forward in 1728 with his greatly enlarged Guide, or Thorough-Bass in Composition, and contributed some thirty signatures to the new fashion, almost all the Organists who had studied WERCKMEISTER'S REMARKS ON THOROUGH-BASS of 1700 [6] till their hair was grey, were struck dumb. . . ."

* * * * * * * * * * * *

"vi". "Finally, when, in 1735, the praiseworthy Herr Mattheson opened his little Thoroughbass-School with actually 70 signatures, the then Organist at —— exclaimed publicly: 'Now the D—l may play the Thoroughbass, and not I! . . .'"

This reminds us of Niedt's picture of the results of a too close adherence to the old German Organ tablature (cf. Ch. i, § 25, II e).

(d) Passing on to the continuation of the *Vorbericht* (written in 1769), we find an eloquent tribute to the merits of a work which cannot, indeed, be praised too much. In Schröter's account of how it came into his possession there is a quaint little personal touch which cannot fail to add to the interest. He writes:

xxxxix. "When I was about to complete my account of the most notable text-books on Thoroughbass (that have appeared in the present century, and are known to me), there was offered to me for sale, by the widow of a Town Musician (*eines Stadtmusikanten*) who had lately died in the neighbourhood, a long and eagerly desired *quarto* volume, of which the full title is as follows: 'Joh. Joach. Quan[t]zens, kőnigl. Preuss. Kammermusicus, VERSUCH EINER ANWEISUNG DIE FLÖTE TRAVERSIERE ZU SPIELEN; mit verschiedenen zur Beförderung des guten Geschmacks in der practischen Musik dienlichen Anmerkungen begleitet, und mit Exempeln erläutert. Nebst 24 Kupfertafeln. Berlin, bey Voss, 1752.' [*Johann Joachim Quantz, Private Musician to the King of Prussia, his Essay at guidance in playing the German Flute; accompanied by various remarks serving to promote the advancement of good taste in practical Music, and illustrated by examples. With 24 copperplates. Berlin, Voss, 1752.*] With the greatest pleasure I payed the money demanded, and found more in it than your cursory page-turner. The praiseworthy author says quite rightly in his preface 'that he has written of good taste in practical Music, not alone as concerns the German Flute, but that his work might be of service to all who make profession, either of singing, or the employment of other instruments, and who desire to cultivate a good style of musical performance. Any one whom it concerns need only select, and make use of, that which applies to his voice or his instrument.' Without flattery, I add that, not only all beginners in Thoroughbass, but sundry Church- and Chamber-Organists known to me, holding posts in large towns, greatly need to lay to heart, principally, the sixth subsection of the seventeenth section [7] of this excellent work. . . . In short: Herr Quan[t]z, who has been known to me for many years, has perpetuated his fame by this work. Enough!"

(e) The arrangement of Schröter's work corresponds exactly with the general scheme outlined by himself soon after 1724 (cf. note 1, xiv), with the further addition of the *Vorbericht* and an Introduction consisting of seven chapters dealing with preliminary matter [8] (cf. note 1, xxxviii), as well as of

---

[6] The first edition of this work appeared in 1698, not 1700 (cf. Ch. i, § 24 *ad init.*).

[7] Cf. Ch. iii, § 11, note 2.

[8] I. *On the harmonic Triad generally.* II. *On the qualifications* (Beschaffenheit) *of*

several miscellaneous chapters incorporated in the third main section, and an excellent Index.

Reference is greatly facilitated by the fact that the numbering of the paragraphs (§§ 1–387) runs continuously from the beginning of the Introduction to the end of the work.

(f) Before proceeding further it will be necessary to look back for a moment.

It must always be remembered that the central idea in Schröter's mind, as is apparent from the title of his work, as well as from the abbreviated abstract of his History of Harmony given above (b), is the *origin of all harmonies in the alteration of "our natural heritage", the Triad.* The first discord (apart from passing notes and certain suspensions) arose, according to his theory, from the addition of the Sixth to the perfect Triad on the fourth degree of the scale, which resulted in a chord, $\frac{6}{5}$, of which all the intervals were consonant with the Bass, though the consonance of the chord, *as a whole*, was *doubtful*. As the first inversion of this he regarded $\frac{6}{4}$, in which there were *two* imperfect consonances, the 6 and 4.[9] Then follow $\frac{7}{5}$ and $\frac{6}{4}$, the latter with *no* perfect consonance.

In support of this order, he advances the following argument (*Vorbericht*, xxx): "Every one admits that, from the inversion of the consonant Triad, there arises FIRSTLY the best three-part chord of the Sixth: 1, 3, 6, 8, with the loss of a single degree of perfection; SECONDLY the best six-four chord: 1, 4, 6, 8, with the loss of two degrees of perfection. Why, then, should the process, in the case of the four-part chords, be reversed or carried out wrongly? Or, to put it more clearly: Why should there be derived from a dissonant harmony $\left[\text{i.e. } \frac{7}{5}\right]$ two similar harmonies which, however, consist only of consonances $\left[\text{i.e. } \frac{6}{5} \text{ and } \frac{6}{4}\right]$? Who would not be astounded at such contradictions!" Schröter adds the following table (ibid., xxxi): [10]

d 6	consonance DOUBT-	f 6	consonance	c 7		a 6	
c 5	FUL on account of	d 4	STILL MORE	a 5	strongly	f 4	still more
a 3	the added fourth	c 3	DOUBTFUL on	f 3	dissonant	c 2	strongly
f 1	part d	a 1	account of	d 1		d 1	dissonant
			the d				

(g) After this clear statement of opinion it will come as a surprise to the reader that, in the main body of his work, Schröter should have classified

a Thoroughbass pupil. III. *On the various positions, the denomination, and circulation of the 12 simple tones.* IIII. *On the number and names of the intervals.* V. *On the Consonances and dissonances.* VI. *On the harmonic and melodic scales.* VII. *On the relationship of the 24 keys.*

[9] Schröter regarded the [perfect] Fourth as a *Consonantia imperfecta* "under limited conditions" (*Vorbericht*, xxviii): as *indisputably* so in a $\frac{6}{4}$, and also a $\frac{6}{3}$ chord (o.c. § 57). The Third (both major and minor) he regards as a *perfect* consonance (*Vorbericht*, xxviii).

[10] The *ratios* of the intervals (as shown on the Monochord), which Schröter gives, are here omitted.

$\frac{6}{5}$, $\frac{4}{3}$, and $\frac{6}{4}$ chords (though as a matter of external arrangement only) as *derivatives of the Seventh.*

It will be remembered that, after 1747, he was in the habit of acquainting his pupils with Sorge's arrangement of the "four four-part chords" as well as his own (cf. note 1, xv). What induced him to adopt this arrangement, contrary to his own deep-rooted conviction, is best related in his own words: "In the years 1745, 46, and 47", he writes (*Vorbericht*, x), "Herr Sorge, Court- and Town-Organist at Lobenstein, came out with a new Guide to Thoroughbass in three successive parts. Let no one hope that I shall institute a detailed criticism of this work, as I have long since been requested to do, to the disadvantage of the author, whom I greatly esteem. No, No! On the contrary, it will transpire in the sequel that, from an inborn love of peace, I have partially retained the now almost universally familiar fashion in the matter of the Seventh (*Septimenmode*), started by a Frenchman, Mr. Rameau by name, and continued by our German Herr Sorge. There are known to me, it is true, various highly placed *connoisseurs* of Harmony who regard the French fashion as a toying with Thirds (*eine Terzentändeley*), in which there is, perhaps, some wit, but no reflection, to be observed. *Ingenium sine judicio.* I cannot, at present, enter into a discussion with the said *connoisseurs*, but must publicly confess to them that, in the present state of the atmosphere (*bey jetziger Witterung*), I do not venture to swim against the strong current that tears me along, as may be clearly seen from chapters 14–17."

(*h*) The following, then, is the basis of Schröter's classification:

"Thoroughbass", he writes (o. c., § 80), "is a constant alteration of the harmonic Triad. . . . There are, altogether, seven ways in which this alteration can take place:

"FIRSTLY by a change in the relative position of the constituents [11] while the Bass (*Grundstimme*) remains the same;

"SECONDLY by a new position of the constituents, with a change of Bass; [12]

"THIRDLY by the displacement (*Versetzung*) of the Bass to the $\left\{\begin{array}{l}\text{Third above}\\ \text{Sixth below}\end{array}\right\}$, whereby the THREE-PART CHORD OF THE SIXTH: 1, 3, 6, 8 arises;

"FOURTHLY by the displacement of the Bass to the $\left\{\begin{array}{l}\text{Fifth above}\\ \text{Fourth below}\end{array}\right\}$, whereby the SIX-FOUR CHORD: 1, 4, 6, 8 arises;

"FIFTHLY by the assumption of a SEVENTH IN PLACE OF THE OCTAVE, thus: $\begin{smallmatrix}7\\5\\3\\1\end{smallmatrix}$. From the inversion (*Versetzung*) of this chord of the Seventh are further derived (in accordance with the French fashion) the following three chords: $\begin{smallmatrix}6\\5\\3\\1\end{smallmatrix}$, $\begin{smallmatrix}6\\4\\3\\1\end{smallmatrix}$, $\begin{smallmatrix}6\\4\\2\\1\end{smallmatrix}$.

"SIXTHLY by the DELAY (*Aufhaltung*) or RETARDATION [*Verzögerung*] (*Re-*

---

[11] *Durch Versetzung seiner Glieder*: *Versetzung*, as is shown by the examples which Schröter gives, here includes, not only *inversion*, but also the change from the close to the extended position of the chord, and vice versâ.

[12] As: (Schröter gives the extreme parts only.)

tardatio) of one, or two, or three parts of the seven PRINCIPAL CHORDS previously mentioned,[13] namely, $\frac{8}{5}, \frac{8}{6}, \frac{8}{6}$; and further $\frac{7}{5}, \frac{6}{5}, \frac{6}{4}, \frac{6}{4}$.

"SEVENTHLY by the ANTICIPATION [*Vorausnehmung*] (*Anticipatio*) of one, two, or three parts of the said SEVEN PRINCIPAL CHORDS."

(*i*) Of these seven 'alterations of the Triad', the first four are illustrated in the first main section (*Hauptabtheilung*) of Schröter's treatise (Chs. viii–xiii), the fifth in the second, and the sixth and seventh in the third. The last chapter of the first main section (Ch. xiii) is devoted to the explanation of transposition by means of imaginary changes of clef.

The second main section (Chs. xiv–xviii) further includes a chapter 'On the harmonized accompaniment of the six intervals still unconsidered' (*Von der harmonischen Begleitung der sechs zurückgelassenen Intervallen*).

These intervals are: (1) the augmented Prime, ×1 or ♮1; (2) the augmented Third, ⚡ or ♮3; (3) the diminished Sixth, 6♭ or 6♮; (4) the diminished Octave, $\hat{8}$; (5) the augmented Octave ×8 or ♮8; (6) the augmented Ninth, ♭9 or ♮9.

The modifications of the "seven principal chords" by the retardation or anticipation of one or more intervals, are treated in the first chapter of the third main section (Ch. xix, §§ 218–80, pp. 114–64), the following chapter being devoted to the illustration of passing harmonies over a stationary Bass.

The remaining six chapters bear the following headings: Ch. xxi, 'On various tables of signatures'; Ch. xxii, 'On the harmonized accompaniment of the various quick Bass notes in even and uneven time'; Ch. xxiii, 'On the harmonious accompaniment of Recitative on the Organ'; Ch. xxiiii, 'On a discreet change of stops on the Organ (*von kluger Abwechselung der Orgelstimmen*) in different kinds of music'; Ch. xxv, 'On the commonest harmonies (*harmonische Sätze*) on the [several] degrees of the major and minor scales'; Ch. xxvi, 'On the *Genus enharmonicum* and its use'.

(*k*) Before bringing this account to a conclusion, certain points of interest remain to be noticed.

Schröter was extremely sensitive in the matter of *hidden consecutives*. With reference to the following (and other similar) examples, all stigmatized as "bad":

[Ex. 1]

he writes (§ 95): "I know very well, it is true, that sundry Composers, as well as *Clavierists*, often use these apparently hidden Fifths, shown above, thereby giving us to understand that their ear has been spoiled from youth upwards, as it might be (*etwa*) by those heartening (*tröstlich*) little trumpeter's pieces in three parts, with or without drums. But can such a (nearly universal, but) quite unfounded usage upset the rule of Nature? As surely as Composers always have space to dispose the middle parts over a stationary

---

[13] Cf. note 1, xiv.

Bass according to rule, so surely are *Clavierists* under an equal obligation to do the same."

With reference to the following:

[Ex. 2]

he writes (§ 101, p. 50): "From this [i.e. a previous, similar example] it can also be seen that, for the avoidance of those most disgusting successive Fifths and Octaves (*der höchst eckeln Quinten- und Octavenfolge*), something more is needed than contrary motion of both hands" . . . [Then, in reference to Ex. 2] "(d) Is actually fundamentally wrong; at (e) it is improved as far as possible."

Schröter does not specify the cases in which hidden consecutives are admissible, but hidden Fifths, between extreme parts, are to be seen, e.g. in the following opening bars of an example, given as a model to the student, both in the matter of melody and harmony (§ 101, p. 49):

[Ex. 3]

(N.B.—In the original only the extreme parts are given.)

At * * there is also found a progression of which, as will be seen, Schröter did not approve.

(*l*) He disliked the particular form of false relation arising through the interval of a *Tritone* between the extreme parts of two successive chords, both in its most familiar form, i.e. a succession of two major Thirds (as in Ex. 4), and also as * * in Ex. 3.

[Ex. 4]

Of the above example he writes (§ 99, p. 47):

"At 'F' I have added a couple of examples of chords from a world-renowned Composer, in order to learn whether any one who can count three in musical matters would venture to justify it."

Of a succession of chords identical with the last five in Ex. 3 (but with strong and weak beats reversed), our author writes (§ 100, note, p. 48): "Should the chords from *e* to *f* not please a Thoroughbass pupil, he can promise himself my approval. It will be shown further on how this age-old Cacophony (*uralter Mislaut*) is to be avoided."

The example 'further on' is probably the following:

[Ex. 5]

8 5 8   3 3 3 3   3   (o.c., p. 49 *e*.)

(*m*) In view of Schröter's sensitiveness in the matter of hidden consecutives, it is the more remarkable that he should have countenanced *apparent* consecutive Fifths of a kind which, e.g., Ph. Em. Bach unreservedly condemned (cf. Ch. iii, § 10 *e*, Ex. 14). The following example is another case in point:

[Ex. 6]

Of this he writes (§ 215, note, p. 112): "In the example at (f) [= Ex. 6] many a person whose intellectual vision is weak (*mancher am Verstande Blödsichtiger*) will think to see apparent consecutive Fifths, which, however, are not noticed by musical ears."

(*n*) Perhaps the most remarkable chapter in Schröter's book is Ch. xix, with which the third main section (*Hauptabtheilung*) of the work opens. It is divided into six sections (*Abschnitte*), as follows:

"i, the one-part ⎫
  ii, the two-part ⎬ retardations in 5, 6, ⁶₄, together with the appropriate
 iii, the three-part ⎭ (*hierher gehörig*) inversions of the same."

"iiii, the one-part ⎫
   v, the two-part ⎬ retardations in 7, ⁶₅, ⁴₃, 2, together with the appropriate
  vi, the three-part ⎭ inversions of the same."

Each retardation, together with any inversions of the resulting chord, are presented in what our author quaintly terms an "harmonic packet" (*harmonisches Packet*); of such the chapter contains no less than forty-three.

These include many unusual harmonies and combinations of figures, rarely to be met with, either in text-books or in actual practice.

In one of the concluding paragraphs (§ 278, p. 160) Schröter writes, in his usual quaint style: "Stop! Many will here think: Assuredly one finds in this chapter, not too little, but rather, often, too much; sometimes UNHEARD-OF RETARDATIONS, and sometimes UNEXPECTED ANTICIPATIONS. I reply: Such an objection is by no means damaging to me. I, thou, he, we, you, they, always much prefer to hear UNHEARD-OF and UNEXPECTED combinations (*Zusammenstimmungen*) rather than the every-day ones. But these new harmonies (*Sätze*) must, undoubtedly, have their foundation in the existing key (*in der vorhabenden Tonart*): Otherwise they can cause no pleasure, and, consequently, receive no approval. . . ."

(*o*) Mention must be made of Schröter's Table of Signatures (*Signatur-Register*), which is like no other known to the present writer.

He writes (Ch. XXI, p. 164 sq.): "Now a COMPLETE TABLE OF SIGNA-TURES will be expected of me, such as Heinichen and Mattheson faithfully provided, in accordance with formerly existing conditions as regards the harmonies already discovered. But as the word COMPLETE seems to me, in this instance, ambiguous, I will proceed to explain myself anent this matter. . . ."

After explaining that he regards the inclusion of figures with prefixed accidentals (♯, ♭, ♮) as superfluous, he proceeds:

"At the same time, I remember with pleasure sundry good pupils in Thorough-Bass, who, instead of a lengthy Table of Signatures, asked for one made as brief as possible. After mature consideration I wrote it down in the following short form, originating, as it does, in the *Ars combinatoria*, or art of inversion, with which I am tolerably familiar:

"New-fashioned Table of Signatures" (*Neumodisches Signatur-Register*)

9 9 9 9 9	9 9 9 9	9 9 9	9 9
4 5 6 7 8	5 6 7 8	6 7 8	7 8
3 4 5 6 7	3 4 5 6	3 4 5	3 4

4 5 6 7 8	5 6 7 8	6 7 8	7 8
3 4 5 6 7	3 4 5 6	3 4 5	3 4
2 2 2 2 2	2 2 2 2	2 2 2	2 2

5 6 7 8	6 7 8	7 8	8
4 5 6 7	4 5 6	4 5	4
3 3 3 3	3 3 3	3 3	3

6 7 8	7 8 8
5 6 7	5 5 6
4 4 4	4 4 4

7 8 8
6 6 7
5 5 5

"The above Table of Signatures has had great light thrown upon it by one of my former pupils, a *Doctorandus Medicinae*. For he wrote down the figurings (*Sätze*) in a considerably extended form (*etwas weitläuftig*), with the number of the section against each, and noted down, not only on which degree of the scale (*Chorda*) either one, 2, or 3 intervals are raised or lowered, but also, in what instances each harmony (*Satz*) was treated, either freely, or as a retardation, or as an anticipation, or as passing. Perhaps I shall make up my mind to publish this excellent commentary (*solche wohlgerathene Er-läuterung*) in the SECOND VOLUME and, at the same time, to display each harmony in extended position; many an addition to the harmonies will, no doubt, result, especially in the chapter on *Point d'Orgue*, or the stationary position of the Bass on I or V in every key."

The conclusion is almost irresistible that Schröter intended his Table as a mild practical joke at the expense of his pupils, and that he could not resist the temptation to record it. He tells us that his pupil, the future Doctor of

Medicine, gave a reference to the section in which each of the signatures was to be found, but after careful and repeated search throughout the entire work (and especially Ch. XIX, described above), thirteen out of the forty-seven signatures in the Table remain unaccounted for, viz. $\frac{9}{3}$, $\frac{9}{7}$, $\frac{9}{6}$, $\frac{9}{5}$, $\frac{9}{4}$, $\frac{4}{2}$, $\substack{8\\7\\2}$, $\substack{8\\6\\2}$, $\substack{8\\5\\2}$, $\substack{7\\3\\2}$, $\substack{8\\4\\3}$, $\substack{8\\6\\5}$, $\substack{8\\7\\5}$.

(*p*) Like Gasparini, Rameau, Heinichen, Kellner, and Mattheson, Schröter presents a scheme, akin to Campion's *Règle de l'Octave*,[14] showing the harmony appropriate to each degree of the major and minor mode (Ch. XXV, § 363).

Like Gasparini [15] (and also Heinichen, as far as the major mode is concerned) he does not carry the ascending scale above the sixth degree.

His reason for this, as he tells us (§ 369), was the desire, for the sake of beginners, to avoid the ambiguity which would arise: (1) by the introduction of the *major* Sixth on the sixth degree of the descending major scale [16] (which he regards, like Heinichen,[17] as involving a modulation to the key of the Dominant), and (2) by the sharpening of the sixth degree of the minor scale in ascending, and the flattening of the seventh degree in descending.

Like Heinichen, Schröter places the leading note at the beginning of the scale. It will be noticed that, although he figures the sixth degree of both modes with a simple 6, he interprets the latter as $\frac{6}{3}$,[18] corresponding (as another inversion of the same fundamental harmony) to the $\frac{6}{5}$ on the fourth degree. For the sake of variety, he tells us (§ 364), the 6 on both the second and the sixth degrees of the scale can be taken as $\frac{6}{3}{8}$ instead of $\frac{6}{4}$, using contrary motion.[19]

In an earlier portion of the work (§ 25, p. 11) Schröter compared the three notes of the Triad to rays of light, and the intervening intervals to shadows; it is in accordance with this idea that, in the following scheme, the former are represented by white notes, and the latter by black (with, or without, tails). Of the scale of A minor only the Bass is given here, as the harmonies are, *mutatis mutandis*, the same as in C major:

---

[14] Cf. § 7 *h*.

[15] Cf. ibid., note 20.

[16] Gasparini, though he does not carry his scales above the sixth degree, sharpens the 6 on the said degree of the major scale, as an *alternative* to the natural 6 (cf. § 5, IV *b*, *sub* Ex. 8).

[17] Cf. ibid., *ad fin*.

[18] Cf. Ch. xxi, 'Incomplete figuring', II, § 2, note.

[19] i.e. because, otherwise, the inclusion of the 8 would involve consecutive 8ves. Although Schröter specifies $\frac{6}{3}{8}$, it can hardly be supposed that he thereby intended to exclude the employment of $\frac{6}{3}$ $\left(\text{or } \frac{6}{3}\right)$. On the second degree of the scale, the 6 can, of course, not be doubled, and Schröter would probably have objected to the employment of $\frac{6}{3}$ on the sixth degree of the descending scale, on account of the hidden Fifths involved:

(Cf. *k*.)

"Scale of the commonest harmonies in C major"

[Ex. 7a]

VII   I   II   III   IIII   V   VI   V   IIII   III   II   I   VII

"The scale of the commonest harmonies in A minor"

[Ex. 7b]

VII   I   II   III   IIII   V   VI   V   IIII   III   II   I   VII

It will be noticed that Schröter's scale includes all the "seven principal chords",[20] except the $\frac{6}{4}$ and the Seventh, and he rightly attached considerable importance to its employment by beginners, as a practical method of acquiring familiarity with the harmonies in most frequent use: "Whoever can play both scales . . . in all the 24 keys, in the three positions, CORRECTLY, IN THE PITCH-DARKNESS OF NIGHT," he writes (§ 368), "can flatter himself that he understands almost the fourth part of the science of Thorough-Bass."

The chapter (Ch. XXV) ends with the important pronouncement (illustrated by a Table), that *every one of the 'seven principal chords' may be employed on every degree of the scale, both major and minor.* In four-part harmony, the diminished Triad on the leading note of the major scale, $\frac{\frac{8}{5}}{\frac{3}{1}}$, can, of course, occur only in the repetition of a sequence, as shown in an example earlier in the work (§ 101, p. 49, bar 5), and, of the imperfect Triad on the leading note of the minor scale, we are told (§ 86, p. 40) that it 'never bears the inclusion of the Octave, and cannot be used without more ado (*so schlechterdings*) in four-part music, [on a Bass moving] either by step or by leap'.

(*q*) It may not be amiss to conclude this account with one of our author's amusing reminiscences.

"I know families belonging to the high aristocracy", he writes (§ 386, p. 202), "who, in choosing a teacher for their young gentlemen and ladies, were chiefly anxious, not only that he should be able to read, write, do a little arithmetic, and explain the catechism, but that he should also be master of various languages and of the *Clavier*, nay, that he should understand horse-breaking and the like, as well! A few weeks ago I was commissioned to examine some highly aristocratic children on the Clavier, as their teacher had been promoted. They seized upon the FREYLINGHAUSEN CHORALE-BOOK, and offered to play me any tunes that I pleased, TOGETHER WITH THE THOROUGH-BASS (*Generalbass-mässig*). Yes, indeed! But, how? Over the Bass notes

[20] Cf. note 1, xiv.

where there was no signature, it is true, they always sounded the full chord. The notes with figures, on the other hand, were accompanied with nothing but shakes (*Fuchstriller*) in the right hand. When I at last inquired, why they did not also render the figures over the notes, I received the following answer: 'Our teacher (*unser Herr Informator*) told us that such figures were only for Organists in large towns (*die grosstädtischen Organisten*), and applied to the pedals.' . . ."

§ 11. *Georg Michael Telemann* (1748–1831).

(*a*) The work which next engages our attention is entitled: "GEORG MICHAEL TELEMANNS, / ehemaligen Accompagnisten am Hamburgischen musikalischen Kirchen-Chor, und / itzigen Candidaten der H. Gottesgelahrt-heit, / UNTERRICHT / im / GENERALBASS-SPIELEN, / AUF DER ORGEL / ODER SONST EINEM CLAVIER-INSTRUMENTE. / HAMBURG, / gedruckt und verlegt von Michael Christian Bock, / 1773."

('Georg Michael Telemann, former accompanist to the Hamburg musical Church Choir, at present Candidate in Theology, his Instruction in Playing from a Thorough-Bass, on the Organ or any other keyed instrument. Hamburg, printed and published by Michael Christian Bock. 1773.')

(*b*) This excellent little treatise, a small quarto of 112 pages, deals with its subject from a purely practical point of view, and, being expressly designed for beginners, all mention of the various adornments, or what Ph. Em. Bach so expressively calls the "niceties" (*Zierlichkeiten*), of accompaniment is avoided.

By 'beginners', as the author is careful to explain (p. 14, note), he means: "not so much beginners of all sorts, as rather (*a*) especially those who make the Art of Music in so far their principal occupation that they intend, some day, to make it their profession; and (*b*), among amateurs, only those who wish to acquire a thorough and connected knowledge of Thoroughbass."

The older treatises, he tells us in his Preface, had ceased to be useful for the purposes of instruction, partly because some of the rules given were out of date, while others were needed in their place; partly on account of the amount of irrelevant matter included—here he, no doubt, had Mattheson in mind—and also because of the perplexity occasioned by the constant employ-ment of Latin, French, Italian, and even Greek words and phrases—and here the reference clearly is to Heinichen. Such works, again, as Sorge's *Vor-gemach der musicalischen Composition* ('Anteroom of musical Composition') and Marpurg's *Handbuch bey dem Generalbass und der Composition* ('Hand-book of Thoroughbass and Composition') were schools of Harmony and not of Accompaniment, while the Second Part of Ph. Em. Bach's *Versuch* was too advanced. Telemann's warmly appreciative description of the latter work, which includes an equally appreciative reference to the subsection in Quantz's great work on the Flute dealing with accompaniment on keyed instruments, has already been quoted.[1]

Telemann mentions "two of the most recent guides to Thoroughbass, which, it is true, provide that which, according to the intention of their accomplished authors, they are meant to provide", but of which, for present purposes, "the one . . . would assuredly be much too lengthy and lacking in

[1] Cf. § 9 *a*.

clearness of plan (*unübersehlich*),[2] and the other, not sufficiently detailed and satisfying".

The intention and scope of Telemann's own work is defined by himself as follows: ". . . in writing it, I have confined myself to the consideration of PLAIN ACCOMPANIMENT (*das simple Accompagnement*) from a correctly figured Bass, and have given the necessary rules, without any prolixity, as briefly as possible and, as I hope, clearly enough, taking the utmost care to illustrate them with abundant examples from accepted authors; at the same time, constantly aiming at order, completeness, precision, and accuracy; but entirely omitting, as irrelevant, all that does not essentially pertain to the doctrine of Thoroughbass, or that transcends the limits of simple accompaniment. Demonstrations of the rules, which, though not indispensable in merely playing from a Thoroughbass, nevertheless conduce to a more thorough comprehension, and other matters, are left for oral instruction. So-called 'useful devices' (*Vortheile*),[3] however, and means of learning to find the chords easily, in employing which, instead of a short cut, one, in point of fact, goes a roundabout way, and, in order to find one chord, has first to remember others,[4] and, worst of all, never attains a clear conviction of the correctness of one's chords without examining each chord in itself: such imaginary 'useful devices', I say, will be sought in vain."

(*c*) The plan of the work (as shown in the Table of Contents at the end) is as follows:

"Introduction. On Thoroughbass generally" (§§ 1–12).

"FIRST SECTION, containing the doctrine of intervals.
   "First chapter. On intervals generally" (§§ 1–10).
   "Second chapter. On the use of the intervals" (§§ 1–9).

"SECOND SECTION, embracing the doctrine of signatures.
   "First chapter, containing the Table of Signatures together with the explanation of the same" (§§ 1–14).
   "Second chapter. On Bass notes without figures; on notes with several figures side by side; on figures over rests; as also of certain signs occurring in a Thoroughbass" (§§ 1–11).

"THIRD SECTION, which contains some further rules to be observed in accompaniment" (§§ 1–8).

(*d*) The second chapter of the first Section contains all that Telemann has to say on the progression of the intervals in the matter of avoiding consecutives, &c., and on the preparation and resolution of discords. The eminently practical character of the book is shown by the advice given at the end of the said chapter: "All the RULES CONCERNING PREPARATION AND RESOLUTION, just given, must be carefully observed AS LONG AS ONE CAN.

---

[2] The work referred to can hardly be any other than Schröter's *Deutliche Anweisung*, last described, though the charge that it is *unübersehlich* (or, in more modern German, *unübersichtlich*), i.e. that it is difficult to obtain at a glance a clear idea of the arrangement of the contents, is certainly not well founded.

[3] Cf. § 6, note 1.

[4] The following, from Ph. Em. Bach (*Versuch &c.*, Part II, Ch. 17, 1, § 6), is a good example of what Telemann means: "If, with the Triad of the Bass note, instead of the Octave, one takes the Ninth, the chord of the Ninth is in the hand. *Whoever knows the Three-two chord* $\left[= \begin{smallmatrix} 5 \\ 3 \\ 2 \end{smallmatrix} \right]$, *knows the chord of the Ninth as well.*" N.B.—The italics are not Bach's.

They extend, therefore, only to what is possible. For since, in accordance with the figures, dissonances are often not prepared, and often not resolved, . . . and since, moreover, dissonances which properly ought to resolve downwards, must sometimes, in accordance with the indication of the figures, resolve upwards, and vice versâ, and so forth, it will easily be seen that there are many exceptions to the above rules. . . . And so, what I say is this: As LONG AS YOU CAN PREPARE, PREPARE; and, again: As LONG AS YOU CAN RESOLVE, RESOLVE! And if any one observes these two rules, he has done his part; and for all else he can leave figurist and composer to answer."

(e) At the beginning of the same chapter (§ 3), in a footnote, Telemann allows himself to be betrayed into a theoretical discussion as to what constitutes a dissonance. His main contention is that intervals, ordinarily (as in his own *text*) classed as dissonances, which on a keyed instrument are *identical in sound* with consonances, should be classed as such. To this category belong (1) the augmented Second = a minor Third, (2) the diminished Fourth = a major Third, (3) the augmented Fifth = a minor Sixth, (4) the diminished Sixth = a perfect Fifth, and (5) the diminished Seventh = a major Sixth. "What a merit", he concludes, "to have made so many intervals, falsely decried as cacophonous, into euphonious ones, and so restored and saved their good name!"

He further desires a distinction between true (*eigentlich*) or essential (*wesentlich*) dissonances, which are dissonant [i.e. with the Bass] *in themselves* [as a Seventh], and *accidental* (*zufällig*) dissonances, which, though inherently consonant, become accidentally dissonant by association with other intervals, as e.g. the perfect Fifth [in a $\frac{6}{5}$ chord] and the minor Third [in a $\frac{4}{3}$].

(f) Telemann's Table of Signatures, given in the first chapter of the second Section (and described in the heading of the chapter as "a list of the most usual figures", &c.), is shown on the opposite page.

It will be observed that no triple figures are included, though they are often necessary. For instance, $\frac{3}{2}\left(=\frac{5}{3}\right)$ is given, but $\frac{5}{4}$, which is of at least equally frequent occurrence, is omitted. There are also other omissions, but, even so, as a means of recapitulating what has been learnt, the Table is a useful one.

(g) In the second chapter of the second Section, the paragraphs "On Bass notes without figures", do not deal, as might be thought, with unfigured Basses, but with those notes, passing or otherwise, which do not bear an independent harmony, or of which the harmony is to be inferred, without the aid of figures, from the context.

In this chapter Telemann gives the rule that, in triplets, and triple time, whether simple or compound, the first *two* notes are *virtualiter* [5] long, and only the third short: "This last statement", he writes (p. 81, note), "contradicts, it is true, the ordinary doctrine of the inherent [relative] length and shortness of the notes; but I could justify my classification with uncontrovertible examples, if it were necessary. . . ."

(h) At the end of the book, in a postscript, Telemann modestly refers those of his readers who desire connected practical examples, "in default of a better work", to his grandfather's "Singe-, Spiel- und Generalbass-Übungen", which have already been described (cf. § 8).

---

[5] Cf. Ch. xviii, "Quick notes in the Bass", § 1 c, note 1.

"Table of Signatures"

"i. Single figures." "ii. Compound figures."

To	is added	and
1	3	8
2	4	6
3	5	8
✕ or: ✕✕ or: +	5	8
♭ or: ♭♭ or: ♭	5	8
♮ or: ♮✕ or: ♮♭	5	8
perfect 4	5	8
augmented 4	2	6
$\widehat{5}$	3	8
diminished 5	3	6
perfect and augmented 5	3	8
minor and major 6	3	8 or: 6 or: 3 or nothing further.
diminished 6	3	nothing further.
augmented 6	3	4 or: 3 or nothing further.
7	3	5 or: 3 or: 8 or nothing further.
8	3	5
9	3	5

*6 (margin note beside $\widehat{5}$)

To	is added
3 1	5
3 2	5
4 2	6
4 3	6
5 2	2 or: 5 or nothing further.
5 3	8
5 4	8
6 2	4
6 3	8
6 4	8
6 5	3
7 2	4 perhaps 5 as well
7 3	5 or: 8 or nothing further.
7 4	5 or: 8
7 5	3
7 6	3
8 3	5
8 5	3
8 6	3
8 7	3
9 3	5
9 4	5
9 5	3
9 6	3
9 7	3 perhaps 5 as well

*7 (margin note beside 6 2)

** For notes 6 and 7 see page 312.

§ 12. *Johann Philipp Kirnberger* (1721–83).

(*a*) In 1781, according to Eitner (though the date does not appear upon the title-page), Kirnberger published a work entitled "GRUNDSÄTZE / des / GENERALBASSES / als erste Linien zur / COMPOSITION" ('Principles of Thoroughbass as the rudiments of [literally: first lines towards] Composition'), Berlin, Hummel.[1]

This little treatise may be said to stand in very much the same relation to the *Kunst des reinen Satzes* as does Mattheson's *Kleine General-Bass-Schule* (according to the author's own statement) to his *Organisten-Probe*.[2]

Kirnberger's object in writing it is explained in the short Preface (*Vorrede*), which is worth quoting at length:

"In my work on the Art of Correct Writing I presupposed [a knowledge of] the fundaments (*die ersten Gründe*) of Music and Thoroughbass: many lovers of the Beautiful, however, have wished for these rudiments (*erste Linien*) as well. This wish, and my earnest desire to follow those doctrines to their source, to form composers, to lay the foundations of a correct accompaniment, and thereby to make the former work more generally serviceable, were strong enough to determine me to make known these elements (*Gründe*) of correct writing into which such zealous inquiry has been made.

"To the amateur, who wants to advance far in a short time, these truths about Music, confirmed by experience, will seem dry, and will sorely try his patience; however, they are written for those who want to learn Music in its entirety (*ihrem ganzen Umfang nach*), to make a real study of it, and to enjoy the delight which attaches to all study, but especially to sound and melody (*Ton und Gesang*); to these lovers of the Beautiful they will not be dry, and he has not deserved the sweet who has not tasted the bitter."

(*b*) It may be gathered from the above that the subject is treated from a purely theoretical point of view; such is, however, far from being the case.

The arrangement of the work is based, it is true, upon a definite system of chord-classification, but the author's object (in spite of the allusion to composition in the title of the work) is, not only to inculcate the laws of harmony, but to teach the pupil to *play* from a figured Bass. To this end the *fingering* of all the scales, major and minor, is given at the outset; for

---

[1] Reprints (likewise undated) were issued by Böhme (Hamburg) and Johann Michael Götz (Munich, Mannheim, and Düsseldorf).

[2] Cf. § 7 *a*.

---

[6] The semicircle ⌢ above the figure 5 always denotes, as Telemann explains (l. c., § 11, p. 61), (1) that the Fifth is *diminished*, and (2) that it is not to be accompanied, as usual, by the Sixth, but by the Octave [unless the chord is taken in three parts only]; cf. Ch. xxiii, 'Varieties of figuring', § 19.

[7] The figuring $\frac{6}{2}$, as the equivalent of $\frac{6}{4}$, should not have been included: (1) because it is not a generally recognized abbreviation of the latter figuring (and the Table professedly includes only the "most usual figures"), and (2) because $\frac{6}{2}$ is used in quite a different way, either in three parts only, or with the 2 doubled, as:

Kirnberger does not appear to share the opinion of Mattheson and Ph. Em. Bach that some time should have been devoted to the study of pieces (*Handsachen*), and some technical proficiency attained, before proceeding to the study of Thorough-Bass (cf. § 7 *b*, *ad init.*). He writes in the Introduction (*Vorbericht*): "It is, indeed, mere prejudice to believe that children must first have control of their fingers, before accustoming their ear to full and pure harmony. As the ear (*Gehör*) is far more sensitive than the touch (*Gefühl*), and can easily be spoilt (*verwöhnt*), and is, primarily, the first means of perception in the art of Music, it is necessary to combine the training (*Ausbildung*) of the same with the practice of the fingers, in order that the pupil may acquire the necessary perfection, strength, and correctness in both at the same time, even though, to begin with, it comes about mechanically and by dint of imitation." For, strange as it may seem to any one perusing the work under discussion, it was for *children* that it was avowedly designed.

Kirnberger advocates the adherence, in the early stages of instruction, to the old German nomenclature, according to which all the black keys, except B flat, were regarded as *sharps*. "One would be acting very wrongly", he writes (o. c., § 20 *c*), "and wasting time in an unjustifiable manner, if one were to torment young children with the different names of one and the same key: [by telling them] e.g. that F sharp (*Fis*) is at another time called G flat (*Ges*), or D, in another case, C double sharp (*cis-is*).

"One may be satisfied, to begin with, if they only give the name C sharp (*Cis*) to the minor Second of C, D sharp (*Dis*) to the minor Third of C, &c."

This is only to apply, however, to the *oral* designation of the notes: their indication by the letters of the alphabet, with a prefixed ♯ or ♭, is invariably correct. Thus the scale of ♭E minor in the right hand (with the fingering given above, and the flat Sixth and Seventh of the descending scale, below) appears as follows (o. c., § 14 *ad fin.*):

" 2 1   1̿   3 1   4 1̿   3 "
♭ē f ♭g ♭a b c̄   d ♭e f ♭g ♭a b c̄   d ♭e
         ♭c ♭d   ♭c ♭d

Kirnberger adds (ibid., § 15): "When the learner has grasped the fingering (*Applicatur*), let him repeat all the hard and soft, or major and minor, scales, ascending and descending, by word of mouth, without letting him play the scales; but only with the twelve different designations, *c*, *c* sharp, *d*, *d* sharp, *e*, *f*, *f* sharp, *g*, *g* sharp, *a*, *b* flat, *b*, *c*; and the true designations, *d* flat, *a* flat, *f* flat, *g* flat, instead of *c* sharp, *d* sharp, &c., should be postponed till the learner can write all the intervals orthographically [?], in which matter the teacher can give the necessary guidance."

It seemed worth while to give the above extracts, as casting an interesting light on the methods of the day.

(*c*) The external arrangement of the *Grundsätze* is based on Kirnberger's theory of harmony, of which the following are important features:

(1) He regards the diminished Triad on the Supertonic of a minor key (on no account to be confused with the "false" Fifth on the leading note) as a *consonant* chord, of which any interval may be doubled.[3]

---

[3] In its first inversion ($^6_3$ on the Sub-dominant of a minor key) the 6 may therefore be freely doubled. This was not fully recognized by musicians of an older generation: even Ph. Em. Bach gives the rule, without any reservation, that a major Sixth, when accompanied by a minor Third, must never be doubled.

(2) He distinguishes sharply between a *consonant* $\frac{6}{4}$, of which any interval may be doubled, and which may be taken without preparation on a weak, as well as on a strong, beat, and a *dissonant* $\frac{6}{4}$, which requires preparation of both intervals, and can only occur on a strong beat. The former he regards as a second inversion, and the latter as a Triad with the 5 and 3 delayed by suspension. He further distinguishes the case in which only the 4 is dissonant and resolves on 3 over the same Bass, in which case the $\frac{6}{4}$ represents a first inversion with the 3 delayed by suspension (o. c., § 169). These three varieties are seen in the following example (*Dritte Abtheilung* [Third Division], Fig. VI) at a, c, and b, respectively. The capital letters below the example denote the root (*Grundton*) of the chord.

[Ex. I]

(3) He divides all discords into two classes, those which are essential (*wesentlich*), and those which are accidental (*zufällig*). The former class (as he explains in the *Kunst des reinen Satzes*) includes only those which resolve on a root (*Grundton*) which rises a Fourth or falls a Fifth (cf. Ch. xi, 'Sevenths', § 1), in other words the Seventh and its three inversions. All other discords therefore originate, according to Kirnberger, in the modification of a concordant or essentially discordant harmony by 'accidental' discords, arising through the retardation of one or more of its intervals; in addition to which, the matter may, of course, be complicated, and the nature of a chord disguised, by the ellipse of a resolution, or by the taking without preparation of an interval which originated in a suspension.

The work, then, is divided into three main sections (*Abschnitte*), of which the first deals (apart from the preliminary matter) with concords, the second with essential, and the third with 'accidental' discords.

At the end of the third *Abschnitt* is appended a subsection (though without any such heading) on a filled-in accompaniment (*Vom vielstimmigen Accompagnement*), and another on certain differences in the method of figuring (cf. Ch. xix, 'On the figuring of transitional notes').

The examples occupy a separate volume in three divisions (*Abtheilungen*) corresponding to the three sections (*Abschnitte*) of the text.

The latter is divided into paragraphs (§§), numbered continuously without regard to the division into sections; by extraordinary carelessness, however, the division into paragraphs ceases abruptly considerably before the middle of the third *Abschnitt*: it is literally impossible to determine (even by the aid of the table of contents) where § 172 is supposed to end! To add to the confusion, the short subsection or appendix, *Vom vielstimmigen Accompagnement*, is divided into §§ 1–12. After § 171, therefore, the only possible reference is to pages, the pagination being the same in the three editions known to the writer.

The first two main sections (*Abschnitte*) are further divided into 'lectures' (*Vorlesungen*), with such absurd inequality that some 'lectures' embrace only a single paragraph of two lines, with reference to but a single example, while others include seven or more long and difficult ones. Added to these defects, the work is marred by extraordinary slovenliness of diction.

The examples, on the other hand, leave nothing to be desired; though here, again, a just proportion is not always observed.[4]

Particularly helpful to a beginner are the recapitulatory examples, which, in some cases, follow the illustration of the individual chords.

(d) Kirnberger's rules for a filled-in accompaniment are of interest.

He differs from Heinichen in *not permitting a discord to be doubled* (cf. Ch. III, "On the general character &c.", § 3, III A 2), but agrees with him in permitting the *resolution of suspended discords to be anticipated* (i.e. in the left hand, though this is not expressly stated). The rules are given as follows (*Vom vielstimmigen Accompagnement*, §§ 10 and 12):

"In the case of essential discords, as in the chord of the Seventh, $\frac{6}{5}$, $\frac{6}{4}$, and the Second $\left[\text{i.e. } \frac{6}{4}\atop{2}\right]$, duplication takes place in exactly the same way as in the case of the Triad, and the chord of the Sixth, and the consonant $\frac{6}{4}$; [5] only the essential discord may not be doubled in any chord: in a chord of the Seventh, therefore, not the Seventh itself, in a $\frac{6}{5}$ chord not the Fifth,[6] in a $\frac{6}{4}\atop{3}$ chord not the Third, and, in the chord of the Second $\left[\frac{6}{4}\atop{2}\right]$ not the Octave of the Bass."

"Note. The chords of the Seventh and of the Second $\left[\frac{6}{4}\atop{2}\right]$, therefore, admit the same duplication as is allowed in the Triad of their root (*Grundton*): the $\frac{6}{5}$ chord the same as the chord of the Sixth; the $\frac{6}{4}\atop{3}$ that which the consonant $\frac{6}{4}$ chord allows.

---

[4] No less than fifty-six examples are given to illustrate $\frac{6}{4}\atop{3}$ on the Supertonic with 4, and not 3, prepared! They are all included in Fig. xxxv of the second *Abtheilung* and are numbered with the letters of the alphabet; when these are exhausted, the rest are (very characteristically) left unnumbered.

[5] In giving rules for the duplication of the intervals of a Triad, Kirnberger proceeds as though he had the composer rather than the accompanist in view, inasmuch as he enumerates the intervals which may be doubled (or trebled) in six-, seven-, and eight-part harmony respectively, whereas Heinichen simply directs that the space between the extreme parts should (at discretion) be filled, so far as the available fingers permit, only taking care to *avoid any considerable gap between the thumbs*, whereby consecutives might become apparent (cf. Ch. iii, 'The general character, &c.', § 3 II, §§ 32–8 of the extract from Heinichen).

With regard to the chords of the Sixth and $\frac{6}{4}$, Kirnberger tells us that the same notes may be doubled as in the Triad.

[6] Kirnberger had previously (l. c. § 4) made a remarkable statement with regard to the chord of the diminished Seventh, in which (as he explains elsewhere) the 7 is an 'accidental' discord, retarding the 6 of $\frac{6}{5}$ on a leading note. "The chord of the diminished Seventh", he writes, "is really a $\frac{6}{5}$ chord, *its Fifth can therefore be doubled*, and the one resolve, while the other rises or falls to the Octave of the Bass [i.e. of the chord of resolution]." (The italics are not Kirnberger's.)

He adds a statement which is worth recording as an example of the obsession under which theorists of the older school (e.g. Heinichen, cf. § 5, III a) laboured in connexion with intervals if *accidentally sharpened*.

"In four-part harmony," he continues, "e.g. in C minor, in which the minor Sixth ♭a is an essential note, while a becomes an accidental note by virtue of the ♮, many composers have preferred, in the case of the unessential (*uneigentlich*) chord of the Seventh on f sharp, to omit the Third a which belongs to it, and, in its place, have doubled the Fifth, and let the one resolve a degree downwards when the Bass pro-

"In the case of accidental discords, the duplication is taken from the consonant chord in which the accidental discords have their resolution, as:

$$\left| \begin{array}{c} 5\; - \\ 4\; 3 \end{array} \right| \begin{array}{c} 9\; 8 \end{array} \left| \begin{array}{c} 6\; 5 \\ 3\; - \end{array} \right|$$

$$\left| \begin{array}{c} 6\; 5 \\ 4\; 3 \end{array} \right| \begin{array}{c} 9\; 8 \\ 4\; 3 \end{array} \left| \begin{array}{c} 7\; 8 \\ 4\; 3 \\ 2\; 1 \end{array} \right| \begin{array}{c} 9 \\ 7 \\ 4\quad 3 \end{array}{>}8 \; \left| \begin{array}{c} 9 \\ 7 \\ 6\quad 5 \\ 4\quad 3 \end{array}{>}8 \right|$$ [discords resolving on a Triad, over the same Bass]

thus, one takes the notes of the Triad of the root (*Grundton*), as indicated by the figures following the accidental figures [i.e. the figures denoting the 'accidental' discords], as in Fig. XLIX a [= Ex. 2 a].[7] The duplication in *b* [= Ex. 2 b] [7] lacks movement in the case of a stationary Bass (*ist beim liegenden Bass ohne Bewegung*). If the Bass were struck [i.e. at the beginning of the 2nd bar] while the notes [i.e. the upper parts] remain stationary, it would be somewhat more tolerable, although the complete repose of a piece is not so well maintained in *b* as in *a*.

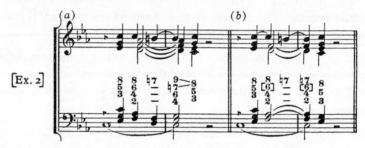

[Ex. 2]

"In the case of the following accidental discords, the figures [8] which arise when resolution on a chord of the Sixth takes place, are doubled, as:

$$7\; 6 \left| \begin{array}{c} 6\; - \\ 4\; 3 \end{array} \right| \begin{array}{c} 9\; 8 \\ 6\; - \end{array} \left| \begin{array}{c} 9\; 8 \\ 7\; 6 \end{array} \right| \begin{array}{c} 9\quad 8 \\ 7{>}6 \\ 5 \end{array}$$ [discords resolving on a Sixth over the same Bass]

likewise in the case of the consonant $^6_4$ chord:

$$\left| \begin{array}{c} 6\; - \\ 5\; 4 \end{array} \right| \begin{array}{c} 7\; 6 \\ 4\; - \end{array} \left| \begin{array}{c} 7\; 6 \\ 3\; 4 \end{array} \right| \begin{array}{c} 9\; 8 \\ 6\; - \\ 4\; - \end{array} \left| \begin{array}{c} 7\quad 6 \\ 5{>}4 \\ 3 \end{array} \right|$$ &c.   [discords resolving on a consonant $^6_4$ chord]

An exception occurs [9] . . . in the case of the Dominant chord [i.e. $^6_4_3$ or $^6_3$ on

ceeds from *f* sharp to *g*, while allowing the second Fifth either to rise a Fifth or fall a Fourth to the Octave of the Bass note *g*."

Ph. Em. Bach makes a similar statement without further comment (*Versuch &c.,* Part II, Ch. 13, II, § 5).

[7] Kirnberger gives three examples *a* (with the same harmony differently disposed) and two examples *b*. Only one of each is given here.

[8] It will, of course, be understood that the dashes (indicating the retention of an interval of the previous chord) count as figures.

[9] The words here omitted correspond to those in italics in the following: "Eine Ausnahme ist *beim Sexten-Accord der aus dem Dreiklange mit der Septime von der Unterquinte entspringt, und* beim Oberdominanten-Accord. . . ."

the Supertonic], in which neither the Sixth, as leading note, nor the Third,[10] as the essential Seventh of the root (*Grundton*), ought to be doubled; nevertheless both are found doubled in the works of the greatest masters.

"Where the Sixth is doubled, the one rises a semitone and becomes the Octave of the following Bass note: $\begin{smallmatrix}6\,b\,8\,\bar{c}\\d\quad c\end{smallmatrix}$, and the other falls a Third and becomes the Fifth of the Bass: $\begin{smallmatrix}6\,b\,5\,g\\d\quad c\end{smallmatrix}$.

"Without these principles no human being can know what to double when the harmony is in more than four parts."

Heinichen's views on the anticipation of the resolution of suspended discords are given at length in the following chapter (§ 3, III A 3).

(*e*) Kirnberger energetically defends the doubling of the major Third of a Triad in four-part harmony except, of course, in the case of the Dominant.

With reference to the following example (*Dritte Abtheilung* [Third division], Fig. I b):

[Ex. 3]

he writes (o. c., § 154): "Theorists (*Tonlehrer*) unanimously forbid the duplication of the major Third; but this rule only applies in the case of the chord of the Dominant, in which this Third is the leading note to the following semitone above; it must also not be doubled, therefore, when it occurs in virtue of an accidental ✕, foreign to the key in which one is, because it then becomes the leading note of the note which follows. In the Triad of the principal note or *Tonique*, and the Triad of the Subdominant, it can be doubled without hesitation, unless special circumstances indicate the contrary."

It may be mentioned in this connexion that Kirnberger, without assigning any reason, forbids the doubling of an *accidentally flattened minor Third*.

He writes (immediately before the passage quoted above): "the duplication of a minor Third is to be avoided only when the latter is accidental, in virtue of a ♭."

(*f*) As will be seen from an example from the *Grundsätze*, given in the following chapter, "On the general character", &c. (§ 9 II, Ex. 10), Kirnberger had no objection to the crossing of parts in a four-part accompaniment, except as a means of excusing what, on a keyed instrument, would have the effect on the ear of a faulty progression (cf. ibid., Ex. 9). With this reservation, however, he countenances the device as a means of escaping

[10] With regard to the doubling of the 3 in $\frac{6}{3}$ on the Supertonic, which Kirnberger regards as an incomplete form of $\frac{6}{4}\vphantom{\frac{}{3}}$, he writes as follows (o. c. § 147, note): "In many writers one finds, both in composition and in playing from a Thorough-Bass, instead of the chord of the Sixth being taken either as $\frac{6}{4}\vphantom{\frac{}{3}}$ or $\frac{8}{6}\vphantom{\frac{}{3}}$, a duplication of the minor Third, which certain strict theorists condemn, because the Seventh of the root is thereby doubled. In our days it is doubled without hesitation, but never the major Sixth because it is the *Ton sensible* which admits of no duplication."

from an occasional difficulty, as in (c) and (d) of the following series of examples (*Dritte Abtheilung* [Third division], Fig. XXVIII (b) (c) (d)):

[Ex. 4]

Of these he writes (p. 77): "In the example at (b) one must be very careful not to take the Sixth on the Bass note preceding the $\frac{7}{4\,3}$ chord as $\frac{8}{6\,3}$, as forbidden Octaves between the middle part [Alto] and the Bass would then be unavoidable. If, however, one has by chance got into the difficult position of having to take this chord of the Sixth as $\frac{8}{6\,3}$, the only remaining remedy is to allow the middle part to cross the upper part and move to the Fifth of the Bass, as in the example at (c).[11]

"If crossing becomes necessary, the downward progression of the middle part *a* to *d* below the prepared Seventh is better: the position of the upper part is thus maintained, as at (d)."

(*g*) Kirnberger gives two examples (major and minor) of transferred resolution (ibid., Fig. XLVIII):

[Ex. 5]

The suspended Dominant Ninth *a* (♭ *a*) in the Bass rises to *g* in the Alto, while the Dominant Seventh *f* in the Alto falls to *e* (♭ *e*) in the Bass.

In taking leave of the *Grundsätze* one cannot help regretting that more care was not bestowed on revision, as it might so easily have been made one of the most useful of existing text-books.

§ 13. *Daniel Gottlob Türk* (1756–1813).

(*a*) The last of the eighteenth-century treatises calling for a detailed notice is the *Kurze Anweisung zum Generalbassspielen* ('Short Guide to Thorough-bass'), by Daniel Gottlob Türk, a small 8vo, published in 1791 at the author's expense, and sold by Schwickert at Leipsic and Hemmerde and Schwetschke at Halle, in which latter town Türk was Director of Music to the University.

A second edition appeared in 1800 (Halle and Leipsic), and three subsequent ones (Halle) in 1816, 1824, and 1841, respectively; besides these a "new and improved edition" (*Neue verbesserte Auflage*) was issued at Vienna

---

[11] It will be noticed that the necessity for the crossing of parts could be avoided by taking the 7 6 on *a* with the Third *c* doubled in the unison:

in 1822 by S. A. Steiner & Co. In this latter the material of the first two chapters has been partially rearranged, and some slight additions have been made in the later chapters, with the result that the numbering of the paragraphs (which runs continuously from the beginning of the work to the end) is entirely changed. In the following pages, therefore, all references will be to the original edition.

(b) Türk explains in a short preface (*Vorerinnerung*) that the work is designed primarily to meet the needs of beginners of small means, to whom a comparatively inexpensive book would be a boon, and that he has therefore compiled "a sort of summary" (*eine Art Auszug*) of a larger and more complete work, already outlined (*entworfen*), and perhaps destined to appear later and to form a Second Part of his larger *Clavier* School (1789). That this idea was never carried out is greatly to be regretted. Like G. M. Telemann, Türk writes only for those who are prepared to take their studies seriously. After telling us of pupils who had attained a considerable knowledge of harmony, and some facility in playing from a Thoroughbass, in six months or a year, he continues: "If any one, with two or, at most, three lessons a week, wants to become a good accompanist in a shorter time, it is not for him that this Guide is written."

He goes on to make a very significant remark, from which it is evident that interest in the art of accompaniment from a Thoroughbass was already very much on the wane. "I shall be uncommonly glad", he writes, "if . . . I have contributed something towards the spread of sound knowledge in regard to Thoroughbass playing. For, if it ever was necessary earnestly to provide for a correct, systematic, and, at the same time, comprehensible exposition of musical principles, that is undoubtedly the case now, when a pretty general neglect of the study of the art causes many rules to be unknown, and therefore, for the most part, not put into practice." [1]

The preface is followed by a short introduction, consisting of "Sundry hints to the teacher", in which very sound advice is given.

(c) The work itself falls naturally, though no such division is actually made, into three parts. (1) The first two chapters contain, besides the necessary definitions and explanations of technical terms, the general rules, both theoretical and practical, for dealing with a Thoroughbass, ending with a summary of the various chords and a "Table of the commonest figurings". [2]

---

[1] How true, and, indeed, almost prophetic, these words were, is shown by the fact, mentioned in the preface to the present work, that to Robert Franz, who was born at Halle only two years after Türk's death (and who was for a time Organist of the Church of St. Ulrich in the same town, at which Türk had formerly been Cantor), the figured Basses in the early volumes of Bach's works issued by the *Bach-Gesellschaft* were almost as much of a revelation as was the Rosetta stone to Egyptologists. And yet, in the early forties of last century, when Franz was conducting performances of Bach's and Handel's works from editions in which the figures were entirely omitted, and was himself *entirely ignorant of the omission*, many men must still have been alive in Halle who remembered Türk, and there may well have been some who had even enjoyed his instruction.

[2] Chapter I, First section (*Abschnitt*): "Explanation of the words Thoroughbass, Harmony, Tone, Interval, Dissonance, and Chord". Second section: "Meaning of the figures and other signs". Third section: "Explanation of the commonest technical terms in reference to Thoroughbass".

Chapter II, First section: "General rules of Thoroughbass". Second section: "General rules, &c., for the Thoroughbass player in particular". Third section: "Survey and names (*Bezeichnung*) of the chords".

(2) Chapters III–IX deal in detail with the chords. Besides the individual examples, each chord, or group of chords, as the case may be, is illustrated by an admirable 'general example' in which the harmonies in question are presented in an appropriate context. Ch. IX concludes with examples illustrating the figuring of changing (i.e. accented passing) notes and pedal points, respectively.

(3) Chapters X–XII deal with details of the accompaniment in which the principal factor is good taste, and also with certain special cases. The headings of these chapters are as follows:

Ch. X. First section (*Abschnitt*): "On accompaniment generally, in so far as account has to be taken of certain incidental circumstances (*Nebenumstände*)."

Second section: "On the accompaniment of Recitative."

Ch. XI. "On playing Chorales."

Ch. XII. "On the accompaniment of unfigured Basses."

(d) Türk's classification of the discords is practically the same as that adopted by Schröter, and is based on the distinction drawn by Kirnberger between essential (*wesentlich*) and accidental (*zufällig*) or substitute (*stellvertretend*) dissonances. To the former class belong (according to Kirnberger) only the Seventh and its three inversions, while all other dissonances are to be regarded merely as temporarily substituted for a consonant interval (as 9 for 8, 4 for 3, &c.) and, therefore, as accidental rather than essential components of the harmony.

It appears, however, that Türk's adoption of this system (like Schröter's) was due to practical considerations rather than conviction. In a long note (o. c., Ch. II, Third section, § 80, pp. 98–101) he gives a sketch of Marpurg's system (derived from Rameau), in accordance with which, as he tells us, "all, or, at all events, most chords with substitute intervals (accidental dissonances) can be derived from three fundamental chords (*Grundaccorde*) of the second class,[3] without assuming suspension".

"The thoroughness of this system," he writes in conclusion, "of which I have given an outline (*Entwurf*), is unmistakable and it deserves, indeed, to be warmly recommended. I should have taken it as a basis throughout the present text-book, were I not writing primarily for beginners (*angehende Generalbassspieler*). Furthermore, too, the different progression, &c., of certain suspensions which are undoubtedly in use now, and have been, in part, accepted [4] by Bach, is perhaps not, in every case, to be determined by this system."

This last sentence is more significant than Türk perhaps quite realized. It is to be regretted that he did not specify the progressions which he found inconsistent with the Rameau-Marpurg theory of chord generation.

Having, then, provisionally adopted Kirnberger's theory of accidental dissonances (or substitute intervals), and having disposed of the 'harmonic Triad', the diminished and augmented Triads, and the chord of the Seventh,

---

[3] By 'chords of the second class' we are told to understand chords of 'supposition', namely, the chord of the Ninth, formed, according to Marpurg, by the addition of a Third *below* a chord of the Seventh, that of the Eleventh, formed by the similar addition of a Fifth (with the intervening Third), and that of the Thirteenth formed by the addition (or 'supposition') of a Seventh (also with the intervening Thirds).

[4] *aufgenommen*: i.e. included by Ph. Em. Bach among the examples in the Second Part of his *Versuch*.

with their respective inversions (Chs. III–V), Türk arranges the remaining chords as follows: those resulting from the retardation of

(1) *one* interval of (*a*) a Triad and its inversions, (*b*) the chord of the Seventh and its inversions (Ch. VI),

(2) *two* intervals of the above (Ch. VII),

(3) *three* (or four) intervals of the above (Ch. VIII),

(4) the Bass of the above (Ch. IX).

These latter chords Türk, in accordance with the common practice of the time, calls *anticipations*,[5] inasmuch as the upper parts do not wait for the belated Bass.

(*e*) The 'Table of the commonest figurings' which Türk gives at the end of his second chapter (cf. note 1) deserves mention on account of the clearness of its arrangement. It makes no pretence at completeness, for (like G. M. Telemann) Türk excludes all triple figures,[6] but it is so arranged as to show the composition of each chord in three- and five-part harmony, respectively.

The following short quotation will suffice to show the arrangement:

	With the signatures:	is taken:	in three parts:	in five parts:
(*a*)	✕ or sharpening ♮	$\frac{8}{5}$ or $\frac{5}{5}$	5 or 8	$\frac{8}{5}_5$ or $\frac{8}{8}_5$
	♭ or flattening ♮	$\frac{8}{5}$ or $\frac{5}{5}$, likewise $\frac{5}{3}$	5 or 8	$\frac{8}{5}_5, \frac{8}{3}$, or $\frac{8}{8}_5$
(*b*)	2	$\frac{6}{4}$	4, rarely 6	$\frac{6}{4}_2$ or $\frac{6}{6}_4$
	&c.	&c.	&c.	&c.

It will be seen from the above that Türk agrees with Heinichen and Kirnberger in not allowing the major Third of a Triad to be doubled when it is accidental.[7]

(*f*) In connexion with the rule forbidding consecutive Octaves and Fifths,[8] a long note is devoted to the consideration of the eternal problem, *why* they— especially the Fifths—are objectionable. Türk appears to accept the theory of Huygens, that consecutive Fifths produce a feeling of uncertainty by suggesting two different keys. He amplifies it, however, in a remarkable way. He holds that consecutive Fifths vary in unpleasantness in proportion to the nearness or remoteness of the relationship of the keys suggested. Thus, $_c^g{}_d^a$ are worse than $_c^g{}_g^d$. He contends, moreover, that the suggested change to a related key on the *sharp side* is less obtrusive than that to one, related in an equal degree, on the *flat side*. Thus $_c^g{}_{b\flat}^f$ are "almost more repulsive" (*fast noch widriger*) than $_c^g{}_d^a$.

(*g*) Türk gives no rules for the reinforcement of the harmony by the doubling, in the left hand, of intervals already present in the right. But, from the little that he says, it is clear that he permits much less liberty than Heinichen, who, as will be seen, disregards consecutives arising between middle parts, or between a middle and an extreme part, provided that the hands are kept close enough together, and also permits discords to be doubled.[9]

---

[5] Cf. § 10, note 1, xiv *ad fin.*   [6] Cf. § 11 *f ad fin.*

[7] Cf. § 5 III (*a*) and § 12 *e*.   [8] o.c., Ch. II, First section, § 43.

[9] Cf. Ch. iii, 'The general character, &c.', § 3 II, §§ 32–8 of the extract from Heinichen.

After advising the student to begin by practising a four-part accompaniment, as being not only more complete, but also easier, than one in fewer parts, Türk continues: [10] "Disproportionately easier is an accompaniment in five or more parts; it presupposes, it is true, somewhat more technical facility, but, for the rest, no such great exactness is observed as regards the middle parts, provided that the progression of the extreme parts is perfectly correct. It is, however, a matter of course that, even with an accompaniment in five or more parts, no bad mistakes, e.g. consecutive Fifths, &c., must be made, and that only the consonances may be doubled."

§ 14. *Conclusion.*

(*a*) In accordance with the intention expressed at the beginning of the present chapter, no description has been given of those purely theoretical works in which little or no account is taken of the art of accompaniment, as such. Other works, too, have been passed over as not being of such importance, either historical or intrinsic, as to make a detailed account of them desirable. Among these, however, there are two which may be regarded as curiosities and, on that account, call for a passing mention.

(*b*) In 1728, the year in which Heinichen's great work appeared, there was published anonymously at Leipsic a tiny 8vo volume entitled *Kurze Anführung zum General-Bass &c.* ('Short Guide to Thorough-Bass'), and was several times reprinted, the edition in the possession of the present writer being dated 1749. It must be admitted that, considering its diminutive compass, it contains no small amount of information, clearly and tersely given. The surprising fact, however, about this little treatise is that it was the work (though hardly, perhaps, the unaided production) of a lady no more than nine years old—a certain Fräulein von Freudenberg. It is mentioned in terms of praise by David Kellner, who writes as follows: [1]

"Before the appearance of Heinichen's work, a young lady some nine years of age, of exceptional intelligence and good education, Freudenberg by name, the daughter of an Hessian colonel, set down on paper, on the occasion of her sojourn here, the so-called most necessary rules of Thorough-Bass which she had learnt in Stockholm . . . and this work of hers has become so popular that many people have made a useful copy of it."

It seems not unlikely that it was by Kellner himself that she was taught at Stockholm, and that she embodied rules, &c., which he had dictated to her in the little book above mentioned.

(*c*) Far more curious is another little treatise (likewise a small 8vo, but containing nearly twice as many pages, and much more closely printed) which appeared in 1739, and which professed to teach the rudiments of Thorough-Bass *with the aid of a machine* invented by the author, Lorenz Mizler (or, to give him his full name, Mizler von Kolof), 1711–78, the founder of an Association for Musical Science of which Bach himself became a member, and editor of the "Neu-eröffnete musikalische Bibliothek" (*Newly opened Musical Library*). The title is as follows: "Anfangs-Gründe / Des / GENERAL / BASSES / Nach / Mathematischer Lehr-Art / abgehandelt, / und / vermittelst einer hierzu erfundenen / *Maschine* / auf das deutlichste vorgetragen / von /

---

[10] o.c., Ch. II, Second section, § 61, note 2, p. 75.
[1] *Treulicher Unterricht &c.*, Ch. III.

LORENZ MIZLERN, / A in Academ. Lips. M. / Leipzig, zu finden bey dem Verfasser, / in der Heustrasse in der Adler-Apotheke."

('Rudiments of Thorough-Bass, treated in accordance with a mathematical method of instruction and set forth with the greatest clearness, by means of a machine invented for the purpose, by Lorenz Mizler, &c., Leipsic, obtainable at the author's lodging at the Eagle Pharmacy in the Heustrasse.')

The price of the machine and book together was 2 *Thaler* 12 *Groschen*, or something over seven shillings.

Mizler seems to have been greatly afraid of literary piracy, for he tells us in the preface that, on its first occurrence, he would at once issue a new edition, augmented by fresh material kept in reserve for the purpose, but that purchasers of the original work would be able to obtain the additions separately, so as not to be put to unnecessary expense. He also stated that his monogram L. C. M. would be attached to the machine, and that his signature would be found on the reverse of the title-page of the book, without which he would acknowledge neither as his work. He seems to have autographed each copy as sold, for the one in the possession of the present writer bears the date 4 May 1741, two years after publication.

The machine, which, according to Schröter,[2] was made of brass, must have been an elaborate affair.[3] "The colours with which the machine is illuminated", Mizler tells us in his preface, "have been arranged by me in accordance with the nature of the tones. For it is well known that optical truths are parallel with musical ones, as the immortal Neuton [*sic*] said long ago. . . ."

As far as the book itself is concerned, it seems to have met with a certain amount of appreciation, for Schröter tells us that "it is certain that this little work was very acceptable to many music-lovers on account of the mathematical method of instruction employed".

[2] *Deutliche Anweisung &c.*, *Vorbericht*, viii.

[3] The following is a specimen of the directions given for its use: "You want to find the harmonies belonging to C major. Proceed as follows. Apply the stave (*Stab*) marked C major to the machine, below, on the left-hand side, so that *Scala ascendens* . . . comes to be below the harmonies (*harmonische Sätze*) headed *Scalae ascendentes*. . . . Move up in a straight line from the first tone C into the uppermost division (*Fach*), and 3, 5, 8 will there be seen one above another. Should you not know what tones these three figures, relating to C, indicate, then turn, in the Circle of Solution (*Auflösungs-Cirkel*), the tone C, marked on the small circle which revolves within the large one, under the figures 8 or 1, headed *Unisonus*, *Octava*. . . . Then look for 3, 5, and 8 in the divisions in which the figures are, and these figures will point to E, g, c on the small circle. Play them on the *Clavier* in the order indicated, and you have the harmony to the first tone of the major scale of C."

CHAPTER III

THE GENERAL CHARACTER OF A FIGURED BASS ACCOMPANIMENT

III

THE GENERAL CHARACTER OF A FIGURED BASS
ACCOMPANIMENT

§ 1. *Introductory.*

The scope of the present chapter cannot be better defined than in the words of Ph. Em. Bach (*Versuch &c.*, Part I, 1762, Introduction, §§ 18, 19):

"The taste of the present day has introduced a quite different use of harmony from that of former days. Our melodies, graces (*Manieren*), and style of performance (*Vortrag*) often demand, therefore, a different harmony from the ordinary. This harmony is now weak, and now strong; consequently the duties of the accompanist nowadays are of a far wider range than formerly, and the familiar rules of Thorough-Bass no longer suffice, and are often liable to modification (*und leiden oft eine Abänderung*).

"An accompanist must therefore, as it were, fit each piece that he accompanies with its *appropriate harmony, properly rendered* ('mit dem rechten Vortrag'), and, moreover, *of the right strength and compass. . . .*"

In Ch. I we followed the development of the art of founding an *ex tempore* accompaniment on a Thorough-Bass from the beginning to the close of the seventeenth century. The purpose of the present chapter is to set forth in detail the general character ('general' as apart from certain details which are best considered separately) of the accompaniment as it is presented to us in the records of the eighteenth century, in the course of which the art in question reached its zenith.

Our chief guides will be Johann David Heinichen and Carl Philipp Emanuel (better known to us as Philip Emanuel) Bach.

§ 2. *The Instruments used.*

(*a*) The most complete list of the instruments used in the middle of the eighteenth century, for the performance of the accompaniment, is that given by Ph. Em. Bach (*Versuch &c.*, Part II, 1762, Introd. §§ 1-9), and, as every word is instructive, it shall be given in full:

(1) "The ORGAN, the HARPSICHORD (*Flügel*[1]), the PIANOFORTE, and the CLAVICHORD [2] are the keyed instruments (*Clavierinstrumente*) most commonly used for the accompaniment."

---

[1] *Flügel* = 'wing'; the term was applied later to the similarly shaped Grand Pianoforte. Of the Harpsichord the term *Kielflügel* (*Kiel* = 'quill') was sometimes used: no doubt in order to distinguish it from the Grand Pianoforte.

It will be observed that the instruments enumerated by Bach (except in the case of a Harpsichord with *only one manual, and without stops*) are such as are capable of a graduated strength of tone, on which he lays great stress.

On a Harpsichord with a single manual, or on a Spinet, such gradation could only be obtained, as he explains later on (ibid., Ch. 29, § 5), by employing fuller harmony or the reverse (in which latter case intervals indicated in the figuring were liable to be omitted), or else by the still less satisfactory method of striking the keys quite shortly in a *piano* passage, in which case we are told that "the rendering (*Vortrag*) suffers in a surprising degree, and very few indeed, even of the *staccato* ('abgestossen') notes, bear this very short pressure".

[2] It is somewhat surprising that Ph. Em. Bach should have included the Clavichord

(2) "It is a pity that HOLFELD's beautiful invention, the BOGENCLAVIER,[3] has not yet come into common use; one cannot, therefore, as yet define its special advantages for the purpose in question (*hierin*). It is certainly to be believed that it will also answer well for accompanying."

(3) "For Church-music the ORGAN is indispensable on account of the Fugues, loud Choruses, and, in general, on account of the syncopations (*Bindungen*).[4] It enhances the grandeur and maintains order."

(4) "But, in Church, whenever Recitatives and Airs are included, especially those in which the middle parts [i.e. the *ripieno* instrumental parts], by dint of a simple accompaniment, leave the voice all possible freedom to make variations, there must be an HARPSICHORD.

"Unfortunately we hear, more than too often, how bare the performance sounds, in such a case, without the accompaniment of the Harpsichord."

(5) "The latter instrument is indispensable in the Theatre, too, and in a room, on account of the said Airs and Recitatives."

(6) "The PIANOFORTE and the CLAVICHORD give the best support to a performance in which the greatest refinements of taste occur. Only certain singers like to be accompanied on the CLAVICHORD or HARPSICHORD rather than on the instrument first named."

(7) "No piece, therefore, can be performed satisfactorily without the accompaniment of a keyed instrument (*Clavierinstrument*).[5] Even in the case

among the instruments suitable for the purposes of accompaniment. In the Introduction (§ 5) to Part I of the *Versuch* (2nd ed., 1759) he speaks of "Clavier-pieces in which there is an accompaniment of other instruments [i.e. such pieces as e.g. J. S. Bach's Sonatas for Clavier and Violin or those for Clavier and *Viol da Gamba*], and which, therefore, *on account of the weakness of the Clavichord*, must be heard on the Harpsichord". (The italics are not Bach's.)

It is true that, in a concerted work for the Clavier and another instrument, the weak tone of the Clavichord would be an even greater drawback than in the case of an instrumental or vocal Solo with a figured Bass, more especially if the Clavier (in the latter case) were supported by a Gamba or Violoncello (see below, 9); but, even so, a Clavichord of exceptional power would be required. Quantz tells us that, as an instrument of accompaniment, the Clavichord possesses the same advantages as the Pianoforte (i.e. gradation of tone) "in playing, but not as regards the effect, because the *fortissimo* is lacking" (cf. § 11 h).

[3] Türk makes the following mention of this instrument, the strings of which appear to have been set in vibration by a contrivance akin to the bow of a Violin: "Der Bogenflügel, ein durch Gleichmann, Ficker &c. in neuern Zeiten wieder bekannt, und (vermittelst wirklicher Pferdehaare) dem Bogenstriche noch ähnlicher gemachtes Geigenwerk, welches Hohlfeld merklich verbesserte" (*Klavierschule*, 1789, Introd., § 2). Ph. Em. Bach mentions Holfeld's (or, as he then spells it, Holefeld's) name in a later chapter (ibid., Ch. 29, § 5) in connexion with a contrivance by means of which all the registers of the Harpsichord could be brought into action, or the reverse, by a light pressure of the foot, without interrupting the playing by the manipulation of draw-stops. This, he explains, was a special advantage in the case of an Harpsichord with only one manual, as the difficulty of playing *piano* was thereby removed.

[4] For the exact definition of *Bindung*, see Ch. i, § 18, note 2.

[5] It is to be hoped that the truth of this may be realized more than has been the case in the past. To take a familiar example, who has not heard an otherwise excellent performance of J. S. Bach's Concerto in D minor for two Violins, with string band and figured Bass, discounted by the omission of the Harpsichord (or Pianoforte) accompaniment?

It is true that the strings, in the main, supply the harmony, but, without the harmonic background of the figured accompaniment, the effect may be likened to that of a chalk drawing on a dead-white surface, as compared with the same on a toned paper.

of music on the largest scale (*bey den stärksten Musiken*), in Operas, even in the open air, when one would feel confident of not hearing the Harpsichord in the very least, one misses it if it is left out. If one listens from a height one can distinctly hear every note. I am speaking from experience, and anybody can make the experiment."

(8) "Some individuals have themselves accompanied, in a Solo, on the Viola, or even on the Violin, without a keyed instrument (*Clavier*). If this is done as a matter of necessity, for lack of good Clavier-players, they must be excused; but, apart from that, many faults (*Ungleichheiten*) occur in a performance of this sort. The Solo becomes a Duet, if the Bass is well written; if it is bad, how jejune (*nüchtern*) it sounds without harmony! A certain master in Italy [6] had, therefore, no need to invent this kind of accompaniment. What mistakes may not result if the parts cross! or is the melody, perhaps, to be mutilated in order to avoid this? Both parts keep closer together than the composer intended. And the chords (*vollstimmige Griffe*) which sometimes occur in the principal part,[7] how thin (*jung*) they sound when not supported by a deep Bass! All the beauties which are brought out by the harmony are lost; a great loss in expressive (*affectuös*) pieces."

(9) "The most complete accompaniment to a Solo, to which nobody can take any exception, is a keyed instrument (*Clavierinstrument*) in conjunction with the Violoncello."

(*b*) Ph. Em. Bach's mention of the Organ in connexion with the performance of sacred music need not be taken as meant to exclude its use for the accompaniment of chamber music of a suitable character.

For instance (to return for a moment to the end of the seventeenth century), in Corelli's *Opera prima* and *terza*, which consist of *Suonate da Chiesa* for two Violins and Bass, the Bass parts are headed: *Basso per l' Organo*, whereas, in the same composer's *Opera seconda* and *quarta*, consisting of *Suonate da camera* (or Suites), they are headed: *Violone ò Cembalo*.

In the latter title, the use of the word *ò* ('or'), rather than *e* ('and'), demands some consideration.

It is very common in the Italian Basses of the eighteenth century, and, in the titles of English works, the words "with a Thorough-Bass for the Harpsichord or Bass Viol" (or "Violoncello", as the case may be) are of frequent occurrence.

This would seem, on the face of it, to suggest the employment of a string Bass as an *alternative*, rather than as an adjunct, to the keyed instrument.

That it sometimes *was* so employed there can be no manner of doubt. There is, indeed, a record of a Violin Solo performed on an important public occasion, the *Festa della Croce* at Lucca, by no less a person than Francesco Veracini, and accompanied only by Lanzetti on the Violoncello.[8]

But the circumstances were quite exceptional: Veracini had presented himself quite unexpectedly, and was, moreover, in an exceedingly (and quite unjustifiably) bad temper at not being allowed to assume the position of First Violin, already occupied by Padre Laurenti. It was, therefore, in all probability, partly out of *bravado*, and partly because he preferred Lanzetti's

---

[6] It is not clear to whom Bach is here alluding.
[7] i.e. on the Violin.
[8] Cf. Burney, *General History of Music*, vol. iii, p. 568.

accompaniment to that of an Organist or Harpsichordist with whose powers he was unacquainted, that Veracini acted as he did.

Such cases are to be judged in the light of what Ph. Em. Bach says (in the eighth of the paragraphs quoted above) to the effect that a defective accompaniment is excusable when employed "as a matter of necessity, for lack of good Clavier-players", and when the title of a work seems to indicate that the accompaniment of a string Bass is intended as an alternative to that of a keyed instrument, we may fairly regard it as a concession to convenience, on the part of the composer, rather than as an indication of his wishes.

It is evident, moreover, that no great stress was laid on the choice of the word *e* or *ò* (as the case might be) in Italian works. For instance, in Antonio Vivaldi's *Opera prima*, and Giuseppe Valentini's *Opera quarta* (both Sonatas for two Violins and Thorough-Bass), the *title-page* bears the description 'Organo *ò* Violoncello', while the *parts themselves* are inscribed 'Organo *e* Violoncello'.

That the co-operation of *both Organ and Violoncello* was intended in these works is sufficiently proved by the fact that in them, as in so many others, the Bass part is *in duplicate*.

This was a matter of convenience, to save the player responsible for the string Bass (Violone, Gamba, or Violoncello, as the case might be) from the necessity of craning his neck and reading his part, as best he could, from the desk of the Organ or Harpsichord, as we see portrayed in a small engraving at the end of (the first edition of) Johann Joachim Quantz's famous Essay on the treatment of the German Flute (*Versuch einer Anweisung die Flöte traversière zu spielen*, Berlin, 1752).

In the duplicate part used by the string Bass the figuring was, of course, superfluous: its inclusion was simply a matter of economy, to avoid the necessity of printing or engraving a separate (unfigured) part.

(*c*) In some instances the Violoncello, instead of merely reinforcing the Clavier Bass, is given a part of its own, not really independent of the former, but a more or less ornate variant of it, long notes being broken up into short ones, others taken in the higher Octave, &c.

This treatment recalls the 'instruments of ornamentation' of the early seventeenth century (cf. Ch. i, § 10 *d*); there is, however, this important difference, that in the present case, the 'ornamentation' was prescribed by the composer instead of being left to the taste and fancy of the performers.

Notable instances of this free treatment of the Violoncello part are to be found, in the late seventeenth century, in the *Canzonas* of Purcell's *Sonnatas of three parts*, 1683, and of the same composer's posthumous *Sonatas in four parts*, 1697.[9]

In the eighteenth century examples are to be found e.g. in the Sonatas for two Violins and Bass of Masciti (or Mascitti) *il Napolitano*, Opera quarta, and in Jean Marie Leclair's Sonatas for Violin and Bass.

---

[9] The Sonatas are, in both cases, for two Violins with a figured Bass and a separate Violoncello part which, in some movements, is free in the manner above described. That the one set should be described as in three, and the other as in four parts, is purely accidental. Indeed, by a curious chance, the only bit of four-part writing in the two sets is to be found in the Largo of the fifth of the 'Sonnatas of *three* parts', in which, for several bars at a time, the Violoncello has a separate imitative part.

The following examples will illustrate the point:

Purcell, *Sonnatas of three parts*, 1683, Sonata III, Canzona, bars 5–7.

N.B.—The *Basso* (which, considering Purcell's supposed antipathy to the Viol tribe, may have been intended for the Violoncello rather than the *Viol da Gamba*) here has the fugal 'subject', following the 'answer' in the 2nd Violin part.

Purcell, *Sonatas in Four Parts*, 1697, Sonata III, Canzona, bars 22–4.

Leclair, *Premier Livre de Sonates à Violon Seul avec la Basse Continue*, Sonata VII.

* * * * * For the use of × (before a *figure*, not before a note) to denote a sharp see Ch. xxiv, 'Varieties of notation', § 2, note 1.

† † For $\text{6} = {}^{6}_{4}{}_{3}$ (found only in Book I of Leclair's *Sonatas for Violin and Bass*) see Ch. xxiii, 'Varieties figuring', §§ 8, 9.

§ 3. *The form of the accompaniment as regards the number of parts and their distribution between the hands.*

I. We have already seen that, in the earlier part of the seventeenth century, the accompaniment was often divided between the two hands,[1] but that, as the century advanced, the practice was gradually established (judging from the

[10] The cross + denotes a trill.

[1] Cf. Ch. I, § 8, Ex. 3 (penult. bar), Ex. 29 (bars 2, 3); § 13, Exx. 5 and 6; § 15, Ex. 3 a.

examples given in the treatises passed under review) of playing only the Bass with the left hand and adding the harmony with the right (cf. Ch. I, § 24, v). We saw also that, in the latter half of the century, many of the examples were given in three parts only,[2] and that there was a great tendency to drop at the slightest provocation, from four-part into three-part harmony.[3]

Saint-Lambert stands alone among his (approximate) contemporaries in his steady adherence to four-part harmony, except in the cases where, as he explains (cf. Ch. I, § 23 f, note 18), the apparent dropping of a part is really due to the coincidence of two parts in the unison.

Niedt gives it as a definite rule that a note figured 6 is to be accompanied by the Sixth and Third only (cf. Ch. I, § 25, III, 8 a), and, in all his examples, as in those of Ebner (ibid., § 19), Locke (ibid., § 21), and Blow (ibid., § 22), all Sixths (and Sevenths resolving on Sixths), as well as any progressions (such as a 5 6 sequence on a rising Bass) in which a four-part accompaniment presents any difficulties, are invariably *taken in three parts only*,[4] with the brilliant exception of two examples of Blow, in one of which as many as five parts are employed (ibid., § 22, Exx. 20, 21).

II. Let us now hear what that most painstaking and sympathetic instructor, Johann David Heinichen (1683–1729), has to say about the form of the accompaniment as practised in his day.

His references to the practice of earlier days are especially interesting and, with their sequel, deserve to be quoted in full.

Writing in 1728 (the year before his premature death) he concludes his chapter on the treatment of common chords (*General-Bass &c.*, 1728, Part I, Ch. II, pp. 119–37) with a description of a 'filled-in' accompaniment, in which the reduplication of the four real parts is limited only by the capacity of the two hands,[5] and with rules for its application to the common chords in question.[6]

---

[2] Cf. Ch. I, § 19, Exx. 4–7; § 21, 'The examples of Precepts in the Rules for playing on a Continued Basse'; § 22, Ex. 4, Exx. 9–11, Ex. 19.

[3] Cf. Ch. I, § 25, III 8, Exx. 2, 5, 6, 7.

[4] Even in later times, when a *succession of Sixths* occurred on a Bass moving either by step or in Thirds, or when, in a Bass rising by step, several notes in succession were figured 5 6, *if the time was quick*, a three-part accompaniment remained the more usual.

Of the former case, taking as examples the following Basses:

Ph. Em. Bach (after showing how they may best be accompanied in four parts) says: "Such passages are most conveniently (*am bequemsten*) accompanied in three parts when the time is quick" (*Versuch &c.*, Part II, 1762, Ch. 3, 1, § 11). Of the latter case he says (ibid., § 15): "If a note is figured 5 6, one strikes the chord proper (*den eigentlichen Accord*) on the entry of the note and passes from the Fifth to the Sixth; the other parts are held. But if this progression (*Satz*) occurs several times in succession, a three-part accompaniment, with the Third alone, is the easiest, and, in pieces which do not in any case require a strong accompaniment, the best."

[5] It will be remembered that, among all the writers passed in review in the first chapter of the present work, Saint-Lambert was the only one who touched upon this subject.

[6] Subsequent chapters contain similar rules, as applying to the particular chord (or chords) treated of in the chapter in question, the examples being given, first with a four-part, and afterwards with a filled-in accompaniment. To such individuals as are fortunate enough to possess an Harpsichord (or even a Spinet) these latter examples are of infinite value.

The numbering of the sections in the following extract, given in brackets, is, of course, Heinichen's.

He writes:

(§ 28) "In concluding this instruction [i.e. the treatment of common chords in four parts] a further important question suggests itself, namely: Whether all the examples given above could not be treated with fuller harmony (*vollstimmiger*), or: Whether the Thorough-Bass must necessarily always abide by a similar four-part accompaniment?"

(§ 29) "To answer this exhaustively, it is well known that the old world treated the Thorough-Bass, after it was first invented, with very meagre harmony (*sehr schwachstimmig* [7]); and, even in the last years of the past century, a three-part accompaniment (in which now the right, and now the left hand took a single part, and the other hand the two remaining ones) was none too rare, because the older generation (*die Alten*), in accompanying on instruments capable of sounding full chords (*bey dem Accompagnement voll-*

---

[7] This statement does not altogether tally with what we have been led to infer from the works discussed in Ch. I. To take the case of Viadana himself, his suggestion that the Organist should prepare an *intavolatura* for his own use (cf. Ch. I, § 4, Rule 6) is almost tantamount to a proof that, in certain cases, he contemplated a four-part accompaniment. Where there were four vocal parts, the *intavolatura* would, most naturally, be in four parts also. What sort of an accompaniment he desired in the *concerti* for a single voice, and in those for two voices, is, of course, purely a matter for conjecture.

To take another case, that of Cavalieri, everything points to the free use of four-part harmony in the accompaniment:

(1) In one instance he used *three* figures, $\overset{10}{\underset{\times 4}{6}}$ (cf. Ch. I, § 8, Ex. 28).

(2) The widely extended harmony, sometimes indicated by the figuring of compound intervals, as e.g. $^{13}_4$ (cf. ibid., Ex. 3, penult. bar), calls imperatively for a fourth part.

(3) As has already been pointed out (Ch. I, § 26, 11), the practice of figuring compound intervals is a strong indication that, where the vocal (or instrumental) writing was in four parts, the accompaniment was intended to be an exact reproduction of the score—played from figures instead of from an *intavolatura* (cf. Ch. I, § 8, Exx. 6 and 14).

Writing in 1607, both Agazzari and Bianciardi give examples of four-part harmony, cf. Ch. I, § 10 c *ad fin.*, and § 11, Ex. 3). In the latter case the number of parts is less regularly maintained, falling in one bar (in which the upper part moves in Thirds with the Bass) to three, while, on the other hand, some chords are taken in five parts.

A little later in the century Praetorius, writing in 1619, gives, as an example, a Bass from one of his own works with the accompaniment in four parts, the final chord (with the Bass doubled in the Octave) being in five (cf. Ch. I, § 15, Ex. 3 a). The distribution of the harmony is irregular. Sometimes the Bass alone (apparently) falls to the left hand (or the pedals of the Organ), sometimes only two parts are within reach of the right hand (as in the first half of bar 9 and on the fifth crotchet of bar 5), while, in the first half of bar 5, the right hand has only a single part.

The most probable explanation of the discrepancy between Heinichen's statement and the facts, as we have envisaged them, would seem to be this: that Heinichen's information, gathered, we must suppose, mainly from tradition (for he was not born till 1683), related mainly to his own fellow-countrymen. We have learnt from Werckmeister and Niedt (cf. Ch. I, §§ 24 and 25) how seriously the German Organists of the seventeenth century (with brilliant exceptions, no doubt) were retarded in their musicianship by their obstinate adherence to the old German Organ-Tablature. Niedt, writing in 1700, mentions, in the discussion which followed the narrative of 'Tacitus' (cf. ibid., § 25, 11 e), that, sixty years earlier, a German Organist was seldom known to play from a Thorough-Bass, or even from the ordinary musical notation. No wonder, then, that, in Germany, the early accompaniments were, for the most part, of a highly primitive description!

stimmiger Instrumente), contented themselves with the *Trias harmonica simplex* [i.e. the Triad *without* the Octave of the Bass] and the most necessary essential intervals of each harmony (*Satz*). Later on, however, more thought was given to the *Trias harmonica aucta* [i.e. $\frac{8}{5}$] and the reduplication of more of the essential intervals of the harmonies (*der musicalischen Sätze*); hence, the four-part accompaniment came more into fashion; at first, it is true, it was divided equally between the two hands (two parts falling to the right, and two parts to the left hand) in order, thereby, to display the arts of a well-regulated *Quatro* (just as is done by celebrated Masters, in certain cases, even at the present day, especially on Organs and when the whole body of sound is small (*bey schwacher Music*). But, as this method was not always applicable, particularly in view of the introduction (contrary to the doctrine of the older generation) of very quick Basses, this four-part accompaniment was, accordingly, divided unequally between the hands, that is to say, three parts [were assigned] to the right hand, and the Bass part alone to the left, which, however, acquired the liberty (as above mentioned) of conducting the Bass in Octaves throughout, when not prevented by the quickness of the notes and of the measure (*Mensur*)." [8]

[8] Writing in 1702, Werckmeister mentions (*Harmonologia*, § 11) that the four-part accompaniment described above (with the Bass alone in the left hand) was then in general use among nearly all the best musicians, but that, in former days, *most of the chords were played with the left hand*, and a single part with the right. The result, he opines, must often have been a 'growl' (*Gemurr*), and far from pleasing. Later on (ibid., § 156) he writes: "But if, in playing a Thorough-Bass, one takes three parts with the left hand, and tootles (*dudelt*) a single part with the right hand in the old fashion, one cannot produce accurate and unbroken (*beständig*) four-part harmony; false progressions will occur, and, if a part be omitted, the harmony will be broken (*unbeständig*) in the higher registers (*in Syrigiis*), while, if the Bass goes low down, the chords will be too clumsy and very unpleasant. . . ."

In a general way this criticism is obviously justified, but, under special circumstances (as, for instance, in the accompaniment of a Solo, when the principal part has a pause of several bars, during which something more elaborate and ornate than usual is expected of the accompanist, and, above all, *when the Bass itself is of a nature to lend itself to such treatment*) the form of accompaniment in question may prove highly effective, and was undoubtedly occasionally used by good musicians long after the period to which Werckmeister alludes, as is suggested e.g. by the two following examples from Johann Mattheson's *Organisten-Probe*, 1719 (*Mittelclasse, Prob-Stück* 18, *Erläuterung; Oberclasse, Prob-Stück* 11, *Erläuterung* [Middle Grade, Test-piece 18, Explanation; Higher Grade, Test-piece 11, Explanation]):

Note the G clef on the lower line of the stave (French Violin clef).

N.B.—The third quaver in the upper part of the left hand is misprinted ♭*b* in the original.

Heinichen himself, too, gives examples of this form of accompaniment (cf. Ch. iv,

(§ 30) "This latter kind, then, is nowadays the most usual and most funda-mental [9] accompaniment, which all beginners are taught, and which we shall consistently carry out in the first section of this book. Those, however, who are already practiced in the art usually seek, and particularly on Harpsichords and the like ('sonderlich auf denen *Clavecins*'), to strengthen the harmony still further, and to accompany with as many parts in the left hand as in the right,[10] which results, according as the two hands find opportunity of employ-ment ('nach Gelegenheit der *Application* beyder Hände'), in an accompani-ment of from 6 or 7, to 8 parts. It is of such persons that we are now thinking, and the question therefore arises as to what these arts consist of."

(§ 31) "To those who have learned to play a Thorough-Bass well, in the manner initiated above [i.e. in four parts, as shown in the earlier part of the chapter], a full accompaniment of this sort is bound to come just as easy as it usually appears difficult to the tyro, provided they observe a simple general rule (*Vortheil*) which we will herewith clearly explain."

(§ 32) "One must be careful, namely, to invent only the extreme [upper] part of the right hand so skilfully that it moves with the Bass without any 5^{ths}, 8^{ves},[11] or other faulty progressions (as has been taught above), but the great distance, or empty space, between the upper part and the Bass should

'On certain niceties of the accompaniment', § 3, Ex. 12 *b*) to be used, he tells us, in cases where the effect of the principal part or parts is not thereby discounted ('so weit es denen dazu componirten Stimmen nicht *Tort* thut'), but especially in the *Ritornelli* of Airs, and during sustained passages in the Solo part (cf. § 5 of the present chapter, A 2).

[9] Heinichen here appends the following footnote, explaining his choice of the word *fundamental*: "Because, in it, beginners must necessarily be taught the essential intervals (*Essential-Stimmen*) of all harmonies, the indispensable resolutions of all dissonances, and the regular progressions of the various parts at the same time; whereas, in a too full accompaniment (of which we shall now at once treat) such arts are, on the one hand, inapplicable, and, on the other, cannot be treated of otherwise than without order and incompletely."

[10] The following footnote is here appended: "On Harpsichords and the like ('auf denen *Clavecins*'), the fuller the accompaniment with both hands, the more har-monious the result. On the other hand, on Organs, especially when the performance is not on a large scale (*bey schwacher Music*), and except in a *Tutti*, one must certainly not become too much enamoured of a too full accompaniment in the left hand, because the continuous rumble (*Gemurre*) of so many deep notes is unpleasant to the ear, and not seldom becomes wearisome to the singer taking the principal part (*con-certirend*). Judgement must here be the best guide."

[N.B.—What Heinichen says of the Organ applies in an almost equal degree to the modern Pianoforte.]

[11] Heinichen here appends the following important footnote: "The question arises: Whether, in music for the Harpsichord and other instruments which sound a number of notes at the same time (*vollstimmige Instrumente*), faulty progressions of the kind in *partibus extremis* may not be excused by the crossing of the parts, familiar in composition? I say No to that, because 5^{ths} and 8^{ves} of the kind strike, not only the eye, but, very plainly indeed, the ear as well, as long, that is to say, as they remain, once and for all, the extreme parts on the instrument itself as well as in the score,* so that, in consequence, one has to picture the pretended exchange between the upper and the nearest middle part in one's imagination only. On the other hand, a *real* interchange [i.e. crossing] of *separate* vocal and instrumental parts is quite another matter, because the ear quite easily allows a deception of the kind to pass *propter differentiam vocum & Instrumentorum, distantiam loci, personarum*, &c. I am speaking, here, with intelligent Musicians, so no long-winded explanation is neces-sary; otherwise a whole chapter might be written on this subject."

* N.B.—Heinichen should rather have said: "*whatever they may be* in the score."

be filled, by both hands, in such a way that the right hand takes all the intervals of the chord [from the upper part] downwards, *as they lie nearest to hand*, and the left hand all the intervals of the chord [from the Bass] upwards, *as they lie nearest to hand*, without troubling in the very least about any 5ths and 8ves which may occur in the middle parts in question; [12] then the accompaniment of the two hands will always turn out to be in from 6 or 7 to 8 parts, without further difficulty. The examples make the matter clear."

(§ 33) "Supposing that we had the following 4 Bass notes: *a. d. g. c.* before us. The 4 notes $\bar{\bar{e}}.\bar{f}.\bar{d}.\bar{e}.$ shall then serve as the upper part of the right hand. Now we find in the empty space (*vacuum*) between these two extreme parts, from the height of the Treble to the depth of the Bass, the following middle parts, indicated by black notes:

[Heinichen then shows two different ways of distributing these chords between the hands: "according as the position (*Application*) of the hands or the convenience of the accompanist permits."]

(§ 34) "If one likes to take high Bass notes low down, both hands get more space, and the accompaniment can, here and there, be fuller, for example:

It may fittingly be mentioned here that Heinichen did not unreservedly condemn consecutives, *not* between extreme parts, which Ph. Em. Bach (for instance) would not have tolerated for a moment.

Of the two following examples:

he says: "In the first two examples of these suspicious and bad progressions the middle part in the right hand moves in 8ves, otherwise forbidden, with the Bass. This can easily be remedied by doubling the 3rd or 6th; nevertheless, this particular kind of 8ves (*diese einzige Arth 8ven*) is still often tolerated, because they are more concealed from the ear by the adjacent parts, and can, therefore, the sooner be excused by the familiar crossing (*Verwechselung*) of parts" (ibid., Ch. III, § 5, pp. 142–4).

[12] The following footnote is here appended: "Because they are covered by the extreme parts, and are, therefore, rightly excused by the usual crossing of parts; as we might say, in accordance with Saint-Lambert's *dictum* in his above-mentioned treatise on Thorough-Bass: *Comme la Musique n'est faite que pour l'oreille, une faute qui ne l'offense pas, n'est pas une faute*: Music is made for the ear alone, that fault, therefore, which does not offend the ear is not to be reckoned as a fault at all [cf. Ch. i of the present work, § 23 *i ad fin.*]. But we must be careful that such faults do not, in fact, offend the ear, i.e. that they are so surrounded by the parts nearest to them or so buried (*überschüttet*) among the multitude of middle parts that it is difficult or impossible for the ear to distinguish them; otherwise they are assuredly to be reckoned (I mean if they are in all innocence committed wholesale) among those very grammatical blunders which do not even admit of the excuse: *errare humanum est*: human fallibility."

(§ 35) "From this it may be seen that the great secret (*die grossen Künste*) of a very full accompaniment depends merely on attention to the two extreme parts, and, consequently, on the fundamental principles of a regular (*regulirt*) four-part accompaniment. . . ."

[§§ 36, 37 are devoted (as explained in the concluding sentences, omitted here, of § 35) to examples of 'full' accompaniment, as applied to successions of Triads given previously in four parts.]

(§ 38) "The same experiment can be made with all the other examples to be found above [i.e. earlier in the chapter], and, in doing so, the following further rule is to be adopted: That, the closer the hands are held together (so that no excessive space or *vacuum* may arise between the middle parts of the right and left hands), the more harmonious an accompaniment will result.[13] Therefore, when, in a musical performance, the Bass is so represented by instruments [14] as to render it unnecessary to strengthen the Thorough-Bass with continuous Octaves in the left hand,[15] it is better to take the deep Bass notes in the higher Octave (*in der Höhe*) [16] with so much the fuller chords (*desto vollstimmiger*), so that the hands may keep closer together, and that the harmony may at the same time be further extended in the *acuta* (high notes). . . ." [Then follows an example.]

(§ 39) "Now, as common chords are treated in a filled-in accompaniment, so, too, all other harmonies (*musicalische Sätze*) are treated, whereof we shall, in each case, give examples in future chapters. . . ."

III. A. It would be of the greatest interest to follow Heinichen through all the examples which he gives of a filled-in accompaniment as applied to all the different chords, did not considerations of space forbid. We must, accordingly, confine ourselves to a survey of the principles which he applies to the treatment of discords (ibid., Ch. III, §§ 54–63, pp. 202–16). They are as follows:

(N.B.—The numbering, &c., of the rules now to be given is independent of Heinichen's. Where his own words are used, they are indicated by inverted commas.)

(1) "All discords in the right hand, *especially in the upper part*, must be treated strictly (*legaliter*). That is to say, they must be prepared and resolved as the rules demand, because any fault would be easily apparent to the ear." [A discord may, however, be *doubled* in the right hand, as in Ex. 4.]

(2) "The reduplications [i.e. of discords] in the left hand, on the contrary, are tied to no such rules, but can be treated, at pleasure, in three different ways":

(*a*) The prepared discord in the right hand may be prepared in the left hand also, subsequently resolving in 8ves with the right hand, as:

[Ex. 3]

---

[13] The great importance of this rule (not yet fully revealed) will presently be made apparent.

[14] i.e. the string and wind Basses (both of 8-ft. and 16-ft. tone) which played from the *Continuo* part.

[15] Cf. § 7.

[16] The liberty to take the Bass an 8ve higher (or lower, as suggested in Heinichen's § 34) was among the 'licences' enumerated by Saint-Lambert (cf. Ch. i, § 23 i, 1 c).

or, again, as Heinichen's examples of a suspended 9 (Ex. 4 *a* and *b*) show (though he does not mention it in his rules), the discord may be doubled in a similar manner *in the right hand itself*, and resolved in 8ves as:

* By a misprint the original has 4.

In these cases it is of the *utmost importance* to observe the injunction that the space (*vacuum*) between the two hands should be as *small as possible* (cf. Heinichen's § 38 quoted in II of the present section), in order that the consecutive 8ves may not become prominent: either between the upper parts of the two hands, as:

or between the thumbs of the two hands, as:

or between the extreme parts of the right hand, as:

(*b*) The discord in the left hand—resolving, as above, in 8ves with the prepared discord in the right hand—may itself be taken unprepared, as:

(c) The discord in the left hand may either:

(α) resolve a degree *upwards*, as:

[Ex. 9]

or (β) "when the convenience of the hand demands it", leap to an interval of the next chord,[17] as:

[Ex. 10]

(3) "In certain cases, the left hand may anticipate the resolutions of the discords occurring in the right hand, in the same way as is sometimes practised by celebrated composers when writing music with full chords (*in vollstimmiger Composition*). The matter needs a lengthy explanation, and may well be passed over by beginners. For the sake, however, of the more experienced we will here describe it in detail."

Heinichen bases his rules, and the examples which he proceeds to give, on what he speaks of as an accepted fact, namely, that in a 9 8 suspension, when played in full harmony [i.e. on a keyed instrument, as described above], the 8 may be included in the middle parts [i.e. in the left hand] in anticipation of the resolution of the 9 in an upper part [i.e. in the right hand].

"It is well known", he says (l.c., § 55), "that, along with the 9 played with full harmony, among other middle parts, the Octave also may be struck,[18] before the aforesaid 9 resolves on its adjacent Octave (9 8); this is, in fact,

---

[17] Heinichen here appends the following characteristic footnote: "The latter liberty seems to be the exclusive privilege (*ein proprium*) of keyed instruments (*vollstimmige Instrumente*); in a score consisting of individual parts (*in denen Partituren separirter Stimmen*) that kind of procedure should not readily be exhibited (*soll man sich mit dergleichen Dingen nicht gerne blicken lassen*). This, however, foreigners do practice: in working out a number of real parts, they resolve e.g. a 4th, 7th, &c., correctly [i.e. downwards] in the voice parts (*vocaliter*), and a degree upwards in the instrumental ones (*instrumentaliter*). Only I should not care often to hear such resolutions in the upper part, and, altogether, I set a higher value on working out a few real parts soundly (*solide*) than on filling an excessive number of real parts with forced and irregular progressions under the pretext that nature admits of nothing else. *Haec obiter*."

[18] "Es ist bekandt, dass man zu der vollstimmigen 9 unter andern Mittel-Stimmen auch die 8[ve] anschlagen kan."

and can be called, nothing else but an *Anticipatio resolutionis Nonae*, or the striking in advance of that note on which the 9 has got to resolve, e.g.:

He then proceeds (l.c., § 56): "If now the ear can tolerate the *Anticipatio resolutionis Nonae*, it must necessarily also be able to tolerate all other *Anticipationes resolutionum* which are derived from the mere inversion of this fully-harmonized (*vollstimmig*) 9, provided that one knows how to treat and prepare them regularly."

The following examples, of 7 6 (as the first inversion of 9 8), and of $^{6}_{5}{}_{4}$ (as the second inversion of the same), with anticipation of the resolution, are then given: [19]

[19] In connexion with the first of these (Ex. 12) Heinichen adds the following warning: "In these examples the suspended 7th above, against the anticipated 6th below, represents the 9 of the previous examples (*machet . . . die vorige* 9 *aus*); consequently, between these parts, all the rules must be observed which are otherwise to be observed in the case of a 9. E.g. the 8ve of the Bass never becomes a 9th by the Bass falling a degree ('Die 8ve zum Bass-*Clave* gehet niemahls *descendendo in Nonam*' [i.e. a 9, resolving on 8, is never prepared by the Octave of the Bass]); consequently the 8ve of the middle part in question [i.e. that in which the anticipation occurs] never becomes a 9th by the descent of the latter. Consequently the first of the two following examples would be wrong, but the second right:

and this observation is to be borne in mind in the case of all future *Anticipationes resolutionum*."

This is an interesting indication of the increasing sensitiveness of musicians in the matter of Octaves (cf. § 10 a).

At the same time, the restriction now imposed by Heinichen is somewhat surprising in view of his express injunction to disregard consecutives (except between extreme parts) in a filled-in accompaniment. It is difficult to see why the preparation of a Ninth, occurring between an upper and a *middle* part, by the upper Octave of the latter (as in Ex. *a* above) should be more objectionable than *simultaneous* consecutive Octaves, between the very same parts, as prescribed by Heinichen (cf. Exx. 3 and 4).

In each of the two following examples (Exx. 14, 15) it will be seen that what Heinichen regards as an *inversion* is really the chord in its root position, while what he calls the 'Chord' is really an inversion:

Of Ex. 14 *b, c* Heinichen tells us (l.c., § 58, note) that "the suspended 4th above, against the anticipated 3rd below, represents the original 9 [as seen in (*a*), between the suspended 9 and its anticipated resolution]", and, as he points out later on, the same applies *mutatis mutandis* to the suspended 6th and its anticipated resolution in Ex. 15 *b, c, d*.

Of the following series he writes (l.c., § 59): "The resolution of a 6th which is merely prepared or tied, even though the 6th itself is not syncopated by the 7th [as in Ex. 15 *b, c, d*], can also be anticipated."

N.B.—In the original the left-hand parts of (*a*) appear as follows:

The misprint in the *second* bar is corrected in the *Errata*, but the one in the first bar remains unnoticed. The conjectural emendation introduced above is based on Ex. 15 *b*.

Of Exx. 15 and 16 Heinichen writes (l.c., § 59, note): "In all these examples the suspended 6th above, against the anticipated 5th below, represents the previous 9 [i.e. in Ex. 15 *a*]."

He then proceeds (l.c., § 60): "The 9 not unfrequently has the 7 with it $\left\{\begin{smallmatrix} 9 & 8 \\ 8 & \\ 7 & 6 \\ 3 & \end{smallmatrix}\right\}$. If, now, we invert (*verwechseln*) this 7th and the bass note, we get an *Anticipatio 3ae syncopatae*, which, it is true, is more serviceable in composing in full harmony (*vollstimmiger Composition*) than in accompaniment; we will, however, include it, now that we are occupied with the investigation of the matter:

"In this inversion the 3rd above, against the 2nd appearing below, represents the previous 9."

[It will be observed that, in this example, the correspondence between the 'Chord' and the 'Inversion' is by no means exact. The latter represents the

progression: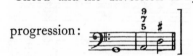

Heinichen also permits the resolution of a *double* suspension to be anticipated in the left hand, as in the following example, of which, however, he says (l.c., § 61): "In the case of double suspensions (*Bey doppelt vorherliegenden Con. und Dissonantien*) one can also introduce double *Anticipationes resolutionum*, but this must be done rarely, and with judgement, that the accumulated dissonances may not be intolerable to the ear:

In connexion with the above example Heinichen reiterates the warning recorded above, in note 19.

Two further important warnings are given (l.c., § 63), of which the following is the substance:

(1) The anticipation of the resolution of the suspended discord (or discords) must never be in the same Octave as the resolution itself. Such examples as the following (selected from the dozen given by Heinichen) would be "absolutely intolerable":

(2) Those *Anticipationes resolutionum* are the best where the suspended discord falls a *whole tone* to its resolution, because the clash of a minor Ninth is harsher than that of a major.

Furthermore, when the suspended discord resolves by falling a semitone to a note *accidentally sharpened* (𝄪 or ♮), the anticipation of the resolution is *absolutely forbidden*.

Thus, of the following examples, *a*, *b*, *c*, *d* are passable (*passabel*), while the remainder are "intolerable and quite forbidden":

B. A careful comparison of Heinichen's numerous examples of a filled-in accompaniment with the original, 4-part versions of the same Basses, given earlier in the work, is most instructive. The following one (given l.c., § 67) must suffice to illustrate the principles set forth in the foregoing pages, and will serve to show how a figured Bass may be treated on the Harpsichord (and, to a very limited extent, on the Pianoforte) when a sonorous accompaniment is appropriate.[20] Heinichen's explanation of the example is appended:

[20] The original, four-part version of the example (given l.c. § 49) is here subjoined for comparison. Note, on the second beat of bar 5 and the fourth beat of bar 8, the

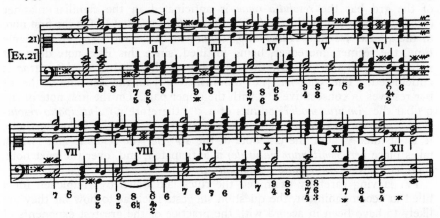

("N.B.—In this example the left hand treats the filled-in (*vollstimmig*) accompaniment as follows: On the first Bass note of the second bar the 7th is resolved in consecutive 8ves with the upper part. On the first Bass note

fifth part taken in at the top (while the lower part is subsequently dropped) for the sake of gaining a higher position (cf. § 4, I, Ex. I):

[21] N.B.—The 5 is not generally included in a $\frac{9}{7}$ suspension (as on the first beat of bar 11) unless present in the previous chord, as in the following example of Ph. Em.

Bach (*Versuch &c.*, Part II, 1762, Ch. 20, § 6):

Bach's rule is as follows:

"When, with this chord $\left[\text{i.e. } \begin{smallmatrix}9&8\\7&6\\3&-\end{smallmatrix}\right]$, instead of the Third, the Fourth is to be taken, it must be expressly indicated. As the latter is likewise [i.e. like the 9 and 7] prepared, the whole chord lies under the hand; so, too, even when the Fifth has to be taken as a fifth part. In this chord the latter may be *perfect, false* [i.e. diminished], and *augmented*, and, as we have just heard [i.e. in the preceding section], is held on from the previous chord (*liegt . . . schon vorher*)."

In a filled-in accompaniment, however, there is naturally more licence, and, in the present case, the inclusion of the 5 is appropriate, if only for the reason sometimes given by Italian theorists of the eighteenth century: *perchè fa buon sentire* ('because it sounds well')!

of the 3rd bar the *resolutio 9nae* is anticipated in the familiar manner (*bekandter Massen*) by the 8^{ve} (*durch die anschlagende* 8^{ve}).[22] On the first note of the 4th bar we find *Anticipatio resolutionis 7mae* and *9nae* at the same time, the former, moreover, being justified, since this Bass note does not naturally bear a 5th.[23] On the first note of the 5th bar *resolutio 4tae* is anticipated. The *5ta min.* [i.e. diminished 5th] on the last note of the 7th bar resolves in consecutive 8^{ves} with the upper part. On the first note of the 9th bar the *Ambitus modi*[24] admits of a 5th, therefore no *Anticipatio resolutionis 7mae* can take place here, whereas, in the case of the following note, it is justified.[25] On the last note of the 10th bar the *resolutio 4tae* (which takes place *per Semitonium naturale*) is anticipated, and, over the next note, there is likewise *Anticipatio resolutionis 4tae.*")

IV. Having carefully examined the rules laid down by Heinichen for a filled-in accompaniment, the question suggests itself as to how far they are likely to have been in accord with the practice of the greatest exponents of the art of accompaniment among his approximate contemporaries.

Unfortunately the question is very difficult to answer with any exactitude, owing to lack of information, since Heinichen is the only notable authority who enters into the matter in detail.

There is, of course, no manner of doubt that a filled-in accompaniment was used, upon occasion, by the best masters.

That point is settled conclusively (if any such confirmation were needed) by the often-quoted testimony of J. S. Bach's pupil, Johann Christian Kittel, in the Third Part (p. 33) of his work on the Organ (*Der angehende praktische Organist*, Erfurt, 1808). He writes as follows: ". . . when Seb. Bach performed a piece of Church Music, one of his most capable pupils always had to accompany on the Harpsichord. It may readily be supposed that it would not, in any case, have done to venture to come forward with a meagre rendering of the Thorough-Bass. Nevertheless, one always had to be prepared often to find Bach's hands and fingers mingling with the hands and fingers of the player, and, without further troubling the latter, adorning the accompaniment with masses of harmony which were even more impressive than the unsuspected proximity of the stern preceptor." (". . . wenn Seb. Bach eine Kirchenmusik auffuehrte, so musste allemal einer von seinen faehigsten Schuelern auf dem Fluegel accompagniren. Man kann wohl vermuthen, dass man sich da mit einer magern Generalbassbegleitung ohnehin nicht vor wagen durfte. Demohngeachtet musste man sich immer darauf gefasst halten, dass sich oft ploetzlich Bach's Haende und Finger unter die Haende und Finger des Spielers mischten und, ohne diesen weiter zu geniren, das Accompagnement mit Massen von Harmonien ausstaffirten, die noch mehr imponirten als die unvermuthete nahe Gegenwart des strengen Lehrers.")

---

[22] The term *anschlagend* (lit. 'striking') is applied to an interval (or chord) struck independently, i.e. not as a passing note (or chord), and without preparation. *Ein anschlagender Accord* is, therefore (to use an old-fashioned term), a *chord of simple percussion*.

[23] The bar in question being in G major, the bass note *B*, as the third degree of the scale, demands a Sixth, rather than a Fifth, as its natural harmony.

[24] The term *ambitus modi* is here used in the sense of the harmony natural to the various degrees of the scale. This is not, however, its original, or only sense (cf. Ch. i, § 24, note 21).   [25] Cf. note 23.

It will at once occur to the reader that this description (in spite of Kittel's wording) applies to a rehearsal rather than a performance; but this is immaterial. It is clear that, upon occasion, when the spirit moved him, Bach played in handfuls. One can almost see him, impatiently thrusting his hands under the arms of the humiliated pupil and, regardless of the discomfort of the posture, revelling in the wealth of his own superb accompaniment!

What it is, alas! impossible to ascertain is, how far his practice coincided with that of Heinichen in two important particulars:

    (1) the free duplication of a discord (or discords),

    (2) the anticipation (in the left hand) of the resolution.

His son, Philip Emanuel, gives us little help in the matter; but the little that he says on the subject of a filled-in accompaniment seems to indicate that his own practice (or, at any rate, his precept) was to duplicate in the left hand the *consonances only*, in which case the anticipation (in the left hand) of the resolution of a discord (in the right) would *a fortiori* be excluded.

His first reference to the matter (*Versuch &c.*, Part II, 1762, Introd., §§ 21 *ad fin.*–24) is as follows:

"... I shall make known the position of certain chords, and, in every case, say which are the indispensable intervals, the less necessary ones, the ones which may perhaps (*allenfalls*) be dispensed with, and the ones which can be doubled.

"This latter information is necessary, because the harmony must sometimes be weak and sometimes strong, and, in the matter of fulness of harmony (*Vollstimmigkeit*), a piece sometimes calls for every variety of accompaniment.

"The accompaniment may be in *one, two, three, four, and more* parts (*ein- zwey- drey- vier- und mehrstimmig*).

"An accompaniment in *four and more parts throughout* is appropriate for performances on a large scale (*starke Musiken*), for pieces in the strict style (*gearbeitete Sachen*),[26] contrapuntal music (*Contrapunkte*), fugues, &c., and, speaking generally, for pieces in which there is merely music, without their affording any special scope for taste (*Stücke wo nur Musik ist, ohne dass der Geschmack besonders daran Antheil hat*)."

This tells us little, and the expression 'in four and more parts' in no way suggests a filled-in accompaniment (with no fixed number of parts, and great laxity of progression except in the extreme parts) of the kind described by Heinichen.

Later in the work, however, a form of accompaniment is described which differs from the latter only in the important particular that the reduplication in the left hand of the chord struck by the right is *restricted to its consonant intervals*. It will be observed that Philip Emanuel agrees with Heinichen in emphasizing the importance of *keeping the hands close together*.

In the course of a chapter (ibid., Ch. 29, § 7) on 'Delivery' or 'Style in performance' (*Vortrag*) he writes:

"Such rules as can be given with regard to *Forte* and *Piano*, in the case of an Organ and an Harpsichord with two manuals, are as follows: The *Fortissimo* and *Forte* are taken on the stronger manual. In the former case

---

[26] The term *gearbeitet* (lit. 'worked') was applied to music in the strict (or *allabreve*) style as opposed to the free style (*der galante Styl*), cf. § 4, IV, note 11.

the consonant chords can be repeated in their entirety by the left hand, and, of the dissonant ones, only their consonant intervals, if the execution of the Bass notes permits (*Bey jenem können die consonirenden Accorde ganz, und bey den dissonirenden, nur die Consonanzen daraus in der linken Hand mitgegriffen werden*, &c.). This duplication must then take place, not low down, but in the neighbourhood of the right hand, in order that the harmony of both hands may be contiguous (*zusammen gränzt*) and that there may be no intervening space, not to mention the fact that, in the contrary case, a disgusting (*ekelhaft*) indistinctness will be occasioned by the rumble of the low notes (*die brummende Tiefe*)."

Ph. Em. Bach had a most fastidious ear, as is proved by his uncompromising condemnation of progressions which were accepted by other authorities,[27] and it is therefore probable that the reduplicated discords (sometimes resolving in consecutive 8ves, and sometimes not resolving at all) permitted by Heinichen were repugnant to his taste.

V. *The use of extended harmony.*

(*a*) The distribution of four-part harmony between the two hands (alluded to by Heinichen in the 29th paragraph of the long extract quoted in II of the present section) was much recommended by Ph. Em. Bach, both as a means of enabling the accompanist to use progressions which would be impracticable in close harmony, and also on purely aesthetic grounds.[28]

In the former case the extended harmony is to be used only for a chord or two, as the exigencies of the case demand. The following examples will make the matter clear:

[Ex.22]

Of the Bass of this example [29] Ph. Em. Bach writes (ibid., Ch. 13, II, § 4): ". . . one cannot, in an undivided accompaniment [i.e. in close harmony],

[27] Cf. § 10 *e*.

[28] He writes (ibid., Ch. 2, II, § 12) as follows: "When chords occur in extended harmony (*im getheilten Accompagnement*), either elegance (*eine Zierlichkeit*) or necessity is the reason (*ist daran Schuld*)."

[29] All Ph. Em. Bach's examples (i.e. in Part II of the *Versuch*) are given on a *single stave*. When the upper parts are given at all, they are often given *after* (instead of *above*) the Bass, in which case they are liable to be noted *an Octave lower than the Bass in question demands*. Thus, the above example appears in the original as follows, showing the Seventh on *d* taken (1) as $\frac{8}{7}$ (in accordance with the text quoted above), and (2) (in extended harmony) as $\frac{7}{5}$:

This must be remembered in connexion with any of Ph. Em. Bach's examples noted on two staves in the present work.

When the upper parts, not being given by the author, have been supplied by the present writer, they are invariably given in smaller print than the Bass.

take the Fifth with the [Bass] note *d* without mistakes; the major Third [♯*f*] must not be doubled: consequently one takes the Octave. Otherwise, one must either accompany this example in three parts or choose the divided accompaniment [i.e. extended harmony]."

In connexion with the above example (which he characterizes as "extra-ordinary in the matter of the figuring") Ph. Em. Bach points out (l.c.) that, if treated in accordance with the existing figuring, instead of the more natural

, the only way to avoid mistakes is by the use of extended harmony (as shown above), unless a temporary fifth part be adopted (cf. § 4, II, Ex. 4).

N.B.—The ugly skip in the upper part in Ex. 23 *b* is quite foreign to Ph. Em. Bach's habit. There can be little doubt that, *in actual practice*, he would either have disregarded the 5 in the $\frac{7}{5}$ on *a*, or have adopted a temporary fifth part:

(*b*) With regard to the use of extended harmony as a means of adding charm to the accompaniment, we cannot do better than quote Ph. Em. Bach, who treats of it in the course of a chapter (ibid., Ch. 32, § 10) "On certain niceties of the accompaniment" (*Von gewissen Zierlichkeiten des Accompagnements*). He writes:

"A divided accompaniment [i.e. two parts to each hand], for which the necessary proficiency is acquired by means of good Clavier pieces previously played, is very often a great adornment. We have already, in the preceding chapters, shown the necessity which sometimes arises for this kind of accompaniment. Apart from this necessity, it is abundantly well known how markedly better the effect of extended harmony (*einer zerstreuten Harmonie*) often is than that of close. We see, for instance, in (*a*) [Ex. 24 *a*], that the usual disposal of the harmony sounds unpleasant (*widrig*) on account of its excessive uniformity, and that it is, therefore, better to take the $\frac{6}{4}{2}$ chord (*Secundenaccord*) in this example, either in a different position, or, best of all, in extended harmony (*im getheilten Accompagnement*) (*b*). If a passage (*Satz*) is repeated, it can be made agreeable by an alternation between an undivided and a divided accompaniment (*c*). In (*d*) the Sixths in the right hand are more telling (*stechen besser durch*), and this tuneful (*sangbar*) progression becomes clearer, if the lowest middle part, which has no tune, but is only there to complete the harmony (*der Vollstimmigkeit wegen*), is made to move [in quavers] with the Bass notes, and is taken in the left hand:

VI. *The fulness of the harmony to be varied according to the circumstances.*

It must always be remembered that the accompanist is at all times free to vary the number of parts at his discretion. This variety is one of the greatest beauties of a good accompaniment.

Johann Joachim Quantz (*Versuch &c.*, 1752, Hauptstück [*Section*] xvii, Abschnitt [*Subsection*] vi, § 4) writes as follows:

"The general rule of Thorough-Bass is to play always in four parts; but, if one wants to accompany really well, it often has a better effect not to adhere too closely to it, but rather to omit some parts, or even to double the Bass in the upper Octave with the right hand [i.e. without harmony]. For, just as little as a composer is able, or obliged, to write a three-, four-, or five-part accompaniment to all melodies alike (unless they are to be rendered unintelligible, or obscured), just as little does every melody bear a continuous full accompaniment on the Clavier; wherefore an accompanist must be guided rather by the nature of the case itself than by the general rules of Thorough-Bass."

[30] All the above examples, except (*d*), are here given *an Octave higher than in the original.*

Ph. Em. Bach's method of notation on a single stave (cf. note 29) obliged him to disregard the question of pitch. In his preface he writes: "I have been obliged to give the examples on a single stave, in order that this work might not become too voluminous and costly: with these examples, therefore, one must always have regard chiefly to the reason for which they are adduced, and not bind oneself to the height and depth prescribed. . . ."

It is therefore a safe rule to imagine them in any key, or at any pitch, which does not cause the part above the Bass (in the close position of the harmony) to go much below the middle of the Tenor Octave, or the upper part to go above *f″*.

§ 4. *The temporary adoption of a fifth part, &c.*

Several cases may be distinguished in which, in a four-part accompaniment, a fifth part may be temporarily included.

In some of these it need be included only in a single chord, while in others its duration is determined by the circumstances to be described.

It must, in the first instance, always be a concordant interval, and one which it is permitted to double.

I. The extra part may be added in order to secure a different (generally a higher) position for the right hand. This may be desirable for two reasons:

(1) The hands may have got too close together, or a higher position of the harmony may be desired on other grounds. In such a case there are two ways out of the difficulty, which Ph. Em. Bach describes as follows (*Versuch &c.*, Part II, 1762, Ch. 2, 1, § 37):

"If the two hands get too close together, or the right hand is too low down, the same chord may be repeated in a higher position over the same [Bass] note, if the latter is not too quick; if there is no time for this, an extra part is taken at the top, and the lowest one [the lower Octave of the new part] abandoned. This device is employed (1) only in case of need, because I think that, otherwise, one must adhere to four regular parts and not lightly exceed them; (2) in the case of consonances, because dissonances limit the accompaniment more."

The following example from Heinichen illustrates both the above-mentioned devices:

[Ex. 1]

General-Bass &c., 1728,
Part I, Ch. III, § 51, p. 199.

The next example, taken from Kirnberger (*Grundsätze des Generalbasses*, Volume of examples, Third Division, Fig. xxiv), is a remarkable one, and illustrates the rule that consecutives are not deemed to arise through the entry of a new part, or the cessation of one previously sounding (cf. Ch. xii, '⁶₅ chords', § 2 *d*, note 2):

[Ex. 2]

N.B.—The entry of the new upper part is marked by the crotchet rests which precede it (as in the original), while the subsequent disappearance of the lower part is shown by the lines added to indicate the progression of the part above it.

Kirnberger explains it as follows (ibid., § 172):

"In this example, from the second half of the first bar to the first half of the second bar, as also from there to the second half of the second bar, there seem to be forbidden progressions of Fifths; these are, however, forbidden progressions in appearance only, for, as soon as the fifth part enters at the top (*in der äussersten Höhe eintritt*), the lowest part ceases to belong to the four-part harmony, and, accordingly, the progression between the first and second bars is not from *a* to *b*, but *d* falls a minor Third to *b*, while *a*, as the now lowest of the three upper parts, falls a tone to *g*. So, too, in the second bar, between the first and second halves."

In spite, however, of the above justification, there can be no doubt but that the device in question is here strained to its limit. Kirnberger presents an alternative method of dealing with what is a very real difficulty,[1] which will be considered later on (cf. § 9, Ex. 10).

(2) A different position of the harmony may be necessary, in order to avoid consecutive Fifths, as in the following example from Mattheson:

Organisten-Probe, 1719, 'Mittel-Classe' (*Middle Grade*), 'Prob - Stück' (Test-piece) 15, bar 42.

N.B.—Only the figured Bass is Mattheson's.

II. A fifth part may be added temporarily (without altering the position of the harmony in the right hand, as in the foregoing examples) in order:
    (1) to avoid consecutive Fifths,
    (2) to cover up a doubtful progression,
    (3) to strengthen a chord by supplying an interval which it would other-
        wise lack:

(1)

[1] The difficulty is the same as in the case of a 7 6 sequence on a rising Bass (cf. Ch. xi, 'Sevenths', IV, § 7).

In default of a special device for keeping the harmony in the right hand at the same relative distance from the Bass, the right hand must take a position, at the beginning of the sequence, high enough to enable it to get to the end of the latter without encountering the left hand, the result being an accompaniment, unpleasing in itself, and with the especial disadvantage that (in the case of a long sequence) one or more of the suspensions may have to be prepared and resolved in the Octave *above* the principal parts, which is always bad, while the converse (though not in itself desirable) is often unavoidable.

In the present instance the accompaniment would be as follows:

[2] The alternative to the extra part (the 5 on *d*), entering at +, is the division of the

Ex.5

M. C. Festing, *Opera sesta* (Sonatas for two Violins and Thorough-Bass), Sonata IV, Largo.

(2)

[Ex.6]

'not good'   'better'

Of this example from Ph. Em. Bach (ibid., Ch. 9, I, § 10) the latter writes: "*To strengthen the harmony* ('zur Verstärkung') one can sometimes double the major and minor Second, also, *apart from that*, in order to cover the bad leap of the augmented Fourth. The major Second when associated with the minor Sixth, and the augmented Second under any circumstances (*überhaupt*), do not bear this duplication."

(3) Two chords which are especially liable, in the midst of four-part harmony, to be taken in five parts are the Dominant Seventh and its second inversion $\frac{6}{4}$ on the Supertonic, particularly when the Seventh (or the 3 of the $\frac{6}{4}$ chord) is in the upper part, as shown in the following examples from Heinichen (ibid., Part I, Ch. III, § 43, p. 191, bar 7 of the example, and § 7, p. 152). It may be mentioned, however, that Ph. Em. Bach's practice in such cases (so far as can be judged by the examples in the *Versuch*) was to adhere to four parts.

[Ex.7]   [a]   [b]   [Ex.8]

Similarly, the chord of the Dominant Seventh is often taken in five parts

accompaniment between the hands, in extended harmony, either in the positions shown in § 3, Ex. 23, or as follows:

[3] Here, again, the only alternative to the fifth part × is extended harmony:

(For the preparation of the discords $\frac{9}{4}$ by notes of shorter duration than themselves, and for their repercussion, instead of being tied to the notes of preparation, see note 11.)

when it either (1) appears over a Tonic Pedal, or (2) is suspended over the Tonic, as in the two following examples from Heinichen and Ph. Em. Bach respectively:

[Ex. 9]   Heinichen, ibid., l.c. § 43, p. 192.

[Ex. 10]   Ph. Em. Bach, ibid., Ch. 13, 11, § 3, Ex. *f* [1].

Of the latter example (of which he gives the Bass only) Ph. Em. Bach says: "the Octave can be taken with [the Bass note] *e* as a fifth part. One then has the Fifth in one's hand with the *a*, and, at the resolution, the Triad is complete."

We will add an example, from the same author (l.c., Ex. *e*), of the Dominant Seventh suspended over the Mediant of the minor key:

[Ex. 11]   (or in any other position).

Of this example (of which only the Bass is given) Ph. Em. Bach writes: ". . . the Seventh on the final *c* must be prepared by the preceding Fifth on *e*. Here the Third is taken with the final *c* as a fifth part [Ex. 11 *a*]. Or it can be taken before as the Octave of *e* [Ex. 11 *b*]."

Further, the common case may be mentioned in which (if a full chord is desired) the 5 is added, as an extra part, to the Tonic chord after $\frac{7}{5}$ on the Dominant (with the leading note in the upper part, and therefore precluded from falling a Third). In such a case the Dominant chord itself can also, of course, be taken in five parts:

Ex. 12

It will be seen that in all the above examples (save in Ex. 8, in which the extra part doubles the Bass) the principle is the same: that of adding to a chord *a consonant interval which it would otherwise lack.*

A different case from those already mentioned is that in which the first inversion of the Dominant Seventh, $\substack{6\\5}$ on the leading note, is taken in five parts, thus *doubling the leading note* by the inclusion of the Octave of the Bass, as: (cf. § 6, Ex. 1, bars 10 and 24).

III. There are many cases in which a fifth part must be added in order to *prepare a subsequent discord*.

Thus, it is obvious that any chord followed, on a bass note rising one degree (or falling a Seventh), by *any harmony which includes a 7*, must itself *contain the Octave of its Bass*.

Similarly, any chord followed by a $\substack{6\\5}$ on the same Bass, or by a 7 on a Bass falling a Third (or Tenth), or rising a Sixth, must itself contain the 5; so, too, any chord followed by a $\substack{6\\5}$ on a Bass *rising* a Third (or Tenth), or falling a Sixth, must itself contain the 7,[4] even though the composer may have *omitted to include the latter in the figuring*.

In the same way, again, a $\substack{6\\5}$ followed by a 4 3 suspension on a Bass rising a Fifth (or falling a Fourth), as in Ex. 22, must itself include the Octave of its Bass.

The following typical examples from J. M. Leclair (1697–1764), in whose Basses the need for five-part harmony (of varying duration) is of especially frequent occurrence, will serve abundantly to illustrate these points:

(1 *a*) $\substack{6\\5}$ resolving on 7 on a Bass rising a degree (or falling a Seventh); $\substack{6\\5} = \substack{8\\6\\3\\5}, 7 = \substack{8\\7\\3\\5}$, as:

Ex. 13

(key example).

Ex. 14

J. M. Leclair, *Sonatas for Violin and Bass*, Book 2, Sonata I, Allegro (Altro), bare 13 sq.

N.B.—The cross + on the second quaver of the Violin part denotes a trill.

[4, 5] For notes 4 and 5 see p. 354.

6)
Ex.15

ibid., Book 3, Sonata I, Aria, 2nd section, bars 18–15 from end.

(1 *b*) $\frac{6}{5}$ resolving on $\frac{9}{7}$ on a Bass rising a degree:

Ex. 16

ibid., Book 1, Sonata VIII, Vivace, 2nd section, bars 28–30.

N.B.—The entry of the new part, *d*, on the last beat of the first bar, is marked by the prefixed cross ×.

(2 *a*) 7 $\frac{6}{5}$ on successive notes of a Bass rising by step; $7 = \frac{7}{5}$, $6 = \frac{6}{5}$:
$$7 = \begin{smallmatrix}8\\7\\5\\3\end{smallmatrix}, \quad 6 = \begin{smallmatrix}8\\6\\5\\3\end{smallmatrix}:$$

Ex. 17

(key example).

N.B.—The fifth part enters at the beginning of the first bar as the (double) Octave of the Bass *; the *part below it* disappears on the third beat of the second bar, appearing last as the 3 (*c*) of the $\frac{6}{5}$ chord on *a*.

---

[4] Except, of course, in cases where the 5 of the $\frac{6}{5}$ can be taken *in transitu*, without preparation, as:

[5] The extra part enters on the second quaver of the first complete bar, as the Octave of the Bass (*c* sharp).

For the Seventh (*b*), on the first quaver of the second complete bar of the suggested accompaniment, *rising* to the 3 on *a* sharp, see Ch. xi, 'Sevenths', II, § 2, Ex. 5.

[6] It must be remembered that the entry of the new part, *d*, at * (on the third

Ex. 18

Leclair, ibid., Book 3, Sonata IV,
Allegro ma non troppo, bars 15-17.

N.B.—The fifth part enters on the third beat of the first complete bar at ×, as the
(double) Octave of the Bass (♭ b).

(2 b) $\frac{9\,6}{7\,5}$ on successive notes of a Bass rising by step; $9 = \frac{7}{5}$, $6 = \frac{6}{5}$: for
illustration see Ex. 16.

(3) $\frac{9}{7}$ resolving on 7 on a Bass falling a Third (or rising a Sixth); $9 = \frac{7}{5}$, $7 = \frac{7}{5}$:

Ex. 19   (key example).

quaver of the first bar of the example), does not give rise to consecutive Octaves
(cf. examples from Marpurg in Ch. xii, '$\frac{6}{5}$ chords', § 2 d, note 2).

⁷ (See p. 356) Two points are to be noted in this example:

(1) The discords $\frac{9}{7}$ on the first crotchet (like the $\frac{9}{4}$ in Ex. 5) are prepared by notes
of shorter duration than themselves, and they are struck afresh instead of being tied
to the notes of preparation (see note 11).

(2) The positions must be avoided in which the consecutive 4ths (between upper

parts) in the last bar appear as 5ths, as [music notation]

The only remedy, if the right position has been missed, is to select this point for
reverting to 4-part harmony and to drop the c sharp (the only part that *can* be
dropped) altogether, thus taking the 6 on f sharp as $\frac{8}{6}$ instead of $\frac{8}{4}$ (for the liberty
to take 6 on the Supertonic as $\frac{6}{4}$, see Ch. xxi, 'Incomplete figuring', II, § 1).

Ph. Em. Bach's instructions as regards similar cases are as follows (ibid., Ch. 34,

In the following example the progression in question occurs sequentially on a Bass which falls a degree from bar to bar. It will be observed that it is only the fall of a Third (in the Bass) in each bar which saves consecutive 5ths, as well as the syncopated 8ves which arise when a 9th is prepared by the 8ve of the preceding Bass note:

Leclair, ibid., Book 2, Sonata I, Allegro (Altro), 2nd section, bars 17–19.

7)
Ex. 20

N.B.—The new part, entering at the beginning of the first bar as the 5 of the $\frac{9}{7}\frac{}{5}\frac{}{3}$ on *a*, is marked by the cross + prefixed.

(4) 9 resolving on $\frac{6}{5}$ on a Bass rising a Third (or Tenth), or falling a Sixth, must include the 7, *whether figured or not*.

The further progression will determine whether (as in the following example) the 5 is also necessary:

Leclair, *Opera Quarta*, Sonatas for two Violins and Bass (Walsh), Sonata II, Allegro, bars 65–71.

8)
Ex. 21

[7] (See p. 355 for beginning of note.)
'On certain precautions in Accompaniment', § 2): "All harmonies (*Aufgaben*) in which progressions of Fourths occur are dangerous, on account of the Fifths if the position is altered. If able, one takes, of course, the *best and safest positions*; sometimes, however, it is impossible. In such case one seeks a good opportunity of escaping from the danger, and into another position, by taking a fifth part through the duplication of a concord, or by the repercussion of the harmony [i.e. in a different position] if the Bass note is fairly long, or is followed by a succession of one or more passing notes [i.e. any notes, not necessarily moving by step, over which the harmony remains unchanged]. If, however, none of these devices can be employed, the *figures* [i.e. intervals] *which occasion mistakes must be omitted*." (These last italics are not Bach's.)

[8] In the second bar the (temporary) leading note, *e* natural, is doubled, as an extra part, in order to prepare the (unfigured) 7, *e flat*, over *f* in the following bar. The preparation of a ♭ by a ♮ (or of a ♮ by a ♯) had its origin in the ellipse of the note to

(5) $\frac{6}{5}$ proceeding to a 4 3 suspension on a Bass falling a Fourth, or rising a Fifth, must include the 8ve of the Bass: for illustration see Ex. 22 (bars 1 and 3).

IV. Some further examples follow in which a fifth part is necessary, either (as in the examples given in III) in order to prepare a subsequent discord, or because, owing to the fixed downward resolution of a discord already present, the *following harmony would otherwise lack a consonant interval.*

For example, if the progression  be modified (as

we find in Ex. 22, bar 3) by a suspended 9 over the bass note *f*, provision must be made for the 6 in the $\frac{6}{5}$ chord which follows.

Being a consonant interval, it can be added, there and then, as an extra part:  or, on the other hand, its presence may be due to

the progression of a part already present.

To effect this, the 9 must be taken as $\frac{9}{7}\frac{}{5}_{3}$ (the 7 being ready to hand from the previous chord) as shown in Ex. 22.

This course is, in the present case (as in subsequent examples), fully justified by the fact that Leclair not unfrequently uses the single figure 9 in cases where (as in Ex. 21) the preparation of a subsequent discord makes the inclusion of the 7 a matter of necessity. Cases will, no doubt, arise in which

which the sharpened note would naturally rise and the anticipation of a flattened downward passing note (*anticipatio transitus per ellipsin*), as:

(cf. Ch. xi, 'Sevenths', I, § 2, extract from Marpurg; also Ch. xxii, 'Inversion and transference of discord &c.', § 7).

it is difficult to decide upon the course to be adopted, and, in such, the accompanist must largely be guided by the practice of the composer in question in the matter of complete or incomplete figuring.

Leclair, *Sonatas for Violin and Bass*, Book 2, Sonata I, Allegro ma poco, 2nd section, bars 9–14.

N.B.—The positions are to be avoided in which the consecutive 4ths between bars 1 and 2 ($_c^f \, _b^e$), and between bars 3 and 4 ($_a^d \, _g^c$), appear as 5ths (cf. note 7).

Ibid., Sonata IX, Adagio, 2nd section *ad fin.*

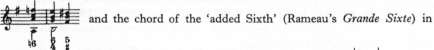

[9] The very remarkable progression shown in bars 1 and 2 of this example is extremely characteristic of Leclair (cf. Ch. xii, '$_5^6$ chords', § 2 d).

It is a sort of hybrid compound of the 'Neapolitan' Sixth (which falls a semitone): and the chord of the 'added Sixth' (Rameau's *Grande Sixte*) in

which the 6 normally rises to the 3 of the following chord: In the

present case the latter progression of the 6 is, of course, impossible (as also between bars 3 and 4) owing to the suspended 4.

[10] For the doubling of the (temporary) leading note (*g sharp*) at *, cf note 8.

Ibid., Book 1, Sonata II, Corrente *ad fin.*

Ex. 24

N.B.—(1) The crosses + over the Violin part denote trills, as in Ex. 23 and other examples. (2) The barred 6̄ (over *a*) was used by Leclair in Book I *only* of his Sonatas for Violin and Bass to denote $\frac{6}{4}$ (*la petite Sixte*), whether the Sixth was *major or minor* (cf. Ch. xxiii, 'Varieties of figuring', §§ 8, 9).

Here, again, it seems probable that Leclair meant the 9 to be taken (as above) as $\frac{9}{7}$, but it can, of course, be taken as $\frac{9}{5}$, adding a fifth part to the next chord:

Ibid., Book 2, Sonata VI, Allegro ma poco, bars 19–23.

Ex. 25

The 9 (in bar 2) has been taken as $\frac{9}{7}$, but the accompaniment might equally well begin as follows (adding the fifth part on the second beat of bar 2):

The preparation of the discord (9) by a note of shorter duration * (as in Exx. 5 and 20), in which case the discord is *not tied*, is a licence permitted in the free style (*der galante Styl* of the German treatises).[11]

---

[11] The 'strict style', on which the rules for the preparation and resolution of discords, &c., were ordinarily supposed to be based (unless the contrary was stated), was variously known in German treatises of the eighteenth century as *Stylus gravis* or *der schwere Styl, der gearbeitete* (lit. 'worked') *Styl*, and *der gebundene* (i.e. 'tied' or 'syncopated') *Styl*. Heinichen speaks of the *Stylus gravis* as synonymous with *Allabreve*. In his chapter 'On the theatrical resolutions of discords' (*General-Bass &c.*, 1728, Part II, Ch. I, § 4, p. 586) he says: "With the *Stylus gravis*, or so-called *Alla-*

§ 5. *The compass of the accompaniment*:

A, in itself.

B, in relation to the principal part.

A. In practically all the text-books of the eighteenth century the rule is laid down that the upper part of the accompaniment should not go above f''; in some cases the rule is added that the lowest of the middle parts should not go below g or f in the Tenor Octave.

Marpurg is slightly more liberal: he tells us that, in the ordinary way, the right hand must not readily go below e or above g'' (*Die Kunst das Clavier zu spielen*, Hauptstück II, Cap. II, § 24, p. 36).

The reason for these rules evidently was: (1) that there should not be too

breve, our predecessors (*die Alten*) invented for us the first rules for a correct (*legal*) resolution of dissonances. . . ."

The *Allabreve*, thus taken as the archetype of strict style, was characterized, as Heinichen explains elsewhere (ibid., Part I, Ch. IV, § 38, p. 333), by two minim beats, and not more than two harmonies to the bar. The quickest notes, generally speaking, were crotchets, moving for the most part by step, and the art of the composer was displayed chiefly in the number of suspensions and syncopations that he was able to introduce (see Ch. xviii, 'Quick notes in the Bass', § 3 *n*).

Contrasted with this was the free style, *der galante* or *leichte Styl*, which was characterized, first and foremost, by its greater laxity in the *treatment of discords*.

Kirnberger (*Kunst des reinen Satzes &c.*, Part I, 2nd ed., 1774, Section V, p. 80) writes: "The former, or strict, style is used chiefly in Church Music, which is always of a serious or solemn character; but the latter belongs chiefly to the stage and to concerted music (*den Concerten*), in which the aim is rather to delight the ear than to awaken serious or solemn feelings. It is, therefore, generally known as the *galant* style, and various elegant departures (*Ausschweiffungen*), and sundry deviations from the rules are conceded to it."

It must not, however, be supposed that it is by any means confined (as Kirnberger seems to suggest) to secular music, of whatever kind. It will be found to predominate in such a work as, for example, J. S. Bach's B minor Mass! To quote Heinichen once more (ibid., Introduction, p. 24):

"And, oh, how beautifully it delights the ears when, in an exquisite piece of Church- or other music, we hear how an intelligent Master (*Virtuose*) has endeavoured from time to time, by his *galant* forms of expression and by their appropriateness to the words ('durch seine *galanten* und dem Text ähnlichen *expressiones*'), to move the feelings of his hearers and thus to attain successfully the true end of Music."

Heinichen appends a note in which the words occur: "Wherefore the practical musicians (*Practici*) of to-day are rightly wont to depart from the unseasoned (*ungesaltzen*) character of a too antique Church-style."

It is, however, Kirnberger to whom we are indebted for a detailed enumeration (following the passage quoted above) of the liberties characteristic of the free style.

His list, freely condensed, and with references to subsequent chapters of the present work in which either Kirnberger's own examples or similar ones are quoted, is as follows:

(1) Certain liberties in the treatment of discords, as:

(*a*) The taking of the Dominant and Diminished Sevenths, and their respective inversions, without preparation (cf. Ch. xi, 'Sevenths', 1, § 2, III, § 2; Ch. xii,

'$^6_5$ chords', §§ 1, 4; Ch. xiii, '$^4_3$ chords', § 1 *ad fin.*, § 3 *a*. 2; Ch. xiv, '$^6_4$ chords',

§ 1 *ad fin.*, § 3, Exx. 1–3, 6, 7, 9, 11).

(*b*) Irregular progressions resulting from

(α) ellipse of the resolution (cf. Ch. xxii, 'Inversion &c.', § 8);

(β) ellipse of the resolution combined with the anticipation of a passing note, *anticipatio transitus per ellipsin* (cf. l.c., § 7).

(*c*) The reappearance and resolution of a Dominant discord (Seventh) in a different part [and in a different Octave] from that in which it first appeared

great a gap between the Bass in the left hand and the chords in the right, and (2) that the general effect of the harmony should not be too ponderous.

> (cf. Ch. xxii, 'Inversion &c.', § 2, Ex. 2), and the passage through successive inversions before resolution (cf. l.c., Ex. 1).
> [Kirnberger omits to mention the parallel case of the Diminished Seventh (Dominant minor Ninth): cf. Ch. xxi, 'Incomplete figuring', v, § 3, Ex. 5.]
> d) The use of a Stationary Seventh (cf. Ch. xi, 'Sevenths', v) on a strong beat, as at * *:

(cf. also l.c., § 4, Ex. 5).

> (e) The corresponding use of its first inversion, as at + in the preceding example (cf. Ch. xii, '$\frac{6}{5}$ chords', § 8, Exx. 1, 2, and note 2).
> (f) The use of unresolving discords arising through the sustention of the same harmony over passing notes (in the Bass) *of greater duration* than would be permitted in the strict style, as:

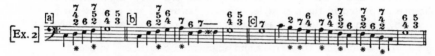

[N.B.—The first crotchet (a) of bar 2 of Ex. b is a particularly bold form of accented passing note, since it 'passes', not to a $\frac{6}{4}$ on g (as in bar 3 of Ex. c), but to *another interval of the same harmony*.]

> (g) The similar use of unresolving discords arising from
>> (α) passing notes of long duration in the upper parts over a stationary Bass, as:

(cf. Ch. xiv, '$\frac{6}{4}$ chords', § 7).

>> (β) passing notes in the Bass, connecting the Dominant Seventh with its first inversion, as:

N.B.—Kirnberger omits to mention the parallel (and not uncommon) case of a similar transition from first to second inversion and vice versâ as:

(2) The preparation of a discord by a note of shorter duration than itself, in which

The chief exception to the restricted upward compass of the accompaniment arose in the case of *Bassetti*, i.e. when C clefs were employed in the Thorough-Bass (cf. § 6).

Apart from this, however, the rules (as regards both the upward and the downward compass) admitted of many exceptions, to be regulated chiefly by the taste and common sense of the accompanist.

The following passages from well-known treatises will illustrate this:

(1) Niedt (cf. Ch. I, § 25), in his *Musicalische Handleitung zur Variation des General-Basses &c.*, 1706, re-edited by Mattheson 1721, writes as follows: (Ch. vi, § 4): "Such *formulae* [i.e. broken chords] may be varied in many

case, however, the discord *is not tied to the note of preparation*, but is struck afresh [cf. Ex. 5 of the preceding section].

(3) The repetition of a discord before resolution.

(4) The use of changing (i.e. accented passing) notes (cf. under 1 *f*, Ex. 2 *b* and *c*).

(5) The use of 'false progressions', i.e. by augmented intervals.

(6) The free use of the consonant $^6_4$ [i.e. on a weak beat], which, in the strict style,

is permitted only in the cadential formula:

From the above list Kirnberger has omitted one very important instance of the licence permitted in the free style, namely, the use of the progression $^5_4$ $^-_3$ with the 4 taken, not in the usual way as a suspended discord, but as a free *appoggiatura*, as in the following examples from Ph. Em. Bach (*Versuch &c.*, Part II, 1762, Ch. 21, § 7 *a, b*) in which both the perfect and augmented Fourth are so used:

We may well conclude with an example of this same licence from J. S. Bach's B minor Mass (*Christe Eleison*, B-G ed., p. 39, bar 4):

Ex. 6

The progression of the harmony in the accompaniment becomes clearer if the unessential notes in the Bass are eliminated:

It will be observed that, *in the voice part*, the ♮ 9 over *b* is taken unprepared, whereas the ♮ 4 over *g* is prepared in the voice part, but not in the accompaniment.

ways, and, with springing chords, one can pass through the whole range of the keyboard, right up to the top *c* [*c'''*].'' To this Mattheson adds: "Any to whom this may seem strange in a Thorough-Bass ... should consider how the matter stands in the case of a 4-foot stop on the Organ; and, although, in a Thorough-Bass, the latter is not used alone, it can, nevertheless, very well be drawn, in the shape of a *Nasat* or Flute, with an 8-foot *Gedackt.* ..."

It must, however, be remembered in connexion with the above, that in the work in question, Niedt was giving directions, not for accompaniment, but for free improvisation on a given Bass. What he here says can, therefore, be applied only to those passages in a figured Bass accompaniment in which a prolonged pause, or sustained notes, in the principal part give the accompanist the liberty to make something of a display.

(2) Heinichen, in the course of a chapter 'On ornate accompaniment' (*Vom manierlichen General-Bass*), gives an example of a form of accompaniment especially suitable (he tells us) in the *Ritornelli* of Airs without instrumental accompaniment, or during *sostenuto* passages in the Solo part ('wozu insonderheit die *cantablen Solo* und leeren *Rittornello* der Arien ohne *Instrumente* die beste Gelegenheit geben'), but also admissible whenever it is not prejudicial to the effect of existing [principal or *ripieno*] parts ('so weit es denen dazu componirten Stimmen nicht *Tort* thut'), namely, an ornate melody in the right hand with plain chords in the left (cf. Ch. IV, 'On certain niceties of the accompaniment', § 3, III, Ex. 12 *b*). The following bar shows the upward extent of the compass employed:

Ex. 1

N.B.—The signs ⟋⟍ and ⫽ here denote a (long) *appoggiatura* and a *mordent*, respectively.

Heinichen appends the following highly instructive footnote (*General-Bass &c.*, 1728, Part I, Ch. vi, § 28, note h, p. 548): "When our predecessors (*die Alten*) gave the rule that the right hand should not readily go above *c''*,[1] and on no account whatever above *e''*, they sought thereby to avoid in their accompaniments, which were then very thin (*schwach*), and usually only in three parts,[2] too large a *vacuum*, or empty space between the hands, and in this they were perfectly justified.

"Indeed, for a similar reason, this very same rule holds good to-day in the case of an accompaniment in four or five parts, in which the parts are equally divided between the hands, and where it would sound bad if, for example, two parts were to be played very high up, in the right hand, and two very low down, in the left. On the other hand, there are two cases in which, to be sure, the old rule lapses naturally (*fällt ... von sich selbst weg*): namely, (1) in a very full accompaniment,[3] in which the two hands cannot, in any

---

[1] Werckmeister gives *c''* as the highest note to be used (cf. *Die nothwendigsten Anmerckungen &c.*, § 56 of the 1715 edition).

[2] Cf. § 3, II, note 7.

[3] Cf. § 38 of the extract from Heinichen quoted in § 3, II, of the present chapter

case, leave a large gap (*vacuum*) between them, and, consequently, the right hand is the more inclined rather to get out of the way of the left into the higher registers; (2) in the above-mentioned melodic variety [of accompaniment], in which one seeks to execute with the right hand, quite alone, a melody, passages, arpeggios, and variations of all kinds, in which case a fancier can go right up to *x'''* if he thinks to achieve anything worth his while by so doing (*welchenfalls ein Liebhaber gleich in das 3 gestrichene x hinauffsteigen mag, wofern er etwas sauberes allda zu hohlen vermeint*)."

(3) Ph. Em. Bach's rule is as follows (*Versuch &c.*, Part II, 1762, Ch. 2 §§ 24, 25):

"With the right hand one does not readily go above *f''*, except the Bass go very high, or the Bass clef be replaced by a higher one, or unless a certain elegance is to find expression in the higher registers (*eine gewisse Zierlichkeit in der Höhe ausgedrückt werden soll*), as, for example, if the position of the chords is to be varied in a repeated passage,[4] &c.

"Further down than the middle of the Tenor Octave the right hand ought not properly to go (*darf die rechte Hand nicht wohl gehen*), except conditions prevail similar to those mentioned in the preceding §" [i.e. unless the Bass is exceptionally low, or (as we shall see later on) an instrument or voice of low pitch is being accompanied].

(4) Türk's instructions (*Kurze Anweisung &c.*, 1791, § 64) are almost identical and need not be quoted.

Instead of speaking of the 'middle of the Tenor Octave', he specifies *g* or *f* as the lowest notes to be taken with the right hand (subject to the exceptions indicated by Bach).

(5) Like Marpurg (see p. 360), G. M. Telemann (*Unterricht im Generalbass-Spielen*, 1773, p. 98) allows the right hand to go up to *g''* ("not readily above *f''*, [or] at most *g''*"), but limits its normal downward compass to *g*.

B. The compass of the accompaniment in relation to the principal part.

I. (*a*) In a general way, two main rules may be said to have found acceptance in the eighteenth century:

(1) The upper part of the accompaniment should avoid playing *continuously* in unison with the principal vocal or instrumental part.

(2) It should keep *below* rather than above it.

The second of these applies, of course, to what may be called the general level of the melodic outline and not, for instance, to the sudden dives into the lower registers so common in Violin music.

The principal treatises of the eighteenth century are somewhat reticent on the subject of the relation of the accompaniment to the principal part, and it is chiefly from stray references that the practice of the best exponents of the art is to be deduced; but there is ample evidence to prove that it was not in accordance with the taste of the eighteenth century to provide an accompaniment comparable with a leafy avenue beneath which (as in some modern examples of accompaniments arranged from a figured Bass) the melody was at liberty to wander in dignified seclusion.

(*b*) Thus, Quantz in his chapter on the duties of the Clavierist (*Versuch &c.*, 1752, Hauptstück [Section] xvii, Abschnitt [Subsection] vi) in which, like

---

[4] Cf. Ph. Em. Bach's recommendation to vary a repeated passage by the alternation of close and extended harmony (§ 3, V, Ex. 24).

Ph. Em. Bach, he betrays a considerable leaning to the *Pianoforte*, which he describes (l.c., § 17) as "uniting all the qualities necessary to a good accompaniment", tells us (l.c., § 21) that it is better for the upper part of the accompaniment to be *below the principal part than in unison with, or even above it.*

He goes on to say that a Violoncello must not be accompanied like a Violin, but that the accompaniment must be kept low. This, however, raises another question which must be dealt with separately.

(*c*) Ph. Em. Bach, in giving the rule that, in a close, the 5 of the Tonic chord must never be in the upper part (ibid., Ch. 2, 1, § 36), goes on to say that, next to the 8, the 3 is the best interval for that position, but that, in such case, the final note of the principal part *must never be below this 3.*

In a later chapter, on delivery, or style in performance (ibid., Ch. 29, 'Vom Vortrage', § 24), he gives some hints which deserve to be quoted: "If there are *ripieno* parts in a piece with a low principal part, one must listen carefully to their pitch (*Höhe und Tiefe*) and take the accompaniment of the *Clavier* within the same compass. The melody (*Gesang*) of the principal part *must never be obscured by middle parts going above it.* For this reason, for the sake of good effect and variety, composers sometimes put the middle part low down when the principal melody moves on that plane (*wenn der Hauptgesang sich daselbst aufhält*), and change with happy effect to the higher pitch in the *Ritornelli.* The accompanist must act in close accordance with all this. . . . Here we will merely recommend to accompanists what we have already frequently insisted upon, namely, that care be taken to secure an agreeable progression (*einen guten Gesang*) in the upper part. To that end, the best positions are, as far as is at all possible, to be selected, and, *if one finds oneself under the necessity of carrying the harmony above the principal part*, those intervals must be put in the upper part which move in Thirds or Sixths (*a*) with other middle parts, or (*b*) with the principal part, or (*c*) with the Bass:

(N.B.—The italics are not Bach's.)

In Ex. *b* an alternative accompaniment is given: in which it will be observed that the upper part is in unison with the Solo part.

Bach continues (l.c., § 25): "*Bad* ('verwerflich') *as is the accompaniment of which the upper part continuously repeats the melody of the principal part*, it is sometimes none the less necessary, and consequently likewise permitted, at the beginning of a *quick* piece, especially if the latter is in two parts [i.e. Solo and Bass]. In this way the players, as it were, join hands (*bieten sich die Hände*) in the matter of the *tempo*. . . . Weak musicians in general, whether accompanying [5] or leading, are allowed this assistance, *even otherwise than at the beginning* [*of a piece*], if by such means they are able to regain the equality of time which they had lost."

N.B.—The italics at the beginning of the paragraph are not Bach's.

II. The compass of the accompaniment in relation to instruments or voices of low pitch.

(*a*) Quantz's assertion that, in accompanying a Violoncello, the pitch of the accompaniment should not be the same as in the case of a Violin, has already been mentioned (I *b*). What he says applies, of course, to any other two instruments or voices which, when playing, or singing, the same piece of music in the same key, differ by an Octave in pitch.

(*b*) Ph. Em. Bach evidently shares Quantz's view on this highly important question. In the section preceding the ones last quoted (l.c., § 23) he says: "When accompanying an instrument of low pitch, a Bassoon, Violoncello, &c., or a low voice, a Tenor or Bass, in a Solo or an Aria, one must never, as regards height, get too far from the principal part, but must pay careful heed to the extent of the compass within which the latter moves (*auf die Weite der Modulation der letztern*). In such a case one does not readily take the harmony above the Octave indicated by a single stroke (*die eingestrichene Octave*, i.e.

). If it is necessary to take the chords quite low down, the harmony must be thinned, as a low position (*die Tiefe*) does not admit of much harmony without loss of clearness."

(*c*) Türk, whose authority is by no means negligible, expresses a view greatly at variance with that of Quantz and Ph. Em. Bach. The paragraph in which he deals with the compass of the accompaniment (*Kurze Anweisung &c.*, 1791, § 198), and in which it will be seen that he is in perfect agreement with the general principles already set forth (cf. B I), is worth quoting *in extenso*:

N.B.—The italics are not Türk's.

"With regard to the position to be chosen in reference to the upward and downward limits of the compass ('in Absicht auf Höhe und Tiefe') the most necessary general information has already been given in § 64. That is to say, the accompanist ('Generalbassspieler') is at least not to go above whatever part is for the time being the principal one ('die jedesmalige Hauptstimme'). Indeed, if it can be avoided, the upper part of the accompaniment is not readily allowed to move in unison with the principal part. That being so, the accompaniment at (*a*) is, from this point of view, already too high [see Ex. 3]. On the other hand, one may, in various cases, *accompany a Bass or Tenor voice, as also the Bassoon, Violoncello, &c., a whole Octave higher*,[6]

[5] i.e. playing *ripieno* parts.
[6] Here Türk appends the following footnote: "This, it is true, is unreservedly forbidden in several good text-books; but, in spite of that, I cannot see how it can always be avoided, e.g. in Recitatives intended for a Bass. For a Bass, as we know, has most notes to sing in the Tenor Octave (*in der sogenannten kleinen oder unge-strichenen Octave*). But how far down would not the accompanist have to carry the middle parts of the accompaniment if he were not allowed on any consideration to

because, namely, middle c ('das eingestrichene c'), for example, sung by a Bass, *is in so far accepted on keyed instruments* ('Klavierinstrumenten') *&c. as the c above.*[7] Consequently, for the bar given at (*b*), the accompaniment added at (*bb*) may perhaps ('allenfalls'), if the circumstances demand, be chosen. In certain passages, e.g. where the composer has left a considerable gap between the Bass and the other parts, it has a good effect to accompany the principal parts an Octave lower, as at (*c*) and (*cc*).[8] For the rest, pieces of cheerful, joyous, lively, &c., character are, in general, accompanied high up rather than low down; but pieces of sad, serious, solemn, &c., character, low down rather than high up:

(*d*) In estimating the difference between the views of Quantz and Ph. Em. Bach, on the one hand, and Türk on the other, the conclusion will probably be reached that the truth, as so often, lies in the middle.

accompany the deeper voices an Octave higher! Just imagine Tenor *d* in the voice, and, below this *d*, some chord or other as accompaniment!"

[7] Türk here raises an exceedingly interesting question in acoustics. It is obvious that one of the objections to accompanying e.g. the Violoncello in the same Octave as the Violin is the danger of Fourths appearing by inversion as Fifths. Supposing the following passage for the Violin, accompanied (in two parts only) on the Pianoforte (*a*), be played an Octave lower on the Violoncello, the result, *as far as absolute pitch is concerned*, is seen at (*b*):

Yet the effect on the ear is quite different, as may readily be ascertained by actual experiment. In fact, the *higher* (but *not* the lower) notes of a Violoncello (or a Bass voice), in their relation to keyed instruments of 8-foot tone, are, for all practical purposes, accepted by the ear (in accordance with Türk's statement) as an Octave higher than their actual pitch as measured by the number of vibrations per second.

[8] Quantz (ibid., l.c. § 22) tells us that, in passages of this sort, "where $\frac{5}{3}\frac{6}{4}\frac{7}{5}\frac{6}{4}\frac{5}{3}$ and the like occur over a stationary Bass", if the *higher* figures (5 6 7, &c.) occur in the principal part, *the order is best reversed in the accompaniment* ($\frac{3}{5}\frac{4}{6}\frac{5}{7}$, &c.), or, better still, the lower figures (i.e. in the reversed order) *may be omitted altogether.* In Türk's example there are *two* principal parts; this being so, Quantz would, no doubt, have wished both intervals to be present in the accompaniment, but in *reversed order*:

Ph. Em. Bach, whose opinions on the details of accompaniment are always well worth recording, mentions an analogous case of which he writes as follows (ibid., Ch. 29, § 22): "When the principal part moves in Tenths with a middle part [as e.g.

From Ph. Em. Bach's words, when he speaks of not getting "*too far* from [i.e. above] the principal part", and, again, of the necessity of taking the chords "quite low down", we may infer that, where the accompaniment of Bass instruments or voices was concerned, he regarded the rules against (1) going above the principal part, and (2) going below *g* or *f* with the right hand, as more or less in abeyance.

At the same time, if the same piece be played alternatively, either on the Violin, or (an Octave lower) on the Violoncello, most musicians will probably agree that, *in a very large number of cases*, the same accompaniment is suitable to either: especially so, where it is the *a*-string of the Violoncello that is chiefly employed.

There is one small point to be noticed in connexion with the second of Türk's examples (Ex. 3 *b*). Although he agrees with the undesirability of allowing the upper part of the accompaniment to move in *unison* with the principal part, he, nevertheless, in this instance, sets it in *Octaves* with the latter. He does not indicate whether the passage in question is to be regarded as belonging to an *Adagio* or an *Allegro*, but, bearing in mind his clearly expressed views on the relation between the *spirit* of the music and the *pitch* of the accompaniment, one might have expected the example to be treated, in the one case, as (*a*) and, in the other, as (*b*):

The *main principle* underlying all the rules for accompaniment that were ever given in the seventeenth and eighteenth centuries, from Viadana on- wards, was that the bread, so to speak, must not be taken out of the mouths of the principal performers, and the fact that Türk did *not* treat the example in question in either of the ways just suggested may probably be taken as an indication of a feeling that, if the accompaniment *had to be* above the principal part, the latter would be *less obscured by an upper part moving in Octaves above it than at some other interval.*

If this is so, Türk was at variance with an older writer already mentioned (Ch. I, § 20), whom it may not be amiss to quote (apropos of the whole question under discussion, and especially of the point just raised), although the seventeenth century is outside the scope of the present chapter.

in a Trio for 2 Violins and Bass], instead of these Tenths, the accompanist takes Thirds low down:

"The doubling of the principal part in Octaves has a better effect here than the doubling of the Tenths."

[With regard to the low pitch of this example, see § 3, note 30.]

Lorenzo Penna writes as follows (*Li Primi Albori Musicali*, 1672, Book III, Ch. 21, Rules 10–13):

10. "In playing with a Soprano or Contralto, one must not play above the [principal] part, or make diminutions."

11. "In playing with a Tenor, one may go above it, and, moreover, remain above it, but *not play in the [upper] Octave the notes which it sings*, nor make diminutions."

12. "With a Bass, one may make some little movement, but if the Bass has passages, it is not good to move at the same rate."

13. "In accompanying a single voice, one must not play more than three or (but very rarely) four parts, and *it is not good to put the Octave* [i.e. of the Bass] *at the top*." (Cf. p. 153, note 60.)

(N.B.—The italics are not Penna's.)

III. The pitch of the accompaniment in relation to discords in the principal part, and other special cases.

(*a*) It is abundantly clear from what has gone before (it is only necessary to refer to Ex. 3 and to note 8) that the question of consecutive 8ves (or unisons) between the principal part and one or other part of the accompaniment, *as a grammatical blunder*, does not arise. It is solely from the point of view of *taste* that it is held to be undesirable for the *upper part* of the accompaniment to reduplicate the melody of the principal part.

The question has, however, been recently raised as to whether the resolution of a *discord* in Octaves with (i.e. below) the principal part is permissible.

Referring to the following passage by Professor Max Schneider (*Bach-jahrbuch*, 1908, p. 101): "that certain ill-sounding progressions (some Fifths) must be avoided is a matter of course; but for this or that part of the accompaniment to coincide with the Solo-part (*wenn diese oder jene Stimme der Begleitung mit der Solo-Stimme geht*) was, and is (even at the present day), perfectly natural; for how could it be avoided without artificial device (*Künstelei*) in a piece with several Solo- or otherwise independent parts?", Herr Johannes Schreyer writes (*Beiträge zur Bach-Kritik*, Dresden, Holze und Pahl, 1910, p. 15): "In my opinion, too, it is perfectly natural for one of the parts in the accompaniment occasionally to move in Thirds or Sixths with the Solo-part (under certain circumstances in Octaves as well, provided that suspensions [*Vorhalte*] are not doubled), wrong, on the other hand, if consecutive Fifths [9] or Octaves of the following kind result:

Ex. 5   (*Grave*, bars 8, 9)

[9] No consecutive *Fifths* between the principal part and the accompaniment occur in either of the two examples quoted by Schreyer (from dall' Abaco, Op. 4, Sonata 3, republished, with an accompaniment set out from the Thorough-Bass, in the *Denkmäler der Tonkunst in Bayern*), of which only the first is given here, as it suffices to illustrate the point at issue.

The Octaves to which Schreyer (presumably) does *not* object, since they remain unmarked in the example, are seen between the Alto of the accompaniment and the Violin, in the last two quavers of the first bar. Of the two pairs which he regards as incorrect, the first occurs in the case of a ♮4 3 suspension over *b* flat, and the second, in that of the resolution of ⁶₅ on the Subdominant in a full close. We may take it, therefore, that his rule is that neither suspended *nor essential* discords in the principal part should be doubled in the (lower) Octave in the accompaniment.

In the present instance this could, it is true, be avoided easily enough, because both the discords in question (in the principal part) happen to be *within the permitted upward compass of the accompaniment* (cf. A).

But let us see what the result would be in other cases, if the rule were carried to its logical conclusion. It would mean either (1) that every discord in the principal part, higher than *f''*, would have to be *omitted altogether* (or else deprived of its legitimate resolution) in the accompaniment, or (2) that the upward compass of the accompaniment would have to be *indefinitely extended*—sometimes beyond the compass of the Spinet, Harpsichord, or Organ!

If any such necessity had existed, would not Heinichen, or Quantz, or Ph. Em. Bach have had something to say about it?

The nearest approach to anything of the kind, so far as the present writer is aware, is Werckmeister's warning to the effect that, in certain cases, e.g. when a singer expresses a particular emotion (*Affectum*) by means of a dissonance, it may be better for that dissonance (even though indicated in the figuring) to be omitted from the accompaniment (cf. Ch. I, § 24, VII, 1 *b*).

Niedt, too, tells us that it is not *necessary* to play an interval (N.B.—he does not specify a *discord*) present in the Solo part, even though figured (cf. Ch. I, § 25, III, 6, Rule 8).

But it is quite clear that both Werckmeister and Niedt were thinking of the *general effect*, not of grammatical rules, and that no idea of forbidden consecutives was, even remotely, present in the mind of either.

That the duplication in the lower 8ve (in the accompaniment) of a discord present in the Solo part is not, in itself, repugnant to a highly developed musical instinct of the very first order, is proved by the following excerpt from Joseph Joachim's realization (in vol. iii of his Violin School) of a figured Bass of Handel ('Twelve Sonatas or Solos for a German Flute, Hautboy, and Violin', No. 3, Allegro, bars 5 and 6 from the end):

(N.B.—In Joachim's arrangement the Bass is in Octaves; these are here omitted, and the original figuring is added.)

It will be observed that Joachim's treatment of the discord in question is precisely the same as that to which Herr Schreyer takes exception in the example from dall' Abaco.[10]

In conclusion we may quote Johann Friedrich Daube (*General-Bass in drey Accorden &c.* ['Thorough-Bass in three chords'], 1756, Ch. xi, 'On Accompaniment', § 7). After saying that, *in soft and delicate passages*, intervals which are present in the Solo part may be omitted from the accompaniment, but that this procedure is often carried to absurd extremes, he continues: "Such bad blunders must be guarded against. They often date from the schoolroom (*den Lehrstunden*), and arise from a too hardly stated rule, never, without any exception, to allow two 5ths or 8ves to be heard in succession. In that way all fulness of harmony is banned, and ignorance is encouraged."

(*b*) There is another case which demands mention. It is that of a series of Sixths in which the 3 and the 6 are present in the principal parts *at a higher pitch than is permissible in the accompaniment.*

If the latter be taken in the lower Octave, consecutive Fifths arise between the upper part of the accompaniment and the lower of the two principal parts, as:

Ex. 7

Are these Fifths objectionable? If so, the 6 would have to be omitted from the accompaniment altogether.[11]

---

[10] If further proof is needed, direct evidence of a similar kind is, fortunately, to be obtained from eighteenth-century sources as well. One of these is G. P. Telemann's *Singe-, Spiel- und Generalbass-Übungen* ('Exercises in singing, playing, and Thorough-Bass'), 1733–4, of which an account has been given in the second chapter (§ 8) of the present work.

A cursory search in the above has revealed five cases of a discord in the voice part reduplicated in the lower 8ve in the accompaniment. These are as follows:

(1) No. 3, ante-penultimate bar, $^6_5$ on leading note.

(2) No. 22, bar 4, $^6_4_3$ on Supertonic.

(3) No. 26, bar 6, $^6_5$ on leading note.

(4) No. 36, bar 6, $^6_5$ on leading note.

(5) No. 37, bar 5, $^6_5$ on leading note.

In all these cases the discord, it will be observed, is an essential one. In the following example from Ph. Em. Bach (*Versuch &c.*, Part II, 1762, Ch. 32, § 8, *n* [3]) we have a 4 3 suspension:

N.B.—This example is here given an 8ve higher than in the original, where it is given piecemeal on a single stave: (1) the Bass and Solo part, (2) the accompaniment (cf. § 3, notes 29 and 30).

[11] The only alternative would be so to arrange the harmony that the 6 never

Here, again, if this had been in accordance with the practice of the best musicians, we should surely have had a hint to that effect from one or other of the authorities already quoted!

Albrechtsberger, a late authority where the best traditions of the 'figured-Bass age' are concerned, does, it is true, unreservedly condemn these Fifths (and Octaves), which he denounces as 'ear-splitting' (*Sämmtliche Schriften über Generalbass &c.*, ed. Seyfried, vol. i, section 36); but he might with equal justice have condemned the use of 16- and 4-foot stops on the Organ, which give rise to consecutives of exactly the same kind!

It need hardly be pointed out that, if the progression $\begin{smallmatrix}13&13\\10&10\\6&6\\3&3\end{smallmatrix}$, shown in Ex. 7, were 'scored' in such a way that the *extreme parts* ($\begin{smallmatrix}13\\3\end{smallmatrix}$) were allotted to (say) *Violins*, and the *inner parts* ($\begin{smallmatrix}10\\6\end{smallmatrix}$) to (say) *Flutes*, or vice versâ, *the Fifths would be intolerable*; but not as long as the $\begin{smallmatrix}13\\10\end{smallmatrix}$ and $\begin{smallmatrix}6\\3\end{smallmatrix}$ are respectively allotted to instruments of the same tone.

Cases may, however, arise when, in a series of Sixths like the above ($\begin{smallmatrix}13&13\\10&10\end{smallmatrix}$, &c., with $\begin{smallmatrix}6\\3\end{smallmatrix}$ in the accompaniment), the temporary silence of the upper instrumental or vocal part (13) causes the Fifths ($\begin{smallmatrix}10&10\\6&6\end{smallmatrix}$) to become apparent, and, in such a case, a vigilant ear is needed to save the accompanist from mistakes if (as is most usual, except in the case of a Solo) he has only the figured Bass before him. The following example from Corelli (*Opera sesta*, Concerto VII, Andante Largo, bar 9 sq.) will illustrate the point:

Ex. 8

If Corelli's figuring is rigidly adhered to, the only way to escape mistakes is to play $\begin{smallmatrix}6\\3\end{smallmatrix}$ on the Bass notes figured 6, and to accompany the intermediate ones (marked *) with 3 only, or, better still, to treat them as though marked *tasto solo*:

On the other hand, there are certain liberties which, if not exactly to be recommended, may, nevertheless, sometimes be taken by a good accompanist on his own responsibility.

For one such we have the paramount authority of Ph. Em. Bach. Of the

---

appeared in the same part in two consecutive chords, by employing a highly artificial and ill-sounding progression, never found in the examples given by the best writers (save as an occasional *pis aller*), such as:

This entails the further disadvantage of having to use 4-part harmony in many cases in which lightness of accompaniment is essential.

following example (*Versuch &c.*, Part II, 1762, Ch. 34, § 2, Ex. *a*) he writes: "instead of 6, it is better to take 7 6 on *b*, in order that no Fifths may occur, if the principal part goes above the accompaniment:

12)
[Ex. 9]

If we feel ourselves justified in applying this recommendation to the somewhat analogous case presented by Ex. 8, it could be accompanied as follows:

Ex. 10

§ 6. *Bassetti.*

(*a*) The term *Bassetto* (Germ. *Bassett, Bassetgen*) was applied to all passages in a Thorough-Bass to which a C- or even a G-clef was prefixed.

The *Bassetto* had its origin in polyphonic compositions, in which, during a silence of the actual Bass, the lowest sounding part (even though it were the Soprano itself) was incorporated in the *Basso continuo* or Thorough-Bass, with or without its appropriate clef.[1] Hence the strict and invariable rule that a *Bassetto* must never be played in Octaves (or, of course, on the pedals of an Organ).

In the case of fugal entries the practice varied considerably. Where the Soprano entered first, the Soprano clef, even without the words *Tasto solo*, would be regarded as a sufficient indication that no harmony was to be played; and the same applies to the G-clef. When the next voice entered, the two parts might appear together (as in Heinichen's example below), to be played without further harmony; or, on the other hand, the lower part only might appear, with such figures as were supposed to enable the accompanist to follow the main outlines of the part above,[2] and with the appropriate change of clef. Thus the first two entries in the example to be given presently might well appear as follows:

[12] Given, in the original, on a single stave, Bass and Solo part only (cf. § 3, notes 29 and 30).

[1] (Cf. Ch. I, § 3 *ad init.*) In some of the earlier Basses of the seventeenth century it was sometimes *the lower Octave of the part in question* which was incorporated in the Thorough-Bass. An example of the kind from one of Viadana's *cento concerti* ('Sanctorum meritis') is given in Ch. I, § 15, III, where some curious comments on the point by Praetorius will be found.   [2] For note 2 see p. 374.

in which case it would be a matter of course that the harmony remained in two parts till the entry of the Tenor.

The rules for the treatment of *Bassetti* cannot be given better than in Heinichen's own words, and if any excuse is needed for giving the whole of his example (a little fugue which, he tells us, he abbreviated for the purpose), it is to be found in the fact that a *real* figured Bass (as opposed to isolated examples illustrating some particular chord or progression) set out, with all the freedom used in actual performance, by a contemporary musician (in this instance, probably, by the actual composer), is such a rarity [3] as to claim especial interest.

Heinichen writes as follows (*General-Bass &c.*, 1728, Part I, Ch. V, §18, p. 515):

(1) "In the said example the words *Tasto solo* are twice found written below. In the Italian language the wooden *Claves* of the Harpsichord (*Clavicembal*), Organ, &c., are called *Tasti*, from *tastare*, to touch or feel; therefore the words *Tasto solo* indicate that one is to continue to play the notes in question

---

[2] Both methods were adopted impartially by Purcell in his *Sonnatas of three parts*, 1683, as the following examples show:

Sonata I, *ad init.*

Sonata II, Allegro.

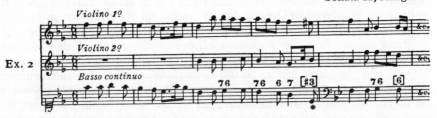

In this latter example it will be remarked that the last note of the *Bassetto* (marked *) is not present in the 2nd Violin part.

[3] The only (authenticated) specimens of which the present writer is aware are:

(a) Telemann's *Singe-, Spiel- und Generalbass-Übungen*, 1733/4 (cf. § 5, note 10).

(b) Kirnberger's setting out (in his *Grundsätze des Generalbasses*) of the *Andante* of J. S. Bach's Sonata in C minor for Flute, Violin, and Bass in the *Musikalisches Opfer* (cf. Ch. xix, 'The figuring of transitional notes', § 7, Ex. 4).

[N.B.—The accompaniment of the other movements, formerly attributed to Kirnberger, was the work of one Röllig, who was clearly not adequately equipped for the task (cf. an article on the Breitkopf and Härtel edition of the compositions of Frederick the Great in the *Allgemeine Musik-Zeitung*, No. 42, 17th Oct. 1890). Röllig's version is to be found in the Peters Edition, No. 287, where even the accompaniment of the *Andante* is not given as Kirnberger wrote it, being carried up, in one place, to ♭ c''', whereas the highest note in Kirnberger's version is ♭ g''.]

(c) Gerber's setting-out of the figured Bass of a Violin Sonata by Albinoni, with corrections attributed to J. S. Bach, given (in an Appendix) in Spitta's *Life of Bach*.

(d) One or two isolated cases like the present one, and also a few bars of the figured Bass of one of his own compositions set out by Praetorius (cf. Ch. I, § 15, Ex. 3 a).

with one key, or finger, at a time,[4] without further accompaniment, till another part, or another clef appears [or until the contrary is indicated by figures [5]]."

(2) "In several cases two parts only, one above the other, are to be seen, which means that, in such cases, not more is to be played than what is there."

(3) "It is to be generally observed, in the case of all Soprano-, Alto-, and Tenor-clefs occurring in a Thorough-Bass, that such *Bassetti* must never (as is permitted in the case of the ordinary Bass-clef) be continuously doubled in the lower Octave."

(4) "The harmony over the *Bassetto* may, however, be taken with both hands (but with a discreet regard to whether there are many or few vocal or instrumental parts co-operating) [6] in as many parts as the available space in the upper Octave of the keyboard permits."

(5) "The countersubject brought in in the last four bars,[7] in the upper part, has been given admittance to shorten the Fugue. Otherwise, however, an accompanist is not bound to divine the whereabouts of suchlike elaborated (*durchgeführt*) *themata, inventiones,* or *variationes* of a composer and to usurp the function of the parts devoted thereto, by imitating them (*und mit Nachahmung derselben, denen dazu gewidmeten Stimmen ins Handwerk zu fallen*). It is in his [*ex tempore*] preludes that a fancier (*Liebhaber*) can with better advantage qualify in such arts: that is really their proper place."

Ex. 1

Tasto solo

---

[4] *Tasto solo* (commonly abbreviated t.s.) must be carefully distinguished from *unisoni*, or *all' unisono*, which indicates, as Ph. Em. Bach tells us (*Versuch &c.*, Part II, 1762, Ch. 22, § 4), that the Bass may be played *in Octaves, with both hands* [or, at all events, with no harmony in the right hand], whereas *Tasto solo* denotes that *only a single key* is to be struck.

[5] If the first bass note following upon a passage marked *tasto solo* (t.s.) or *unisoni*, bears a Triad (which, in the ordinary way requires no indication), *one*, at least, of the intervals must be figured ($\frac{5}{3}$, 5, 3) to indicate the resumption of the harmony (cf. Ph. Em. Bach, l.c., § 10, and Ch. 23, § 9).

[6] This reservation is a very important one. In a fugal composition (for voices or instruments) *in four parts* only, if the chordal accompaniment begins (as in Heinichen's example) with the entry of the Tenor, it is clearly more natural that the harmony should, *in a general way*, not exceed three parts, though the necessity for a fourth may often arise.

Quantz tells us (without mentioning the change of clef) that: "When the Bass leaves its proper register (*Lage*) for that of the Tenor, the accompaniment must be in few parts, and quite close to the left hand" (*Versuch &c.*, 1752, XVII, vi, § 27).

[7] The counter-subject in question will first be found in bars 11–17; and afterwards, in combination with the main subject, from bar 25 onwards.

(*b*) The above example will be found amply to repay the trouble of a detailed analysis. From what has gone before, the reader will be able to detect where a new part is taken at the top, to secure a higher position, and a corresponding one dropped below (cf. § 4, 1); also to distinguish the real parts, forming the living tissue of the harmony, from those which have been added for the sake of fulness; some consecutives, too, will be found, besides those which, as Heinichen expressly tells us, may be disregarded in a filled-in accompaniment (cf. § 32 of the extract from that author, given in § 3, II, of the present chapter).

Thus, if we mark the entry of a new part by a rest before it, and the dropping of a part by a rest after it, and the coincidence of two parts in the unison by a double tail to the note in question (where it has been omitted by Heinichen), the harmony of the first bars will appear as follows:

In bar 8, on the third beat, the 8ve of the Bass *e* is added as a new part, which finally disappears after the second beat of the following bar. The harmony, though in five parts, is hardly full enough (one would have thought) to excuse the 8ves (Alto and Bass) between bars 8 and 9, which would almost certainly not have been passed by Ph. Em. Bach:

Marpurg, however, would possibly have excused them on the ground of a hypothetical crossing of parts, $^c_a \times ^{bb}_g$ (cf. § 9, 1, Exx. 3 and 4).

Apart from this, a remarkable feature of the harmony (in bar 9) is the coincidence of the two lowest middle parts in the unison *on the leading note* *e*,[8] which immediately afterwards appears, as a semiquaver, in the Bass also (thus, incidentally, giving rise to more Octaves).

The Bass of bar 9, stripped of passing notes, is:

G is the Supertonic, and it has always been accepted that 6 on the Supertonic may, at discretion, be taken as $^6_3$, the second inversion of the Dominant Seventh (cf. Ch. xxi, 'Incomplete figuring', II, § 1). In the present case, since Heinichen has included the 5 in the suspended Seventh on *g*, the resolution $^{7\,6}_{5\,4}_{3\,-}$ would be particularly natural, in which case the chord must *change from*

---

[8] The double tail, marking the unison, though omitted in the original, in the first instance, *is expressly added* in Heinichen's long list of *Errata*.

second to first inversion on the following note *e*, as indicated above in brackets, *in order to avoid 8ves with the Bass* in proceeding to the resolution on *f*. This kind of change has often to be made without being indicated in the figuring.[9]

In the first chord of bar 10, ⁶₅ on *e*, we again find an irregular duplication of the leading note by the inclusion among the upper parts of the 8ve of the Bass with a view, no doubt, to adding fulness to the chord.

Among the authorities of the eighteenth century Ph. Em. Bach is perhaps the most inexorable champion of correct progression, especially in the matter of avoiding consecutives. If, then, we sum up the points mentioned above, by attempting to reconstruct the accompaniment as we believe he would have approved it (picking up Heinichen's harmony, minus the extra part, in the middle of bar 8) we arrive at something like the following:

Bass in 8ves

The consecutives in bar 16 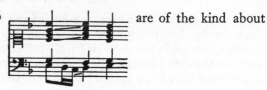 are of the kind about

which Heinichen expressly told us (in the passage before alluded to) that they could be disregarded in a filled-in accompaniment; and, if the latter is employed, it is obvious that they are unavoidable.

On the other hand, the 8ves (Alto and Bass) between bars 21 and 22

 seem entirely gratuitous.

Why did Heinichen not avoid them?

It must have been because they seemed to him the lesser evil as compared, on the one hand, with the loss of a sounding part (*a*), or, on the other, with a

more monotonous upper part (*b*):

The fact of the matter seems to be that, when Heinichen tells us that, in a filled-in accompaniment, all consecutives save those between extreme parts may be disregarded, *provided the hands are kept close enough together*

---

[9] Ph. Em. Bach (ibid., Ch. 32, § 8) writes: "Many mistakes can be avoided by interchanging the intervals of a middle part with passing notes in the Bass." (For his examples, see Ch. iv of the present work, § 5 *f*, Ex. 17.)

(cf. § 3, III, Exx. 8–10), *he is understating the case from his own point of view.*

Even apart from a filled-in accompaniment (in which the left hand reinforces the harmonies of the right) he seems to have, to a large extent, disregarded consecutive Octaves between a middle and an extreme part, generally the Bass, provided that (to use his own expression) there was no *vacuum* between the parts in question, and also provided that there was something to be gained, either in the way of sonority or what not! [10]

Finally, in the ⁶₅ chord on *e* (the leading note) in bar 24, we see the Octave of the Bass included as an extra part, although the Bass proceeds direct from leading note to Tonic without the intervention of the Dominant (as a passing quaver) as in bar 10.

In irregularities of this sort, a great factor (in accompaniments designed for the Harpsichord or Organ) was, no doubt, the rule (given most explicitly by Quantz, cf. § 11 *b*) that a discord (like a long *appoggiatura*) must be played *more loudly than its resolution.*

On the Pianoforte the need for an extra part disappears.

(*c*) The reader may well ask: why all this elaborate criticism of a simple example?

It is, assuredly, inspired by no wish to depreciate Heinichen, for whose earnest teaching, indeed, no sincere student can do otherwise than feel gratitude and admiration.

The object was merely to call attention to the kind of liberties (liberties which in a harmony exercise would rightly provoke the severest censure) which, at this period, were taken in the treatment of a figured Bass, not by the ignorant or unskilled, but by one of the soundest musicians of his day, a man whose name we never find mentioned without respect, and of whom Mattheson wrote in such terms as the following: "The work . . . of Herr Johann David Heinichen, Director of Music (*Capellmeister*) to the King of Poland and Elector of Saxony, rightly deserves to rank first, and it would be only superfluous here to spread the fame of this work, since it must already be in the hands of all, and it would be a real disgrace, both to a musician and to every proper connoisseur and amateur, not to possess it, or to value it as it deserves." [11]

It may not be inapposite to mention in this connexion that, in setting out an accompaniment from the figures, it is very easy to give the appearance of incorrectness where none exists. For instance, in employing the device of taking in a new top part (for the sake of gaining a higher position) and subsequently dropping its lower Octave, it is not always convenient to indicate the entry of the new part and the exit of the old one by placing a rest before the one and after the other. A glance at § 4, I, Ex. 2 (in which Kirnberger has, it is true, indicated the entry of the new part, *but not the converse process*), will make the matter clear.

The writer was present at a Bach Festival, held at Duisburg in 1910 under the auspices of the *Neue Bach-Gesellschaft*, and, at an informal congress of the members, at which matters connected with forthcoming publications of Bach's works were discussed, a desire was expressed for fully-set-out accom-

---

[10] Cf. Ch. IV, § 3, II, Ex. 3, note 6.

[11] Cf. *Grosse General-Bass-Schule*, 1731 (the 2nd edition of the *Organisten-Probe*, 1719), *Vorbereitung* (Introduction), § xiv.

paniments in place of, or in addition to, Bach's figured Basses. Various
reasons against this were advanced: buildings differed in their acoustical
properties, and so forth, and the accompaniment required to be modified
accordingly. But the writer had little doubt that the *real* (if subconscious)
reason in the minds of those concerned was the wise reflection that, in playing
from a figured Bass, it is often convenient to do things *which do not look well
on paper.*

(*d*) The subject of *Bassetti* may well be brought to a conclusion with the
following most remarkable example from Corelli (*Opera sesta*, Concerto VI,
Largo) in which the principal part (2nd Violin) actually goes below the
Thorough-Bass. In fact, for the space of half a bar, the Violin part forms
the Bass of what may best be described as an independent *stratum* of harmony.
The *same discord* is present in both *strata*, but in a different form, appearing,
over the Harpsichord Bass, as 7 6, and, over the Violin Bass, as $\frac{4}{2}$ ♭ 5, so
that the Violin Bass contains the *discord itself and its resolution.* The 7 6 in
the upper parts must, therefore, perforce *move in Octaves with the said Bass.*

The accompaniment is set out to make this clearer.

The Violin Bass in bar 2 is:

Ex. 2

We find a remarkable parallel to the above example (indeed the identical
duplicated harmonies) in Mattheson's *Organisten-Probe*, 1719 (or *Grosse
General-Bass-Schule*, 1731), *Mittel-Classe* [Middle Grade], *Prob-Stück*
[Test-piece] 13, for two *Cembali.*

The passage in question is as follows:

Ex. 3

In the Bass of *Cembalo I* the third quaver from the end of the bar (marked*)
is (in the wider sense) a passing note, not, indeed, belonging to the harmony
above it, but anticipating that which follows (cf. Ch. xviii, 'On quick notes in
the Bass', § 1 k). The final quaver is also a passing note (cf. l.c., § 1 h); the

outline of the Bass is therefore: an exact transposition of

Corelli's *Cembalo*-Bass  while the Bass of *Cembalo II* corre-

sponds almost exactly [12] with the Violin-Bass:

§ 7. *The use of Octaves in the Bass.*

Except when the Bass clef is replaced by a C (or even G) clef (cf. § 6), and except, of course, when the harmony is divided between the two hands, the Bass may always, *so far as is convenient and appropriate*, be played in Octaves.

It is not necessary to do more than produce the necessary authority for this statement.

(*a*) We have already had occasion to quote Heinichen's references to the matter [cf. (1) § 29 *ad fin.* of the extract given in § 3 II of the present chapter, (2) Rule 3 *ad fin.* in the extract given in § 6 *a*].

(*b*) Ph. Em. Bach, in speaking of *forte* and *fortissimo* passages, writes (*Versuch &c.*, Part II, 1762, Ch. 29, § 7): [1] "The mere doubling of the Bass in the left hand likewise has a penetrating effect, and is indispensable in cases where the notes are not very quick and can be easily brought out, but at the same time have a certain melodic progression of some duration (*dabey aber einen gewissen Gesang enthalten, welcher eine ziemliche Weile einnimmt*). In Fugues, when the subject enters [i.e. in the Bass], and imitations which call for a strong delivery, this doubling of the Bass is very effective. But if a subject, or, indeed, any phrase (*Gedanke*) demanding special expression, contains sundry florid figures (*bunte Figuren*) which cannot well be brought out in Octaves with one hand, then the principal notes, at least, are doubled, and the others played singly:

Example

(*c*) George Michael Telemann, grandson of the better-known George Philip, writes to much the same effect (*Unterricht im Generalbass-Spielen &c.*, 1773, Introd. § 8):

"As for the left hand, its sole concern, excepting the above-mentioned case [i.e. when the harmony is divided equally between the hands] is with the

---

[12] The correspondence would be perfect if (1) the last crotchet (*a*) in the Bass of *Cembalo II* were figured $^6_{5\flat}$ instead of 6, and (2) if the $^4_2$ and 5♭ in the Violin-Bass each included the 6 (*b* flat and *a* respectively). This would be the case if the 7 6

over *e*, in the Harpsichord-Bass of Ex. 2, were taken as $^{7,\,6}_{5\flat\,4}$, as:
$^{}_{3\,3}$

(for the inclusion of the diminished Fifth in the case of a suspended Seventh see Ch. xi, 'Sevenths', IV, § 5, and for the treatment of 6 on the Supertonic as $^6_4$ see $^{}_3$ Ch. xxi, 'Incomplete figuring', II, § 1).

The details do not, however, affect the remarkable parallelism between Exx. 2 and 3.

[1] The passage here quoted is the direct continuation of the extract given in § 3 IV *ad fin.*

Bass. This it can double in the lower Octave if the notes are slow. If the Bass is too low to double in the lower Octave, one either does not double it at all, or does so in the Octave above.[2] In any case this doubling is not a necessity, save when a loud accompaniment is wanted."

It would be easy, but is quite unnecessary, to multiply references to the same effect.

(d) From the above it will be seen that the employment of Octaves in the Bass (save in the case of *Bassetti*) was entirely at the discretion of the player, and that the two main considerations were (1) feasibility and (2) expression.

As far as the latter is concerned, it is obvious that the nature of the instrument employed is an all-important factor.

On Spinets, and Harpsichords with a single manual (and no stops), the only means of playing softly (besides a gentle touch, which does not of course, make approximately the same difference as on the Pianoforte) is to reduce the number of sounding parts,[3] and, in such a case, it is obvious that, in a *piano* passage, Octaves in the Bass are absolutely ruled out.

It must also be remembered that, on *quilled* instruments, whatever their appliances in the shape of a second manual and of stops, the resonance of the lower strings is very marked. On a Pianoforte, therefore, even a very soft passage might, in some cases, be played with a doubled Bass, whereas, on a Harpsichord, the same treatment would be highly inappropriate.

§ 8. *How far the accompaniment is expected to possess independent interest.*

(a) The question is often asked, how far an accompaniment extemporized (or set out) from a figured Bass is expected to be contrapuntal, or even imitative in character.

Before attempting to answer this question, it must be assumed that the reader has fully realized what has already more than once been pointed out, namely, that any display on the part of the accompanist must be strictly limited to the cases in which it can be indulged in without in any way competing with, or even obscuring, the activities of the principal part or parts (cf. e.g. Ch. I, § 24, VII 1 *a*; ibid., § 25, III 8 *d*; § 5, A of the present chapter, text preceding Ex. 1; ibid., § 5 B II *d*, *sub* Ex. 4).

Such cases arise primarily (1) *during prolonged pauses of the principal part or parts*, and (2) *during sustained notes occurring in the latter*. It is evident that both these cases are more likely to occur in a Solo than when two or more principal parts are employed.

(b) If we pass in review what is to be found in the pages of the principal authorities on the employment of contrapuntal devices in the accompaniment, it will turn out to be surprisingly little, which circumstance in itself almost

---

[2] This is sometimes a great convenience as a means of avoiding too great a space between the hands without, at the same time, getting too far down with the right hand. It must also be remembered that on the older Harpsichords and Spinets the lowest note ordinarily available was the 8-foot C. The 'short Octave', of course, imposed further limitations.

[3] Quantz tells us in § 17 of the Subsection referred to earlier in the present chapter (§ 5 B I *b*) that, on a Harpsichord with one manual, a *piano* is obtained by a gentle touch, and by reducing the number of parts; *mezzo forte*, by playing the Bass in 8ves; *forte*, in the same way, and also by doubling some of the concords in the left hand; *fortissimo*, by also breaking the chords rapidly upwards.

amounts to a proof that such devices were never recognized as, in any way, a necessary feature of a good accompaniment.

(c) Saint Lambert tells us (*Nouveau Traité &c.* 1707, Ch. IX, 12) that, *in accompanying a single voice*, and in cases where the music lends itself to such treatment, imitations may be introduced on the Harpsichord. He adds (very significantly): "But this demands consummate science, and, to be a success, must be of the first order" (cf. Ch. I, § 23 *k*, 12).

(d) Heinichen devotes an entire chapter to the subject of the embellishment of the accompaniment (*General-Bass &c.*, 1728, Part I, Ch. VI, 'Vom manierlichen General-Bass', &c. [On an ornate accompaniment, &c.]. In this he shows how an accompaniment may be adorned and made interesting in various ways (cf. Ch. IV, 'On certain niceties of the accompaniment', § 3), but as regards any form of imitation, the little that he says on the subject is in the sense of warning players against exploiting their skill in this direction, save under quite exceptional circumstances.

We have already heard his views on the employment, in accompanying a Fugue from the figured Bass, of a counter-subject taken therefrom (cf. § 6 *a*, fifth paragraph of extract preceding Ex. 1).

In the chapter referred to above (l.c. § 4) he concludes his list of the embellishments at the disposal of the accompanist with the words: "And, along with the others, we will further include imitation as a special form of embellishment (*Wobey wir noch die Imitation als eine besondere Manier mit anhängen wollen*)" (cf. Ch. IV, 'On certain niceties of the accompaniment', § 3, 1).

Later on (l.c. § 40) he returns to the subject, and what he says is so illuminating that no excuse is needed for quoting it *in extenso*:

"Finally, the second class of our embellishments was brought to a conclusion with imitation, which differs from the said embellishments in that it does not, as they do, depend on our own ideas, but must be derived from the text of the composition itself (*aus der vorgeschriebenen Composition selbst*). So, what is here called imitation is when the accompanist seeks to copy the beginning of a figure or invention of the composer (*eine angefangene Clausul oder Invention des Componisten*) in places *where the composer himself has not introduced it*. Now, since one must never thus get in the way of the singer or instrumentalist with this figure (*Clausul*), whenever he has it himself; and since, on the other hand, it is to be supposed that the composer is likely himself to have occupied with it the points where the beginning of an imitation (*seine angefangene Imitation*) is appropriate, and, consequently to have left the accompanist little scope for imitating, it is clear from all this that, on the *Clavier*, this form of embellishment is the most miserable of all (*die allerarmseeligste*).[1]

"But since, here and there, rare cases may occur in which, in a composition (particularly in Cantatas and Arias without instruments), there is a spot left where a clever accompanist might repeat a figure, given in the Thorough-

---

[1] Heinichen here adds the following footnote: "It is a different matter when one purposely puts before beginners, for practice and to sharpen their wits, the Thorough-Bass only of a piece previously well worked out in several parts, and lets them try to find out for themselves where the particular figure (*Clausul*), appearing here and there in the Thorough-Bass, may be introduced anew in the upper parts. Which good training (*Exercitium*) is carefully carried out throughout the whole of Mattheson's *Organisten-Probe*."

Bass or in the *Solo* part, more often than the composer himself has done, the following example may serve as something of an illustration; in it this further point is specially to be noted, that the right hand inclines to seek to accompany the *Solo* part in 3rds and 6ths, and, as it were, to form a concerted *Duetto* with it. This kind of imitation turns out particularly well in vocal pieces (*cantablen Sachen*), and is the easier to accomplish since, in Chamber- and Operatic music, it is possible, from the part generally written above [the Bass], to keep a close watch on the singer, to avoid encroaching on him, and, again, to follow in his steps (*nachgehen*):

[Ex. I]

Tu sei la speranza.

Larghetto

(1)   (2)   (3)

[Words discontinued in the original]

'Imitation in the right hand'

(4)   (5)   (6)

(7)   (8)   (9)

(10)   (11)

The above masterly little example is most instructive. In bar 4 we have a genuine imitation of the preceding vocal phrase; in the second half of bar 5 and the beginning of bar 6, and, again, in the second half of bar 8 and in bar 9, we have the 'concerted *Duetto*' of which Heinichen speaks, first in Sixths and then in Thirds; in bar 7 and the first half of bar 8 is found a most important device, which Heinichen does not specially mention, namely, *the establishment of a rhythmic figure* (which serves to maintain a balance between the principal part and the accompaniment) by means of an *ornamental resolution* of the suspended discords 9 and 4. Finally, in the short *Ritornello* (bars 10 and 11), we find the original theme most appropriately utilized in the upper part of the accompaniment in the second half of bar 10, as an imitation of the Bass in the first half. It must be clearly understood that in such a case as this (namely, where the principal part is silent), what Heinichen says against the employment of imitation does not apply. If there were *ripieno* instrumental parts, in which the composer might have introduced the imitation in question had he been so minded, the case would, of course, be different.

It is hardly necessary to mention that, where the right hand has to execute a definite theme, especially when wide intervals occur in it (as, for instance, the skip of an Octave with which the imitation in bar 4 begins), great care is needed to avoid undue curtailment of the harmony indicated by the figures, and also (perhaps more difficult still) to make a workman-like 'join' with the ordinary chordal accompaniment (where the latter is quitted and resumed), so far as is possible under the given circumstances.

(*e*) Ph. Em. Bach has a chapter (*Versuch &c.*, Part II, 1762, Ch. 33) entitled 'Imitation' (*Nachahmung*), but the imitation therein described is, for the most part, of an entirely different character from that with which we are now concerned.[2]

---

[2] The cases with which Ph. Em. Bach deals in six out of the seven sections which constitute the chapter, are those in which an imitation *already exists between the Solo part and the Bass*. The accompanist is then expected to follow (or even, when the point of imitation occurs first in the Bass, to precede) the Soloist in an *ex tempore* variation or embellishment of it. As Ph. Em. Bach points out, a perfect understanding between the two is necessary to success. He was, no doubt, thinking chiefly of cases where composer and performer were one, as he speaks elsewhere (ibid. Ch. 29, § 2) of a "piece which, according to the present fashion, he [i.e. the Soloist] must have produced himself".

His examples will make the matter clear. In Exx. 1 and 2 the Soloist leads with the point of imitation, and, in Ex. 3, the Bass. In all these examples, the first half shows *the composer's text*, as performed in the first instance, while the second half presents the same point of imitation, *as modified by either performer on repetition*. Bach's words, "Imitations are among those phrases (*Gedanken*) which are commonly varied *on repetition*," apply equally to the recurrence of an individual phrase in the course of a movement or section (as in Ex. 1), and also to the recurrence of a phrase or theme owing to the repetition of an entire section (or to a *da capo*), as in Exx. 2 and 3.

N.B.—Two points in the above require explanation: (*a*) The ornament ⁓ over *g* sharp was a favourite one of Ph. Em. Bach, called by him *prallender Doppelschlag*

At the end of the chapter, however, he gives two examples in which a kind of imitation is introduced, alternating with, and balancing, the rhythmic figure in the principal part.

They are given, as usual, on a single stave, and the suggested accompaniment is given separately. In order the better to visualize the relation between the latter and the principal part, they are here given on three staves, and an Octave higher than in the original.[3]

It will be seen that each example contains two alternative Solo parts, (*a*) and (*b*), over the same Bass, whereas only a single form of accompaniment is given; it is also evident that the latter was conceived with a view to the Solo part (*b*) rather than (*a*).

(i.e. a turn with a snap). The sharp (𝕏) above it (omitted in the Bass, by a misprint, in the

original) denotes *f* sharp, and the execution, with the *appoggiatura*, is:

(*b*) The diagonal stroke ╱ under the penultimate quaver of the second bar (a changing, or accented passing, note) indicates the striking with it of the harmony indicated by the following figure ($\frac{5}{3}$ on *a*). The alternative would be the figuring $\frac{7}{4}$ (cf. Ch. xix, 'The figuring of transitional notes', § 5).

[Ex. 2]

It will be observed that, in the above example, the variation of the Bass is attended by a slight change of harmony: $\frac{6}{4}$ (instead of $\frac{6}{3}$) on *b* flat &c.

[Ex. 3]

In this example, as above mentioned, *the accompanist has the lead*.

In such a case, Bach recommends extreme caution on his part: "in order that he may know how much to expect from the person following his lead (*seinem Nachfolger*) in the matter of variations." "If", he continues, "he cannot absolutely rely on his skill in this particular, he must give up his desire for variation and adhere to the plain notes."

He adds further cautions of which the two following are the most important:

(1) "Likewise, at the end of the variations, a return to simplicity must be made in the accompaniment, in order that the principal part may bring what follows, particularly if it consists of a number of figures (*Figuren*), to an especially brilliant conclusion (*damit die Hauptstimme ihre Nachfolge . . . ausnehmend endigen könne*)."

(2) "If the *Clavier*-player has several Basses associated with him, he must hold back with his variations, unless he is perfectly certain that the others can follow him."

Certain cases are then mentioned, passages which can be accompanied *with Thirds only*, in which the middle part, too, can share the variation of the point of imitation with the Bass.

One example only, of the three given, will serve to illustrate this:

[Ex. 4]

Then follow the examples (to be given in our text) in which a species of imitation *not already present in the composition*, may be introduced in the accompaniment.

[3] Cf. § 3 v, notes 29 and 30.

Ph. Em. Bach prefaces the examples as follows (l. c. § 7):

"Any one who possesses a good insight into the art of composition can, also, occasionally invent a middle part which elegantly imitates the principal part. Passages in which a number of Sevenths and $\frac{6}{5}$ chords occur, while the Bass notes rise and fall, are the most convenient for the purpose. The time must, however, not be very quick, or one falls into the error of indistinctness:

It is not quite clear whether Ph. Em. Bach intended the accompaniment to be in two parts only, or whether he merely omitted a third part as being unessential to the point at issue. The latter seems the more probable.

If this is so, and if the accompaniment be taken in three, rather than in four parts, the $^6_5$ chords in Ex. 3 may well be taken as $^6_3$, as the 5 is present in the Solo part, whereas the 3 would, otherwise, be entirely absent.

Besides the instances given above, Ph. Em. Bach makes a reference to imitation, illustrated by an example, in the preceding chapter (ibid., Ch. 32, 'Von gewissen Zierlichkeiten des Accompagnements' [*On certain niceties of the accompaniment*], § 9).

In enumerating the cases in which "certain skips with the harmony in the right hand" are admissible, he includes "certain phrases (*Gedanken*) which bear imitation".

The example is here given an 8ve higher than in the original, where it appears, as usual, on a single stave (cf. § 3, v, notes 29 and 30):

[Ex. 4]

(*f*) The last reference to the subject under discussion that need be quoted here is from Ch. XI, 'Vom Accompagniren' [*On Accompaniment*], of Johann Friedrich Daube's *General-Bass in drey Accorden* ['Thorough-Bass in three chords], 1756. The reference which he makes to J. S. Bach seemed a fitting conclusion to what has hitherto been said, and may be accepted as an excuse for departing slightly from chronological order by dealing first with examples from Ph. Em. Bach's *Versuch*.

It will be necessary to follow Daube through his somewhat lengthy, but highly interesting, classification of the different ways in which (according to him) the accompaniment may be treated.

He seeks to establish three varieties (l. c. § 1): (1) "die simple oder gemeine" (*the simple or ordinary*); (2) "die natürliche, oder die der Eigenschaft einer Melodie oder eines Stücks am nächsten kommt" (*the natural, or that which comes nearest to the character of a melody or of a piece*); (3) "die Künstliche oder zusammengesetzte" (*the artificial or composite*).

"The first", he tells us (l.c. § 2), "is the easiest. It is used in Solos, Trios, Airs, &c. The second is used in Recitatives, likewise when the principal part has long notes with little melody (*Gesang*)." [4]

"The third kind is only for a skilled master and composer. Its real purpose is, however, to give help to the upper melody [i.e. the Solo part], either by imitation or by the conduct of a second part (*Sie besteht aber eigentlich darum:*

---

[4] Daube here adds the following note: "Here the breaking of chords is appropriate, both in the upper and lower part, as is to be seen in the variations in the preceding chapter." Among the examples there given are the following:

*dem obern Gesang entweder durch Nachahmen, oder durch die zweyte Stimm-
führung aufzuhelfen*). This variety can be used in all pieces with few performers (*schwach besetzt*) or in few parts. Here, a good delivery (*Bespielung*)
and imitation of the melody, together with the appropriate embellishments
(*nebst den gehörigen Zierrahten*), contribute much to the maintenance of fulness of harmony (*Vollstimmigkeit*), and to the repair of mistakes arising in
this or that part. Altogether, this kind is calculated to preserve balance. But
it is rarely to be met with in perfection (*selten gut anzutreffen*)."

By the 'simple or ordinary' accompaniment Daube evidently means a plain
3- or 4-part chordal accompaniment, without any embellishment, or 'breaking'
of the chords, and without using the left hand to 'fill in' the harmony, except
in isolated cases, either for special expression or, as Daube himself phrases
it, as a "musical note of exclamation" (cf. l.c. §§ 3–9).

The second kind, he tells us, is derived from the first, and *differs little from
it*. Its special use is in the accompaniment of Recitatives, and its chief
characteristics are: (1) the greatest possible fulness of harmony (in both
hands), and (2) occasional (upward) breaking of the chords; "but this", we
are told, "must be done rapidly and with distinctness" (cf. l.c. § 10).

Elegant forms of arpeggio are a great feature, and are appropriate in Solos
when the two parts (Solo and Bass) move in equal long notes. Daube compares
this form of accompaniment with that of a Lute or Theorbo (cf. l.c. § 11).

"The third kind",[5] he continues (l.c. § 12), "arises: (1) When, by a skilful
alternation with the first kind, one sometimes tries to bring in syncopations
(*Bindungen*) [6] where the composer has not put them or expressed them by
figures. (2) When the principal part pauses:[7] here one can sometimes intro-

---

[5] Daube here adds the following note: "The excellent Bach possessed this third
kind in the highest degree. Through him the principal part was bound to shine
(*brilliren*). He gave it life by his perfect accompaniment, when it had none. He knew
how to imitate it so skilfully with the right or left hand, or unexpectedly to bring in
a countersubject, that his audience could have sworn that it had been so composed
with all care. At the same time the regular accompaniment [i.e. the harmonies indicated by the figures] was very little curtailed. Altogether, his accompaniment always
resembled a *concertante* part, elaborated with the greatest care, and taking its place
beside the principal part; at the right moment, the principal part was bound to shine
(*Überhaupt sein Accompagniren war allezeit wie eine mit dem grössten Fleiss ausgear-
beitete und der Oberstimme zur Seite gesetzte concertirende Stimme, wo zu rechter Zeit
die Oberstimme brilliren musste*). This privilege was also accorded to the Bass, without
prejudice to the principal part. Enough! Whoever has not heard him has missed
much (*hat sehr vieles nicht gehört*)."

The above enthusiastic account of Bach's accompaniment has a striking parallel
in the following well-known passage from Lorenz Mizler's *Musikalische Bibliothek*
(Part 4, 1738, p. 48):

"Any one who wants to get a real idea of delicacy in [playing from] a Thorough-
Bass, and of what good accompaniment means, need only trouble himself to hear our
Capellmeister Bach here, who plays any Thorough-Bass to a Solo in such a way that one
imagines that it is a Concerto, and that the melody which he plays with his right hand
has been composed like that beforehand. I can bear witness, for I have heard it myself."

In this account, however, no mention is made of *imitation*, but only of the beautiful
and elaborate melody.

[6] The syncopations here meant are evidently those arising in the case of suspensions
(4 3, 7 6, 9 8, &c.).

For the distinctive meaning of the term *Bindung* see Ch. i, § 18, note 2.

[7] It may be mentioned here that Daube consistently uses the term '*Ober*stimme',
usually applied to the upper part of the accompaniment, as the equivalent of '*Haupt*-
stimme' or principal part.

duce sundry melodic figures (*melodiöse Gänge*). (3) One can also move in 3rds or 6ths with the principal part.[8] (4) When one attempts to imitate the theme of the principal part, or even, at discretion, to let a countersubject be heard. (5) As it sometimes happens, too, that, even with a good principal part, the Bass is badly written: whether it be that it might have imitated [the principal part], but that this has been omitted from carelessness or ignorance, or that, where it might have moved in quick or slow notes, the very opposite is done. In such a case the accompanist might well take the liberty of trying to correct this without pausing in his accompaniment (*unter währendem Accompagnement*). But, in such case, regard must be had to the person whom one is accompanying. For such a procedure great insight and knowledge of composition, and exceptional caution, are required."

(*g*) What is now the conclusion to be drawn from the evidence produced? It may seem, at first, as though Heinichen and Daube were completely at variance on the subject of the employment of imitation in the accompaniment, while Ph. Em. Bach appears, perhaps, to occupy an intermediate position. But, upon closer examination, it will become apparent that no such great difference of opinion need be assumed.

It must be clearly kept in mind that at least two kinds of imitation are mentioned: (1) more or less *canonic* imitation, where one part follows the other, and (2) one in which a part of the accompaniment moves simultaneously, in Sixths or Thirds, with the principal part.

To these might almost be added a third variety, namely, the establishment of a sequential rhythmic figure in the accompaniment, following, and balancing, one present in the principal part. In this variety the actual intervals employed in the principal part *may* be more or less accurately reproduced in the accompaniment (as in Exx. 2 and 3), but the more important factor is the rhythmic balance, to which attention has already been called in connexion with the ornamental resolutions in bar 7 *sq.* of Ex. 1.

It is the first of these varieties which is now under discussion: that in which, as Heinichen expresses it, "the accompanist seeks to copy the beginning of a phrase or invention of the composer in places where the composer himself has not introduced it". It will be noted that this definition, 'the beginning of a phrase, &c.', does not apply to the sequential, and, as has just been pointed out, predominantly rhythmic imitation in Ph. Em. Bach's examples.

It is of this quasi-canonic imitation, then, that Heinichen tells us that "here and there rare cases may occur", &c., &c., while Daube, on the other hand, seems to regard it as a device which a sufficiently gifted accompanist (a *rara avis*, as he admits) might frequently employ with advantage.

He takes the opportunity of alluding to J. S. Bach's phenomenal mastery of this form of accompaniment (cf. note 5).

But what were the occasions on which Bach elected to display his powers in this direction? They arose, on the evidence before us, when a composition, *weak and devoid of charm in itself*, invited (or provoked) a gifted musician to lend it such interest as he was able by the subtlety of his accompaniment. "He gave it life", says Daube, "when it had none."

It will be remembered, too, that, among the devices characteristic of his third variety of accompaniment, Daube included the enrichment of the

---

[8] This is in accordance with Heinichen's recommendation (cf. Ex. 1, bars 5, 6 and 8, 9).

harmony by the addition of suspensions *not indicated in the figuring*, and even the *extemporaneous alteration of an unsatisfactory Bass*,[9] from which it is evident that he was thinking, not so much of the legitimate devices of a normal accompaniment, as of the means whereby the various faults of an unsatisfactory composition (such as poor harmony, or a lifeless melody) might, in some measure, be remedied.

When such an occasion arose, J. S. Bach may very well have amused himself by exercising his unrivalled contrapuntal skill in the good-natured endeavour to show a poor composition in the most favourable light, and we can well believe Daube's statement, that those who heard him thought that what he played must have been composed beforehand.

Apart, however, from such an abnormal occasion (and, more particularly, such a supernormal accompanist!) there seems to be no reason to distrust Heinichen's view, namely, that the introduction of a countersubject derived from the composition itself, though appropriate in an improvised prelude, is *out of place in accompaniment*,[10] and that the occasions when (canonic) imitation may be employed with advantage are very few and far between.

(*h*) Besides the purely contrapuntal devices discussed above, there are various ways in which the monotony of a purely chordal accompaniment may be relieved, and independent interest added to it, wherever this is appropriate: in other words, wherever it is *compatible with due subordination to the principal part or parts*. As has already been pointed out, such opportunities occur chiefly in *Ritornelli*, and during prolonged pauses of the principal part; also where the latter has long sustained notes, or is otherwise lacking in melodic interest.

Quite apart from all this, however, there is (as is only natural) an enormous difference between one Bass and another in the opportunity which they respectively afford for any sort of embellishment. This difference is, of course, to a large extent, inherent in the Basses themselves; but it also depends, in a very large measure, on the amount of detail presented by the figuring: *especially in the matter of passing notes to be introduced.*

Let any one take, for instance, the *Allemande* of J. S. Bach's Sonata in E minor for Violin and figured Bass (*B. G.* ed. xliii, Part I). If Bach's figures are adhered to, it will be found that, beyond the position in which the first chord is taken, *very little indeed is left to the fancy of the accompanist.*

It was, no doubt, similar fastidiousness in the matter of detail, on the part of composers, which eventually caused the whole system of figuring to fall

---

[9] Of such cases Ph. Em. Bach writes as follows (ibid. Introd., § 27): "In faulty and unskilled compositions, where there is very often no possibility of a correct middle part, on account of the falseness of the Bass from which they [i.e. the middle parts] ought to flow, one covers the mistakes, so far as is possible, with a thin accompaniment; one is sparing with the harmony; at a pinch, an interval [not indicated in the figuring] is included (*man greift zur Noth eine Ziffer*); . . . if one is accompanying alone [i.e. without string, or other, Basses] one alters the Bass on the spur of the moment and thereby gains correct and fluent (*natürlich fliessend*) middle parts just as surely as by adopting the same procedure with wrong figures. How often is not this latter expedient necessary!"

[10] Heinichen expressed this view in connexion with a *fugal* composition (§ 6 *a*, Ex. 1), whereas Daube, in speaking of a countersubject (*Gegenthema*), was probably thinking of one, to be invented by the accompanist, in a composition not necessarily fugal. Heinichen makes no special mention of this device, but it seems probable that he would have regarded its employment as on a par with that of canonic imitation, since what he says of the one applies, very largely, to the other.

into disuse. If a figured Bass was to become a sort of Tablature in disguise, its purpose, as a musical short-hand, was gone.

The practical details of the embellishment of the accompaniment are more conveniently treated separately and will form the subject of the next chapter.

As far as the general principle which governs the employment of such devices is concerned, it is well stated by Mattheson in the following words (*Organisten-Probe*, 1719, *Mittel-Classe* [Middle Grade], *Prob-Stück* [Test-piece] 9, *Erläuterungen* [Explanations], § 1):

"In this connexion the observation must again be made that, in a Thorough-Bass, there is rarely scope for ornate and florid playing (*das manierliche und bunte Spielen . . . selten Raum habe*) where the foundation [i.e. the Bass itself] is designedly written in an ornate and florid manner (*wo das Fundament selbst, mit Fleiss manierlich und bunt gesetzet ist*). If, on the other hand, the Bass is without special embellishment (*Zierath*), and one is playing alone, either at the beginning of an Air, in the middle, or wherever else there is a pause [in the principal part], it is then and there that these graces (*Manieren*), these figures, these fancies (*Einfälle*), these adornments (*Ausschmückungen*), which have been, amongst others, the principal objects in view in the present work, find their proper field (*ihren bequemen Ort*), nay, their almost necessary place."

§ 9. *The crossing of parts.*

I. *As a means of evading consecutives.*

Very little mention is made in the treatises of the eighteenth century of the crossing of parts in an accompaniment from a figured Bass, but there is enough evidence to show that the employment of this device as a means of escaping faulty progressions (*not* between extreme parts) in four- or five-part harmony, quite apart from those in a filled-in accompaniment (cf. § 3 II, note 12), was countenanced by such an authority as Mattheson, to a certain very limited extent by Heinichen, and, at a somewhat later period, subject to well-defined restrictions, even by Marpurg, but not, either for the purpose named or for any other, by Ph. Em. Bach.

The only reference which the latter makes to the practice, so far as the present writer is aware, is in connexion with Pedal Points, of which he writes (*Versuch &c.*, Part II, 1762, Ch. 24, § 5):

"The arrangement of the harmony is often such that one part rises above (*übersteiget*) another, which is liable to occasion a crossing (*Verwechselung*) of the parts in a Thorough-Bass, *which is not allowed, as otherwise many mistakes might be defended without the ear after all being satisfied.*" [The italics have been added.]

Heinichen, on the other hand, who, as we have seen, was quite uncompromising in his refusal to admit the possibility of justifying consecutives between *extreme* parts by any such device (cf. § 3 II, note 11), does not *unreservedly* condemn certain Octaves between Alto and Bass (i.e. neither between extreme nor *adjacent* parts) as in the following example:

Ex. 1

It is true that he condemns these 'suspicious and bad progressions', but he adds that "this particular kind of Octaves [i.e. between Alto and Bass] is *still often tolerated*, because they are more concealed from the ear by the adjacent parts and can, therefore, the sooner be *excused by the familiar crossing of parts*." [The italics are not Heinichen's.]

We have here a plain record of a growing sensitiveness in the matter of progressions which in 1728 (the date of Heinichen's treatise, published when he was 45 years of age) were evidently regarded as a relic of an obsolescent practice.

Mattheson, on the other hand, suggests the following treatment of a part of one of his Basses (*Organisten-Probe*, 1719, *Mittel-Classe* ['Middle Grade'], *Prob-Stück* ['Test-piece'] 22, *Erläuterung* [Explanation], § 4:

Ex. 2

Of this he remarks (l.c. § 8): "Should some critical creature perhaps think to detect Octaves (*Octaven zu erjagen*) in the second bar, he must allow himself to be informed what is meant by the crossing (*Abwechselung*) of parts." [1]

We see from this that Mattheson's standard was precisely that to which Heinichen (only two years his junior) alludes, in connexion with the progressions shown in Ex. 1, as being "still tolerated".

Marpurg, who goes most carefully and minutely into the subject of consecutives (*Handbuch bey dem Generalbasse* [Part I], 1755, 2nd ed. 1762, II Abschnitt: 'Von der harmonischen Fortschreitung der Intervallen' [*Section* II: *On the harmonious progression of the intervals*]), and whose views on this matter are eminently sane, combining strictness, on the one hand, with freedom from pedantry, on the other, disallows the assumption of a crossing of parts (i.e. on a keyed instrument) as a palliation of consecutive Octaves when (1) the harmony is not full enough [i.e. in less than (presumably) four parts], (2) both chords are consonant, (3) the Octaves are in extreme parts, (4) most of the parts progress by similar motion.

[Thus Exx. 1 and 2 above would be disqualified by rules 2 and 4.]

The same, he tells us later, applies to Fifths.

Apart from these conditions, however, Marpurg sanctions the device in question, as a means of saving consecutives, as in the following examples, two of which, as will be seen, are in five parts:

Ex. 3      Tab. VII (2nd ed. Tab. V), Fig. 5.

---

[1] Mattheson's *Kleine General-Bass-Schule*, 1735, contains instances of the most bare-faced consecutives without comment or explanation. We can only suppose that the author would have justified them in the same way as in the above case.

For examples of consecutive Fifths and Octaves (as well as of the forbidden progression of an augmented Second) from the above-mentioned work, see Ch. ii ("The principal treatises", &c.), § 7 i, Exx. 4–11).

Ex. 4   Tab. VIII (2nd ed. Tab. VI), Fig. 20.

II. *Crossing of parts as a means of maintaining a higher position in the right hand than the necessary preparation and resolution of a discord would otherwise permit.*

We have already seen how Dr. John Blow used the device now under discussion in a sequence of Sevenths $\left(\begin{smallmatrix}7&6&5\\5&6\end{smallmatrix}\right)$ on a rising Bass (cf. Ch. i, § 22, Ex. 20); it is, however, with the eighteenth century that we are at present concerned.

Mattheson's *Kleine General-Bass-Schule*, 1735, already referred to, provides several examples in which a discord makes its appearance, as such, in a different part (or, at all events, in a different position in relation to the other parts) from that in which it was prepared.

No mention is made of a crossing of parts, but there is no other way in which the progressions in question can be explained, as will be seen from the following examples:[2]

Ex. 5a    *Höherer Classe, 6ste Aufgabe,* § 6, bars 3 and 4, p. 212 (p. 191).

Ex. 5b    ibid., *7de* [sic] *Aufgabe,* § 3, bars 13 and 14, p. 215 (p. 193).

Aufsteigender Classe, 6ste Aufgabe, Erste Abtheilung (First Division), § 5, p. 176 (p. 160).

Ex. 6

---

[2] For the explanation of the page-references in brackets, and the method of figuring, see above, Ch. ii, § 7 (a) note 1, and (c).

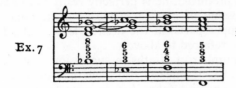

Ex. 7

ibid. *Zweite Abtheilung* (Second Division), § 5, bars 6–9, p. 178 (p. 162).

Ex. 8

Höherer Classe, 2te Aufgabe, § 6, bars 11–13, p. 195 (p. 177).

It is important to observe that, in all the above examples, the same end can be obtained by the employment of a device which Ph. Em. Bach recommends more than once, and which has already been described in the present chapter (§ 4 I), that of *taking in a fifth part* (above the others) and *immediately dropping its lower Octave*.[3]

We have seen that Ph. Em. Bach apparently regarded the crossing of parts as inadmissible in playing from a figured Bass. Such was, however, by no means the attitude of Kirnberger, also a pupil of John Sebastian, and the recognized upholder of a high standard where correctness of harmonic progression is concerned.

The latter, as might be expected, disallows the crossing of parts (which, on a keyed instrument, is not, as he points out, to be recognized as such by the hearer) *wherever the actual effect upon the ear is that of consecutives*,[4] as in the following example,[5] in which he tells us that the bad effect of Octaves $_d^d{}_c^c$ between Alto and Bass is to be avoided by omitting the 8ve of the Bass in the last chord and doubling the 3 (*b*) or the 5 (*c*) instead:

Ex. 9

---

[3] It is only necessary to compare Ex. 5 *a* with the following (in which the new upper part is indicated by an asterisk and the dropping of the lower part by a rest) in order to realize how small is the actual difference between the two procedures:

[4] *Grundsätze des Generalbasses*, in the section entitled 'Von denen beim Accord vorkommenden Dissonanzen', following § 172.

[5] Volume of examples, Part (*Abtheilung*) III, Fig. xxv.

But where no such ill effect is produced, he is perfectly ready to sanction (indeed, to recommend) the crossing of parts as a means of keeping the accompaniment (i.e. the three upper parts) at the desired level, instead of resorting to the alternative device referred to above.

He writes: "In the case of a number of Ninths in succession, instead of entering with a fifth part [cf. § 4 1, Ex. 2], one can also allow the parts to cross without detriment to purity of progression (*ohne dass der reine Satz dadurch verletzet wird*). . . . In this way the four-part harmony is maintained, and since, in any case, in Duets,[6] two voices of equal compass, and, in Trios, two Violin- or Flute-parts cross each other in many of these sequences of Ninths, that accompaniment sounds best of all in which the parts are allowed to rise one above another, exactly as in the following example, Fig. XXVI [7] [Ex. 10], whereas, in the contrary case, if the Ninth were allowed to remain where it was prepared (*wenn man die None an der Stelle wo sie gelegen, liegen liesse*) and were resolved in the same part [or rather in the position in the same position in the chord in relation to the other parts], one would (1) not only get too low down with the right hand, but would also (2) bring about Octaves with the principal parts [8] (while, by crossing, the latter maintain themselves at the same level), in addition to which a very bad melodic progression (*ein sehr schlechter Gesang*) in the upper part would result."

Ex. 10.

It is extremely important thoroughly to understand the above example.

It will be seen that two procedures are adopted: over the first minim the Tenor rises above the Alto and Treble *simultaneously with the resolution of the 9*; over the second minim the crossing of parts (Alto over Treble) *precedes* it, and, in this latter case, *the 3 has to be doubled* (omitting the 5) *in order to avoid consecutive Fifths*.

It follows, then, that (in a similar sequence) when the chord in question has a *major Third*, it is better to adopt the progression *which does not involve its duplication*, and that when that Third happens to be a leading note

---

[6] The *Duets* referred to are, of course, for two voices and a figured Bass and are, therefore, exactly on a par with the *Trios* next mentioned (for 2 Violins, or Flutes, and Bass).

[7] i.e. in Part (*Abtheilung*) III of the volume of examples.

There can be little doubt of the superiority of this form of accompaniment to the alternative treatment of the same Bass shown in § 4 1, Ex. 2. In the latter, with all due deference to what Kirnberger says about the lowest of the upper parts ceasing to belong to the four-part harmony as soon as the fifth part enters at the top, many musicians would feel that the effect upon the ear was still that of consecutive Fifths.

[8] It has been shown (§ 5 B, III *a*) that the resolution of a discord in the accompaniment in Octaves with (i.e. below) a principal part, though not in itself to be desired, is not always to be avoided. In the present case, however, it is especially undesirable, as the effect of one Ninth resolving in unison with a principal part, and the next in the lower Octave, would be particularly bad.

(especially if accidentally sharpened) it is imperative to do so. Otherwise the choice between the two alternatives is purely a matter of taste.[9]

The following example from the works of Giovanni Ravenscroft (*Sonate a tre*, Sonata I, second *Grave*, bars 5–10) will serve further to illustrate what Kirnberger says concerning the relation of the accompaniment (as prescribed by him in Ex. 10) to the principal parts, and also the result of resolving each Ninth in the same relative position in the chord as that in which it was prepared (as in Ex. 11 *a*):

§ 10. *Consecutives.*

(*a*) During the first half of the eighteenth century a considerable change took place in the attitude of musicians towards certain kinds of consecutives in a figured Bass accompaniment, as well as in actual composition. We have seen that Mattheson was ready to excuse a progression (consecutive 8ves between Alto and Bass) which neither Ph. Em. Bach, nor Marpurg, nor Kirnberger would have tolerated for an instant, on the plea of a crossing of parts, wholly imaginary as far as the effect upon the ear is concerned (cf. § 9, Ex. 2, note 1).

Octaves, too, saved only by the retardation of one of the parts concerned (described in German treatises by the very convenient term *nachschlagende Octaven*), also ceased by degrees to be tolerated.

At the close of the seventeenth century such a musician as Purcell did not hesitate to prepare a Ninth (resolving on the *Octave*) with the Octave of the Bass, as:

[9] Thus, the above example might equally well be treated as follows. It is, of course, desirable, for the sake of variety, to alternate between the two methods:

Ex. 1

'Sonatas in four parts', 1697.
Sonata III, Canzona, antepenult.
bar.

In the earlier part of the eighteenth century this usage still survived.

Godfrey Keller, in his *Compleat Method for attaining to play a Thorough Bass*, 1707, writes:

"The ninth is generally prepared by a third or a fifth, and it may be by a sixth or eighth, but not so naturally," and gives the following example:

Ex. 2

N.B.—Keller regularly omits the 3 from the chord of the Ninth; it was, therefore (presumably), not with any idea of partially concealing the consecutive 5th $_{g\ c}^{a\ d}$ that he employed this procedure in the present instance.

By the middle of the century, however, such progressions had ceased to be tolerated.

Marpurg stigmatizes the preparation of a 9, resolving on 8, by the Octave of the Bass as "An ugly breach of the rule against Octaves" (*Ein hesslicher Fehler wider das Verbot der Octaven*).[1]

Ph. Em. Bach gives the rule as follows:[2]

"The Ninth must never be prepared by the Octave of the preceding Bass note; consequently the following example would be wrong:

Ex. 3

"It is the resolution of the Ninth on the Octave that has occasioned this rule: if the resolution is not on the Octave, this prohibition lapses."[3]

In connexion with the above, Ph. Em. Bach adds the following illustration

---

[1] *Handbuch bey dem Generalbasse* [Part I], 1755 (2nd ed. 1762), Abschnitt II, 'Von der harmonischen Fortschreitung der Intervallen' (Section II, *On the harmonious progression of the intervals*).

[2] *Versuch &c.*, Part II, 1762, Ch. 17 II, § 3.

[3] Bach, however, goes on to say that "the preparation of the 9 by the 8 is never a beauty, and must be avoided (1) in the extreme parts, (2) when the harmony is thin, and (3) apart from contrapuntal necessity".

In such a progression as the following, therefore, the 9 must not be in the upper part:

of an obsolete standard: "Musicians of an older generation (*die Alten*)", he writes, "composed such examples without scruple:

Ex. 4

It is not, however, necessary to go to an earlier source than Mattheson (born only four years earlier than J. S. Bach) in order to find Octaves very much on a par with those in Ex. 2, the only difference being that the retardation, in the present instance, is in the *Bass*:

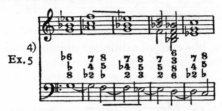

Ex. 5

(*b*) Another point in which the authorities of the earlier part of the eighteenth century differed from those of a somewhat later date is in connexion with consecutives arising between an upper part and a passing note in the Bass.

Mattheson's attitude in this matter can only be conjectured, because, in the *Organisten-Probe*, 1719 (and the second edition of the same work, entitled *Grosse General-Bass-Schule*, 1731), only the Basses are given, except in the case of certain excerpts from them dealt with in the 'Erläuterungen' (*Explanations*), in which latter suggestions are made with regard to the form of accompaniment to be adopted (cf. § 9, Ex. 2), while, in the *Kleine General-Bass-Schule*, 1735, the Basses are entirely in semibreves and minims, so that the case does not arise.

Heinichen's examples, on the other hand, in all of which the accompaniment is fully set out, abound with consecutive Octaves (in four-part harmony) arising as aforesaid.

In order to realize the difference between his standard in this matter and that of Ph. Em. Bach it is only necessary to refer to Ch. xviii, 'Quick notes in the Bass', and to examine the following examples (all from Heinichen): Ex. 29, 1, 2, 4, Ex. 30, Ex. 44, No. 3, Ex. 46, 4, Ex. 60, bars 23–4 (in all of which the passing note is *another interval of the same harmony*, reached by the leap of a Third), also Ex. 58, bars 13 and 14, Ex. 64, 2nd section, bar 3 (in which the Bass moves by step), and then to compare with them a series of examples of Ph. Em. Bach given in Ch. iv, 'On certain niceties of the accompaniment' (§ 5 *f*, Ex. 17).

(*c*) A special case arises when the Bass itself is in broken two-part harmony which includes discords and their resolutions.

Here we find a difference of opinion comparatively early in the eighteenth century.

---

[4] J. Mattheson, *Kleine General-Bass-Schule*, 1735, 'Höherer Classe' (*Higher Grade*), '5te Aufgabe' (*5th Lesson*), § 7, bars 4–8, p. 207 (p. 187).

For the double page-reference, and for the method of figuring, see § 9, note 2.

David Kellner, whose excellent little treatise on Thorough-Bass attained great popularity, writes as follows:[5]

"The Bass sometimes makes, as it were, an incursion (*Ausfall*) into an inner part; the accompanist, however, must take no notice, but adhere to his ordinary accompaniment. And, although, in the following example, the intervals figured above it are included in the Bass (*und obgleich im folgenden Exempel die darüber stehende* [sic] *Signaturen schon im Basse mit anschlagen*), the right hand must none the less play its complete chords:

Ex. 6

N.B.—In the original the last note is given (almost certainly by a misprint) as F.

G. P. Telemann is, however, of a different opinion. In his *Singe-, Spiel- und Generalbass-Übungen*, Hamburg, 1733/4,[6] the following passage occurs (No. 21, bar 17), the 7 (which appears in the figuring) being omitted in the right hand:

Ex. 7

Telemann makes the following comment:

"in the case of broken notes, that is to say, where the Bass includes one or more intervals which are really in the province of the right hand as at (*b*) and (*c*), these may, it is true, be struck in one of the middle parts with the same progression [i.e. as in the Bass], but hardly (*nicht leicht*) in the upper part; to that end we have here preferred to omit the 7 which is, in any case, heard in the Bass, rather than introduce two 8ves, namely, *b* and ♯ *a*."

Ph. Em. Bach, as might be expected, is in perfect agreement with Telemann.

He tells us that, in the following example,[7] "where the Bass resolves dissonances in broken harmony, a change must be made in the accompaniment [i.e. the harmony indicated by the figures], in order that the disgusting lagging Octaves (*die nachschlagenden ekelhaften Octaven*) may be avoided. The dissonances included in the figuring in the first bar may, therefore, be omitted with a good conscience."

Ex. 8

[For the notation of the example see § 3 v, note 29, in the present chapter.]

[5] *Treulicher Unterricht im General-Bass* ('Faithful tuition in Thorough-Bass'), 1732, Ch. I, XVI.   [6] Reprinted 1914, Berlin (Liepmannssohn), ed. Max Seiffert.
[7] *Versuch &c.*, Part II, 1762, Ch. 34, 'On certain precautions in the accompaniment', § 2 *f*.

(d) The fullest and clearest exposition of the rules relating to consecutives is to be found in Marpurg's *Handbuch* in the section already referred to (see note 1).

The author distinguishes carefully between the various circumstances which make for greater or less strictness: the number of parts employed, the speed, &c.

It has to be taken into account, he tells us, "Whether one is composing or accompanying on the Clavier. In the former case many things are mistakes which are not so in the latter."

The following will serve as an illustration:

In *compositions* of more than two parts, we are told, Octaves are saved by the interposition of an imperfect consonance (Third or Sixth) in *contrary motion* (Ex. 9), but *not* by one in *similar motion* (Ex. 10):

Ex. 9   Tab. VI (2nd ed. Tab. IV), Fig. 9.

8)
Ex. 10   ibid. Fig. 10.

In a figured Bass accompaniment, on the other hand, such a progression as in Ex. 11 *a* "can be tolerated", though (*b*), we are told, is *better*:

Ex. 11   ibid. Fig. 11.

Marpurg's eminently sane attitude towards 'tolerated' progressions is admirably expressed in the following words:

"I maintain that harmony (*ein Satz*) which is free from all those Octaves and Fifths which can be excused is better than that in which these excusable Octaves and Fifths are to be found."

(e) The following is an interesting instance of varying sensitiveness to consecutive Fifths on the part of three recognized (and approximately contemporary) authorities of the eighteenth century, Ph. Em. Bach, Marpurg, and Christoph Gottlieb Schröter.

In a sequence of Ninths $\left(\begin{smallmatrix}9\\5\\3\end{smallmatrix}\right)$, alternating with $\begin{smallmatrix}6\\5\end{smallmatrix}$ on a Bass note a Third below, it is evident that consecutive Fifths will arise except when the 9 is below the 5 so that the interval between them appears as a *Fourth*.

---

[8] The imperfect consonance (Third) is here obscured by the intervening (first) semiquaver.

In close harmony, therefore, there is only one position of the chords by which Fifths may be avoided, namely, with the 9 in the lowest of the upper parts, as:

Ex. 12

Of the above sequence Ph. Em. Bach, from whom the Bass is taken, writes (*Versuch &c.*, Part II, 1762, Ch. 17 I, § 8):

"The Fifths which arise in the other two positions,[9] however much they may be defended, *are, and remain, disgusting to the ear*." [The italics are not Bach's.]

Marpurg, in the context already referred to (cf. note 1), writes of these, and other similar Fifths (which, it will be noted, he disposes between the two inner parts), as follows:

"There are certain sequences of harmonic progressions in which consecutive Fifths *between the inner parts* are fairly tolerable. See Fig. 24 [Ex. 13].

[9] With regard to alternative treatments Bach writes: "It is better, if the good position is not obtainable, to omit the Sixth from the ⁶₅ and to double the Third instead (a). Besides that, the treatment (b) in extended harmony (*im getheilten Accompagnement*) is to be noted and occasionally used."

He says nothing about another alternative in extended harmony (c) (the only one in which the 9 need not be in the lowest of the upper parts), but he would, presumably, have sanctioned its occasional use, if desired:

Bach does not mention, though he can hardly have overlooked the fact, that in the particular Bass (as regards its position in the scale) which he has selected as an illustration, *no special device is called for* in the case of the first two of the three pairs of Fifths.

We have, first, a perfect Fifth falling to an imperfect one ($^{g\,f}_{c\,b}$), which, as Bach himself tells us (ibid. Ch. 2 II, § 22), is permitted between *any two parts*. Next we have an imperfect Fifth falling to a perfect one ($^{f\,e}_{b\,a}$), which, we are told (l.c. § 23), "is permitted only in case of need and hardly (*nicht leicht*) between extreme parts". These conditions may be said to be fulfilled here, even if the Fifths are not kept between the two inner parts. [N.B.—Our author himself, in one of his examples, uses the progression in question *between extreme parts* (cf. Ch. iv, 'On certain niceties of the accompaniment', § 5, Ex. 12, note 3).]

There is, therefore, no reason, from Ph. Em. Bach's own strict point of view, why this particular Bass should not be accompanied as follows (taking only the last ⁶₅ as $^{6}_{3}_{3}$):

If, however, the sequence is continued (as in Ex. 14), we of course get a succession of perfect Fifths, except under the conditions described above.

The dissonance here stifles the annoyance to the ear which would otherwise arise from the succession of Fifths."

In the *first* edition of his work (1755) Marpurg continues:

"For the rest, any one who does not care so to use them is at liberty to write *(setzen)* the three upper parts differently and to transform the Fifths into Fourths. This much is certain, that it would betray either recklessness *(Verwegenheit)* or ignorance to be constantly using such progressions without discrimination. But it would be no less reckless to forbid them without discrimination. This is the opinion of the celebrated Capellmeister Graun. At the least, *they can be used without fear in accompanying.*" [The italics are added.]

In the *second* edition (1762), however, Marpurg cancels the above passage (though it may be doubted whether his personal conviction had changed) and substitutes the following:

"However, it is better to write *(setzen)* the three upper parts differently and to transform the Fifths into Fourths." [10]

Ex. 13

Tab. VIII (2nd ed. Tab. VI), Fig. 24.

Of the same progression as that shown in Ex. 13 *a* Christian Gottlieb Schröter *(Deutliche Anweisung &c.*, 1772, § 234, p. 123) merely says: "Mock Fifths *(Scheinquinten)* are not real Fifths."

It seems probable from the above that he would not have objected to the Fifths in question between Alto and Treble, though, in the following example, he disposes them (like Marpurg) between the inner parts:

Ex. 14

We see from the foregoing that Ph. Em. Bach and Schröter represent diametrically opposite, extreme views, between which Marpurg holds the balance.

It is not quite without significance that Schröter (1699–1782) belonged to a somewhat older generation than either Ph. Em. Bach (1714–88) or Marpurg (1718–95), and that his treatise (of which the concluding paragraph is dated: *Nordhausen, am 30 December 1754*) was completed eighteen years before publication, and, therefore, earlier than that of either of the others.[11]

---

[10] It will be noticed (from the use of the word *setzen*=to compose rather than *einrichten*=to arrange or dispose) that the above refers to *composition*; it need not, therefore, be assumed that Marpurg intended to withdraw his full sanction of the progressions in question *in a figured Bass accompaniment*, in which he was prepared, as we have seen, to concede greater licence than in composition.

[11] None of the later authorities (as far as the present writer is aware) support

(f) Instances occur sometimes in which consecutive Fifths between an upper part and the *Bass* (so that no inversion, whereby the Fifths could be changed into Fourths, is possible) cannot be avoided (except, indeed, by the artificial device of an 'ornamental' resolution of a discord) without omitting an interval from the prescribed harmony.

The accompanist must decide for himself whether to do so, or to accommodate himself to the standard (and carry out the evident intentions) of the composer.

In both the following examples from the works of Jean-Marie Leclair (1697–1764) the fixed downward resolution of the 5 in the $\frac{6}{5}$ chord makes it impossible to omit the 5 from the Seventh on the following Bass note a degree below.

Schröter's view, or even that of Marpurg: they all assume the necessity of avoiding the consecutive Fifths.

Türk (*Kurze Anweisung &c.*, 1791, Ch. 5 ii, § 131, Ex. e, pp. 178 sq.) agrees with Ph. Em. Bach in recommending the omission of the Sixth from the $\frac{6}{5}$ chord and the doubling of the Third instead (cf. note 9).

So, too, W. A. Mozart, in a little treatise published under his name, though its authenticity has been disputed (*Kurzgefasste Generalbass-Schule*, Vienna (Steiner), Ch. 7, 'Von den sechs gefährlichen Gängen' [*On the six dangerous progressions*], 'Sechster Gang' [*Sixth progression*]).

Albrechtsberger, who likewise enumerates 'Six dangerous progressions' (*Sämmtliche Schriften über Generalbass &c.* ['Complete works on Thorough-Bass &c.'], ed. Seyfried, Vienna (undated), vol. i, § 37 f, pp. 77 sq.), advises:

(1) (a) in a *minor* key the omission of the imperfect [i.e. diminished] Fifth from the chord of the Ninth [i.e. on the Supertonic] and the doubling of the Third instead, as:

Ex. A

or (b) in a *major* key (in the progression corresponding to the preceding one) the doubling the 3 of the $\frac{6}{5}$ chord, *letting the 6 follow*, as:

Ex. B

(2) A *three*-part accompaniment (whereby each $\frac{6}{5}$ chord loses the 6).

(3) *Motus contrarius* (whereby the 5 of the chord of the Ninth is temporarily omitted and the 3 doubled), as:

Ex. C

[N.B.—In the case of the first Ninth, on *a* (the Supertonic), Albrechtsberger adopts the same procedure as in Ex. A.]

Apart, therefore, from the doubtful expedient of an ornamental resolution, consecutive Fifths cannot be avoided except by omitting the 5 from the $^6_5$ chord and doubling the 3 or 6 instead.

In Ex. 16 the harmony has to be in five parts for reasons explained earlier in the present chapter (cf. § 4 III, Ex. 14).

Leclair, Sonatas for Violin and Bass, Book I, Sonata VII, Adagio, bars 5 and 6.

N.B.—As the entire passage is in C major, there can be no doubt but that the 5 in the Seventh on *e* is *b natural*, and that both Fifths are, therefore, *perfect*. Strictly speaking, this should have been indicated by the figuring $\natural^7_5$ (or, in Leclair's notation, $\times^7_5$).

ibid. Book II, Sonata X, Allegro ma non troppo, 2nd section, bars 23, 24 from end.

In the following example, from Antonio Vivaldi, Fifths with the Bass are implied by the figuring, $^6_5$ on *a* followed by $_{[5]}^{7}$ on *g*. The real resolution, however, of the $^6_5$, whereby the Fifths are narrowly saved, is on $^4_3$ over the same Bass, $^{6\,-}_{5}\,^{-}_{4}.^{13)}$
$^{3\,-}$

The missing figures have here been supplied in brackets, and the

---

[12] If the consecutives are to be avoided by the artificial device of an ornamental resolution of the 5 in the $^6_5$ chord on *f*, the progression will be as follows:

and so, *mutatis mutandis*, in other similar cases.

[13] This is shown by the progression of the 2nd Violin part. The 5 in the $^6_5$ chord is a suspension: the essential discord (which occurs in the principal parts only as a passing semiquaver *c* in the 2nd Violin) is the 3, a Seventh on *d* in its second inversion.

accompaniment arranged accordingly, in order to make the progression clear: [14]

Antonio Vivaldi, Opera Prima, Sonatas for two Violins and Bass, Sonata III, Adagio, bars 12–14.

Ex.17

In the remaining example, in which the ellipse of the resolution of the suspended 4 on *b* flat serves to limit the freedom of progression,[15] consecutive Octaves and Fifths $_{bba}^{bba}$ $_{fe}$ can best be avoided by (1) omitting the 8 over ♭ *b* (doubling the 5 instead), and (2) omitting the 5 of the following Triad till the entry of the second quaver *g*, as:

Ex.18

Corelli, Opera quinta, Follia, Var. 20, bars 13 sq.

The only alternative is the temporary employment of extended harmony, involving the bad progression of an augmented Fourth ♭ *b e*:

Ex. 18ª

[14] It is, of course, open to the accompanist, and, in this instance, *perhaps best*, to omit the 5 altogether, and to double the 6 instead:

This is just one of the cases to which Werckmeister's recommendation, with regard to the occasional omission of a discord indicated in the figuring (cf. Ch. i, § 24 VII, 1 *b*) may well be applied.

[15] If the 4 resolved in the normal way, it would be possible (though the progression would not be an elegant one) to save the consecutives by contrary motion:

§ 11. *Gradation of tone.*

(*a*) It was an accepted principle that a *discord should be played louder than a concord.*

Ph. Em. Bach, in speaking of the common practice of alternating between *forte* and *piano* in the case of repeated phrases, adds: "It may, however, be noted that dissonances are generally played more loudly and consonances more softly, because the former stimulate and accentuate the emotions (*die Leidenschaften mit Nachdruck erheben*), while the latter calm them." [1]

The author does not further elaborate this point in the Second Part of his *Versuch*, in which he treats of Accompaniment, but it is obvious that the principle enunciated above applies to the latter as much as to the performance of music composed for the Clavier.

(*b*) Johann Joachim Quantz, however, in his celebrated treatise on the Flute, goes into the matter in great detail.[2]

He bases his instructions on the assumption that a discord is, in itself, unpleasant to the ear, and that, the harsher the discord, the more it requires to be emphasized, in order that the gratification caused by the subsequent concord may be proportionately enhanced. This principle he illustrates by an admirable example, a short Adagio for a solo instrument (presumably the Flute) and figured Bass, in which every gradation of tone in the accompaniment is carefully indicated.

(*c*) Certain discords, which do not, as it were, hold the ear in suspense, are exempted from the need for emphasis. Thus, we are told (l.c. § 15), a Seventh alternating with $\frac{6}{4}$ (cf. Ex., bar 19), and a Seventh arising on a passing note in the Bass (cf. Ex., bar 40) "demand no particular expression".

[The same is evidently meant to apply, though Quantz does not expressly mention it, to a Seventh taken *in transitu*, 8 7 [3] (as we see from bar 38 of the example, in which the Seventh on the last beat of the bar is marked *pp* while the preceding Triad on the same Bass is *p*), also to $\frac{4}{2}$ (without the 6) taken *in transitu*, $\frac{3\ 4\ 5}{1\ 2\ 3}$, as in bar 30 of the example.]

It is, perhaps, a little surprising to find certain *suspended* discords included in the same category.

---

[1] *Versuch &c.*, Part I, 2nd ed. 1759, Hauptstück [Section] 3, 'Vom Vortrage' [On Delivery], § 29.
N.B.—The full context is quoted at the end of the present section.

[2] *Versuch &c.*, 1752, Hauptstück [Section] xvii, 'Von den Pflichten derer, welche accompagniren, oder die einer concertirenden Stimme zugesellten Begleitungs- oder Ripienstimmen ausführen' [On the duties of those who accompany or execute the complementary or *ripieno* parts associated with a *concertante* part], Abschnitt [Subsection] vi, 'Von dem Clavieristen insbesondere' [Of the Clavierist in particular], §§ 12–17.

[3] It might, perhaps, be expected that any inversion of the same harmony, e.g. $\frac{6}{4}$ arising on a *passing note in the Bass*, would experience the same treatment; but, in bar 6 of the example, $\frac{4}{2}$ on ♭ *a*, following a major Triad on ♭ *b*, is marked *mf* (following *p*), and, in bar 26, $\frac{6}{2}$ on *f*, following a minor Triad on *g*, is marked *f* (following *mf*). On the other hand, in bar 11, $\frac{6}{5}$ on ♭ *b*, following $\overset{6}{\underset{♭}{}}$ on the same Bass $\left(\overset{6\ 5}{\underset{6\ -}{♭\ -}}\right)$, is not emphasized in any way.

It would seem, therefore, that Quantz regarded a passing discord in the *Bass* as more appreciably discordant than the same discord in an upper part.

Quantz writes (l.c. § 13): "The Ninth, the Ninth and Fourth, the Ninth and Seventh, the Fifth and Fourth, are not so harsh (*sind dem Gehöre nicht so empfindlich*) as the Fifth with the major Sixth, the false Fifth with the minor Sixth, the false Fifth with the major Sixth, the minor Seventh with the minor or major Third, the major Seventh, the diminished Seventh, the [major] Seventh with the Second and Fourth, the augmented Sixth, the major Second with the Fourth, the minor Second with the Fourth, the major and augmented Second with the augmented Fourth, the minor Third with the augmented Fourth.

"For this reason, then, the former do not demand anything like as much emphasis [4] in the accompaniment as the latter.

"But, among these latter, there is again a distinction to be made.

"The minor Second with the Fourth, the major and augmented Second with the augmented Fourth, the false Fifth with the major Sixth, the diminished Seventh, the [major] Seventh with the Second and Fourth, demand still more emphasis than the others, and must, therefore, be played still louder by the accompanist, by dint of a more vigorous touch."

This passage is here given *in extenso* because two discords are mentioned, the minor Seventh with the major Third (Dominant Seventh) and the *minor* Second with the Fourth [and minor Sixth], which Quantz inadvertently omits from his subsequent classification.

(*d*) Quantz proceeds (l.c. § 14) to divide the discords into three classes according to the amount of emphasis which they require: (1) *mezzo-forte*, (2) *forte*, (3) *fortissimo*.

He explains, however, that these degrees of loudness are not to be regarded as *absolute* but as *relative*, that is to say, proportionate to the degree of loudness prevailing at the moment. Thus, in a passage marked *pianissimo*, discords of the 3rd (*fortissimo*) class will be played no louder than *mezzo-forte* [and, of course, if the passage is already *mezzo-forte*, or even *forte*, the converse will be the case].

This principle will be found to account for apparent discrepancies in the example (cf. notes 6, 11, 21).

The *normal* level of the concords in the accompaniment of an Adagio, Quantz tells us (l.c. § 14), is *mezzo-piano*; it is upon this assumption, therefore, that his classification is based.

He tells us, furthermore (l.c. § 15), that when discords of various kinds follow each other, and discords resolve on discords, the *intensity of expression must be kept on the increase* by strengthening the tone and increasing the number of parts.[5]

---

[4] A little later on (l.c. § 15) Quantz tells us that three of the suspensions mentioned above, the Fifth and Fourth $\left(\frac{5}{4}\right)$, the Ninth and Seventh $\left(\frac{9}{7}\right)$, the Ninth and Fourth $\left(\frac{9}{4}\right)$ [and he, no doubt, intended to include the Ninth $\left(\frac{9}{5}{\scriptstyle 3}\right)$ as well], like the passing discords already mentioned (cf. *c ad init.*), demand '*no* particular expression'. Thus, in the example, neither $\frac{5}{4}$ (cf. bars 2, 10), nor $\frac{9}{7}$ (cf. bar 17), nor $\frac{9}{4}$ (cf. bars 8, 16), are in any way emphasized.

[5] It follows naturally from this that if two discords, which *individually* demand the same degree of loudness, occur in *succession*, there are two alternatives: either the first one must be played less loudly than usual (in order to allow for the increase), or the second one more loudly, as the circumstances seem to dictate. Thus, in bar 6 of the example, $\frac{4}{2}$ (with the augmented Fourth) resolves on $\flat\frac{6}{5}$ (minor Sixth with diminished Fifth. *Both* are normally *forte*, but, in this case, the $\frac{4}{2}$ is to be played *mf*, to allow for

(e) The classes are as follows:

I. *Mezzo-forte:*
   "Second with [perfect] Fourth." [6]
   "Fifth with major Sixth" [and major or minor Third].[7]
   "Major Sixth with minor Third." [8]
   "Minor Seventh with minor Third." [9]
   "Major Seventh." [10]

II. *Forte:*
   "Second with augmented Fourth." [11]
   "False Fifth with minor Sixth." [12]
   [Minor Seventh with major Third.] [13]
   [Minor Seventh with false (i.e. diminished) Fifth and minor Third.] [14]
   [Major Third with augmented Fourth and major Sixth (the second inversion of the preceding chord).] [15]
   [Minor Second with Fourth and minor Sixth.] [16]

N.B.—The last four chords are omitted by Quantz from his classification, but occur in the example.

the *crescendo*. On the same principle, in bars 15 and 37, where a diminished Seventh (*fortissimo*) resolves on $\flat\,^6_5$, the latter (though ordinarily only *forte*) remains *fortissimo*, in order that there may, at least, be *no decrease* of intensity.

[6] Cf. Ex., bars 3 and 26. In bar 26 the indication *f* is accounted for, in accordance with the principle explained above (cf. *d*), by the fact that the preceding notes are already *mf*.

[7] Cf. Ex., bar 23. In bar 25, doubtless by inadvertence, no indication is given; we may safely assume that *mf* was intended. In bar 11, in which the chord in question remains *piano*, the discordant interval (the 5) is taken *in transitu* (cf. note 3).

[8] It is clear from the example (cf. bars 5, 12, 22) that $^6_4\!{}_3$ on the Supertonic (the 2nd inversion of the Dominant Seventh) is meant. In bars 9 and 11 the major Sixth with the minor Third on the Subdominant minor is marked *p*.

For the figuring $6 = ^6_4{}_3$ see Ch. xxi, 'Incomplete figuring', ii, § 1.

[9] In bar 9 of the example this chord occurs with the 7 suspended over the Subdominant minor. In bar 43 the Seventh (on the Supertonic) is essential (resolving on a Dominant Seventh), and here it is not clear why Quantz has marked it *f* instead of *mf*.

N.B.—The description 'minor Seventh with minor Third' does not include the minor Seventh with minor Third and diminished Fifth on the leading note (or sharpened Subdominant) which Quantz omits to mention, but which, as we see from bar 5 of the example, belongs to the second (*forte*) class.

[10] In the penultimate bar of the example a major Seventh on the Subdominant (not resolving on 6, but followed by $^6_4$ on the Dominant) is marked *pp*, showing that Quantz is not a slave to his own rules.

[11] Cf. Ex., bars 4, 12, 34 (in all of which the preceding chord is *piano*). In bar 6 the $^4_2$ chord is marked *mf* (cf. note 5), and in bar 24, in which the preceding discord ($^6_5$ with perfect Fifth and major Sixth) is already *mf*, the $^{4\sharp}_2$ is marked *ff* (cf. *d*).

[12] Cf. Ex., bars 7, 9, 17, 27, 32 (in which latter the preceding chord is *mf*), and 41 (in which the preceding chord is *pp*). In bars 15 and 37 the $^6_5$ is *ff* (cf. note 5); in bars 33 and 40 it is *mf*. In the latter case it will be observed that the discordant note (the diminished Fifth) is taken *in transitu* (cf. note 3).

[13] Though not included by Quantz in his classification, we see from bars 29 and 43 of the example that this chord belongs here, except, of course, when alternating with $^6_4$ on the same Bass (cf. bar 19), or when taken *in transitu* (cf. bar 38) as above mentioned (cf. *c*).   [14] Cf. Ex., bar 5.   [15] Cf. Ex., bar 42.

[16] In bar 11 of the example this chord is marked *ff* and not *f*, but that is, no doubt, because the preceding Triad is already *f*.

From the fact that Quantz mentions it *first* among those discords which require

III. *Fortissimo:*

"Augmented Second with augmented Fourth." [17]

"Minor Third with augmented Fourth." [18]

"False Fifth with major Sixth." [19]

"Augmented Sixth." [20]

"Diminished Seventh." [21]

"Major Seventh with Second and Fourth." [22]

[It will be noted that the first three of the above chords are, respectively, the 3rd, 2nd, and 1st inversions of the chord of the diminished Seventh.]

(*f*) Quantz then proceeds:

"In order to make the matter still plainer, I will add an example illustrating the above-mentioned dissonances and the difference of expression as regards diminution and increase [of tone], from which any one will be able to see clearly that, in execution, the *piano* and *forte* are one of the most indispensable factors in an adequate expression of sentiment (*um die Affecten gehörig aus-zudrücken*). Let any play this example a few times in exact accordance with the indications *piano, pianissimo, mezzo-forte, forte,* and *fortissimo*; then let them repeat it without any variation in the strength of tone, and take careful note, the while, both of the difference between the figures [i.e. the harmonies indicated thereby] and of their own feeling. I am convinced that, when once they have accustomed themselves a little, without prejudice, to this manner of accompanying: when they learn to recognize the various effects of the dissonances: when they take careful note of the repetitions of phrases, of the sustained notes which interrupt the animated flow of the music (*welche die Lebhaftigkeit unterbrechen*), of the *inganni* (*Betrugsgänge*) which often occur in the cadences [cf. Ex., bars 35÷36], and of the notes which lead to a new key, and which are raised by a sharp or a natural, or lowered by a flat: I am convinced, I say, that they will then be able very easily to divine the *piano, mezzo-forte, forte,* and *fortissimo,* without their being indicated."

Example (ibid. Tab. xxiv)

greater emphasis (i.e. than *mezzo-forte*) it seems probable that he intended it to belong to the *forte* class.

[17] No instance in the example.

[18] Cf. Ex., bar 21.

[19] No instance in the example.

[20] Cf. Ex., bar 39. N.B.—Quantz does not specially mention the augmented Sixth in conjunction with the augmented Fourth and major Third ('French Sixth'), or with the perfect Fifth and major Third ('German Sixth'), but they are, of course, meant to be included.

[21] Cf. Ex., bars 15, 27, 37. In bar 20, the preceding notes being *pianissimo*, the chord is only *forte* (cf. *d*).

[22] Cf. Ex., bar 31.

N.B.—*Mezzo-forte* is to be understood to apply (Quantz tells us) to the note above the *f*, not to that above the *m*.

(*g*) An important factor in expression, apart from the loudness or softness of the tone, is the *position* in which the chords are taken.

Discords sound harsher, as Quantz points out (l.c. § 16), when the dissonant intervals are close together than when they are apart. For example, in the first or second inversion of a Seventh, $\frac{6}{5}$ or $\frac{4}{3}$, the effect of the discord is less marked when the dissonant intervals, 6 and 5, or 4 and 3, are taken as a Seventh than when they are heard as a Second.

Therefore the position of the chords must, as far as possible, be carefully chosen, as Quantz tells us, to suit the requirements of the occasion ('wie es jedesmal der Sache Beschaffenheit erfordert').

(*h*) With regard to the delicate gradations of tone in the accompaniment which Quantz demands, particularly in music of an expressive character, it is obvious that the instrument employed is an all-important factor. Of the Organ Quantz says nothing, but on an Harpsichord with one manual, a *piano* is to be obtained, he tells us (l.c. § 17), by a gentle touch and a reduction of the number of parts, *mezzo-forte* by playing the Bass in Octaves, *forte* in the same way, and also by doubling some of the consonant intervals of the harmony in the left hand, and *fortissimo* by the further device of *rapidly breaking the chords from the Bass upwards*.

"On an Harpsichord with two manuals", Quantz continues, "one enjoys the further advantage of being able to use the upper manual for a *pianissimo*.[23] But it is on a Pianoforte that all requirements can best be satisfied; for this instrument, of all those known by the name of Clavier, possesses in the highest degree the qualities requisite for a good accompaniment (*hat vor allem, was man Clavier nennet, die zum guten Accompagnement nöthigen Eigenschaften am*

---

[23] It would appear from this that Quantz contemplated a change of manual in the course of the same passage (as e.g. between bars 28 and 29, and bars 30 and 31 of the example. Ph. Em. Bach, on the other hand (speaking, it is true, not of accompaniment, but of pieces composed for the Clavier), writes as follows, in a context already referred to (cf. note 1): "If these Test-Pieces are played on an Harpsichord with more than one manual, one must remain on the same one for the *forte* and *piano* which occur in the case of individual notes; a change in this particular must not be made until entire passages are distinguished from one another by *forte* and *piano*."

meisten in sich): with this instrument it is merely a question of the player and his discrimination. On a good Clavichord, it is true, the conditions are precisely the same in playing, but not as regards the effect, because the *fortissimo* is lacking."

(*i*) The reader who has followed the above exposition of Quantz's rules and, above all, compared them with the example, will at once realize that they were not intended to be applied blindly and without great discrimination. Quantz himself writes as follows (l.c. § 14):

"But it is true that, with this manner of accompanying on the Harpsichord, good judgement and sensitiveness of soul must also play a large part (*Es muss aber freylich auch, bey dieser Art mit dem Clavicymbel zu accompagniren, die gute Beurtheilungskraft, und eine feine Empfindung der Seele, ein vieles wirken*). Whoever lacks these two qualities will never achieve any great success in it: unless indeed he make himself competent by earnest endeavour and much experience: for, by industry, we may gain perception (*Erkenntniss*); and, by perception, we may assist nature."

That Quantz was guided, first and foremost, by his musical instinct is clear, e.g., from the penultimate bar of the example in which a major Seventh, which according to his rule should have been *mezzo-forte*, is marked *pp*: actually less loud than the preceding concord which is marked *p*.

A valuable comment is furnished by Ph. Em. Bach in a passage from which a single sentence has already been quoted (cf. *a*): though written in reference to compositions for the Clavier, it bears equally upon accompaniment. It is significant that the First Part of Ph. Em. Bach's *Versuch* (from which it is taken) was first published in 1753, a year after the appearance of Quantz's work; it seems not improbable, therefore, that he had the latter in mind in writing as follows:

"It is not really possible to determine the cases in which *forte* and *piano* are appropriate, *because even the best rules suffer exceptions as numerous as the cases which they establish*; the special effect of this light and shade depends on the ideas (*Gedanken*), on the combinations of ideas, and, in general, on the composer, who can, with a reason, just as well introduce a *forte* where at another time there was a *piano*, and who often marks a phrase, *together with its consonances and dissonances*, now *forte* and now *piano*.

"For that reason repeated phrases, whether they reappear at the same pitch (*in eben derselben Modulation*), or at another one (particularly if they are accompanied by different harmonies), are generally apt to be differentiated by *forte* and *piano*. It may, however, be noted that the *dissonances are generally played more loudly, and the consonances more softly*, because the former stimulate and accentuate the emotions while the latter calm them. A special flight of fancy (*Schwung der Gedanken*), designed to arouse violent emotion (*einen heftigen Affect*) must be powerfully expressed. The so-called *inganni* (*Betrügereyen*), therefore, since it is often with that object that they are introduced, are usually played *forte*. The following rule, too, which is not without foundation, may perhaps be noted, namely, that those intervals in a melody which are external to the scale of the key are apt to bear being played *forte* ('gerne das forte vertragen'), *regardless of whether they are consonances or dissonances*, and, on the other hand, that the intervals which are in the scale of the key are apt to be played *piano*, *whether they are consonant or dissonant*."

N.B.—The italics have been added.

It is evident from this that Ph. Em. Bach, while endorsing *up to a certain point* the prevailing practice of playing discords more loudly than concords (even, it would appear, in the case of repeated phrases marked respectively *forte* and *piano*), was not prepared to carry this differentiation to anything like the same lengths as Quantz, far less to attempt to reduce it to a system.

§ 12. *Unisoni (all' unisono) and tasto solo.*

(*a*) The distinction between the above terms is often overlooked, but is, nevertheless, a very important one. It is this: in both cases there is an absence of any harmony in the accompaniment, but when the Bass is marked *unisoni*, or *all' unisono*, it is played, as Ph. Em. Bach expressly tells us (*Versuch &c.*, Part II, 1762, Ch. 22, § 4), *with both hands, in Octaves*, whereas, when it is marked *tasto solo*, it is played *with the left hand alone, without either the lower or the upper Octave*, and if string or other Basses are associated with the Clavier or Organ, those of 16-foot tone are silent.

In both cases the resumption of the harmony is indicated by the reappearance of figures, and if the first harmony is a *Triad*, it must, under these circumstances, contrary to the usual custom, be *figured*.

With regard to the *tasto solo*, Bach writes (ibid. Ch. 23, § 8):

"With our kind of accompaniment [i.e. the *tasto solo*, which is the subject of the chapter in question] the Bass notes are never doubled by the left hand, except the execution of the phrase were so vigorous (*es sey denn, dass der Vortrag des Gedanken so stark . . . wäre*), and the *Clavier* so extraordinarily bad, that a due proportion had to be sought in this way. It is, however, always better, and more in accordance with the nature of the *tasto solo*, not to employ this expedient. It is precisely in this that the essential distinction between the *tasto solo* and *unisono* consists, that with the latter there is duplication, but not with the former."

(*b*) Ph. Em. Bach does not expressly tell us that the duplication of the Bass *all' unisono* is in the *upper* Octave; it is, however, clear from what he says that, *normally*, this is the case, but *not without exception*.

In the two chapters devoted, respectively, to the *unisono* and *tasto solo*, Bach gives directions for the treatment of a number of cases in which we are left to infer that inadequate or incorrect indications on the part of the composer oblige the accompanist to use his own discretion. Of one such case Bach writes (ibid. Ch. 22, § 7): "If, for certain reasons, a composer assigns to the Bass a phrase which is accompanied by the other parts *literally* [1] in the unison ('im *eigentlichen* Einklang'), and which consequently bears no duplication in either the upper or the lower Octave, because it is to be executed at precisely the pitch indicated and at no other, then one allows the right hand to pause and plays this illusory [2] unison in single notes (*einstimmig*) with the left hand alone."

It is quite clear from this that, with the *unisono*, the Bass (as written) falls to the left hand, and the reduplication in the Octave to the right.

---

[1] Bach had previously explained (l.c. § 1) that, in this connexion, the term *unison* includes the 8ve.

[2] Bach calls it *illusory* ('verführerisch') because the composer, as we are led to infer, has wrongly marked the passage *all' unisono* instead of *tasto solo*.

On the other hand, after giving examples of passages which may most appropriately be accompanied *tasto solo*,[3] he continues (ibid. Ch. 23, § 4):

"But if such phrases are to be played loud, and the Thirds and Sixths [i.e. between the *Solo* part and the Bass] are not too close together [i.e. if they appear as compound intervals, Tenths and Thirteenths, &c.], the accompaniment with the unison (*unisono*) may be used, and the Bass notes doubled. If the latter do not go too low down, it is better to take this duplication *in the lower rather than in the upper Octave*. This case sometimes arises in Symphonies and Concertos, where the two Violins, and the Viola and Bass, respectively, move in unison with each other."

(*c*) It is important to realize that composers often fail to give the necessary indication *all' unisono* and *tasto solo*, especially the former, and that cases are therefore liable to arise in which the accompanist is justified in disregarding the figuring and substituting one or other of the above-named forms of accompaniment at his own discretion. Ph. Em. Bach gives a graphic description of such a case, which deserves to be quoted. He writes as follows (ibid. Ch. 23, §§ 2, 3):

"We do not need to extol the effect of this mode of performance [i.e. *all' unisono*], which derives its beauty from the omission of the harmony; numerous musical compositions by good Masters bear witness to this.

"None the less, it has been remarked with surprise that some composers, in noting their Basses, do not always indicate these progressions in the unison. We sometimes find figures placed over the Bass, where none ought to be played. The result of this cannot be otherwise than displeasing. Just imagine! A composer works out a piece with much care; he lavishes on it, as it were, every melodic and harmonic artifice and combines them in the most charming fashion. He now thinks that it is time to arouse the attention of his hearers by something fresh; to that end he seeks for a phrase (*Gedanke*) with a sort of enthusiasm; the splendour and nobility of this phrase is to stand forth and be felt. He therefore, as it were, renounces the beauties of harmony for a time; his phrase is to remain in single notes (*einstimmig*); it alone is to occupy

---

[3] Bach's description of the passages in question is as follows:

"We use the *tasto solo*, when necessary, with great advantage. When, for example, the Bass moves in a number of successive Thirds and Sixths with the principal part, without the addition of any middle part, then our kind of accompaniment is in place. The piece may be in two or more parts. When these Bass notes are to be played softly, if the Thirds and Sixths lie quite close together [i.e. appear as Thirds and Sixths rather than as their compounds], and are, consequently, not doubled in the Octave in either part, then no other accompaniment but ours is, in the nature of the case, possible; the Double-Bass (*Contraviolon*) is then silent, and the other Basses play the notes quite softly, literally in unison, with the Clavier. The following examples are of this kind:

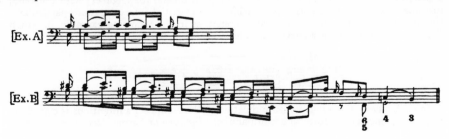

[Ex. A]

[Ex. B]

alike the thoughts and fingers of all the accompanists at once (*er soll allein der Gedanke und die Beschäftigung aller Begleiter zugleich seyn*). His piece is completed. It is performed. In the midst of the most pleasurable expectation of the desired effect of this phrase, the accompaniment of the *Clavierist* disturbs him. The latter prepares and resolves the intervals indicated, as honestly and regularly as possible; at another time with much credit, only now giving rise to annoyance. Luckily for the accompanist, the composer remembers that he has made a mistake in his presentment of the Bass (*Grundstimme*), and is overjoyed when the former, in disgust at his wrong accompaniment, abandons the harmony of his own accord, pays no further regard to the figures, and helps to reinforce the phrase in question in the unison, as far as is necessary, because the first principle of accompaniment, which we have stated in the 19th section of the Introduction, at once occurs to him: To every piece which he accompanies the accompanist must, as it were, fit the appropriate harmony, *of the right strength.*"

(*d*) Bach goes on to describe certain typical cases in which the accompaniment *all' unisono* (i.e. with the Bass doubled in the upper Octave by the right hand) is desirable (l.c. §§ 6–9):

(1) In the case of passages in which all the parts are in unison [which term, as above mentioned, includes the 8ve][4] with the Bass and with each other.

In such cases, we are told, the indication *unisoni* or *all' unisono* is generally to be found.[5]

(2) "The second case in which the unison accompaniment is beneficial", writes Bach (l.c. §§ 8, 9), "includes all brilliant passages in the Bass in which the composer has had a particular object in view; whether they consist of skips, runs, broken harmony, chains of shakes, or who knows what other figures. In dealing with them, our object is that these passages should stand out clearly, which object is not so successfully attained by an harmonized accompaniment as by one in unison. It has not yet become customary in such cases to use the indication *unisoni* or *all' unisono*; it is therefore left to the discretion of a good accompanist. I am sufficiently convinced, by experience, of the good effect of this accompaniment in the case of such passages.

"It is only in the case of a *piece in two parts* [i.e. principal part and Bass],

---

[4] To be distinguished from this is the case, mentioned above (cf. *b*), in which the other parts are *literally* in unison with the Bass, and in which, as Bach tells us, the accompaniment must be in single notes without the upper Octave, i.e. *tasto solo* [whatever indication may be given].

[5] Bach mentions a further case in which it is appropriate to accompany *all' unisono*, namely, when the Solo part has either a melodic progression of its own, or simply a sustained note, while the *ripieno* parts move in unison [or Octaves] with the Bass, in some form of broken harmony in which the essential intervals, more particularly the discords and their resolutions, are present, as in the following example, in which the *Solo* part consists of a sustained note:

In such a case, Bach tells us, an indication of the composer's intentions is especially necessary, since either form of accompaniment (*unisono* or harmonized) is admissible.

an instrumental or vocal *Solo*, that these brilliant Basses are, for the most part, accompanied in harmony."

(*e*) In his chapter on the *tasto solo* Bach mentions a very characteristic case. His advice, though directed rather to the composer than to the accompanist, is, none the less, worth recording. He writes (ibid. Ch. 23, § 6):

"The *tasto solo* is also employed in the case of Bass notes over which the melody is maintained at a low pitch, without there being any accompaniment [i.e. of *ripieno* instrumental parts] at a higher pitch (*in der Höhe*). If this low-pitched melody is accompanied, in harmony, by several [instrumental] parts at a low pitch, one can, it is true, put figures over the Bass, which figures an intelligent accompanist, who at once grasps the character of the piece, will not take otherwise than in the same low position; but as the discretion of the accompanist (*Generalbassspieler*), who is very often an amateur, cannot always be relied on, it is better to put *t. s.* over the Bass, and, it may be, to lose the harmony on the *Clavier*, rather than suffer an accompaniment which drowns (*überschreyet*) everything by its high pitch and spoils the effect. It is in Concertos in general, especially if they are written for Bass instruments, in Arias for low voices, &c., that these low-pitched melodies with low-pitched harmony sometimes occur."

(*f*) Of more practical value to the accompanist are some examples given by Bach, in which a single bass note is to be taken *tasto solo, even though it be figured*, in which case the indication *t. s.* will, of course, be lacking.

In the first example, the principal part begins in actual unison with the Bass. The bass note in question is to be played without the lower Octave, and the harmony (a Triad) omitted. In all the other examples the effect of the entry, after a rest, of the principal part would be discounted (especially in slow time) if the change of harmony which it introduces were *anticipated* in the accompaniment. The notes in question are marked *t. s.*, and the figuring possibly to be found (but to be disregarded) has been added in square brackets:

§ 13. *Anticipating the Bass in the right hand.*

(*a*) It is often conducive, indeed necessary, to a good effect to strike a chord over a short rest, in anticipation of the Bass (cf. Ch. xviii, 'Quick notes in the Bass', § 3 *d*, Ex. 33); sometimes, too, over a dot, or its equivalent in the shape of a short tied note (cf. Ex. 11).

In the first-mentioned case, some composers place the figure belonging to the following bass note over the rest (*a*), or (much more rarely) place a dash over the rest, to connect it with the following figure (*b*):

In the majority of Basses, however, especially the older ones, no such help is given.

The anticipation of the following harmony over a short rest in the Bass is appropriate only in the absence in any other part, during the rest, of any note discordant with the harmony in question. The accompanist, therefore, enjoys a great advantage in the case of a *Solo*, in which the principal part is usually printed over the Bass.

The following series of examples is from Ph. Em. Bach (*Versuch &c.*, Part II, 1762, Ch. 36, § 4), and the explanation of them is best given in his own words.[1]

(*b*) Cases in which the anticipation of the harmony over a short rest is necessary or admissible.

Bach writes: "In *e* [= Ex. 1] the striking of a chord in advance (*das Vorschlagen*) over the rest is indispensable, especially if this example occurs with a large and full orchestra (*bey einem weitläuftigen und stark besetzten Orchester*), in which all the parts enter simultaneously with these short notes. . . . Here the *Clavierist* must lead, and give the signal at the rest by striking as loud a chord as possible:

"In *b* [= Ex. 2] there is no alternative to the necessity of striking a chord over the rest, unless the entire half-bar is to be allowed to pass without accompaniment. In a quick measure this assistance in keeping time is very necessary to the principal part as well as to the accompanist. This example must not be quicker than *Andante* if the chord is not to be struck by the right hand till after the rest, as this would otherwise give rise to a dislocation of the time (*eine widrige Bewegung im Tacte*):

"In *a* [= Ex. 3] it is permitted to a beginner to strike the Triad of *C* over the rest, in order to make sure of the time; a practiced accompanist waits to

---

[1] The order of the examples has here been altered in order to separate the cases in which the anticipation of the harmony over a rest is more or less called for from those in which the reverse is the case. Bach numbers the examples with the letters of the alphabet (*a–l*); his references to these letters, in the passages quoted, will show the original order.

In those examples here given on three staves, the right-hand part and the *Solo* part are given *an Octave higher than in the original* for reasons already explained (cf. § 3, notes 29 and 30).

enter with a chord of the Sixth in the right hand over *e*, and allows both the rest and the *c* to pass:

"In *d* [=Ex. 4] it is necessary, on account of the stationary nature of the principal part, and on account of the syncopation in the Bass, that the harmony, even in a slow measure, should be struck in slow quavers. The first quaver may, perhaps, pass without harmony, in order not to obscure the *piano* with which a sustained note usually begins:

(*c*) Cases in which the anticipation of the harmony over a short rest would give rise to a clash with the principal part.

"In *c* [=Ex. 5], be the *tempo* what it may, the Triad of *c* cannot be struck before the entry of the first Bass note, because this Triad does not harmonize with the *f* in the principal part:

"In *k* [=Ex. 6] the *appoggiatura* [i.e. the semiquaver *c* in the Solo part] does not admit of a Triad over the rest; it is therefore best for the right hand to pause for the duration of a quaver:

"In example *g* [=Ex. 7], too,[2] with dotted notes, the accompanist does not strike a chord in advance, because there is an *appoggiatura* in the principal part which does not resolve till after the short note in the Bass:

[2] The word 'too' (*ebenfalls*) was meant by Bach to refer to Ex. 8, but with the present arrangement of the examples (cf. note 1) it remains equally appropriate.

[Ex. 7]

(d) Cases in which the anticipation of the harmony is excluded by considerations of taste.

"In f [=Ex. 8], where the notes which follow the quaver rest are not as short as in the previous example [i.e. Ex. 1 in the present arrangement, see note 1], and where all the parts likewise enter simultaneously in unison [4] [which term here includes the 8ve] after a general silence (*Generalpause*), there is no anticipation:

[Ex. 8]

"Example h [=Ex. 9], with the pathetic Bass after the French taste, must be accompanied without striking the harmony in advance, as, otherwise, it loses much of its defiant character:

[Ex. 9]

"The illustration at i [=Ex. 10] shows a case where the composer sometimes puts a certain weight into the expression of the principal part, and, at the same time, requires that the latter should begin by itself where the change of harmony takes place [5] (*mit der Veränderung der Modulation*)."

[Ex. 10]

---

[3] The semicircle ⌒ over the figure 5♭ ('Telemann's sign') warns the accompanist against taking the 5♭ as $^6_{5♭}$ (cf. Ch. xxiii, 'Varieties of figuring', § 19).

[4] The bass notes in question were doubtless intended to be marked *unisoni* or *all' unisono* (cf. § 12 d, 1); this indication has therefore been added in square brackets.

[5] i.e. by the operation of a new ♭ or ♯. This case is exactly parallel with the one illustrated at the end of § 12 (Exx. 2–5).

(*e*) Cases in which a chord is struck in advance over a dot or short tied note in the Bass.

"In *l* [= Ex. 11] a chord is struck over the dots and tied notes:

§ 14. *Modifications of the figured harmony necessitated by ornaments &c. in the principal part.*

I. *Introductory.*

(*a*) It often happens that a retardation in the principal part, by an appoggiatura or other ornament, of one, or even two intervals of the harmony is ignored in the figuring.[1]

Ph. Em. Bach devotes four chapters (*Versuch &c.*, Part II, 1762, Chs. 25–8) to the modifications of the accompaniment necessitated by the retardation of the harmony in the principal part. He deals successively with the long or variable appoggiatura (i.e. that of which the time-value stands in a definite relation to that of the main note), with driving notes (*rückende Noten* or *Rückungen*), with the dotted *Anschlag* (for which term we have no English equivalent), and, finally, with that most arbitrary of ornaments the dotted slide (*Schleifer*).

It must suffice here to select a few characteristic examples from among the great number presented by Bach.

(*b*) It will be readily understood that, in all the cases mentioned above, the procedure as regards the accompaniment is governed not so much by any hard and fast rule as by considerations of taste, and that it therefore varies in accordance with circumstances, as represented by the pace and character of the music. Here, as always, the main principle is to avoid discounting the effect of the principal part, and therefore, the greater the emotion expressed by the latter, the more guarded must be the accompaniment. Ph. Em. Bach writes as follows (ibid. Ch. 25, § 8 *ad fin.*): "In a piece in which there is great feeling (*Affect*), and in which a slow *tempo* is taken, one must endeavour to throw into a still brighter light by means of the accompaniment, or at all events not to obscure, all beauties of the melody (*Gesang*) and of its execution, whether they consist in chromatic intervals (*Intervallen wider die Modulation*), in retardations or anticipations of the resolution, or in driving notes (*Rückungen*). The former object is best attained by means of rests, the latter by thinning the harmony. Were one to join in expressing all such refinements on the *Clavier*, the hearers would no longer know whether a piece was merely being accompanied or being played by some second person (*mitgespielt*)."

---

[6] Only the Bass is given in the original.

[1] This is, no doubt, owing to the fact that such ornaments are usually indicated by small notes, in such a way that their time-value and that of the main note which follows them are not apparent to the eye.

II. *The Appoggiatura.*[2]

(*a*) Of this ornament Ph. Em. Bach writes (l. c. §§ 2, 3):

"Appoggiaturas can rarely be disregarded in the accompaniment; they generally affect it considerably (*sie haben mehrentheils einen grossen Antheil daran*). They are of most frequent occurrence in pieces in which taste is dominant, as they are one of its principal graces.

"Appoggiaturas retard the harmony which the Bass note really (*eigentlich*) bears. It is well known that, according to the rules of good taste, the appoggiatura is executed loud, and the main note (*Abzug*) softly. Consequently people are doubly wrong when they disregard it in their figuring; when that is done, the accompaniment cannot, for the most part, fail to prove displeasing."

In one case, however, we are told (l. c. § 5), a figuring in which no account is taken of an appoggiatura in the principal part may be adhered to, and the accompaniment, if required, be in four parts: namely, when the appoggiatura and the main note are either simultaneously compatible with the figured harmony,[3] or are actually contained in it, as in the following examples selected from those given by Ph. Em. Bach. The former case is illustrated by Ex. 1, the latter by Ex. 2:

(*b*) With regard to the cases in which the above-mentioned conditions are not fulfilled Bach writes as follows (l. c. § 6):

"But when the appoggiatura is not compatible with all the intervals of the chord prescribed, because the latter is calculated with a view to the harmony of the main note which follows, the appoggiatura is included in the accom-

---

[2] In accordance with the usual practice of the eighteenth century the variable (or long) appoggiatura occupies half the time of a note divisible into two parts, and two-thirds of the time of one divisible into three, as:

Written:

Played:

[3] This case arises e.g. when the appoggiatura represents the 4, and the main note the 3, of a chord which is figured 6 (or 6), *but which is equally capable of being taken as* $\frac{6}{4}$ (cf. Ch. xxi, 'Incomplete figuring', II, §§ 1–3), and in all other instances in which the appoggiatura represents an interval not actually present in the figured harmony, but one which may be added to it without detriment to the progression.

paniment (*mitgespielt*),[4] and, in addition, as many of the intervals indicated in the figuring as the degree of loudness of the performance and the harmony of the appoggiatura permit. When [however] the latter is played with great feeling (*Affect*), and softly, its duration depending only on the good pleasure of the principal performer, then the accompanist does not play it too, but takes one, or, at most, two other intervals of the harmony. This is also frequently done in the case of appoggiaturas which are chromatically raised a semitone (*welche wider die Modulation einen halben Ton zu hoch sind*). *Double* appoggiaturas are included in the accompaniment and are, accordingly, disposed of in three parts.[5] Certain appoggiaturas do not admit of any harmony at all. All this leads to the general observation that, the more feeling there is in a piece, the more subtle (*fein*) must the accompaniment be. This subtlety is manifested in the choice, the entry, the economy (*Menagement*), often, too, in the omission of the harmony. Examples of all kinds will further explain my meaning."

(*c*) Bach gives numerous examples of each of the essential harmonies (Triads and Sevenths, with their respective inversions) with one or other of their intervals retarded by an appoggiatura, from above or below, in the Solo part.

Among these examples four different treatments may be distinguished:

(1) If the *tempo* is not too slow [and the resulting discord not too harsh], the appoggiatura may be disregarded, and the accompaniment played in accordance with the figuring, as at * in the following examples: [6]

Ex. 3   (l. c. § 8 *k*)

---

[4] Examples are, however, given in which, *presupposing a fairly quick time*, the appoggiatura may be disregarded in the accompaniment in spite of the resulting discord (cf. Exx. 3, 4).

[5] As an alternative to this procedure, a passage in which several double appoggiaturas occur in succession may also be accompanied *tasto solo* (cf. Ex. 19).

[6] In the original the examples are given, with an entire disregard for pitch, on a single stave (cf. § 3, notes 29, 30): first the Solo part and Bass (the latter figured *in the way that Bach condemns*, i.e. without regard to the ornament in the Solo part) and then the accompaniment (in which the Bass is sometimes noted an 8ve lower than in the original example, in order to make room for the upper parts on the single stave) *with the figuring that Bach regards as correct*. Thus Ex. 11 in the present section appears in the original as follows:

In some few instances Bach does not supply the accompaniment (cf. Exx. 3, 26, 27, 28, 32, 38).

Here most of the examples are noted on three staves, in many cases an 8ve higher than in the original, and in four instances (Exx. 11, 12, 22, 32) the Solo part has been *raised an 8ve in relation to the Bass*.

[7] The harmony has been supplied in accordance with Bach's instructions, to the

Ex. 4

N.B.—In the above example, and in all subsequent ones in the present section, the figures here shown *above* the Bass are those given by Bach *without reference to the appoggiatura in the Solo part*, while those *below* represent what he regards as the proper figuring (cf. note 6).

(2) The harmony may be modified to a greater or lesser degree in order to avoid too harsh a clash with the appoggiatura.

In the second bar of Ex. 5, and in Ex. 6, a Triad is taken *without the 8ve of the Bass*, so that the appoggiatura (2 rising to 3) clashes with the 3 (like the 9 in a $\frac{9\ 8}{5\ -}$ suspension) but not with the 8 as well: [8]

Ex. 5   (l. c. § 8 a)

effect that, *when the time is not too slow*, the appoggiaturas are to be disregarded and Triads played. For the treatment in slow time see Ex. 13.

   [8] In neither of these two examples could the appoggiatura 2, if included in the accompaniment, be treated as 9 resolving on 8, as is sometimes possible (cf. Ex. 13): in Ex. 5 the 9 would be incorrectly prepared by the 8ve of the Bass (cf. § 10 a, Ex. 3), while, in Ex. 6, the Bass rises a semitone to *f* sharp. Concerning the latter example Bach tells us that the 6 of the $\frac{6}{5}$ chord must be omitted over the first *f* sharp, *in order to avoid consecutive Fifths*. This is a remarkable instance of his extreme aversion to consecutives, since the Fifths in question (between Solo part and accompaniment) arise only on the assumption that the accompaniment is in four parts from the beginning, with the Alto and Tenor coinciding in the unison till the $\frac{6}{5}$ chord (*a*), instead of the 6 entering as a new part on the second crotchet of the bar (*b*):

for we have Marpurg's authority for the axiom that consecutives do not arise through the entry of a new part, or the cessation of one previously sounding (Ch. xii, '$\frac{6}{5}$ chords', § 2 d, note 2).

Ex.6   (l. c. § 8 *i*)

In Ex. 7 only the 6 of a $\frac{6}{3}$ chord is taken during the appoggiatura ♩, the 3 being added when the latter rises to the main note:

Ex.7   (l. c. § 8 *o*)

In Ex. 8 Bach prefers to accompany the appoggiatura with the Bass alone:

Ex.8   (l. c. § 8 *n*)

In bar 4 of Ex. 5 (where the appoggiatura occupies two-thirds of the time of the dotted note, and its resolution one-third) it will be observed that the entry of the harmony is gradual: with the first half of the appoggiatura the Bass alone is sounded, with the second half the 5 is added, and with its resolution the Triad is completed by the addition of the 3. This is a good instance, in a small way, of what Bach calls the *Menagement* of the harmony (cf. II *b ad fin.*).

(3) The appoggiatura may be duplicated in the accompaniment.

In this case its resolution may either be the same (upward or downward) as in the Solo part, or, in the absence of any reason to the contrary,[10] it may be treated in the accompaniment as a prepared discord with a downward resolution, while it rises in the Solo part. The fulness of the harmony will of course vary in accordance with the character and sentiment of the passage.

[9] The semicircle ⌒ over the $\frac{5}{3}$ below the Bass, like those in Exx. 14, 18, 21 (corrected Bass), 35, and 38, denotes that no interval other than those figured is to be included (cf. Ch. xxiii, 'Varieties of figuring', § 19).

[10] Cf. note 8 *ad init.*

In the four following examples (Exx. 9–12) the progression of the appoggiatura is the same in the accompaniment as in the solo part:

In the next two examples the appoggiatura in the Solo part *rises*, while the corresponding interval in the accompaniment *falls*.

In Ex. 13 the 3 of three Triads in succession is retarded, in the Solo part, by 2 which, in the accompaniment, is treated as a suspended 9.

[11] Of this example Bach tells us that the appoggiatura in the Solo part may be accompanied in three different ways: (1) with the 5 only, (2) with the 5 and 3, and (3) with the 8 as well, as above.

In Ex. 14 *a* the 5 of a ⁶₅ chord on the leading note is retarded in the Solo part by 4 which, in the accompaniment, falls to 3 :

(l. c. § 8 *k*)

(l. c. § 13 *a*)

(4) The *second half only* of the appoggiatura may be duplicated in the accompaniment.

It is evident (though Bach does not expressly tell us so) that this form of accompaniment is especially suitable when the duration of the appoggiatura is *double that of the main note*, as in the following examples.

Of Ex. 15 Bach writes : "... where so many chromatic appoggiaturas occur (*wo so viele Vorschläge wider die Modulation vorkommen*), one must make the harmony quite thin and intersperse it with rests, in order that the clashes (*Zusammenklänge*) may not be too harsh and that the appoggiaturas may stand out well."

Ex.15

(l. c. § 8 *l*)

Of the next example Bach writes : "If, in a Solo, or in any piece in which the accompaniment has to be very subtle (*fein*), a number of appoggiaturas occur in succession in the principal part, the time being somewhat slow, one does not duplicate them all in the right hand, in order that the effect of the principal part may not be obscured. If these appoggiaturas cannot very well be passed over (*Wenn man diese Vorschläge ohne Zwang nicht vorbey gehen kann*), variety should at least be introduced by means of rests, whereby the

---

[12] The treatment of the same Solo part and Bass *in quick time* is seen in Ex. 3.

principal part is differentiated in performance (*so machet man wenigstens durch Pausen eine Veränderung, wodurch der Vortrag der Hauptstimme unterschieden wird*). In this way we concede to it the advantage of being the first to let the ornament be heard, unaccompanied, and we then echo it in the accompaniment. The variety which results from these rests is the more agreeable, the longer the uniform movement of the Bass has already been going on, and the longer it is subsequently continued."

It will be observed that the appoggiaturas in this example are not noted as such, but are incorporated in the time of the bar; this is generally the case when an appoggiatura is itself preceded by another ornament, as in the second bar of the example:

(l. c. § 17)

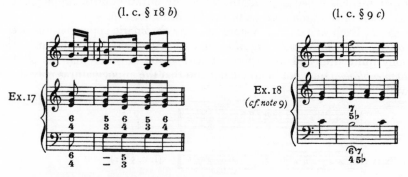

Ex. 16

(*d*) Double appoggiaturas in the Solo part are usually included in the accompaniment (cf. II *b*), either with the two intervals in the same relative position (Ex. 17), or inverted (Ex. 18):

(l. c. § 18 *b*)   (l. c. § 9 *c*)

Ex. 17   Ex. 18
                         (*cf. note* 9)

Of this last example Bach writes:

"If the accompaniment is to be slight, the appoggiatura is omitted, substituting a crotchet rest and taking the $\frac{7}{5b}$ afterwards."

Of Ex. 19 we are told that, by way of accompaniment, "one either plays the whole example, just as it stands, or lets the right hand rest."

(l. c. § 18 *e*)

Ex. 19

(e) Bach gives several examples (of which it must suffice to quote only two) of cases in which the proper duration of the appoggiatura has been ignored by the composer himself ("for which", we are told, "absence of mind or ignorance may be to blame"), and the Bass itself, in consequence, incorrectly noted, i.e. in even, instead of dotted, notes. "If appoggiaturas were written out", Bach writes (l. c. § 18), "and properly incorporated in the bar in accordance with their time-value, such mistakes would not occur. The result of the performance of these appoggiaturas is an insufferable harshness in relation to the Bass instead of the ingratiating effect which is ordinarily the object in view with all appoggiaturas. Often one cannot even get out of the difficulty by dint of pauses pending the resolution or *Abzug* of the appoggiaturas, the right hand joining in again at this resolution. The appoggiatura, the main note (*Abzug*), everything, is dissonant owing to the progression of the Bass. No middle parts at all, at least no natural and therefore good ones, derive themselves (*fliessen*) from these examples. A sure sign of bad, or at least not well-considered writing! Whoever wants to think correctly in composing, must think melody and harmony at the same time. Examples cannot easily be found in which it is so easy to get so many consecutive Fifths as here.[13] But if the Bass is dotted, the figuring and accompaniment become natural and easy."

The Bass as corrected by Bach is appended to each example. For the sake of clearness the principal part, as actually played, has been added by the present writer:

[13] It will be observed that, in Ex. 20, consecutive Fifths, avoided in Bach's accompaniment by the rests, arise between the principal part and the 3 of the first and second, and third and fourth chords of the bar.

[14] Here it will be seen that, besides correcting the Bass so as to avoid the ugly con-

With regard to the accompaniment given with the uncorrected Bass, omitted in the case of two examples not quoted here, Bach writes: "In the case of the examples where only one bearable accompaniment is possible, I have added the latter, which, however, must never go above the principal part."

Nevertheless, it will be observed that, at the beginning of Ex. 21, this latter condition is not fulfilled.

Bach continues: "In the examples where no accompaniment is given, the *tasto solo* must be adhered to."

(*f*) A short (or invariable) appoggiatura in a Solo part, Bach tells us (l.c. § 19), is not played in the accompaniment, or in any way regarded.

Nevertheless, he gives examples in which short notes (though not, in the strict sense of the term, short appoggiaturas)[15] of which the figuring takes no account, call for a modification of the accompaniment *when the time is slow*. Among them are the following:

Of these examples Bach writes: "In (*b*) and (*c*) [=Exx. 22, 23] the rests have a good effect; in (*b*) [=Ex. 22] they introduce variety into the movement, and the appoggiaturas at the same time become distinct; in (*c*) [=Ex.

secutive Ninths with the Solo part, Bach has improved the harmony by introducing a retardation, 6 5 over *a*, in addition to the 2 3 already present in the Solo part:

---

[15] The short or invariable appoggiatura *comes out of the time of the main note*, but its duration (generally very short) stands in no definite relation to that of the latter. In the present examples the notes in question, though short in themselves, are of equal duration with their resolution and are therefore, technically, variable or long appoggiaturas. Bach had, however, explained earlier in the chapter (l.c. § 4) that the shortest variable appoggiaturas [i.e. the shortest to be considered in the accompaniment] must not be quicker than a quaver in *Allegretto*.

23] the rests are necessary, because the Thirds, if struck simultaneously with the bass notes, give rise to disgusting Fifths [cf. note 13]. In (*d*) [=Ex. 24], where a number of appoggiaturas occur in succession, the unpleasant clashing is likewise diminished by rests."

Ex. 24

Of the following example, with double appoggiaturas, Bach tells us that rests are required for the same reason as in Ex. 22. He gives two alternative accompaniments:

Ex. 25

or

III. *Driving notes (Rückende Noten, Rückungen).*

(*a*) "Driving notes", Ph. Em. Bach writes (ibid. Ch. 26, § 1), "either *anticipate* or *retard* the ordinary harmony."

(*b*) In the former case, we are told, no difference is made in the accompaniment, the chords being struck in exact accordance with the figuring, as:

16)
Ex. 26

(l. c. § 2)

When the *time is quick*, this applies even when the driving notes *are in the Bass*:

16) 17)
Ex. 27   *Allegro*

(l. c. § 3)

16 The chords, not given by Bach, have here been added for clearness' sake.
17 Cf. Ch. xviii, 'Quick notes in the Bass', § 3 *d*, Ex. 40, and the text immediately preceding.

(c) When, on the other hand, the driving notes in the principal part *retard* the harmony, it is evident that they are exactly on a par with the long (or variable) appoggiatura (cf. II c, Exx. 3, 13).

When, therefore, *the time is quick,* they are disregarded in the accompaniment, as:

Ex. 28
(*cf. note* 16)

(l. c. § 3)

But when the time is slow, the accompaniment is subject to the same kind of modification (irrespective of the figuring) as in the case of the appoggiatura. In the following example, after the first two chords, the accompaniment is in two parts only:

Ex. 29

(l. c. § 2)

In Ex. 30 there is no reduction of the harmony, but it is so modified as to avoid clashing with the Solo part. At the beginning of the first bar the retardation (4 3) in the Solo part is included in the accompaniment (with the addition of 9 8), and in the remainder of the example, up to the last bar, in which the Solo part anticipates instead of retarding the harmony (cf. III b), the latter is skilfully modified in such a way as to fit in perfectly with the principal part. Bach also presents an alternative accompaniment (b):

(l. c. § 2)

Ex. 30

In Ex. 31, we are told, the right hand must be raised with the entry of the *d* sharp in each bar of the Solo part, as shown at the end of the example:

(l. c. § 2)

Ex.31

(*d*) When the progression is by semitones, Bach tells us, the accompaniment of driving notes must be particularly delicate (*fein*), "in order that the said semitones may retain their distinctness, and cacophony not be promoted". In the following examples (two out of the three given by Bach) a slow (or at all events moderate) *tempo* is presupposed.

In Ex. 32 the driving notes anticipate the harmony in the Bass (cf. Ex. 27). Bach warns us that the Triad on *f* * must be taken without the 8ve:

Ex.32
(*cf. note* 16)

(l. c. § 4)

In Ex. 33 the progression by semitones is imitated in the right hand. If a fuller accompaniment is desired, Bach tells us, the notes belonging to the principal part can be included in it, as indicated by the figuring below the example:

Ex.33

(l. c. § 4)

IV. The dotted 'Anschlag' and dotted Slide.

(*a*) With regard to the dotted *Anschlag* and the dotted slide (*Schleifer*), to the accompaniment of each of which Ph. Em. Bach devotes an entire chapter, it must suffice to say that the modifications of the accompaniment (and of the figuring) which may be entailed by them depend on exactly the same principles as in the case of the long appoggiatura.

Both ornaments are characteristic of pieces in which sentiment predominates, and both, but more especially the latter, are liable to be arbitrarily prolonged as a means of intensifying the expression.[18]

---

[18] Ph. Em. Bach's rules for the execution of these ornaments (given in Part I of the *Versuch*), together with his examples, are given in full in Dannreuther's *Musical Ornamentation* (Novello & Co.), Part II, Chapters vi, vii.

(b) The dotted *Anschlag*, as Ph. Em. Bach explains,[19] originates in the interposition, between a long appoggiatura from below and the main note, of a short appoggiatura from above. The main note, therefore, loses *a fraction more of its value* than when preceded by a long appoggiatura only. At first, no doubt, the interposition of this short appoggiatura depended entirely on the fancy of the performer, for Bach tells us that the dotted *Anschlag* is indicated, either *by a simple appoggiatura from below*, or as in the following example:

One point that emerges from Bach's numerous examples of the accompaniment of the dotted *Anschlag* is worth noticing, though he himself makes no mention of it: When it precedes a dotted note, its first note may either occupy *two-thirds* of the time of the latter (as is normally the case with a long appoggiatura), or only *one-third*.

In Ex. 35 the former is the case, in Ex. 36 the latter. This is clearly shown by the figures *below* the Bass, which, as in previous examples, represent what Bach regards as the correct figuring, as opposed to that which may ordinarily be expected (here given *above* the Bass):

---

[19] *Versuch &c.*, Part I, Hauptstück (Section) II, Abtheilung (Subsection) VI, § 9.
[20] This example, which is given in the 3rd edition 1787 of Part I of the *Versuch* (l. c. § 8), does not appear in the 2nd edition 1759.
[21] It will be observed that, doubtless as a concession to established custom, Bach

(c) The dotted slide is indicated by two small notes, of which the first is dotted. Unlike the appoggiatura and the dotted *Anschlag* it starts *two* degrees below the main note, the interval being bridged by the short note following the dot. No other ornament, Bach tells us, is so variously interpreted in the matter of the time-value assigned to it and to the main note, respectively. The frequent prolongation of the first note, and proportionate curtailment of what follows, is determined primarily by the sentiment to be expressed by the passage in question and is, therefore, to a very large extent, purely arbitrary.

Two examples must suffice:

(ibid. Ch. 28, § 4 *f*)

(l. c. § 4 *i*)

Of this example Bach writes: "If, in this last example, the first note of the slide is held longer than usual, the Third is not struck till the last quaver of the bar, and the Sixth is repeated with it, as we have shown in the final version."

employs what he himself stigmatizes as the *incorrect* notation of the dotted *Anschlag* (cf. Ex. 34). The interpretation of the ornament has here been added by the present writer for the sake of clearness.

²² The interpretation of the ornament, added by the present writer, is based on the following example from the rare folio volume in which Ph. Em. Bach illustrates the First Part of the *Versuch* ('Exempel und Probestücke', &c., Tab. VI, Fig. xciii):

(a) The figured bass is indicated by the small notes, of which (at the

CHAPTER IV
ON CERTAIN NICETIES OF THE ACCOMPANIMENT

ON CERTAIN NICETIES OF THE ACCOMPANIMENT

§ 1. *Introductory.*

(*a*) The above heading is borrowed from Ph. Em. Bach, whose chapter 'Von gewissen Zierlichkeiten des Accompagnements' (*Versuch &c.*, Part II, 1762, Ch. 32) is, in importance, second to none of our few sources of information on the subject.

(*b*) The first attempt to tabulate the means, over and above the literal interpretation of the figures, by which life and interest may be given to the accompaniment, was made, so far as the present writer is aware, by Michel de Saint Lambert, and has already been recorded (cf. Ch. i, § 23 *k*).

(*c*) Much may be learned from Mattheson's *Organisten-Probe* ('Organists' Test'), 1719, of which a second edition appeared in 1731 under the title *Grosse General-Bass-Schule* ('Great Thorough-Bass School').

It must, however, be remembered that this work is in no sense a School of *Accompaniment*. The forty-eight 'Test-Pieces' (twenty-four, of moderate difficulty, constituting the 'Mittel-Classe' or Middle Grade, and twenty-four of greater difficulty the 'Ober-Classe' or Higher Grade) are designed to afford opportunities for the display of an Organist's powers of improvization (on the Harpsichord) on a given figured Bass, and, in so far, they are an excellent preparation for the occasions where the principal part is either silent, or so devoid of interest as to give the accompanist a legitimate opportunity for display (cf. Ch. iii, § 8 *h*).[1]

(*d*) By far the most systematic treatment of the subject is to be found in the sixty-two pages which Heinichen devotes to it in his most illuminating chapter: 'Vom Manierlichen GENERAL-BASS und fernern *Exercitio* eines *Incipienten*'[2] (*General-Bass &c.*, 1728, Part I, Ch. VI).

(*e*) Besides this, a most interesting and important source of information is Part II of Geminiani's *Opera* 11: 'The ART of ACCOMPANIAMENT [*sic*] . . . on the HARPSICHORD', published in 1755.

(*f*) In each case, however much the details may differ, the main principle is the same, namely, to make the accompaniment flow, instead of presenting a series of perpendicular blocks of harmony, the isolation of which is far more marked on the Harpsichord than on the Organ on account of the evanescent tone of the former.

(*g*) Furthermore (apart from Mattheson, who did not deal with the problem of accompaniment at all), there is complete agreement in the most important principle of all, namely, that no embellishment of the accompaniment must ever be allowed in any way to obscure the principal part or to discount the interest attaching to it.

---

[1] What Geminiani says of his own examples (cf. *g*) may equally well be said of Mattheson's.

[2] *On the embellishment of a Thorough-Bass and the further practice of a beginner*: a literal translation of the title is impossible, the adjective *manierlich* being used, not in the modern sense of 'well mannered', but in direct correspondence with the technical meaning (as applied to Music) of the noun *Manier*, namely, any kind of grace or embellishment (French *agrémen*).

Geminiani, who gives a number of examples (briefly explained in his Introduction) of the free and varied treatment of simple Basses, expresses himself
on this point with admirable clearness, as follows:

"It will perhaps be said that the following Examples are arbitrary Compositions upon the Bass; and it may be asked how this arbitrary Manner of
accompanying can agree with the Intention and Stile of all sorts of Compositions. Moreover a fine Singer or Player, when he finds himself accompanied
in this Manner, will perhaps complain that he is interrupted, and the Beauties
of his Performance thereby obscured, and deprived of their Effect. To this I
answer, That a good Accompanyer ought to possess the faculty of playing all
sorts of Basses in different Manners, so as to be able, on proper Occasions,
to enliven the Composition, and delight the Singer or Player. But he is to
exercise this Faculty with Judgement, Taste, and Discretion, agreeable to the
Stile of the Composition, and the Manner and Intention of the Performer. If
an Accompanyer thinks of nothing but satisfying his own Whim and Caprice,
he may perhaps be said to play well, but will certainly be said to accompany ill."

Ph. Em. Bach expresses himself to the same effect (l.c. § 3):

"The commonest expression by which a good accompanist is characterized
is generally the following: *he accompanies with discretion.* . . . He seeks, with
the greatest modesty, to share in gaining the desired credit for those whom
he accompanies, regardless of the fact that his powers sometimes exceed
theirs. . . . Furthermore, he always takes into consideration the intentions of
the Composer and the performers of a piece; he seeks to further and uphold
their intention; he seizes upon all possible beauties of performance, and
accompaniment generally, as often as the nature of a piece demands; but, at
the same time, he uses the necessary caution in the employment of these
beauties, in order not to hamper (*einschränken*) any one; to that end he uses
his powers, not continually, but sparingly, and only when they enhance the
general effect (*wenn sie die gute Ausnahme befördern*). . . . In a word, a discreet
accompanist must possess a good musical soul, which has much understanding
and good will."

(*h*) With regard to the means to be employed with a view to the embellishment
of the accompaniment, the two most important points are, broadly: (1) the
avoidance of monotony in the upper part, and (2) the establishment of a certain
continuity by means of connecting links between the successive harmonies.

In the attainment of both objects great use is made of passing notes,
bridging the interval of a Third, in any of the upper parts, or even, as in
one of Heinichen's examples (§ 3, Ex. 2 *a*, bar 1), in the Bass itself.

Sometimes, when the Bass lends itself to such treatment, and when the
effect of the principal part is in no way discounted thereby, an upper part
may move in Thirds (or occasionally Sixths) with the former, thereby con-
tributing to a general fluency of effect.

Sometimes, too (though this is not specially mentioned by the authorities
here quoted), an ornamental resolution of a discord may be used to establish
rhythmical balance between the accompaniment and the principal part (cf.
Ch. iii, § 8, Ex. 1, bars 7 sq., and Ex. 2).

Sometimes, again, the harmonies may be broken up in some form of
arpeggio.

Characteristic examples from the authorities above mentioned will be given
in the sequel.

§ 2. *Mattheson.*

(*a*) It has already been mentioned that the forty-eight figured Basses, given as 'Test-Pieces' in Mattheson's *Organisten-Probe*, 1719 (*Grosse General-Bass-Schule*, 1731), are designed as the foundations of independent improvizations, and not, like most of the examples given by Heinichen and Ph. Em. Bach, as subservient to imaginary principal parts.

It is not surprising, therefore, that Mattheson, in the explanatory notes (*Erläuterungen*) which follow each 'Test-Piece', makes a great point of a form of imitation, namely, the employment in the upper part of a phrase or figure which has occurred, or is about to occur, in the Bass.

It may be remembered that Heinichen excused himself for the employment of this very device in the last four bars of his setting-out of the figured Bass of a short Fugue (Ch. iii, § 6, Ex. 1), expressly stating that such devices were not required of an *accompanist*, whereas they were especially appropriate in a *Praeludium*, that is to say, a free improvization (founded on a given Bass, or wholly independent, as the case might be).

It has, however, been pointed out more than once, that a prolonged silence of the principal part, or even the occurrence of long sustained notes (or other figures devoid of melodic interest), sometimes provides the accompanist with a legitimatè opportunity for a display which would otherwise be inappropriate (cf. Ch. iii, § 8 *a ad fin.*). No excuse, therefore, is needed for giving examples of Mattheson's procedure in the matter in question.

It may be mentioned incidentally that his Basses were evidently carefully designed to provide the opportunities for imitation to which he calls attention (cf. Ch. iii, § 8 *d*, note 1), and are, therefore, of an highly artificial character.

(*b*) The following is a characteristic example (o.c. *Ober-Classe, Prob-Stück* 4, bars 23 sqq.):

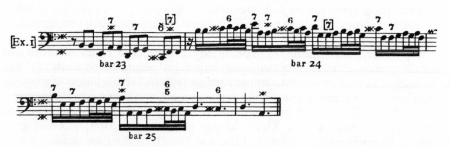

Here Mattheson directs us (l. c. *Erläuterungen*, § 6) to use the Bass of bar 24, a Third (or rather a Tenth) higher, as the upper part of bar 23.[1]

---

[1] With regard to the Bass of bar 23, it would naturally be played in Octaves (cf. Ch. iii, § 7), and Mattheson expressly indicated this treatment in similar passages earlier in the piece. In the present case, however, the usual duplication in the *lower* Octave is impossible, owing to the limited compass of the Harpsichord; we must, therefore, either double the Bass in the upper Octave (cf. Ch. iii, § 7 *c*, note 2) or

take some other interval of the harmony in the left hand, as:

When a florid upper part is assigned to the right hand, Mattheson frequently recommends that the left hand should be made responsible for the harmony, but this would not be convenient or effective in the present case.

With regard to bar 24, and the first half of bar 25, no special direction is given; plain chords may, therefore, be used. On the other hand, Mattheson so frequently recommends us to follow the Bass in Thirds (he sometimes refers to this as a kind of standing order) that it seems likely that he would have preferred that this should be done in the present case, as shown in Ex. 1 *a* below.

The last four notes of the example are a transposition of the beginning of

the phrase with which the Test-Piece opens: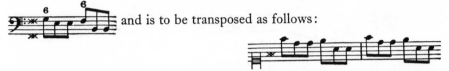

With regard to these we are told (l.c. § 7) that the 'suitable countersubject' is to be derived from a phrase which appears in the Bass (in bar 4):

and is to be transposed as follows:

"From which one sees", as Mattheson adds, with a touch of his usual self-complacency, "that these pieces are no mere whims, empty compositions (*Sätze*), disorderly wild ideas, or dry Basses either; but that everything hangs together, and that there is hardly a note to be found which has not a definite relation to the others."

If, then, we follow Mattheson's directions, we arrive at something like the following:

Ex. 1a

N.B.—At *, on the fourth quaver beat of the second bar of the example we see a fifth part added at the top, its lower 8ve being subsequently dropped (cf. Ch. iii, § 4 1).

In the case of the next example (ibid. *Ober-Classe, Prob-Stück* 10, bars 33–6) Mattheson's directions are as follows (l.c. *Erläuterungen,* § 3):

"The thirty-third bar starts a new invention and demands that the right hand should follow the left in canonic fashion, that is to say, note for note, as soon as the latter has a start of three steps [i.e. quavers]; and so it goes on till the thirty-seventh bar. . . ."

In accordance with the above, the example will appear, in the main, as follows:

4)
[Ex.2]

bar 33   34   35

36   37

(c) Two examples of Mattheson's melodic treatment of the upper part have already been given (cf. Ch. iii, § 3 II, note 8, Exx. A and B).

Of the following example (ibid. *Mittel-Classe, Prob-Stück* 22, bars 21 sqq., *Erläuterungen,* § 7) he writes (l.c. § 8):

"Suchlike *cantabile* methods (*Sing-Arten*),[5] however, are in place only when some one is playing alone, or playing such pieces as these examples by way of a test; also, to be sure, when the Bass gives the singer occasion to pause and take breath. . . ."

He further adds: "What has several times been said about full harmony (*Vollstimmigkeit*) in the Bass, or left hand,[6] holds good: otherwise it would

[4] Apart from the countless misprints and omissions in the figuring of his examples, it would appear that Mattheson sometimes purposely refrained from indicating accidentals, as above, on the first quaver of bar 36, where the correct figuring is supplied in brackets.

In his explanatory notes to the 12th 'Test-Piece' of the 'Higher Grade' he writes (l. c. *Erläuterungen,* § 4): "Only the Seconds [i.e. the 2 of a $\frac{6}{4}$ chord] are written over the notes, nothing more; the rest a pupil who has advanced from the Middle to the Higher Grade must by this time know for himself, namely, whether the Fourth belonging to the chord should be augmented or perfect (*gross oder klein*), in accordance with the nature and property of each harmony (*Klang*) and of the key to which it belongs. If, having regard to the melody, the key changes, one generally puts in the required figures as clearly as possible; if not, some of them can be omitted with every justification, since the player must know the conditions (*Bewandniss*) and nature of his key, beyond which nothing is here required. . . ."

[5] This applies, of course, only to the first seven bars of the example.

[6] This is not to be taken as meant to imply that the entire chord (with the exception of the upper part) is necessarily to be taken by the left hand, but merely that the latter

not be a Thorough-Bass at all. Only print did not admit of the possibility of indicating all the parts." [7]

8)
[Ex. 3]

N.B.—The ⤬ prefixed to the first bass note of the example, being already in the key-signature, denotes a *double* sharp (cf. Ch. xxiv, 'Varieties of notation', § 3).

is to be responsible for the completeness of the harmony, and must therefore take any interval indicated by the figures which cannot conveniently be taken by the right hand.

[7] The inner parts, indicated by small notes, have been added by the present writer. In this, as in other similar examples, it is a thousand pities that Mattheson did not place his intentions with regard to them beyond the reach of doubt, in spite of the typographical difficulties of the early eighteenth century.

It is very probable that, in the present instance, he intended the harmony to be fuller than as shown here. In bars 5 and 7, in particular, the ♭ 5 in the figuring, due to be struck on the second crotchet of the bar over the Bass *b* sharp (which, though actually silent at the moment, is present in the imagination, and is as much the Bass of the new harmony indicated by the ♭ 5 as if it were sounded) appears here only as an unaccented semiquaver in the upper part.

Very possibly something like the following was intended:

The consecutive 8ves, $\sharp f \sharp e$, are such as are bound to occur in a case of this kind if, as Mattheson frequently insists, the completeness of the harmony is to be maintained, which would evidently not be the case if an important interval, like ♭ 5, only appeared (after it was due) as a transitory note in the upper part.

Between bars 3 and 4 similar consecutives, $\frac{b}{b} \frac{\sharp a}{\sharp a}$, have been introduced between the upper part and one of the added inner parts. Here, however, they are slightly veiled by the crotchet's rest in the latter. [*Cont. on p.* 444.

[8] See note on p. 444.

(d) A device which Mattheson is very fond of recommending, as an alternative to plain chords, is some form of what is known in German as *Brechung*, a term which denotes, not only a true *arpeggio*, but any form of harmony in which the respective intervals are not struck simultaneously, so that the chord (as the term in question implies) may be said to be 'broken'. The following examples [9] will serve for illustration.

Of the first of them (Ex. 4) Mattheson naïvely says:

"This way of syncopating [10] is quite easy and makes as much of a to-do as if it were something quite out of the way (*und macht ein Aufsehen, als wenn es was rechtes wäre*): accordingly one can often make use of it with particular advantage and but little trouble."

It must be remembered that the florid upper part in bars 1–7 of the example is practically a *Solo* (such as might have been played on a Violin) while the remaining parts represent the real figured Bass accompaniment. Consecutive 8ves between the one and the other are, therefore, almost on a par with those discussed in Ch. iii (§ 5 B III a).

[8] In bar 11 of the example it is possible that the second quaver (♯ d) is due to a misprint and that ♯ c was intended. It is more probable, however, that Mattheson anticipated the 6 (which he omitted to figure) in order to maintain the pattern set in the two preceding bars.

[9] Cf. ibid. *Ober-Classe, Prob-Stück* 2, *Erläuterungen*, § 2; l. c. § 4; *Prob-Stück* 9, *Erläuterungen*, §§ 2 and 3.

[10] The term (*syncopiren*) is here used as the equivalent of *brechen*.

N.B.—The figures in the above (with the exception of those added in square brackets) are as given in the text of the *Prob-Stück* itself: in the example as it appears in the *Erläuterungen* there are several omissions.

In Ex. 6 (which comprises bars 37–43 of the *Prob-Stück* from which it is taken) the upper part follows the pattern of the Bass of adjacent bars, though not quite so closely as was the case in Ex. 1.[11]

The last three examples (Exx. 4–6) are unaccompanied by the directions for the completion of the harmony by the left hand which Mattheson gave in connexion with Ex. 3, and in other similar cases. On the other hand, these directions are omitted in a case [12] in which there can be *no possible doubt* but that they were intended to apply, and, when given, it is sometimes in terms which convey the idea that Mattheson regarded them as a standing order.[13]

[11] The Bass of the three bars immediately preceding the example is:

[12] Cf. ibid. *Ober-Classe, Prob-Stück* 22, *Erläuterungen*, § 2:

[13] With reference to an example (ibid. *Ober-Classe, Prob-Stück* 1, *Erläuterungen*, § 2) beginning as follows—

Mattheson writes: "That, with this adornment [i.e. the florid upper part], the left hand must share in playing the figures and chords (*die Zieffern und Accorde mitgreiffen müsse*) has been said, it is to be hoped, often enough; and I should frequently have liked to note the Bass [i.e. the left-hand part] exactly as it is to be played, if combinations of notes could be printed as easily as they can be written or engraved on copper (*wenn die Noten so wol in einander könnten gedruckt, als geschrieben, oder auff Kupffer gestochen werden*)."

We may, therefore, safely add a part to all three examples.[14]

(e) Ornaments in the shape of appoggiaturas, trills, &c., are rarely mentioned by Mattheson, but it will be seen from the following that he attached considerable importance to their employment, not only in the upper part (as in the extract given in note 12), but *in the Bass itself*.

It is hardly necessary to remind the reader that nothing of the sort would be appropriate except during pauses in the principal part, or when the latter is of such a nature that the chief interest lies in the accompaniment (cf. Ch. iii, § 8 *a ad fin.*).

In § 5 of the explanatory notes (*Erläuterung*) to *Prob-Stück* 19 of the *Ober-Classe* Mattheson writes: "In the twenty-third bar a grace (*Manier*) occurs to me which can often be employed in the left hand, the more so since, generally speaking, a great lack of ornamentation (in the shape of good sharp trills, appoggiaturas, accents, and the like) is to be noticed in the playing of

[14] Exx. 4 and 5 (left hand only) will appear as follows, the right-hand part remaining unaltered:

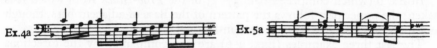

In the case of Ex. 6 there will be a slight crossing of parts in the first three bars which will, however, cause no inconvenience to the player.

The example will appear, in the main, as follows:

Of course, if desired, three parts can be taken in the left hand:

a Thorough-Bass. What I require here concerns the upward leap of a Third, where one can generally make a vigorous slide (*Schleuffer*), and thereby give uncommon force to the high note. The slide in question must not, however, be drawn out (*gezogen*), as, for instance, in singing, but must be short and executed with some violence, as though one put all three fingers down at once and only raised them one by one. It can better be shown in playing

than described." The bar in question is: [Ex.7] (musical notation) to be

executed approximately as follows: [Ex. 7a] (musical notation)

From what Mattheson says we may infer that he regarded this treatment as applicable in all similar cases in which it is desired to give emphasis to the higher note.

The next example (ibid. *Ober-Classe, Prob-Stück* 22, *ad init.*) concerns the

downward leap of a (minor) Third: [Ex. 8]

Of this Mattheson writes (l. c. *Erläuterung,* § 1):

"At the very beginning, where *c* sharp falls to *a* sharp, it is to be noted that, between the two, *b* must be struck as an appoggiatura with a short trill (*dass zwischen beyden das* h *an- und mit einem kurzen Triller vorschlagen muss*)."

It is impossible to say with certainty exactly how this is to be interpreted, but it seems probable that the following is approximately what was intended:

[Ex. 8a] (musical notation)

The last instance to be quoted is a particularly interesting one, as it makes it probable that, under the circumstances in question, a shake, whether indicated or not, was a matter of established tradition.

In the 4th *Probstück* of the *Ober-Classe* (from which Ex. 1 was taken) the opening phrase recurs twice, in different keys:

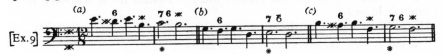

[Ex.9]

In all these cases Mattheson directs (l.c. *Erläuterung,* §§ 1, 3, 5) that the fifth note (marked * above) should be played with a shake (what he describes as a *sharp trill*) in the *lower* Octave,[15] the Bass, as its nature demands, being played in Octaves (cf. Ch. iii, § 7).

In the third case (Ex. 9 *c*) Mattheson adds: "If any one cares to attempt

---

[15] Except in the case of a very large hand, the upper Octave will, of necessity, have to be temporarily abandoned.

this trill with the right hand, on the Sixth, at the same time, it can do no harm." [16]

Now, it is extremely interesting to note that the two cases embodied in Ex. 9 (*a* and *c* being identical except in pitch) are the very ones in which Michel de Saint-Lambert tells us that a *tremblement* is always introduced in the Bass (cf. Ch. i, § 23 *k* 15).

He, too, mentions the possibility of making a shake on the Sixth instead of, or even in addition to, that on the bass note, though he does not advocate it. Of the latter alternative, indeed, he says: "but I should not like it done with either of these two kinds of cadence. It would be too affected."

Mattheson was evidently very familiar with Saint-Lambert's *Nouveau Traité*, which he often quotes; generally, it is true, in a disparaging tone. It is, therefore, possible that, in the matter of these shakes, he was merely following Saint-Lambert; but it seems more probable that their employment in the cases in question was a matter of tradition both in France and in Germany.

§ 3. *Heinichen.*

I. In the chapter mentioned above (cf. § 1 *d*) Heinichen states his programme as follows (l.c. §§ 2 and 4):

"The art of embellishing a Thorough-Bass (*die Kunst eines manierlichen* [1] *General-Basses*) consists in not always merely striking plain chords (*dass man seine Accorde nicht überall platt niederschlage*), but in occasionally introducing a grace (*Manier*) in all the parts (especially in the extreme part of the right hand, which is most prominent) and thereby giving more elegance (*Grace*) to the accompaniment; this can be done with every comfort in an accompaniment of four, and, upon occasion, from five to six parts."

"As the basis of our enterprise we will choose from innumerable graces only the following ones, and divide them, in order the better to distinguish them, into two classes. The first class shall include those small graces which always remain invariable, just as one learns them from one's teacher, and these are (1) the Shake (*Trillo*), (2) the *Transitus* to the Third [i.e. a passing note bridging the interval of a Third], (3) the Appoggiatura (*Vorschlag*), (4) the Slide, (5) the Mordent, and (6) the so-called Acciaccatura. The second class embraces those kind of graces which must be invented by ourselves, and which depend on the fancy of the individual; these are (1) Melody, (2) Passages, and (3) Arpeggios or broken harmonies [2] (*gebrochene Sachen*). And, along with the others, we will further include Imitation [3] as a special form of embellishment."

II. (*a*) With regard to the ornaments of the first class above mentioned,

[16] If this is done, the execution will be as follows:

or, of course, the chords can be taken in another position.

[1] Cf. § 1, note 2.   [2] Cf. § 2 *d ad init.*

[3] Heinichen's views on this subject have already been given fully (cf. Ch. iii, § 8 *d*).

it is unnecessary to give the whole of Heinichen's example illustrating the use of the Shake, as the latter occurs so frequently in his other examples to be given presently. It will, of course, be understood that the shake begins with the auxiliary and not, as in later times, with the main note:

[Ex. 1]

In some cases, however (e.g. in the last bar of Ex. 2 *a*), it seems probable that the sign *tr.* was used by Heinichen to indicate a *Pralltriller* or Inverted Mordent, afterwards denoted by the sign ⌣.

We shall see later on, from what Heinichen says about the execution of the Mordent, that he had no pedantic inclination to regard one particular interpretation of an ornament as the one and only way to salvation.

(*b*) Of the grace next mentioned on his list Heinichen says (l.c. § 6):

"The *Transitus* to the Third has not, in itself, the effect of an embellishment on the *Clavier*.[4] But if, in the case of somewhat slow notes, it is accompanied by a trill, it sounds much more elegant (*zierlicher*), and can be introduced both in the parts falling to the right hand and also in the Bass itself. For, instead of a plain (*schlecht*) accompaniment, such as:

[Ex. 2]

the following will prove far more elegant:

[Ex. 2a]

---

[4] "Der *Transitus* in die 3ᵉ ist an sich selbst auf dem *Clavier* von schlechten *Effect*." It is important to note that in the German of Heinichen's time (and even later), the word *schlecht* was still used in its old sense of 'simple', 'unadorned', without necessarily implying any disparagement. The meaning of the above is, therefore, that the effect is *plain* as opposed to *ornate*.

[5] Heinichen explains in a footnote (l.c. § 5) that these examples are designed to illustrate as fully as possible the use of the *Manier* in question, and that they are not to be taken as indicating that it is to be employed so often, to the exclusion of others, within the compass of a few bars.

(c) The following example (l.c. § 7) illustrates the use of the Appoggiatura, which Heinichen does not indicate in the usual way, but by the *custos* ᴧ:

With regard to the execution of the Appoggiatura, Heinichen tells us (l.c. § 9, note *a*) that it is *not the same in playing as in singing*. In playing, the ornament is *anticipated by a short note*, as in the following examples:

Thus, the third bar of Ex. 3 (right hand) is to be played as follows:

(d) Of the Slide Heinichen says (l.c. § 9):

"The well-known Slide (*Schleiffung*) with 3 fingers has a good effect in *cantabile* pieces, and can be used in the case of all upward leaps, as also in the case of a rising 2nd. Only one must be careful that the note on which the slide begins, always marked with a ✕ in the following examples, does not give rise to faulty progressions with the Bass. [It will be seen that Heinichen's method of executing the slide makes this caution doubly necessary.] Thus in the following three first examples (Ex. 5 (a) (b) (c)) the Slide would be improperly introduced, because it occasions 8ves and 5ths with the Bass. On the other hand, in the extended example which follows, the effect is good throughout. It is to be noted at the same time that this grace is best introduced in the upper part; thus, the right hand cannot well play more than two parts, and the rest of the accompaniment must be relegated to the left:

[6] The consecutive 8ves (Treble and Tenor) in the first and penultimate bars, like those (Alto and Bass) in Ch. iii, § 6, Ex. 1 (between bars 21 and 22), are not excused

[Ex.6]

Heinichen's way of executing the ornament in question was very different from that described and illustrated some years later by Ph. Em. Bach. He tells us, moreover, in the note referred to above (below Ex. 3), that in *playing*, but not in singing, the ornament is to be anticipated by a short note, as:

[Ex. 7]   (as written)

[Ex.7a]   (as sung)

[Ex.7b]   (as played) [7]

(*e*) Of the Mordent, which he indicates by two small parallel strokes ⸜ pointing obliquely upwards at the note to which they are prefixed, Heinichen tells us (l.c. § 11) that it can be executed in three different ways.

Following his description of the ornament in question on *c″*:

we arrive at: Ex.8

The time-values here assigned are, of course, only approximate, since the duration of the ornament is in no definite proportion to that of the main note.[8]

by the fulness of the accompaniment. Compare what is said elsewhere (Ch. iii, § 6 *b ad fin.*) about similar cases.

[7] In subsequent examples, however, the sign ✕ is thrice used in a context which makes the above interpretation impossible (cf. Ex. 12 *a*, bars 3 and 7; Ex. 12 *b*, bar 7). In each case the figure is the same, though at a different pitch:

Three possible renderings suggest themselves, of which the third (*c*) comes nearest to Heinichen's explanation of the ornament, as shown in Ex. 7 *b*:

[8] Of (*a*) Heinichen tells us that the two notes *b c* are to be struck almost simul-

It will be noticed that (a) is simply a short *appoggiatura*. This mode of execution, Heinichen tells us, is in accordance with the description given by Gasparini,[9] who says that the ornament in question is called *Mordente* (from *mordere* = to bite) because it resembles the bite of a small animal which at once lets go without inflicting any wound.

Of (c) we are told that the ornament is thus executed by some people in the case of *slow* notes, and that the repercussion takes place *once or oftener*.

Heinichen goes on to say (l.c. § 12) that it is a matter of indifference how a pupil has been taught to execute the Mordent, and that he is at liberty to vary the execution as circumstances seem to demand. The important question, he tells us, is *whether the interval between the auxiliary and the main note is to be a semitone or a whole tone*, and this is to be settled in accordance with the *Ambitus modi*,[10] or key: in other words, the ornament is to be strictly diatonic.[11]

[Ex. 9]

This example, we are told, is equally applicable to the Harpsichord and to the Organ (*so wohl auf Saiten- als Pfeiffwerck*).

Particular attention is called to the ⁜ prefixed by Heinichen to the ⸝, as a guide to the student, on the third beat of bar 2 and the second beat of bar 4.

Some interesting details are given (l.c. §§ 14, 15) concerning Gasparini's use of the ornament which he called a *Mordente* (Ex. 8 a), which differed considerably, we are told, from that illustrated above, and is very effective *on the Harpsichord*, particularly in Recitatives and music of a pathetic character.

These are best considered in connexion with the *Acciaccatura* (from *acciaccare* = to crush).

(f) Heinichen bases his lengthy description of the *Acciaccatura* (l.c. §§ 16–25) entirely on that of Gasparini. A very brief account must suffice here. Gasparini makes only a very slight distinction between the *Mordente* and the *Acciaccatura*: he applies the former term to those cases only in which the auxiliary is a *semitone* below the main note, and the latter to all others.

In both cases, the chord in which these ornaments occur (and Gasparini

taneously ("fast in einem *Tempo*"); of (b) he says that it is to be executed "with such rapidity that all three percussions give the *c*, as it were, but one accent".

[9] *L'armonico pratico al cimbalo*, Venice (Bortoli), 1708.

[10] For the definition of this term, in its stricter and wider senses, see Ch. i, § 24 VII 3, note 21. In the present instance the term includes, not only the key in which a piece is written, but attendant keys.

[11] In the minor key (whether it be the main key of the piece, or only temporary), when the Mordent falls on the first degree of the scale, *accompanied by Tonic harmony*, the auxiliary, as the leading note of the scale, is, of course, sharpened, as may be seen in Ex. 9, bars 2 and 4. In the first of these two instances it will be noticed that the temporary key (E minor) is not established till the following bar.

does not appear to employ them otherwise than in a chord) is slightly spread ('mit einem gelinden *Arpeggio*'), that is to say, the notes are struck in rapid upward succession, each note being retained, as struck, *except the ornaments themselves*, which are instantly released.

In the examples given (borrowed from Gasparini), the printing of the notes in succession denotes the spreading of the chord, while the black notes indicate the ornaments, as:

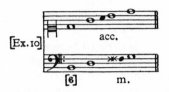

A further twofold distinction between the two ornaments is noticeable in Gasparini's examples quoted by Heinichen, to which, however, no reference is made: (1) the Acciaccatura may be above (instead of below) the main note, and (2), when two notes of a chord are separated by the interval of a Fourth, the *two* intervening notes may constitute the *Acciaccatura*, as:

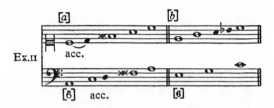

N.B.—The slur at the beginning of Ex. *a* (in the upper stave) would seem to indicate (as it clearly does in another example, not quoted here), that the two notes are to be struck with the thumb of the right hand.

Heinichen gives the following *recipe* for ascertaining when these ornaments can be introduced: the beginner is to notice when the interval of a Third in a chord coincides with an unoccupied finger, which is forthwith to strike the intervening note, "whether a *Mordente* or an *Acciaccatura* happens to result".

Three precautions are to be observed: (1) Suchlike dissonant chords are not to be used too often, but only by way of variety. (2) Not more than three or four adjacent notes are ordinarily to be struck at once. (3) The chord is to be slightly spread, but only the "false notes" should be at once released.

On a modern Pianoforte the Acciaccatura is not a success, but on an Harpsichord it can be extraordinarily effective. Any one fortunate enough to possess the latter instrument will find opportunities of testing this assertion in Longo's (unexpurgated) edition of Domenico Scarlatti's works.

III. We now come to the second class of embellishments (as tabulated by Heinichen): those depending on the fancy and inventiveness of the player.

(*a*) As an example of the material from which a melody may be evolved, our author takes a simple Bass, moving in unbroken quavers till the last two bars. This he furnishes with the plainest chordal accompaniment.

It is unnecessary to give more than the beginning and end:

In the next two examples we see the same Bass furnished with a melodic upper part.

In the first, the harmony is divided between the two hands, and the Bass itself is adorned with an occasional trill or mordent; in the second, the chords are relegated to the left hand, and all embellishments to the right.

In both examples we meet with all the embellishments described above (cf. II) except the *Acciaccatura*.

[12] Heinichen calls attention to the third note (a demi-semiquaver) in the upper part

In the next example, which, we are told, illustrates a form of accompaniment particularly appropriate in the *Ritornelli* of Airs without instrumental accompaniment (cf. Ch. iii, § 8 *h ad fin.*), Heinichen points out that the deeper bass notes are best taken an 8ve higher [cf. Ex. 12 *a*, bars 5 and 9] to avoid the unpleasant effect, especially on the Organ, of full chords taken so low down:

Ex.12b

(*b*) Passages, by which we are to understand all kinds of quick notes, moving either by step or by leap (except Arpeggios, which are treated separately), are appropriate, we are told (l.c. § 29), in quick and lively pieces, whereas it is chiefly in slow, *cantabile* pieces of an emotional character that melody can be introduced with advantage.

of bar 1, and a similar one (the sixth note) in bar 2, as a little ornament, known as *Superjectio* (Germ. *Ueberschlag*), which can often be used in the melody with good effect, especially in the case of a falling Second.

The method of executing the Slide in bars 3 and 7 (and in bar 7 of Ex. 12 *b*) has already been discussed (cf. 11 *d*, note 7).

When the Bass itself contains passages, especially when the latter are of considerable compass, one may proceed in Thirds or Sixths with the Bass, omitting most, or all of the other parts [i.e. those indicated by the figures], and this, Heinichen tells us, is usually very effective. [It is hardly necessary to point out that such an accompaniment, illustrated by the following example, must not be used in such a way as to discount the effect of the principal part or parts.]

Ex.13

Heinichen proceeds (l.c. § 30): "If, however, the Bass itself has no passages, the right hand may seek to introduce such passages wherever it can be done without damaging the effect of the principal parts (*wo es denen concertirenden Stimmen keinen Eintrag thut*), and here, again, the left hand alone maintains, as far as possible, the full accompaniment."

Four examples are given, all on the same Bass; two of these must suffice here.[13]

[Ex.14]

[13] The two omitted here (the second and third) are very similar in character to Ex. 14, from which Ex. 14 *a* differs, as will be noticed, in the use of broken chords as well as runs.

(c) Heinichen devotes a great deal of space (l.c. §§ 31–8) to the explanation and illustration of the use of Arpeggios in playing from a figured Bass.

It is important to note at the outset that, under certain circumstances, he sanctions their use in the left hand, *as a substitute for the plain bass notes actually written*.[15]

In this case, however, an important reservation is made: when an Arpeggio (in 2, 3, or 4 parts, as the case may be) is used in the right hand, the order in which the respective intervals are taken is purely a matter of taste, but when it occurs in the left hand, *the Bass of the chord must always be the first note struck*.

Heinichen's examples accordingly fall into two main groups, showing: (1) Arpeggios,[16] in (a) two, (b) three, and (c) four parts, in the *right hand*; (2) the same in the *left hand*.

This second group, again, contains two sets of examples: in the first of these, the right hand has plain chords (of varying fulness); in the second, it has Arpeggios of the same pattern as, but sometimes in contrary motion with, those in the left hand.[17]

The examples, of some of which only the beginning is here given, will, for the most part, explain themselves:

[14] From the end of bar 1 to the third beat of bar 2 the Bass is taken an 8ve lower than in Ex. 14.

[15] "Not all composers", he tells us (l.c. § 38, note k), "approve of suchlike variations of the Bass. But when such things are introduced appositely and with discretion, e.g. in a *Solo*, a *Cantata a voce sola*, and the empty *Ritornello* [i.e. without *ripieno* instrumental parts], they adorn the accompaniment and are quite admissible. Only one must not irritate the singer with this kind of thing, or turn the accompaniment into a Prelude [i.e. a free improvisation]."

[16] Heinichen uses the term *Arpeggio* (also *Harpeggio* and *Harpeggiatur*) in a somewhat wider sense than usual, in making it include broken two-part harmony (as in Ex. 15), and also the three-part figure (shown in Ex. 16 b) too familiar in the so-called 'Alberti Bass'.

[17] Of the form of accompaniment shown in these latter examples Heinichen tells us (l.c. § 38) that "in quick pieces of a stately character (*bey pompös und lebendig gesetzten Sachen*) it gives no little brilliance (*Lustre*) to the Harpsichord". "On the Organ (*Pfeiffwerck*)", he adds, "one must walk much more warily in such matters."

Of the case illustrated by the above example Heinichen tells us (l.c. § 36) that the accompaniment in the left hand "does not always really need to be so very full, as a 3-part Arpeggio in the right hand can make noise enough".

"The 4-part Arpeggio", he continues (l.c. § 37), "is not so rich in good inventions [i.e. so capable of variety] or so convenient (*applicabel*) as the 3-part one. . . . Here, again, the left hand has the remainder of the accompaniment, in many or few parts according to circumstances, as the following example will further serve to illustrate:

In the examples which follow, illustrating the use of Arpeggios (and the other broken harmony which Heinichen includes under that name) in the left hand, as a variation of the written Bass, the latter is given on a third stave, below the variation.

In connexion with some of these examples (as also Ex. 17 *a*) it must be remembered that, between Arpeggios, *consecutives are not deemed to exist.*[18]

[18] Cf. Marpurg, *Handbuch &c.*, Part I, 1755, Abschnitt [Section] I, Tab. VI (2nd ed. 1762, Tab. IV), Fig. 14 (Octaves), and Tab. VIII (2nd ed. Tab. VI), Fig. 23 Fifths).

Ex.18

"2 = part *Harpeggiaturas*"

[Ex.19]

"3 = part *Harpeggiaturas*"

In the remaining examples we see the broken harmony in both hands which Heinichen tells us is so particularly effective on the Harpsichord when appropriately used (cf. note 17):

N.B.—In Ex. 21 b, on the middle stave, the third group of four semiquavers (marked * *) is given as: ![notation], and the fifth group as: ![notation], thus omitting the Seventh from the harmony. This has been assumed to be a misprint, though not included in Heinichen's long list of *Errata*.

(d) Heinichen adds some further examples, which need not be quoted here, showing how the devices described above (Melody, Passages, and Arpeggios) may be applied to Basses consisting of repeated notes, as:

the treatment naturally varying with the pace and character of the music.

He also illustrates devices to be substituted for the rapid repercussion of bass notes. This, being a matter of convenience rather than of embellishment, need not occupy us here.

(e) Heinichen's views on the subject of Imitation, with which he concludes his list of the embellishments depending on the fancy and inventiveness of the player, have already been quoted (Ch. iii, § 8 d).

(f) The concluding paragraph of Heinichen's long chapter (l.c. § 41) deserves to be quoted: "Thus much have we seen fit to write on the embellishment of the Thorough-Bass (vom manierlichen General-Bass). Now it would certainly be useful, and necessary, to illustrate the application of all the embellishments hitherto mentioned in entire Thorough-Basses, and also to give the principal part as well, in order, as it were, to point out to the beginner where this or that embellishment has a happy effect or the reverse; but any one with a knowledge of Music will easily see that, for such exhaustive examples, not a single chapter, as here, but an entire book would be needed.[19] To make up for this deficiency we ought, it is true, to recommend other authors who have treated, ex professo, the matter in question; but, at the moment, I do not know of a single author who has taken much trouble in the matter, or [any work which] is better adapted for the practice of an embellished (manierlich) Thorough-Bass than the Organisten-Probe, just mentioned,[20] of Capellmeister Mattheson. This book possesses great merits in making a beginner, who has previously mastered the fundamenta of Thorough-Bass, secure (Sattel-feste) in all sorts of ways, and in imparting to him (1) the difficulties of all the keys (Modi Musici), (2) a dexterous hand, and (3) all kinds of embellishments (Galanterie) of the Thorough-Bass.[21] And, for my part, I am of opinion (without empty boasting) that whoever uses the above-mentioned Organisten-Probe in conjunction with the present Treatise, will not need a third author, either for the theory or the practice of Thorough-Bass. Wherefore, instead of an extension of the present chapter, I hereby recommend the said Organisten-Probe, and herewith conclude the first part of this work."

§ 4. Geminiani.

(a) Something has already been said (cf. § 1 g) about the character of Geminiani's examples.

The main principle which he endeavours to inculcate may be said to be economy of the evanescent tone of the Harpsichord.

In his Explanation of the Examples prefixed to Part the first (sub Example I)

---

[19] Heinichen here appends a note, for which see § 5 n ad fin.

[20] Cf. Ch. iii, § 8 d, note 1.

[21] Mattheson took an early opportunity of handsomely returning Heinichen's compliment (cf. Ch. iii, § 6 c, note 11 and the text above). Heinichen somewhat qualified his praise by appending the following note, which will surprise no one who knows Mattheson's Organisten-Probe: "I am here reasoning a potiori. There are, however, certain harmonies and progressions (harmonische Sätze und Gänge) for which the author must himself be answerable, concerning which I cannot here enter into a dispute. . . ."

he writes: "I repeat here, what I have said in my Preface, that the Art of Accompagniament [*sic*] chiefly consists in rendering the Sounds of the Harpsichord lasting, for frequent Interruptions of the Sound are inconsistent with true Melody. The Learner is therefore to observe not to exhaust the Harmony all at once, that is to say, never to lay down all his Fingers at once on the Keys, but to touch the several Notes whereof the Chords consist in Succession."

Nearly all the examples take the form of figured Basses, varying in length from one to thirty bars (but generally quite short), repeated over and over again, so as to show the different methods of treatment of which they are capable, the variation being, in some cases, extended to the Bass itself.

Very free use is made both of passing and changing (i.e. accented passing) notes, and of appoggiaturas, *but no shake or other similar ornament* is used throughout the entire work.

Geminiani makes frequent use of a peculiar notation designed, partly, it would appear, to facilitate the printing by reducing the number of rests, and partly to help the learner to distinguish at a glance between essential and unessential notes.[1] In the examples now to be given, however, it seemed better to employ the ordinary notation.

[1] Geminiani's notation is as follows (cf. Part I, *Explanation of the Examples*, s.v. Example 9, also Part II, *Introduction*):

(1) Round black notes without tails, over or under minims, are to be played as crotchets, and "are to be struck in the Middle of the Time of the Notes under or over them", that is to say, *as though preceded by a crotchet rest.* For example,

is to be played thus:

(2) Similarly: "Quavers under or over Crotchets are to be struck in the Middle of the Time of those Crotchets under or over them", that is to say, *as though preceded by a quaver rest.*

In the following example this rule will be found to apply also to quavers (marked *), not over crotchets, but each one over two quavers:

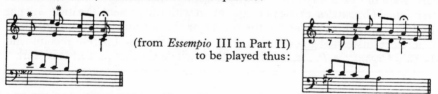

(from *Essempio* III in Part II)
to be played thus:

(3) Minims with a stroke across their tails "are to be played as Crotchets, and the Crotchets immediately following [are to be] played in the latter Half of the Time [i.e. as one crotchet after another]. They are written in this Manner for the sake of Distinction, the Minims with a Stroke across their Tails being Concords,* and the following Crotchets passing Discords."

Sometimes, though Geminiani omits to mention it, the crotchet *precedes* the minim. In either case, the two are connected by a slur (often accidentally omitted). Thus:

(Part I, *Essempio* XII, 1⁰ *Modo di suonare*, bars 6, 7.)

* It is evident from the examples that, by *concords*, Geminiani meant the *essential harmony note* (which might happen to be a discord).

(b) One of the most instructive examples in the entire work, as illustrating Geminiani's method of "rendering the Sounds of the Harpsichord lasting" is *Essempio* XXIV with which Part the first concludes.   It consists of sixteen separate examples, all based on the *Scala Fondamentale* of C major, all differently harmonized, and all in triple time.

It is from these that the two following have been selected, one on a descending, and the other on an ascending Bass.   In them it is fortunately unnecessary to alter Geminiani's notation.[2]

[Ex. I]

Note 1 *continued.*
stands for:

(4) The same applies, *mutatis mutandis*, to crotchets with a stroke across their tails followed [or preceded] by quavers, as in the following examples (from *Essempio* III in Part II):

stands
for:

N.B.:—In the first half of Ex. *a* the notation of the upper part might have been expected to be as follows, since it is the *d* and *b* which are the essential harmony notes:

 (cf. in Ex. *b*).

[2] With the trifling exception that, in the original, the figuring is given over a separate Bass instead of under the example itself.   Geminiani uses the old *signum cancellatum* ✕ in the text, and the modern ♯ in the figuring, thus exactly reversing the practice of Ph. Em. Bach in his *Versuch.*

[3] There is one not unimportant point, in the above example, in which Geminiani's,

(c) *Essempio* XI in Part the second consists of a number of variations on the following Bass, which, in the course of the example, is transposed into B flat major:

Of the three of these variations (the fourth, fifth, and seventh) selected for presentation here, the first, though purely chordal, deviates from the ordinary rule of the text-books, to the effect that each chord should be taken in the position nearest that of the preceding one.

In the second, we have an exceedingly free use of appoggiaturas, which, needless to say, could not be employed in actual accompaniment, save under special conditions already described (cf. Ch. iii, § 8 *a ad fin.*). Apart from this, a comparison with the above figured Bass will reveal, in both variations, certain small deviations from the prescribed harmony. These are indicated by the figures in brackets below the Bass, as also in the third variation.

In the latter Geminiani reveals himself as a Violinist by the passages in semiquavers, first in the Tenor, and then in the upper part.

and, presumably, the Italian practice generally, differs from the German as represented by Ph. Em. Bach. In the figuring of the first bar a dash is placed after the 5 to indicate that the $\sharp^6_4$ comes on the third, instead of the second, beat. In the third, sixth, and seventh bars (where there is no dash) the 7 resolves on the second beat. Ph. Em. Bach's rule, on the other hand, is as follows (*Versuch &c.*, Part II, 1762, Ch. 1, § 47): "When a note of three equal, or, what comes to the same thing, two unequal parts, has two consecutive figures over it, the larger part, or two-thirds, falls to the first figure, and the small part, or one-third, to the second." Any deviation from this, we are told, is indicated by a dash. Ph. Em. Bach would, therefore, have omitted the dash in the first bars of Geminiani's example, whereas, in the third, sixth, and seventh bars, the figuring would have been 7 6 —. In actual practice, a composer's intentions in this matter can generally be ascertained by a careful examination of the principal part or parts.

[Ex. 3]

One or two small points are to be noted in connexion with the above:
(1) In (a), at the beginning of the penultimate bar, the downward resolution
of the suspended 9 involves the crossing of the two upper parts:

(2) In the corresponding bar of (b) the 9 has an extremely free and unusual ornamental resolution, while, in (c), it does not appear at all, except as a passing semiquaver.

(3) In the fourth and fifth bars of (b), the quavers in the Alto echo the Bass in the higher Octave.

(d) Geminiani's examples are characterized by singular freshness and spontaneity, and many more no less interesting ones might be given did not space forbid. In taking leave of him it is worth pointing out that, in one respect, his work differs from all others dealing with the same subject: in all the others (save only that of Quantz, who, however, gives no examples of a set-out accompaniment) we are taught by Accompanists how to accompany, but Geminiani, the pupil of Corelli, speaks as a Soloist, telling us how he likes to be accompanied!

"The Art of Accompagniament [sic]", he tells us in his Preface, "consists in displaying Harmony, disposing the Chords, in a just Distribution of the Sounds whereof they consist, and in ordering them after a Manner that may give the Ear the pleasure of a continued and uninterrupted Melody. This Observation, or rather Principle, is the Ground of my Method, which teaches the Learner to draw from the Harmony, he holds under his Fingers, diversified and agreeable Singings."

§ 5. *Ph. Em. Bach.*

(a) Ph. Em. Bach differs materially from Heinichen in his conception of the means which may be employed with a view to adding interest and elegance to the accompaniment, as will be gathered from the opening words of the chapter from which the heading of the present one is borrowed (cf. § 1 a). Indeed, it would almost seem as though it were against Heinichen, with whose work he must have been familiar, that they were directed. He writes (l.c. § 1):

"Here we remind [the reader] once again that it is not in florid figures and ornaments, inappropriately devised, with which some actually disfigure the melodic progression of the Bass (*in bunten Figuren und Manieren, welche man zur Unzeit erfindet, und wodurch einige sogar den Gesang der Grundnoten entstellen*), that the elegance of the accompaniment must consist."

From this we gather that he disapproves, in a general way, of the introduction of ornaments and passage-work, and, in particular, of any alteration of the Bass itself, either by any kind of grace-notes (cf. § 3, Exx. 2 a, 12 a), or by the substitution of broken harmony in the left hand (cf. § 3, Exx. 18–23). On the other hand, we shall see that he is guided by the principle, tacitly adopted by Mattheson and Heinichen, and admirably defined by Geminiani when he says that "the Art of Accompagniament [sic] chiefly consists in rendering the Sounds of the Harpsichord lasting".

It is in obedience to this principle that he prescribes the following of the Bass in Thirds (or Tenths), sometimes alternating with Sixths, in the right hand, and also the use of passing notes and chords connecting successive harmonies.

Bach's examples, as has already been explained, are all given on a single stave, and with an entire disregard for pitch (cf. Ch. iii, § 3 v, notes 29 and 30).

They will be given here as seems most convenient, and, in some cases (which will be duly noted), an Octave higher than in the original.[1]

---

[1] A certain proportion of Bach's examples must reluctantly be omitted here.

(*b*) Before proceeding to the actual subject of the chapter under discussion, Bach mentions a case in which special watchfulness is demanded of the accompanist. The principal performer, he tells us (l.c. § 5), may so far yield to the inspiration of the moment, in varying and embellishing his part, as to involve a slight departure from the harmony prescribed by the figures. Guided by his ear alone, the accompanist may have to choose between alternatives such as those indicated in the following examples.

In the first ones (Ex. 1) there is an actual difference in the harmony; in the others (Ex. 2) it is merely a question of a delayed progression:

(*c*) Continuous movement in Thirds (or Tenths) with the Bass.

It will be remembered that Niedt was familiar with this principle (cf. Ch. i, § 25 III, Ex. 3 *b*).

"One of the principal niceties (*Zierlichkeiten*) of the accompaniment", writes Bach (l.c. § 6), "is the progression in Thirds with the Bass. The right hand, in such case, is never bound to an equal fulness of harmony. An accompaniment in four parts throughout [Ex. 1] is seldom used, and that only in the case of slow notes, as the Thirds cannot be brought out well if the time is quick. A three-part accompaniment, and, in the great majority of cases, one in two parts, in which only the Thirds are played with the Bass, are the best. From all the examples given below we shall see that, under certain circumstances, notes moving by step, and by the leap of a Third, are best adapted for this accompaniment in Thirds. . . . Certain introductory figures (*Einleitungsclauseln*) [i.e. preceding a repeat, &c.] can likewise be accompanied in Thirds only [Exx. 6, 7]. If the latter example occurs in the minor key, the accompaniment must be changed [Ex. 8]:

(given an 8ve lower in the original).

[2] This same example (with the Bass an 8ve lower) is given later on with an accompaniment in which Tenths alternate with Sixths (cf. Ex. 16 *b*).

The following examples are given by Bach later on in a paragraph (l.c. § 8) devoted mainly to the illustration of an accompaniment in which one part follows the Bass in Thirds (which term, in the present connexion, of course includes Tenths) alternating with Sixths.

As the examples in question exhibit no such alternation, it seemed better to include them here:

Of the above example Bach remarks that: "As the accompaniment is in four parts, the *tempo* must not be very quick."

The two following examples are not quite so regular in pattern as the preceding, but both of them exhibit the same characteristic progression in Thirds with the Bass:

In both the above examples the upper part of the accompaniment is seen to reduplicate the principal part; in Ex. 13, moreover, the accompaniment goes *above* the principal part (cf. Ch. iii, § 5 B 1). Yet it will be found that in neither case could a much better accompaniment be devised.

At the end of the first bar of Ex. 13, where the accompaniment first rises above the principal part, two things will be noticed: (1) the principal part is itself *only a Third above the Bass*, and (2) the accompaniment sets in *after* the lower note (*f* in the principal part) has been heard, and this makes all the difference!

(*d*) Certain precautions to be observed.

Bach utters a very necessary caution against the indiscriminate employment of the device described above. He writes (l.c. § 7): "If, in a piece in two parts [Solo and Bass],[5] the Bass notes are such as to admit of being accompanied with continuous Thirds in the right hand, but the principal part has to play, either these very Thirds, or other *continuous* intervals *of the same*

---

[3] Of the progression (shown in the above example) of a diminished Fifth descending to a perfect one, between extreme parts, Ph. Em. Bach himself says that: "it is allowed only in case of need, and not easily between extreme parts" (ibid. Ch. 2, 1, § 22).

[4] The penultimate note in the upper part of the accompaniment (*b*) is, of course, treated, in accordance with the custom of the time, as a *demi-semiquaver*, so as to coincide exactly with the demi-semiquaver *d* in the Bass.

[5] We are not expressly told that it is, generally speaking, chiefly in such compositions (i.e. Solo and Bass) that the accompaniment in question is appropriate, but it almost follows if we consider: (1) that, the greater the number of principal parts, the less need is there to depart from a perfectly plain accompaniment, and (2) that the necessary precautions cannot be adequately observed if the accompanist has to rely on his ear alone; for, as a rule, it is only a *Solo* part that is printed over a figured Bass.

time-value as the Bass notes, plain chords are to be played, and the progression in Thirds omitted. Otherwise, in the first case, one would be duplicating notes which belong to the principal part alone, while, in the second, one would obscure the melodic progression (*Gesang*) of principal part and Bass by an adventitious (*neu hinzugekommen*) third movement of the same kind [i.e. in notes of the same value]."

The accompaniment in Thirds (or Tenths) is, therefore, most appropriate (we are told) when the principal part has either a sustained note [as in Exx. 3 and 5], or (2) notes (of whatever time-value) repeated in the unison or 8ve,

as: 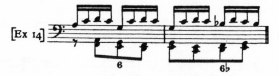 or (3) notes *slower* than those in the Bass [as in

Ex. 9], or (4) notes *at least twice as quick* as the bass notes, as:

[Ex 14]

"In the latter case", writes Bach, "the caution which is always necessary in the employment of these Thirds must be redoubled, lest any unpleasant clashes [Ex. 15 *a*] or forbidden progressions [Ex. 15 *b*] should be occasioned:

[Ex.15]

N.B.—The offending Thirds, omitted in the original, have been added in small notes, to make Bach's meaning plainer to the eye.

(*e*) Thirds (Tenths) with the Bass alternating with Sixths.

"Sometimes", we are told (l.c. § 8), "the Thirds in question are mixed with Sixths:

[Ex.16]

Solo

Acc

[6] In (*b*) and (*c*) all the notes in the Bass and in the accompaniment are *harmony notes*, whereas in (*a*) (where the horizontal dashes in the figuring denote the retention of the same harmony throughout) the second and sixth quavers in the Bass *a* are, in the wider sense, passing notes, and the fourth and eighth quavers *f* are also passing notes. The accompaniment shown above, however, treats the Bass as though figured

as follows:

We have already had (*b*) with an accompaniment in Thirds only (cf. Ex. 4).

(f) A special case.

A particular case, incidentally involving the alternation of a Third (Tenth) with a Sixth, between the Bass and an upper part, arises when the former rises or falls a Third (with or without an intermediate passing note) *to another interval of the same harmony.* If, then, an upper part (the one which has the same interval as that to which the Bass moves) *itself proceeds to the interval abandoned by the Bass* (thus effecting an exchange of intervals, or inversion), it not only greatly enriches the harmony and tends, as Geminiani expresses it, to "make the Sounds of the Harpsichord lasting" (cf. § 4 a), but, as Ph. Em. Bach points out (l.c. § 8), it is often *necessary*, in order to avoid consecutive 8ves with the Bass, and, in such case, the inversion must be effected, *even though not indicated in the figuring.* Bach's examples will make the point abundantly clear:

N.B.—The figures added in square brackets indicate the inversion of the harmony; the asterisks show where consecutives would otherwise have occurred.

(g) Bach gives examples illustrating the light accompaniment suitable when the time is quick. In these the Bass rises and falls a Third, or vice versâ, while the harmony remains unchanged. The accompaniment is in three parts, one of which is sustained, while the other moves in Thirds (or Tenths) with the Bass, or Tenths alternating (in contrary motion) with Sixths. The quickness of the time, as Bach points out, makes the harmony sound fuller than it actually is:

The following example (in which the harmony changes on each quaver) illustrates the same principle. In this example, it will be noticed, the recurring note *a* is not sustained but reiterated with each harmony:

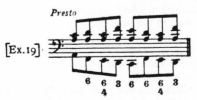

⁷ In (e), at the beginning of the bar, the semiquaver *a* in the Alto, over the passing semiquaver *f* in the Bass, is one of the most familiar instances of the practice of

The next example admirably illustrates the use of three-part harmony, interspersed at pleasure with fuller chords. "The lightness of delivery", Bach writes (l.c. § 8 g), "would suffer if a four-part accompaniment were used throughout." Incidentally, too, the good melodic progression (*guter Gesang*) in the upper part, on which Bach always lays great stress, is shown:

[Ex. 20]

"We see from these examples", Bach continues, "how easy (*bequem*) one can make these quickly moving Basses for oneself, partly by Thirds and Sixths, partly, too, and more especially, by the sustention (*Liegenlassen*) of the intervals already to hand. Consequently, this sustention is good for many reasons: it binds and sings more, and is also easier and more harmless [8] than repercussion. The latter is almost impossible in quick time, especially with a four-part accompaniment, and has a bad effect."

(*h*) Bach gives a few characteristic examples (from which, he tells us, we can draw our own conclusions with regard to other similar cases) in which the sole accompaniment consists of Thirds or Sixths, not with the Bass, but with (i.e. below) the principal part. This accompaniment, we are warned, can only be used in compositions in which the Solo part appears above the figured Bass:

[Ex. 21]

N.B.—In these examples the middle part *only* (together with the Bass) represents the accompaniment.

(*i*) Skips in the harmony.

N.B.—All the examples still to follow, in the present section, except Exx. 26 and 29, are given an 8ve higher than in the original.

following the Bass in Thirds or Tenths. If this were, in the present instance, required by the composer, the *f* in the Bass would have to be figured $\frac{7}{5}$.

[8] Bach more than once alludes to the injurious effect of rapidly reiterated notes (especially in the Bass, where they are most liable to occur) in stiffening the hands (cf. *Versuch &c.*, Part I, Introd., § 9, note). It would almost seem that this must be what he has in mind here. Nevertheless, it will be noted that, in Ex. 19, the recurrent note *a* is reiterated.

In certain cases, Bach tells us, skips with the harmony (generally to be avoided as much as possible) have a good effect.

Such cases may occur:

(1) When a suitable occasion arises for the imitation of a phrase occurring in the principal part (see Ch. iii, § 8, Ex. 4).

(2) During a sustained note in the principal part (cf. Ex. 22 below).

(3) In the case of passages *dwelling mainly on the same note or notes*, repeated sequentially (cf. Ex. 23), or actually reiterated (cf. Exx. 24–6).

Of these last Bach writes: "When such passages occur, an intelligent accompanist can quite easily, and with great freedom, satisfy the just claims which, by reason of their excessive uniformity, the ear makes to variety. It may be, in a general way, that it is the phrase (*Gedanke*) containing but little variety in itself which most conveniently admits of a change in the disposal of the harmony. Much, however, as such a phrase can be assisted by a subtle (*fein*) accompaniment, proportionate care is, nevertheless, needed to prevent this beauty, too, of the accompaniment from being used too often and out of season."

(k) What Bach says about the use of extended harmony (*das getheilte Accompagnement*), as a means of lending both charm and variety to the accompaniment, has already been given, in another connexion, together with his examples (cf. Ch. iii, § 3 v, Ex. 24) and the text immediately preceding.

(l) How the gaps between slow notes in the Bass may be filled.

It is interesting to note that this is the only case in which Bach prescribes the use of any *ornament* in the accompaniment.

In all his examples (to be given presently) except the last, the principal part either *has a sustained note*, or *is silent*, which renders it possible to disregard the figuring to some extent, as will be seen in Exx. 28 and 29.

The first case to be dealt with is that of a Bass in dotted notes, moving in such a way as to admit of being accompanied in Thirds or Tenths, whatever other parts might be added. Here we are told that, *if the time is slow*, the interval of time following each dotted note may be occupied with a turn (*Doppelschlag*) in the upper part, *but not in the Bass itself*, as this would be prejudicial to clearness:

The next example is best described in Bach's own words: "As the sound of an Harpsichord does not always continue (*nachklingt*) long enough [after the note is struck], and as long and sustained notes, generally speaking, sound somewhat empty on this instrument, one can, if the time is slow, choose an

---

[9] The sign ⌒ over the figures at the beginning of bar 2 denotes the omission of the 3 (cf. Ch. xxiii, "Varieties of figuring", § 19.

accompaniment which fills out the dotted notes in the Bass. This example represents an introductory figure (*Einleitungsclausel*),[10] during which the principal part is silent, thereby placing the accompanist under the necessity of inventing something, in order that the ear may not remain too unsatisfied. If, in such a case, the principal part is itself associated with the Bass in leading to whatever follows, and moves in Thirds or otherwise with it, the accompanist adheres to a plain accompaniment.[11] But, apart from that, these introductory figures are very well suited to call forth the inventive spirit of the Clavierist; only, in such a case, he must adapt his inventions to the feeling and character of the piece. If it is then possible to introduce something taken from the preceding phrases (*aus den hervorgegangenen Gedanken*), so much the better, and in that case, *if it is necessary*, the Bass notes may be altered, and the transition (lit. 'introduction') effected in a different way." Bach adds the following footnote, which is to be understood as a reference to the liberties sometimes taken by a Soloist with the composer's text (cf. *b*): "In this case a reasonable supremacy (*eine vernünftige Souverainität*) must likewise be conceded to the accompanist, the more so, the less the principal part is hampered thereby."[12]

[10] Cf. Exx. 6–8.
[11] In accordance with the figuring, the plain accompaniment would, in this instance, be:

The oblique stroke preceding the figures (and pointing from them to the note before), misplaced by a misprint in the original, indicates that the harmony ($\frac{4}{3}$ on *d*) is to be struck with the changing (i.e. accented passing) note *e*, which would otherwise be figured $\frac{3}{2}$ $\left(=\frac{5}{3}\right)$ (cf. Ch. xix, "The figuring of transitional notes in the Bass", § 5, Ex. 1 *b*, and § 6, Ex. 6 *b*).

It will be seen that, in Ex. 28, Bach has treated the Bass as though figured as follows:

[12] It is hoped that no excuse is needed for quoting so high an authority in full on so important a subject.

In the next example, the principal part, we are told, may either consist of a sustained note or be altogether silent. The accompanist can, therefore, use his discretion in the treatment of the harmony, in whichever of the three following ways the Bass is figured:

The second of the following versions requires, we are told, a slower time than the first:

The final example serves to illustrate once more the vigilance sometimes called for by the vagaries of the Soloist.

If the principal part is played as written, it is better to avoid duplicating the chromatic progression in the accompaniment, which may then be taken in either of the two ways shown below at (*a*) and (*b*); but if the Soloist chooses to linger (with or without a shake) on the first note of each bar, to the exclusion of the two remaining notes, this must be supplied in the accompaniment as indicated by the figuring, as shown at (*c*):

(*m*) Passing notes and chords linking successive harmonies.

There is no device which tends more than this to enliven the accompaniment and to give it, so to speak, a quasi-contrapuntal character.

The passing notes in question, we are told, may either follow the striking of a Bass note, or may coincide with passing notes in the Bass itself, irrespective of the transient discords thus arising, which need no resolution. "In

[13] The execution of the ornament $\overset{\times}{\underset{\sim}{\sim}}$ (in which the sharp $\times$ denotes the sharpening of the lower auxiliary note) in the two versions is, respectively: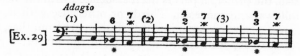

the employment of these harmonic beauties," Bach adds, "great caution is needed, in order that the principal part may not be hampered or obscured."

N.B.—In the examples which follow, the figures *above* the Bass represent the usual figuring; those *below* are added (as in the original) to indicate the free treatment illustrated by the example in question.

In the following series of examples the passing notes in each case serve to bridge the interval of a Third (*transitus in tertiam*), as described by Heinichen (cf. § 3 II *b*):

In certain cases the interval of a Third may also be bridged by a changing (i.e. accented passing) note, as:

[14] In (*f*) and ʼ(*g*) the second quaver of the Bass is a passing note. The figures, therefore, 2+ and 7, respectively, simply denote the resolution of the foregoing suspended discord, without reference to the remaining intervals of the harmony. The

essential Basses of the two examples are:

In the first case, the diminution of the interval between the Bass and the upper part, caused by the rising passing note in the former, causes the ♯ (=♯ 3) shown above to become 2+; in the second, 6 becomes 7 by the reverse process. Such progressions are made much clearer by the use of horizontal dashes indicating the intervals retained from the previous chord, as:

[15] In a full close, it is an accepted licence to include the 7 in the Dominant chord at discretion, even though not figured (cf. Ch. xxi, 'Incomplete figuring', II, § 5). The

In the following series, we have an ornamental anticipation of the resolution of a discord:

In the next series of examples, a note common to two successive chords, instead of remaining stationary, falls a degree (in (*a*) a chromatic semitone), and rises again in time to take its place in the second chord. In one instance (*e*) the process is reversed. In (*d*), the falling note synchronizes with a passing semiquaver in the Bass, and rises again in Sixths with the latter:

In the next example, we see three changing (i.e. accented passing) notes combined to form a chord. It will be noted that the harmony indicated by the dash over the second quaver in the Bass (i.e. $\frac{6}{4}$ on *f*) is *never struck*, $\frac{8}{6}$ being substituted: [18]

7 may, of course, either be struck *with* the chord $\left(\begin{smallmatrix}8\\7\\3\end{smallmatrix}\text{ or }\begin{smallmatrix}7\\5\\3\end{smallmatrix}\right)$ or follow it $\left(\begin{smallmatrix}8&7\\5&-\\3&-\end{smallmatrix}\text{ or }\begin{smallmatrix}8&-\\5&7\\3&-\end{smallmatrix}\right)$, subject to such modifications as shown in the above example.

[16] In (*b*) the second quaver in the Bass is a passing note, *followed in Thirds by the upper part*; the main progression is:

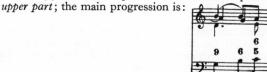

[17] In (*b*) and (*c*), the second quaver in the Bass (a passing note) might with advantage to clearness have been figured $\frac{4}{2}$ $\left(=\begin{smallmatrix}6\\4\\2\end{smallmatrix}\right)$. The main progressions are, respectively:

[18] There are, of course, other ways in which the effect of movement in the upper parts may be obtained, as:

[Ex.35]

All the examples hitherto given in the present section are in four-part harmony.[19] Bach's last four examples (from which the two following are selected) are mainly in three parts.

In the first of the two, the upper part rises a Third (bridged by an accented passing note) to the interval ($5\flat$) required to complete the harmony indicated by the figures. In the second, which is masterly in its freedom, the harmony belonging to the last note of the first bar ($\frac{6}{4}$ on d) is never struck; instead we have $\frac{8}{6}$ approached by changing (i.e. accented passing) notes, somewhat after the manner of Ex. 35; this 8, in its turn, serves to prepare 2 on the following c, treated as a rising *appoggiatura* (2 3), while the 7, struck simultaneously, has its proper downward resolution:

[Ex. 36]

(*n*) Readers, whose patience may have been taxed by the length of the chapter just brought to a conclusion, are reminded that the purpose of this work would not be fulfilled if any material evidence, bearing on so vital a subject, were wittingly passed over.

The writer cannot do better than quote the excuse made by Heinichen at the end of the chapter which formed the subject of § 3 (l.c. § 41, note *n*):

"I am sorry, as it is, that the examples in the above chapter have taken up so much space in print, although the entire chapter in question is a very useful little work for the necessary practice of a beginner, which, on account of the method once adopted, could not well have been made shorter."

[19] The cases in which the continuity of a part is interrupted for the space of a single quaver are probably due to Bach's cramped notation of the examples on a single stave, which sometimes makes it difficult to distinguish the time-values of a crotchet and quaver struck simultaneously. Moreover, as Bach had the Harpsichord, rather than the Organ, in mind in noting the examples, he was not likely to trouble the printer much about a distinction non-existent except on paper. Thus Ex. 31 c should most

probably appear as follows: [music], though it is possible that quaver

rests in the Alto were intended: [music]

The same applies, *mutatis mutandis*, to Ex. 31 *d* (first half-bar), Ex. 32, and Ex. 34 *d* (second half-bar).